Digital Forensics Playbook

Practical recipes for investigating enterprise Windows and Linux system artifacts

Nishant Krishna

www.bpbonline.com

First Edition 2026

ISBN: 978-93-65891-515

Distributors:

BPB PUBLICATIONS
20, Ansari Road, Darya Ganj
New Delhi-110002
Ph: 23254990/23254991

DECCAN AGENCIES
4-3-329, Bank Street,
Hyderabad-500195
Ph: 24756967/24756400

MICRO MEDIA
Shop No. 5, Mahendra Chambers,
150 DN Rd. Next to Capital Cinema,
V.T. (C.S.T.) Station, MUMBAI-400 001
Ph: 22078296/22078297

Published by Manish Jain for BPB Publications, 20 Ansari Road, Darya Ganj, New Delhi-110002 and Printed by him at Repro India Ltd., Rewari.

www.bpbonline.com

Dedicated to

My late mother and father:

Dr. Usha Krishna

and

Dr. K. P. Krishna

About the Author

Nishant Krishna is an entrepreneur, writer, and inventor who loves exploring and using new ways to solve complex problems in cybersecurity, cyber forensics, system programming, cognitive computing, computer vision, and product scaling to hyper-scale levels.

In his 25+ year software development career, he has created many software products from scratch, working in various technical roles across architecture, cybersecurity, API development, anti-counterfeiting technologies, cloud and virtualization, the **Internet of Things (IoT)**, and machine learning. Apart from his day-to-day work, he also works on core research in cybersecurity and cognitive computing. In cybersecurity, his focus is on cyber forensics and vulnerability assessment.

In his consulting role, he advises many companies on making their enterprises ready for cyber forensics evidence collection, product development, threat-surface reduction, database and application scalability, and the use of standard processes to deliver high-quality products.

As a leader, he works with, manages, and influences people across organizations to deliver high-quality products and services. He has been working with multiple large teams at any given time and bringing out the best in them to support the organization's success.

Nishant is also an adjunct professor teaching cybersecurity, cyber forensics, cognitive computing, and databases to students and faculty in multiple prestigious institutions. As part of his teaching assignments, he seeks innovative, hands-on ways to teach complex concepts.

About the Reviewers

- **Brijesh Kapadiya** is a digital forensics professional and vice president - **digital forensics and incident response (DFIR)** with strong experience in cyber incident investigations, ransomware response, and digital forensics. He has worked extensively with enterprise clients, law enforcement and government agencies on handling data breaches, ransomware investigations and advanced cyber threats.

  His expertise includes forensic analysis across endpoints and mobile devices, clouds, emails, incident response, and ensuring legal admissibility through proper evidence handling practices. He is passionate about building DFIR capabilities, developing cyber forensic labs and strengthening organizational cyber resilience.

  He is currently serving as vice president - DFIR at Drona Cyber Solutions Pvt Ltd.

- **Suneeth Maraboina** is a senior audio engineer and technologist with over 18 years of experience designing and delivering large-scale audio and media systems across consumer, enterprise, and automotive platforms. His work spans digital signal processing, spatial and immersive audio, real-time communication, and system-level audio architecture. Over the course of his career, he has held critical technical roles at globally recognized technology companies, including Apple, Dolby Laboratories, Microsoft, Qualcomm, Intel, and Roku, contributing to widely deployed products used by millions of users worldwide.

  At Apple, Suneeth focuses on advanced in-vehicle audio systems, including CarPlay, Spatial Audio, and next-generation media frameworks. His prior work includes Dolby Atmos speaker systems, VoIP and conferencing audio pipelines, Bluetooth and wideband audio drivers, and multimedia streaming platforms. He has authored and reviewed technical papers, served as a peer reviewer and judge for academic and industry forums, and is an active member of professional engineering societies.

  Suneeth is passionate about mentoring engineers, translating complex audio concepts into practical systems, and advancing the future of immersive sound through both industry practice and technical writing.

- **Akhilesh Bhangepatil** is a cybersecurity operations leader who helps global organizations strengthen cyber defense across enterprise, critical infrastructure, and **operational technology (OT)** environments. He leads security operations programs spanning detection engineering, incident response, and digital forensics/forensic readiness, developing repeatable investigative procedures, disciplined evidence handling, and rapid containment workflows. Akhilesh advises executive and operational leaders on incident response strategy, forensics-informed decision-making, and OT/industrial control system cyber defense, aligning technical actions to business risk, safety, and operational continuity while supporting the resilience of national critical infrastructure. He holds CISSP and CISA credentials, along with GIAC certifications including GICSP, GCIP, and GRID. An invited speaker at the **American Petroleum Institute (API)** Cybersecurity Conference, a leading forum for the energy sector's cybersecurity community with international participation, he also contributes to ISA/IEC 62443 standards development working groups advancing security for industrial automation and control systems.

Acknowledgement

I want to express my deepest gratitude to my family and friends for their unwavering support and encouragement throughout this book's writing, especially my wife Parimita. I will always be thankful to my late father, Dr. K. P Krishna, who, as a prolific writer himself and researcher in psychology and criminology, inspired me greatly to write a book on this topic. I will also be thankful to my late mother, Dr. Usha Krishna, who, as a lawyer, made me aware of some of the challenges faced while investigating crimes.

I am thankful to Dr. Rashmi Agrawal, Dr. Shinu Abhi, and Dr. J. B. Simha, all excellent researchers in their respective areas. They helped me steer my cyber forensic research towards a clear goal, which greatly aided me while writing this book.

Topics like Windows Forensics are vast areas in their own right. I am thankful to Dr. Praveen Misra and Arjun Bollepelly for some of the deep brainstorming we did as early as 2023.

I am also grateful to BPB Publications for their guidance and expertise in bringing this book to fruition. It was a long journey of revising this book, with the valuable participation and collaboration of reviewers, technical experts, and editors.

I would also like to acknowledge the valuable contributions of my colleagues and coworkers during many years working in the tech industry, who have taught me so much and provided valuable feedback on my work.

I would also like to acknowledge the valuable contribution of the technical reviewers of this book. They have reviewed the book for technical errors and provided important suggestions to improve its quality.

Finally, I would like to thank all the readers who have taken an interest in my book and for their support in making it a reality. Your encouragement has been invaluable.

Preface

Digital forensics is not just for police departments and crime labs anymore. Today, every type of organization creates massive amounts of digital information around the clock. Whether you're looking at a tech startup that runs everything in the cloud or a huge company owning different computer systems, they all face the same challenge. When bad things happen, like hackers stealing data, employees going rogue, ransomware attacks, or sensitive information getting leaked, companies need to know how to handle the digital evidence properly. This means finding it, keeping it safe, collecting it properly, analyzing what happened, and presenting the findings clearly. How well they do this affects the level of business continuity and whether they can defend their actions when auditors, insurance companies, lawyers, or law enforcement come asking questions.

This book takes you through digital forensics step by step, starting with the basics and working up to complex real-world situations you would actually face in a business setting. The main goal is teaching you a structured way to investigate problems that covers finding evidence, following proper procedures to handle it, keeping detailed records of who touched what and when, and producing results that will hold up under intense scrutiny.

Everything in this book focuses on hands-on learning with clear, detailed instructions and practical recipes you can use in real investigations. This includes setting up your forensic workspace, gathering digital artifacts from different computer systems, analyzing logs and network data, examining computer memory and running processes, and investigating malware attacks. The book also covers how to integrate forensics into your organization through proper preparation, meeting regulatory requirements, maintaining thorough documentation, and treating every investigation as a formal case rather than just another tech problem to solve.

When you finish this book, you should feel confident handling digital forensics investigations and security incidents. You will know what evidence matters, how to collect it properly, how to analyze it systematically, and how to document everything clearly. This book works for all types of readers, including students building their foundation, people studying for CHFI certification, incident response professionals expanding into digital forensics, or experienced investigators who want a solid framework to follow. You can use it both as a reference when you need to look something up and as a hands-on lab manual for practicing techniques.

Chapter 1: Introduction to Digital Forensics – This chapter introduces digital forensics as a discipline, its principles, phases, and how it aligns with the cyber breach response lifecycle. Establishes what constitutes digital evidence, why evidence integrity matters, and how ethics and defensibility shape every investigation.

Chapter 2: Digital Forensics for Enterprises – This chapter explains how digital forensics fits into enterprise security, covering forensic readiness, evidence types in organizations, attack vectors, legal/compliance considerations, and reporting expectations. This chapter also covers beginning with hands-on work by setting up a practical forensic environment to support investigations.

Chapter 3: General Digital Forensics Techniques – This chapter builds the core evidence lifecycle: identification, acquisition/preservation, analysis, and reporting. It covers practical techniques such as log inspection, email and browser artifacts, file change evidence, SQLite analysis, and structured documentation to ensure repeatability.

Chapter 4: Development Environment for Digital Forensics – This chapter guides you in creating a safe, repeatable development and test environment for forensic work, so you can validate tools, automate tasks, and experiment without contaminating evidence. It also covers also covers setting up Python and PowerShell toolsets (including editors and virtual environments) for scripting and analysis.

Chapter 5: Linux Forensics – This chapter covers Linux-specific evidence collection and analysis across file systems, logs, auditing, integrity validation, partitions, deleted-file recovery, history artifacts, and configuration traces. It emphasizes practical techniques that apply across distributions in real enterprise server environments.

Chapter 6: Windows Forensics – This chapter focuses on collecting and analyzing forensic evidence from Windows endpoints and servers, e.g., event logs, system information, user accounts, Registry, file systems, metadata, and key built-in/third-party utilities. This chapter is designed to help you detect suspicious activity and gather defensible artifacts quickly.

Chapter 7: Networks Forensics – This chapter explains network evidence sources in enterprise and cloud contexts, and how to analyze both live and offline artifacts, such as PCAPs, flow logs, firewall/proxy logs, DNS/DHCP, and SIEM data. It includes practical Wireshark-based workflows and extends into voice forensics and IOC-driven investigations.

Chapter 8: Memory Forensics – This chapter introduces memory forensics and live response, covering techniques such as capturing volatile evidence (processes, connections, injected code, credentials, keys) and analyzing memory dumps using tools like Volatility and other utilities. It also connects memory evidence with reverse engineering concepts and IOC/IOA-based behavioral analysis.

Chapter 9: Malware Forensics – This chapter provides a practical malware-focused investigation workflow, covering common malware types and how to identify and analyze them using techniques such as static analysis, reverse engineering, process investigation, log analysis, and threat intelligence. It includes hands-on tooling such as REMnux, oletools, PeStudio, Ghidra, Sysinternals, and VirusTotal-based triage.

Chapter 10: Working with Digital Forensics Cases – This chapter shows how to handle investigations as a structured case by introducing concepts like triage, evidence organization, chain of custody, timeline creation, visualization, and reporting. It covers the use of tools such as Autopsy and the Sleuth Kit to ingest artifacts, correlate findings, and produce investigation outputs that support legal and enterprise needs.

Chapter 11: Mobile Forensics – This chapter covers why mobile devices are critical evidence sources and how to acquire and analyze artifacts from Android and iOS. You will learn mobile OS architectures, acquisition approaches, and hands-on workflows using tools such as Autopsy, Android Studio, Logcat, and MobSF, including analysis of APK/AAB structures and recovery challenges.

Chapter 12: Imaging Techniques – The chapter explains forensic imaging as the foundation of defensible evidence acquisition, including live vs. dead imaging and integrity verification using hashes. It provides practical disk and partition imaging workflows in Linux (dd and variants) and Windows (FTK Imager), plus best practices for preparing and organizing images for examination.

Chapter 13: Digital Forensics and Incident Response – This chapter introduces DFIR as the combined practice of investigating incidents while preserving evidence for legal, regulatory, and business use. It focuses strongly on accurate reporting, DFIR report structure, and generating reports from common tools (FTK Imager, Autopsy, and others) to support containment, recovery, and defensible conclusions.

Chapter 14: Cloud Forensics – This chapter builds the cloud fundamentals needed for investigations, including service/deployment models and shared responsibility, and explains why traditional forensic methods fall short in virtualized, distributed cloud environments. Includes hands-on, CLI-driven evidence collection recipes for AWS and Azure, including snapshotting volumes and automating acquisition via cloud CLIs.

Code Bundle and Coloured Images

Please follow the link to download the
Code Bundle and the ***Coloured Images*** of the book:

https://rebrand.ly/150621

The code bundle for the book is also hosted on GitHub at
https://github.com/bpbpublications/Digital-Forensics-Playbook.
In case there's an update to the code, it will be updated on the existing GitHub repository.

We have code bundles from our rich catalogue of books and videos available at **https://github.com/bpbpublications**. Check them out!

Errata

We take immense pride in our work at BPB Publications and follow best practices to ensure the accuracy of our content to provide an indulging reading experience to our subscribers. Our readers are our mirrors, and we use their inputs to reflect and improve upon human errors, if any, that may have occurred during the publishing processes involved. To let us maintain the quality and help us reach out to any readers who might be having difficulties due to any unforeseen errors, please write to us at: **errata@bpbonline.com**

Your support, suggestions and feedback are highly appreciated by the BPB Publications' Family.

Piracy

If you come across any illegal copies of our works in any form on the internet, we would be grateful if you would provide us with the location address or website name. Please contact us at **business@bpbonline.com** with a link to the material.

If you are interested in becoming an author

If there is a topic that you have expertise in, and you are interested in either writing or contributing to a book, please visit **www.bpbonline.com**. We have worked with thousands of developers and tech professionals, just like you, to help them share their insights with the global tech community. You can make a general application, apply for a specific hot topic that we are recruiting an author for, or submit your own idea.

Reviews

Please leave a review. Once you have read and used this book, why not leave a review on the site that you purchased it from? Potential readers can then see and use your unbiased opinion to make purchase decisions. We at BPB can understand what you think about our products, and our authors can see your feedback on their book. Thank you!

For more information about BPB, please visit **www.bpbonline.com**.

Join our Discord space

Join our Discord workspace for latest updates, offers, tech happenings around the world, new releases, and sessions with the authors:

https://discord.bpbonline.com

Table of Contents

Chapter 1
Introduction to Digital Forensics

Introduction

Digital forensics is a branch of forensic science that focuses on identifying, preserving, collecting, analyzing, and presenting digital evidence in a court of law. It involves the application of standard methods and procedures to recover, examine, and document digital evidence from various sources. Digital forensics tools and techniques are extensively used in solving conventional crime and cybercrime alike due to the prevalent digital trail everywhere in today's world.

Digital forensics and cyber forensics are synonymous and are used interchangeably. In this book, we will use digital forensics to refer to forensics for data stored electronically.

In this chapter, we will become acquainted with the basic concepts of digital forensics, its needs, and use cases.

Structure

In this chapter, we will cover the following topics:

- Pre-requisites to effectively use this book
- Understanding digital forensics
- Similarities with conventional forensics
- Principles of digital forensics
- Phases of digital forensics
- Cyber breach response lifecycle
- Use cases of digital forensics
- Understanding what constitutes digital evidence
- Role of digital forensics in cybercrime investigation
- Digital forensics tools and techniques
- Ethical considerations of digital forensics
- Job roles in digital forensics

Objectives

In this opening chapter, we will first understand what digital forensics is and what the needs of digital forensics are. After that, we will look at the similarities with conventional forensics to give a good analogy to the readers. This is followed by the main working principles of this field. We will then look at various phases involved in digital forensics and, as a practitioner, how you would use the cyber breach response cycle to work with cybersecurity incidents necessitating the need for digital forensics. There are various use cases of digital forensics in the context of crime solving and prevention. We will look at them next. This will be followed by getting an understanding of what constitutes digital evidence. We will then look at the role of digital forensics in cybercrime investigation. Toward the end of the chapter, we will briefly discuss digital forensics tools and techniques. Finally, we will end the chapter with a discussion about the ethical considerations of digital forensics. After finishing this chapter, you should have become familiar with the key concepts of cyber forensics.

Pre-requisites to effectively use this book

Digital forensics is a vast area in itself, even though it is considered a subset of cybersecurity. While this book covers the concepts of digital forensics from the basics, the readers of this book need to know about working with Windows and Linux operating systems. You should be able to download software and install on Windows and Linux operating systems. You should also be able to run commands on these operating systems by following the examples given in the respective recipes.

A fundamental knowledge of cybersecurity is a must to get into digital forensics. You should be able to visualize the various ways an attacker can compromise a system and how various security controls can be put in place to take care of such vulnerabilities.

Finally, since a lot of work around digital forensics requires experts to work with networking and protocols, a basic knowledge of these areas will go a long way to bring a successful career in digital forensics.

Understanding digital forensics

Let us first understand what digital forensics is. The **International Criminal Police Organization** (INTERPOL), which facilitates police cooperation and crime control across country borders, has a succinct definition of digital forensics. As per them:

Digital forensics is a branch of forensic science that focuses on identifying, acquiring, processing, analysing, and reporting on data stored electronically.

As per the preceding definition, it is evident that digital forensics deals with data stored electronically. This is also referred to as a digital asset. Examples of digital assets can differ greatly. For an organization, such digital assets can be their know-how, company secrets, competitor information, their copyrighted material, etc. For an individual, such digital assets may constitute their private information, including their financial details, their private photos, their medical records, and so on. There is a wide range of such digital assets that may be considered important for one, so if they are lost, leaked, or compromised, it may result in serious loss for the party.

Hence, when a crime happens, they can directly focus on stealing or compromising such digital assets. However, even in a conventional crime nowadays, there is always a digital trail. Hence, digital evidence plays a role in nearly every modern criminal case, making digital forensics an essential part of law enforcement investigations.

This type of evidence can come from various devices and platforms, including computers, smartphones, cloud storage, drones, maritime systems, and more.

The main function of digital forensics, hence includes the following:

Function	Details
Collecting evidence from the cybercrime scene	Collecting all the information from the scene of cybercrime Includes everything that can have digital information.
Preservation of the collected evidence	Preserving the collected data so that they cannot be tampered with.
Analysis by cyber forensics experts	Analyzing the information to understand how the cybercrime was committed and a possible motivation behind the crime. Finding out the evidence from the collected data.

Documentation and presentation	Creating documentation like **digital forensics and incident response** (**DFIR**). Presenting the documentation and evidence to a court of law for prosecution or use it for insurance claim purposes.

***Table 1.1**: Main functions of digital forensics*

In a nutshell, the primary objective of digital forensics is to extract data from these sources, analyze it, and transform it into actionable intelligence, which is then used to support legal proceedings. Throughout the process, forensic experts employ rigorous methods to guarantee that the evidence is admissible in court.

Interesting fact: **The term digital forensics was first used in the late 1980s and early 1990s to refer to crimes with a digital footprint, with the proliferation of digital assets that are connected to or accessible from the outside world.**

Similarities with conventional forensics

Experts use conventional forensics techniques to collect evidence and analyze them to solve complex crimes of all sorts. Such forensic techniques used by forensic experts may range from very old and conventional methods like fingerprint analysis to recent methods like DNA analysis.

Digital forensics is similar to forensics in the following aspects:

- Both deal with evidence left by criminals during the course of a criminal investigation.
- Both use scientific methods for identifying, preserving, analyzing, and presenting the evidence.
- Both follow a strict chain of custody approach while transferring evidence from one investigator to another.
- Both use similar concepts and terminologies.
- They have similar approaches to reporting and presenting the evidence in court.

Principles of digital forensics

There are a few key principles of digital forensics we need to be aware of. These principles help to guide the way specific digital forensics activities are carried out during the cybercrime investigation.

The following table lists these key principles of digital forensics:

Principle	Details
No change in the original data	This principle states there should not be any change in the original data that was collected from the scene of the crime. The integrity of the original data must be maintained to be used it as evidence in a court of law. Without this, the evidence may not be permissible in a court of law.
Competency in accessing original data	Original data must be accessed and worked with by experienced experts who are competent in handling such data. Even by the act of opening or printing a file, one can change something (for example, it is metadata), and hence it is not the same anymore with the originals.
Requirement for audit trail/chain of custody	Similar to traditional forensics, an audit trail is needed in digital forensics too. This audit trail can consist of a mix of a paper trail and digital trail. An audit trail is important to keep track of how the evidence is used, accessed, transferred internally and externally, and how new evidence is added. This is an important aspect of keeping the chain of custody intact and admissible in a court of law.
Preserving the evidence	One of the key principles of digital forensics deals with preserving the evidence. Extreme attention should be given to make sure the evidence is not tampered with intentionally or unintentionally. Write blocking device should be used without exception to access and acquire data from the electronic media so that the date remain unmodified.

***Table 1.2**: Principles of digital forensics*

Phases of digital forensics

Let us look at the phases of cyber forensics. There are 5 distinct phases of cyber forensics that enforce a structure to the entire cybercrime investigation. This specific way to handle the digital evidence is required so that it is permissible in a court of law and cannot be tampered with between identification and presentation.

The following table lists the phases of cyber forensics:

Phase	Details
Identification	This includes things like what evidence is present in the system, where the pieces of evidence are stored, and how they are stored. They can be stored in various personal computers, servers, mobile phones, networking devices, thumb drives, SSD drives, and so on.
Preservation	The evidence is preserved and secured after isolating them so that their physical and digital states are preserved. This is important for presenting it in a court of law, as any changes in the evidence may not hold it in the court of law.
Analysis	Understand the evidence which is found and reconstruct how cybercrime was committed using fragments of data found. The analysis step is a complex operation and can take multiple iterations. Moreover, analysis is done on a copy of the evidence while the original evidence is preserved.
Documentation	Document everything, including the data found, the correlation understood, and even what is not clear. Documentation is an important step to help the cyber forensic team recreate the scene of the cybercrime.
Presentation	The evidence found, and the result of analysis and documentation is presented in a form that anyone can understand. It can also be present in a court of law during prosecution.

***Table 1.3:** Phases of digital forensics*

Cyber breach response lifecycle

A cyber breach is an incident where an organization's (or an individual's) personal and confidential information is lost, exposed intentionally or unintentionally, or disclosed by threat actors without authorization.

Cyber breach response is an important area of cybersecurity that deals with formal incident response to minimize or prevent the damage from such security breaches or cyberattacks. Most enterprises have a formal team that works on the cyber breach response due to its criticality and compliance requirements from the government. It is a continuous process that consists of the following high-level steps:

Step	Details
Preparation	**Get ready**: Establish a clear plan, train your team, and test your strategy to handle any cyberattack.
Detection and analysis	**Spot the intruder**: Identify the incident, assess its scope, and gather evidence to figure out what happened.
Containment, eradication, and recovery	**Stop the spread**: Wall off the infected systems, eliminate the threat, and restore affected data and operations.
Post-incident activities	**Learn from the experience**: Analyze the incident, update your plan to prevent future breaches, and keep everyone informed.

***Table 1.4:** Cyber breach response lifecycle*

The following figure shows the cyber breach response lifecycle:

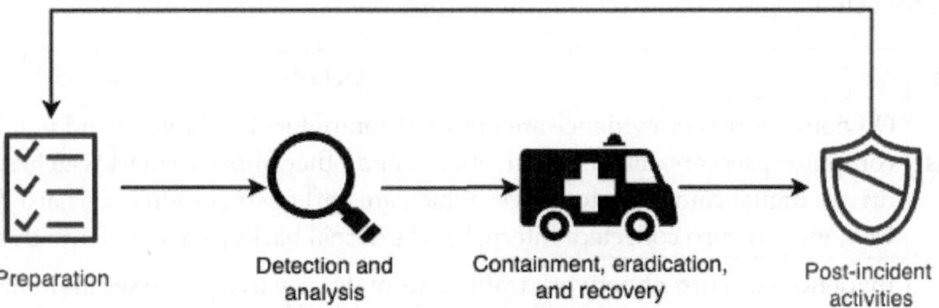

Figure 1.1: *Cyber breach response lifecycle*

It is evident from this figure that the cyber breach response lifecycle is an ever-in-progress cycle, with the learning from post-incident activities feeding back into the system to avoid future incidents.

Use cases of digital forensics

In today's digital era, when we cannot imagine our lives without all the applications and benefits that come with being digital, digital forensics is playing an ever-increasing role. There are a large number of use cases where digital forensics is useful.

Let us look at a few top use cases of digital forensics:

- Investigating cybercrimes, like cyberattacks, implanting malware, phishing, etc.
- Analyzing compromised systems (for example, servers, networking devices, endpoints, etc.) in incident response.
- Supporting criminal investigations connected with fraud, terrorism, human trafficking, espionage, etc.
- Collecting evidence for litigation or regulatory compliance.
- Identifying insider threats and data breaches.
- Examining network intrusions and unauthorized access.
- Verifying digital signatures and document authenticity.
- Investigating intellectual property theft.
- Ensuring evidence integrity for court proceedings.
- Recovering deleted or hidden data from critical systems for crime investigation or for business continuity.

If you look at the preceding list, a very interesting pattern emerges. While digital forensics is important for crime investigation and prevention, it is also used by organizations to make sure their business continues as usual in case of an incident. For example, the same techniques used by digital forensics experts to recover deleted and hidden data from seized media from the crime scene can also be used to recover deleted data from a critical computer system that has not been backed up. Accidents related to data deletion or wiping do happen, and digital forensics, in such cases, can act as a lifeline to ensure business continuity.

Hence, the strategic digital forensics processes in an enterprise help implement their **business continuity process** (**BCP**) goals as well, which ensures that the business continues to operate in adverse conditions too.

Understanding what constitutes digital evidence

As we discussed, digital forensics focuses on identifying, preserving, collecting, analyzing, and presenting digital evidence. When digital evidence is collected by the first responders, the group of people who are the first to come into action in case of a cybercrime, a wide range of possibilities are considered. When in doubt, everything is collected.

Let us understand what constitutes such digital evidence. The following table, at a high level, lists the types of evidence that can be collected:

Types of evidence	Details
Everything which is stored digitally	Obvious sources or evidence are personal computers like laptops and notebooks, desktop computers, servers, tablets, smartphones and other phones, smart watches, thumb drives, flash drives, digital cameras, etc. Drives which are part of such sources as hard drives, flash drives, CDs, etc., are also collected. Internal and external backups also fall into this category.
System information and status	Evidence like current network traffic information, active processes and their details, logged-on user details, open external connections, open files, etc., are also collected. Please note this is volatile information, and hence as much as possible should be collected as they will not be available afterwards. A dump of the memory can also be taken in case such information needs to be analyzed in depth later. Swap files that may contain a part of the memory can also invaluable information.
Sources that are critical in analysis	They include network web-based emails, temporary internet files, internet history, audio and video files, and equipment like routers, switches, hubs, etc. They may even include printers, firewalls, **intrusion detection systems (IDSs)**, **intrusion prevention systems (IPSs)**, and other such specialized devices.
Other sources	Malware and other such security threats found on the system are also part of the digital evidence. They are implicitly collected as part of the collection of digital storage media.

***Table 1.5:** Types of digital evidence*

The following figure shows a few examples of digital evidence that can be collected from the scene of a cybercrime:

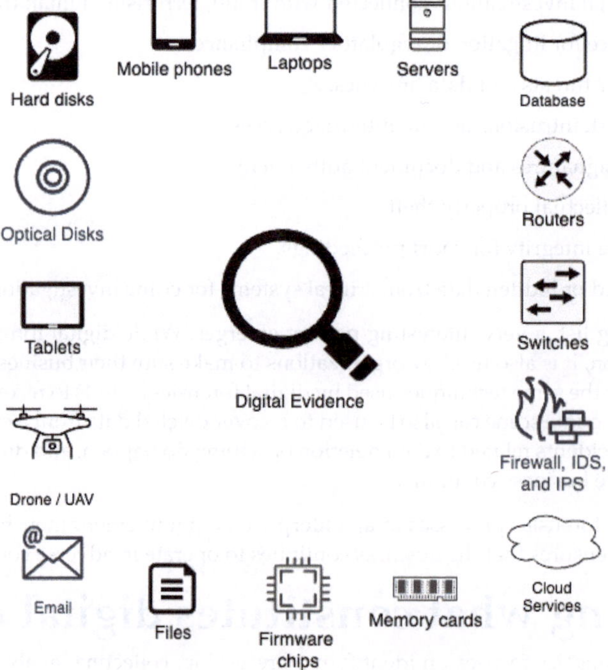

***Figure 1.2:** Examples of digital evidence*

Note: Due to the advent of new technologies, sources for digital evidence now include drones and unmanned aerial vehicles (UAVs) too, as applicable in the context of cybercrime or cyber incidents.

There is also a classification done on live vs. dead evidence:

- Live evidence is that which can be collected from running systems, for example, open applications, open files, memory, process status, etc. Such evidence is extremely important as they provide.
- Dead evidence includes those pieces of evidence that are components that mostly constitute secondary storage, for example, hard disks, memory cards, flash drives, CDs, internal firmware chips, etc.

Role of digital forensics in cybercrime investigation

Let us elaborate on a few of our use cases from a previous section to understand the role of digital forensics in cybercrime investigation. In this section, with the help of these use cases, we will look at how digital forensics is absolutely a must for cybercrime investigation.

Investigating cyber crimes

Digital forensics plays a pivotal role in investigating all sorts of cyber crimes due to their digital origins and digital trails.

In the case of cyberattacks, digital forensics is used to collect and analyze evidence. Such evidence can be collected even while such cyberattacks are in progress. If a cyberattack has already happened, digital forensics techniques can be used to collect information for further analysis.

If malware is found on the system, it can be traced back to one or more attack vectors resulting from weak security. Additionally, digital forensics techniques can be used to reverse engineer malware as well as run them in a sandbox to analyze their behavior, thereby uncovering how they work and which external systems they contact.

Phishing scams are becoming a nuisance to society as unsuspecting people are tricked by social engineering methods to provide their private and confidential information to the threat actor. They can also benefit significantly from digital forensics.

Moreover, in all these circumstances, digital forensics can also help us uncover the attacker's methods, the tools used, and their probable objectives.

Analyzing compromised systems in incident response

When an incident (for example, a cyberattack or intentional data exposure) happens, digital forensics techniques are used to analyze the compromised systems in terms of how they were breached by attackers and the extent of the damage done. Such compromised systems can be at the periphery / perimeter of the organization's networks as well as in the core network.

Using digital forensics, the nature of the attacks, the entry points (attack vectors), and the extent of the damage done can be assessed. The analysis can also help guide remediation efforts and prevent similar future incidents.

However, the system should be ready for forensic evidence collection beforehand; otherwise, such an assessment is not always possible.

Supporting criminal investigations

There are all sorts of unthinkable crimes being committed around the world that can benefit greatly from digital forensics techniques. Such crimes can be committed by individuals or by organized groups. A few such crimes include various types of fraud, various forms of terrorism and human trafficking, and even espionage by spies. Digital forensics can help law enforcement agencies build strong cases by linking suspects to criminal activity.

When such crimes surpass the boundaries of countries, digital forensics plays a pivotal role in getting insights about the threat actors and their intentions, facilitated by international organizations like INTERPOL.

Collecting evidence for litigation or regulatory compliance

When an organization detects an incident like cybercrime, it may be their obligation to collect as much digital forensics evidence as possible. This is important, as such evidence can be used for litigation purposes and even for regulatory compliance purposes. Governance and regulatory frameworks worldwide, like Europe's **General Data Protection Regulation** (**GDPR**) and the US's **Health Insurance Portability and Accountability Act** (**HIPAA**), may enforce such regulatory needs.

Moreover, it may also become the organization's safety net as they can prove that the incident happened even with all types of security controls in place. Such types of proof are important for insurance claim purposes in many cases.

All of these can help the organization demonstrate compliance during audits and investigations by regulatory bodies.

Identifying insider threats and data breaches

Many incidents happen due to insider threats, where an actor intentionally or unintentionally carries out a data breach. While it may not always be easy to pinpoint such incidents to the correct person, digital forensics techniques can use the digital trail left by the perpetrator to identify them. Evidence like system logs, email exchanges, and file access patterns can be used to understand if the incident happened due to an insider threat.

In unintentional data leaks, even if there may not have been an insider threat involved, digital forensics can still be used to identify the sources of such data leaks and the weaknesses in the system that caused them.

Examining network intrusions and unauthorized access

Digital forensics can help in the examination of network intrusions and unauthorized access by analyzing network traffic and logs. Most attacks on any organization happen using its networks as attack vectors. Hence, it is an obvious choice to emphasize analyzing how the security was bypassed, how the attacker gained access, and how lateral movement in the network happened.

Evidence like network traffic dumps, server access logs, firewall logs, data from event management systems, etc., can be used to track how attackers gained access to the systems and compromised them.

This can help tighten the security of weak and vulnerable network devices that are wide open to attacks once the attacker gains access to the network.

Verifying digital signatures and document authenticity

Digital signatures provide a failsafe mechanism for establishing the authenticity of documents and other artifacts. For example, a signed code can be used to establish its authenticity.

Digital signatures are also used in official documents as a seal of authenticity. In today's world, where unauthorized copying of anything electronic is widespread, digital signatures provide a way to prove the source of such documents. For example, in a legal dispute, digital forensics experts can use such tools and techniques to confirm whether an agreement signed digitally has been modified since it was signed.

In such instances, digital forensics experts may use digital forensics techniques like hashes, cryptographic algorithms, timestamps, and metadata to establish if the attacker altered the document.

Investigating intellectual property theft

Digital forensic experts can help track how intellectual property, such as patents, blueprints, or confidential designs, was stolen or leaked. For example, in cases of industrial espionage, forensic examination might reveal that a former employee emailed sensitive design files to a competitor or transferred proprietary information to an external device like a USB drive before leaving the company.

System administrators may be unable to create a timeline and collect enough evidence to provide a legal basis for taking action against such perpetrators. Digital forensics techniques can, in such instances, be used to provide enough evidence to take legal action. Findings from such investigations can also be used to add security controls to help prevent future IP thefts.

Ensuring evidence integrity for court proceedings

Digital evidence must be handled according to strict protocols to maintain its integrity and admissibility in court. This involves preserving the chain of custody, ensuring no data is altered during analysis, and documenting every step of the process. This chain must demonstrate who had access to the evidence and how it was handed over to the next person in the chain. For instance, in high-profile cybercrime cases, forensic experts present their findings in court, detailing how the evidence was collected and ensuring it has not been tampered with. This confirms the integrity and admissibility of the evidence in the court.

This is an important aspect of digital forensics as a whole, as tampered or altered evidence will most probably not be accepted by the court of law.

Recovering deleted or hidden data from critical systems

Forensic experts can use specialized tools to recover deleted files, hidden partitions, or encrypted data from devices crucial to ongoing investigations or business operations. For example, in a criminal case where a suspect tried to wipe their device, forensic recovery techniques could retrieve critical files showing evidence of illegal activity. Similarly, after a cyberattack, a company may use forensics to recover critical business data to ensure continuity of operations.

The same techniques can be used to restore business operations after a data loss due to system crashes or disasters like fire, flood, earthquakes, etc. Recovering business-critical files using such techniques can ensure that the business returns to normal without much disruption.

Digital forensics tools and techniques

While the approach and experience of digital forensics professionals are very important, their tools and techniques are equally important. For complex use cases, it is almost impossible to make progress without the use of a few of these tools.

Note: **While it is not possible to discuss all these tools and techniques in this book, we will be covering many of them, especially the ones available in open-source. We will also cover at least one or more tools from each of the digital forensics areas, for example, network forensics, mobile forensics, and so on.**

Digital forensics tools

Let us become familiar with a few of the well-known tools in no particular order of their popularity and classification, and the operating systems they are available for in the following table:

Digital forensics tool	Operating system	Purpose
OpenText EnCase	Windows, Linux, macOS	Forensic data recovery and analysis platform
Forensic Toolkit (FTK)	Platform independent–runs as a virtual machine	Comprehensive forensics tool for analyzing data from devices
Autopsy	Windows, Linux, macOS	Open-source digital forensics platform for investigating hard drives and devices
FTK Imager	Windows	Tool for creating forensic disk images and previewing data
Tableau	Windows	Forensic hardware and software tools for digital evidence acquisition
Splunk	Platform independent	Data analytics and security monitoring platform
Wireshark	Platform independent	Online and offline network protocol analyzer for inspecting traffic and identifying anomalies
IDA Pro	Platform independent	Disassembler used for reverse-engineering software and malware
Ghidra	Platform independent	Open-source reverse-engineering framework for analyzing software and malware
OllyDbg	Windows	Debugging tool for reverse-engineering and analyzing binaries
Magnet AXIOM	Windows	Forensic tool for recovering and analyzing digital evidence from computers, mobiles (Android, iOS) and cloud data
Cellebrite	Windows	Leading tool for mobile device data extraction and forensic analysis. Also used for data extraction and analysis from cloud services, as well as drones/UAVs
XRY	Windows	Mobile forensics tool for extracting data from smartphones and tablets
Oxygen Forensics	Windows	Mobile forensics tool for data extraction from mobile devices and cloud services
CaseWare IDEA	Windows	Data analysis tool for investigating financial data and identifying irregularities
X1 Social Discovery	Windows	Tool for collecting and analyzing social media and web-based data. Part of X1's suite of products
Relativity	Windows	E-discovery platform for managing electronic documents in legal cases
Nuix	Windows	Data processing tool and investigative analytics for handling large-scale document review and e-discovery
Logikcull	Windows, macOS	E-discovery and legal holds software for legal document review and management
Bro/Zeek	Linux, macOS	Network analysis tool for monitoring traffic and detecting intrusions
NetFlow Analyzer	Windows, Linux	Tools for analyzing network traffic flows and identifying anomalies

Table 1.6: *Popular digital forensics tools*

While many of the tools mentioned in the preceding table are platform independent, the majority of digital forensics tools use Windows as the operating system of their choice. However, they need high-end machines in a digital forensics lab setting.

Note: **The operating system information in the above table is as per the information available on their respective websites at the time of writing this book. Tools are supported on other operating systems all the time. Hence, this information may change. It is suggested to refer to their websites and user guides to get the latest operating system supported.**

Digital forensics techniques

Now, let us understand various digital forensics techniques that are used by experts. We will cover most of these techniques in detail in the subsequent chapters:

- **File recovery**: Techniques for recovering deleted or hidden files from storage in digital devices.
- **Data carving**: An advanced technique for extracting files from raw disk images or unallocated disk space.
- **Live data capture**: Capturing volatile data (RAM, processes, open files, swap space, temporary files, cache, etc.) from live systems.
- **Reverse engineering**: Analyzing malware code and payloads to understand their behavior, which may include converting machine code to a human-readable form or using specialized software to read machine code.
- **Network traffic analysis:** Inspecting network packets and logs for abnormal activity and traffic patterns, live or offline.
- **Deep packet inspection (DPI)**: Examining the contents of network packets beyond headers to identify malicious data.
- **Incident containment**: Strategies to isolate and neutralize ongoing cyber incidents.
- **Log analysis**: Reviewing system and network logs to identify suspicious or unauthorized activity, or identify anomalies.
- **Encryption bypass**: Cryptoanalysis and other automated techniques to break or bypass encryption to access secure data.
- **Chain of custody management**: Ensuring secure handling and documentation of digital evidence as it is passed from person to person.
- **Metadata analysis:** Examining file metadata (data about data) to assess document authenticity and forensic relevance.
- **Malware behavior analysis**: Tracking how malware interacts with a system, including network communications and file changes.
- **Digital signature verification**: Verifying the authenticity and integrity of digital signatures and documents with embedded digital signatures.
- **Packet capture**: Capturing real-time network traffic with tools like Wireshark for live or offline analysis.
- **Disk imaging**: Creating forensic disk images for investigation without altering original data.
- **Document review**: Managing and analyzing large sets of digital documents for litigation or compliance.
- **Traffic flow analysis**: Monitoring network traffic patterns to identify unauthorized activity or anomalies.

Ethical considerations of digital forensics

Digital forensics, like any branch of dealing with crimes, may sometimes blur the lines when it comes to ethics. While not intentional, due to human biases and even unintentional misses on the part of the stakeholders involved, the ethical part of digital considerations is put to the test. Let us look at a few ethical considerations of digital forensics:

- **Invasion of privacy**: One of the most important ethical considerations regarding digital forensics is the probable invasion of privacy. In a typical criminal case, a search warrant or other similar sort of approval from law enforcement may be required to search and seize personal property or property belonging to the organization. If there are sensitive data pieces of evidence collected during the search or during the raid, there are clear guidelines for who can access the evidence and how it can be accessed.

  However, such a process may not be followed in digital forensics. Digital forensics investigators may access sensitive data and often private data without obtaining proper consent from the owner of the data, and also without a warrant. This may be an invasion of privacy and may also violate an individual's right to privacy.

- **Accuracy and integrity of data**: How accurate the data collected from the scene of the crime is always the question. Accuracy may be affected if key pieces of evidence are not collected. It may also be affected if false data is planted by criminals or someone with a vested interest in derailing the investigations. Moreover, someone may intentionally plant the names of innocent individuals, which can lead to serious consequences for victims. Such acts may change the integrity of data.

  Such instances are not unheard of, and hence, the data must be analyzed by forensic experts who are trained on the legal and ethical aspects of cyber forensics. Another option is to have at least one or two such individuals as part of the cyber forensics team who very tightly control how and what information is shared among the team based on the information's level of sensitivity.

- **Discrimination and bias**: It has also been seen that there is a potential for discrimination and bias in the collection and analysis of digital evidence. Such discrimination and bias are more evident for racial and gender bias, and bias related to socioeconomic status. There are cases of people of color and women of color being subjected to more extensive digital evidence collection than other individuals. In general, such discrimination and bias may lead to a collection of more evidence or the collection of selective evidence, unknowingly favoring or discriminating against such individuals. Many ethnic minorities and immigrants may also be subject to such discrimination and bias, even though they may be law-abiding individuals who are trying to comply.

  This may lead to errors in the forensic analysis and, finally, a biased trial and prosecution. This may also lead to wrongful arrests and jail time for innocent individuals. Especially for a non-citizen, this may create a complex situation and may also lead to severe consequences for their career, job prospects, and personal relationships.

Interesting fact: **Humans, by nature, may be biased. But what about artificial intelligence (AI) based crime analysis systems? It turns out that bias is one of the key aspects of such AI systems that researchers worldwide are working on to take care of. Hence, law enforcement and cyber forensic experts are very cautious when using such AI systems to solve crimes. At best, they should be used at this point in time to get more insights into where to look for clues than for the final verdict. However, things are meant to improve in the future based on the current pace of development of such AI systems.**

Job roles in digital forensics

Digital forensics is a vast field with many opportunities for aspirants to move up the ladder as they gain experience. Moreover, due to its vastness, there is something for everyone, irrespective of their interests. Let us look at a few of the job roles in digital forensics:

Job role	Job level	Details
Digital forensics analyst	Entry to mid-level	Digital forensics analysts recover and analyze data from digital devices using tools like EnCase, FTK, and Autopsy. They follow strict forensic procedures to ensure evidence is admissible in court. Their work includes file recovery, data carving, and analysis of system logs.
First responders	Mid to senior level	They are the first to respond in case of an incident. They may be sent to the crime site to collect digital evidence. In case of a cyberattack, they may do the same remotely. They are the first set of experts whose expertise help the rest of the teams get as much digital evidence as possible for further analysis.
Forensic investigator	Entry to mid-level	Forensic investigators collect and preserve digital evidence from crime scenes using tools like write blockers and imaging software such as FTK Imager or Tableau. They ensure a proper chain of custody and often work on-site to capture live data. Their role involves meticulous documentation and safe transportation of digital media.
Incident response specialist	Mid to senior level	Incident response specialists use tools like Splunk, Wireshark, and FireEye to detect, analyze, and mitigate cybersecurity incidents. They focus on real-time analysis of compromised systems, investigating network traffic, and identifying attack vectors. Their role includes developing containment strategies and coordinating recovery efforts.
Malware analyst	Mid to senior level	Malware analysts reverse-engineer malicious software using tools like IDA Pro, Ghidra, and OllyDbg. They analyze malware behavior, disassemble code, and identify **indicators of compromise** (**IOCs**) to understand threats. Their work is critical in developing detection signatures and defensive measures.
Digital forensics consultant	Senior level	Forensic consultants advise organizations on digital forensics processes and incident handling, often using a broad range of tools such as Magnet AXIOM, Cellebrite, and X1 Social Discovery. They help design forensic readiness plans and provide expert testimony or analysis for legal cases. Their focus is on ensuring best practices and legal compliance.
Mobile forensics expert	Mid-level	Mobile device forensics experts use tools like Cellebrite, XRY, and Oxygen Forensics to recover data from smartphones and tablets. They specialize in bypassing encryption, extracting app data, and analyzing communication logs. They often work on recovering deleted messages, call logs, and location data for investigations.
Forensics auditor	Mid to senior level	Forensic auditors use tools like ACL Analytics, IDEA, and EnCase to trace financial transactions, audit digital records, and detect fraudulent activities. They analyze accounting data and transaction logs to uncover irregularities. Their work is critical in financial fraud investigations and regulatory compliance.
Network forensics specialist	Mid to senior level	Network forensics specialists analyze network traffic using tools like Wireshark, Zeek, and NetFlow analyzers. They focus on identifying malicious traffic, tracing unauthorized access, and reconstructing network events. Their techniques involve deep packet inspection and traffic flow analysis to detect intrusions.
Forensic software developer	Mid-level	Forensic software developers create specialized tools for forensic investigations using programming languages like Python, C++, PowerShell, shell scripts, Java, etc. They develop automation for data recovery, file analysis, and evidence reporting. Their tools often integrate with established forensic suites like Autopsy or custom-built solutions.
Cybercrime investigator	Mid to senior level	Cybercrime investigators use a variety of tools like Maltego, Splunk, and forensic suites such as **Forensic Toolkit** (**FTK**) to investigate online crimes such as hacking, fraud, or identity theft. They gather digital evidence, trace cybercriminal activities, and build cases for prosecution. Their techniques often involve tracking digital footprints and analyzing communication patterns.

***Table 1.7**: Job roles in digital forensics*

While digital forensics is considered a subset of cybersecurity, it is in itself a pretty vast area. You may start as an analyst and then slowly work on other, more complex areas like reverse engineering and malware analysis. Each of these areas has a lot of learning opportunities, and the work is never dull due to the diversity of the cases you may have to deal with. Hence, working in this area leads to a rewarding career and a lifelong learning opportunity.

Conclusion

In this chapter, we understood that digital forensics involves identifying, preserving, collecting, and analyzing digital evidence from various devices such as computers, smartphones, and cloud storage. This evidence is often used to support criminal investigations, cybersecurity incidents, or regulatory compliance.

We also discussed that forensic experts employ specialized tools throughout an investigation to ensure that the evidence remains intact and legally admissible in court. These tools help experts uncover digital trails left behind in crimes, from cyberattacks and fraud to human trafficking and espionage.

Later, we understood that digital forensics is not limited to law enforcement. It also plays a significant role in corporate investigations, where it helps identify insider threats, recover lost data, and verify document authenticity.

Hence, we can conclude that digital forensics is indispensable today, helping solve a wide range of criminal cases and protecting organizations from cyber threats. Advanced tools and techniques allow experts to recover critical evidence, ensuring that justice is served while maintaining ethical standards.

In the next chapter, we will look at various aspects of digital forensics in the context of enterprises.

Questions

1. What is digital forensics?
2. What types of digital devices can provide digital evidence?
3. What are the main functions of digital forensics?
4. How does digital forensics compare to conventional forensics?
5. Why is preserving the integrity of digital evidence important?
6. What is the chain of custody in digital forensics, and why is it important?
7. What are the five phases of digital forensics?
8. What are some everyday use cases of digital forensics?
9. How does digital forensics help investigate cybercrimes like phishing or malware attacks?
10. What role does digital forensics play in analyzing compromised systems?
11. How can digital forensics be used in cases of intellectual property theft?
12. What are some tools used by digital forensics experts?
13. What is the difference between live evidence and dead evidence in digital forensics?
14. How does digital forensics help in recovering deleted or hidden data?
15. What are some ethical considerations in digital forensics investigations?

Points to remember

- Digital forensics involves identifying, preserving, collecting, analyzing, and presenting digital evidence stored electronically, which is essential for modern criminal and cyber investigations.
- Digital evidence can be collected from various devices like computers, smartphones, cloud storage, drones, and more.

- The core functions include collecting, preserving, analyzing, and documenting digital evidence for legal or investigative purposes.
- Both digital and conventional forensics rely on scientific methods, follow strict chains of custody procedures, and aim to maintain the integrity of evidence.
- The five phases of digital forensics include identification, preservation, analysis, documentation, and presentation of evidence.
- The four key steps in the cyber breach response cycle include preparation, detection and analysis, containment and eradication, and post-incident activities.
- Common use cases of digital forensics include investigating cybercrimes, supporting fraud and terrorism investigations, collecting evidence for compliance, and analyzing network intrusions.
- Important ethical issues include the potential invasion of privacy, maintaining data accuracy, and avoiding bias or discrimination during forensic investigations.

Key terms

- **Digital forensics**: The branch of forensic science focused on identifying, preserving, collecting, analyzing, and presenting electronic data as evidence.
- **Digital evidence**: Information or data stored electronically that can be used as evidence in legal or investigative contexts.
- **Chain of custody**: The documented process concerned with how the evidence is handled and transferred, and tracks the handling of digital evidence from its collection to its presentation in court to ensure it remains untampered.
- **Forensic tools**: Software or hardware tools used to collect, recover, analyze, and preserve digital evidence (for example, EnCase, FTK, Wireshark).
- **File recovery**: A technique used in digital forensics to retrieve deleted or hidden data from storage devices.
- **Data carving**: A forensic technique used to extract files from unallocated disk space or raw disk images.
- **Live evidence**: Data collected from a system that is running, including processes, memory, and network connections.
- **Dead evidence**: Data stored in non-volatile storage such as hard drives, flash drives, or CDs, collected after a system is powered off.
- **Incident response**: The structured process of identifying, containing, eradicating, and recovering from cybersecurity incidents like cyberattacks.
- **Malware analysis**: The process of reverse-engineering malicious software (malware) to understand its functionality, logic, behavior, and potential threat.
- **Audit trail**: A record of all actions and interactions with digital evidence, used to track how it has been handled throughout an investigation.
- **Preservation**: The process of securing and maintaining the integrity of digital evidence so it can be used in legal proceedings.
- **Network traffic analysis**: The process of inspecting network data packets to identify malicious activity, unauthorized access, or cyberattacks.
- **Digital signature**: A cryptographic method used to verify the authenticity and integrity of digital documents or messages.

CHAPTER 2
Digital Forensics for Enterprises

Introduction

While digital forensics is important in most areas, it has become an important consideration for enterprises. Enterprises are prone to cyberattacks and data exposure. Hence, they need to be prepared to collect evidence in case of a cyberattack and mitigate the threat as soon as possible.

In this chapter, we will look at various aspects of digital forensics in the context of enterprises. We will also get started with hands-on recipes for fundamental concepts so that you can get experience with these concepts while you work on them.

Structure

In this chapter, we will cover the following topics:

- Digital forensics test and analysis environment
- Recipe 1: Getting started with simple digital forensics environment
- Role of digital forensics in enterprise
- Types of digital evidence collected in an enterprise
- Recipe 2: Simple fingerprinting techniques
- Forensic readiness
- Recipe 3: Logging login and logout activities
- Understanding various attack vectors for cyberattacks
- Estimating an organization's attack surface
- Legal framework for digital forensics
- Understanding compliance requirements for digital evidence collection
- Maintaining chain of custody and preserving evidence integrity
- Documenting findings and preparing reports for legal proceedings
- Forensic analysis of various operating systems

Objectives

Now that you know the basics of digital forensics, in this chapter, we will look at the digital forensics concepts for enterprises. We will start with understanding the role of digital forensics in the enterprise. We will then look at the types of evidence that can be collected when a cyberattack or any other security incident occurs and how we can make sure that the enterprise is ready for the evidence to be collected in such scenarios. We will then look at various attack vectors that threat actors use for cyberattacks on an enterprise, and how estimating the attack surface can help us manage it better. We will then look at the legal framework for digital forensics around the world. Finally, we will look at the aspects related to compliance, maintaining the chain of custody, documenting the findings, and preparing reports for legal proceedings. After finishing this chapter, you will become familiar with the fundamentals of how digital forensics fits into an enterprise setting.

Digital forensics test and analysis environment

Due to the diversity of the tools used in the digital forensics landscape, it is important to work with both Linux and Windows. While you can work with a digital forensics environment in just one operating system, it is suggested that you get a working knowledge of both Linux and Windows to have better coverage.

Two-thirds of all the computers worldwide are running Windows, and hence, there is a high probability that when a cyberattack or a similar incident happens, a Windows-based system is affected.

Moreover, many digital forensics tools are exclusively available for Windows or Linux. If you look at the section *Digital forensics tools and techniques* of the previous chapter, the table lists a mix of tools across the operating systems. Hence, to gain an in-depth knowledge of all these tools, working with both Linux and Windows is suggested.

Let us look at our test and analysis environment for working with the recipes in this book based on the type of operating systems you are using right now. This can be used not only for working with recipes in this book but also much beyond during a career in digital forensics:

Type of user	Additional suggested environment
If you are a Windows user	Windows + digital forensics tools Linux VMs running on Oracle VirtualBox + digital forensic tools
If you are a macOS user	Linux VMs running on Oracle VirtualBox + digital forensic tools Another Windows computer + digital forensic tools
If you are a Linux user	Linux + digital forensic tools Another Windows computer + digital forensic tools
Any other operating system user	Windows + digital forensics tools Linux VMs running on Oracle VirtualBox + digital forensic tools

***Table 2.1**: Digital forensics test and analysis environment options*

This means that you may have to invest in another computer apart from what you have if you are using either Linux or macOS exclusively.

Note: **VirtualBox can also run the Windows operating system inside macOS or Linux. However, in order to do so, you will have to buy a Windows license.**

Recipe 1: Getting started with simple digital forensics environment

In this recipe, we will look at getting started with a Linux environment to work on other recipes. We assume that you know how to install a Linux virtual machine on a hypervisor like VirtualBox.

Note: **In case you need to get up and running with VirtualBox and install VMs quickly, refer to the Oracle VirtualBox user guide available at https://www.virtualbox.org/wiki/Documentation. It has excellent details about installing VirtualBox on your preferred operating system and creating virtual machines.**

In this recipe, we will install Kali Linux. Kali Linux is a Debian-based distribution that is preferred for digital forensics work. It is preferred mainly due to the reinstalled tools for digital forensics and cybersecurity that come along with it.

Kali Linux has come up with a distribution called Kali Purple that has additional tools for defense security, apart from the regular offensive security tools in the existing distributions. Some of these tools are important for cyber forensic work, and hence, this can be considered as a viable distribution to start with. You can still continue with any distribution and then install the tools as you go. However, Kali Purple provides a simple way to start with pre-packaged defensive security tools.

Note:

- **Compatibility: Kali Linux**
- **License considerations: Free software used**

Recipe

Let us install Kali Linux on Oracle VirtualBox. Refer to the following steps to complete this recipe:

1. First, let us download Kali Linux from its website **https://www.kali.org/get-kali**. As mentioned before, you could use Kali Linux or Kali Purple. Moreover, you can plan to install it using an ISO-based installer, or you can download virtual machine images for VirtualBox, VMware, and Microsoft Hyper-V. In this book, we will use VirtualBox for all our recipes.
2. Create the VM by following the following steps:
    a. Click on the **New** button or **Machine** to start creating a new VM. Fill in all the information required in the **Virtual machine Name and Operating System** screen, as shown in the following figure:

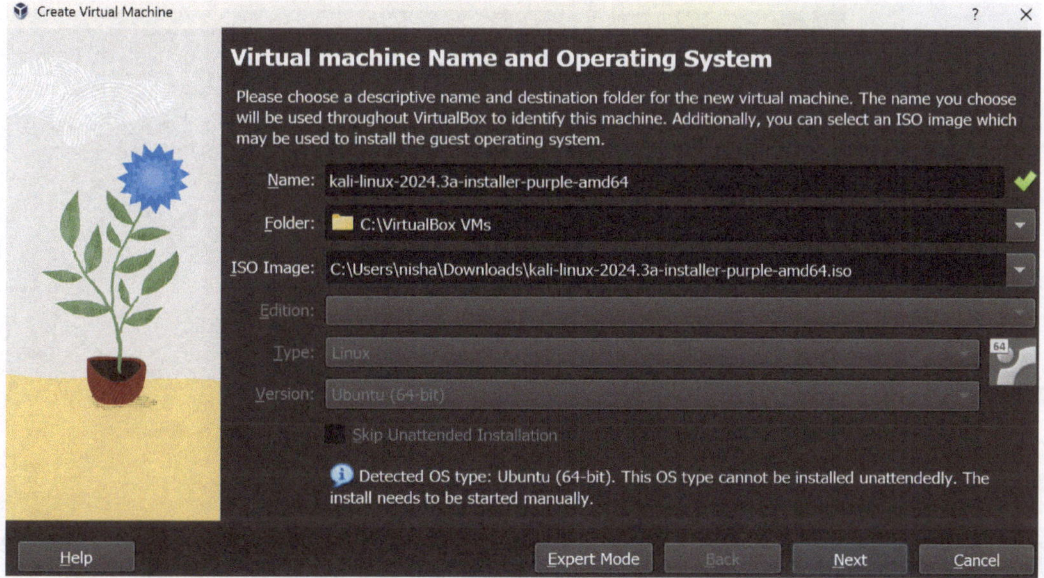

***Figure 2.1**: Installing Kali Linux, Virtual machine Name and Operating System screen*

    b. In the next screen, provide the memory and processor details. For most digital forensics work, 8 GB RAM and 4 vCPUs should be enough. You may be able to start with less than this resource, but be ready to increase them later if required:

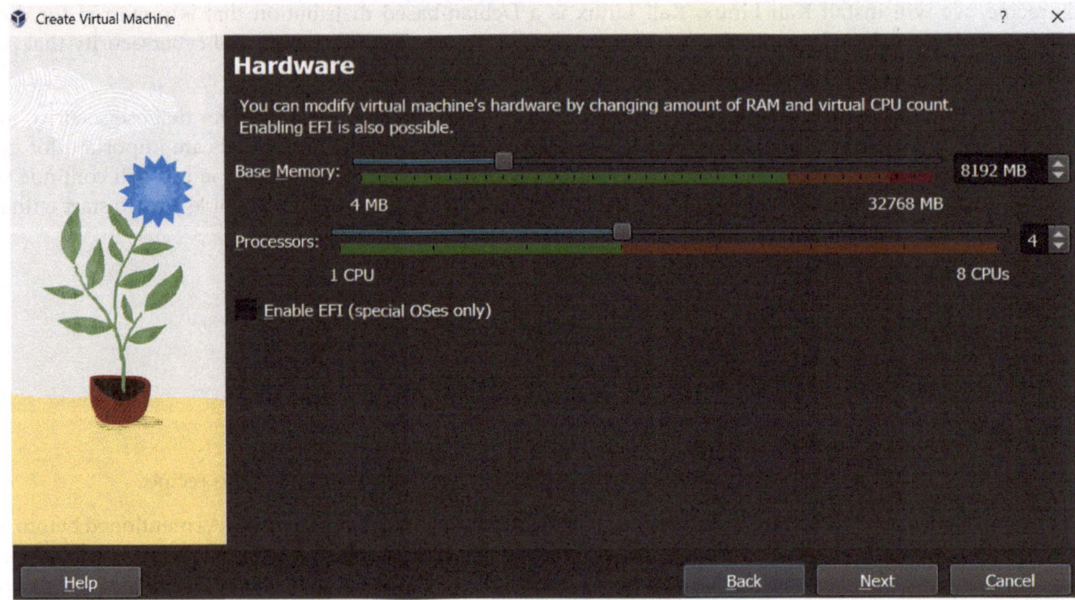

Figure 2.2: Installing Kali Linux, Hardware screen

c. In the next screen, **Virtual Hard disk**, configure the hard disk allocation for this virtual machine. 50 GB or above can be used as a starting size, as shown in the following figure:

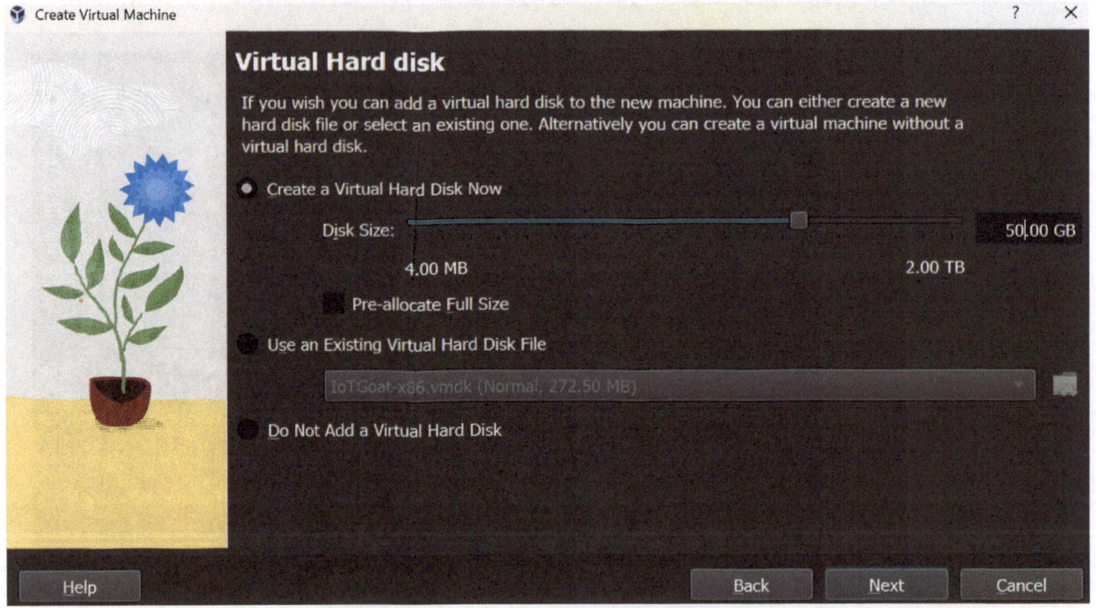

Figure 2.3: Installing Kali Linux – Virtual Hard disk screen

d. Confirm that you have entered all the details properly in the **Summary** screen after you click **Next**, and then click **Finish** to finish creating the VM.

3. Once the VM is created, you need to power on the VM and then follow the instructions to install the Kali Linux operating system. This includes the creation of the user, selecting what to install, the hard disk the VM is going to use, and so on.

   If you are using Kali Purple as part of install, you will get a window with the options shown as follows. Make sure to go ahead with the default options already selected to get all the defensive security tools also installed:

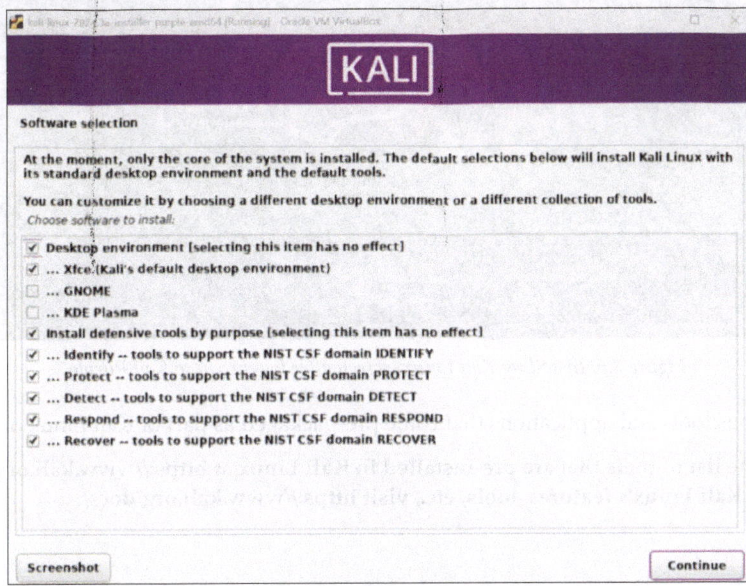

Figure 2.4: *Installing Kali Linux, Software selection screen*

4. Once the installation is complete, login to Kali Linux with the user and password you configured during the installation.

Your first screen after login may look like the following if you installed Kali Linux:

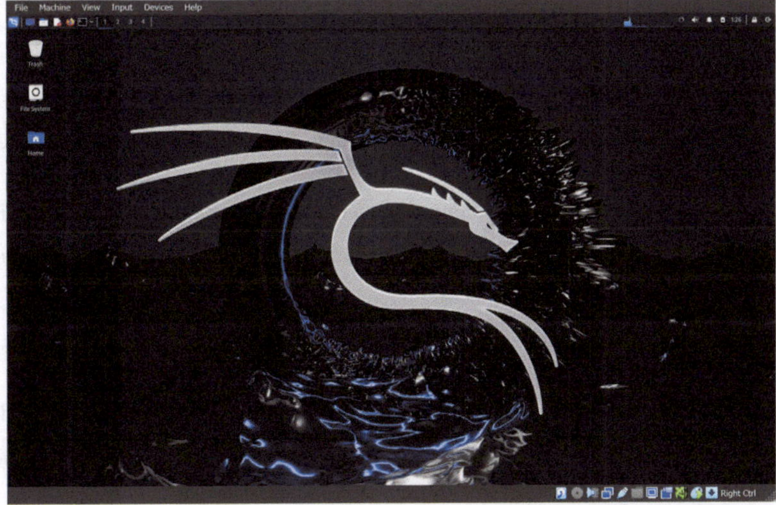

Figure 2.5: *Installing Kali Linux, screen after logging in to Kali Linux*

Your first screen after login may look like the following if you installed Kali Purple:

Figure 2.6: *Installing Kali Linux, screen after logging in to Kali Purple*

You can explore various tools and applications that come pre-packaged as part of Kali Linux or Kali Purple.

Note: **You can find the list of tools that are pre-installed in Kali Linux at https://www.kali.org/tools/. If you want to know more about Kali Linux's features, tools, etc., visit https://www.kali.org/docs/.**

Activity

Attempt the following activities before the next recipe:

- In Kali Linux, can you determine which digital forensic tools are installed by looking at its application menu?
- Are there any that you can relate to with the concepts covered in *Chapter 1, Introduction to Digital Forensics*?
- Look at Kali Linux documentation to understand the list of digital forensics tools available and their functionalities.

Role of digital forensics in the enterprise

Digital forensics plays an important role in enterprises of any size. Here are the key roles of digital forensics in any enterprise:

- Investigate and respond to security incidents such as breaches, data theft, or insider threats.
- Preserve and analyze digital evidence to support legal, regulatory, or HR investigations.
- Provide insights into the root cause of incidents, helping to enhance security measures.
- Ensure compliance with industry standards and regulatory requirements by maintaining secure and traceable evidence handling.
- Support threat intelligence and proactive defense measures by learning from past incidents.

Let us understand various facts about digital forensics' role in the enterprise and how it varies based on the size, type of work, and client relationships.

Changes based on enterprise size

The following table lists the changes in the role of digital forensics based on the enterprise size:

Enterprise size	Change in the role of digital forensics
Large enterprises	Have dedicated forensics teams and advanced tools for comprehensive, ongoing investigations and compliance management.
Small and medium enterprises (SMEs)	Often rely on external forensics services due to limited in-house resources; focus may be on incident response rather than proactive investigations.
Startups/small businesses	Limited forensic capabilities, may rely heavily on external consultants, and often prioritize essential incident response due to budget constraints.

Table 2.2: *Changes in the role of digital forensics based on enterprise size*

Changes based on the type of work

The following table lists the changes in the role of digital forensics based on the type of work these enterprises do:

Type of work enterprise do	Change in the role of digital forensics
Highly regulated industries (e.g., finance, healthcare)	High demand for rigorous forensic processes to comply with data protection laws (e.g., HIPAA, GDPR) and industry standards.
Technology and SaaS companies	Strong emphasis on forensic readiness, especially around protecting intellectual property and securing customer data.
Manufacturing/Retail	Focus may be more on incident response for ransomware or supply chain attacks, with forensics supporting business continuity.

Table 2.3: *Changes in the role of digital forensics based on the type of work*

Changes based on client and partner relationships

The following table lists the changes in the role of digital forensics based on the client and partner relationships:

Client and partner relationship	Change in the role of digital forensics
B2B enterprises with MNCs or government clients	Require more robust forensic processes, as these clients often have strict compliance, security, and reporting requirements.
Enterprises handling sensitive client data (e.g., law firms, healthcare providers)	Need rigorous digital forensics practices to protect client confidentiality and meet regulatory mandates.
SMEs working with large clients	May need to bolster forensic capabilities to meet client-mandated security and incident response standards, even if internal resources are limited.

Table 2.4: *Changes in the role of digital forensics based on client and partner relationship*

Types of digital evidence collected in an enterprise

As we have been discussing, collecting digital evidence is important to analyze any cyberattack or incident in an enterprise. Such evidence may span across network devices, servers, endpoints, and even cloud infrastructure.

Let us look at the types of digital evidence that can be collected in an enterprise in case of a cyberattack or incident by first responders and other digital forensics experts. We will also look at most of the details in the subsequent chapters.

System logs

System logs are probably one of the first evidence to be collected in case of an incident. They include:

Digital evidence	Details
Operating system logs	For Windows, logs from Windows Event Viewer, and for Linux, logs under **`/var/log`** can be collected. They provide a lot of details about login attempts, application activities, installation activities, system updates, etc.
Firewall logs	Firewall logs can be collected from all the various firewalls in use in the enterprise. They provide network traffic information and security events like port scanning, suspicious connection attempts, and blocked traffic.
IDS/IPS log	Specialized security components like **intrusion detection system (IDS)/intrusion prevention system (IPS)** provide extra layers of security in enterprise. Their logs may record suspicious network activity, attempted exploits, and successful or failed attacks.
Antivirus and endpoint detection logs	The logs from **endpoint detection and response (EDR)** systems and antivirus may give us a lot of insights in the form of malware detections, quarantined files, and remediation actions performed by endpoint protection software.

Table 2.5: *Digital evidence – system logs*

Network traffic logs, dumps, and other artifacts

Since most attacks happen through networks, collecting network traffic and other related artifacts is important. Such evidence includes:

Digital evidence	Details
Packet capture	Raw network traffic data captured during or after the attack, showing packets exchanged between devices on the network. This can reveal IOCs like malware communication, exfiltration attempts, or attack vectors.
Network flow logs	Records of metadata about the network traffic (e.g., source/destination IP addresses, ports, and data volumes) help understand patterns of data flow and identify anomalous activity. These can be captured at various locations and devices, especially at gateways, routers, reverse proxies, etc.
Proxy logs	Capture details about internet activity in an enterprise, showing websites accessed, file downloads, or possible exfiltration points. These can be captured in network proxies, reverse proxies, etc.

Table 2.6: *Digital evidence, traffic logs, dumps, and other artifacts*

Disk and file artifacts

Digital forensics experts use the evidence collected around disk and file artifacts to understand how the threat actor compromised the security, where their payload was transferred, the malware was installed, **advanced persistent threat** (**APT**) software was installed, etc. They include:

Digital evidence	Details
Disk images	Full or partial images of hard drives are collected for deep forensic analysis. These images contain deleted files, hidden partitions, and remnants of malware or artifacts from executed programs.

Memory dumps	Capturing the contents of volatile memory (RAM) at the time of the incident provides insight into running processes, active network connections, and any in-memory malware or rootkits.
File system metadata	Information about file creation, modification, and access times (MAC times) helps create timelines for the attack.
Registry entries	Windows Registry contains information about system configurations, installed software, and recently accessed files, which may provide clues about persistence mechanisms or malware installation.
Temporary files	Cache, cookies, and other temporary files can reveal browser activity, downloaded files, and remnants of malicious activity.

***Table 2.7**: Digital evidence, disk and file artifacts*

Application logs

Logs at the application layer can be the last in line, which means they help us analyze what happened during the incident, including the sequence of events. This, however, works only if the applications generate sufficient logs to give us such insights. Such logs include:

Digital evidence	Details
Web server logs	Logs from web servers (e.g., Apache, NGINX, IIS) record incoming requests, failed login attempts, **structured query language** (**SQL**) injections, and other attack attempts targeting web applications.
Database logs	Logs from web servers (e.g., Apache, NGINX, IIS) record incoming requests, failed login attempts, SQL injections, and other attack attempts targeting web applications.
Email server logs	These logs provide information about email communications, possible phishing attempts, or compromised email accounts.
Application-specific logs	Custom or off-the-shelf application logs that track user activity, transaction data, or system errors within the application.
Audit logs	Audit logs are helpful in understanding what was intentionally or unintentionally changed during the incident. They can also be used to create a timeline of the incident.

***Table 2.8**: Digital evidence, application logs*

User and authentication logs and data

In case of an intrusion, it is quite possible that a user's account was compromised, and the perpetrator came inside the system using such a compromised account. User and authentication logs and data can help us identify such instances. They include the following:

Digital evidence	Details
Active Directory (**AD**) logs	In an enterprise with Windows-based infrastructure, AD logs contain records of user authentication attempts, group policy changes, and access to shared resources.
VPN logs	These logs capture remote access connections, including the source IP addresses and login times, which may reveal unauthorized or malicious access.
Authentication logs	Information about user login attempts, successful logins, or failed **multi-factor authentication** (**MFA**) can indicate compromised accounts or brute force attempts.

***Table 2.9**: Digital evidence, user and authentication logs and data*

Cloud platform logs

If one or more systems are on the cloud, cloud logs must be collected. This is becoming more important as more and more applications are moving to the cloud. They include:

Digital evidence	Details
Cloud managed service logs	Logs from cloud providers (e.g., AWS CloudTrail, Azure Monitor) that track activities like API calls, virtual machine launches, storage access, and user authentication in the cloud.
Cloud security logs	These logs may come from security services like AWS GuardDuty or Azure Sentinel and can detect anomalous behavior or malicious activities within cloud environments.
Cloud resource metadata	Information about the virtual machines, storage, and network settings within the cloud environment that may have been tampered with during the attack.

***Table 2.10**: Digital evidence, cloud platform logs*

Endpoint logs and artifacts

Endpoints are devices that users use. They are often the first to be attacked by the attackers. Logs that can be collected from the endpoints include:

Digital evidence	Details
Mobile device logs and artifacts	On mobile devices, forensic experts may collect application logs, call history, SMS/MMS messages, and GPS location data to identify potential breaches through mobile platforms.
Workstation logs	Logs and data from endpoints such as workstations or laptops, including browser history, downloaded files, and recently opened documents, help trace user activity related to the incident.
Remote desktop session logs	These logs track remote sessions, including access times and activities performed on a remote system, and can be collected from the target machine, i.e., the machine to which the remote desktop was done.

***Table 2.11**: Digital evidence, endpoint logs and artifacts*

Malware dumps and artifacts

When a system gets infected with malware, one of the ways to know more about the malware, its behavior, and if it is based on existing malware is to dump the malware in memory. Apart from that, all the malware files found in the system can be collected. Such files include the following:

Digital evidence	Details
Executable files	Any malicious executables, scripts, or code fragments identified during the investigation may be isolated for further malware analysis (reverse engineering).
Email attachments and links	Phishing emails and malicious attachments, as well as any malware downloaded through compromised links, may provide insight into the initial infection vector.
Payload left by malware	These include anything left by the attacker while installing malware, for example, executable packages and other installers, scripts, configuration files, etc.

***Table 2.12**: Digital evidence, malware dumps, and artifacts*

Evidence from physical devices

When attackers use USB devices to gain access to the system or any other types of hardware are compromised, evidence from these devices should be collected. Irrespective of the suspicion, it is always good to collect logs from all the devices in the network, as they may contain valuable information that one may not consider useful at the time of collection. Such evidence includes:

Digital evidence	Details
USB device logs	Many operating systems track the use of USB storage devices. Logs related to USB devices can indicate the use of external drives for data theft or introduction of malware.
Hardware forensics	Forensic experts may examine hardware such as routers, switches, or even physical access control systems (RFID, keycards) for tampering or abnormal access patterns. Data from such systems and other biometric-based access control systems can be collected in such instances
Security camera footage	In case of physical compromise of a facility, security camera footage can also be collected. These when combined with other evidence can create a strong case against the perpetrator.

***Table 2.13**: Digital evidence, evidence from the use of other physical systems*

Metadata and artifacts from collaboration tools

Due to the proliferation of collaboration tools teams use, they are also being used as possible attack vectors by threat actors. Some of the evidence that can be collected can be seen in the following figure:

Digital evidence	Details
Chat logs	Messages from tools like Slack, Microsoft Teams, WhatsApp, or other collaboration platforms can provide evidence of social engineering, insider threats, or unauthorized access.
Social media platforms	Messages, posts and artifacts from social media platforms like Meta, Telegram, Instagram can also provide evidence of the suspicious activities of the threat actor.
File sharing logs	Logs from file sharing services (e.g., OneDrive, Google Drive, Dropbox) can show file uploads/downloads, file sharing links, and potential data exfiltration attempts.

***Table 2.14**: Digital evidence, metadata and artifacts from collaboration tools*

Backup and snapshots

If there are automatic backups and snapshots are configured, chances are they may also end up taking backups of the malicious content on the system. Such backups and snapshots can provide a lot of valuable information, as digital forensic professionals can compare them to find out when the incident happened or when the cyberattack was done. Such evidence includes:

Digital evidence	Details
Backup files	Backups of critical systems, databases, or virtual machines may be examined to identify changes made by attackers or to retrieve files that were deleted or altered.
Backup logs	Backlog logs with the list of files backed up can provide valuable information, as this can be compared with older logs to understand the files that were changed or added.
Virtual machine snapshots	These snapshots may capture system states before or during an attack, useful for forensic analysis or system restoration.

***Table 2.15**: Digital evidence, backup and snapshots*

Recipe 2: Simple fingerprinting techniques

In this recipe, we will use various checksum tools to understand how simple fingerprinting techniques can be implemented. While it may look like a very simple recipe, this same technique is used by sophisticated audit, antivirus, and other security software to understand if the file has changed intentionally or unintentionally.

A checksum is a value generated from a set of data to verify its integrity. It is calculated using algorithms such as MD5, SHA-256, or CRC32, which process the input data and produce a fixed-size hash value. The checksum ensures that the data is not altered during storage or transmission. Even a small change in the data results in a drastically different checksum, making it an effective way to detect errors or tampering.

Interesting fact: **The most important aspect of checksum is that even a small change in the data results in a drastically different checksum, making it an effective way to detect errors or tampering. Hence, a file's checksum before and after download can be compared using various checksum algorithms available for most operating systems. If they match, the file is unaltered. If not, then the file is altered.**

Common uses of checksums include:

- **File verification**: Used to ensure that the files downloaded from the Internet or shared by someone are intact (e.g., comparing a file's SHA-256 checksum against the one provided by the source).
- **Data integrity checks in networks**: Used to verify that the packets sent over a network (e.g., TCP/IP uses checksums to detect corrupted packets) are not corrupted or not changed on the way.
- **Integrity checks in database and storage systems**: Can be used to ensure that stored data remains consistent and uncorrupted. Such data may include database files, backups, snapshots, archived data, etc.

Note:

- **Compatibility: Linux**
- **License considerations: Free software used**

Recipe

Let us understand how the checksum is used to verify file integrity checks by a simple example.

Refer to the following steps to complete this recipe:

1. In your home directory, create a directory called **work** or any other directory of your choice. Create a file with a simple string:

   ```
   mkdir work
   cd work
   echo "This is a line of confidential text!" > secret.txt
   ```

   Check the content of the file by using **cat** command:

   ```
   cat secret.txt
   ```

   The file you just now created will be printed.

2. Now, we need to find out the file's checksum so that we can use it to confirm any intentional or unintentional changes in the file. For this, first, we will create a checksum of the file.

   ```
   [nishant@forensics Work]$ sha1sum secret.txt
   c9b453e4a88fc6ac813fc1f7aa7391234a5f99c2  secret.txt
   ```

sha1sum tool calculates and prints the checksum of the file on the screen. If you want to save this for later use, you can use the > redirection operator.

```
sha1sum secret.txt > checksum_secret.txt
```

3. Now, let us make a small change in the file. Open the file in your favorite editor, e.g., vi, nano, or any other text editor, and add a space at the end of the line. If you print the file again on the console, you will not find any perceivable differences, but this new file is no longer the same as the original file. We can verify this by checking the checksum of the modified file:

```
sha1sum secret.txt > checksum_changed_secret.txt
```

Let us print both files to see if there are changes in the checksum:

```
[nishant@forensics Work]$ cat checksum_secret.txt checksum_changed_secret.txt
c9b453e4a88fc6ac813fc1f7aa7391234a5f99c2  secret.txt
a84aa16770a449f9d5d34f357baa8c24df0af12e  secret.txt
```

The first checksum value is of the original file, and the second one is of the modified file. You can see that a trivial change, i.e., adding an extra space, led to a very large change in the checksum value. Hence, this technique can be used to determine if the files are modified with high confidence.

Activity

Attempt the following activities before the next recipe:

- In this example, we used sha1sum to calculate the checksum for a text file. *Can a checksum be applied to all the other file types?* Verify it by trying on other file types.
- Try out other checksum tools and verify the size of the checksum they create. A few of the checksum tools you can try are md5sum, sha256sum, and sha512sum.

Forensic readiness

One of the key issues the first responders and cyber forensics experts encounter in most cyberattacks and incidents where confidential data is lost or exposed is the unavailability of enough evidence to collect.

We understand by now that every piece of evidence is vital for understanding how the malicious actors conducted the attack and what attack vectors were used. That is the reason it is important to make one enterprise ready for cyber forensics evidence collection.

Let us look at some key ways to prepare any enterprise for cyber forensics evidence collection in the following table:

Way to ensure readiness	Details
Log everything	Log everything important, using access logs, security logs, event logs, audit logs, etc. These logs are important to understand everything that is happening in the enterprise.
Enable audit logging	Enable audit logs to catch changes in critical files and even log access to confidential files. Audit logs can also be used to create Audit Trails that can be used to trace everything that has been done with critical digital assets.
Enable logs in specialized security components	All the important security equipment and components should produce logs, e.g., firewalls, IDSs, and IPSs. These components can see everything passing through the network. Hence, they can log a lot more critical things that may not be logged by other systems, e.g., general-purpose servers.

Way to ensure readiness	Details
Backup, backup, and backup…	Backup device configurations on a periodic basis. Also, backup important system configuration files. This gives a way to quickly go back to a good configuration in case of an intentional or unintentional change.
Create network baselines	Create network baselines on regular basis against which the changes can be compared. If there are unauthorized changes, then the baseline can be used to revert the changes.
Use SIEM	Use **security information and event management** (**SIEM**) solutions to send all the logs in near real time to a central location that can then be analyzed and alerts can be generated.
Archive logs	Periodically archive logs and other potential evidence to a centralized system. Historical logs are essential when one has to look into the past in case of an incident.

Table 2.16: *Ways to ensure forensic readiness*

Recipe 3: Logging login and logout activities

In this recipe, we will use various commands to check the user activities on the system. While collecting digital evidence, the output of these commands should also be collected, especially if it is a live system. Collecting such logs gives us a good view of users who have logged in the system and their duration of stay inside the system.

Linux uses various logs for logging user activities:

Log file	Purpose
`/var/log/wtmp`	Logs of last login sessions
`/var/log/utmp`	Logs of the current login sessions
`/var/log/btmp`	Logs of the bad login attempts
`/var/log/auth.log`	Logs all the login and logout activity
`/var/log/secure`	Logs for various security events with lot more details than other logs
`/var/log/audit/audit.log`	Logs for system and file audit
`/var/log/wtmp`	Logs of last login sessions

Table 2.17: *Important logs in Linux for user activities*

Many of these logs are in binary format and are not human-readable. Depending on the system, not all the logs mentioned in the preceding table may be available. If available, all these logs should be collected while collecting digital evidence. Using these logs can help us establish the timeline of events that happened on the system leading to an incident or a cyberattack.

Note:

- **Compatibility: Linux**
- **License considerations: Free software used**

Recipe

Let us first look at the **`last`** command on Linux that provides valuable information about the user activity. If you run into permissions issues while running any of the following commands, make sure you run them as **`root`** or any other privileged user:

Command	Purpose
`last`	Prints a list of recently logged in users.
`last <username>` e.g., `last nishant`	Prints login history of a particular user.
`last -f /var/log/btmp` `lastb`	Prints bad login attempts on the server.

Table 2.18: Important last commands

Now, let us look at the content of other log files. You can text the editor like **vi**, **cat** or **tail** command to view the content of these log files:

```
cat /var/log/secure | more
tail /var/log/secure
tail /var/log/auth.log
tail /var/log/audit/audit.log
```

Activity

Attempt the following activities before the next recipe:

- Are there any other logs than those we discussed that should be collected? What about the differences in the logs across various Linux distributions?
- If you bring up a system using a forensic image, will these commands still give you the same result as when the system was live?
- What do **tty** and **pts/0** mean in the output of the **last** command?

Understanding various attack vectors for cyberattacks

Attack vector is a way for attackers to enter a system or network – it can be a specific method, scenario, or path. Malicious actors use such attack vectors to attack a system and plant malicious code to compromise a system for later exploitation. Such systems can be used to steal information over time and launch **distributed denial-of-service (DDoS)** attacks. Minimizing the number of attack vectors is a key component in improving the security posture.

Note: We can think of attack vectors as weaknesses or entry points through which an attacker can launch their assault.

The following table lists a few of the common attack vectors:

Attack vector	Details
Malware	Malicious software like viruses, worms, ransomware, etc., can infect devices through infected attachments, downloads, or drive-by downloads.
Phishing	Deceptive emails, messages, or websites designed to trick users into revealing sensitive information or clicking malicious links.
Social engineering	Techniques used to manipulate individuals into giving up confidential information or taking actions that compromise security.
Unpatched vulnerabilities	Software flaws or bugs that have not been addressed by security updates, allowing attackers to exploit them.

Attack vector	Details
Weak passwords	Easy-to-guess passwords or reused passwords across multiple accounts are easily compromised and used for unauthorized access.
Misconfigured systems	Improperly configured network devices, servers, or applications can create vulnerabilities for attackers to exploit.
Lack of encryption	No encryption or weak encryption that are considered obsolete.
No 2FA or MFA	No **2-factor authentication (2FA)** or **multi-factor authentication (MFA)** for remote login, and directly accessing the network with password only.
Internal threats	Threats from internal individuals who intentionally harm the network's security.

Table 2.19: *Common attack vectors*

Estimating an organization's attack surface

Attack surface is the sum of all the attack vectors leading to the system that signifies weakness or vulnerability, and threat actors can exploit that. There is a direct correlation between the attack vector and the attack surface. The more the number of attack vectors, the larger the attack surface. The attack surface also directly correlates to types of technologies, types of devices, how employees connect from remote locations, the level of encryption on devices, etc.

A larger attack surface provides more potential attack vectors for malicious actors to exploit. Reducing the attack surface, like patching vulnerabilities, removing unused applications, and implementing strong authentication, minimizes the opportunities for successful attacks.

Note: **We can think of an attack surface as the entire landscape that attackers can potentially exploit.**

When estimating an organization's attack surface, the following aspects can be used:

Factor	Details
Number of devices and systems	More devices (laptops, desktops, mobile phones, servers, etc.) connected to a network increase potential entry points.
Software applications	Each application running on a system adds to the attack surface, potentially containing vulnerabilities.
Network connections	Exposed ports, weak network access controls, and connections to untrusted networks enlarge the surface.
Human factors	User behavior like clicking suspicious links, opening unsafe attachments, or falling for social engineering tactics can create openings.
Remote working	Remote working poses unique challenge by greatly increasing the attack surface of the organization.

Table 2.20: *Factors increasing an organization's attack surface*

Legal framework for digital forensics

Let us now understand the legal framework for digital forensics. We will also discuss when it may be illegal to collect evidence. We will also talk about various grey areas around the legality of digital forensics.

The legal framework for digital forensics varies by jurisdiction, but generally includes laws and regulations designed to ensure that digital evidence is collected, handled, and used in ways that respect individuals' rights while upholding justice. Let us look at some of the key points regarding the legal framework, rights against evidence collection, restrictions, jurisdictional differences, and other related concepts.

The legal framework for digital forensics is complex and highly dependent on the jurisdiction. Individuals' rights against evidence collection protect their privacy, limiting the unauthorized gathering of personal data. However, in public safety cases, law enforcement can bypass these rights with proper legal authorization. Understanding these jurisdictional differences is crucial for forensic professionals to ensure that evidence collection remains lawful and admissible.

Digital forensics operates under a framework that includes national and international laws, standards, and guidelines that govern the collection, analysis, and admissibility of digital evidence. Common regulations include data protection laws, such as the GDPR in the European Union, and cybersecurity laws, like the **Computer Fraud and Abuse Act** (**CFAA**) in the United States, which restrict unauthorized access to digital information. Cybercrime and digital evidence handling are also covered by international treaties like the Budapest Convention on Cybercrime, which seeks to harmonize cybercrime laws across countries. Compliance with these laws ensures that forensic processes are legally sound and that evidence can be admissible in court.

Rights against forensic evidence collection

Individuals have rights that protect their privacy and personal information against unauthorized collection. Most democratic legal systems provide protections against unreasonable searches and seizures under privacy or constitutional rights, such as the Fourth Amendment in the U.S. or Article 8 of the European Convention on Human Rights. In many jurisdictions, these rights mean that digital forensic evidence cannot be collected without proper authorization, typically a warrant or consent from the individual concerned. If evidence is gathered unlawfully or without a proper warrant, it may be inadmissible in court.

In a nutshell, individuals have rights against invasive or unlawful evidence collection:

- **Right to privacy**: Investigators must ensure that data collection does not infringe upon a person's privacy without proper legal authorization.
- **Due process**: Evidence must be collected in a manner consistent with legal procedures to ensure fairness.
- **Exclusionary rule (certain jurisdictions)**: Evidence obtained unlawfully may be inadmissible in court.
- **Legal recourse**: Individuals can challenge the collection or use of forensic evidence that violates their rights.

Illegal evidence collection without consent

Certain types of data are illegal to collect without explicit consent or a court order. This includes personal communications (emails, messages), private documents, and sensitive personal data, like financial records or health information. In most jurisdictions, it is illegal to intercept electronic communications, monitor devices, or access personal accounts without the owner's permission or a legal warrant. Violating these restrictions can result in criminal charges against the collector, and the evidence may be excluded due to violations of privacy laws.

Additionally, if we need to understand these in easy-to-understand points, here are the key points for illegal evidence collection without consent:

- **Unauthorized data collection is illegal**: Collecting personal communications (emails, messages), private documents, or sensitive data (financial or health records) without explicit consent or a legal warrant is prohibited in most jurisdictions.
- **Interception and monitoring restrictions**: Unauthorized interception of electronic communications, monitoring of personal devices, or accessing private accounts without permission constitutes a violation of privacy laws and may lead to severe legal consequences.
- **Legal consequences for isolators**: Engaging in illegal evidence collection can result in criminal charges, civil penalties, and liability for damages caused to the affected individuals.

- **Exclusion of illegally obtained evidence**: Courts often exclude evidence obtained through illegal means, deeming it inadmissible due to violations of privacy and due process rights.
- **Exceptions through legal authorization**: In certain cases, law enforcement agencies and authorized entities may collect such data legally if backed by a valid court order, warrant, or specific regulatory permissions.

Exceptions when evidence collection is permissible

There are situations where digital evidence collection is permissible without consent. For instance, law enforcement agencies can collect evidence without consent if they obtain a warrant based on probable cause. In certain cases, such as imminent threats to national security or cases of suspected terrorism, some jurisdictions permit warrantless searches. Additionally, in corporate settings, employers may have the right to monitor company-owned devices and networks if proper policies are in place and employees are notified of potential monitoring, though this varies by jurisdiction.

In other words, forensic evidence collection is permissible under specific conditions:

- **Warrants and legal orders**: Evidence must often be obtained through proper legal channels, such as court-issued warrants.
- **Consent**: Voluntary consent from the individual or organization being investigated.
- **Exigent circumstances**: In emergencies (e.g., imminent harm or destruction of evidence), evidence can be collected without a warrant, subject to later judicial review.
- **Good faith exceptions**: In some jurisdictions, evidence collected in good faith but with minor procedural errors may still be admissible.

Jurisdictional differences

Jurisdiction plays a critical role in determining the legality of evidence collection in digital forensics. Each country has specific privacy laws, standards, and thresholds for when digital evidence can be collected. For example, the U.S. has a relatively broad scope for digital evidence collection under federal law, while the EU has stricter requirements under the GDPR, emphasizing user consent and data minimization. Additionally, certain countries have broad data localization laws, meaning that digital evidence collected within their borders must not be transferred internationally without meeting specific legal requirements.

To summarize, here is how jurisdiction impacts how cyber forensics is conducted:

- **Local laws**: Different countries have unique legal systems, affecting what is considered permissible evidence.
- **Cross-border challenges**: Digital crimes often span multiple jurisdictions, complicating evidence collection and prosecution.
- **Conflicts of law**: A country's laws may conflict with another's, requiring international cooperation (e.g., **Mutual Legal Assistance Treaties** (**MLATs**)).
- **Example**: A server in one country might host data related to a crime in another, raising questions of sovereignty and access.

Understanding compliance requirements for digital evidence collection

We have seen so far that digital forensics techniques aid greatly in investigating incidents in general and cyberattacks in particular. However, other aspects of digital forensics may compel enterprises to collect evidence on an ongoing basis. Hence, they are, in such cases, compelled to be ready for cyber forensic analysis in case of incidents or cyberattacks.

The questions that enterprises need to ask themselves are as follows:

1. Do we have data critical in nature that may cause adverse effects to the business if exposed, including loss of reputation?
2. Do we have a large attack surface due to the nature of our business?
3. Do we have data that moves around geographies due to the nature of our business?
4. Are there many associates who are non-employees, e.g., contractors or temporary workers, who have access to confidential and sensitive data?
5. Are there 3rd party groups and vendors who have access to confidential and sensitive data?
6. Are we in a business that deals with data of such a type that has an illegal/black market that attackers may be interested in selling in?
7. Are we working with the government, including on projects of national interest and defense projects?

If the answer to one or more of the preceding questions is yes, then there may be compliance requirements from the respective jurisdictions to collect forensically sound digital evidence. This is because the enterprise's attack surface is very large. Well-known global standards like ISO 27001-2022, SOC2 Type 2, **National Institute of Standards and Technology Cybersecurity Framework** (**NIST CSF**), etc., have implicit requirements when complied with, resulting in a reduction of attack vectors. Such standards also have requirements around the collection of evidence. While they are not directly cyber forensic standards, compliance with them ensures that the enterprise is both protected and ready for cyber forensic analysis.

Moreover, the more the business diversifies and expands, the greater the risk of an increase in the attack surface. In such cases, it may not be easy for the enterprise to confidently prove that all the attack vectors were unknown beforehand and a conscious effort was not taken to close them.

Enterprises may need to navigate a complex compliance landscape when collecting digital evidence and balancing legal requirements, privacy rights, industry standards, and internal policies. Proper compliance ensures legal defensibility and builds trust with employees, customers, and stakeholders by respecting privacy and security standards.

Let us look at a few aspects of what compliance would mean for enterprises.

Data protection laws

Enterprises must comply with data protection laws such as the **General Data Protection Regulation** (**GDPR**) in the European Union, the CCPA in the U.S., and others based on operating locations. These regulations require that digital evidence collection respects individuals' privacy rights, minimizes unnecessary data collection, and ensures transparency. For example, under GDPR, data collection must be limited to what is necessary, and subjects may have the right to access or object to the processing of their personal data. Any evidence gathered should align with these principles, and proper consent or legal justification should be in place.

Example: A European e-commerce company collecting customer transaction logs for forensic investigation must ensure compliance with GDPR. If a fraud investigation requires access to customer browsing history, the company must justify the data collection under legitimate interest or obtain explicit consent. Failure to comply can result in heavy fines, as seen in cases where companies were penalized for excessive data retention.

Lawful interception and monitoring

Enterprises are often subject to lawful interception and monitoring regulations, which govern the conditions under which they can monitor communications and activities on their systems. For instance, employers may monitor corporate devices if employees are informed, typically via a consent policy that clarifies the scope and nature of monitoring. Compliance involves adhering to these policies and notifying employees, customers, or users about monitoring, often documented through *Acceptable Use Policies* and privacy notices.

Example: A multinational corporation implements employee monitoring on company-issued devices. To comply with U.S. laws like ECPA and EU regulations, they include a clause in the employee contract and provide an **Acceptable Use Policy** (**AUP**) explaining the scope of monitoring. If an employee disputes the monitoring in court, the policy serves as legal justification.

Industry standards and regulations

Certain industries have specific compliance standards for data handling and evidence collection, such as the **Health Insurance Portability and Accountability Act** (**HIPAA**) for healthcare, which mandates stringent measures for protecting patient data. Financial institutions may follow guidelines under the **Sarbanes-Oxley Act** (**SOX**) or the **Payment Card Industry Data Security Standard** (**PCI DSS**), which require secure handling and documentation of sensitive financial data. Compliance involves securing data access, limiting exposure to sensitive information, and ensuring evidence collection meets industry-specific regulations.

Example: A healthcare provider under HIPAA compliance needs to investigate a breach of patient records. While collecting evidence from hospital systems, they must ensure encryption, access logs, and minimum data exposure. Violating these requirements, such as failing to log access to patient data, could result in non-compliance penalties.

Chain of custody requirements

To ensure admissibility in legal proceedings, enterprises must establish a clear chain of custody for digital evidence. This involves detailed logging of who accessed the evidence, when, how, and any transfers or analyses it underwent. Maintaining this chain is crucial for ensuring that digital evidence is legally defensible and has not been tampered with. Enterprises should implement standardized chains of custody procedures and regularly audit compliance to ensure adherence.

Example: A bank investigating internal fraud collects digital evidence from employee workstations. They implement a chain of custody by documenting who accessed the forensic images, timestamps of evidence transfer, and hashes of the collected files. If the case reaches court, the documented chain ensures evidence integrity and admissibility.

Employee and insider privacy rights

Compliance also involves respecting employee privacy rights, especially when monitoring workplace activities. While some monitoring is permissible, it must be balanced with employees' expectations of privacy and be legally justifiable. Regulations such as the **Electronic Communications Privacy Act** (**ECPA**) in the U.S. limit employer monitoring of private communications. Enterprises should have clear policies and procedures that respect these rights and limit collection to only work-related data unless otherwise legally mandated.

Example: A tech company detects data exfiltration by an employee. Before reviewing employee communications, the company must ensure that monitoring is restricted to work-related data. If personal communications are accessed without consent, the employee may sue for privacy violations under laws like ECPA (US) or GDPR (EU).

Cybersecurity frameworks and incident response protocols

Enterprises often follow cybersecurity frameworks like NIST, ISO 27001, or CIS Controls, which outline data collection, evidence preservation, and incident response guidelines. Compliance with these frameworks includes implementing protocols to securely collect, store, and analyze digital evidence in response to incidents while ensuring the evidence is appropriately documented and protected from unauthorized access.

Example: A retail company following NIST CSF detects a malware attack on its payment processing system. To comply with forensic readiness policies, they capture network traffic logs, system snapshots, and audit trails. These logs help in understanding attack vectors and ensure regulatory compliance, e.g., PCI DSS for payment security.

Internal policies and procedures

Enterprises should have internal compliance policies governing evidence collection, including documented protocols for evidence handling, storage, and analysis. These policies define roles and responsibilities, establish criteria for evidence collection, and outline the approval processes required for accessing sensitive data. Regular training and audits are also essential to ensure employees understand and follow these policies.

Example: A global enterprise sets up an internal compliance policy for handling forensic evidence. They require pre-approval from legal and security teams before accessing sensitive employee data. If an HR dispute requires access to logs, the policy ensures that actions follow legal and ethical guidelines.

Cross-border data transfers

When operating internationally, enterprises may face restrictions on cross-border data transfers due to data localization laws. Certain jurisdictions require data collected within their borders to remain local unless specific requirements are met, such as obtaining user consent or following approved transfer mechanisms. Enterprises need to be aware of these restrictions and ensure that evidence collected across borders is handled in compliance with international data transfer regulations.

Example: A U.S.-based tech company collects forensic evidence related to a cyberattack in China. Due to China's data localization laws, such as the **Personal Information Protection Law** (**PIPL**), they cannot transfer data outside the country without government approval. Instead, they set up localized forensic analysis within China to comply with regulations.

Maintaining chain of custody and preserving evidence integrity

Chain of custody is a documented process that tracks the handling of digital evidence from its collection to its presentation in court to ensure it remains unaltered. In simpler terms, it decides what happens when the evidence passes from one hand to another and from one location to another.

Let us understand a few aspects of this mandatory process in forensics that ensure that an audit trail is maintained throughout the entire digital forensic evidence investigation:

- Chain of custody is the meticulous process of documenting each step that digital evidence undergoes, from its initial collection to its final presentation in a legal setting.
- This process includes tracking who has handled the evidence, when, where, and under what conditions, and the precise manner in which it was transferred or analyzed.
- This chain ensures that the digital evidence remains unaltered and is preserved in a way that maintains its integrity.
- Much like in conventional forensics, where evidence such as fingerprints, fibers, or physical objects undergo similar tracking, digital forensics demands rigorous attention to documenting each transfer and change in custody.

- This parallel exists because both digital and conventional forensics are concerned with evidence that may be presented in a court of law; therefore, maintaining a verifiable record is crucial to ensure the evidence remains credible and admissible.

In both digital and traditional forensic investigations, any breach in the chain of custody or failure to document the handling process can call the validity of the evidence into question, potentially leading to its exclusion in court. If there is any indication that the evidence may have been tampered with, lost, or accessed by unauthorized individuals, the defense may argue that it is unreliable, thus undermining the investigation and prosecution efforts. The chain of custody is crucial in preventing this by ensuring that each individual handling the evidence is accountable and that every action taken on the evidence is documented, limiting opportunities for contamination, alteration, or loss.

Preserving the integrity of digital evidence is essential in upholding the credibility of an investigation and maintaining fairness in judicial processes. Digital evidence can be particularly volatile and can degrade or change easily, either intentionally or unintentionally, through improper handling, environmental factors, or technical interference. For instance, actions such as powering a device, connecting it to a network, or using software to examine it can inadvertently alter or delete important information. By preserving evidence integrity, investigators ensure that the evidence remains in the same state as when it was initially discovered, which is crucial for accurate analysis and reliable findings. Any alteration, even if minor, can impact the investigation's outcome, potentially leading to misinterpretation of data or wrongful conclusions. In legal contexts, evidence integrity guarantees that the material presented reflects an authentic and unaltered form, allowing all parties to trust its accuracy and relevance.

Ultimately, the chain of custody and evidence integrity are cornerstones in digital forensics, ensuring that the truth of the evidence remains intact from initial discovery through to court proceedings. These practices provide the foundation for forensic work, enabling digital evidence to meet the high standards required for legal admissibility and maintaining public confidence in the judicial process.

Documentation and reporting for legal proceedings aspects

We will discuss the entire process of documenting the findings and preparing reports for legal proceedings in later chapters when we talk about **digital forensics and incident response** (**DFIR**). For now, let us discuss some basic concepts about how digital forensic professionals document their findings as part of their analysis and use this evidence to prepare reports that are admissible in a court of law.

As part of any cybercrime or major security incident investigation, documenting findings and preparing reports for legal proceedings are critical steps that require accuracy, clarity, and a systematic approach. These aspects form the backbone of presenting digital evidence in a court of law and help ensure that the evidence is credible, understandable, and admissible. Proper documentation and reporting support the forensic investigation by creating a clear narrative that can be used to explain the findings to non-technical audiences, including judges, juries, and attorneys.

Documentation of findings in cyber forensics involves recording all steps taken during the investigation, including the tools used, procedures followed, and data uncovered. This documentation begins at the moment evidence is collected and continues throughout every phase of the analysis. For example:

- A forensic investigator must log information about each piece of evidence collected, detailing aspects such as device identifiers, locations, timestamps, and hash values.
- Even as simple as powering on a device or running a command, each action should be documented meticulously to provide a complete, traceable account of the evidence's handling.
- When a handoff is done between various investigators at the end of the shift, the action of what is being passed from one investigator to another must be logged.

Such detailed documentation prevents gaps in the investigation's history, ensuring that all processes can be verified if scrutinized in a legal context.

Another critical aspect is documenting the methodology and tools used during the investigation. This includes specifying the exact software versions, hardware configurations, and algorithms used, as digital forensic tools can vary significantly in their accuracy and reliability. Documenting these details enables others to replicate the results or verify the validity of the findings if questioned in court. It also demonstrates that industry standards and best practices were followed, reinforcing the forensic investigator's credibility.

Preparing the report for legal proceedings involves compiling all findings into a structured, easily understandable document that clearly explains what evidence was collected, how it was analyzed, and the conclusions drawn. The report should be tailored to a non-technical audience, avoiding jargon while ensuring technical accuracy. It should provide a concise yet thorough account of the evidence, beginning with an overview of the investigation's scope, objectives, and any limitations encountered. Sections typically include an introduction, evidence collection methods, forensic analysis steps, findings, and conclusions. Importantly, each piece of evidence should be presented objectively, without bias, allowing the legal team to interpret it in alignment with their case strategy.

In the legal context, the clarity and impartiality of the report are paramount. An effective forensic report must stand up to cross-examination, meaning it should withstand scrutiny on both the technical and procedural fronts. Forensic reports often include visual aids like charts, timelines, and screenshots to help convey complex information visually, making it easier for legal professionals to understand critical data points. Additionally, a forensic report often ends with an expert opinion section, where the investigator may summarize the implications of the findings, though this must remain within the bounds of objective analysis.

Forensic analysis of various operating systems

In digital forensics, a general approach across all operating systems involves identifying, preserving, analyzing, and presenting evidence while maintaining data integrity. Analysts capture forensic images, which are exact replicas of the storage medium, and employ hashing techniques to ensure data integrity throughout the analysis. They then proceed to examine system logs, user activity, installed applications, and specific files to identify evidence of suspicious activities, such as unauthorized access, data exfiltration, or malware infections. Each operating system, however, has unique structures, file systems, and log types that require specialized techniques for effective forensic analysis.

Each operating system, Linux, Windows, and macOS, has unique structures, tools, and methodologies for forensic analysis. Linux forensics emphasizes log files, shell histories, and open-source command-line tools, while Windows forensics relies heavily on the Registry, event logs, and file artifacts like prefetch files. macOS forensics, on the other hand, focuses on **Property List** (**PLIST**) files, **Apple File System** (**APFS**) snapshots, and Unified Logs, using specialized tools to navigate Apple's proprietary systems. By understanding these operating-system-specific approaches, forensic analysts can more effectively investigate incidents and uncover evidence tailored to the unique environments within each OS.

Linux forensics

In Linux forensics, analysts primarily focus on system logs, file permissions, user accounts, and configuration files, foundational to tracking activities and identifying potential threats. Linux stores crucial logs in the `/var/log` directory, which includes authentication logs (`auth.log` or secure), system logs (`syslog`), and application-specific logs, all valuable for identifying anomalies in user actions or unauthorized access attempts. Analysts carefully examine user histories, including shell history files like `.bash_history`, to understand the commands executed by each user. Network configurations and access details, such as network interfaces and IP tables, are typically stored in configuration files in `/etc`, which provide insight into network-related activities. By examining these files, forensic investigators can determine whether unauthorized connections were established or malicious configurations were applied.

Linux forensics also benefits from the extensibility of the Linux command line, where native tools such as **`grep`**, **`awk`**, **`find`**, and **`strings`** are used extensively to extract, filter, and analyze evidence from text-based logs and system files. Additionally, analysts often use dd to create forensic images, preserving evidence to maintain data integrity and prevent contamination. Linux file systems, especially Ext4, provide valuable metadata that helps recover deleted files or track modifications, thanks to unique structures like inodes and journaling capabilities. Specialized tools such as **The Sleuth Kit (TSK)** and Autopsy are commonly used to analyze Linux file systems, examine partitions, and recover hidden or deleted data.

Another critical area in Linux forensics is analyzing malware and rootkits, which are more prevalent in Linux environments than other OSes. Tools like chkrootkit and rkhunter are specifically designed to identify rootkits and suspicious system alterations that might indicate compromise. Analysts can identify persistent malware that may have embedded itself into system processes by examining startup scripts, scheduled cron jobs, and library paths. Understanding the open-source nature of Linux is crucial, as investigators can tailor scripts or modify tools to suit specific forensic needs, allowing them to dig deeper into evidence and perform thorough investigations tailored to the Linux ecosystem.

Windows forensics

Windows forensics is heavily centered around analyzing the Windows Registry, which acts as a comprehensive database for user activities, software installations, and system configurations. The Registry stores vital forensic artifacts across various hives, including **`SYSTEM`**, **`SOFTWARE`**, **`SECURITY`**, and **`NTUSER.DAT`**, each containing valuable data such as login information, USB device connections, installed programs, and recently accessed files. Investigators use tools like Registry Explorer, RegRipper, and **Forensic Toolkit** (**FTK**) to parse Registry keys and extract artifacts that reveal user actions, software installations, and possible malicious modifications. By analyzing the Registry, forensic investigators can build a timeline of user behavior and system interactions, which is crucial in understanding the sequence of events leading to a security incident.

Windows event logs, stored in the Event Viewer, are another vital source for forensic analysis. These logs contain detailed records of system events, including application crashes, login attempts, user activities, and network connections. By examining event logs, analysts can uncover behavior patterns, identify unauthorized login attempts, and pinpoint specific times when suspicious actions occurred. For example, security event logs track successful and failed logins, while application event logs provide insights into software behavior, which can help detect and analyze malicious activities. Tools like Event Log Explorer and Sysinternals' suite enable investigators to filter and analyze logs efficiently, allowing them to identify anomalies that may signal breaches or unauthorized access.

Windows also generates unique artifacts like prefetch files, which record application launch information and are invaluable for tracking program usage and timeline analysis. Windows shadow copies and **Volume Shadow Service** (**VSS**) snapshots allow investigators to recover deleted or altered files and restore previous states of the system. These artifacts, along with the NTFS file system's journaling feature, are powerful resources in forensic investigations, helping analysts recover lost data and reconstruct file access history. Combining Registry, event log, and file system analysis, Windows forensics provides a comprehensive view of user activities, making it possible to track, analyze, and correlate user behavior and system events effectively.

macOS forensics

macOS forensics requires specialized knowledge due to the unique architecture, file systems, and log structures inherent to Apple's operating system. macOS relies on PLIST files, found throughout the system in locations like **`/Library/Preferences`** and **`/Users/<username>/Library/Preferences`**, which store user preferences, system settings, and application data. These files are valuable for forensic investigations as they reveal user activity, such as recently opened files, configured devices, and application usage. By examining PLIST files, forensic analysts can reconstruct user actions and analyze program interactions, shedding light on the events that took place on the device.

The introduction of the APFS, designed for SSDs, adds new layers of complexity and features such as snapshots, encryption, and copy-on-write functionality, which impact forensic analysis. APFS snapshots provide point-in-time captures of the file system, which are useful for restoring previous states and examining system changes over time. Analyzing APFS requires specialized tools that can navigate its unique structure, such as BlackBag's BlackLight, which is designed for macOS forensic analysis. Additionally, macOS's native tools, like `fs_usage` for file activity tracking and log show for system logs, provide real-time insights and historical records of system and application events, allowing investigators to trace actions and detect potential malicious activity.

Another critical component in macOS forensics is the Unified Log system, which stores detailed records of system operations, errors, and diagnostics across different system modules and applications. These logs provide an in-depth view of the system's activities and are invaluable for tracking both normal user behavior and unauthorized access. Unlike traditional log files, Unified Logs are highly detailed and cover a wide range of system events, making them useful for reconstructing an incident timeline. Investigators often employ Magnet AXIOM or macOS-specific forensic tools to parse these logs, enabling them to comprehensively view user actions, network connections, and system-level events that may be relevant to an investigation.

Conclusion

In this chapter, we discussed a comprehensive overview of digital forensics in enterprise settings. We discussed setting up basic forensic environments, roles of digital forensics in enterprises, types of evidence, attack vectors, legal frameworks, compliance requirements, and chain of custody practices.

We also discussed that some of the key aspects of digital forensics for enterprises include creating forensic readiness, maintaining evidence integrity, and documenting findings. While doing so, an emphasis on the importance of compliance with data protection laws and understanding jurisdictional differences was also discussed.

As a part of the recipes in this chapter, we look at how to set up a Kali Linux-based forensic environment and fingerprinting techniques using various checksum tools available in Linux, and which are the important logs for checking user activity in the system.

By the end of this chapter, we were able to gain hands-on experience and the ability to integrate a few key concepts of digital forensics into enterprise incident response and legal processes, ensuring readiness for cyberattacks and compliance with legal standards.

In the next chapter, we will look at the general digital forensics techniques.

Questions

1. What is the role of digital forensics in enterprises of different sizes?
2. Name three types of digital evidence typically collected in cyber incidents.
3. How does forensic readiness benefit an enterprise?
4. Explain the concept of a checksum and its applications.
5. What are the key components of a chain of custody?
6. How do attack vectors differ from an attack surface?
7. Discuss the legal frameworks governing digital forensics.
8. What are the unique challenges of forensic analysis in macOS systems?
9. Why is documenting findings crucial for legal admissibility?
10. How can SIEM systems enhance forensic evidence collection?

Points to remember

- Forensic readiness ensures an organization can effectively collect, preserve, and analyze digital evidence during incidents.
- System, application, and network logs are crucial for reconstructing incident timelines and identifying unauthorized activities.
- Attack vectors represent specific exploitation methods, while the attack surface is the totality of potential vulnerabilities.
- A chain of custody tracks evidence handling from collection to court presentation, ensuring integrity and legal admissibility.
- Checksums detect data alterations by generating unique hash values and verifying file integrity during transmission or storage.
- Each operating system (Linux, Windows, macOS) requires specialized forensic techniques due to its unique structures and tools.
- SIEM systems centralize log collection and analysis, enhancing anomaly detection and forensic investigations.
- Regular backups of critical data and configurations protect against loss and support recovery during incidents.
- Digital forensics adheres to jurisdiction-specific laws like GDPR and CCPA, ensuring privacy and legal compliance.
- Compliance with standards like ISO 27001 and HIPAA guides evidence collection and regulatory adherence.
- Platforms like Kali Linux and tools such as Autopsy enable thorough forensic investigations.
- Clear and systematic documentation of investigative steps ensures evidence credibility and supports legal processes.
- Maintaining evidence integrity prevents contamination or alteration, preserving its original state.
- Reducing attack surfaces and preparing for incidents proactively minimizes vulnerabilities and enhances defense.
- Cross-border compliance ensures evidence handling adheres to laws governing data localization and transfer.

Key terms

- **Checksum**: A unique value generated to verify data integrity using algorithms like SHA-256.
- **Chain of custody**: The process of documenting evidence handling to ensure its integrity.
- **Attack vector**: A specific method or entry point that attackers use to compromise systems.
- **Attack surface**: The sum of all possible vulnerabilities in a system.
- **SIEM**: A centralized real-time monitoring and log analysis solution.
- **Forensic readiness**: Preparation to collect and preserve digital evidence systematically.
- **APFS**: A macOS-specific file system designed for SSDs, incorporating encryption and snapshots.
- **Unified Logs**: Detailed, centralized logs in macOS for tracking system and application events.
- **Compliance**: Adherence to legal, regulatory, and organizational standards in digital evidence collection.

CHAPTER 3
General Digital Forensics Techniques

Introduction

Digital forensics techniques used by experts in digital forensics labs and by individual digital forensics practitioners involve general and domain-specific methods. They include techniques that cover email forensics, browser forensics, and many other aspects of digital forensic analysis. Many of these techniques, when acquired, can be used across multiple operating systems and domains.

In this chapter, we will look at a few general digital forensic techniques that can be used by digital forensics experts across operating system and domain.

Structure

In this chapter, we will cover the following topics:

- Evidence lifecycle in digital forensics
- Techniques for evidence identification
- Recipe 4: Techniques for evidence acquisition – emails
- Recipe 5: Techniques for evidence acquisition – browsing history
- Techniques for evidence acquisition – network logs
- Recipe 6: Techniques for evidence acquisition – details about changed files
- Recipe 7: Techniques for evidence acquisition – changed files using find
- Recipe 8: Techniques for evidence acquisition – cookies
- Techniques for evidence analysis
- Recipe 9: Analyzing SQLite database files
- Techniques for documentation and reporting the findings

Objectives

In this chapter, we will look at the evidence lifecycle in digital forensics with its distinct phases, identification, acquisition, analysis, and report. We will look at each of these phases in detail and reinforce our learning with the help of hands-on recipes. By the end of this chapter, you should have become familiar with the evidence lifecycle in digital forensics, and should be able to identify and use other techniques in these lifecycle steps.

Evidence lifecycle in digital forensics

The evidence lifecycle can be broadly classified into four stages, evidence identification, evidence acquisition and preservation, evidence analysis, and documentation and reporting.

Evidence identification

This includes things like what evidence is present in the system, where the pieces of evidence are stored, and how they are stored. They can be stored in various personal computers, servers, mobile phones, networking devices, thumb drives, SSD drives, and so on. Such evidence identification can be done in a hybrid approach, using conventional processes where manual skills are required and specialized software that can do it automatically to a great extent.

In scenarios when a raid is done at the place of cybercrime or conventional crime, there may be seizure of digital assets like computers, phones, and other devices that may store digital data. In such cases, there may not be time to perform evidence identification, but the first responders may need to collect as much evidence as possible.

Evidence acquisition and preservation

The evidence is acquired from various sources that could be classified as live or dead sources. Once acquired, the evidence is preserved and secured after isolating it, so that its physical and digital states are preserved. Often, a forensically sound copy of evidence is created without altering the original evidence for analysis purposes. The original evidence is preserved using a chain of custody to ensure that there is no scope for damage, corruption, or contamination of data, i.e., the integrity of the original evidence is preserved. These aspects are important for presenting it in a court of law, as any changes in the evidence may not hold up in the court of law.

Evidence analysis

This stage includes understanding the evidence that is found and reconstructing how cybercrime was committed using fragments of data found is part of this phase. The analysis step is a complex operation and can take multiple iterations involving a team of investigators with specialized skills. This stage results in important insights, like timeline reconstructions. Moreover, analysis is done on a forensically sound copy of the evidence while the original evidence is preserved.

Documentation and reporting

As part of this phase, everything is documented, including the data found, the correlation understood, and even what is not clear. The documentation is done using standardized templates and processes that are admissible in a court of law. This documentation is an important step to help the digital forensic team recreate the scene of the cybercrime. Such documentation includes the result of analysis using various digital forensics methods by digital forensic experts and hence can provide a deep insight into the crime based on the evidence collected.

Finally, the evidence found and the result of analysis and documentation are presented in a form that anyone can understand. It can also be present in a court of law during prosecution.

Techniques for evidence identification

Digital forensic first responders and investigators use various techniques to identify evidence effectively. These techniques focus on locating potential sources of evidence, understanding the context, and ensuring the evidence is relevant to the investigation. These techniques ensure the systematic identification of evidence while preserving its integrity and providing a sound foundation for effective forensic investigations of cybercrime or cyber incidents being investigated.

Let us look at the general techniques first responders and investigators use for the identification of forensic evidence in the following table:

Technique	Description	Purpose	Examples
Visual inspection	Physically examining the digital environment for potential evidence sources.	Identify devices (e.g., computers, USB drives, mobile phones) and unusual hardware.	Spotting hidden USB drives, network cables connected to suspicious devices, identifying damaged hardware, locating external hard drives.
System inventory	Cataloging all hardware and software present at the crime scene or investigation site.	Establish baseline data for analysis and identify potential evidence sources.	Listing installed applications, checking connected peripherals, reviewing system configurations, identifying unauthorized software.
Network scanning	Using tools to map active devices and connections in the network.	Detect unauthorized devices or rogue systems.	Using nmap for IP discovery, identifying open ports, detecting rogue Wi-Fi networks, locating unauthorized network devices.
Log inspection	Examining system and application logs for signs of suspicious activity.	Identify timestamps, user actions, and possible intrusion points.	Reviewing authentication logs, scanning error logs, analyzing audit logs, inspecting web server logs for anomalies.
Email header analysis	Inspecting email headers for routing, authentication, and sender information.	Identify spoofing, phishing, or malicious email activity.	Tracing IP addresses, analyzing **sender policy framework** (**SPF**) and **DomainKeys Identified Mail** (**DKIM**) records, reviewing X-Headers, identifying anomalies in return-path addresses.
File signature analysis	Comparing file extensions with actual file signatures.	Detect anomalies or tampering.	Identifying renamed executables, checking for disguised malware, detecting mismatched file types, verifying integrity of transferred files.
Browsing history review	Examining web browsing history for evidence of user activity.	Identify visited websites, search queries, and potential malicious activity.	Reviewing bookmarked sites, detecting interactions with phishing domains, identifying cloud storage access, analyzing browser cache and download history, analyzing cookies and session data, analyzing autofill data, detecting third-party plugins, checking search engine queries, reconstructing search intent.
Keyword and string search	Searching systems and storage for specific keywords or strings.	Locate files or communications related to the investigation.	Searching for passwords in email dumps, locating encrypted archives, identifying specific user IDs, finding references to sensitive projects.
Network traffic monitoring	Capturing live network traffic for analysis.	Identify ongoing malicious activity or data exfiltration.	Monitoring real-time packet captures, detecting unauthorized file transfers, analyzing C2 communications, identifying DDoS patterns.

Table 3.1: *General techniques for evidence identification*

Now, let us look at the advanced techniques first responders and investigators use for the identification of forensic evidence in the following table:

Technique	Description	Purpose	Examples
Volatile data identification	Capturing data that resides in system memory or active processes before it is lost.	Preserve ephemeral data for further analysis.	Capturing RAM contents, identifying active sessions, preserving unsaved data from applications, analyzing network connections in real time.
Metadata analysis	Inspecting file metadata to identify creation, modification, and access details.	Establish the origin and authenticity of files.	Analyzing EXIF data in images, checking document timestamps, verifying author details in PDFs, comparing modification times.
Device and media examination	Inspecting storage devices for suspicious files or directories.	Locate hidden or deleted files.	Searching for hidden partitions, identifying encrypted volumes, locating steganographic files, examining USB contents for suspicious activity.
Hash matching	Generating and comparing hash values of files against known hashes.	Detect known malicious or unauthorized files.	Using VirusTotal for hash matching, verifying integrity of system images, detecting duplicates, matching malware signatures.
Memory analysis	Analyzing volatile memory for active processes, network connections, and malware.	Gather evidence of in-memory attacks.	Analyzing process trees, extracting credentials from RAM, identifying injected DLLs, isolating encryption keys.
Triage tools	Using specialized tools to quickly assess and identify evidence.	Expedite identification during time-critical investigations.	Using **Forensic Toolkit** (**FTK**) Imager for live preview, identifying large files with WinHex, locating browser caches, detecting mounted virtual drives.

***Table 3.2:** Advanced techniques for evidence identification*

Recipe 4: Techniques for evidence acquisition – emails

Email is one of the key modes of communication in today's world. It is so widely used that sending an email is considered mundane without understanding how much information is being sent as part of the email. What we see in the email using an email client like Microsoft Outlook or a web-based client is the formatted body of the email plus some metadata.

However, there is a lot more information that is sent along with the actual email content or body. All this information is important evidence. Not only that, but when a large number of emails are inspected, they can provide a complete picture of the entire sequence of events and the threat actors behind it.

Let us look at a few things that we may be interested in an email. First, let us look at what is visible to the recipient:

Visible information to the recipient	Details
Email content	This includes things like subject line, body text, embedded images, attachments, etc. This can also include embedded hyperlinks.
Sender and recipient details	This includes the sender's display name and email address, and the recipient's email address. It can also include the recipient's display name.
Timestamp	This is basically the date and time when the email was sent or received.

Visible information to the recipient	Details
Attachments	Depending on email client, attachments can be shows as file type icons or just clip icons. The email client may also show the file name, size and type.

Table 3.3: Email information visible to recipients

Most things that are visible to the recipients may be harmless and may not evoke suspicion. Plenty of what is visible can be spoofed by the malicious actor or made to look like trusted or useful content.

However, let us now look at the hidden information in the email that is not visible to the recipient:

Hidden information to the recipient	Details
Information in email headers	Every email has an email header that has a lot of information invisible to the recipient and is used for various purposes during the transport and for rendering of the email by the email client. This includes: • **Message ID**: A unique identifier assigned by the originating server • **Return-path**: The actual email address to which bounces or replies might go, often different from the "From" address. • **Received chain**: A list of servers through which the email passed, including timestamps and IP addresses.
Routing information	This information are used to route the email from the source to destination. They include: • **Simple mail transfer protocol (SMTP) servers**: Servers involved in relaying the email. • **Relaying IPs**: Can indicate the geographic origin of the email. • **SPF, DKIM, DMARC results**: Authentication information to determine if the email is genuine.
X-Headers	They are custom headers that can be added by added by email servers or security tools, such as spam filters, antivirus checks, or company-specific systems. A few examples include X-Spam-Score, X-Mailer, X-Originating-IP, etc.
Hidden information in attachments	Attachments, though may look harmless, may have a lot more content than what is visible. Information like creation and modification dates, author or owner information, file type and extensions, and hidden or embedded objects, such as macros in Microsoft Office files, can be included in the attachments. They can also have malicious code like macros, embedded executables, or scripts.
Hidden information in the email content	The email content can also have hidden information that is not right away visible to the recipients. They may include embedded tracking tools like tracking pixels or web beacons to identify if the email was opened, and links containing tracking codes for click monitoring. They may also Base64 encoded content like hidden scripts or files that can be decoded.
Other information	Emails can also contain embedded geolocation information, time zone information, and encryption indicators.

Table 3.4: Email information hidden from recipients

Note:

- **Compatibility: Cross-platform**
- **License considerations: Free software used**

Recipe

Let us inspect a spam email in your Gmail account. First, login to your Gmail account and go to the **Spam** folder. From here, you can click on any email to see the content on the right side.

Caution: Do not click on any link embedded in the spam email, as it may be a phishing email that can compromise your personal information.

Following is a sample of one of such spam emails:

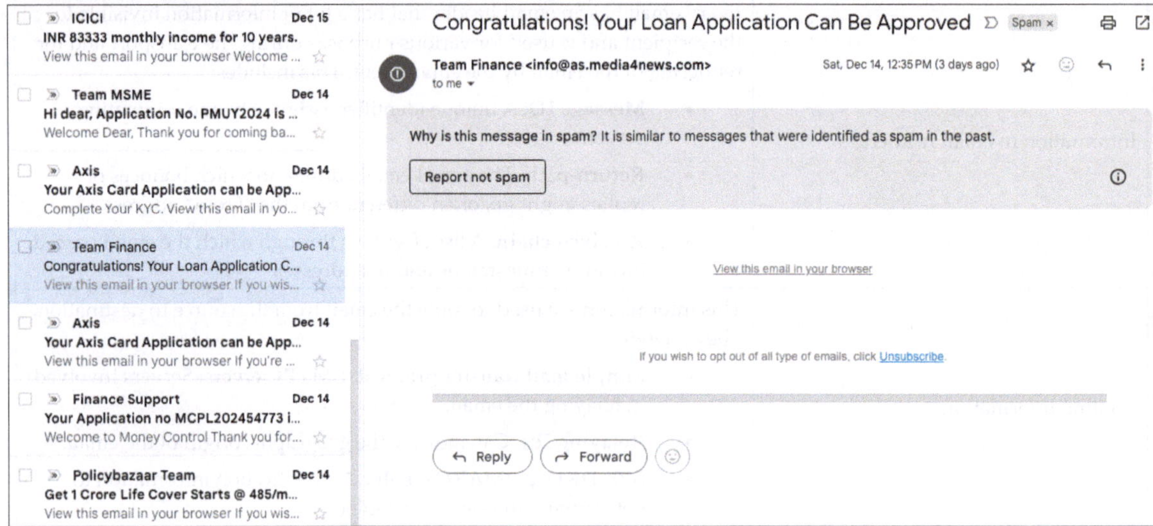

Figure 3.1: Email forensics, spam email shown in Gmail

Now, click on the three dots on the right side and then click on the option **< > Show original**. This will open the email in a new tab with all the details like the header information, embedded content, and the email body.

The header information will look like the following:

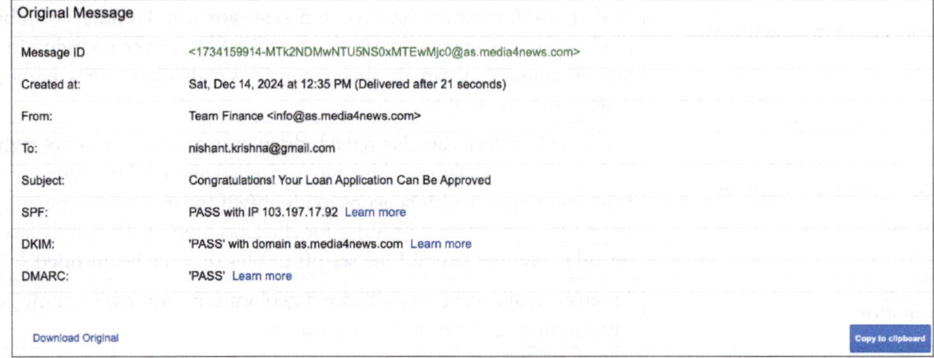

Original Message

Message ID	<1734159914-MTk2NDMwNTU5NS0xMTEwMjc0@as.media4news.com>
Created at:	Sat, Dec 14, 2024 at 12:35 PM (Delivered after 21 seconds)
From:	Team Finance <info@as.media4news.com>
To:	nishant.krishna@gmail.com
Subject:	Congratulations! Your Loan Application Can Be Approved
SPF:	PASS with IP 103.197.17.92 Learn more
DKIM:	'PASS' with domain as.media4news.com Learn more
DMARC:	'PASS' Learn more

Download Original

Copy to clipboard

Figure 3.2: Email forensics, email header

This header information itself has a lot of information to infer that this email is spam and is part of a mass campaign. While the **SPF**, **DKIM**, and **DMARC** are set to **PASS** by *Google*, the email can still not be trusted.

Let us look at the content of the body to see if we can find anything suspicious. All the ones that are marked in bold are worth noting and require further analysis to rule out the email being a spam/phishing email or otherwise:

```
Delivered-To: nishant.krishna@gmail.com
Received: by 2002:a05:7000:b9cd:b0:5dc:327c:9a8a with SMTP id gh13csp896032mab;
        Fri, 13 Dec 2024 23:05:35 -0800 (PST)
X-Google-Smtp-Source: AGHT+IHSPvdFKANBAkgKH8Ju2+EcBRvk/czP3A/qN+P7hrjWj86UYTIx5+Bd3xAP5zF/ytWXiVJ+
X-Received: by 2002:a05:6214:23c9:b0:6d8:f0d2:f472 with SMTP id 6a1803df08f44-6db0f3e0ca2mr1090970
66d6.10.1734159935615;
        Fri, 13 Dec 2024 23:05:35 -0800 (PST)
ARC-Seal: i=1; a=rsa-sha256; t=1734159935; cv=none;
        d=google.com; s=arc-20240605;
        b=kCST7n1JmRA2+mWjQ+xfykqcT38obNnrvQcW/QAVIGRjXdtU4outU2jqd8JsMZvWT7
         fuiEh/eX2M7DspmxodICzad9MO2dsqb7CKk1qSOcR/gDdqrCY2oU6zzFanhEWdRIpDTV
         RXqkLIrPOvGkU4OSnDFMhpIIJLtOltYDlNccFl/XmZcENffl65Rs2Yo1vE1w/tMfGmJE
         Zl7hh0+9Ga0ILYh4rC6UjITfFSKViqqD6LxNPwwqvXIK/b6Y9OAin7E8Gjk90XnG8dus
         UvfCeKuY5xQC6Jz1w0NbtFLFMicN8Pg/rjFBzvRuGpeO62J3je6twbjehKVZxMB4died
         uIUA==
ARC-Message-Signature: i=1; a=rsa-sha256; c=relaxed/relaxed; d=google.com; s=arc-20240605;
        h=mime-version:feedback-id:list-unsubscribe-post:list-unsubscribe
         :reply-to:to:from:subject:message-id:date:dkim-signature;
        bh=/w3IxX6kxWhAsRqBbIKtlPuSNts/zMi1OM3y6WKaGt0=;
        fh=qPj1P8RDejPhuC+/oeHIp/giVytazfUAlNPDcQPx5wA=;
        b=XfrA6BxREMLRNTSZkGu1oWI/T5hIyKwBakYYvO9JPw2ZGH8nZJJeGNrfOotEmVfxrz
         N18X4rLO9Q/zHkackmvR9ytSKOFuCsuYxFYfP0OY/0V/R6mR51ufVKO8MwsavmGNUSc8
         M6kuwnM/Qn5IyWeknhfnCOZxKcYyMzLgKY/afMnE7Dmbi2uR9AJ+N6AnXhAJ4oW+qixK
         SO9mYEfxaEdFjCDq22ULp0UAPmReNNsGAVbLViIyLA6Fri/i6w3O8x01v394oFCvFZhj
         U8ir9ZVhnxZEvYwXZ5tziRLtcOCPK76ddgJKt2zAoztGavbcPbfSv2xw3DZie9M6RRc1
         NdLg==;
        dara=google.com
ARC-Authentication-Results: i=1; mx.google.com;
       dkim=pass header.i=@as.media4news.com header.s=trade header.b=IUYqKWiQ;
       spf=pass (google.com: domain of bounce.cli2547-1110274-1110274-1964305595-2565-19825-43117-
66-p1887@as.media4news.com designates 103.197.17.92 as permitted sender) smtp.mailfrom=bounce.
cli2547-1110274-1110274-1964305595-2565-19825-43117-66-p1887@as.media4news.com;
       dmarc=pass (p=NONE sp=NONE dis=NONE) header.from=as.media4news.com
Return-Path: <bounce.cli2547-1110274-1110274-1964305595-2565-19825-43117-66-p1887@as.media4news.
com>
Received: from m1004.media4news.com (m1004.media4news.com. [103.197.17.92])
        by mx.google.com with ESMTPS id 6a1803df08f44-6dccd1c6582si1398745
```

```
6d6.129.2024.12.13.23.05.35
        for <nishant.krishna@gmail.com>
        (version=TLS1_2 cipher=ECDHE-ECDSA-CHACHA20-POLY1305 bits=256/256);
        Fri, 13 Dec 2024 23:05:35 -0800 (PST)
Received-SPF: pass (google.com: domain of bounce.cli2547-1110274-1110274-1964305595-2565-
19825-43117-66-p1887@as.media4news.com designates 103.197.17.92 as permitted sender) client-
ip=103.197.17.92;
Authentication-Results: mx.google.com;
       dkim=pass header.i=@as.media4news.com header.s=trade header.b=IUYqKWiQ;
       spf=pass (google.com: domain of bounce.cli2547-1110274-1110274-1964305595-2565-19825-43117-
66-p1887@as.media4news.com designates 103.197.17.92 as permitted sender) smtp.mailfrom=bounce.
cli2547-1110274-1110274-1964305595-2565-19825-43117-66-p1887@as.media4news.com;
       dmarc=pass (p=NONE sp=NONE dis=NONE) header.from=as.media4news.com
DKIM-Signature: v=1; a=rsa-sha256; q=dns/txt; c=relaxed/relaxed; s=trade; d=as.
media4news.com; t=1734159914; h=subject:from:to; bh=/w3IxX6kxWhAsRqBbIKtlPuSNts/
zMi1OM3y6WKaGt0=; b=IUYqKWiQd7E7XVDTKFMgFz8k2KbtlgOXxFBPjY88XanHZdcwxlW0D3YIFCDb2fk37aV2hv
EhZZ6jRWYS4pJLiQgHinPudlC/h4Op24VHAOiyzjITvzlIenvRpra2mAygcOAAc33kOQzn
kH6Qbo8iU88ZwjON1XzwCML3PWVk8ZJSqXq/9YxFXOHHKhuoyTpf2f2s+9QejzeMHXsgRZ
XxA+epcuYX7I6Ea5+xmX98XTvxtWbDj/7Bw5kX9OVXinu4+Ki7x+Vjfc1IjbjEeDkFKIFZ
MIhLLRyZoXx2pXYpQzo4qzCrhRQ1h/JDwzqBNgSRvDrw4OPm3uLdyAikOuzTZQ==
Date: Sat, 14 Dec 2024 07:05:14 +0000
Message-ID: <1734159914-MTk2NDMwNTU5NS0xMTEwMjc0@as.media4news.com>
Subject: Congratulations! Your Loan Application Can Be Approved
From: Team Finance <info@as.media4news.com>
To: nishant.krishna@gmail.com
Reply-To: info@as.media4news.com
List-Unsubscribe: <https://email.media4news.com/us/
cfEXMbfBfPBKbaCxvMbjgvdaffzFMKKbAchvlcfWfMedKBHMsBBAjqKMkIYH>, <mailto:unsub.cli2547-1110274-
1110274-1964305595-2565-19825-43117-66-p1887@as.media4news.com?subject=unsubscribe>
List-Unsubscribe-Post: List-Unsubscribe=One-Click
X-campaignid: 1110274
X-SentFromServer: 103.197.17.92
X-Subscriber-ID: 1964305595
Feedback-ID: 6633:1964305595:2547:asmedia4ne
Mime-Version: 1.0
Content-Type: multipart/alternative;
boundary=68dd10cbb2880fbc6f2f7a2b1d6945f1dab63200527154f441a3ef7bf5c5
.
.
.
    <span style=3D"display:none !important;" class=3D"preheader"><img src=
=3D"https://email.media4news.com/opens/cfEXMbfBfPBKbaCxvMbjgvdaffzFMKKbAchv=
lcfWfMedKBHMsBBAjqKMkIYH/blank.gif" alt=3D"open track" width=3D"0" height=
```

```
=3D"0" style=3D"display:none !important;" /></span><div style=3D"display:no=
ne"><a href=3D"https://email.media4news.com/a/SfExqbkbAsHVnkzGVdaFfzf" styl=
e=3D"display:none !important;">.</a></div>
  </body>
</html>

--68dd10cbb2880fbc6f2f7a2b1d6945f1dab63200527154f441a3ef7bf5c5--
```

The above output has been truncated to show only the important parts.

Note: While you collect all the details previously discussed, do not forget to collect the content of the email, attachments, and other embedded images themselves. They are all important when looked into in their entirety.

Activity

Attempt the following activities before the next recipe:

- Inspect a non-spam email and highlight the differences with what we saw for a spam email.
- Find out a few of the header information in the spam email based on the information provided in this recipe.
- Do you see a tracking pixel in any of the spam emails? If yes, what do they look like in the code?
- We discussed SPF, DKIM, and DMARC as part of the routing information in the email. Find out what they are and what each of them is used for.
- What are the other ways the Message ID of the email metadata can be used for?
- We checked the email header and other information in the email from the Gmail web interface. Can you also do this using an email client on your personal computer?

Recipe 5: Techniques for evidence acquisition – browsing history

Browsing history from laptops, desktops, phones, tablets, and other devices is extremely valuable information for digital forensic investigators. Browsing history can provide a wealth of information for forensic investigators, often serving as critical evidence in digital forensics cases.

Note: Collecting and analyzing browsing history is one of the key aspects of browser forensics and is something that can be used during an investigation irrespective of the cybercrime.

Let us look at what browsing history can reveal:

Category	Details
User activity and intent	**Visited websites**: Insights into interests and activities **Search queries**: Reveals user intent and focus—Bookmarks and saved links. Highlights ongoing interests
Timeline of events	**Access times**: Browsing history includes timestamps, allowing investigators to construct a timeline of user activity. **Corroboration with other evidence**: Timeframes can be cross-referenced with other data (e.g., chat logs, emails) to confirm or refute claims.

Category	Details
Data exfiltration and malicious activity	**File downloads**: Logs of files downloaded, including file types and URLs, can indicate attempts to exfiltrate data or acquire malicious tools. **Cloud activity**: Access to cloud storage sites may show data upload or download activity. **Phishing and scam interactions**: Reveals if the user fell victim to phishing or visited fraudulent sites.
User behavior and patterns	**Daily routines**: Regular patterns of web usage (e.g., social media usage, news sites) help create a user profile. **Digital footprint**: Identifies whether the user regularly uses anonymizing tools like VPNs, Tor, or private browsing modes.
Evidence of malicious tools or illegal activities	**Dark web usage**: Browsing history may indicate **The Onion Router (Tor)** usage and interactions with onion websites. **Suspicious searches**: Queries related to illegal activities (e.g., hacking tools, contraband).
Context of the device usage	**Session analysis**: Helps determine who was using the device at a specific time. **Associated devices**: Can identify if data or sites were accessed through other devices (e.g., syncing).
Indicators of obfuscation or data destruction	**Cleared history**: Gaps in browsing history may suggest intentional deletion of data. **Private browsing and extensions**: Reveals if privacy-focused tools were employed, such as incognito mode or history-cleaning extensions.
Network and technical evidence	**IP addresses and sessions**: Some logs capture IPs, which can trace physical or virtual locations. **Browser fingerprints**: Unique configurations of browsers may help tie browsing history to specific users or devices.
Legal and organizational implications	**Policy violations**: Identifies activities violating company or organizational policies. **Intellectual property concerns**: Shows potential leaks of sensitive or proprietary information through browsing.

Table 3.5: Information that can be revealed from browsing history

Note:

- **Compatibility: Windows (similar tools are available for other operating systems)**
- **License considerations: Free software used**

Recipe

Let us look at a few Windows-based standalone tools that can help us to collect all the details from well-known browsers.

https://www.nirsoft.net has a large number of tools for browser forensics that include browsing history. Some of the browser forensics tools that are useful are the following:

Tool	Details
ChromeCacheView	Utility that reads Chrome browser's cache and displaying the list and details of all the files like URL, content type, file size, last accessed time, expiration time, server name, server response, etc.

Tool	Details
ChromeHistoryView	Utility that reads the Chrome browser's history and displays the list of all the visited web pages.
BrowsingHistoryView	Utility that shows history data of four browsers—Internet Explorer, Mozilla Firefox, Google Chrome, and Safari.

Table 3.6: *A few browser forensics tools*

Caution: While working with third-party applications It is suggested to use them on a Windows machine other than your regular machine. Using a portable app is more preferable as this does not result in the installation of the application and changing the Registry.

Let us try **ChromeCacheView**. When you run the utility, you will see a screen similar to the following:

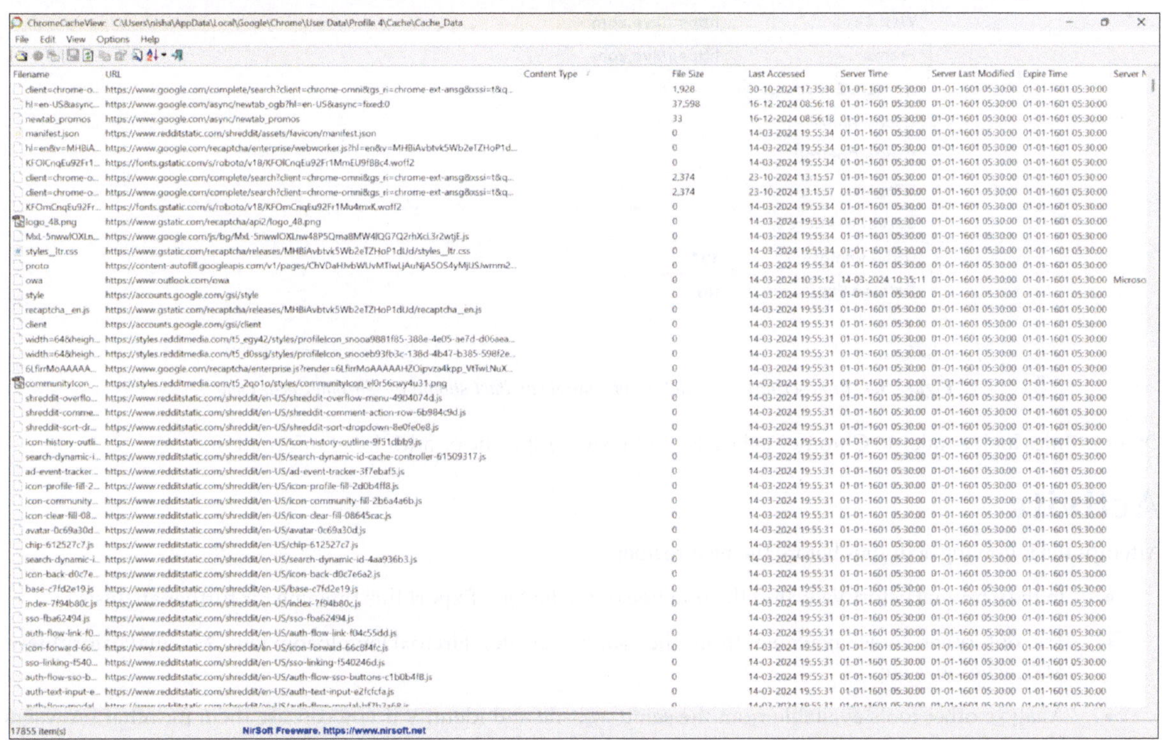

Figure 3.3: *Browser forensics, details shown by ChromeCacheView*

As you can see in this screenshot, this utility shows all the recently visited sites with their details. If you want to see details for a specific entry in a simpler to read format, double-click on any entry. You will see a screen similar to the following figure, which shows all the details of that entry:

Figure 3.4: *Browser forensics, details of a single artifact shown by ChromeCacheView*

Other utilities look similar to ChromeCacheView but provide specific or additional information.

Activity

Attempt the following activities before the next recipe:

- In the ChromeHistoryVew, find the timeline of the history. Export this timeline for further analysis.
- Try out other tools available from the same website, FirefoxDownloadsView, MozillaHistoryView, MZCacheView, etc.
- Analyze other tools available from the same website and identify if you can use them for other browsers (e.g., Safari, Opera) and other operating systems (e.g., Linux, macOS).

Techniques for evidence acquisition – network logs

Since a majority of attack vectors are related to the network, it is important to collect evidence from the network. The most important evidence one can collect from the network is network logs.

Let us look at the important network logs one can collect as evidence in case of a cyberattack or any other cybersecurity incident:

Log type	Description	Location (Linux/Windows)	Location/Collection on network devices
Firewall logs	Logs traffic allowed or denied by firewall rules, including source/destination IPs and ports.	Depends on the firewall software (e.g., **/var/log/ufw.log** on Linux, Windows Event Viewer for software firewalls).	Access through firewall web **graphical user interface (GUI)** or **command line interface (CLI)** (e.g., Cisco ASA devices: show logging).
IDS/IPS logs	Detects and logs suspicious activities or policy violations (e.g., Snort, Suricata).	**/var/log/snort/** or **/var/log/suricata/** on Linux. Suricata is a well-know open-source software with IDS and IPS capabilities	Access through IDS/IPS management console or CLI.
Proxy logs	Logs HTTP/S requests made via proxy servers, showing URLs, timestamps, and user agents.	Varies by proxy software (e.g., **/var/log/squid/access.log** for Squid on Linux).	Retrieve via proxy server management interface (e.g., Bluecoat or Palo Alto Panorama).
Web server logs	Tracks web access and error logs (e.g., Apache, NGINX), showing client IPs, URLs accessed, and errors.	**/var/log/apache2/access.log** or **/var/log/nginx/access.log** on Linux; IIS logs in **%SystemDrive%\inetpub\logs**.	Not applicable (these are usually server-side logs).
DHCP logs	Tracks IP lease activity, associating MAC addresses with IP addresses.	**/var/log/syslog** on Linux (for ISC DHCP), Event Viewer | System Logs on Windows Server.	Routers: Access via web GUI or CLI (e.g., show ip dhcp binding on Cisco devices).
DNS logs	Logs DNS queries and responses, helping trace domain resolution activity.	**/var/log/named.log** for BIND DNS on Linux, Windows DNS Server logs in Event Viewer.	Routers: Enable DNS logging in the device configuration or collect via DNS server management interface.
VPN logs	Logs VPN connection details, such as user logins, source IPs, and duration.	**/var/log/openvpn.log** or similar for Linux VPNs; Event Viewer for Windows VPN solutions.	VPN devices: Access logs via management interface (e.g., Cisco ASA devices: show **vpn-sessiondb**).
Netflow/PCAP data	Tracks flow-level traffic details, including source/destination IP, port, and protocol.	Captured using tools like tcpdump, Wireshark, or nfdump.	Export NetFlow data from routers/switches (e.g., Cisco: export flow data to a collector).
Router logs	Logs routing activity, interface status, and access attempts.	Not applicable (router logs are collected on devices).	Access via CLI (e.g., show logging on Cisco routers) or through SNMP/syslog configuration.
Switch logs	Tracks port activity, VLAN assignments, and spanning tree events.	Not applicable (switch logs are collected on devices).	Access via CLI or web GUI (e.g., Cisco: show logging or configure syslog).

Log type	Description	Location (Linux/Windows)	Location/Collection on network devices
Email server logs	Tracks email delivery, including sender, recipient, timestamp, and errors.	`/var/log/mail.log` for Postfix on Linux; Exchange Server logs in Event Viewer or specific Exchange paths.	Not applicable (email logs are server-side).
SIEM logs	Aggregated logs from multiple sources for correlation and analysis (e.g., Splunk, ELK, QRadar).	Centralized in SIEM systems, with paths varying by software.	Logs are collected and processed by the **security information and event management** (**SIEM**) server directly from network devices or endpoints via agents or connectors.
Authentication logs	Tracks user login/logout events, including successful and failed attempts.	`/var/log/auth.log` or `/var/log/secure` on Linux, Windows Security Event Logs in Event Viewer.	Not applicable (authentication logs are typically on servers, not network devices).
Syslog	Centralized log messages from network devices, including error, warning, and info messages.	`/var/log/syslog` on Linux.	Devices configured to send logs to a centralized syslog server (e.g., configure logging host on Cisco devices).

***Table 3.7:** Techniques for network logs collection*

As you see, many of these logs cannot be collected directly as we do from Linux or Windows servers. Many specialized network devices, like routers, gateways, firewalls, etc., may have their own proprietary interfaces to download the latest and archived logs.

This table gives a snapshot of a few of the important logs that can be collected. In real life, you need to keep adding to this list and collect all the logs that are generated. Additionally, it is extremely important to automate the collection process using a home-grown solution/script or a third-party utility, as collecting these logs may be a tedious and time-consuming process.

Now that you know the location of some of these logs, you can automate the collection of the log process as follows:

Log	Methods to collect them
Linux logs	Most of the logs can be collected directly. Even the logs that are not directly readable can be collected and parsed using well-known tools.
Windows logs	A few of the Windows logs can be collected directly. However, logs that are not present in a parseable fashion in a file, e.g., event logs, can be collected using PowerShell. We will look at this method in a later chapter.
Network devices (e.g., router, gateway, switch, etc.)	Some of them can be collected from the file system. However, a lot of them can be collected only through their user interface or using another method (e.g., REST method). Automation using Python and Selenium can be used to collect these logs.

***Table 3.8:** General methods to collect logs*

Recipe 6: Evidence acquisition – changed files using auditctl

A threat actor in the process of compromising the system would most certainly end up modifying files. For example, such modifications can be done to gain access to certain resources or to get higher privileges.

Discovering the changed file information is an important aspect, as it can help digital forensics investigators create a timeline as well as focus on the files that have been changed.

In this recipe, we will understand how to collect the list of modified files as part of the overall evidence collection using Linux's auditctl utility.

Note:

- **Compatibility: Linux**
- **License considerations: Free software used**

Recipe

We have discussed in the last chapter that Linux's audit log, which is stored at `/var/log/audit/audit.log`, provides valuable information about important files being accessed (read), changed, or deleted.

The auditctl utility can be used to create default audit rules that generate audit logs whenever the file is read, written to, executed, or its attributes are changed.

Before you use auditctl, install the following commands:

```
apt-get update
apt-get upgrade
apt-get install auditd
```

Once you have installed the auditctl, refer to the following step to complete option 1 of this recipe:

1. Start the auditd service:

   ```
   systemctl start auditd
   ```

   You can verify if it is running by executing the following command:

   ```
   systemctl status auditd
   ```

   You will get an output similar to the following:

   ```
   root@Debian-12:/home/nishant/Work# systemctl status auditd
     auditd.service - Security Auditing Service
        Loaded: loaded (/lib/systemd/system/auditd.service; enabled; preset: enabled)
        Active: active (running) since Sun 2024-12-22 12:01:51 IST; 4min 25s ago
          Docs: man:auditd(8)
                https://github.com/linux-audit/audit-documentation
       Process: 3428 ExecStart=/sbin/auditd (code=exited, status=0/SUCCESS)
       Process: 3432 ExecStartPost=/sbin/augenrules --load (code=exited, status=0/SUCCESS)
      Main PID: 3429 (auditd)
         Tasks: 2 (limit: 9390)
        Memory: 652.0K
           CPU: 11ms
        CGroup: /system.slice/auditd.service
                └─3429 /sbin/auditd

   Dec 22 12:01:51 Debian-12 augenrules[3442]: enabled 1
   Dec 22 12:01:51 Debian-12 augenrules[3442]: failure 1
   ```

```
Dec 22 12:01:51 Debian-12 augenrules[3442]: pid 3429
Dec 22 12:01:51 Debian-12 augenrules[3442]: rate_limit 0
Dec 22 12:01:51 Debian-12 augenrules[3442]: backlog_limit 8192
Dec 22 12:01:51 Debian-12 augenrules[3442]: lost 0
Dec 22 12:01:51 Debian-12 augenrules[3442]: backlog 8
Dec 22 12:01:51 Debian-12 augenrules[3442]: backlog_wait_time 60000
Dec 22 12:01:51 Debian-12 augenrules[3442]: backlog_wait_time_actual 0
Dec 22 12:01:51 Debian-12 systemd[1]: Started auditd.service - Security Auditing Service.
root@Debian-12:/home/nishant/Work#
```

2. Now, create a text file where we are going to store something secret. This text is a representation of other secret/confidential files we want to protect.

   Use your favorite text editor, like **vi**, **nano**, or **gedit**, to create the text file **secret.txt**. After making sure the file is created, refer to the following:

   ```
   cat secret.txt
   ```

   You will get an output similar to the following:

   ```
   root@Debian-12:/home/nishant/Work# cat secret.txt
   This is a secret line!
   root@Debian-12:/home/nishant/Work#
   ```

3. In order to configure auditing for this file to ensure that we are notified in case the file is accessed, changed, or deleted, we will add audit rules for this file. The audit rules need to be added using the full path of the file:

   ```
   auditctl -w /home/nishant/Work/secret.txt
   ```

   In order to verify if the audit rules are indeed added, the following command can be used:

   ```
   root@Debian-12:/home/nishant/Work# auditctl -l
   -w /home/nishant/Work/secret.txt -p rwxa
   root@Debian-12:/home/nishant/Work#
   ```

   The **-l** option of **auditctl** lists all the rules. The **rwxa** means the audit is set for the following operations:

   a. – **r**: The file is read, accessed, opened, or printed
   b. – **w**: The file is written to
   c. – **x**: The file is executed
   d. – **a**: The files attribute is changed, e.g., when its permissions, date, and time, etc.

4. Now, open additional tabs in the terminal. In one tab, run the following command to monitor the log files as the logs are being added to it:

   ```
   tail -f /var/log/audit/audit.log
   ```

   In the second tab, let us now try a few operations that may result in audit logs being generated.

   First, print the file by using **cat**:

   ```
   cat secrets.txt
   ```

In the tab, where we are monitoring the file, you will see logs like the following in the **auditd.log** file:

```
type=SYSCALL msg=audit(1734853374.437:88): arch=c00000b7 syscall=56 success=yes exit=3
a0=ffffffffffffff9c a1=ffffc1b05e8d a2=0 a3=0 items=1 ppid=3218 pid=3682 auid=1000 uid=0 gid=0
euid=0 suid=0 fsuid=0 egid=0 sgid=0 fsgid=0 tty=pts0 ses=3 comm="cat" exe="/usr/bin/cat"
subj=unconfined key=(null)ARCH=aarch64 SYSCALL=openat AUID="nishant" UID="root" GID="root"
EUID="root" SUID="root" FSUID="root" EGID="root" SGID="root" FSGID="root"

type=CWD msg=audit(1734853374.437:88): cwd="/home/nishant/Work"

type=PATH msg=audit(1734853374.437:88): item=0 name="secret.txt" inode=3028133 dev=103:02
mode=0100644 ouid=0 ogid=0 rdev=00:00 nametype=NORMAL cap_fp=0 cap_fi=0 cap_fe=0 cap_fver=0
cap_frootid=0OUID="root" OGID="root"

type=PROCTITLE msg=audit(1734853374.437:88): proctitle=636174007365637265742E747874
```

Let us see now if we can track whether any files are being changed.

Open the file, add one more line, or even just one character, and save it. As soon as you save the file, you will see a bunch of logs like the following in the **auditd.log** file, which include logs that show the file is being opened (read) and then modified:

```
type=SYSCALL msg=audit(1734866129.565:102): arch=c00000b7 syscall=8 success=no exit=-61
a0=aaab1ff03380 a1=ffff9f0f5dd8 a2=ffffc9f3aed0 a3=84 items=1 ppid=3218 pid=4080 auid=1000 uid=0
gid=0 euid=0 suid=0 fsuid=0 egid=0 sgid=0 fsgid=0 tty=pts0 ses=3 comm="vi" exe="/usr/bin/vim.
tiny" subj=unconfined key=(null)ARCH=aarch64 SYSCALL=getxattr AUID="nishant" UID="root" GID="root"
EUID="root" SUID="root" FSUID="root" EGID="root" SGID="root" FSGID="root"
type=CWD msg=audit(1734866129.565:102): cwd="/home/nishant/Work"

type=PATH msg=audit(1734866129.565:102): item=0 name="secret.txt" inode=3028133 dev=103:02
mode=0100644 ouid=0 ogid=0 rdev=00:00 nametype=NORMAL cap_fp=0 cap_fi=0 cap_fe=0 cap_fver=0 cap_
frootid=0OUID="root" OGID="root"

type=PROCTITLE msg=audit(1734866129.565:102): proctitle=7669007365637265742E747874

type=SYSCALL msg=audit(1734866129.565:103): arch=c00000b7 syscall=56 success=yes exit=3
a0=ffffffffffffff9c a1=aaab1ff03380 a2=0 a3=0 items=1 ppid=3218 pid=4080 auid=1000 uid=0 gid=0
euid=0 suid=0 fsuid=0 egid=0 sgid=0 fsgid=0 tty=pts0 ses=3 comm="vi" exe="/usr/bin/vim.tiny"
subj=unconfined key=(null)ARCH=aarch64 SYSCALL=openat AUID="nishant" UID="root" GID="root"
EUID="root" SUID="root" FSUID="root" EGID="root" SGID="root" FSGID="root"

type=CWD msg=audit(1734866129.565:103): cwd="/home/nishant/Work"

type=PATH msg=audit(1734866129.565:103): item=0 name="secret.txt" inode=3028133 dev=103:02
mode=0100644 ouid=0 ogid=0 rdev=00:00 nametype=NORMAL cap_fp=0 cap_fi=0 cap_fe=0 cap_fver=0 cap_
frootid=0OUID="root" OGID="root"

type=PROCTITLE msg=audit(1734866129.565:103): proctitle=7669007365637265742E747874

type=SYSCALL msg=audit(1734866129.565:104): arch=c00000b7 syscall=56 success=yes exit=3
a0=ffffffffffffff9c a1=aaab1ff03380 a2=41 a3=1a4 items=2 ppid=3218 pid=4080 auid=1000 uid=0 gid=0
euid=0 suid=0 fsuid=0 egid=0 sgid=0 fsgid=0 tty=pts0 ses=3 comm="vi" exe="/usr/bin/vim.tiny"
subj=unconfined key=(null)ARCH=aarch64 SYSCALL=openat AUID="nishant" UID="root" GID="root"
EUID="root" SUID="root" FSUID="root" EGID="root" SGID="root" FSGID="root"

type=CWD msg=audit(1734866129.565:104): cwd="/home/nishant/Work"

type=PATH msg=audit(1734866129.565:104): item=0 name="/home/nishant/Work" inode=3027982 dev=103:02
mode=040755 ouid=1000 ogid=1000 rdev=00:00 nametype=PARENT cap_fp=0 cap_fi=0 cap_fe=0 cap_fver=0
cap_frootid=0OUID="nishant" OGID="nishant"

type=PATH msg=audit(1734866129.565:104): item=1 name="secret.txt" inode=3028133 dev=103:02
```

```
mode=0100644 ouid=0 ogid=0 rdev=00:00 nametype=NORMAL cap_fp=0 cap_fi=0 cap_fe=0 cap_fver=0 cap_
frootid=0OUID="root" OGID="root"
type=PROCTITLE msg=audit(1734866129.565:104): proctitle=7669007365637265742E747874
type=SYSCALL msg=audit(1734866129.565:105): arch=c00000b7 syscall=52 success=yes exit=0 a0=3
a1=81a4 a2=0 a3=1 items=1 ppid=3218 pid=4080 auid=1000 uid=0 gid=0 euid=0 suid=0 fsuid=0 egid=0
sgid=0 fsgid=0 tty=pts0 ses=3 comm="vi" exe="/usr/bin/vim.tiny" subj=unconfined key=(null)
ARCH=aarch64 SYSCALL=fchmod AUID="nishant" UID="root" GID="root" EUID="root" SUID="root"
FSUID="root" EGID="root" SGID="root" FSGID="root"
type=CWD msg=audit(1734866129.565:105): cwd="/home/nishant/Work"
type=PATH msg=audit(1734866129.565:105): item=0 name=(null) inode=3028133 dev=103:02
mode=0100644 ouid=0 ogid=0 rdev=00:00 nametype=NORMAL cap_fp=0 cap_fi=0 cap_fe=0 cap_fver=0 cap_
frootid=0OUID="root" OGID="root"
type=PROCTITLE msg=audit(1734866129.565:105): proctitle=7669007365637265742E747874
```

This means if there are audit rules like this set on important files in critical servers, we can find out instantaneously if these files are being changed. Not only that, but the logs also have important information like user ID (UID), group ID (GUID), the name of the program that was used to change the file, when the file was modified, and so on. This can also help us identify the attack vector being used by the cybercriminal.

Enabling audit logs for such important files is one of the key aspects of making the systems ready for forensic evidence collection.

When are you done with testing and do not need the audit rules anymore for the file, you can delete them using the following command:

```
auditctl -D
```

The preceding command will delete all the rules. Ideally, you should delete the specific rules if. They are not needed.

Note: In this recipe, the activities were done using the Debian Linux distribution. Well-known operating systems like Ubuntu and Kali Linux are based on Debian. While you may comfortable with just using Kali Linux for forensics and may not feel a need to use any other distribution, it is good to use a variety of distributions to get a feel of the changes that come along with these distributions.

Activity

Attempt the following activities before the next recipe:

- We discussed that a part of the audit rule gets triggered when a file attribute is changed. Run the following commands and verify if they result in the generation of audit logs: `touch secrets.txt`, `chmod 644 secrets.txt`, and `chown root:root secrets.txt`. Explain the attributes changed by each of these commands that might have resulted in the audit logs.
- Write a simple Python program to parse the logs in **auditd.log** to show them in a much more readable way that can be used in a report.
- Read the auditctl documentation (man pages) to find out how you can delete a specific audit rule.
- Read the auditctl documentation (man pages) to find out if you can create just a `w` rule instead of a default `rwxa` rule.

Recipe 7: Techniques for evidence acquisition – changed files using find

The **find** command in Linux is a versatile command that is used to search for files in the Linux filesystem. One of the important features of the find command is that it can help to find based on the timestamp of the file.

In this recipe, we will look at using find commands to find details about changed files.

Note:

- **Compatibility: Linux**
- **License considerations: Free software used**

Recipe

Let us see how we can use the **find** command to discover recently changed files.

The following command can list all the files that were changed in the last one day:

```
find . -mtime 1 -type f
```

When you execute this command in your home directory, the output will look similar to the following:

```
root@Debian-12:/home/nishant/Work# find . -mtime -1 -ls
  3027982      4 drwxr-xr-x   3 nishant  nishant      4096 Dec 22 16:45 .
  3028133      4 -rw-r--r--   1 root     root           24 Dec 22 16:45 ./secret.txt
root@Debian-12:/home/nishant/Work#
```

Now, let us create another file in the same directory and run the following command again:

```
touch test_forensics.txt
find . -mtime -1 -ls
```

The output will look similar to the following:

```
root@Debian-12:/home/nishant/Work# find . -mtime -1 -ls
  3027982      4 drwxr-xr-x   3 nishant  nishant      4096 Dec 22 17:11 .
  3028133      4 -rw-r--r--   1 root     root           24 Dec 22 16:45 ./secret.txt
  3028143      0 -rw-r--r--   1 root     root            0 Dec 22 17:11 ./test_forensics.txt
root@Debian-12:/home/nishant/Work#
```

Activity

Attempt the following activities before the next recipe:

- In the **find** command, sort the output so that the result is printed in reverse chronological order, i.e., the most recently modified file gets printed first.
- **find** command also provides a way to find files changed between a time interval. Modify the commands discussed in this recipe to find files that were changed between the third day and the second day in the past.

Recipe 8: Techniques for evidence acquisition - cookies

Before we get into the details of acquiring cookies from a target system, let us understand a bit about cookies in the context of digital forensics. Cookies are small text files stored by web browsers containing data from visited websites, and store information like session data, browsing history, timestamp, tracking date, and many identifiers (e.g., user IDs, preferences, shopping carts, etc.). They serve as evidence of user activity, preferences, and interactions, aiding in timeline reconstruction and user behavior analysis.

Due to the types of information they store. Cookies can be used for the following purposes in digital forensics:

- Identifying user interaction with specific websites.
- Reconstructing timelines for investigations.
- Linking cookies to user accounts or malicious activity.

Interesting fact: **Cookies can also be stored in SQLite databases. Hence, while collecting evidence from the browsers, collect everything. You never know which piece of artifact may get you additional and valuable information.**

Note:

- **Compatibility: Windows (similar tools are available for other operating systems)**
- **License considerations: Free software used**

Recipe

Let us check what are the cookies that are stored by Chrome on our machine. For this, we will use another utility called **ChromeCookiesView**. This utility can also be downloaded from **https://www.nirsoft.net**. As usual, while working with 3rd party applications for digital forensics purposes, it is advisable to use another machine that is not used for any other critical purpose and does not store critical data.

If you have the Chrome browser running, close the browser, otherwise the cookies may be locked by the browser, and **ChromeCookiesView** will not be able to open them.

Let us run the **ChromeCookiesView** and analyze what you see. You will see a Window like this, where all the cookies that are in the Chrome Cache are shown. You can also export them and create a report for them.

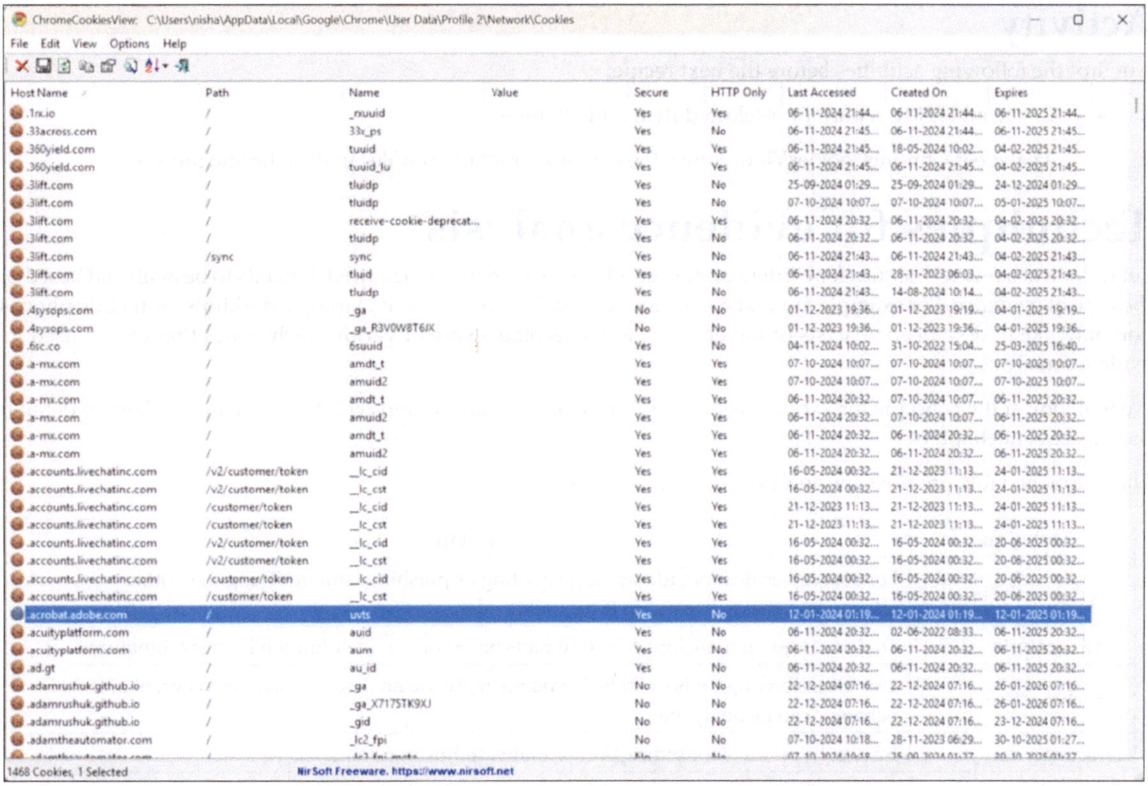

Figure 3.5: Browser forensics, list of cookies shown by ChromeCookiesView

The **ChromeCookiesView** shows a lot of information, including who created the cookie (hostname of the site), when it was created, when it was last accessed, and so on.

If you double-click on any of the selected cookies, the details are shown in an easy-to-read format in a pop-up:

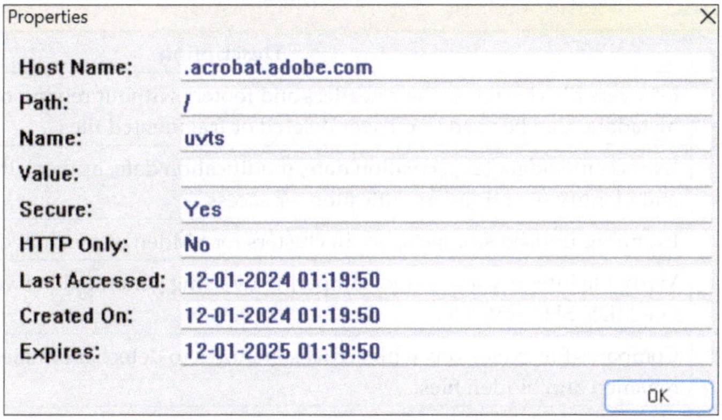

Figure 3.6: Browser forensics, details of a single cookie shown by ChromeCookiesView

Activity

Attempt the following activities before the next recipe:

- Create an HTML report for a selected item and all items.
- Analyze if ChromeCookiesView shows the cookies for all the profiles in the Chrome browser.

Techniques for evidence analysis

Let us look at a few techniques for evidence analysis. Once the evidence is acquired, it needs to be analyzed based on the type of evidence. For example, if you have collected emails from the seized laptops, desktops, or mobile phones, you may like to do a deep analysis of the emails. Let us become aware of various techniques that can be used for evidence analysis.

We will look at the concepts for various techniques for evidence analysis and will discuss many of them in detail in the subsequent chapters.

The following table provides the analysis techniques for emails:

Technique	Details
Header analysis	For source verification, identifying spoofing or phishing, and verifying may other information that is present in the email header.
Hash analysis	To detect known malicious files or emails based on the well-known hashes/signatures.
Attachment analysis	Using sandboxing tools or static/dynamic malware analysis, attachment content and their behavior can be analyzed
Link analysis	Inspect hyperlinks for redirection or malware-hosting domains.
Correlation analysis	Cross-referencing metadata with known threat intelligence feeds.
Spam analysis	Examines spam emails for phishing or social engineering attempts, and for detecting emails trying to perform fraud or data theft.

***Table 3.9**: Techniques for email evidence analysis*

The following table provides the analysis techniques for file systems:

Technique	Description
File carving	Recovers files based on their headers and footers without relying on the file system metadata. Can be used to recover deleted or fragmented files.
Metadata analysis	Extracts metadata (e.g., creation date, modification date, author). It can be used to analyze and identify file origin, modification, or access.
Unused space analysis	Examines unused storage space in clusters for hidden or residual data.
File hashing	Verify file integrity and detect tampering by using generated has values using algorithms like MD5, SHA-256, etc.
File signature analysis	Compares file extensions with actual signatures to detect anomalies, and identify renamed and hidden files.

***Table 3.10**: Techniques for file systems evidence analysis*

The following table provides the analysis techniques for network-based evidence:

Technique	Description
Packet analysis	Analyzes network traffic using tools like Wireshark and can be used to reconstruct network activity and detect anomalies.
NetFlow analysis	Examines flow-level data (source/destination IPs, ports, protocols) to trace network communication patterns and detect anomalies and threats.
Log analysis	Reviews network device logs (firewalls, proxies, routers) to identify unauthorized access or data exfiltration.
DNS query analysis	Investigates DNS logs for suspicious queries and can be used to detect command and control (also known as C2) communication or phishing attempts.
Deep packet inspection	Inspects payload content within packets. Can be used to extract sensitive information or malware payloads.

Table 3.11: Techniques for network-based evidence analysis

The following table provides the analysis techniques for memory evidence:

Technique	Description
Memory dump analysis	Analyzes **raw memory dumps** (**RAM**) for processes and artifacts, and to recover encryption keys, credentials, and get more insights into malware.
Analysis using tools like Volatility	Uses specialized tools to extract processes, DLLs, network connections, etc., and analyze running processes and malware activity.
String search	Searches for readable strings in memory dumps, to extract important information like plain-text credentials or keywords.
Dynamic-link library (**DLL**) injection detection	Identifies malicious DLLs injected into processes, and can be used to detect malware or rootkits in memory.

Table 3.12: Techniques for memory evidence analysis

The following table provides the analysis techniques for disk evidence. Some of them are used over and above the evidence for file systems we discussed previously:

Technique	Description
Disk imaging	Creates an exact copy of storage media, preserving evidence integrity for analysis.
Partition analysis	Examines partition tables for hidden or deleted partitions, to recover hidden or deleted data.
Data decryption	Attempts to decrypt encrypted drives or files, to access encrypted evidence. Can be used to access encrypted volumes too.
Deleted file recovery	Recovers files marked as deleted in the file system for intentionally or accidentally deleted files.
Hexadecimal analysis	Analyzes raw disk sectors using hex editors to hidden data or verify file integrity.

Table 3.13: Techniques for disk evidence analysis

The following table provides the analysis techniques for mobile device (phone, tablet, smart watch, etc.) evidence:

Technique	Description
Logical extraction	Extracts user-accessible data using software tools, to access app data, call logs, SMS, and media.
Physical extraction	Extracts complete raw data from device memory, to retrieve deleted or hidden data.
Cloud data analysis	Analyzes data synced with cloud services, to access remotely stored backups or accounts.
SIM card analysis	Extracts data stored in SIM cards, to retrieve SMS, contacts, or subscriber details.
App data analysis	Examines app-specific data like chats, usage logs, and cached files, for reconstruction of user activities.

***Table 3.14**: Techniques for mobile device evidence analysis*

The following table provides the analysis techniques for evidence collected in the form of application logs:

Technique	Description
Log parsing	Extracts structured data from application logs to reconstruct user or system activities.
Timestamp analysis	Verifies timestamps to create event timelines, to establish sequence of events.
Error code analysis	Interprets error codes in logs for identifying attempts or attacks.
Correlation analysis	Links related log entries across multiple sources, coordinated or complex activities.

***Table 3.15**: Techniques for application logs, based evidence analysis*

The following table provides the analysis techniques for multimedia evidence. Using various advanced techniques, multimedia files can also reveal a lot and aid in digital forensics analysis:

Technique	Description
Image metadata analysis	Extracts **exchangeable image file format** (**EXIF**) data from images (e.g., camera model, geolocation) and can be used to trace the source or location of photos. EXIF is a standardized way to store various technical information and metadata about digital images.
Video frame analysis	Analyzes individual video frames for hidden details to identify anomalies or tampered content.
Audio spectrogram analysis	Inspects audio files for hidden messages or anomalies to detect steganography or tampering.
Steganography detection	Scans files for hidden data embedded in multimedia to reveal hidden messages and payloads.

***Table 3.16**: Techniques for multimedia evidence analysis*

Recipe 9: Analyzing SQLite database files

SQLite is a lightweight, self-contained, serverless database engine. It stores data in a single file on disk and is widely used due to its simplicity, portability, and minimal configuration requirements. It is often embedded in applications, browsers, mobile devices, and IoT systems.

Note: DB-engines has a very informative page for SQLite at https://db-engines.com/en/system/SQLite that provides a lot of details about this very versatile database.

Analyzing SQLite database is important as it is used to store data by web and mobile applications. The data may include logs, attachments, timestamps, user settings, app-specific settings, file usage history, configuration data, and much more. Attackers may also use SQLite database for temporary data storage when the attack vectors are through browsers or mobile apps. Hence, analyzing SQLite databases is crucial in cyber forensics as they often contain critical evidence about user activities, application data, and potential malicious behavior.

Let us quickly understand a few key points about the structure of a typical SQLite database. This will help you understand what to look for in case a database file is collected as part of the evidence:

- A SQLite database is a single `.sqlite`, `.db`, or `.sqlite3` file on disk.
- The database file contains all the data (e.g., tables, indexes, triggers, and the entire schema) and is portable. This means you can just copy the single DB file to another system and work with it.
- SQLite is a relational database. Hence, its schema would look similar to other relational databases. Just like other relational databases, a SQLite database can have tables, indexes, views, triggers, etc.
- Internally, the SQLite database is organized into pages with a typical page size of 4 KB or 1 KB, which is configurable. Pages are the smallest units of **input/output** (**I/O**) in the SQLite database.
- Tables and indexes are stored using the B-Tree data structure. This is very common in other relational databases as well.
- Rows in the tables are stored as key-value pairs.
- SQLite supports variable-length records. However, rows only take up the required space and are not fixed-width.
- There are a few system tables that include `sqlitemaster` and `sqlitesquence`.
- SQLite uses additional temporary files for transactional consistency that include rollback journals (`.journal` files), write-ahead logging (WAL, or `.wal` files), and shared memory files (`.shm` files).

In this recipe, let us look at how we can use a small utility, SQLiteDatabaseBrowser, to browse the content of a SQLite database. You can download sample SQLite databases from various GitHub projects.

Note:

- **Compatibility: Windows (similar tools are available for other operating systems)**
- **License considerations: Free software used**

Recipe

In order to work with the SQLite database, we can either create a database or work with an existing database. You can use various SQLite tutorials and samples available on the web to create a database. However, when it comes to digital forensics, the investigators need to work with an existing database that has been collected as part of the evidence. We will use one of such publicity available database sample.

Note: **In order to inspect a SQLite database, you will need a database manager. There are multiple freeware options available. One of them is DB Browser for SQLite Portable which is available at the Portable Apps site at https://portableapps.com/apps/development/sqlite_database_browser_portable. However, feel free to use any well-know SQLite database manager.**

We will use DB Browser for SQLite Portable for analyzing the SQLite database file. Start the **DB Browser for SQLite**. The first screen would look like the following:

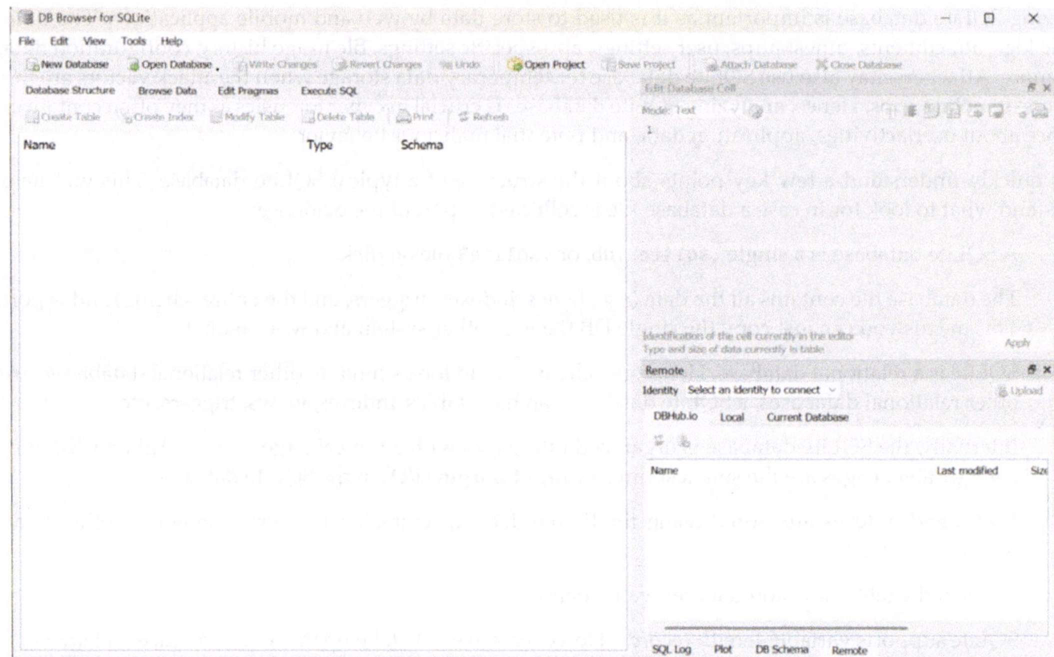

Figure 3.7: SQLite database forensics, DB Browser for SQLite opening screen

Click on **Open Database** on the top bar and select the sample database you have downloaded from the Internet, i.e., the company's database. The application now shows the details about the database.

The following screenshot shows the database structure:

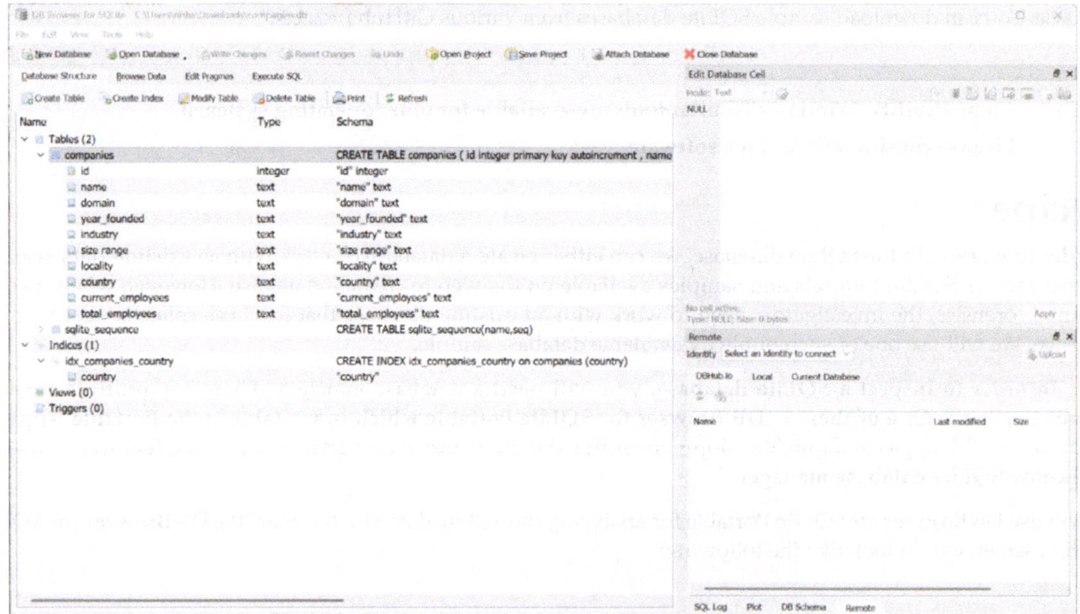

Figure 3.8: SQLite database forensics, SQLite database structure

The following screenshot shows the **Browse Data** tab. In this tab, you can select the table you want to browse from the **Table** dropdown:

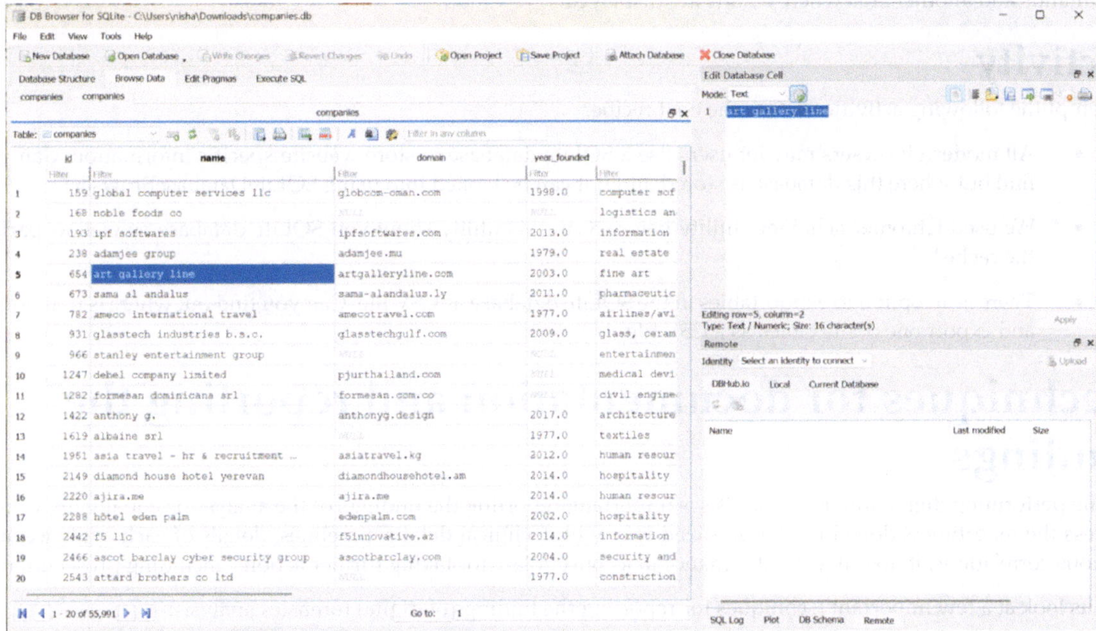

Figure 3.9*: SQLite database forensics, browsing tables of the SQLite database*

The following screenshot shows how we can run SQL queries on various tables, similar to other such tools:

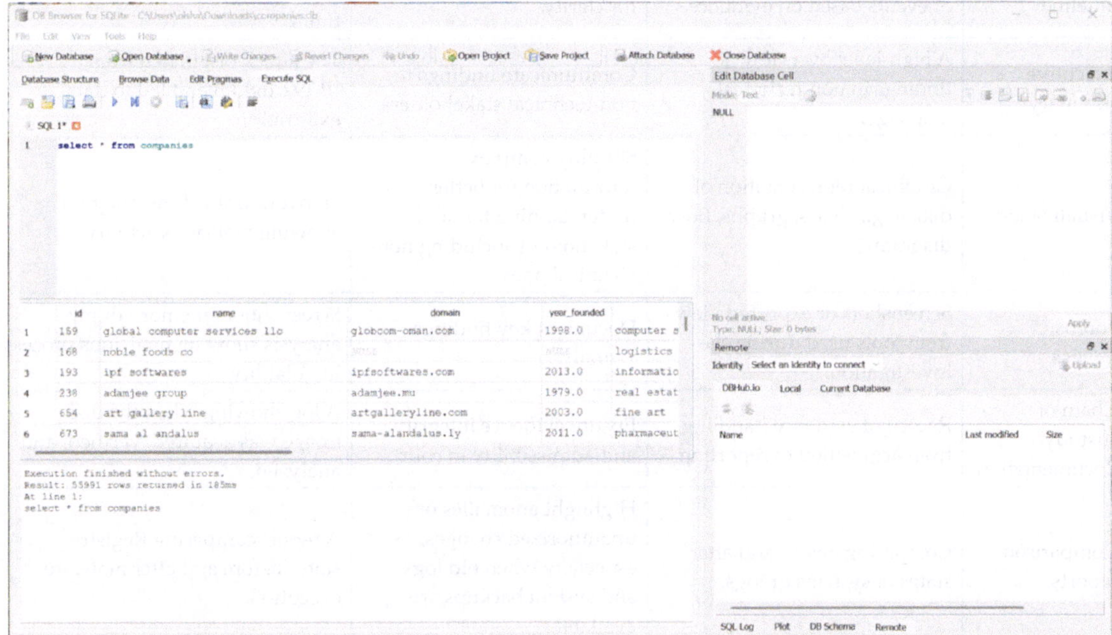

Figure 3.10*: SQLite database forensics, running SQL queries on the tables in the database*

If you are already familiar with other such applications that are used for relational databases like MySQL and MS SQL Server, you would right away understand how to use it. It has a similar area for typing and executing SQL commands and another area where results are displayed.

Activity

Attempt the following activities before the next recipe:

- All modern browsers may let users use a SQLite database to store website-specific information. Can you find out where this database is stored and if it can be looked into using SQLiteDatabaseBrowser?
- We used ChromeCacheView utility before. Can this utility show you SQLite database as well as part of the cache?
- There is an option to export tables in the SQLite database as CSV file. Can you find out where is that option and export one of the tables as a CSV file.

Techniques for documentation and reporting the findings

While performing digital forensics analysis is important, reporting the findings of the analysis is equally important. Unless the reporting is done in a standardized way with technical details, timelines, details of each evidence, and various correlations, it does not stand a chance in a court of law for taking further actions, including prosecution.

Let us look at a few important techniques for reporting the findings of digital forensics analysis:

Technique	Description	Purpose	Example
Incident timeline	Chronological reconstruction of events based on evidence.	Show sequence of activities for clarity.	A timeline of login events, file access, and malware execution times.
Executive summary	A high-level overview of findings in non-technical language.	Communicate findings to non-technical stakeholders.	The attack originated from IP 192.168.1.5 and led to data exfiltration.
Visualization	Graphical representation of data (e.g., charts, graphs, flow diagrams).	Simplify complex information for better understanding for all the stakeholders including non-technical ones.	Network traffic flow diagram showing malicious activity.
Forensic images	Screenshots or exported views from tools used during the investigation.	Document key findings visually.	Screenshot of memory dump analysis showing malicious process in Volatility.
Chain of custody documentation	Record of evidence handling from acquisition to reporting.	Ensure evidence integrity and admissibility in court.	A log showing when the disk image was acquired, verified, and analyzed.
Comparison reports	Comparing before and after states of systems or logs.	Highlight anomalies or unauthorized changes, especially when old logs and system backups are available.	A report comparing Registry states before and after malware execution.

Technique	Description	Purpose	Example
Log summaries	Consolidated summaries of logs analyzed during investigation.	Identify patterns or anomalies quickly.	Summary of firewall logs showing repeated access attempts from the same IP address.
Hash verification report	Documentation of hash values used to verify file integrity.	Confirm authenticity and integrity of evidence.	MD5 and SHA-256 hash comparison for acquired disk image.
Malware analysis report	Details of malware behavior and associated IOCs.	Document malicious activity and its impact.	A report detailing malware persistence techniques and communication with a C2 server.

***Table 3.17**: Reporting the findings of digital forensics analysis*

All of these can be part of a detailed technical report that documents evidence, tools, and methods used comprehensively, and provides detailed documentation for legal or technical audiences. It is worth noting that many commercial digital forensic tools already generate highly detailed reports that can be customized for court and various stakeholders.

Note: **Digital forensics and incident response (DFIR) which is a highly specialized sub-field of cybersecurity focusing on identifying, remediating, and investigating cyber security incidents, uses such reports for detailed analysis and reporting of incidents.**

Conclusion

In this chapter, we looked at general digital forensic techniques applicable across domains, emphasizing the evidence lifecycle, identification, acquisition, analysis, and reporting. We also got insights into acquiring various evidence types, including emails, browsing history, network logs, and cookies. With these, we discussed analyzing diverse evidence, such as email headers, file metadata, network logs, and SQLite databases. We discussed a few advanced concepts in this chapter that highlighted the importance of reporting findings using structured methods like timelines, visualizations, and technical reports.

Digital forensic investigators, after mastering these techniques, can ensure evidence integrity, comprehensive analysis, and legally admissible reporting.

In the next chapter, we will discuss the development environment for digital forensics that digital forensic investigators and analysts can use.

Questions

1. What are the main phases of the evidence lifecycle in digital forensics?
2. Why is preserving the original evidence important?
3. What techniques can be used for email evidence acquisition?
4. What hidden information can be extracted from email headers?
5. How can browsing history aid in digital forensics investigations?
6. What tools can be used to analyze browsing history?
7. What are the critical types of network logs collected in forensic analysis?
8. How can auditctl be used to monitor file changes?

9. What are the advantages of using SQLite databases in digital forensics?
10. What metadata can be extracted from files during forensic analysis?
11. How does packet analysis help in network-based evidence analysis?
12. What is the role of DNS query analysis in detecting phishing attempts?
13. What is memory dump analysis, and what can it reveal?
14. Why is file carving crucial in forensic investigations?
15. How can multimedia evidence be analyzed for hidden data?
16. What is the significance of chain of custody documentation?
17. What is the difference between logical and physical data extraction for mobile devices?
18. How are hash values used to verify evidence integrity?
19. What are the key components of a forensic investigation report?
20. How do tools like ChromeCookiesView assist in cookie analysis?

Points to remember

- Digital forensics involves the systematic process of identification, acquisition, analysis, and reporting.
- Evidence must be preserved in its original state to maintain integrity.
- Emails contain both visible and hidden data crucial for investigations.
- Browsing history reveals user intent, activities, and potential malicious actions.
- Network logs provide insight into unauthorized access and data exfiltration.
- auditctl helps monitor file changes in Linux systems.
- SQLite databases are widely used and store critical application data.
- File metadata reveals creation, modification, and access details.
- File carving is used to recover deleted files without relying on file system metadata.
- Memory dumps uncover active processes, malware, and encryption keys.
- DNS logs trace suspicious queries and C2 communications.
- Visualizing data helps non-technical stakeholders understand forensic findings.
- Chain-of-custody records ensure evidence admissibility in court.
- Logical extraction retrieves accessible data; physical extraction retrieves all raw data.
- Steganography detection scans multimedia for hidden data.
- Packet analysis reconstructs network activity for threat identification.
- Tools like Wireshark and tcpdump aid in network evidence analysis.
- Reporting findings with timelines ensures clarity and completeness.
- Hash values like MD5 and SHA-256 confirm evidence integrity.
- Logs from network devices like firewalls and routers provide critical evidence.

- Timestamp analysis establishes the sequence of events.
- Dark web interactions can be identified through browsing history.
- Emails often include tracking pixels and hidden scripts.
- Commercial forensic tools generate comprehensive, court-ready reports.
- Forensic analysis techniques must align with legal standards to be admissible.

Key terms

- **Evidence lifecycle**: The process of identifying, acquiring, analyzing, and reporting evidence.
- **Auditctl**: A Linux utility to create audit rules for monitoring file activity.
- **SQLite**: A lightweight, serverless database engine used for storing application data.
- **EXIF**: Metadata embedded in images, including camera details and geolocation.
- **Packet analysis**: Inspecting network packets to reconstruct activity or detect anomalies.
- **Chain of custody**: A documented process ensuring evidence integrity from collection to reporting.
- **Steganography**: The process and art of concealing data within multimedia files like photos, audio files, and video files.
- **DNS query analysis**: Examining DNS logs for suspicious activity or malicious domains.
- **Hash values**: Cryptographic values used for verifying data integrity (e.g., MD5, SHA-256).
- **Forensic image**: A bit-for-bit copy of storage media for analysis.
- **Deep packet inspection**: Analyzing payloads of network packets for sensitive data or malware.
- **Tor**: Tor is a privacy-focused network that enables anonymous communication by routing internet traffic through multiple encrypted relays.
- **Logical extraction**: Retrieving user-accessible data from devices.
- **Physical extraction**: Retrieving all raw data, including deleted or hidden data.
- **Volatility**: A well-known tool for analyzing memory dumps for processes and malware.
- **NetFlow**: Flow-level network data summarizing communication patterns.
- **File carving**: Recovering files without relying on file system metadata.
- **Timeline**: Chronological representation of events for clarity in reporting.
- **Visualization**: Graphical representation of data to simplify complex information.
- **Metadata**: Information describing a file's attributes, such as creation date.
- **Syslog**: A standard for message logging from network devices and systems.
- **Spam analysis**: Examination of emails for phishing, fraud, or social engineering attempts.
- **Cookies**: Small text files storing user session and interaction details.
- **SQL injection**: An attack manipulating SQL queries to gain unauthorized access.

CHAPTER 4

Development Environment for Digital Forensics

Introduction

A personalized development environment is essential for every cybersecurity professional working on digital forensics. Such environments allow professionals to try various tools and techniques in an isolated environment. They also help professionals work with advanced concepts that are destructive in nature without fear of adversely affecting anyone else.

A development environment like this can allow digital forensics professionals to write custom code for specialized investigation needs. It can also help them study code for open-source tools and reverse-engineered code.

In this chapter, we will set up the development environment so you can complete all the hands-on activities and assignments in this book. These recipes are in addition to the virtualized environment using Kali Linux or Kali Purple in *Chapter 02, Digital Forensics for Enterprises*.

Structure

In this chapter, we will cover the following topics:

- Importance of development and test environments
- Recipe 10: Configuring your Python development environment
- Recipe 11: Configuring important libraries using pip3 and apt-get
- Recipe 12: Setting up your Python virtual environment or venv
- Recipe 13: Testing sample programs to confirm that everything is configured well
- Recipe 14: Configuring your PowerShell development environment on Windows
- Recipe 15: Understanding the PowerShell ISE editor
- ISE editor versus other editors on Windows
- Recipe 16: VS Code for Python and PowerShell scripting
- Recipe 17: Testing a PowerShell script filter-based logs
- Secure environment for working with digital forensic evidence
- Additional considerations for the development environment

Objectives

In this chapter, we will understand the importance of developing and testing environments for digital forensics and configure our digital forensics environments for both Linux and Windows. As part of this, we will configure a Python development environment, including a virtual environment for Python. We will also configure and test the PowerShell development environment for Windows. After that, we will understand the PowerShell ISE editor by running a few sample programs. We will also look at how the ISE editor compares to other popular PowerShell editors for Windows.

By the end of this chapter, you should be comfortable with using Linux and Windows for various development and scripting needs of digital forensics.

Importance of development and test environments

In digital forensics, development and test environments play a critical role in ensuring the reliability, accuracy, and credibility of forensic tools, methodologies, and processes. A well-structured development and test environment in digital forensics is essential for ensuring tool reliability, process validation, skill development, and legal defensibility. It provides a risk-free space to test new tools, train investigators, and simulate real-world forensic cases. This practice ultimately strengthens the accuracy, repeatability, and integrity of digital forensic investigations.

The following tables list the importance of development and test environments in digital forensics:

Key objectives	Details
Tool testing and validation	Ensures forensic tools are reliable, accurate, and do not alter digital evidence. Helps maintain different versions of tools and dependencies with projects.
Methodology validation	Validates new forensic techniques and methodologies for repeatability and accuracy.
Minimizing errors and false positives	Helps identify errors and misconfigurations to avoid false positives or missing data.
Minimizing false negatives	Helps identify errors and misconfigurations to avoid false negatives or absence of a condition or data when it is actually present.
Training and skill development	Provides a controlled environment for investigators to hone digital forensic skills.
Replication of cyber incidents	Simulates cyber incidents to study digital traces and refine investigative strategies.
Legal defensibility	Ensures tools and methods meet legal standards for evidence admissibility.
Test methods and tools without affecting anyone else	Ensure that advanced techniques that may lead to other parties getting affected are tested without the fear of any repercussions.
Better collaboration	Helps proper collaboration between team when they share a common environment.
Replicable environments	Helps replicate the environment as well as going back to a clean state. Easy to recreate if the environment is corrupted.

***Table 4.1**: Importance of development and test environment for digital forensics*

There are a few important considerations for the creation of a test environment for digital forensics. The following table lists a few of them:

Key test environment considerations	Details
Hardware and software setup	Dedicated systems with various OS and file systems for diverse test cases.
Isolation and segmentation	Isolated (often air-gapped) systems to avoid contamination of test environments.
Data sources and test data sets	Standard datasets (e.g., NIST CFReDS—https://cfreds.nist.gov/) and synthetic data for controlled testing.
Forensic tools and utilities	Mix of open-source (e.g., Autopsy) and commercial (e.g., EnCase) forensic tools.

Documentation and standardization	Detailed documentation for repeatable testing and compliance.
Test reports and results	Ability to securely fetch the results or upload the results into other environments like AWS and Azure.

***Table 4.2**: Key considerations for a test environment for digital forensics*

The added advantage of such environments is that they can be used to train new and experienced investigators in complex and new scenarios. Such a test environment that can also serve as a training environment has many essential features, a few of which are listed in the following table:

Training environment features	Details
Controlled lab setup	Virtual or physical setups for trainees to practice forensics tasks.
Scenarios and case studies	Simulated cases such as insider threats, IP theft, and data destruction.
Forensic images and artifacts	Sample forensic images (e.g., E01, AFF) for data acquisition and analysis.
Capture the flag (CTF) setup	CTF events for hands-on forensic challenges and skill testing.
Tools for practical exposure	Variety of tools like FTK Imager, EnCase, Autopsy for practical learning.

***Table 4.3**: Desired features for training environment for digital forensics*

While one takes care of most of these aspects, there are a few aspects that are important for any cyber forensic lab and cyber forensic professionals. They include the ability to write custom forensic scripts and study/analyze the reverse-engineered code. These are summarized in the following table:

Custom scripting and study need	Details
Custom scripting	Need to do scripting in Python and PowerShell to automate cyber forensic evidence collection and analysis.
Reverse engineering	Using Python and PowerShell code to revere engineer dumps, binary files, of standard and proprietary format.
Analyze reverse engineered code	Environment for studying, analyzing and even changing the reverse engineered code to understand its functionality and behavior.

***Table 4.4**: Custom scripting and study needs for digital forensics*

In this chapter, we will primarily focus on setting up the Python and PowerShell environments, which complement the rest of the cyber forensic lab tools and software. Other related topics will be implicitly covered in the upcoming chapter as part of the relevant recipes.

Note: INTERPOL's Global guidelines for digital forensics laboratories provides an excellent insight into various aspects of building digital forensics labs for investigation and testing purposes.

Recipe 10: Configuring your Python development environment

While digital forensics mostly requires working with specialized tools, knowledge of Python provides a significant advantage. Python is a versatile language that can be used to create simple tools during the analysis phase and to generate various reports. Regardless of the operating system you use, proficiency in Python will help you work more efficiently and with greater accuracy.

In this recipe, we will focus on setting up the Python development environment on a Linux system. A similar procedure can be followed for Windows and macOS.

Note:

- **Compatibility: Cross-platform**
- **License considerations: Free software used**

Recipe

Python is installed by default in Kali Linux and other Linux distributions. In order to check if it is installed, run the following commands:

```
┌──(root㉿forensics)-[/home/nishant]
└─# which python3
/usr/bin/python3

┌──(root㉿forensics)-[/home/nishant]
└─# python3 --version
Python 3.11.9

┌──(root㉿forensics)-[/home/nishant]
└─#
```

The `which` command in Linux shows where Python is installed. The `python --version` commands show the version of Python.

If you can run the preceding commands, that means you are good to go. If you do not see Python installed on your machine, then you can install Python using the following command:

```
apt-get install python3
```

Activity

Attempt the following activities before the next recipe:

- Try running `apt-get install python3` on your Kali Linux machine when it is already installed. What do you see?
- Find out the `apt-get` syntax for upgrading your Python installation.
- Read the `tcpdump` documentation to understand how it works and how it can be used to capture network packets.
- Explore more about how Python can be installed on other operating systems like Windows and macOS.

Recipe 11: Configuring important libraries using pip3 and apt-get

Python has its own package installer called PIP, written generally as `pip` and `pip3` (an alias to be used with Python 3). It is a tool written in Python that is used for installing Python applications and their dependencies. Pip automatically connects to an online Python Package Index and downloads the required packages.

Note:

- **Compatibility: Cross-platform**
- **License considerations: Free software used**

Recipe

As part of the network packets capture, we will be using Python binding for Wireshark (a network packet capture tool), called **pyshark**.

Let us first check if the package **pyshark** is installed:

```
┌──(root㉿forensics)-[/home/nishant/forensics-playbook]
└─# pip3 list | grep pyshark


┌──(root㉿forensics)-[/home/nishant/forensics-playbook]
└─#
```

The preceding command executes without any output. The **pip3 list** command lists all the Python packages installed. The **grep pyshark** part of the command checks **pyshark** in the output.

Let us now install the **pyshark** package. You will see an output as follows:

```
┌──(root㉿forensics)-[/usr/bin]
└─# pip3 install pyshark
error: externally-managed-environment

× This environment is externally managed
╰─> To install Python packages system-wide, try apt install
    python3-xyz, where xyz is the package you are trying to
    install.

    If you wish to install a non-Debian-packaged Python package,
    create a virtual environment using python3 -m venv path/to/venv.
    Then use path/to/venv/bin/python and path/to/venv/bin/pip. Make
    sure you have python3-full installed.

    If you wish to install a non-Debian packaged Python application,
    it may be easiest to use pipx install xyz, which will manage a
    virtual environment for you. Make sure you have pipx installed.

    See /usr/share/doc/python3.12/README.venv for more information.

note: If you believe this is a mistake, please contact your Python installation or OS distribution
provider. You can override this, at the risk of breaking your Python installation or OS, by
passing --break-system-packages.
hint: See PEP 668 for the detailed specification.
```

If you get the preceding error, that means that your environment is being managed by the **apt** package manager, which stands for APT. Hence, you can proceed to install this Python package as follows:

```
┌──(root㉿forensics)-[/home/nishant]
└─# apt-get install python3-pyshark
Reading package lists... Done
Building dependency tree... Done
Reading state information... Done
The following packages were automatically installed and are no longer required:
  ibverbs-providers libboost-iostreams1.83.0 libboost-thread1.83.0 libcephfs2 libgfapi0 libgfrpc0
libgfxdr0
  libglusterfs0 libibverbs1 libpython3.11-dev librados2 librdmacm1t64 python3-lib2to3 python3.11
python3.11-dev
  python3.11-minimal samba-vfs-modules
Use 'sudo apt autoremove' to remove them.
The following NEW packages will be installed:
  python3-pyshark
0 upgraded, 1 newly installed, 0 to remove and 2044 not upgraded.
Need to get 26.4 kB of archives.
After this operation, 144 kB of additional disk space will be used.
Get:1 http://kali.download/kali kali-rolling/main amd64 python3-pyshark all 0.6-0kali1 [26.4 kB]
Fetched 26.4 kB in 1s (32.3 kB/s)
Selecting previously unselected package python3-pyshark.
(Reading database ... 396817 files and directories currently installed.)
Preparing to unpack .../python3-pyshark_0.6-0kali1_all.deb ...
Unpacking python3-pyshark (0.6-0kali1) ...
Setting up python3-pyshark (0.6-0kali1) ...

┌──(root㉿forensics)-[/home/nishant]
└─#
```

The preceding command installed `python3-pyshark` package for us. On systems where you do not get the error, the following command would still work:

```
pip3 install pyshark
```

Interesting fact: PIP is a recursive acronym that stands for Pip Installs Packages. This is a geeky way to describe the purpose of this tool, which repeats in the expansion. Other well-known recursive acronyms in the technology world are GNU means GNU's Not Unix, WINE is Wine Is Not an Emulator and YAML means YAML Ain't Markup Language.

Activity

Attempt the following activities before the next recipe:

- The example we saw in this recipe installs the latest version of that package. Find out how to install a specific version of a package.
- Can you also install all the packages matching a wildcard, e.g., *. If yes, how can you do that?

Recipe 12: Setting up your Python virtual environment or venv

Let us first understand why we need a Python virtual environment or **venv**. A Python virtual environment, created using the **venv** module, is an environment that helps manage dependencies and isolate Python projects. It ensures that the dependencies and libraries installed for one project do not interfere with those of another project.

The following table shows the main uses of Python **venv**:

Function	Details
Dependency isolation	Each virtual environment has its own installation directory for Python packages, separate from the global or system-wide Python environment. This prevents version conflicts and ensures that the libraries required for one project do not affect others.
Reproducibility	Virtual environments make it easier to replicate a specific development environment by storing dependencies in a **requirements.txt** file. Others can recreate the exact environment using **pip install -r requirements.txt**.
Version management	We can use different versions of Python packages or modules in different virtual environments, which is helpful when working on multiple projects with varying requirements.
Ease of testing and development	Virtual environments are ideal for testing, allowing developers to work in isolated spaces and experiment with packages or settings without risking other projects.

***Table 4.5**: Important uses of a Python virtual environment (venv)*

Note:

- **Compatibility: Cross-platform**
- **License considerations: Free software used**

Such a virtual environment, thus, is very useful for digital forensics use cases when one has to test multiple versions of a tool or develop something that should have its own dependencies different than other tools.

Recipe

In this recipe, we will create a Python virtual environment. A **venv** can be created irrespective of the operating system, like:

```
python3 -m venv <environment name>
```

E.g.:

```
python3 -m venv digital-forensics
```

When you run this command, you will notice that Python creates a directory with the same name given and a directory hierarchy inside it. The output will look similar to the following:

```
┌──(root㉿forensics)-[/home/nishant]
└─# python3 -m venv digital-forensics
The virtual environment was not created successfully because ensurepip is not
available.  On Debian/Ubuntu systems, you need to install the python3-venv
```

```
package using the following command.

    apt install python3.12-venv

You may need to use sudo with that command.  After installing the python3-venv
package, recreate your virtual environment.

Failing command: /home/nishant/digital-forensics/bin/python3

┌──(root㉿forensics)-[/home/nishant]
└─#
```

If you get preceding output, then make sure you install the package **python3-venv** and retry the command:

```
rm -rf digital-forensics
python3 -m venv digital-forensics
yum install python3-venv
```

In the preceding commands, we first removed the directory that was created, then installed the **python3-venv** package, and then recreated the **venv**.

The last command will exit silently now, that confirms that our **venv** is created successfully:

```
┌──(root㉿forensics)-[/home/nishant]
└─# python3 -m venv digital-forensics

┌──(root㉿forensics)-[/home/nishant]
└─#
```

Once the **venv** is created, you need to activate it. Activation makes the environment your current Python environment.

In order to activate it, you can use the following command on Windows:

```
.\<environment\_name\>Scriptsactivate
```

E.g., you can run the following command to activate the **venv** on Windows:

```
.\digital-forensics\Scripts\activate
```

On Linux or macOS, the following command is used to activate the venv:

```
source <environment_name>/bin/activate
```

For example, you can use the following command to activate the **venv** on Linux:

```
┌──(root㉿forensics)-[/home/nishant]
└─# source ./digital-forensics/bin/activate

┌──(digital-forensics)─(root㉿forensics)-[/home/nishant]
└─#
```

The preceding command now activates your own virtual environment (**venv**) and uses its own dependencies and binaries. In order to check if that is true, run the following command:

```
┌──(digital-forensics)-(root㉿forensics)-[/home/nishant]
└─# which python
/home/nishant/digital-forensics/bin/python

┌──(digital-forensics)-(root㉿forensics)-[/home/nishant]
└─#
```

The command **which python** now should point to the Python in your virtual environment rather than the system's Python

Activity

Attempt the following activities before the next recipe:

- Explore each of the directories inside your **venv** and list down what you find in each of them.
- Describe how you will confirm if you have multiple **venv**.
- You can create shareable Python environments by using **pip3 freeze > requirements.txt**. Try this to create a **requirement.txt** and then use this file to create another environment.

Recipe 13: Testing a Python program to check configuration

Let us know use a simple Python program to check if everything is configured properly. This recipe will also get you started with Python if you have not programmed in Python before.

Note:

- **Compatibility: Cross-platform**
- **License considerations: Free software used**

Recipe

In order to check if your Python environment is set properly, let us try a simple program to run **tcpdump** as a subprocess to capture network packets and then print the captured packets:

```
# tcpdump.py

import subprocess
import time

class TcpDump:
    def do_capture(self):
        # Use -l option for line buffered pipe so that we can print them as the output is generated. -c can be
        # used to limit the number of packets being captured
        tcpdump_subprocess = subprocess.Popen(
            ('tcpdump', '-l', '-c 5'), stdout=subprocess.PIPE)
```

```
        # Print until the program is interrupted
        for output in iter(tcpdump_subprocess.stdout.readline, b''):
            print(output.rstrip())


if __name__ == "__main__":
    print('Capturing packets using tcpdump. Press Ctrl+C to stop...')
    time.sleep(1)
    tcpdump = TcpDump()
    tcpdump.do_capture()
```

Execute this program in your Kali Linux environment as follows and wait for some time:

```
python3 tcpdump.py
```

The output will look similar to the following:

```
┌──(root㉿forensics)-[/home/nishant/forensics-playbook]
└─# python3 tcpdump.py
Capturing packets using tcpdump. Press Ctrl+C to stop...
tcpdump: verbose output suppressed, use -v[v]... for full protocol decode
listening on eth0, link-type EN10MB (Ethernet), snapshot length 262144 bytes
b'12:24:21.156637 IP 192.168.19.1.mdns > mdns.mcast.net.mdns: 0 [1n] ANY (QM)? e20dda8f-9132-4f1a-afc8-ebae06cf971b._acdseems._tcp.local. (111)'
b'12:24:21.231862 IP 192.168.19.139.59825 > 192.168.19.2.domain: 8485+ PTR? 251.0.0.224.in-addr.arpa. (42)'
b'12:24:21.247685 ARP, Request who-has 192.168.19.139 tell 192.168.19.2, length 46'
b'12:24:21.247720 ARP, Reply 192.168.19.139 is-at 00:0c:29:05:a1:6b (oui Unknown), length 28'
5 packets captured
11 packets received by filter
b'12:24:21.248281 IP 192.168.19.2.domain > 192.168.19.139.59825: 8485 1/0/0 PTR mdns.mcast.net. (70)'
0 packets dropped by kernel

┌──(root㉿forensics)-[/home/nishant/forensics-playbook]
└─#
```

As part of this program, we captured five packets and confirmed that our Python environment is working properly. We will discuss network packet capture in details in the later part of the book.

Activity

Attempt the following activities before the next recipe:

- Update this program to use **pyshark** instead of **tcpdump** to dump the network packets.
- Specify what happens when you use a Python package that is not installed yet. Do you get enough error details?
- Explore how you can dump packets in a similar way in Windows.

Recipe 14: Configuring PowerShell development environment on Windows

PowerShell is a powerful task automation and configuration management framework from Microsoft. It includes a command-line shell and an associated scripting language, designed for managing systems and automating administrative tasks. Originally developed for Windows, it is now cross-platform, supporting Windows, macOS, and Linux.

Interesting fact: **PowerShell was first introduced in 2006 as part of the release of Windows PowerShell 1.0. It was initially included as an optional component for Windows XP SP2, Windows Server 2003, and Windows Vista. Since then, it has gone through tremendous changes to become a de-facto standard for task automation in Windows environments.**

In this recipe, we will check if PowerShell is installed on your Windows machine and will configure it if it is not installed. This example is taken from Windows 11. Other Windows flavors have similar ways of enabling PowerShell configuration.

Note:

- **Compatibility: Windows**
- **License considerations: Part of the operating system**

Recipe

First, check if PowerShell is installed on your system by clicking on the **Start** menu and then typing `powershell`. If you see the result like the following, then it is installed on your system:

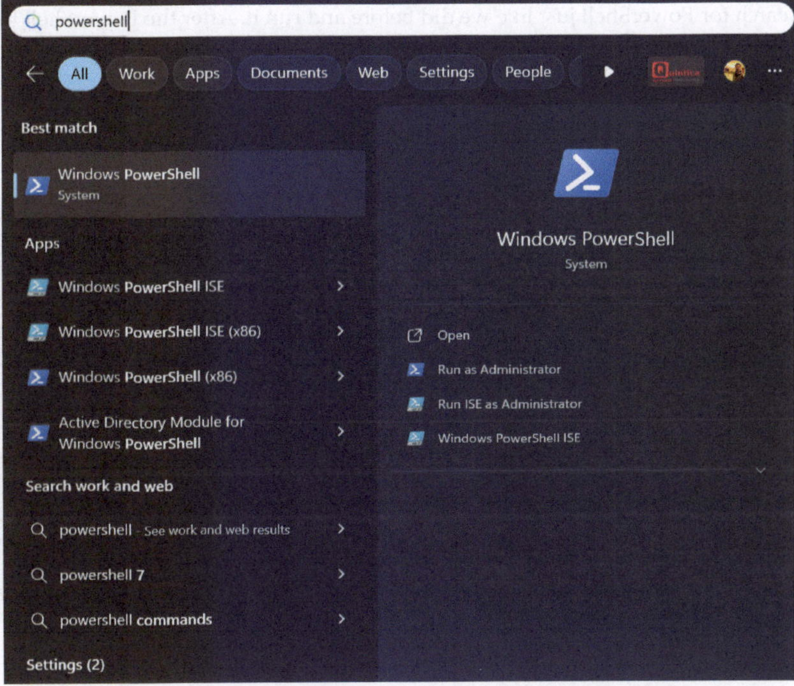

Figure 4.1: Checking if PowerShell is installed on the Windows system

If you do not see it, it is installed from Windows optional components. To install it, go to **Start menu | Settings | System | Optional features**, and click on **More Windows** features. From the dialog you get, you can now enable PowerShell, and then Windows will automatically install it:

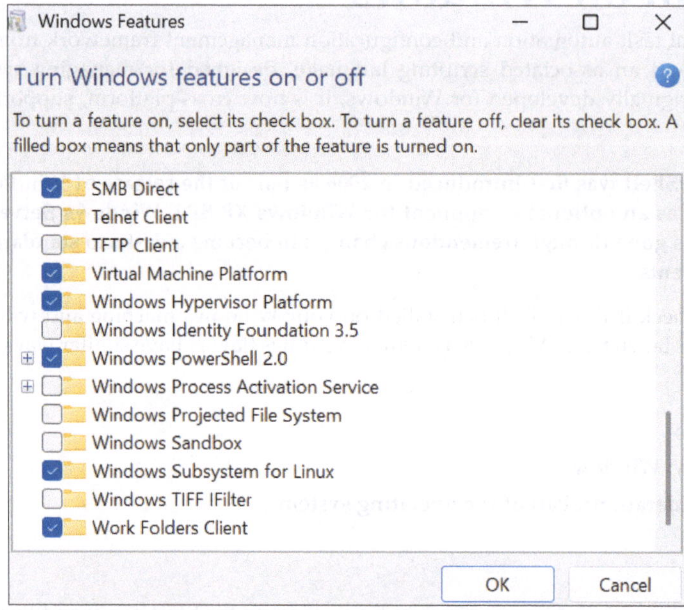

Figure 4.2: Enabling Windows PowerShell from optional features

In order to verify, search for PowerShell just like we did before and run it. After the PowerShell terminal opens, run the following command to check the version of the PowerShell:

```
$PSVersionTable
```

If your output looks like the following (PSVersion may vary), it means that your PowerShell environment is configured properly:

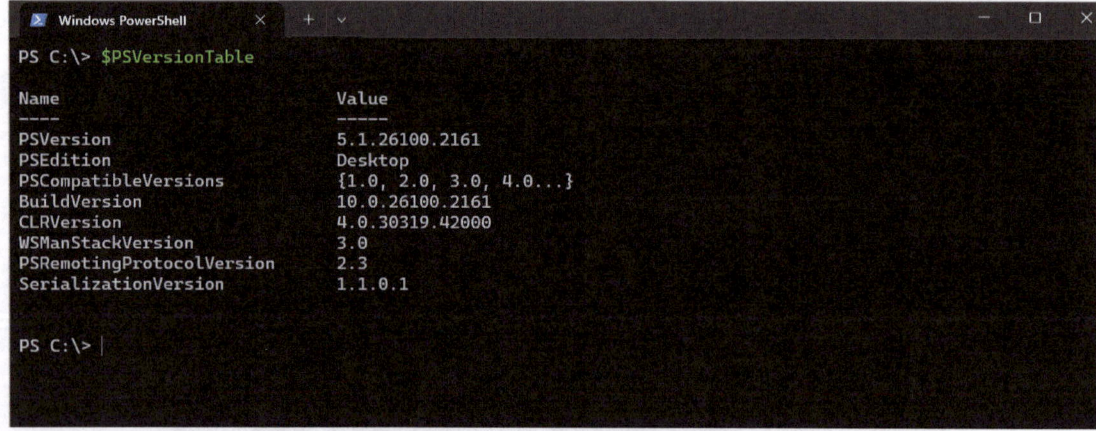

Figure 4.3: Checking if PowerShell works with a simple command

The preceding command prints details about the version of PowerShell and other dependent installed components.

Activity

Attempt the following activities before the next recipe:

- Try running PowerShell by clicking on **Run as Administrator,** and notice the difference you see in the PowerShell terminal that opens up.
- Bring out the differences between Windows command prompt and Windows PowerShell.

Recipe 15: Understanding the PowerShell ISE editor

The **integrated scripting environment** (**ISE**) editor is a host application for Windows PowerShell, specifically designed to help users write, test, and debug PowerShell scripts. It is included as part of Windows PowerShell 2.0 through 5.x. ISE provides a user-friendly interface with features to simplify script development, especially for users who are new to scripting or need an integrated environment.

ISE editor provides a host of features for PowerShell development needs in Windows. ISE may also not be installed by default and can be enabled using Windows optional components, as we did before for PowerShell.

Note:

- **Compatibility: Windows**
- **License considerations: Part of the operating system**

Recipe

Check if the ISE editor is installed on your system by searching for `powershell` or `ise` on your Start menu. If you do not find it, enable it by going to **Start menu** | **Settings** | **System** | **Optional features** and then enabling **Windows PowerShell ISE**:

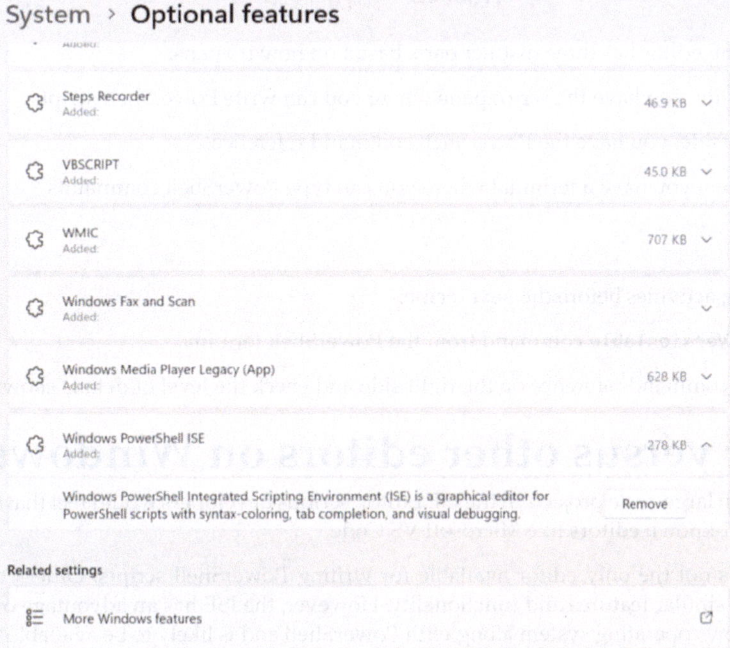

Figure 4.4: *Enabling PowerShell ISE from optional features*

Once you enable it, launch ISE from the **Start** menu. You will see the ISE Window, as shown in the following figure:

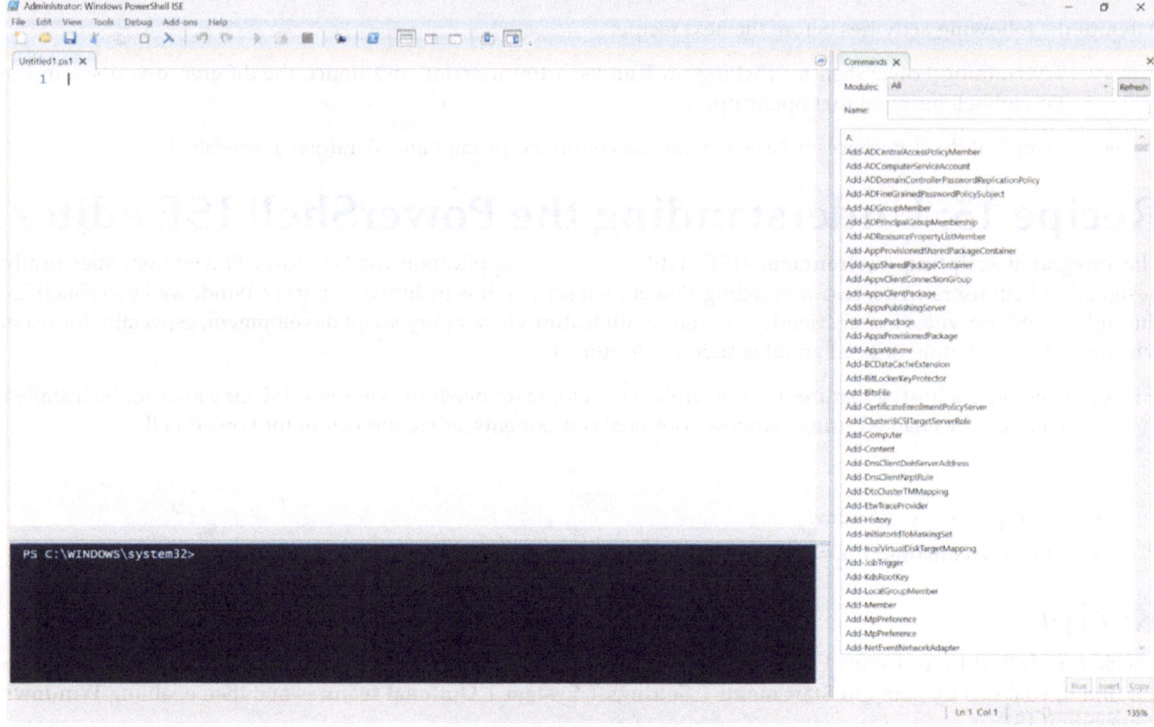

***Figure 4.5:** ISE opening screen*

You can see that the ISE editor has three distinct parts based on how it opens:

- On the left side, you have the script pane where you can write PowerShell scripts.
- On the right side, you have the PowerShell command reference.
- On the bottom, you have a terminal where you can type PowerShell commands.

Activity

Attempt the following activities before the next recipe:

- Run the `$PSVersionTable` command from the PowerShell terminal.
- Explore the command reference on the right side and check the level of details shown for each command.

ISE editor versus other editors on Windows

While one can work on large-scale projects in the ISE Editor, serious developers would feel that it lacks many features available in other well-known editors like Microsoft VS Code.

The PowerShell ISE is not the only editor available for writing PowerShell scripts. Other editors, such as Visual Studio Code, provide similar features and functionality. However, the ISE has an advantage over other editors. It is installed in the Windows operating system along with PowerShell and is likely to be available wherever PowerShell is. This is especially useful when you are working on a remote system where any additional software cannot be installed apart from what is already shipped with the operating system. Additionally, the ISE provides a simpler and more powerful editing experience than some other editors.

It is strong in the following areas:

- Easy to use and built into Windows, making it accessible without additional installations.
- Ideal for beginners and simple scripts.
- Lightweight with a clean and intuitive interface.
- Integrated command and API reference.

However, it has many weaknesses, the most important ones are the following:

- Limited features compared to modern editors like VS Code.
- No active development (deprecated in favor of VS Code).
- Lacks advanced debugging and integration capabilities.

Let us compare a few PowerShell editors for Windows on the most important parameters. The following table summarizes the well-known PowerShell editors:

Editor	Platform	Debugging	Ease of use	Advanced features	Free/Paid
Windows PowerShell ISE	Windows-only	Basic	Beginner-friendly	Limited	Free
Visual Studio Code	Cross-platform	Advanced (with plugins)	Versatile	Extensible, multi-language support	Free
PowerShell Studio	Windows-only	Advanced	Professional grade	GUI designer, script packaging	Paid
ISE Steroids	Windows-only	Advanced	Familiar to ISE users	Enhances ISE functionality	Paid (one-time fee)
Notepad++	Windows-only	None	Lightweight	Simple syntax highlighting	Free
JetBrains Rider	Cross-platform	Advanced	Developer-oriented	Professional IDE features	Paid

Table 4.6: *Comparison of features of well-known PowerShell editors*

While a few PowerShell editors may come out on top, it is more about one's preference. So, choose one that you think suits your needs. Once you become comfortable working with the editor of your choice, it does not matter much which editor you use, unless you need to use advanced features like debugging.

Another important consideration when using such editors for digital forensics work is to ensure compliance with licensing terms. Some of them, though free for personal use, may not be free for commercial use. Moreover, editors that are operational during an indefinite trial period may not be used for commercial purposes.

Interesting fact: PowerShell is no longer confined to Windows. It is now supported on Linux as well. Many developers like to keep their development environment consistent across various operating systems. There is a high chance that one would end up using a much more advanced IDE like VS Code in Linux than anything else while working with PowerShell. Hence, ISE is losing its acceptance among developers.

Recipe 16: VS Code for Python and PowerShell scripting

As we understood in the last recipe, VS Code is one of the widely used code editors and IDEs. The best part about VS Code is that it supports the most popular programming and scripting languages with the help of extensions. It even supports features like code formatting, context-sensitive help, and many more with such extensions that are published by large publishers like Microsoft and other individual publishers.

In this recipe, let us look at setup VS Code on a minimum of two operating systems, e.g., Windows and Linux.

Interesting fact: **While VS Code is an open-source software under the MIT License, the VS Code product binary itself is licensed under a separate Microsoft Software License that can use telemetry/tracking for data collection. Hence, a project called VSCodium (https://vscodium.com/) has come into existence that provides a community-driven, freely licensed binary distribution of Microsoft's editor VS Code.**

Note:

- **Compatibility: Cross-platform**
- **License considerations: Free software used**

Recipe

Let us try to install VS Code on at least two operating systems so that we are comfortable working with it irrespective of the operating system. VS Code can be installed on Windows, Linux, and macOS as follows:

Operating system	Installation options
Windows	By downloading the VS Code binary installer from its download page and installing it.
Linux	For Kali Linux, Debian, and Ubuntu: By downloading the VS Code binary installer from its download page in the form of a `.deb` package, and then running the following commands: **`sudo apt install ./<file>.deb`** For Red Hat, Fedora, and SUSE: **`sudo dnf install code`** Look at **https://code.visualstudio.com/docs/setup/linux** for detailed instructions for installing VS Code on Linux.
macOS	By downloading the VS Code binary installer from its download page and installing it

Table 4.7: Installing VS Code in different operating systems

The download page of VS Code (**https://code.visualstudio.com/Download**) also provides the binaries for x64 (e.g., Intel and AMD) and Arm64 architectures. Hence, no matter what machine and operating system you are using, you will be able to run VS Code on it.

If you are using VSCodium, then it can be installed by directly downloading it from its download page or by using platform-specific package managers. Such package managers provide a simple way to install many commonly used software and keep them updated using simple command line options, rather than the need to install and update each of the software separately. Two of such widely used package managers are:

- Chocolatey on Windows
- Homebrew on macOS

Once you install them by following these instructions, launch them and try to run Python and PowerShell code. Do not forget to click on the **Extension** icon on the left side and install the Python and PowerShell extensions.

The following figure shows the PowerShell extension that needs to be installed. Ensure the published is Microsoft before installing it:

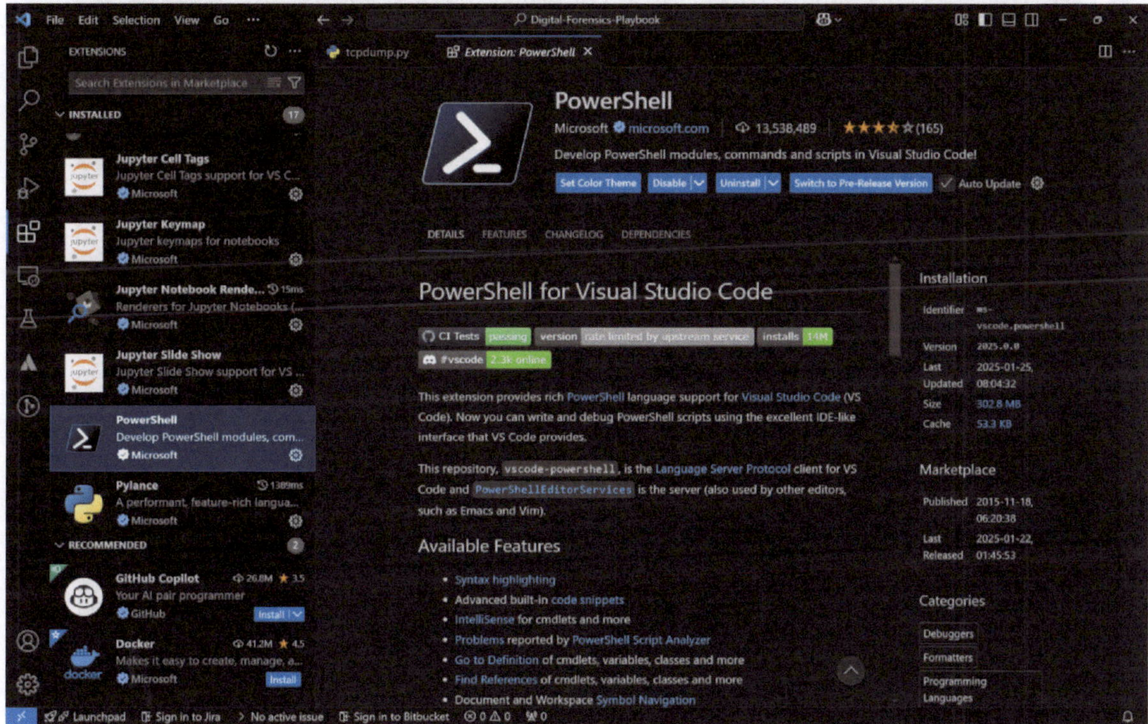

***Figure 4.6:** Installing PowerShell extension in VS Code*

The following figure shows VS Code running on Windows with PowerShell code open:

```
function Get-SecurityEventLogs {
    <#
        .DESCRIPTION
        Get a list of security logs from Windows event logs.

        .PARAMETER NumberOfLogs
        Number of logs.
    #>
    [CmdletBinding()]
    Param
    (
        [Parameter(mandatory = $true)]
        [ValidateNotNullOrEmpty()]
        [uint16]
        $NumberOfLogs
    )

    $EventLogs = Get-EventLog -LogName Security -Newest $NumberOfLogs

    return $EventLogs
}

# Call the function for getting a list of security event logs
Get-SecurityEventLogs -NumberOfLogs 5
```

```
PowerShell Extension v2025.0.0
Copyright (c) Microsoft Corporation.

https://aka.ms/vscode-powershell
Type 'help' to get help.

PS C:\Work\Digital-Forensics-Playbook>
```

Figure 4.7: *VS Code running on Windows*

The following figure shows VS Code running on Kali Linux with Python code open:

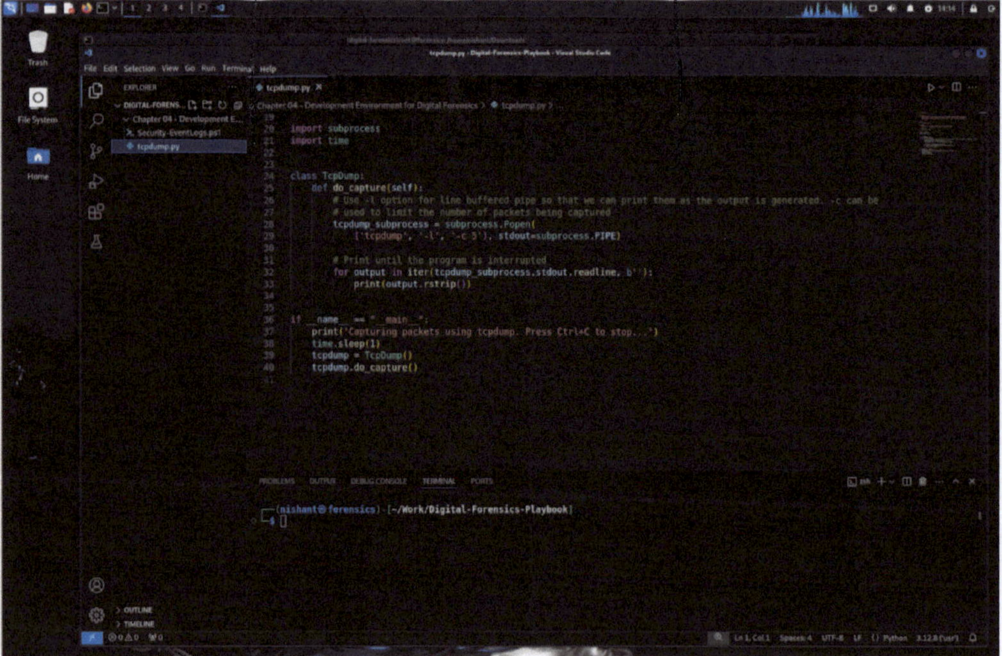

Figure 4.8: *VS Code running on Kali Linux*

Note: VS Code may automatically ask to install the well-known extensions for the code type when the code file is opened.

Activity

Attempt the following activities before the next recipe:

- While working on Linux, do you need to take care of running with the correct privileges? Observe what you encounter if you have copied the files on Linux as the **root** user but edited the files as a regular user.
- Study the documentation for VS Code to check how you can work with multiple Python versions.

Recipe 17: Testing a PowerShell script filter-based logs

Windows logs are one of the best ways to understand what happened on the system as part of a forensic analysis. Windows generates a lot of logs by default that are classified into different categories. These logs can be accessed in an easy-to-understand format using Windows Event Viewer. Moreover, additional logs can be enabled for specific requirements like file audits.

In *Chapter 6, Digital Forensics for Windows System*, we will go deep into Windows Event Viewer. In this recipe, we will look at how we can use PowerShell to access security logs that are part of the event logs.

Note:

- **Compatibility: Windows**
- **License considerations: Part of the operating system**

Recipe

In this recipe, we will use the PowerShell command **Get-EventLogs** to get the list of security event logs.

The following PowerShell program gets a number of the most recent event logs. This needs to be executed as an administrator.

```
# Security-EventLogs.ps1

function Get-SecurityEventLogs {
    <#
        .DESCRIPTION
        Get a list of security logs from Windows event logs.

        .PARAMETER NumberOfLogs
        Number of logs.
    #>
    [CmdletBinding()]
    Param
    (
        [Parameter(mandatory = $true)]
        [ValidateNotNullOrEmpty()]
```

```
        [uint16]
        $NumberOfLogs
    )

    $EventLogs = Get-EventLog -LogName Security -Newest $NumberOfLogs

    return $EventLogs
}

# Call the function for getting a list of security event logs
Get-SecurityEventLogs -NumberOfLogs 5
```

Let us understand this PowerShell script a little better:

- The function **Get-SecurityEventLogs** is called by the main program.
- **Get-SecurityEventLogs** expects a mandatory argument **NumberOfLogs**.
- The function **Get-SecurityEventLogs**, calls the PowerShell command **Get-EventLogs** with the parameters **LogName** and passes it **Security** as the log name. It also uses the parameter **Newest** and passes the number of logs to signify how many logs it has to fetch.
- This result is stored in a variable **EventLogs**, which is then returned to the main program.

When you run this program, you will see an output similar to the following:

```
PS C:\Work\Digital-Forensics-Playbook>
PS C:\Work\Digital-Forensics-Playbook> . 'C:\Work\Digital-Forensics-Playbook\Chapter 04 - Development Environment for Digital Forensics\Security-EventLogs.ps1'

   Index Time          EntryType   Source                 InstanceID Message
   ----- ----          ---------   ------                 ---------- -------
  607180 Jan 26 11:55  SuccessA... Microsoft-Windows...         4624 An account was successfully logged on....
  607179 Jan 26 11:46  SuccessA... Microsoft-Windows...         4624 An account was successfully logged on....
  607178 Jan 26 11:44  SuccessA... Microsoft-Windows...         4624 An account was successfully logged on....
  607177 Jan 26 11:43  SuccessA... Microsoft-Windows...         4624 An account was successfully logged on....
  607176 Jan 26 11:43  SuccessA... Microsoft-Windows...         4624 An account was successfully logged on....


PS C:\Work\Digital-Forensics-Playbook>
```

As you see, it has returned the five most recent security logs from Windows Event Logs.

This information is extremely useful during digital forensic evidence collection from the Windows system, as it can provide details of many activities like login, logout, user creation, user deletion, group assignment, etc.

Activity

Attempt the following activities before the next recipe:

- Modify the preceding script to get a list of the newest 10 application logs.
- Modify the script to get a list of the newest 5 logs of each type of system, security, and application logs.
- Explore the other parameters `Get-EventLog` accepts by going through the documentation and context-sensitive help in ISE and VS Code.

Secure environment for working with digital forensic evidence

A secure environment for working with digital forensic evidence is a controlled and protected space, physical, virtual, or both, and is designed to ensure the confidentiality, integrity, and availability of the evidence while preventing tampering, contamination, or unauthorized access. It ensures the evidence remains admissible in court and complies with legal, regulatory, and organizational standards.

Hence, creating a secure environment for working with digital forensic evidence is crucial for any cyber forensics professional to maintain the integrity of the evidence, ensure compliance with legal and regulatory frameworks, and prevent contamination or tampering.

Let us look at a few key considerations for such an environment:

Consideration for secure environment	Details
Controlled physical environment	The servers, desktops and other hardware need to be inside a secure premises that are access controlled. Moreover, access to these hardware should be based on **role-based access control** (**RBAC**) methods
Controlled virtual environment	A lot of working environments in a digital forensic lab consists of virtual machines and virtual networks. Such environments should also be controlled under multiple layers of security
Backup considerations	Every cyber forensic professional should be well versed with the backup considerations of their environments. At any point in time, a lack of backup shouldn't come in the way of their work. A good backup strategy includes a combination of VM snapshots, OS restore points, onsite backups and offshore backups.
Strong chain of custody implementation	A proper chain of custody implementation ensures that we have detailed logs of who accessed the evidence, when, and for what purpose. This is important for a second layer of security within the team, as not everyone may have been cleared to access the evidence

Table 4.8: Considerations for a secure digital forensic environment

Note: The publicly available document from INTERPOL, global guidelines for digital forensics laboratories, provides a list of guidelines for creating digital forensic labs. While this is a little old document, it provides comprehensive guidelines for cyber forensics professionals.

Additional considerations for the development environment

So far in this chapter, we have created and configured development environments for Python and PowerShell-based scripting and automation work. We focused on making them work across the operating system so that, irrespective of the primary operating system of your choice, you should be able to work with them.

We also looked at creating a virtualized environment using Oracle VirtualBox and Kali Linux or Kali Purple in *Chapter 02, Digital Forensics for Enterprises*. A virtualized environment like this goes a long way to repeatedly testing the evidence without the fear of getting wrong results due to the contamination of the environment.

With these, you should be ready to work efficiently with the recipes in this book. However, to be really comfortable, focus on the following:

- Try out a few Python programs from a minimum of two operating systems, e.g., Linux and Windows, by running them from the command line as well as from VS Code.
- Look at how to share the Python environment configurations with others and use the configuration from others using `requirements.txt`.
- Run a couple of simple PowerShell scripts from ISE and from VS Code. Also, understand how it is different between running them without administrator privileges and with administrator privileges.
- Create a minimum of two Linux virtual machines, one with Kali Linux and another with any distribution of your choice. You can use Windows or Linux-based hypervisors to create these virtual machines.
- A lot of the time, you may get an image of the hard disk as forensic evidence of a dead system that needs to be mounted either on your operating system as a volume or as a hard disk in a new virtual machine. Having practiced this can help you work with such types of evidence in a much more efficient way.
- There are other environments and package managers that practitioners of digital forensics may consider. Two of such noteworthy environments are: Homebrew for macOS and Chocolatey for Windows. Both of them provide simple ways to install well-known tools and packages along with their dependencies.

Conclusion

A robust development environment is fundamental for digital forensics professionals. Such a developed environment ensures reliability, efficiency, and security while handling evidence. A development environment, as we discussed in this chapter, allows writing custom code for specialized investigation needs and also helps digital forensics professionals study code for open-source tools as well as reverse-engineered code.

In this chapter, we explored the importance of a secure and isolated setup for testing and training, emphasizing the need for accuracy and compliance with legal standards. We looked into configuring Python and PowerShell environments across platforms, leveraging tools like virtual and VS Code editors. We looked at practical examples of the use of Python for network packet capture and PowerShell for retrieving event logs, showcasing real-world forensic scenarios. We also examined the significance of virtualization and secure lab environments in preventing contamination and maintaining chain-of-custody integrity.

In the next chapter, we will discuss digital forensics for Linux systems.

Questions

1. Why is an isolated development environment important in digital forensics?
2. What are the key components of a secure physical environment for handling forensic evidence?
3. How does the Python virtual environment (venv) help manage dependencies?
4. What is the role of hashing in evidence integrity?
5. Compare PowerShell ISE and VS Code for scripting.
6. What are the advantages of using air-gapped systems in digital forensics labs?
7. Explain the significance of chain of custody logs in forensic investigations.
8. What is the purpose of apt-get and pip3 commands in setting up a Python environment?
9. How can you verify if Python is installed on a Linux system?
10. What is the function of the Get-EventLog command in PowerShell?
11. Describe the benefits of using virtual machines in forensic analysis.
12. What are the steps to create and activate a Python virtual environment?
13. What is the importance of testing forensic tools in a controlled lab?
14. How does PowerShell scripting facilitate forensic evidence collection in Windows?
15. What are the backup considerations for a secure forensic environment?

Points to remember

- Development environments should be isolated to prevent contamination.
- Strict physical and virtual access controls should be maintained in a digital forensic lab setup.
- Cryptographic hashing is used to ensure evidence integrity.
- Forensic tools need to be tested in controlled environments before deployment.
- Python's virtual environments prevent dependency conflicts.
- PowerShell is ideal for automating system tasks and evidence collection on Windows systems, but can be used on other operating systems too.
- Virtualization enables repeated testing of forensic images and evidence.
- VS Code is cross-platform and extensible, making it ideal for forensic scripting.
- ISE is user-friendly but lacks advanced features found in modern editors.
- Secure backups are critical to prevent data loss during investigations.

Key terms

- **Forensic evidence**: Digital artifacts collected for analysis during investigations.
- **Python virtual environment (venv)**: Isolated Python environments for managing dependencies.
- **PIP**: Stands for Pip Installs Packages and is a standard package manager for Python, and is available for all the platforms where Python is available.
- **PowerShell ISE**: Integrated scripting environment for writing and debugging PowerShell scripts.
- **VS Code**: A cross-platform code editor developed by Microsoft with extensive features for Python and PowerShell.
- **Air-gapped system**: A network-isolated system to enhance security.
- **Hashing**: A method to verify evidence integrity using algorithms like SHA-256.
- **Advanced Package Tool (APT)**: A Linux utility for managing software packages.
- **Chain of custody**: Documentation of evidence handling to ensure legal compliance.
- **Get-EventLog**: PowerShell command to retrieve Windows event logs.
- **ISE steroids**: An add-on to enhance PowerShell ISE with advanced features.
- **Virtualization**: Using virtual machines to simulate environments for testing and analysis.
- **Backup strategy**: A combination of snapshots, restore points, and off-site backups for data protection.

Join our Discord space

Join our Discord workspace for latest updates, offers, tech happenings around the world, new releases, and sessions with the authors:

https://discord.bpbonline.com

CHAPTER 5
Linux Forensics

Introduction

In an enterprise setting, most servers may be running Linux. Linux systems may also be used by developers, testers, and sysadmins for their work, in the form of virtual machines, given the proliferation and easy access to virtualization techniques. In case of a cyberattack, a digital forensics expert should be able to work with such systems and collect forensic evidence. This process should be carried out regardless of the Linux distribution in use (e.g., Debian, Fedora, etc.). Given the rich and diverse set of tools and utilities available in Linux, a variety of methods are often required to effectively conduct forensic investigations. In this chapter, we will understand how such forensic evidence can be collected from Linux systems.

Structure

In this chapter, we will cover the following topics:

- Recipe 18: Understanding Linux file systems
- Recipe 19: Working with file system
- Recipe 20: Important Linux tools for digital forensics
- Understanding important logging systems on Linux
- Recipe 21: Enabling audit logs
- Recipe 22: Using audit logs to capture file changes
- Recipe 23: Sending logs to a syslog destination
- Recipe 24: Implementing best practices for log management in Linux
- Recipe 25: Validating file integrity using checksum
- Recipe 26: Analyzing disk partitions
- Recipe 27: Identifying deleted files
- Recipe 28: Examining swap files
- Recipe 29: Analyzing file system structure
- Recipe 30: Recovering lost data from deleted files
- Recipe 31: Checking timestamp changes
- Recipe 32: Working with history and last commands
- Recipe 33: Working with sudoers file
- Recipe 34: Verifying login without passwords
- Recipe 35: Verifying changes in environment variables
- Recipe 36: Analyzing Linux packages

Objectives

In this chapter, we will explore a wide range of tools and techniques for conducting digital forensics on Linux systems. Using practical, recipe-based examples, we will address the diverse complexities of Linux environments.

By the end of this chapter, you will be equipped to work with various forensic tools and methods to identify signs of exploits or misconfigurations and to collect the necessary evidence for further analysis.

Recipe 18: Understanding Linux file systems

Linux uses the **extended file system** (**ext**). It was implemented in April 1992 as the first file system created specifically for the Linux kernel. Since then, it has been superseded by other file systems, such as ext2, ext3, and ext4.

If you look at your Linux system, you will find a bunch of directories at the root (/) of your file system. Many of these directories are standard directories that are present in every Linux system, even across various distributions.

Let us look at the most important directories and understand their purpose:

Directory	Content
`/`	Root directory of the entire file system
`/home`	Home directory of users
`/bin`	Essential user command binaries. Generally linked to `/usr/bin`
`/etc`	Configuration files for the system
`/sbin`	Essential system binaries
`/usr`	User application support data and binaries. Further divided into `/usr/bin`, `/usr/sbin`, `/usr/include`, `/usr/lib`, `/usr/local`, `/usr/share`, etc.
`/var`	Variable data files. Further divided into `/var/cache`, `/var/lib`, `/var/lock`, `/var/log`, `/var/spool`, etc.
`/dev`	Devices files
`/opt`	Add-on/optional application software packages
`/mnt`	Mount files for temporary file systems, e.g., external hard disks and optical disks
`/lib`	Libraries and kernel modules
`/boot`	Boot loader files – Contains kernel images (`vmlinuz`), initial RAM disk (`initrd`), and bootloader configuration (GRUB, LILO).
`/media`	Removable media mount points – Temporary mount location for CDs, USB drives, external disks.
`/tmp`	Temporary files – Temporary storage cleared at reboot, world-writable but with restricted permissions (sticky bit).
`/run`	Runtime process information – Stores temporary data about running processes since boot.
`/root`	Root user's home directory – The administrator's personal space, separate from `/home`.

***Table 5.1**: Important directories in Linux and their purpose*

Note:

- **Compatibility: Linux**
- **License considerations: Free software used**

Recipe

Let us look at the file system of Kali Linux. You do not have to be a root user to look around most of the directories. First, change the directory to the root directory by running the following command:

```
┌──(nishant㉿forensics)-[~]
└─$ cd /
```

Once you are on root directory, run the following command to list all the directories under `/`:

```
┌──(nishant㉿forensics)-[/]
└─$ ls -l
```

When you run the preceding command, you will see the following output:

```
┌──(nishant㉿forensics)-[~]
└─$ cd /

┌──(nishant㉿forensics)-[/]
└─$ ls -l
total 64
lrwxrwxrwx   1 root root     7 Dec  2 18:38 bin → usr/bin
drwxr-xr-x   3 root root  4096 Dec  2 18:58 boot
drwxr-xr-x  17 root root  3320 Jan 25 12:00 dev
drwxr-xr-x 183 root root 12288 Jan 27 06:05 etc
drwxr-xr-x   3 root root  4096 Dec  2 18:58 home
lrwxrwxrwx   1 root root    28 Dec  2 18:39 initrd.img → boot/initrd.img-6.8.11-amd64
lrwxrwxrwx   1 root root    28 Dec  2 18:39 initrd.img.old → boot/initrd.img-6.8.11-amd64
lrwxrwxrwx   1 root root     7 Dec  2 18:38 lib → usr/lib
lrwxrwxrwx   1 root root     9 Dec  2 18:46 lib32 → usr/lib32
lrwxrwxrwx   1 root root     9 Dec  2 18:38 lib64 → usr/lib64
drwx------   2 root root 16384 Dec  2 18:38 lost+found
drwxr-xr-x   3 root root  4096 Dec  2 18:38 media
drwxr-xr-x   2 root root  4096 Dec  2 18:38 mnt
drwxr-xr-x   3 root root  4096 Dec  2 18:46 opt
dr-xr-xr-x 339 root root     0 Dec  3 00:33 proc
drwx------   4 root root  4096 Jan 26 14:17 root
drwxr-xr-x  36 root root   880 Dec  3 00:33 run
lrwxrwxrwx   1 root root     8 Dec  2 18:38 sbin → usr/sbin
drwxr-xr-x   3 root root  4096 Dec  2 18:48 srv
dr-xr-xr-x  13 root root     0 Dec  3 00:33 sys
drwxrwxrwt  17 root root   360 Jan 27 06:05 tmp
drwxr-xr-x  16 root root  4096 Dec  2 18:46 usr
drwxr-xr-x  12 root root  4096 Dec  3 00:31 var
lrwxrwxrwx   1 root root    25 Dec  2 18:39 vmlinuz → boot/vmlinuz-6.8.11-amd64
lrwxrwxrwx   1 root root    25 Dec  2 18:39 vmlinuz.old → boot/vmlinuz-6.8.11-amd64

┌──(nishant㉿forensics)-[/]
└─$
```

Figure 5.1: *List of the / (root) directory in Kali Linux*

If you notice, there are many other directories than what we discussed in the preceding table. They have specific functions that you can find out more about.

You will also notice a combination of code as the first column for each of the directories and files. They determine the permissions for each of these directories or files. Let us understand what they mean.

Let us look at two of the entries in the root directory:

```
drwxr-xr-x  12 root root  4096 Dec  3 00:31 var
lrwxrwxrwx   1 root root    25 Dec  2 18:39 vmlinuz -> boot/vmlinuz-6.8.11-amd64
```

You will notice that the string in the first column consists of 10 characters. This string represents the following:

1. File type—first character
2. Owner permissions—characters 2 to 4
3. Group permissions—characters 5 to 7
4. Other permissions—characters 8 to 10

The permission codes are as follows:

- **Read (r)**: Allows viewing the contents of a file or listing a directory's contents.
- **Write (w)**: Allows modifying the contents of a file or adding/removing files in a directory.
- **Execute (x)**: Allows running a file as a program or entering a directory (cd).

Hence, each set of three characters (e.g., `rwx`) represents these permissions:

- r: Read
- w: Write
- x: Execute
- -: No permission

The first character in this permission string is very versatile and indicates the file type:

Code	Meaning
-	Regular file
d	Directory
l	Symbolic link
b	Block device file
c	Character device file
s	Socket file
p	Named pipe (FIFO)

Table 5.2: *Various options for the first character in the permission string*

Hence, for the following entries, we can break down the permissions as follows:

```
drwxr-xr-x  12 root root  4096 Dec  3 00:31 var
```

We can decipher the permissions in the preceding code as follows:

- d: Directory
- **rwx**: Owner can read, write, and execute
- **r-x**: Group can read and execute
- **r-x**: Others can read and execute

For the following entry, we can break down the permissions as follows:

```
lrwxrwxrwx   1 root root    25 Dec  2 18:39 vmlinuz -> boot/vmlinuz-6.8.11-amd64
```

We can decipher the permissions in the preceding code as follows:

- l: Symbolic link
- **rwx**: Owner can read, write, and execute

- **rwx**: Group can read, write, and execute
- **rwx**: Others can read, write, and execute

Interesting fact: **Linux enforces security through its least privilege philosophy, where new files are created with restrictive default permissions—files are not executable, and access is limited unless explicitly granted. This ensures malicious files cannot accidentally execute, and sensitive data remains protected. Combined with strict user, group, and other permission separation, Linux inherently minimizes security risks. Linux's permission model is at the core of it for creating a secure operating system.**

Activity

Attempt the following activities before the next recipe:

- Find out more about other additional directories in the root of the file system.
- The **PATH** variable determines in which order the files will be executed. Find out how you can change the value of this variable to add more directories.

Recipe 19: Working with file system

Now that we understand the basic philosophy behind the Linux file system, let us use a few simple commands to become comfortable working with it. Even if you are not a user of Linux, you can use the previous and this recipe to become comfortable working with the Linux file system.

Note:

- **Compatibility: Linux**
- **License considerations: Free software used**

Recipe

If you look at the directory listing, it shows that **/bin** is linked to **/usr/bin**, and **/sbin** is linked to **/usr/sbin**. In fact, several other directories are also linked to locations within the **/usr** directory. If you want to know where some well-known commands are stored, you can use **which** command. Let us find the details about one of such commands, as shown:

```
┌──(nishant㉿forensics)-[~]
└─$ which cat
/usr/bin/cat

┌──(nishant㉿forensics)-[~]
└─$
```

cat is short for concatenate and is an easy-to-use utility for printing the file on the standard output. While many commands in Linux are built into the shell itself, most of the commands are distributed as separate executables.

As we can see from the earlier list of directories, more than one directory path may have executables. The **PATH** variable determines the order in which these executables are accessed in the sequence. You can check the value of the **PATH** variable as follows:

```
┌──(nishant㉿forensics)-[~]
└─$ echo $PATH
/usr/local/sbin:/usr/local/bin:/usr/sbin:/usr/bin:/sbin:/bin:/usr/local/games:/usr/games
```

```
┌──(nishant㉿forensics)-[~]
└─$
```

While working with the Linux file system, if you want to find out in which directory you are, then use `pwd` command as follows, which prints the name of the current directory:

```
┌──(nishant㉿forensics)-[~]
└─$ cd /bin

┌──(nishant㉿forensics)-[/bin]
└─$ pwd
/bin

┌──(nishant㉿forensics)-[/bin]
└─$
```

Kali Linux's default shell prompt already shows the directory you are in. Hence, it may not feel like a very important thing to learn. However, it is absolutely valuable when such an informative prompt is not used.

Also, you would have already guessed by now that the `cd` command is used to change the directory. There is a trick to using `cd` to quickly change the directory to your home directory. The home directory is a personal workspace for each user on the system. It is typically located at **/home/<username>** and serves as the user's private area to store files, settings, and configurations. Let us learn how to use it, as shown:

```
┌──(nishant㉿forensics)-[/bin]
└─$ cd /usr/sbin

┌──(nishant㉿forensics)-[/usr/sbin]
└─$ pwd
/usr/sbin

┌──(nishant㉿forensics)-[/usr/sbin]
└─$ cd

┌──(nishant㉿forensics)-[~]
└─$ pwd
/home/nishant

┌──(nishant㉿forensics)-[~]
└─$
```

The simplest way to get help in Linux is by using the `man` command. For example, `man cat` shows you manual pages for `cat`. Let us see the `man` command in action:

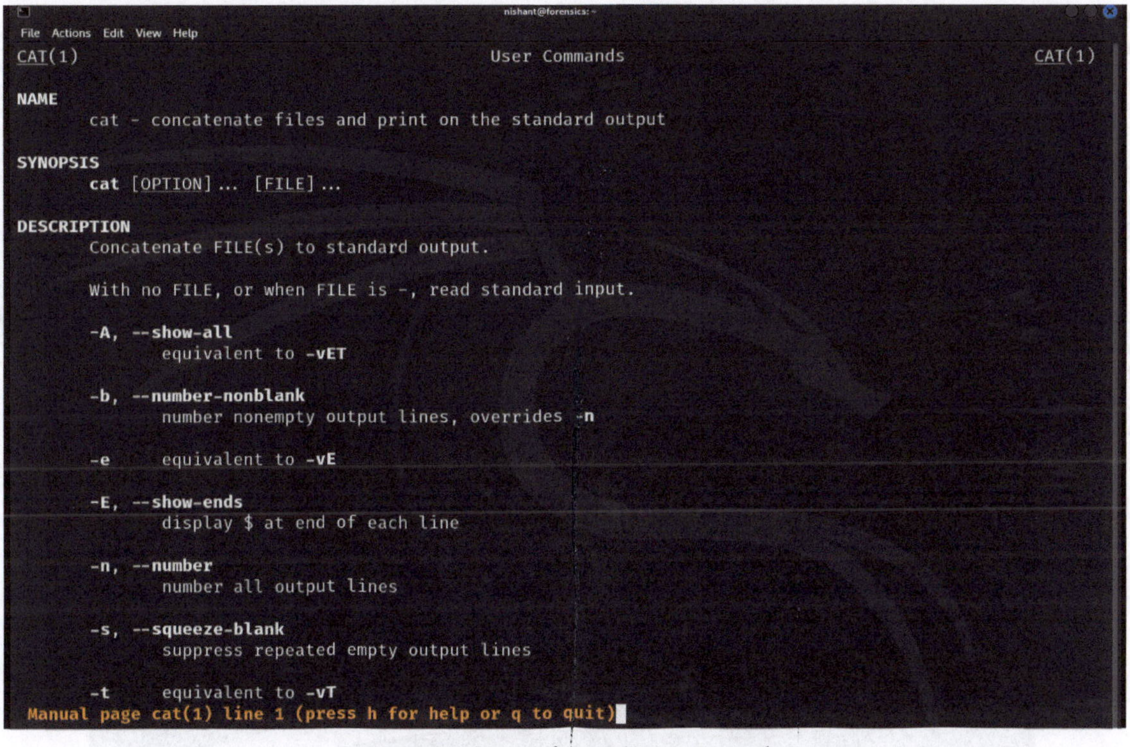

```
nishant@forensics: ~
File  Actions  Edit  View  Help
CAT(1)                          User Commands                          CAT(1)

NAME
       cat - concatenate files and print on the standard output

SYNOPSIS
       cat [OPTION]... [FILE]...

DESCRIPTION
       Concatenate FILE(s) to standard output.

       With no FILE, or when FILE is -, read standard input.

       -A, --show-all
              equivalent to -vET

       -b, --number-nonblank
              number nonempty output lines, overrides -n

       -e     equivalent to -vE

       -E, --show-ends
              display $ at end of each line

       -n, --number
              number all output lines

       -s, --squeeze-blank
              suppress repeated empty output lines

       -t     equivalent to -vT
 Manual page cat(1) line 1 (press h for help or q to quit)
```

Figure 5.2: Output of a sample man command

The preceding command shows the manual pages for **cat**. There are multiple pages of the manual content for this command, and you can use arrow keys to move up and down and *Ctrl+f* and *Ctrl+b* to move down and up one page at a time, respectively.

Note: If you are not already working with Linux, try out the basic Linux commands like `ls`, `mkdir`, `rmdir`, `rm`, `cp`, `mv`, `head`, `tail`, `find`, `sudo`, `whoami`, `chmod`, and `ps`. We will discuss the commands that are used in forensics at the relevant places. However, it is important to be comfortable finding your way around the Linux file system using these basic commands. You can use man to know everything about these commands.

Activity

Attempt the following activities before the next recipe:

- Check if you see the **cat** command in both **/bin** and **/usr/bin**? How do you infer the observations?
- Can you create a directory as the root user and delete it using a non-root user? What error do you receive when you try to do that?

Recipe 20: Important Linux tools for digital forensics

Linux has an extensive set of tools that can be used in various aspects of digital forensics and aid in collecting and analyzing forensic evidence. These tools are not only used for working with evidence from the underlying Linux system but are valuable for working with any evidence collected from other systems during the analysis.

When we work with Kali Linux, there are a large number of tools that are part of this distribution by default. This ensures that digital forensics professionals already have access to the most widely used tools.

> **Note:**
>
> - **Compatibility: Linux**
> - **License considerations: Free software used**

Recipe

Clicking on the Kali Linux icon in the top-left corner will display a menu with numerous options. The tools most commonly used by cybersecurity professionals are neatly organized into various categories. Throughout this book, we will work with many of these tools. For now, click on the **Forensics** category to view tools used in the different stages of digital forensics:

Figure 5.3: Commonly used digital forensics tools in Kali Linux

Sleuth Kit is one of the suites of widely used tools that we will learn in this chapter.

As is known, all these tools come with man pages. For example, you can run the command `man autopsy` to view detailed information about the autopsy tool:

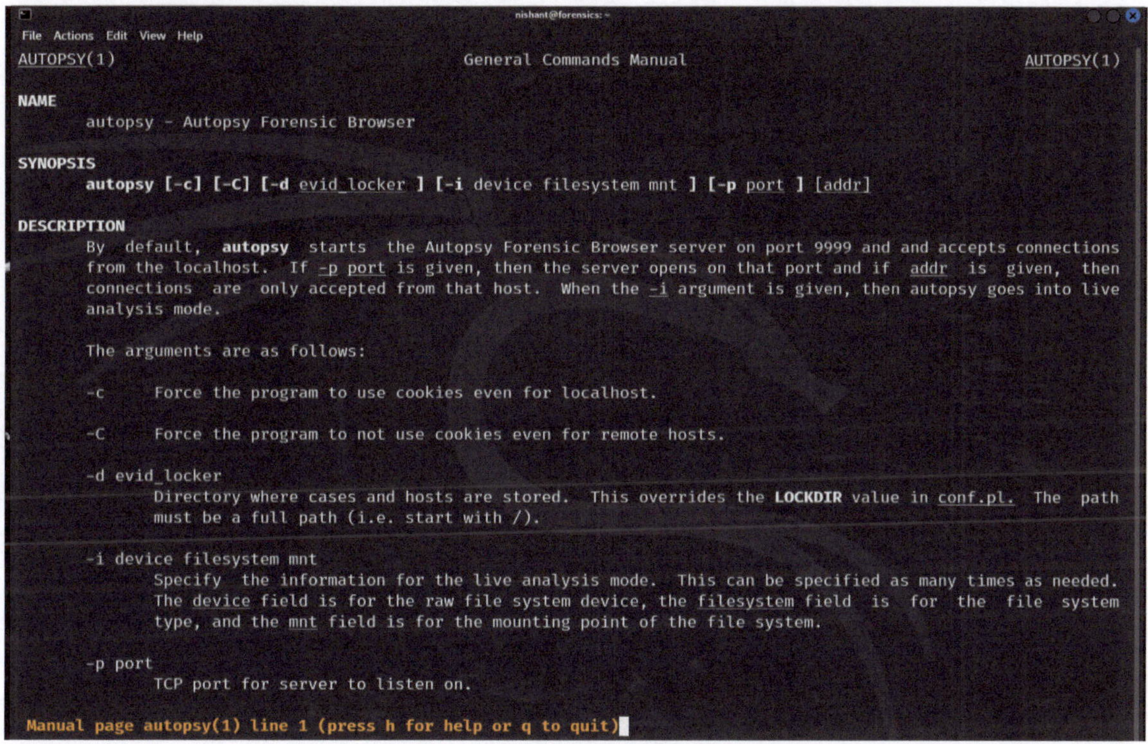

Figure 5.4*: An example of man pages for a digital forensics tool in Kali Linux*

While all these tools are pre-packaged as part of Kali Linux, there are many other tools that are available as part of Linux or can be easily installed using one of the package managers like yum (Fedora, CentOS, RHEL, etc.) or apt (Debian, Kali Linux, Ubuntu, etc.). The following table lists a few of these tools that every digital forensic professional should master:

Tool	Details	Usage
`dd`	Disk cloning and imaging tool for creating raw disk images.	It can be used to create a forensic image of a disk volume or a file by cloning the volume to the destination file and is used for data acquisition. **Example**: The following command copies the entire disk volume **`/dev/sda`** to another volume **`/dev/sdb`**: **`dd if=/dev/sda of=/dev/sdb`** `if` stands for *input file* and `of` stands for *output file*.
`tcpdump`	Command-line packet capture and analysis tool.	`tcpdump` is part of network forensics to dump network packets into a file. The dump can be used to analyze what was happening in the network. **Example**: The following command dumps the packets from the network interface eth0 to a file: `tcpdump -w network_capture.pcap -i eth0` The `-w` is used for the capture file name and `-i` is used for the interface name.

Tool	Details	Usage
`lsof`	Lists open files.	As part of a live system forensics, **`lsof`** can be used to list all the open files and the command that opened that file. **Example**: The following command lists all the open files and can result into a very long output: **`lsof`** There are many options supported by **`lsof`**. For example, the option **`-u`** lists all the files by a specific user.
`ps`	`ps` stands for process status and lists all the running processes.	**`ps`** is widely used for checking the running processes. It can be piped to **`grep`** to look for specific text in the command for the running process. **Example**: The following command lists all the process that has the word **`network`** in it: **`ps -eaf | grep -i network`**
`parted`	`parted` is a disk partition manipulation program that can be used to create and recover disk partions.	**`parted`** is used to check the disk partition as well as for recovery of the disk partitions as part of disk forensics. **Example**: The following command lists the partition layout of all the block devices: **`parted -l`**

Table 5.3: Important digital forensic tools

Note: We will discuss many more tools throughout this book for data acquisition, file system analysis, memory forensics, disk and partition analysis, timeline and metadata analysis, malware analysis, and even live system forensics. This recipe is intended to make you familiar with a few of the widely used tools.

Activity

Attempt the following activities before the next recipe:

- Do all the tools under the Forensics menu have a **graphical user interface** (GUI)? If not, find out how to interact with them.
- Look at the man pages for the dd command to back up an entire partition/volume to a file. The command will look like this **`dd if=/dev/hda1 of=/home/<user>/hda1.img`**. Ensure you use a smaller volume for this activity, as it can take up a lot of space.
- Write a command to capture only 10 packets using the **`tcpdump`** command.
- What are the other options that can be supplied to the **`ps`** command?

Understanding important logging systems on Linux

Linux provides many powerful logging mechanisms that are crucial for monitoring system activity, detecting security incidents, and conducting forensic investigations. Let us examine a few of them that are important for digital forensics.

syslog

syslog, or system logging, is a standard logging system used in Linux to collect and manage logs from various applications and services. It allows logs to be categorized and sent to different locations, such as files, remote servers, or databases.

At a high level, this is how syslog works:

- On the client machine, various logs are generated, e.g., security logs, audit logs, syslog, etc.
- These logs can then be logged to specific files using routing and storage rules.
- Finally, the logs can be sent to an external syslog server or a tamper-proof and secure **security information and event management** (**SIEM**) for storage.

A few important log files that are used and processed for syslog are as follows:

Log file	Purpose
`/var/log/syslog`	This log file is used in Debian-based distributions (e.g., Ubuntu). This is used to log general system activity, including startup messages and error details.
`/var/log/messages`	The purpose of this log is similar to **`/var/log/syslog`** for Red Hat-based distributions (e.g., CentOS, RHEL).
`/var/log/auth.log` or / **`var/log/secure`**	Both the logs are used to log authentication-related events such as login attempts and access control. Debian-based systems use auth.log, while Red Hat-based systems use secure.
`/var/log/kern.log`	This log captures kernel messages and helps diagnose issues at the system's core.
`/var/log/boot.log`	This log is useful for troubleshooting startup problems as it tracks system initialization and boot-time events.

***Table 5.4**: Important Linux logs that are processed as part of syslog*

Audit log

Audit logs are primarily used for security event monitoring by auditing what is happening on the system. **Audit daemon** (**`auditd`**) is a highly detailed security auditing framework in Linux that tracks system calls, file access, and user activity. The main files for **`auditd`** are as follows:

File	Purpose
`/var/log/audit/audit.log`	The file to which all the audit logs are sent by **`auditd`**.
`/etc/audit/auditd.conf`	Configuration file for **`auditd`** to fine tune the audit logging properties.

***Table 5.5**: Main auditd files*

Access log and authentication logs

Access logs track user interactions with services such as web servers (e.g., Apache, NGINX), and remote login services like SSH or Secure Shell.

Each of the applications, like web servers, can have its own access, which looks like the following:

- **Apache server**: **`/var/log/apache2/access.log`**
- **NGINX server**: **`/var/log/nginx/access.log`**

Apart from them, SSH logs are created in standard files like the following:

- **Authentication logs**: `/var/log/auth.log` (for Debian, Kali Linux, Ubuntu, etc.)
- **Secure log**: `/var/log/secure` (for RHEL, CentOs, Fedora, etc.)

Each of these logs provides useful information about who has accessed the system or resources, making them important evidence for digital forensic investigation.

Event logs

Linux also has the provision of event logs that capture kernel activity, system errors, and application behavior. The two most important event logs are as follows:

- **Kernel events**: `/var/log/kern.log`
- **Systemd logs (for systemd-based systems)**: Stored in binary format and accessible via the `journalctl` command

Both logs provide important information to reconstruct the timelines of a cybersecurity incident, such as a cyberattack.

Recipe 21: Enabling audit logs

Audit logs can be used to create an audit trail in Linux, which is important evidence for digital forensics investigations. Access to the audit trail of the system is one of the important aspects of being able to perform Forensic analysis. Audit logs in Linux can be used to track any changes in the system. For example, audit logs can be used to log every attempt to modify system files like `sshd_config`, `passwd`, changes in the system date and time, etc. Linux's `auditctl` utility is used to create an audit trail.

Let us understand how to create a simple audit trail for an important file on Linux.

Note:

- **Compatibility: Linux**
- **License considerations: Free software used**

Recipe

`/etc/passwd` file along with `/etc/shadow` file store all the user details and their password. When a user is added, removed, or modified (e.g., changes in the user's group), then these files are modified. Hence, we can assume that if a threat actor is trying to create a user, we would get audit logs for these files if enabled.

`auditd` needs to be installed before we can enable audit logs on the system. Run the following command to install `auditd`:

```
apt-get install auditd
```

Once it is installed, start the `auditd` service by running the following command:

```
systemctl start auditd
```

Verify that the `auditd` service is running by using the following command:

```
systemctl status auditd
```

You will get an output similar to the following:

```
┌──(root㉿forensics)-[~]
└─# systemctl status auditd
● auditd.service - Security Audit Logging Service
     Loaded: loaded (/usr/lib/systemd/system/auditd.service; disabled; preset: disabled)
     Active: active (running) since Sun 2025-02-02 09:02:17 IST; 5h 32min ago
 Invocation: aa9687fb2f5f423da4d359f6e4989f46
       Docs: man:auditd(8)
             https://github.com/linux-audit/audit-documentation
    Process: 369009 ExecStart=/usr/sbin/auditd (code=exited, status=0/SUCCESS)
   Main PID: 369018 (auditd)
      Tasks: 2 (limit: 9393)
     Memory: 860K (peak: 1.4M)
        CPU: 402ms
     CGroup: /system.slice/auditd.service
             └─369018 /usr/sbin/auditd

Feb 02 09:02:17 forensics systemd[1]: Starting auditd.service - Security Audit Logging Service...
Feb 02 09:02:17 forensics auditd[369018]: No plugins found, not dispatching events
Feb 02 09:02:17 forensics auditd[369018]: Init complete, auditd 4.0.2 listening for events (startup
state enable)
Feb 02 09:02:17 forensics systemd[1]: Started auditd.service - Security Audit Logging Service.

┌──(root㉿forensics)-[~]
└─#
```

The previous output shows that the audit service is running. Now, we are ready to work on our important files, which we need to monitor for changes.

Activity

Attempt the following activities before the next recipe:

- When you installed and enabled **auditd**, do you see logs already getting generated in **/var/log/audit/audit.log**? If yes, what types of logs are getting generated?
- Specify the encryption algorithm used to store the passwords in **/etc/shadow** file.

Recipe 22: Using audit logs to capture file changes

We saw how to configure **auditd** in the previous recipe. Let us now configure audit logging for an important file, **/etc/passwd**. Configuring an audit for this file will help us understand if the file was tampered with, or if any user was added, modified (e.g., change in the user's group), or deleted.

Note:

- **Compatibility: Linux**
- **License considerations: Free software used**

Recipe

We will first use **auditctl** to create default audit rules that generate audit logs whenever the file is read, written to, executed, or its attributes are changed:

```
┌──(root㉿forensics)-[/var/log/audit]
└─# auditctl -w /etc/passwd
```

In the preceding command, we created a **rwxa** rule that stands for read, write, execute, and attribute changes. This is created by default by the command we use. Let us verify by running the following command:

```
┌──(root㉿forensics)-[/var/log/audit]
└─# auditctl -l
-w /etc/passwd -p rwxa

┌──(root㉿forensics)-[/var/log/audit]
└─#
```

The preceding command shows that there is an **rwxa** rule created on **/etc/passwd**. Now, let us see if any audit logs are generated just by the action of reading this file.

Open two terminals in Kali Linux. On the first terminal window, run the following command to monitor the audit. log file:

```
tail -f /var/log/audit/audit.log
```

In the second terminal window, run the following command to print the content of the **passwd** file:

```
cat /etc/passwd
```

When you run this command, you will see something similar to the following in the terminal window where **audit.log** was being monitored:

```
type=SYSCALL msg=audit(1738482962.399:249): arch=c000003e syscall=257 success=yes exit=3 a0=ffffff9c a1=7fff200865eb a2=0 a3=0 items=1 ppid=245647 pid=414020 auid=1000 uid=0 gid=0 euid=0 suid=0 fsuid=0 egid=0 sgid=0 fsgid=0 tty=pts1 ses=2 comm="cat" exe="/usr/bin/cat" subj=unconfined key=(null) ARCH=x86_64 SYSCALL=openat AUID="nishant" UID="root" GID="root" EUID="root" SUID="root" FSUID="root" EGID="root" SGID="root" FSGID="root"

type=CWD msg=audit(1738482962.399:249): cwd="/var/log/audit"

type=PATH msg=audit(1738482962.399:249): item=0 name="/etc/passwd" inode=2231251 dev=08:01 mode=0100644 ouid=0 ogid=0 rdev=00:00 nametype=NORMAL cap_fp=0 cap_fi=0 cap_fe=0 cap_fver=0 cap_frootid=0OUID="root" OGID="root"

type=PROCTITLE msg=audit(1738482962.399:249): proctitle=636174002F6574632F706173737764
```

In the preceding logs, the following information can be found:

- exe: The command used to read this file, **/usr/bin/cat**.
- **AUID**: The audit user ID of the user.
- **UID**: The UID of the user, in this case root.
- **GID**: The group ID of the user.
- **EUID**: The effective user ID of the user.
- **SUID**: The set user ID of the user.
- **FSUID**: The file system user ID of the user.

You can also see that the file being audited is also printed. This means we have all the information necessary to determine which file was read, which command was run to read the file, and all the properties of the user who read the file.

The same will apply for other operations like write, delete, and attribute change. The simplest way to test a write operation on **/etc/passwd** is to create a new user or change the group of an existing user.

When audit logging, like that seen in this recipe, is enabled for important system files and any other files, it helps understand the attack vector and creates a timeline of the cyberattack or incident.

Note: **The /etc/passwd file is read frequently by the Linux system. Hence, you may not want to create an audit rule for read. However, it makes sense to use other rule types that help you determine other types of intentional actions by the threat action, like creating a user, elevating the permission of a user, deleting a user, and so on.**

Activity

Attempt the following activities before the next recipe:

- Create a modification-only rule on the **/etc/passwd** file. After that, create a user and check if you get the audit logs.
- If a read rule is present on the **/etc/shadow** file, does logging in as any user trigger an audit log?
- Create an audit rule on a file in your home directory and confirm that audit rules are in place. Now, use the **touch** command in the format of **touch <file name>** to change the timestamp to the current time and date. Do you observe logs getting generated in audit logs? Why did it do so?
- Look at **auditctl** documentation and delete selected rules and all the rules.

Recipe 23: Sending logs to a syslog destination

We have so far looked at many logs in this chapter. Many of them are configured by default, like access logs and security logs, while others may need to be configured explicitly, like audit logs.

While, as part of digital forensics evidence collection, it is important to collect all of them from the target systems, it is a big hassle to collect logs from 100s or even 1000s of systems in a typical enterprise. Hence, it is equally important to be able to send these logs to a centralized location.

Security information and event management (**SIEM**) is a specialized security system that collects logs from numerous systems in a centralized location. Furthermore, a SIEM system can perform functions such as event correlation, log analytics, incident monitoring, compliance management, reporting, and even uncover hidden insights from the logs. With the advent of **artificial intelligence** (**AI**), SIEM systems have become more powerful. SIEM is an essential technology for any enterprise and is widely utilized across various domains, including finance, banking, retail, and critical infrastructure.

Although the installation and configuration of a SIEM system are beyond the scope of this book, its functionality can be simulated using a syslog server. Nevertheless, as a cyber forensic professional, it is important to develop a thorough understanding of how SIEM systems operate, including their configuration and effective use, particularly with open-source solutions.

Note:

- **Compatibility: Linux**
- **License considerations: Free software used**

Recipe

Let us use a syslog server to simulate sending the logs from one Kali Linux machine to another Linux machine. For this, we will need two Linux machines:

1. Kali Linux machine that will act like the source machine from where the logs are getting generated and forwarded using syslog.
2. Ubuntu machine that will receive the logs using a syslog server using **syslog-ng**.

Note: **Ensure that both the Kali Linux and Ubuntu machines are on the same subnet and that their firewalls are turned off. However, in real-world situations, they can be located anywhere as long as the target machine is reachable from the source machine. Additionally, it is not advisable to turn off the firewall in a production system, and you should adhere to the enterprise's security policies.**

Once you are ready with another VM running Ubuntu, let us get started. Refer to the following steps to send access logs from the source machine (syslog client) to the target machine (syslog server):

1. Install and configure **syslog-ng** on the Ubuntu system (syslog server):

```
apt-get install syslog-ng
systemctl start syslog-ng
```

After this, you can check if the **syslog-ng** process is running by using the following command:

```
systemctl status syslog-ng
```

The configuration of syslog-ng is in the file **/etc/rsyslog-ng/rsyslog-ng.conf**. Search the file for lines that match the following pattern:

```
##########################
# Sources
##########################
# This is the default behavior of sysklogd package
# Logs may come from unix stream, but not from another machine.
#
source s_src {
       system();
       internal();
};
```

The preceding lines are used to define where the logs may come from. In this case, it says that the logs can come only from the system and applications internal to this system.

We need to add a new log source in this file to enable logs from our source system, i.e., the Kali Linux machine. We can also enable logs from specific IP addresses for added security. However, for now, we will enable logs from all the source systems. Add a source to this file so that it looks like the following:

```
##########################
# Sources
##########################
# This is the default behavior of sysklogd package
# Logs may come from unix stream, but not from another machine.
#
```

```
source s_src {
        system();
        internal();
};

source s_external {
        udp(ip(0.0.0.0) port(514));
};

destination d_external {
        file ("/var/log/remote.log");
};

log {
        source(s_external);
        destination(d_external);
};
```

The preceding changes will now allow **syslog-ng** to receive logs from any syslog clients (hence 0.0.0.0) as far as they are sent to this syslog server on **user datagram protocol** (**UDP**) port 514. Also, the logs from remote syslog clients will be stored in **/var/log/remote.log**.

Now restart the **syslog-ng** by running the following command:

```
systemctl restart syslog-ng
```

If no errors are encountered, **syslog-ng** will restart successfully. To verify that it is operating correctly, run the following command:

```
systemctl status syslog-ng
```

Now, the **syslog-ng** server is ready to receive logs from the external syslog clients.

> **Note: Syslog supports sending logs using UDP and TCP, which stand for User Datagram Protocol and Transmission Control Protocol, respectively. The former is a connectionless protocol, while the latter is a connection-oriented protocol. In order to add security, you can also consider using Transport Layer Security (TLS) for sending syslog messages.**

2. Install and configure **rsyslog** on the Kali Linux system (syslog client). Use **apt-get** to install **rsyslog** on Kali Linux:

```
apt-get install rsyslog
systemctl start rsyslog
```

We can always obtain the status of the **rsyslog** process using below command:

```
systemctl status rsyslog
```

Once you have confirmed that the **rsyslog** process is running, configure the syslog configuration to send logs to our target system. Before we move forward, note the IP address of the target system by running the **ifconfig** command on the target system, i.e., the Ubuntu system on which we installed **syslog-ng**.

The configuration file for **rsyslog** is **/etc/rsyslog.conf**. Add the following lines at the end of the file:

```
auth.*,authpriv.*,local6.* @192.168.19.132:514
```

In the preceding example, this line implies that we need to forward all the logs of type auth to the syslog server recognized by the IP address on port 514. To make it work, replace the IP address with the IP address of your machine.

Once you are done, restart the **rsyslog** service by running the following command:

```
systemctl restart rsyslog
```

With this, we are ready to send logs from the Kali Linux machine, that is, our source machine or syslog client.

3. Let us now test if we can receive all the authentication logs in our syslog server.

   On the target machine, i.e., the Ubuntu machine, run the following command to create an empty file:

   ```
   touch /var/log/remote.log
   ```

   Monitor this file by running the following command:

   ```
   tail -f /var/log/remote.log
   ```

   On the source machine, i.e., Kali Linux machine, perform the following operations:

   - Lock your Kali Linux desktop and unlock it by providing the password.
   - Open a new terminal and then become root by using **sudo su**.
   - Run **exit** to exit from your root session.

If everything is configured well, you will see logs similar to the following getting generated in the target system, i.e., Ubuntu system, running syslog server using **syslog-ng**:

```
Feb  2 16:25:47 192.168.19.139 lightdm: pam_unix(lightdm-greeter:session): session closed for user lightdm
Feb  2 16:25:47 192.168.19.139 lightdm: pam_systemd(lightdm-greeter:session): New sd-bus connection (system-bus-pam-systemd-496821) opened.
Feb  2 16:25:47 192.168.19.139 lightdm: pam_unix(lightdm-greeter:session): session closed for user lightdm
Feb  2 16:25:47 192.168.19.139 lightdm: pam_systemd(lightdm-greeter:session): Failed to release session: Transport endpoint is not connected
Feb  2 16:25:47 192.168.19.139 systemd-logind[802]: Removed session c23.
Feb  2 16:25:57 192.168.19.139 (sd-pam): pam_unix(systemd-user:session): session closed for user lightdm
Feb  2 16:25:57 192.168.19.139 systemd-logind[802]: Removed session 183.

Feb  2 16:28:26 192.168.19.139 sudo:  nishant : TTY=pts/3 ; PWD=/home/nishant ; USER=root ; COMMAND=/usr/bin/su
Feb  2 16:28:26 192.168.19.139 sudo: pam_unix(sudo:session): session opened for user root(uid=0) by nishant(uid=1000)
Feb  2 16:28:26 192.168.19.139 su[503509]: (to root) root on pts/6
Feb  2 16:28:26 192.168.19.139 su[503509]: pam_unix(su:session): session opened for user root(uid=0) by nishant(uid=0)
Feb  2 16:28:26 192.168.19.139 su[503509]: pam_systemd(su:session): New sd-bus connection (system-bus-pam-systemd-503509) opened.

Feb  2 16:29:10 192.168.19.139 su[503509]: pam_unix(su:session): session closed for user root
Feb  2 16:29:10 192.168.19.139 sudo: pam_unix(sudo:session): session closed for user root
```

The above output has logs for all three scenarios and is demarcated by a new line for easy understanding.

Activity

Attempt the following activities before the next recipe:

- We discussed SIEM systems in this recipe. There is another set of specialized security systems called **security orchestration, automation, and response** (**SOAR**) systems. Can you read about SOAR systems and understand their role in cybersecurity in general and in digital forensics in particular?
- We used the UDP protocol to send logs from the source machine to the syslog server. Can we do the same using the TCP protocol? Look at the documentation of syslog-ng to understand how this can be done.
- You can also use the **`logger`** command on Kali Linux to simulate sending logs to **`/var/log/syslog`**. Use this utility to create a few simple logs and understand how this can be used in scripts written using Python or Shell Scripts.
- What does the log of type **`local6`** signify in the **`rsyslog.conf`** on our source machine?

Recipe 24: Implementing best practices for log management in Linux

Logs are at the core of evidence collection for digital forensics in Linux. However, the effectiveness of the evidence that can be collected also depends on implementing the best practices for log management. In this recipe, we will look at a few of them and also try them out on your Kali Linux and Ubuntu machines.

Note:

- **Compatibility: Linux**
- **License considerations: Free software used**

Recipe

Let us look at a few of the log management best practices:

1. **Centralized logging**: Use a centralized log server to collect important logs from multiple machines. This is the same principle that is used by a syslog server or a SIEM system. We just tried this out in the last recipe, where we used **`rsyslog`** on one machine as a client and syslog-ng on a remote server to collect authentication logs.
2. **Use log rotation**: Log rotation keeps a specified set of logs for any Linux applications. This helps prevent logs from consuming too much disk space.

   Global log rotation configurations are present in **`/etc/logrotate.conf`** and look like the following:

```
# see "man logrotate" for details

# global options do not affect preceding include directives


# rotate log files weekly
weekly


# keep 4 weeks worth of backlogs
```

```
rotate 4

# create new (empty) log files after rotating old ones
create

# use date as a suffix of the rotated file
#dateext

# uncomment this if you want your log files compressed
#compress

# packages drop log rotation information into this directory
include /etc/logrotate.d

# system-specific logs may also be configured here.
```

You can also create configurations for specific files like below, in this case for **/var.log/auth.log**:

```
/var/log/auth.log {
    weekly
    rotate 4
    compress
    missingok
    notifempty
}
```

3. **Secure log files**: Log files themselves are prone to injection attacks, where a threat actor, as part of the compromise, can either add specific logs to mislead the investigators or delete logs. This can be mitigated by restricting access to logs that may be sensitive.

   The following examples show how this can be done:

```
sudo chmod 600 /var/log/auth.log
sudo chown root:adm /var/log/auth.log
```

4. **Use journaling to view logs for a specific time interval**: The **journalctl** service in Linux is used for journaling and, hence, a very important tool to retrieve important system logs. It can be used to view all the logs or logs for a specific process.

   The following command shows logs for the last hour:

```
journalctl --since "1 hour ago"
```

5. **Monitoring logs in real time**: If you noticed, we have already used **tail -f** to monitor log files as the logs are added to them. This is a very simple yet powerful way to monitor logs in real time. It can be done by the following command:

```
tail -f <log file>
```

   Example:

```
tail -f /var/log/audit/audit.log
```

6. **Use external tools like logwatch to automate log analysis**: Tools like **logwatch** provide a powerful way to watch logs. It also analyzes the logs and reports specific areas of interest. To use **logwatch**, first install it using the following command:

   ```
   apt-get install logwatch
   ```

   Copy the **logwatch** configuration file to **/etc/** directory:

   ```
   cp /usr/share/logwatch/default.conf/logwatch.conf /etc/logwatch/conf/
   ```

   Once done, you can use it to watch logs like the following:

   ```
   logwatch --detail high
   ```

   The preceding command will print a detailed report. logwatch is highly configurable for watching logs for a large number of services. The services are again present under **/usr/share/logwatch/scripts/services**. They can be copied to the **/etc/share/logwatch/script/services** to watch the logs for the services as per your requirements.

7. **Enable remote log backup**: While you can send a subset of logs to the central log server using syslog, not everything can be sent to the remote server, as a typical Linux system may generate a large amount of logs. In such cases, **rsync** (remote sync) comes in handy:

   ```
   rsync -avz /var/log/ <remoteuser>@<logserver>:/backup/logs/
   ```

   With some clever tweaks, the preceding command can be modified to store logs in a specific directory on the remote server.

8. **Implement a log retention policy**: Deleting logs after a pre-specified time period is also one of the best practices of log management. This helps clean the old logs:

   ```
   find /var/log -type f -mtime +30 -exec rm -f {} \;
   ```

   The preceding command cleans all the logs under **/var/log** that are older than 30 days. This method can be used in conjunction with **rsync** to ensure that no logs are lost.

Activity

Attempt the following activities before the next recipe:

- Find out if you can configure the size of the logs that are created in **logrotate.conf**?
- Restrict access to **/var/log/audit/audit.log** to the user root belonging to the group root.
- How can you use **journalctl** to view logs for a specific process?
- Create a **rsync** command to backup logs to a remote server in a directory named after the IP address of the source server.

Recipe 25: Validating file integrity using checksum

A hash code is a fixed-length alphanumeric string generated by applying a cryptographic hash function to data (e.g., a file). It uniquely represents the contents of the file and changes completely if even a single byte is altered. This means that even a minor change in the file by a threat actor can easily be detected if the hash code (also known as a checksum) is stored for the file. In this recipe, let us examine an example of how a checksum can be used to validate the integrity of a file.

Note:

- **Compatibility: Linux**
- **License considerations: Free software used**

Recipe

Let us first create a file with simple content as follows:

```
┌──(root㉿forensics)-[/home/nishant]
└─# cat testsum.txt
This is a file with confidential information.

┌──(root㉿forensics)-[/home/nishant]
└─#
```

Now, let us find the checksum of the file using **sha1sum**:

```
┌──(root㉿forensics)-[/home/nishant]
└─# sha1sum testsum.txt
7924265ef66d7fc5f4ff8a726ef6697b8f4a9e74  testsum.txt

┌──(root㉿forensics)-[/home/nishant]
└─#
```

The string printed represents the checksum of the file's content. It is a fixed-size string regardless of the size of the file's content.

Now, we will make a tiny change to the file that otherwise would not be noticeable. Let us edit the file and add a space after the first line. When you run **sha1sum** on the file again, you will observe that the checksum has changed drastically:

```
┌──(root㉿forensics)-[/home/nishant]
└─# sha1sum testsum.txt
05c32190eef895aebbedf489c81b846ec75ea2b2  testsum.txt

┌──(root㉿forensics)-[/home/nishant]
└─#
```

This method can now be used to verify whether anything has changed in the file. When combined with methods like file auditing, it provides a powerful way to verify the integrity of the file.

Interesting fact: **You can even create a file with a checksum of multiple files and then create a checksum of this file. This cascading style checksum can be used to quickly check a group/directory of files for modification instead of checking the integrity of the files one by one.**

Activity

Attempt the following activities before the next recipe:

- Specify the other ways/ algorithms to create checksums.
- Does the checksum of the file change if the file is renamed or copied to another location?

Recipe 26: Analyzing disk partitions

A disk partition is a logically separated section of a physical storage device. It allows better management of disk space and can have different file systems.

The common partition types in Linux are shown in the following table:

Partition type	Details
Primary partition	Bootable partition. There can be up to 4 primary partitions.
Extended partition	A container for logical partitions.
Logical partition	A partition inside an extended partition, with no limit on the number.
Swap partition	A partition that can be used as a virtual memory for swapping memory pages between the main memory and disk.

Table 5.6: Common partition types in Linux

In this recipe, let us look at a few ways to analyze disk partitions. The disk partition information is important to be collected during the digital forensic evidence collection.

Note:

- **Compatibility: Linux**
- **License considerations: Free software used**

Recipe

We have discussed before in this chapter in *Recipe 20, Important Linux tools for digital forensics,* that parted can be used to create and recover disk partitions. For example, the following command lists the partition layout of all the block devices:

```
┌──(root㉿forensics)-[~]
└─# parted -l
Model: VMware, VMware Virtual S (scsi)
Disk /dev/sda: 53.7GB
Sector size (logical/physical): 512B/512B
Partition Table: msdos
Disk Flags:

Number  Start   End     Size    Type      File system     Flags
 1      1049kB  52.7GB  52.7GB  primary   ext4            boot
 2      52.7GB  53.7GB  1022MB  extended                  lba
 5      52.7GB  53.7GB  1022MB  logical   linux-swap(v1)  swap

┌──(root㉿forensics)-[~]
└─#
```

In this example, you can easily see that there are primary, extended, and logical partitions in the partition table. Also, since this VM is running on a hypervisor, which in turn is running on the Windows host, the main partition table is shown as `msdos`.

We can view a different representation of the same information using **`fdisk`** as follows:

```
┌──(root㉿forensics)-[~]
└─# fdisk -l
Disk /dev/sda: 50 GiB, 53687091200 bytes, 104857600 sectors
```

```
Disk model: VMware Virtual S
Units: sectors of 1 * 512 = 512 bytes
Sector size (logical/physical): 512 bytes / 512 bytes
I/O size (minimum/optimal): 512 bytes / 512 bytes
Disklabel type: dos
Disk identifier: 0x0d9f8707

Device     Boot     Start       End   Sectors  Size Id Type
/dev/sda1  *         2048 102856703 102854656   49G 83 Linux
/dev/sda2       102858750 104855551   1996802  975M  f W95 Ext'd (LBA)
/dev/sda5       102858752 104855551   1996800  975M 82 Linux swap / Solaris

┌──(root㉿forensics)-[~]
└─#
```

The preceding command gives a little bit deeper details of the partition table including the start and end sectors and the number of sectors that are used for the virtual machine.

Note: parted and fdisk should be used with caution as they can change the partition table and hence cause irrecoverable loss of data. It is a good practice to back up your system before working with these tools.

If you want to know the details of all the block devices, then the **lsblk** command can be used:

```
┌──(root㉿forensics)-[~]
└─# lsblk
NAME   MAJ:MIN RM  SIZE RO TYPE MOUNTPOINTS
sda      8:0    0   50G  0 disk
├─sda1   8:1    0   49G  0 part /
├─sda2   8:2    0    1K  0 part
└─sda5   8:5    0  975M  0 part [SWAP]
sr0     11:0    1 1024M  0 rom

┌──(root㉿forensics)-[~]
└─#
```

The command displays all the block devices connected to the system in a hierarchical structure, providing valuable information. If multiple physical disks are present in the system, they will be displayed accordingly.

Finally, let us try to print the metadata for one of the disk partitions **/dev/sda1**. As per the above outputs, we can easily infer that **/dev/sda1** is the disk where the entire Linux system resides. We can print the metadata associated with this disk as follows using **dumpe2fs** command:

```
┌──(root㉿forensics)-[~]
└─# dumpe2fs /dev/sda1
dumpe2fs 1.47.1 (20-May-2024)
Filesystem volume name:   <none>
Last mounted on:          /
Filesystem UUID:          77078c82-745f-4970-a3d7-f920eabddcb4
Filesystem magic number:  0xEF53
```

```
Filesystem revision #:    1 (dynamic)
Filesystem features:      has_journal ext_attr resize_inode dir_index orphan_file filetype needs_
recovery extent 64bit flex_bg metadata_csum_seed sparse_super large_file huge_file dir_nlink extra_
isize metadata_csum orphan_present
Filesystem flags:         signed_directory_hash
Default mount options:    user_xattr acl
Filesystem state:         clean
Errors behavior:          Continue
Filesystem OS type:       Linux
Inode count:              3219456
Block count:              12856832
Reserved block count:     642841
Overhead clusters:        280954
Free blocks:              8820884
Free inodes:              2751643
.
.
.
Journal features:         journal_incompat_revoke journal_64bit journal_checksum_v3
Total journal size:       256M
Total journal blocks:     65536
Max transaction length:   65536
Fast commit length:       0
Journal sequence:         0x00003c8e
Journal start:            34554
Journal checksum type:    crc32c
Journal checksum:         0x8caff99f


Group 0: (Blocks 0-32767) csum 0x262c [ITABLE_ZEROED]
  Primary superblock at 0, Group descriptors at 1-7
  Reserved GDT blocks at 8-1031
  Block bitmap at 1032 (+1032), csum 0x793217e3
  Inode bitmap at 1048 (+1048), csum 0x79eee880
  Inode table at 1064-1575 (+1064)
  21548 free blocks, 8171 free inodes, 2 directories, 8171 unused inodes
  Free blocks: 11220-32767
  Free inodes: 22-8192
.
.
.
Group 392: (Blocks 12845056-12856831) csum 0x59af [INODE_UNINIT, ITABLE_ZEROED]
  Block bitmap at 12582920 (bg #384 + 8), csum 0x6ec77c90
```

```
Inode bitmap at 12582929 (bg #384 + 17), csum 0x00000000
Inode table at 12587026-12587537 (bg #384 + 4114)
52 free blocks, 8192 free inodes, 0 directories, 8192 unused inodes
Free blocks: 12850171-12850175, 12854796-12854826, 12856816-12856831
Free inodes: 3211265-3219456
```

The preceding output is truncated in this example as it prints a large amount of metadata. However, just by looking at the output, you can realize this gives deep level information about the disk including its properties, allocation details, journal features, block groups, and much more.

Activity

Attempt the following activities before the next recipe:

- Refer to the man pages for `parted` and `fdisk` to learn how to create partitions.
- Next, consider what the disk partition output would look like if these commands were executed on a bare-metal server running Kali Linux directly on the hardware.
- Finally, review the initial set of properties in the output of the `dumpe2fs` command and explore the meaning of each.

Recipe 27: Identifying deleted files

Files deleted from the file system are not completely deleted. They are only marked for deletion. It is possible that, over time, some of the disk sectors used by the file have been reclaimed by other files. Regardless of these aspects, knowing that there are deleted files in the file system can help digital forensics investigators recover those files.

In this recipe, we will explore a few ways to identify deleted files. We will also discuss how to recover a deleted file as a new file for further analysis. This recipe provides the essential details on how deleted files are identified. However, digital forensic investigators may employ advanced tools that can fully automate the process of identifying and recovering deleted files.

Note:

- **Compatibility: Linux**
- **License considerations: Free software used**

Recipe

If you remember, we have used the `lsof` command before to list all the open files. The `lsof` command can also be used to find deleted files that were open before and are now claiming disk space, as follows:

```
lsof -nP | grep -i deleted
```

When you run this command, the output will look similar to the following:

```
—(root㉿forensics)-[~]
└─# lsof -nP | grep -i deleted
lsof: WARNING: can't stat() fuse.gvfsd-fuse file system /run/user/1000/gvfs
      Output information may be incomplete.
lsof: WARNING: can't stat() fuse.portal file system /run/user/1000/doc
      Output information may be incomplete.
pipewire    1217                        nishant   35u      REG                   0,1       2312
```

```
3092 /memfd:pipewire-memfd:flags=0x0000000f,type=2,size=2312 (deleted)
pipewire     1217                    nishant   38u      REG                0,1       2312
2080 /memfd:pipewire-memfd:flags=0x0000000f,type=2,size=2312 (deleted)
.
.
.
qterminal 245496 245497 QXcbEvent    nishant    22u      REG               0,41      53712
1122 /tmp/#1122 (deleted)
qterminal 245496 245498 QDBusConn    nishant    19u      REG               0,41     214848
1120 /tmp/#1120 (deleted)
qterminal 245496 245498 QDBusConn    nishant    21u      REG               0,41   67884224
1121 /tmp/#1121 (deleted)
qterminal 245496 245498 QDBusConn    nishant    22u      REG               0,41      53712
1122 /tmp/#1122 (deleted)

┌──(root㉿forensics)-[~]
└─#
```

The preceding output is truncated in this example, as it prints a large amount of data even when we are only looking for deleted files.

Let us understand another way to list the inodes (addresses on the disk where the file is actually present) for the deleted file. Tools like **debugfs** can be used to undelete the files whose disk space is not yet claimed. We can use **debugfs** as follows:

```
debugfs /dev/sda1
```

Once in **debugfs**, run **lsdel**. **lsdel** given you a list of inodes corresponding to deleted files.

```
debugfs: lsdel
```

After that, you can use **cat** to print the content of the file:

```
debugfs: cat <inode number>
```

In the preceding command, include angle brackets while running the command.

You can now **dump** the inode into a file on the file system as follows:

```
debugfs: dump <inode number> /<directory>/<filename>
```

Activity

Attempt the following activities before the next recipe:

- Create a file, add some content, and delete that file. What are the ways you can find the details of the files that were deleted?
- Try identifying the deleted files after a few days. Is the information about the deleted file still available?
- What are the other tools that can be used to identify deleted files?

Recipe 28: Examining swap files

A swap file or swap partition is a space on the disk used as virtual memory when RAM is full. It helps the system handle memory overflow but may store sensitive data, including passwords, encryption keys, and other artifacts.

Swap files are used in most modern operating systems for this purpose. Since they contain a portion of the memory in the form of serialized memory pages, they can be used to discover a subset of what was running in the main memory or RAM.

Note:

- **Compatibility: Linux**
- **License considerations: Free software used**

Recipe

Let us first understand which partition is used to store the swap file. We can do that using the **swapon** command as follows:

```
┌──(root㉿forensics)-[~]
└─# swapon --show
NAME      TYPE      SIZE USED PRIO
/dev/sda5 partition 975M   0B   -2

┌──(root㉿forensics)-[~]
└─#
```

We now know that **/dev/sda5** is being used as a swap partition. We can now use the **dd** command to dump this partition into a file to create a forensic image:

```
dd if=/dev/sda5 of=swap_image.dd bs=4M status=progress
```

The preceding command will show the progress of the dumping and then show the final results of the operation. The output will look similar to the following:

```
┌──(root㉿forensics)-[/home/nishant]
└─# dd if=/dev/sda5 of=swap_image.dd bs=4M status=progress
994050048 bytes (994 MB, 948 MiB) copied, 11 s, 90.0 MB/s
243+1 records in
243+1 records out
1022361600 bytes (1.0 GB, 975 MiB) copied, 11.4523 s, 89.3 MB/s

┌──(root㉿forensics)-[/home/nishant]
└─#
```

The generated file is now a forensic image of the swap volume. This can now be used for performing various analysis tasks by using tools that are part of Kali Linux, as well as advanced image analysis tools.

Note: **Be careful when dumping an entire partition into a file, as the file size will match the disk partition size. If you do not have enough space, you may run out of disk space, which can disrupt applications.**

We can use the **strings** command to examine for any readable text as follows:

```
strings swap_image.dd | less
```

We can also use the **strings** command to look for specific keywords as follows:

```
strings swap_image.dd | grep -i password
```

There are other advanced tools that can be used to examine the swap file. For example, we can use **binwalk** to look for hidden data as follows:

```
binwalk --run-as=root -e swap_image.dd
```

This operation can take a lot of time and CPU resources.

Finally, we can also use foremost to recover files from the swap as follows. This may not result in complete files, but anything recovered could be significant for forensic examination:

```
foremost -i swap_image.dd -o recovered_files
```

If foremost is not installed on your Kali Linux system, then you can install it using the following command:

```
apt-get install foremost
```

Note: Tools like swap_digger that are available for free on GitHub can provide a much deeper analysis ability of swap files. Look for such tools and add them to your toolset due to the importance of swap file analysis.

Activity

Attempt the following activities before the next recipe:

- Read more about how **strings** command can find out the string literals from a binary file like a swap file.
- Is there any other binary file analysis tool that can be used to analyze a dump of swap files?

Recipe 29: Analyzing file system structure

While working with a Linux system, it is important to understand the file system structure in addition to the partition and disk volume details. We aim to capture aspects such as mounted volumes, the total number of volumes, their disk utilization, and many others, all of which are important during a digital forensic examination.

Let us examine a few simple ways to analyze the file system structure of a Linux system, using Kali Linux as an example.

Note:

- **Compatibility: Linux**
- **License considerations: Free software used**

Recipe

The first tool we will use is **df,** which stands for *disk free* and provides details of the file system space usage. However, it also provides the list of all the fixed volumes and mounted volumes and hence is a very useful tool. We can run **df** as follows:

```
┌──(root㉿forensics)-[/home/nishant]
└─# df -h
Filesystem      Size  Used Avail Use% Mounted on
udev            3.9G     0  3.9G   0% /dev
tmpfs           792M  1.5M  790M   1% /run
/dev/sda1        48G   15G   32G  32% /
tmpfs           3.9G     0  3.9G   0% /dev/shm
tmpfs           5.0M     0  5.0M   0% /run/lock
tmpfs           1.0M     0  1.0M   0% /run/credentials/systemd-journald.service
```

```
tmpfs           1.0M     0  1.0M   0% /run/credentials/systemd-udev-load-credentials.service
tmpfs           1.0M     0  1.0M   0% /run/credentials/systemd-tmpfiles-setup-dev-early.service
tmpfs           1.0M     0  1.0M   0% /run/credentials/systemd-sysctl.service
tmpfs           1.0M     0  1.0M   0% /run/credentials/systemd-tmpfiles-setup-dev.service
tmpfs           3.9G  592K  3.9G   1% /tmp
tmpfs           1.0M     0  1.0M   0% /run/credentials/systemd-tmpfiles-setup.service
tmpfs           1.0M     0  1.0M   0% /run/credentials/getty@tty1.service
tmpfs           792M  124K  792M   1% /run/user/1000

┌──(root㉿forensics)-[/home/nishant]
└─#
```

This output will vary based on your system. `df -h` shows a much more readable output than just using `df`.

The second useful command is `tree`, which provides the tree structure of the current directory in a recursive way. The `tree` command can be used as follows:

```
┌──(root㉿forensics)-[/home/nishant]
└─# tree
.
├── Desktop
├── Documents
├── Downloads
│   └── code_1.96.4-1736991114_amd64.deb
├── Music
├── Pictures
├── Public
├── Templates
├── Videos
├── Work
│   └── Digital-Forensics-Playbook
│       └── Chapter 04 - Development Environment for Digital Forensics
│           ├── Security-EventLogs.ps1
│           └── tcpdump.py
└── forensics-playbook
    └── tcpdump.py

13 directories, 4 files

┌──(root㉿forensics)-[/home/nishant]
└─#
```

You can also use `tree` to get the tree structure of a specific directory as follows:

```
tree /home/nishant
```

We have used **lsblk** before to check the partition structure. We can use it to get additional information about the mounted partitions as follows:

```
┌──(root㉿forensics)-[/home/nishant]
└─# lsblk -f
NAME   FSTYPE FSVER LABEL UUID                                 FSAVAIL FSUSE% MOUNTPOINTS
sda
├─sda1 ext4   1.0         77078c82-745f-4970-a3d7-f920eabddcb4   31.2G    30% /
├─sda2
└─sda5 swap   1           989b594c-abd5-4842-910d-0f707abc583e                [SWAP]
sr0

┌──(root㉿forensics)-[/home/nishant]
└─#
```

A file system type can also be inspected using **file** command as follows:

```
┌──(root㉿forensics)-[/home/nishant]
└─# file -s /dev/sda1
/dev/sda1: Linux rev 1.0 ext4 filesystem data, UUID=77078c82-745f-4970-a3d7-f920eabddcb4 (needs journal recovery) (extents) (64bit) (large files) (huge files)

┌──(root㉿forensics)-[/home/nishant]
└─#
```

How the file systems are mounted can be checked using the **/etc/fstab** file. **/etc/fstab** is a special Linux file that is used to mount disk volumes:

```
┌──(root㉿forensics)-[/home/nishant]
└─# cat /etc/fstab
# /etc/fstab: static file system information.
#
# Use 'blkid' to print the universally unique identifier for a
# device; this may be used with UUID= as a more robust way to name devices
# that works even if disks are added and removed. See fstab(5).
#
# systemd generates mount units based on this file, see systemd.mount(5).
# Please run 'systemctl daemon-reload' after making changes here.
#
# <file system> <mount point>   <type>  <options>       <dump>  <pass>
# / was on /dev/sda1 during installation
UUID=77078c82-745f-4970-a3d7-f920eabddcb4 /               ext4    errors=remount-ro 0       1
# swap was on /dev/sda5 during installation
UUID=989b594c-abd5-4842-910d-0f707abc583e none            swap    sw              0       0
/dev/sr0        /media/cdrom0   udf,iso9660 user,noauto     0       0

┌──(root㉿forensics)-[/home/nishant]
└─#
```

If you want to understand the details about inodes that are used by a file, then you can use **ls** command as follows. We will first create a file and then find out its inode information:

```
┌──(root㉿forensics)-[/home/nishant/Work]
└─# touch inode-file

┌──(root㉿forensics)-[/home/nishant/Work]
└─# ls -i /home/nishant/Work/inode-file
1966197 /home/nishant/Work/inode-file

┌──(root㉿forensics)-[/home/nishant/Work]
└─#
```

Activity

Attempt the following activities before the next recipe:

- Specify if you can use **ls** command to print similar details as given by **tree** in a recursive fashion?
- What is the significance of **Universally Unique Identifier** (UUID) in the disk volumes that we have seen in the output of the **lsblk** and **/etc/fstab** file?

Recipe 30: Recovering lost data from deleted files

We saw an example of how to recover deleted files using **debugfs**. However, this tool is a little cryptic to use, and using it manually may be extremely time-consuming. In this recipe, we will use a few other ways to recover lost data from deleted files.

Note:

- **Compatibility: Linux**
- **License considerations: Free software used**

Recipe

The first tool we will use to recover lost data from deleted files is **extundelete**. **extundelete** is not installed by default in Kali Linux and needs to be installed as follows:

```
apt-get install extundelete
```

Once you install it, you can execute it as follows to recover all the deleted files:

```
extundelete /dev/sda2 --restore-all
```

The deleted files are restored under the current directory under **RECOVERED_Files/path**.

extundelete provides you with many other ways to restore in a selective way. You can just run **extundelete** without any parameters to check various options.

Note: **Do not run extundelete on the current active partition. Ideally, you should mount a volume as a new volume and then run this command to be safe.**

There is another utility that comes with Kali Linux called **photorec**. This is a text-based, easy-to-use interface that can be used to recover deleted files. When you run **photorec**, you will see a screen like the following:

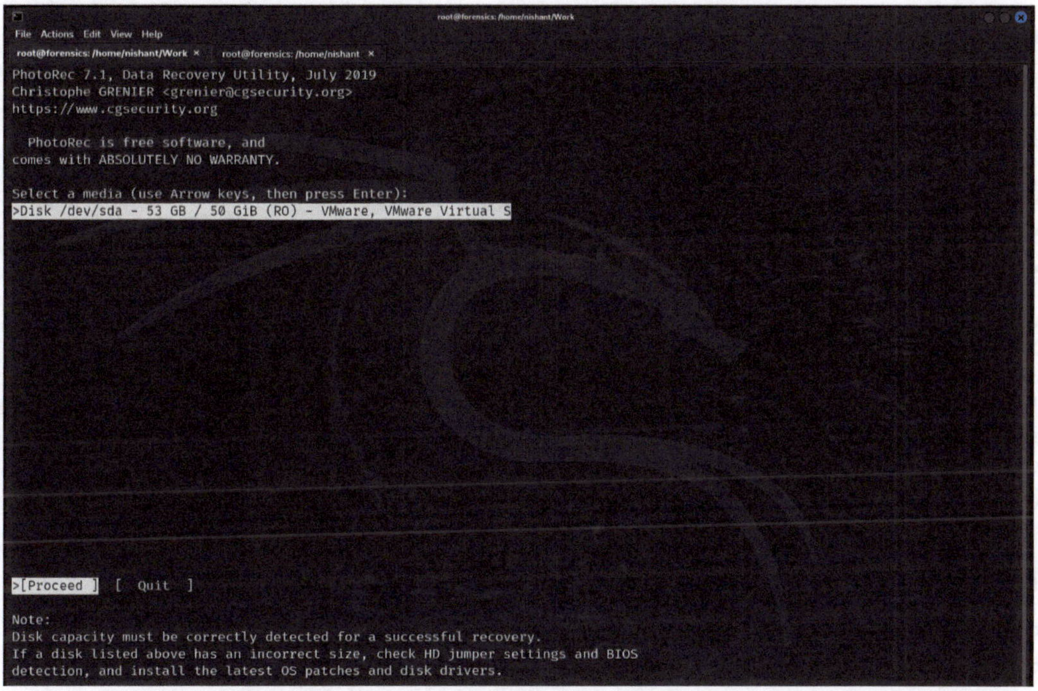

Figure 5.5: File recovery utility photorec in action

Once you drill down the disk and then start the recovery process by following the instructions, it takes a while to recover the files. The output will look similar to the following:

```
PhotoRec 7.1, Data Recovery Utility, July 2019
Christophe GRENIER <grenier@cgsecurity.org>
https://www.cgsecurity.org

Disk /dev/sda - 53 GB / 50 GiB (RO) - VMware, VMware Virtual S
     Partition                  Start        End    Size in sectors
 1 * Linux                    0  32 33  6402 136  6  102854656


2920 files saved in /home/nishant/Work/recup_dir directory.
Recovery aborted by the user.
```

Note: `PhotoRec` can recover a large number of files, including temporary files, packages, and other types. The recovered files can take up a large amount of disk space.

Activity

Attempt the following activities before the next recipe:

- Try to recover all the deleted files in your partition using the **`PhotoRec`**.
- Open a few recovered files and observe what you see there. Do you see anything that can be understood without using any specialized tools?

Recipe 31: Checking timestamp changes

In digital forensics, the concept of MACB timestamps refers to modified, accessed, changed, and born. These attributes are attached to every file in the file system and can help understand various aspects of how and when files are created, modified, deleted, and accessed.

Note:

- **Compatibility: Linux**
- **License considerations: Free software used**

Recipe

Earlier in this chapter, we discussed how to use Linux's file auditing facility to track various operations performed on a file, such as accessing or reading it. When such audit logs are enabled, we can retrieve the complete log history for that file and analyze it to understand the changes and activities that have occurred over time, as shown in the following:

```
cat /var/log/audit/audit/log | grep <file name or pattern>
```

The ls command also has an option to list the files and directories based on the timestamp as follows:

```
ls -lt
```

We can then use the stats command to get a lot of details of the MACB attributes as follows:

```
┌──(root㉿forensics)-[/home/nishant/Work]
└─# stat test-file
  File: test-file
  Size: 0               Blocks: 0          IO Block: 4096   regular empty file
Device: 8,1     Inode: 1966195     Links: 1
Access: (0644/-rw-r--r--)  Uid: (    0/    root)   Gid: (    0/    root)
Access: 2025-02-02 20:12:35.629302058 +0530
Modify: 2025-02-02 20:12:35.629302058 +0530
Change: 2025-02-02 20:12:35.629302058 +0530
 Birth: 2025-02-02 20:12:35.629302058 +0530

┌──(root㉿forensics)-[/home/nishant/Work]
└─#
```

The next thing we may want to do as part of digital forensics analysis is to find files by timestamp. There are multiple ways the find command can be used. The following table gives a few examples:

Purpose	Command
Find file modified in the last 24 hours or 1 day	`find /path/to/directory -type f -mtime -1`
Find files accessed in the last 7 days	`find /path/to/directory -type f -atime -7`
Find files with metadata changed in the last 7 days	`find /path/to/directory -type f -ctime -6`
Find files modified in the last 1 hour	`find /path/to/directory -type f -mmin -60`

Table 5.7*: Various options to find files by timelines using the find command*

Execute each of these commands and understand their outputs. In a production machine, these commands can return a large number of files. Hence, it is important to use filters, such as the **grep** command, to restrict the list to the ones that we are interested in.

Activity

Attempt the following activities before the next recipe:

- Use auditctl to create a rule for modification of the file.
- Execute the find commands to check various MACB attributes along with filter using **grep**.
- What do you see when you use **stat** command with a directory?

Recipe 32: Working with history and last commands

One of the key tasks performed with any system during digital forensics is to check what was run on the system and which users last logged in. In this recipe, we will use the history and last commands to examine these aspects.

Note:

- **Compatibility: Linux**
- **License considerations: Free software used**

Recipe

The history command shows the list of all the commands that were executed. In order to check history, we can use it in the following way:

```
history
```

The output of this command can contain hundreds or even thousands of lines for a long-running system. Therefore, history can also be used with a filter, providing a much more manageable list of the last commands run. The following example shows which **find** commands were run:

```
┌──(root㉿forensics)-[/home/nishant]
└─# history | grep find
  422  find . -type f -mtime -1
  423  find . -type f -atime -7
  424  find . -type f -ctime -7
  425  find . -type f -mmin -60

┌──(root㉿forensics)-[/home/nishant]
└─#
```

The actual history entries are stored in the home directory of each of the users under the home directory, based on the shell that is being used. It could be a file like **.bash_history** or **.zsh_history**. These files must be collected as part of evidence collection.

Interesting fact: **History is different for every user in Linux and can be used even when analyzing a dead system. That means if a digital forensic examiner has the image of the system, they can create a new system out of that image and can still check the history.**

The **last** command provides a list of the last users who logged on to the system. If the last command does not work on your system, you can install it using the following command:

```
apt-get install wtmpdb
```

After installation, it will log every user who logs onto the system. Running it immediately after installation may result in an error related to the **wtmp.db**. However, if you execute a **sudo su** to switch to root, it will provide details of the last users, specifically the root user:

```
┌──(nishant㉿forensics)-[~]
└─$ last
open_database_ro: Cannot open database (/var/lib/wtmpdb/wtmp.db): unable to open database file

┌──(nishant㉿forensics)-[~]
└─$ sudo su
[sudo] password for nishant:
┌──(root㉿forensics)-[/home/nishant]
└─# last
root     pts/2                        Sun Feb  2 20:56 - still logged in

/var/lib/wtmpdb/wtmp.db begins Sun Feb  2 20:56:28 2025

┌──(root㉿forensics)-[/home/nishant]
└─#
```

This utility provides you with a list of all recent logged-in users in a system that has been running for a while. Hence, it is important to install it in every Linux system. This ensures the system is ready for this important piece of digital forensic evidence collection.

Activity

Attempt the following activities before the next recipe:

- Is there a configuration that decides how many previous commands are stored in history? If yes, can you change it to automatically purge the old commands?
- Find out if the output of the **last** command changes based on which user runs it.

Recipe 33: Working with sudoers file

The **/etc/sudoers** file controls which users or groups can execute commands as root or other users using **sudo**. It enforces privilege escalation rules while maintaining system security.

If a user is granted unrestricted access without a password, an attacker with access to their account can escalate privileges. Hence, auditing **sudoers** file should also be done without fail.

Note:

- **Compatibility**: **Linux**
- **License considerations: Free software used**

Recipe

Let us first look at how to open the **sudoers** file. While you can open the **sudoers** file directly from **/etc/sudoers** location, it is not recommended to do so. The proper way to open and work with **sudoers** file is using **visudo** command as a root user:

```
visudo
```

One of the reasons to use **visudo** is that it prevents syntax errors that could lock users out if the file is modified directly.

This command opens an editor where you can modify the file as per your need. In order to know more about **sudoers** file, you can check the man pages as follows:

```
man sudoers
```

Once you are comfortable with how various permissions in the **sudoers** file is defined, analyze the file from the following perspective:

Key section	Details	Example
User privileges	Defines which users can run sudo.	**alice ALL=(ALL) NOPASSWD: ALL** Alice can run all commands without a password.
Group privileges	Grants permissions to a user group.	**%admin ALL=(ALL) ALL** Anyone in the admin group has full **sudo** access.
Command restrictions	Limits what commands can be executed.	**bob ALL=(ALL) /usr/bin/systemctl restart apache2** Bob can only restart Apache server.
Aliases	Used to simplify rule management.	**Cmnd_Alias NETWORKCMDS = /sbin/ifconfig, /usr/sbin/tcpdump** **jack ALL=(ALL) NETWORKCMDS** Jack can only run network-related commands in the list.

Table 5.8: *Various permissions in the sudoers file*

Common ways by which a threat act can exploit the sudoers file are as follows:

Key section	Details	Example
Misconfigured NOPASSWD entries	If a user is granted unrestricted access without a password, an attacker with access to their account can escalate privileges.	What attacker adds to the file: **attacker ALL=(ALL) NOPASSWD: ALL** After this, attacker can run this command to become superuser (root): **sudo su** Attacker can even modify the PATH environment variable to add malicious paths: **echo "export PATH=/tmp/malicious:$PATH" >> /.bashrc**
Running commands as root	If a user can run commands as root, an attacker can exploit this to gain a root shell.	What attacker adds to the file: **attacker ALL=(ALL) NOPASSWD: /bin/bash** After this, attacker can run this command run shell as root: **sudo /bin/bash**

Key section	Details	Example

Editing system files	If a user is allowed to run text editors with sudo, they can edit system files (like **/etc/passwd** or **sudoers**) to escalate privileges.	What attacker adds to the file:
		`attacker ALL=(ALL) NOPASSWD: /usr/bin/nano`
		After this, attacker can run this command to open the **sudoers** file and then add themselves as root:
		`sudo nano /etc/sudoers`

Abuse of wildcard () in sudoers	If wildcards (*) are used improperly, attackers may execute unintended commands.	What attacker adds to the file:
		`attacker ALL=(ALL) NOPASSWD: /bin/rm`
		After this, attacker can run a destructive command like this to delete everything:
		`sudo rm -rf /`

Exploiting writable directories in sudoers	If a user can run scripts or binaries from a writable directory, an attacker can replace them with malicious versions.	What attacker adds to the file:
		`attacker ALL=(ALL) NOPASSWD: /home/attacker/script.sh`
		After this, attacker can exploit it in the following way to execute a root shell:
		`echo "/bin/bash" > /home/attacker/script.sh`
		`chmod +x /home/attacker/script.sh`
		`sudo /home/attacker/script.sh`

***Table 5.9**: Various ways sudoers file can be exploited by threat actors*

A digital forensic examiner should look for these types of patterns in the **sudoers** file to understand how the attacker escalated their privileges or ran privileged commands.

Activity

Attempt the following activities before the next recipe:

- Create a user and give it permission to only run a few commands by modifying the **sudoers** file using **visudo**.
- If the user or its group is not defined in the **sudoers** file, what error message do you get when you use the **sudo** command?
- Can you think of how to mitigate each of these exploits or misconfigurations in the **sudoers** file?

Recipe 34: Verifying login without passwords

First, let us understand a very important file in the Linux system called **sshd_config**. This file is the configuration file for the OpenSSH server (**sshd**) and is located under **/etc/ssh**. It defines the behavior of how the user logs on to the system and gives various users permissions.

Note:

- **Compatibility: Linux**
- **License considerations: Free software used**

Recipe

In the **/etc/ssh/sshd_config**, we need to look for the following to verify that login without passwords is enabled:

1. Enabling passwordless login using the **PermitRootLogin** directive:

   ```
   PermitRootLogin yes
   ```

   If SSH key-based authentication is disabled (**PasswordAuthentication yes**), an attacker can brute force the root password as follows:

   ```
   hydra -l root -P password_list.txt ssh://<IP Address>
   ```

2. Allowing empty passwords using **PermitEmptyPasswords** directive:

   ```
   PermitEmptyPasswords yes
   ```

   If this is enabled, attackers can scan for accounts with empty passwords and log in without credentials using **nmap** as follows:

   ```
   nmap --script ssh-auth-methods -p 22 <target-IP>
   ```

Activity

Attempt the following activities before the next recipe:

- Investigate how these directives can weaken the security of the system and can help identify the attack vectors—**PasswordAuthentication**, **AllowUsers**, **AllowGroups**, **AllowAgentForwarding**.
- Is there a way an attacker can weaken/downgrade the encryption of host key algorithms and then perform an **adversary-in-the-middle** (AiTM) attack?

Recipe 35: Verifying changes in environment variables

Environment variables are key-value pairs used by the Linux shell and applications to store system configurations, user settings, and process-specific data.

Note:

- **Compatibility: Linux**
- **License considerations: Free software used**

Recipe

One of the simplest ways to check the changes in the environment variables is to check the values with a baseline, i.e., a standard set of configurations defined by the enterprise.

For example, we can check the number of lines and characters in the environment variables by running the following command:

```
┌──(root㉿forensics)-[/home/nishant]
└─# set | wc
   215     678   25899

┌──(root㉿forensics)-[/home/nishant]
└─#
```

The **wc** command in this performs a count of newlines, words, and characters to the output of the **set** command. The **set** command itself prints all the environment variables.

Now, next time, if there is a change in the output of the preceding command, it signifies a change in the environment variables.

Apart from this trick, you can use the following methods to detect changes in the environment variables:

- By checking the history for any **export** command that is used to export changes to the environment variables for the current session
- By checking if the history file by using **echo $HISTFILE** to verify if it has been modified to **/dev/null** to not record any operations.
- By checking if the permissions of important files like **.bashrc**, **.profile**, and **/etc/profile** are modified.

Note: **Environment variables may be different for different users. Hence, they should be checked for discrepancies for all users.**

Activity

Attempt the following activities before the next recipe:

- The command **env** also prints a list of environment variables. What is the difference between the output of the **set** command with that of **env**?
- How can the modification of permission for an important configuration file signify that an attacker might have used it to their advantage?

Recipe 36: Analyzing Linux packages

In Linux, the software is installed using well-known package managers like **yum** (for RHEL, CentOS, Fedora, etc.) or **dpkg** (for Kali Linux, Ubuntu, Debian, etc.). The software packages themselves have a standard structure that contains the binary, metadata, and other information like dependencies. A threat actor can change the dependency information to inject malicious packages into the system that can then be used to exploit other weaknesses in the system. In this recipe, let us look at how to analyze Linux packages.

Note:

- **Compatibility: Linux**
- **License considerations: Free software used**

Recipe

Let us look at ways to analyze an important package like **openssh-server**.

First we will use **dpkg -l** command to list basic details of the package:

```
┌──(root㉿forensics)-[/home/nishant]
└─# dpkg -l | grep openssh-server
ii  openssh-server                              1:9.7p1-7                              amd64
secure shell (SSH) server, for secure access from remote machines

┌──(root㉿forensics)-[/home/nishant]
└─#
```

After this, we will find more details about this package, including its dependencies:

```
┌──(root㉿forensics)-[/home/nishant]
└─# dpkg -s openssh-server
Package: openssh-server
Status: install ok installed
Priority: optional
Section: net
Installed-Size: 1807
Maintainer: Debian OpenSSH Maintainers <debian-ssh@lists.debian.org>
Architecture: amd64
Multi-Arch: foreign
Source: openssh
Version: 1:9.7p1-7
Replaces: openssh-client (<< 1:7.9p1-8), ssh, ssh-krb5
Provides: ssh-server
Depends: adduser, libpam-modules, libpam-runtime, lsb-base, openssh-client (= 1:9.7p1-7), openssh-sftp-server, procps, ucf, debconf (>= 0.5) | debconf-2.0, runit-helper (>= 2.14.0~), libaudit1 (>= 1:2.2.1), libc6 (>= 2.38), libcom-err2 (>= 1.43.9), libcrypt1 (>= 1:4.1.0), libgssapi-krb5-2 (>= 1.17), libkrb5-3 (>= 1.13~alpha1+dfsg), libpam0g (>= 0.99.7.1), libselinux1 (>= 3.1~), libssl3t64 (>= 3.0.0), libwrap0 (>= 7.6-4~), zlib1g (>= 1:1.1.4)
Pre-Depends: init-system-helpers (>= 1.54~)
Recommends: default-logind | logind | libpam-systemd, ncurses-term, xauth
Suggests: molly-guard, monkeysphere, ssh-askpass, ufw
Breaks: runit (<< 2.1.2-51~)
Conflicts: sftp, ssh-socks, ssh2
Conffiles:
 /etc/default/ssh 500e3cf069fe9a7b9936108eb9d9c035
 /etc/init.d/ssh 3649a6fe8c18ad1d5245fd91737de507
 /etc/pam.d/sshd 72487a556c4f0e23fd25ce21fc294ca8
 /etc/ssh/moduli 366395e79244c54223455e5f83dafba3
 /etc/sv/ssh/.meta/installed d41d8cd98f00b204e9800998ecf8427e
 /etc/sv/ssh/finish f5f032f6f3e569c821346294d410b636
 /etc/sv/ssh/log/run 63e0ec3e1080dafc68d6d71d42b150a9
 /etc/sv/ssh/run 411f69ac55d12f0c98998552846b1c78
 /etc/ufw/applications.d/openssh-server 486b78d54b93cc9fdc950c1d52ff479e
Description: secure shell (SSH) server, for secure access from remote machines
```

```
 This is the portable version of OpenSSH, a free implementation of
 the Secure Shell protocol as specified by the IETF secsh working
 group.
 .
 Ssh (Secure Shell) is a program for logging into a remote machine
 and for executing commands on a remote machine.
 It provides secure encrypted communications between two untrusted
 hosts over an insecure network. X11 connections and arbitrary TCP/IP
 ports can also be forwarded over the secure channel.
 It can be used to provide applications with a secure communication
 channel.
 .
 This package provides the sshd server.
 .
 In some countries it may be illegal to use any encryption at all
 without a special permit.
 .
 sshd replaces the insecure rshd program, which is obsolete for most
 purposes.
Homepage: https://www.openssh.com/

┌──(root㉿forensics)-[/home/nishant]
└─#
```

Next, we will user another **apt-cache** command to find the dependencies of this package:

```
apt-cache show openssh-server
```

The preceding command provides even more verbose information about the package including its dependencies.

Let us understand why this information is important. In Linux, when a package is installed, its dependencies are automatically installed as well. A threat actor can alter the dependencies of a package to compel the system to install malicious packages automatically. This may not occur with packages from reliable sources. However, it can easily happen if a threat actor compromises the build system of a critical utility. In such cases, updating the package through the package manager could inadvertently install malicious code, potentially creating a backdoor into your system.

Activity

Attempt the following activities before the next recipe:

- Analyze the dependencies using the given method or a few other Linux packages for Kali Linux.
- How are the details provided for Kali Linux packages different than the details shown for Fedora packages?

Conclusion

Digital forensics for Linux systems is a crucial aspect of cybersecurity. It helps investigators collect, analyze, and interpret forensic evidence in the event of a cyberattack. Given the complexity and diversity of Linux distributions, forensic experts must be familiar with different tools, logging mechanisms, and system behaviors.

In this chapter, we learned about Linux file systems, forensic tools, auditing logs, best practices for log management, integrity validation techniques, and advanced forensic methods like disk partition analysis and recovery of deleted files. We also examine essential forensic capabilities, such as utilizing audit logs to identify unauthorized modifications, sending logs to centralized locations for secure storage, and validating file integrity through checksums. Furthermore, examining Linux permissions, user authentication mechanisms, and previous command execution logs enables investigators to effectively reconstruct an attack timeline.

We understand that by combining multiple forensic techniques, such as analyzing system logs, monitoring system integrity, and utilizing built-in Linux utilities, digital forensic investigators can uncover malicious activities, prevent further damage, and ensure a strong incident response. As cyber threats evolve, mastering Linux digital forensics becomes an essential skill for security professionals, allowing for the timely detection and mitigation of security breaches.

In the next chapter, we will discuss digital forensics for Windows systems.

Questions

1. What is the purpose of digital forensics in Linux systems?
2. How does the Linux file system structure help in forensic investigations?
3. What is the difference between syslog and audit logs?
4. How can file permissions in Linux be used to prevent unauthorized access?
5. What are the three main categories of Linux permissions?
6. What is the significance of /var/log/auth.log and /var/log/secure in forensic investigations?
7. How can auditctl be used to track file changes?
8. What is a swap file, and why is it important in digital forensics?
9. What are the ways by which you recover lost data from deleted files in Linux?
10. What role does journalctl play in log analysis?
11. How does rsyslog differ from syslog-ng?
12. Why is remote logging important for digital forensics?
13. How can an attacker exploit misconfigured sudoers file entries?
14. How does dumpe2fs help in understanding file system metadata?
15. How can an attacker manipulate Linux environment variables for privilege escalation?

Points to remember

- Linux uses hierarchical file system structures, with / as the root directory.
- Important system logs are stored in /var/log/.
- syslog collects general system logs, while auditd provides audit-related logs.
- File permissions in Linux control read (r), write (w), and execute (x) privileges.
- Remote logging to a syslog server secures logs against tampering.
- rsyslog and syslog-ng are used for centralized log management.

- The /etc/sudoers file controls user permissions for executing privileged commands.
- Deleted files are often recoverable until overwritten by new data.
- Swap files may contain sensitive data like passwords and encryption keys.
- Log rotation (logrotate) prevents log files from consuming excessive disk space.
- The last command displays previous login attempts.
- ps and top monitor running processes in a live forensic analysis.
- Linux enforces the least privilege principle for security.
- Wildcard misconfigurations in the sudoers file can lead to privilege escalation.
- SIEM systems aggregate logs for analysis.

Key terms

- **Digital forensics**: The process of collecting, analyzing, and preserving electronic evidence.
- **Linux file system**: The structure that Linux uses to organize and store files (e.g., ext4, XFS).
- **syslog**: A logging system used to store system messages and logs.
- **rsyslog**: An advanced syslog implementation with remote logging capabilities.
- **auditd**: The Linux Audit Daemon that tracks security-related system events.
- **auditctl**: A command-line utility for managing audit rules.
- **Checksum**: A hash-based method to verify file integrity (e.g., sha256sum).
- **sudoers file**: The /etc/sudoers file that controls user privileges for executing commands as root.
- **Swap file**: A disk-based extension of RAM that may contain sensitive data.
- **SIEM**: Security information and event management system for log analysis.
- **Log rotation**: The practice of archiving and rotating logs to manage disk space.
- **Deleted file recovery**: The process of retrieving files marked as deleted using forensic tools.
- **Journalctl**: A command used to query and display logs stored in systemd's journal.
- **Forensic image**: A bit-for-bit copy of a storage device, preserving all data for analysis.
- **Live forensics**: The process of analyzing a running system without shutting it down.
- **Dead forensics**: The analysis of forensic images from offline or disk-cloned systems.
- **MACB timestamps**: Modified, accessed, changed, and born timestamps are used in forensic investigations.
- **Adversary-in-the-middle (AiTM)**: A type of attack where an adversary intercepts and manipulates communications.
- **Process analysis**: Monitoring running processes using tools like ps and top.
- **Disk partitioning**: Dividing a disk into sections to organize data efficiently.
- **Environment variables**: System-wide or user-specific settings stored in key-value pairs.

Chapter 6
Windows Forensics

Introduction

Even though Linux is widely used, most companies still run many of their servers on Windows. On top of that, employees often use Windows on their personal computers. During a cyberattack, a digital forensics expert needs to know how to handle these systems and gather evidence from both servers and personal machines. It is also important to collect evidence not just from the systems that were directly compromised, but from others on the same network. In this chapter, we will look at how forensic evidence can be collected from Windows systems.

Structure

In this chapter, we will cover the following topics:

- About the version of Windows
- Recipe 37: Checking system information
- Recipe 38: Listing user accounts
- Recipe 39: Understanding other net commands
- Recipe 40: Understanding Windows Event Viewer
- Understanding important logs on Windows
- Recipe 41: Fetching security, system, and application logs
- Recipe 42: Enabling audit logs in Windows
- Recipe 43: Logging file changes with audit logs
- Recipe 44: Checking audit log policies
- Recipe 45: Configuring log management best practices
- Understanding Windows file systems
- Recipe 46: Identifying file system type
- Recipe 47: Checking directory and file metadata
- Recipe 48: Working with MACB timestamps
- Recipe 49: Examining disk partitions
- Recipe 50: Identifying deleted files
- Recipe 51: Performing hash calculations
- Recipe 52: Working with Windows File Recovery tool
- Recipe 53: Recovering lost data and deleted files using WinHex
- Recipe 54: Exploring Windows Registry

- Recipe 55: Listing Registry keys and values
- Recipe 56: Generating logs for Registry changes
- Recipe 57: Checking USB device history from Registry
- Recipe 58: Working with users and groups
- Recipe 59: Working with the Device Manager
- Recipe 60: Working with Windows Services
- Recipe 61: Working with certificates
- Recipe 62: Working with keystores
- Recipe 63: Analyzing update history

Objectives

In this chapter, we will learn a wide range of tools and techniques for working with and learning digital forensics for Windows systems. With the help of recipes, we will learn almost every aspect of Windows systems, which are varied in complexity. We will look at not only the built-in tools that are part of Windows, but we will also look at the ones that can be installed as add-ons for free, as well as tools from third parties.

By the end of this chapter, you should be able to work with various tools and techniques in Microsoft Windows operating systems that are used to identify the signs of exploits and misconfigurations and collect the necessary evidence for further analysis.

About the version of Windows

All the recipes in this chapter were created and tested using Windows 11 Pro. However, all of them should work on Windows 11 Home Edition with PowerShell enabled. Moreover, they should also work on the Windows Server family of operating systems.

The Windows Server family has many additional important commands and widgets that digital forensics professionals use to collect Windows server-specific evidence. While they are not covered as part of this chapter, we strongly believe that once you are familiar with one of the Windows distributions, it is simple to look for additional evidence that can be collected. The same holds true for any new versions of Windows that are released in the future.

Note: **Most commands in this chapter that are run in command prompt or PowerShell need you to have administrative privileges on your system.**

Recipe 37: Checking system information

One of the first steps in collecting forensic evidence from a Windows system is gathering basic system information. Windows provides a simple way to do so from the command line using a tool called `systeminfo`. Let us see how this tool can be used to capture key details about the system.

Note:

- **Compatibility: Windows**
- **License considerations: Part of the operating system**

Recipe

To get a summary of system information, run the following command:

```
Systeminfo
```

The output may look similar to the following:

```
C:\>systeminfo

Host Name:                 INFIKNIT
OS Name:                   Microsoft Windows 11 Pro
OS Version:                10.0.22631 N/A Build 22631
OS Manufacturer:           Microsoft Corporation
OS Configuration:          Standalone Workstation
OS Build Type:             Multiprocessor Free
Registered Owner:          < redacted >
Registered Organization:
Product ID:                00330-80000-00000-AA388
Original Install Date:     19-01-2024, 09:12:29
System Boot Time:          16-03-2025, 07:43:22
System Manufacturer:       VMware, Inc.
System Model:              VMware20,1
System Type:               ARM64-based PC
Processor(s):              1 Processor(s) Installed.
                           [01]: ARMv8 (64-bit) Family 8 Model 0 Revision   0 Apple ~2000 Mhz
BIOS Version:              VMware, Inc. VMW201.00V.21805430.BA64.2305221830, 22-05-2023
Windows Directory:         C:\Windows
System Directory:          C:\Windows\system32
Boot Device:               \Device\HarddiskVolume1
System Locale:             en-us;English (United States)
Input Locale:              00004009
Time Zone:                 (UTC+05:30) Chennai, Kolkata, Mumbai, New Delhi
Total Physical Memory:     8,187 MB
Available Physical Memory: 4,463 MB
Virtual Memory: Max Size:  8,699 MB
Virtual Memory: Available: 5,175 MB
Virtual Memory: In Use:    3,524 MB
Page File Location(s):     C:\pagefile.sys
Domain:                    WORKGROUP
Logon Server:              \\INFIKNIT
Hotfix(s):                 5 Hotfix(s) Installed.
                           [01]: KB5049624
                           [02]: KB5027397
                           [03]: KB5033055
                           [04]: KB5053602
                           [05]: KB5052107
Network Card(s):           1 NIC(s) Installed.
                           [01]: vmxnet3 Ethernet Adapter
```

```
                                 Connection Name: Ethernet
                                 DHCP Enabled:    Yes
                                 DHCP Server:     172.16.135.254
                                 IP address(es)
                                 [01]: < redacted >
                                 [02]: < redacted >
Hyper-V Requirements:      VM Monitor Mode Extensions: No
                           Virtualization Enabled In Firmware: No
                           Second Level Address Translation: No
                           Data Execution Prevention Available: No

C:\>
```

Please note that a few personal/confidential pieces of information indicated with **<redacted>** have been redacted in the preceding output.

If you review the preceding output, you can immediately see how useful it is to have the basic information about the system. This can be a good starting point for any digital forensic analysts or investigators working on a case.

Note: **When run on the command prompt, the set command provides a list of all the environment variables for the current user, including many details of how the system is configured. This is important information that should be collected.**

Activity

Attempt the following activities before the next recipe:

- Run the command **systeminfo /?** and understand what additional information you can find out about the Windows system.
- Find out if there is a way to export this information in a format that can be used by other programs.

Recipe 38: Listing user accounts

One of the key ways we can find out if there are threats present on the system is to look for user accounts. Threat actors can add additional user accounts to use them as a way to perform illegal activities or install **advanced persistent threats** (**APTs**), including backdoors. Hence, we need to look for such users on a regular basis. Moreover, while collecting digital forensics evidence, it is important to collect the details about the user accounts from the system.

Note:

- **Compatibility: Windows**
- **License considerations: Part of the operating system**

Recipe

To get a list of all the user accounts, run the following command:

```
net user
```

The output may look similar to the following:

```
C:\>net user

User accounts for \\INFIKNIT

-------------------------------------------------------------------------------
Administrator            DefaultAccount           Guest
nishant                  WDAGUtilityAccount
The command completed successfully.

C:\>
```

Activity

Attempt the following activities before the next recipe:

- `net user` only shows the local user accounts. Find out how the list of user accounts can be configured in Active Directory.
- Add a new user and re-run the command. Check if you can see the new user on the list.

Recipe 39: Understanding other net commands

We saw one example of the `net` command in the last recipe. This is a simple-to-use yet powerful command that has many other options. In this recipe, we will look at a few other options of the `net` command that are invaluable for any digital forensic analyst.

Note:

- **Compatibility: Windows**
- **License considerations: Part of the operating system**

Recipe

Let us understand what other information can be gathered using `net` commands. The following table lists a few useful commands for digital forensics:

net command	Purpose
`net share`	Lists the network shares from this machine.
`net start`	Lists all the Windows services that are started.
`net accounts`	List various password policies related to the user account, e.g., maximum password age, minimum password length, lockout threshold, etc.
`net group`	Lists all the local user groups present on this system.

net command	Purpose
`net session`	Lists the sessions between the local computer and others on the network.
`net localgroup administrators`	Lists all the local administrator on the computer.

Table 6.1: Various important net commands

Activity

Attempt the following activities before the next recipe:

- Go through the **`net`** command's help and find out if any options only apply to a computer with the role of Windows Domain Controller.
- What is the use of the **`net time`** command? Can this be used by threat actors to confuse digital forensics professionals?

Recipe 40: Understanding Windows Event Viewer

Windows Event Viewer is a built-in utility or widget in Windows operating systems that allows users to view detailed information about system events, including errors, warnings, and informational messages. It provides a centralized location for accessing logs from various sources, such as system components, applications, and security-related events. Through Event Viewer, users can diagnose system issues, track security incidents, and monitor system performance by analyzing the recorded events.

By examining these logs, administrators and investigators can gain insights into system activities, identify potential problems, and take corrective actions to maintain system stability and security. The same logs can be used by cybersecurity professionals in general and digital forensics professionals, in particular, to perform investigations in case of a cybercrime or a cyber incident.

In this recipe, let us become familiar with Windows Event Viewer.

> Note:
>
> - **Compatibility: Windows**
> - **License considerations: Part of the operating system**

Recipe

Let us understand how to use the features of Windows Event Viewer. Refer to the following steps:

1. In order to launch Event Viewer, search for the **Computer Management** widget in Windows and launch it. A screen similar to the following can be seen:

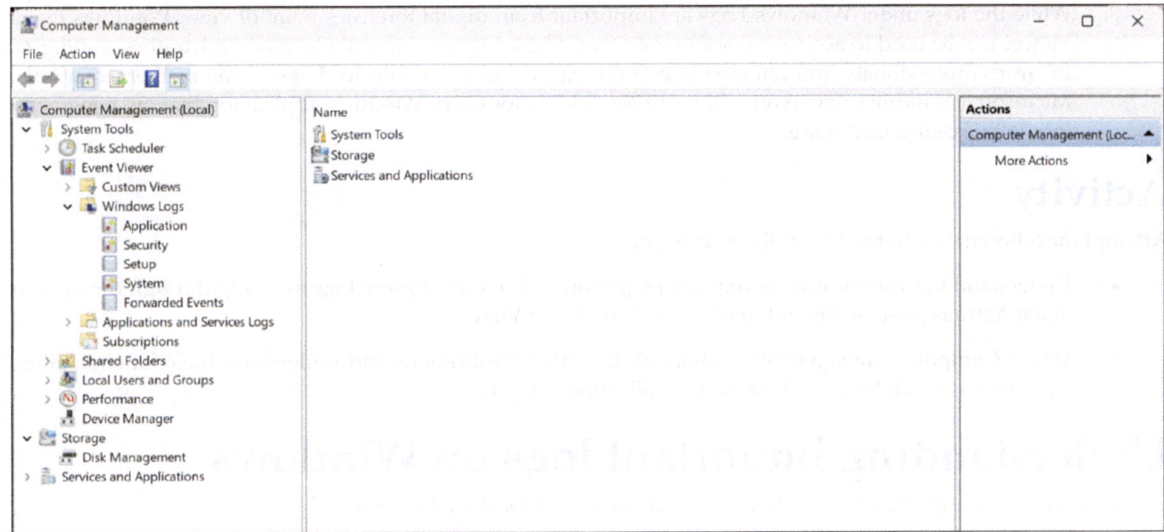

Figure 6.1: Computer Management widget

The **Computer Management** widget in Windows aggregates many applications that can also be launched individually. For example, you can launch Event Viewer by directly searching for it in the **Start** menu.

2. Now, if you click on any of the logs under Windows Logs, you will see a list of logs on the right-side table. Clicking on any of the logs shows further details in the bottom pane, as shown in the following figure:

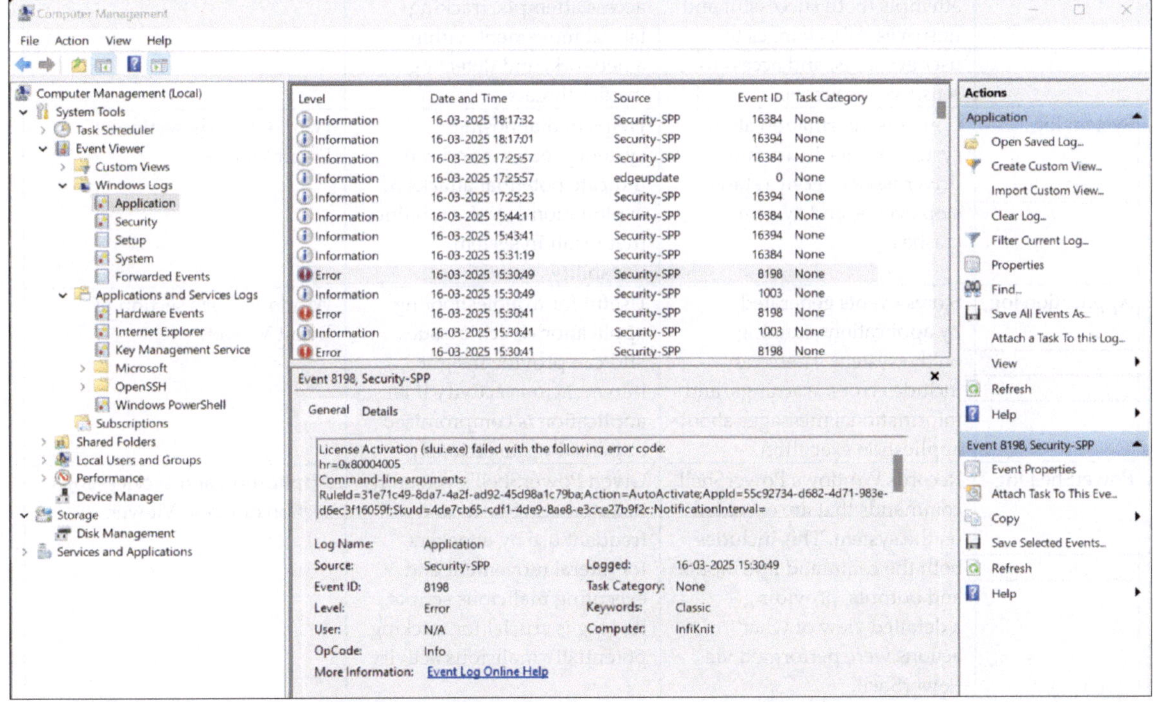

Figure 6.2: Various Windows Logs under Event Viewer

3. While the logs under Windows Logs are important from digital forensics point of view, Windows Event Viewer can be used to access and see many other. These logs are important for administrators and digital forensics professionals. You can see these under **Application** and **Service Logs**. If you further expand the Microsoft | Windows item, you will find 100+ folders for every Windows application that are generating logs to this centralized place.

Activity

Attempt the following activities before the next recipe:

- Understand the various actions that can be performed on one or more logs by going through the options in the **Actions** pane on the rightmost side of the Event Viewer.
- Under **Computer Management**, explore all the other applications and understand their functionalities. Also, try to launch them as standalone application widgets.

Understanding important logs on Windows

Let us look at a few important logs on Windows that are useful for digital forensics.

Windows generates numerous log files that can be crucial in digital forensic investigations. These logs can help investigators understand system activities, identify potential security breaches, and track user behavior. Following is an overview of the most important Windows logs, their descriptions, and their usefulness in digital forensics:

Log	Details	Usefulness	Location
Security log	Records events related to security, such as login attempts (both successful and unsuccessful), changes to user accounts, and access to sensitive resources.	Extremely valuable for identifying unauthorized access attempts, tracking lateral movement within a network, and detecting insider threats.	Windows Logs section of Event Viewer.
System log	Contains information about system events, including driver issues, service start/stop events, and system crashes.	Helps in diagnosing system problems and can indicate potential attacks or exploitation of vulnerabilities that result in system instability.	Windows Logs section of Event Viewer.
Application log	Stores events generated by applications running on the system. These can include errors, warnings, and informational messages about application execution.	Useful for troubleshooting application-specific issues and can provide insight into malicious activity if an application is compromised or behaving suspiciously.	Windows Logs section of Event Viewer.
PowerShell log	Records Windows PowerShell commands that are executed on the system. This includes both the command line inputs and outputs, providing a detailed view of what actions were performed via PowerShell.	Given PowerShell's versatility in automating tasks and its frequent use by attackers for lateral movement and executing malicious scripts, this log is crucial for tracking potentially malicious activity.	Application and services logs section of Event Viewer.

Log	Details	Usefulness	Location
Task Scheduler log	Contains events related to the Task Scheduler service, including task creations, deletions, and executions.	Helps in identifying scheduled tasks that may be used by attackers to maintain persistence on a compromised system or execute malware at specific times.	Application and Services Logs section of Event Viewer | Microsoft | Windows | TaskScheduler | Operational.
DNS Client log	Records DNS queries made by the system, which can help trace communication with **command and control (C2)** servers or other malicious domains.	Valuable for network traffic analysis and identifying potential connections to malicious servers.	Application and Services Logs section of Event Viewer | Microsoft | Windows | DNS Client Events | Operational.
Windows Update log	Records events related to Windows updates, including successes and failures in updating the operating system.	Helps in understanding if a system is up-to-date with security patches, which can indicate vulnerabilities that could be exploited by attackers.	Application and Services Logs section of Event Viewer | Microsoft | Windows | WindowsUpdateClient.
Windows Defender logs	Records malware detection, scans, and remediation activity.	Helps in understanding various malware activities on the system, and also provide details about the scans that were done and any issues found.	Application and Services Logs section of Event Viewer | Microsoft | Windows | Windows Defender | Operational.

***Table 6.2**: Important Windows logs that can be used in digital forensics*

Windows setup logs that capture operating system installation, upgrade, and feature updates are also of great interest and can be found in `C:\Windows\INF` and `C:\Windows\Logs`.

Note: **The logs, like security, system, application logs, and most of the logs mentioned above, can also be accessed from `%SystemRoot%\System32\winevt\Logs\`. All of these logs are also visible in Event Viewer.**

Recipe 41: Fetching security, system, and application logs

Now that we understand Windows Event Viewer, let us understand how we can fetch various Windows logs using PowerShell. Fetching logs in this way helps us automate the evidence collection process regularly or during an incident.

Note:

- **Compatibility: Windows**
- **License considerations: Part of the operating system**

Recipe

In this recipe, let us look at how we can use PowerShell to fetch the default Windows logs. We will fetch the security logs for the last 10 minutes. After that, you can modify the command to fetch application and system logs, too.

Refer to the following steps to use PowerShell for fetching the default Windows logs:

1. First, run PowerShell as administrator. After that, run the following command in PowerShell:

```
PS C:\> Get-EventLog -LogName Security -InstanceId 4624, 4625, 4634 -After (Get-Date).
AddMinutes(-10)
```

   The output will look similar to the following:

```
PS C:\> Get-EventLog -LogName Security -InstanceId 4624, 4625, 4634 -After (Get-Date).
AddMinutes(-10)

   Index Time          EntryType   Source                 InstanceID Message
   ----- ----          ---------   ------                 ---------- -------
  108802 Mar 16 12:14  SuccessA... Microsoft-Windows...         4624 An account was
successfully logged on....
  108800 Mar 16 12:13  SuccessA... Microsoft-Windows...         4624 An account was
successfully logged on....


PS C:\>
```

   Let us understand what this command does as follows:

   - `-LogName` signifies the category of log we want to read, in this case, `Security`. You can use `System` and `Application` to read system and application logs, respectively.
   - `-InstanceID` signifies the specific types of logs we want to read.
   - The rest of the command is used to add `-10` minutes to the current date to fetch the logs for the last 10 minutes.

2. While the preceding output is very useful, there could be cases where we want to see all the details the way it is shown in the Event Viewer. In that case, we need to change the command a bit as follows, where we are getting the newest security log and then printing all the properties:

```
PS C:\> Get-EventLog -LogName Security -newest 1 | Select-Object -Property *
```

   The output of the preceding command will look similar to the following:

```
PS C:\> Get-EventLog -LogName Security -newest 1 | Select-Object -Property *


EventID            : 4672
MachineName        : InfiKnit
Data               : {}
Index              : 108803
Category           : (12548)
CategoryNumber     : 12548
EntryType          : SuccessAudit
Message            : Special privileges assigned to new logon.

                     Subject:
```

```
                Security ID:            S-1-5-18
                Account Name:           SYSTEM
                Account Domain:         NT AUTHORITY
                Logon ID:               0x3e7

            Privileges:                 SeAssignPrimaryTokenPrivilege
                                SeTcbPrivilege
                                SeSecurityPrivilege
                                SeTakeOwnershipPrivilege
                                SeLoadDriverPrivilege
                                SeBackupPrivilege
                                SeRestorePrivilege
                                SeDebugPrivilege
                                SeAuditPrivilege
                                SeSystemEnvironmentPrivilege
                                SeImpersonatePrivilege
                                SeDelegateSessionUserImpersonatePrivilege
Source             : Microsoft-Windows-Security-Auditing
ReplacementStrings : {S-1-5-18, SYSTEM, NT AUTHORITY, 0x3e7...}
InstanceId         : 4672
TimeGenerated      : 16-03-2025 12:14:39
TimeWritten        : 16-03-2025 12:14:39
UserName           :
Site               :
Container          :


PS C:\>
```

3. With the above information, you should also be able to experiment with more complex **Get-Event** queries. For example, the following PowerShell command will check all the security logs for Event ID:

```
Get-WinEvent -LogName Security | Where-Object { $_.Id -eq 4672, 4788 -and $_.Message
-match "Configure-SMRemoting.exe" }
```

Commands like this are used frequently by incident response teams and digital forensics analysts to understand what had happened on the system, in this case giving us insights into whether someone configured remote management by running the command **Configure-SMRemoting.exe** with relevant options.

Activity

Attempt the following activities before the next recipe:

- Modify the PowerShell command in Activity 1 to print system logs for the last 1 hour.
- Find out what else you can print by using the security log events reference at **https://www.ultimatewindowssecurity.com/securitylog/encyclopedia/.**
- Find out the instance IDs you should be checking if you need to monitor local groups.

- Lock your Windows desktop and unlock it. After that, run the preceding command. Do you see additional security logs?

Recipe 42: Enabling audit logs in Windows

File auditing is the process of tracking and recording access and modifications to important files within a system or network. It is crucial for digital forensics because of the following:

Advantages	Details
Detecting unauthorized access	It identifies when sensitive files are accessed or altered by unauthorized users, helping to catch insider threats or compromised accounts.
Monitoring suspicious file activities	Tracking changes to files, especially critical or sensitive ones, helps detect ransomware, data exfiltration attempts, and other malicious activities.
Ensure compliance	File auditing supports compliance with regulations like **General Data Protection Regulation** (**GDR**) and **Health Insurance Portability and Accountability Act** (**HIPPA**) by providing evidence of data-handling practices and security controls for sensitive information.
Forensic analysis and incident response	Detailed audit logs provide a trail of actions that can be invaluable during investigations, helping to understand the scope and impact of security incidents.

***Table 6.3**: Advantages of file auditing in the context of digital forensics*

In this recipe, we will enable audit for a file and then understand how various operations to the file can generate logs.

File auditing can help audit operations with files in Windows, similar to what we did using **`auditctl`** in Linux in the previous chapter.

Note:

- **Compatibility: Windows**
- **License considerations: Part of the operating system**

Recipe

Let us enable file auditing for a file of our interest by following the below steps:

1. To enable audit for files and folders, first run **Local Group Policy Editor** (**`gpedit.msc`**) and go to **Computer Configuration** | **Windows Settings** | **Security Settings** | **Advanced Audit Policy Configuration** | **System Audit Policies**, as shown in the following figure:

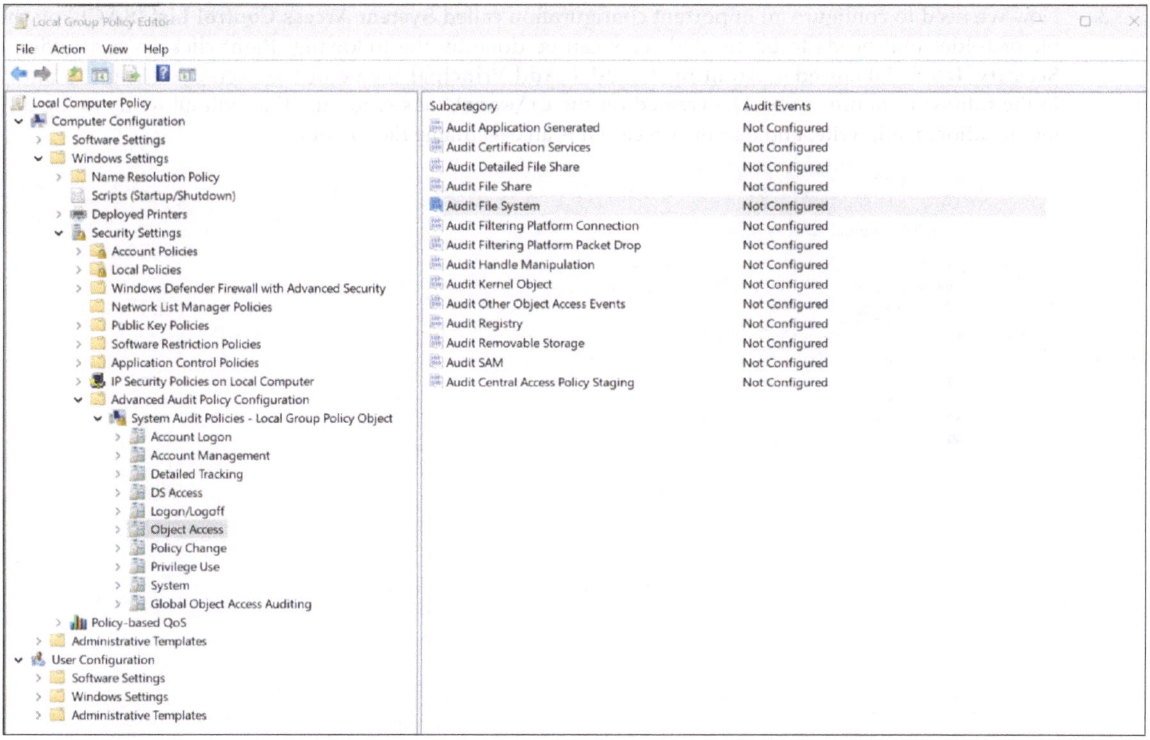

Figure 6.3: *Working with Audit Policies using Local Group Policy Editor*

2. Next, double-click on **Object Access** and then enable **Audit File System**. This ensures that whenever a file object within the specified folder is accessed, the action is recorded in the logs:

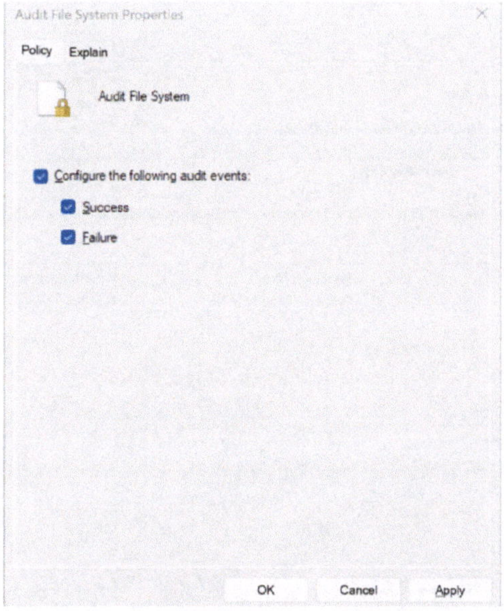

Figure 6.4: *Audit File System Properties*

3. Now we need to configure an important configuration called **System Access Control List** (**SACL**) on the file or folder that needs to be audited. This can be done by the following: Right-click on file/folder | **Security Tab** | **Advanced** | **Auditing** | **Add** | **Add Principal** (name of the users) you want to audit. In the following figure, a SACL is created on the `C:\Word\Passwords` file that will allow us to log any modification, read, write, and execute (in case it is an executable file) on our file:

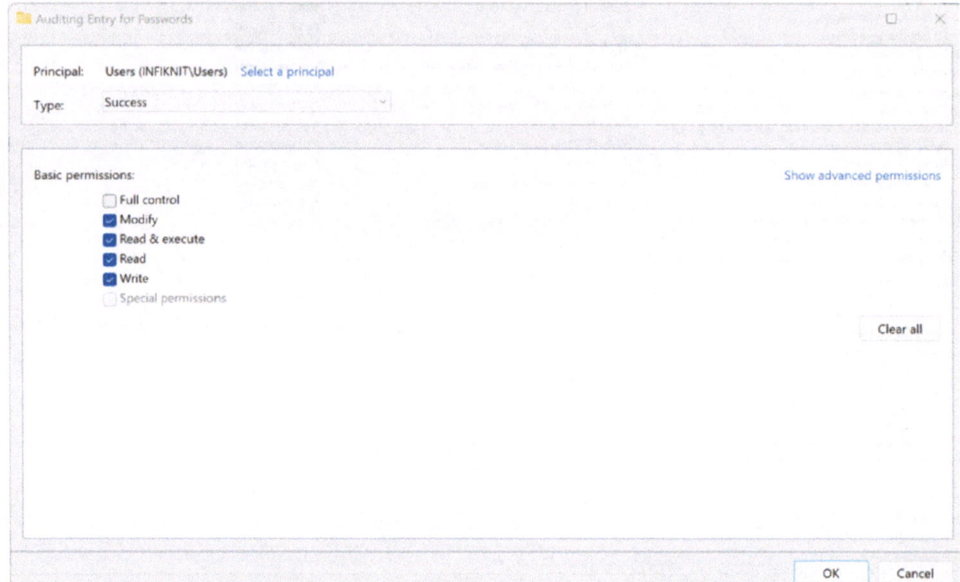

***Figure 6.5**: SACL: Configure basic permissions for the file to be audited*

Once you save these basic permissions by clicking on **OK**, you will be back to the previous screen where the access for the principal is added:

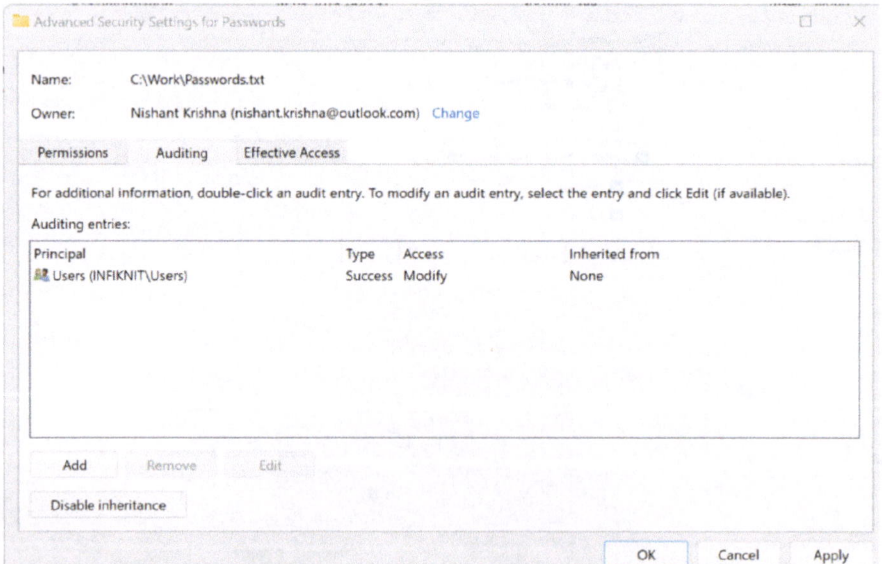

***Figure 6.6**: SACL: Advanced Security Settings for Passwords window after SACL configured*

After we have gone through the preceding steps, we have successfully configured auditing for a specific file or a folder.

Caution: **Folder auditing can generate a large number of logs based on the number of files present in the folder, which will be tough to manage, as most of them may be noise. Hence, it is important to strike a balance between security and the number of logs that can be processed. Also, remember that generated logs frequently impact the system's performance.**

Activity

Attempt the following activities before the next recipe:

- Under the **System Audit Policies**, go through all the other types of audits we can do and analyze if a few more of them can be used in digital forensics.
- Go through other features of **Local Group Policy Editor** and understand the features it can provide for security in general and digital forensics in particular.

Recipe 43: Logging file changes with audit logs

File auditing is the process of tracking and recording access and modifications to files within a system or network. It is crucial for cybersecurity because of the reasons we saw before. We have enabled file audit in the previous recipe. Let us now check Event Logs for logs related to the audit after any operation done on the file/folder object.

Note:

- **Compatibility: Windows**
- **License considerations: Part of the operating system**

Recipe

Once the SACL on a file is created, as we saw in the last recipe, any attempt to access the file, e.g., opening it in a program like Notepad or modifying the file, will result in the creation of an audit log that can give us insights into what was done by the attacker.

To check if we can get the audit logs for our file, perform a few operations like opening the text file in Notepad and then modifying the file by changing its content.

In both cases, you can check that there are audit events generated under the Security section of Windows Logs.

Activity

Attempt the following activities before the next recipe:

- Try to rename the file. Check if you see audit logs getting generated.
- Try to delete the file. Check if you see audit logs getting generated.
- Check the **Full Control** option while creating the SACL. Now, check once more what operations are logged for this file.

Recipe 44: Checking audit log policies

Although you can enable audit logs as needed, reviewing them through the **Local Group Policy Editor** can be tedious. Let us explore a simpler way to check the status of audit policies across different categories.

Note:

- **Compatibility: Windows**
- **License considerations: Part of the operating system**

Recipe

To check if an audit is enabled on all the categories, we can use the following command:

```
Auditpol /get /category:*
```

When you run this command, you will see an output similar to the following:

```
C:\>Auditpol /get /category:*
System audit policy
Category/Subcategory                      Setting
System
  Security System Extension               No Auditing
  System Integrity                        No Auditing
  IPsec Driver                            No Auditing
  Other System Events                     No Auditing
  Security State Change                   No Auditing
Logon/Logoff
  Logon                                   No Auditing
  Logoff                                  No Auditing
  Account Lockout                         No Auditing
  IPsec Main Mode                         No Auditing
  IPsec Quick Mode                        No Auditing
  IPsec Extended Mode                     No Auditing
  Special Logon                           No Auditing
  Other Logon/Logoff Events               No Auditing
  Network Policy Server                   No Auditing
  User / Device Claims                    No Auditing
  Group Membership                        No Auditing
Object Access
  File System                             Success and Failure
  Registry                                Success and Failure
  Kernel Object                           No Auditing
  SAM                                     No Auditing
  Certification Services                  No Auditing
  Application Generated                   No Auditing
  Handle Manipulation                     No Auditing
  File Share                              No Auditing
  Filtering Platform Packet Drop          No Auditing
  Filtering Platform Connection           No Auditing
  Other Object Access Events              No Auditing
```

```
  Detailed File Share                       No Auditing
  Removable Storage                         No Auditing
  Central Policy Staging                    No Auditing
Privilege Use
  Non Sensitive Privilege Use               No Auditing
  Other Privilege Use Events                No Auditing
  Sensitive Privilege Use                   No Auditing
Detailed Tracking
  Process Creation                          No Auditing
  Process Termination                       No Auditing
  DPAPI Activity                            No Auditing
  RPC Events                                No Auditing
  Plug and Play Events                      No Auditing
  Token Right Adjusted Events               No Auditing
Policy Change
  Audit Policy Change                       No Auditing
  Authentication Policy Change              No Auditing
  Authorization Policy Change               No Auditing
  MPSSVC Rule-Level Policy Change           No Auditing
  Filtering Platform Policy Change          No Auditing
  Other Policy Change Events                No Auditing
Account Management
  Computer Account Management               No Auditing
  Security Group Management                 No Auditing
  Distribution Group Management             No Auditing
  Application Group Management              No Auditing
  Other Account Management Events           No Auditing
  User Account Management                   No Auditing
DS Access
  Directory Service Access                  No Auditing
  Directory Service Changes                 No Auditing
  Directory Service Replication             No Auditing
  Detailed Directory Service Replication    No Auditing
Account Logon
  Kerberos Service Ticket Operations        No Auditing
  Other Account Logon Events                No Auditing
  Kerberos Authentication Service           No Auditing
  Credential Validation                     No Auditing

C:\>
```

Now, you can see in one glance the status of each of the categories of the audit logging. You can now easily understand from the preceding output that audit is enabled for the File System and Registry. You can also use this information to automate checking the deviation from the expected policies.

Activity

Attempt the following activities before the next recipe:

- Auditpol provides you the option to back up and restore the policies. Look at the help of Auditpol to understand how to do that.
- Write a command to use Auditpol for printing the audit policies for a single category, e.g., Object Access.

Recipe 45: Configuring log management best practices

While Windows provides a comprehensive log management system, they can only serve their purpose if configured properly. In order for an enterprise to be ready for digital forensic evidence collection for Windows systems, many best practices need to be put together in a log management strategy.

Note:

- **Compatibility: Windows**
- **License considerations: Part of the operating system**

Recipe

Let us now look at a few important log management policies and best practices that can be used to monitor the system as follows:

Best practice	Details
Enable and configure audit logging	Go to **Local Group Policy Editor** (`gpedit.msc`) and go to **Computer Configuration** | **Windows Settings** | **Security Settings** | **Advanced Audit Policy Configuration** | **System Audit Policies**, and enable audit logging as per the requirements.
Check if the audit log is enabled	Use the following command to periodically check if an audit is enabled as per the enterprise's policies. This ensures an audit of the audit log policies: **`Auditpol /get /category`**:
Enable Logon/Logoff auditing	This ensures that all the logon and logoff events are logged. This can be done from the **Logon/Logoff** section of **System Audit Policies.**
Update log retention	Generally, most enterprises set log retention to 90 to 180 days. You can update this as per your policies using the following command using the Event Manager's command line utility, `wevtutil`: **`wevtutil sl Security /ms:1073741824`** The preceding command sets the maximum-security log size to 1 GiB. You can set it to the required size based on the logs generated daily.
Monitor critical event IDs	Every event log in Windows is generated using an event ID. This is extremely useful to understand what this log is about. Every digital forensic professional working with Windows forensics should understand how to decipher these event IDs. Look at the Event Manager for the events generated and then understand from the events documentation about their purpose. For example, the following event IDs provide details about logon: • **4624**: An account was successfully logged on. • **4625**: An account failed to log on.

Best practice	Details
Detect log clearing	An attacker may clear the logs to wipe their trails. The following event ID can be monitored for such an event: • **1102**: The audit log was cleared.
Regularly review and archive logs	Logs can be reviewed using a scheduled task using Task Scheduler. One way to do that is to run a PowerShell script every fixed amount of time (e.g., 10 minutes) to review the generated logs. In the same way, logs can be archived daily/weekly by either exporting them or copying the `.evtx` files.
Forward the logs as they are generated	Logs can also be forwarded as they are generated (in real time) to a centralized log management system.
Use time synchronization	**Network time protocol** (**NTP**) synchronizes the system's clock with a reliable time source. Attackers can change the time to make the logs generated that are out of sync and may not be helpful in forensic investigation. Hence, network time synchronization is an important best practice for log management. The following command can be used to check that the system is synching to a trusted NTP server: `w32tm /query /status`

Table 6.4: Log management best practices

Note: A regular audit of these configurations would ensure that they are not tampered with by the attacker, undermining the digital forensic readiness of the enterprise.

Activity

Attempt the following activities before the next recipe:

- Check other options provided by `wevtuntil` and find out the way to list all the logs names.
- You can also use a config file to set the retention of logs by Event Manager using `wevtutil`. Refer to `wevutil` help to understand how this can be done.
- List the important attributes printed by the `w32tm` command we saw previously.

Understanding Windows file systems

Understanding the file systems supported by an operating system can help digital forensics professionals in several ways, as follows:

- It can provide knowledge of how data is organized and stored on different file systems, allowing forensic analysts to effectively recover deleted files or examine file structures.
- It can build awareness of specific features and limitations and can help identify vulnerabilities or misconfigurations that might have been exploited during a cyber incident.
- Cyber forensics professionals can use this knowledge to understand compatibility issues between different file systems and aids in investigating incidents involving multiple devices and operating environments.

Let us understand in brief the various file systems used with Windows as follows:

File system	Details
NTFS	**New Technology File System (NTFS)** is a journaling file system developed by Microsoft. It has become the default file system of Windows operating systems, including Windows 10 and Windows 11. NTFS supports features like encryption, compression, file permissions, journaling, support for large files, and advanced features like permissions, encryption, disk quotas, and shadow copies.
FAT	**File Allocation Table (FAT)** is an older file system compatible with a wide range of devices and operating systems but has limitations such as a maximum file size of 4GB.
exFAT	**Extended File Allocation Table (exFAT)** is designed for flash drives, offering larger file sizes than FAT32 without the overhead of NTFS.
ReFS	**Resilient File System (ReFS)** is a file system that is found in the Windows Server family of operating systems.

Table 6.5: Various file systems in Windows operating systems

Interesting fact: A journaling file system is a file system that keeps track of changes not yet committed to the file system's main part by recording the goal of such changes in a data structure known as a journal, which is usually a circular log. In the event of a system crash or power failure, such file systems can be brought back online more quickly with a lower likelihood of becoming corrupted.

Analyzing file system structure

A forensic analysis of the Windows file system involves examining metadata, deleted files, timestamps, system logs, and hidden artifacts. A few of the important aspects of such analysis include the following:

- Identifying file system type, e.g., NTFS, exFAT, etc.
- **Master file table** (**MFT**) analysis.
- NTFS change journal analysis.
- File slack space and unallocated space analysis.
- Deleted file identification and recovery.
- Recycle bin forensics.
- Timeline analysis using **modified, accessed, created, and born** (**MACB**) timestamps.
- **Volume shadow copy** (**VSS**) analysis.

We will look at many such methods in the upcoming recipes in this chapter. A few other related concepts are left to explore.

Recipe 46: Identifying file system type

We understood the types of file systems Windows can support across various flavors of personal and server operating systems. Identifying the file system type provides important information for further analysis, e.g., when the system image needs to be analyzed.

In this recipe, let us look at the various information we can get about the file system of a drive that can help us identify the file system type.

Note:

- **Compatibility: Windows**
- **License considerations: Part of the operating system**

Recipe

Windows has a handy utility called **`fsutil`**, which stands for **file system utility**. This tool can be used to get a lot of details about the file system. You can run this from both the command prompt and PowerShell.

Let us use the following command to get the volume information about a volume, in this case **`C:`** drive:

```
fsutil fsinfo volumeinfo C:
```

When you run this command, you will get an output similar to the following:

```
PS C:\logs> fsutil fsinfo volumeinfo C:
Volume Name :
Volume Serial Number : 0x40432530
Max Component Length : 255
File System Name : NTFS
Is ReadWrite
Not Thinly-Provisioned
Supports Case-sensitive filenames
Preserves Case of filenames
Supports Unicode in filenames
Preserves & Enforces ACL's
Supports file-based Compression
Supports Disk Quotas
Supports Sparse files
Supports Reparse Points
Returns Handle Close Result Information
Supports POSIX-style Unlink and Rename
Supports Bypass IO
Supports Case-Sensitive Directories
Supports Object Identifiers
Supports Encrypted File System
Supports Named Streams
Supports Transactions
Supports Hard Links
Supports Extended Attributes
Supports Open By FileID
Supports USN Journal
PS C:\logs>
```

Now, let us run this command on a USB drive (**`D:`**) and see what we get:

```
C:\>fsutil fsinfo volumeInfo D:
Volume Name : USB DISK
Volume Serial Number : 0x6474dbfc
Max Component Length : 255
File System Name : exFAT
Is ReadWrite
```

```
Not Thinly-Provisioned
Preserves Case of filenames
Supports Unicode in filenames
Returns Handle Close Result Information
Supports Encrypted File System
```

As you can see, the file system for USB drives is exFAT, while the one for fixed drives in the previous output was NTFS.

If the file system is FAT, other commands can be used to analyze it further.

Activity

Attempt the following activities before the next recipe:

- Execute the command `fsutil fsinfo drives` to list all the drives. Confirm if you see only the fixed drives or also the USB drives.
- Execute the command `fsutil fsinfo statistics C:` and analyze the type of statistical information you get.
- Check other commands supported by `fsutil`, e.g., `usn` for **Update Sequence Number** (**USN**) Journal, and volume for volume commands.

Recipe 47: Checking directory and file metadata

`Get-ChildItem` in PowerShell is a versatile PowerShell command that can provide many more details, and we have been using it in many recipes. We can use the same command to get a lot more details about the file or the metadata of the file. Metadata is data about data and provides context and information about a file, such as its creation date, author, and file type, which helps in organizing, finding, and understanding the file's content.

Note:

- **Compatibility: Windows**
- **License considerations: Part of the operating system**

Recipe

To test this recipe, follow the following steps:

1. First create a folder and then a few files inside the folder, similar to the following:

```
PS C:\logs> tree /F
Folder PATH listing
Volume serial number is 00000153 4043:2530
C:.
├──input
│       input_log.txt
│
└──output
        output_log.txt

PS C:\logs>
```

2. Now, we can find out the metadata of these two **.txt** files using the following command:

```
Get-ChildItem -Path C:\Logs\ | Select *
```

In this command, we are getting all the child items of **C:\Logs** and then printing all the properties for each of the items. The output may look similar to the following:

```
PS C:\logs> Get-ChildItem -Path C:\Logs\ | Select *

PSPath            : Microsoft.PowerShell.Core\FileSystem::C:\Logs\input
PSParentPath      : Microsoft.PowerShell.Core\FileSystem::C:\Logs
PSChildName       : input
PSDrive           : C
PSProvider        : Microsoft.PowerShell.Core\FileSystem
PSIsContainer     : True
Mode              : d-----
BaseName          : input
Target            : {}
LinkType          :
Name              : input
FullName          : C:\Logs\input
Parent            : Logs
Exists            : True
Root              : C:\
Extension         :
CreationTime      : 20-02-2024 20:54:40
CreationTimeUtc   : 20-02-2024 15:24:40
LastAccessTime    : 16-03-2025 23:14:17
LastAccessTimeUtc : 16-03-2025 17:44:17
LastWriteTime     : 20-02-2024 21:08:52
LastWriteTimeUtc  : 20-02-2024 15:38:52
Attributes        : Directory

PSPath            : Microsoft.PowerShell.Core\FileSystem::C:\Logs\output
PSParentPath      : Microsoft.PowerShell.Core\FileSystem::C:\Logs
PSChildName       : output
PSDrive           : C
PSProvider        : Microsoft.PowerShell.Core\FileSystem
PSIsContainer     : True
Mode              : d-----
BaseName          : output
Target            : {}
LinkType          :
Name              : output
FullName          : C:\Logs\output
```

```
Parent            : Logs
Exists            : True
Root              : C:\
Extension         :
CreationTime      : 20-02-2024 20:54:45
CreationTimeUtc   : 20-02-2024 15:24:45
LastAccessTime    : 16-03-2025 23:14:19
LastAccessTimeUtc : 16-03-2025 17:44:19
LastWriteTime     : 20-02-2024 21:24:52
LastWriteTimeUtc  : 20-02-2024 15:54:52
Attributes        : Directory
```

3. If you analyze the output properly, you will see that we got the metadata of the folders but not the files themselves. Let us now check all the metadata of files as well using the following command:

```
Get-ChildItem -Path C:\Logs\ -recurse | Select *
```

The output will be similar to the following, which not only prints the metadata of the folders but also the files inside them:

```
PS C:\logs> Get-ChildItem -Path C:\Logs\ -recurse | Select *

PSPath            : Microsoft.PowerShell.Core\FileSystem::C:\Logs\input
PSParentPath      : Microsoft.PowerShell.Core\FileSystem::C:\Logs
PSChildName       : input
PSDrive           : C
PSProvider        : Microsoft.PowerShell.Core\FileSystem
PSIsContainer     : True
Mode              : d-----
BaseName          : input
Target            : {}
LinkType          :
Name              : input
FullName          : C:\Logs\input
Parent            : Logs
Exists            : True
Root              : C:\
Extension         :
CreationTime      : 20-02-2024 20:54:40
CreationTimeUtc   : 20-02-2024 15:24:40
LastAccessTime    : 16-03-2025 23:14:17
LastAccessTimeUtc : 16-03-2025 17:44:17
LastWriteTime     : 20-02-2024 21:08:52
LastWriteTimeUtc  : 20-02-2024 15:38:52
Attributes        : Directory
.
```

```
.
.

PSPath            : Microsoft.PowerShell.Core\FileSystem::C:\Logs\input\input_log.txt
PSParentPath      : Microsoft.PowerShell.Core\FileSystem::C:\Logs\input
PSChildName       : input_log.txt
PSDrive           : C
PSProvider        : Microsoft.PowerShell.Core\FileSystem
PSIsContainer     : False
Mode              : -a----
VersionInfo       : File:             C:\Logs\input\input_log.txt
                    InternalName:
                    OriginalFilename:
                    FileVersion:
                    FileDescription:
                    Product:
                    ProductVersion:
                    Debug:            False
                    Patched:          False
                    PreRelease:       False
                    PrivateBuild:     False
                    SpecialBuild:     False
                    Language:
.
.
.
PSPath            : Microsoft.PowerShell.Core\FileSystem::C:\Logs\output\output_log.txt
PSParentPath      : Microsoft.PowerShell.Core\FileSystem::C:\Logs\output
PSChildName       : output_log.txt
PSDrive           : C
PSProvider        : Microsoft.PowerShell.Core\FileSystem
PSIsContainer     : False
Mode              : -a----
VersionInfo       : File:             C:\Logs\output\output_log.txt
                    InternalName:
                    OriginalFilename:
                    FileVersion:
                    FileDescription:
                    Product:
                    ProductVersion:
                    Debug:            False
```

```
                    Patched:          False
                    PreRelease:       False
                    PrivateBuild:     False
                    SpecialBuild:     False
                    Language:

BaseName          : output_log
Target            : {}
LinkType          :
Name              : output_log.txt
Length            : 285
DirectoryName     : C:\Logs\output
Directory         : C:\Logs\output
IsReadOnly        : False
Exists            : True
FullName          : C:\Logs\output\output_log.txt
Extension         : .txt
CreationTime      : 20-02-2024 21:24:52
CreationTimeUtc   : 20-02-2024 15:54:52
LastAccessTime    : 16-03-2025 23:16:13
LastAccessTimeUtc : 16-03-2025 17:46:13
LastWriteTime     : 20-02-2024 21:25:38
LastWriteTimeUtc  : 20-02-2024 15:55:38
Attributes        : Archive

PS C:\logs>
```

The above output has been truncated to show the important parts due to the length of the output.

Activity

Attempt the following activities before the next recipe:

- List all the properties of interest that can be used by a digital forensic analyst while working on a case.
- Think of ways these properties can be used during the investigation of a cybercrime case.

Recipe 48: Working with MACB timestamps

In the previous chapter, we learned the concept of **MACB** timestamps, which stand for **modified, accessed, changed, and born**. These are attributes attached to every file in the file system and can be used to understand how and when files are created, modified, deleted, and even accessed.

MACB timestamps can be used to reconstruct user activity or timelines in Windows using PowerShell as well. Many other digital forensics tools can help create timelines. One such well-known tool is Plaso or log2timeline, which is a Python-based engine used by several tools for the automatic creation of aggregated timelines from multiple artifacts. MFTECmd is another tool that can be used in Windows. We will discuss more about these tools in *Chapter 12, Imaging Techniques*.

Note:

- **Compatibility: Windows**
- **License considerations: Part of the operating system**

Recipe

Let us check the MACB timestamps of all the files inside a folder using the following command:

```
Get-ChildItem -Path C:\Logs\ -Recurse | Select Name, CreationTime, LastAccessTime, LastWriteTime
```

The output will look similar to the following:

```
PS C:\> Get-ChildItem -Path C:\Logs\ -Recurse | Select Name, CreationTime, LastAccessTime,
LastWriteTime

Name           CreationTime        LastAccessTime      LastWriteTime
----           ------------        --------------      -------------
input          20-02-2024 20:54:40 16-03-2025 23:14:17 20-02-2024 21:08:52
output         20-02-2024 20:54:45 16-03-2025 23:14:19 20-02-2024 21:24:52
input_log.txt  20-02-2024 19:32:30 05-11-2024 11:08:55 20-02-2024 21:25:37
output_log.txt 20-02-2024 21:24:52 20-02-2024 21:25:38 20-02-2024 21:25:38


PS C:\>
```

In this example, we saw the MACB timestamp of only 2 files inside a folder. If you have more files, it will recursively provide the details.

Interesting fact: MACB timestamps can be used to detect an intentional change by an attacker called timestomping, where the attacker alters the timestamp of the files accessed or modified to cause confusion. The MACB timestamps can be used to detect such anomalies.

Activity

Attempt the following activities before the next recipe:

- Check what other details `Get-ChildItem` can provide in terms of MACB timestamps.
- Analyze how MACB timestamps can be used to find the anomalies.

Recipe 49: Examining disk partitions

A disk partition is a logical division of a physical storage device (HDD, SSD, USB drive) that appears as a separate drive to the operating system. In Windows, partitions help organize data and manage storage efficiently.

There are two main partition types in Windows as follows:

Partition type	Details
Master Boot Record (MBR)	Supports up to 4 primary partitions (or 3 primary + 1 extended). Uses a partition table (512-byte sector) stored in the first sector of the disk.
GUID partition table (GPT)	Supports 128 partitions and drives larger than 2TB. It uses a protective MBR for backward compatibility and stores multiple copies of the partition table for redundancy.

***Table 6.6:** Main partition types in Windows*

A typical system may have the following partitions, which may vary from system to system:

Partition	Description	Use case
System reserved (100MB—500MB)	Stores boot manager and **Boot Configuration Data (BCD)**.	Required for booting.
EFI system partition (ESP)	GPT partition storing bootloader and **Unified Extensible Firmware Interface (UEFI)** firmware.	Required for UEFI booting.
Primary partition (C:, D:, etc.)	Stores OS and user data	Main storage.
Recovery partition	Contains Windows recovery tools and data.	Used for system restore in case of corruption or resetting the OS.
Unallocated space	Free space that can be partitioned or used for extending existing partitions.	May contain deleted partitions.

Table 6.7*: Partitions present on a system*

Interesting fact: **UEFI, or Unified Extensible Firmware Interface, is a modern firmware interface that replaces the traditional BIOS, providing a standardized interface between the operating system and the platform firmware, enabling features like faster boot times and improved security.**

Note:

- **Compatibility: Windows**
- **License considerations: Part of the operating system**

Recipe

Let us see a few ways to examine disk partitions. First, we will use the **diskpart** utility from the Windows command prompt:

```
diskpart
```

This will bring you to the **diskpart** utility prompt, from where you can examine the partitions as follows:

```
C:\>diskpart

Microsoft DiskPart version 10.0.22621.1

Copyright (C) Microsoft Corporation.
On computer: INFIKNIT

DISKPART> list disk

  Disk ###  Status         Size     Free     Dyn  Gpt
  --------  -------------  -------  -------  ---  ---
  Disk 0    Online           64 GB  1024 KB        *

DISKPART> select disk 0

Disk 0 is now the selected disk.
```

```
DISKPART> list partition

  Partition ###  Type              Size     Offset
  -------------  ----------------  -------  -------
  Partition 1    System             100 MB  1024 KB
  Partition 2    Reserved            16 MB   101 MB
  Partition 3    Primary             63 GB   117 MB
  Partition 4    Recovery           888 MB    63 GB

DISKPART>
```

You can finally use **exit** command to exit DiskPart.

Caution: DiskPart is a system utility that can be used to perform operations with partitions that can cause unrecoverable data loss. Hence, be very careful when experimenting with DiskPart.

There are a few other ways to get information about disk partitions. We can use **wmic** as follows:

```
C:\> wmic partition get Name, BootPartition, Size, Type
BootPartition  Name                   Size         Type
TRUE           Disk #0, Partition #0  104857600    GPT: System
FALSE          Disk #0, Partition #1  67663560704  GPT: Basic Data
FALSE          Disk #0, Partition #2  931135488    GPT: Unknown
```

We can also use the PowerShell command **Get-Disk** to get similar information:

```
PS C:\> Get-Disk / Get-Partition

   DiskPath: \\?\scsi#disk&ven_nvme&prod_vmware_virtual_n#5&14eaf08e&0&000000#{53f56307-b6bf-11d0-
94f2-00a0c91efb8b}

PartitionNumber  DriveLetter Offset                                                    Size Type
---------------  ----------- ------                                                    ---- ----
1                            1048576                                                 100 MB System
2                            105906176                                                16 MB
Reserved
3                C            122683392                                             63.02 GB Basic
4                            67786244096                                              888 MB
Recovery


PS C:\>
```

As we saw before, you can get a lot more information about the object (in this case, the disk) by using **Select-Object** as follows:

```
PS C:\> Get-Disk | Select-Object *

DiskNumber             : 0
PartitionStyle         : GPT
ProvisioningType       : Fixed
OperationalStatus      : Online
HealthStatus           : Healthy
BusType                : NVMe
UniqueIdFormat         : SCSI Name String
OfflineReason          :
ObjectId               : {1}\INFIKNIT\root/Microsoft/Windows/Storage/Providers_v2\WSP_Disk.
ObjectId="{bfa9a4a6-b6ed-11ee-b79f-806e6f6e6963}:DI:
                         \?\scsi#disk&ven_nvme&prod_vmware_virtual_n#5&14eaf08e&0&000000#{53f56307-
b6bf-11d0-94f2-00a0c91efb8b}"
PassThroughClass       :
PassThroughIds         :
PassThroughNamespace   :
PassThroughServer      :
UniqueId               : eui.8C41B3D4997995B2000C296EE1759051
AdapterSerialNumber    : VMware NVME_0000
AllocatedSize          : 68718428160
BootFromDisk           : True
FirmwareVersion        : 1.3
FriendlyName           : VMware Virtual NVMe Disk
Guid                   : {15505fc8-18c4-43ea-9fd3-44732fad2b20}
IsBoot                 : True
IsClustered            : False
IsHighlyAvailable      : False
IsOffline              : False
IsReadOnly             : False
IsScaleOut             : False
IsSystem               : True
LargestFreeExtent      : 1048576
Location               : PCI Slot 224 : Bus 17 : Device 0 : Function 0 : Adapter 1
LogicalSectorSize      : 512
Manufacturer           :
Model                  : VMware Virtual NVMe Disk
Number                 : 0
NumberOfPartitions     : 4
Path                   : \?\scsi#disk&ven_nvme&prod_vmware_virtual_n#5&14eaf08e&0&000000#{53f56307-
b6bf-11d0-94f2-00a0c91efb8b}
PhysicalSectorSize     : 4096
SerialNumber           : 8C41_B3D4_9979_95B2_000C_296E_E175_9051.
```

```
Signature                 :
Size                      : 68719476736
PSComputerName            :
CimClass                  : ROOT/Microsoft/Windows/Storage:MSFT_Disk
CimInstanceProperties     : {ObjectId, PassThroughClass, PassThroughIds, PassThroughNamespace...}
CimSystemProperties       : Microsoft.Management.Infrastructure.CimSystemProperties

PS C:\>
```

Activity

Attempt the following activities before the next recipe:

- Try DiskPart on other systems and analyze if the output is different than what you saw.
- Observe if you see USB drives too in the DiskPart output.
- Think of ways these properties can be used during the investigation of a cybercrime case.

Recipe 50: Identifying deleted files

When a file is deleted in Windows, it is not immediately erased. Instead, the file system marks it as deleted, making it recoverable until overwritten. For forensic analysis, we can investigate **master file table** (**MFT**) records, USN Journal ($J), Recycle Bin (**`$Recycle.Bin`**), Shadow Copies, and unallocated disk space to identify and recover deleted files.

In this recipe, we will look at these ways to identify deleted files. While there are many free and commercial tools available that provide advanced capabilities to identify (and recover) deleted files, understanding the ways in this recipe can provide you with much deeper insights into how deleted files can be identified and recovered.

Note:

- **Compatibility: Windows**
- **License considerations: Part of the operating system**

Recipe

Let us look at various ways to identify deleted files.

Check the $Recycle.Bin for recently deleted files

When a user deletes a file from Windows Explorer, it moves to the **`$Recycle.Bin`** until emptied. The recycle bin is stored in the path **`C:\$Recycle.Bin\S-1-5-21-\ (user-specific)`**.

Inside the recycle bin, the **`$I`** files contain metadata, such as the original filename and deletion timestamps, while the **`$R`** files store the actual deleted file data.

Let us use **`Get-ChildItem`** to get the list of all the deleted files as follows:

```
Get-ChildItem -Path 'C:\$Recycle.Bin' -Recurse -Force
```

The output of this command will look similar to the following:

```
PS C:\> Get-ChildItem -Path 'C:\$Recycle.Bin' -Recurse -Force


    Directory: C:\$Recycle.Bin
```

```
Mode                 LastWriteTime         Length Name
----                 -------------         ------ ----
d--hs-        20-01-2024     14:44                S-1-5-18
d--hs-        17-03-2025     01:18                S-1-5-21-378136081-2435938798-3280355894-1001


    Directory: C:\$Recycle.Bin\S-1-5-18


Mode                 LastWriteTime         Length Name
----                 -------------         ------ ----
-a-hs-        20-01-2024     14:44            129 desktop.ini


    Directory: C:\$Recycle.Bin\S-1-5-21-378136081-2435938798-3280355894-1001


Mode                 LastWriteTime         Length Name
----                 -------------         ------ ----
-a----        17-03-2025     01:18             96 $IAP5WDM.txt
-a----        17-03-2025     01:18             96 $IJ51SV1.txt
-a----        05-11-2024     11:08            444 $RAP5WDM.txt
-a----        05-11-2024     11:08            644 $RJ51SV1.txt
-a-hs-        19-01-2024     23:07            129 desktop.ini


PS C:\>
```

Once you understand that there are deleted files, you can recover them using tools like FTK Imager.

Extracting deleted file information from the USN journal

Windows USN journal logs file creation, deletion, and modifications.

We can use the following command to read the USN journals:

```
fsutil usn readjournal C:
```

The output will look similar to the following:

```
PS C:\> fsutil usn readjournal C:
USN Journal ID     : 0x01da4afa8408fbb0
First USN          : 1166016512
Next USN           : 1207624912
Start USN          : 0
Min major version : Supported=2, requested=2
Max major version : Supported=4, requested=4
```

```
Usn                 : 1166016512
File name           : d2d1.dll
File name length    : 16
Reason              : 0x00001000: Rename: old name
Time stamp          : 16-03-2025 07:40:05
File attributes     : 0x00000080: Normal
File ID             : 00000000000000000006000000023e65
Parent file ID      : 00000000000000000006000000023e60
Source info         : 0x00000000: *NONE*
Security ID         : 0
Major version       : 3
Minor version       : 0
Record length       : 96
Usn                 : 1166016592
File name           : d2d1.dll
File name length    : 16
Reason              : 0x00002000: Rename: new name
Time stamp          : 16-03-2025 07:40:05
File attributes     : 0x00000080: Normal
File ID             : 00000000000000000006000000023e65
Parent file ID      : 00000000000000000002000000048042
Source info         : 0x00000000: *NONE*
Security ID         : 0
Major version       : 3
Minor version       : 0
Record length       : 96

Usn                 : 1166016672
File name           : d2d1.dll
File name length    : 16
Reason              : 0x80002000: Rename: new name / Close
Time stamp          : 16-03-2025 07:40:05
File attributes     : 0x00000020: Archive
File ID             : 00000000000000000006000000023e65
Parent file ID      : 00000000000000000002000000048042
Source info         : 0x00000000: *NONE*
Security ID         : 0
Major version       : 3
Minor version       : 0
Record length       : 96
```

```
Usn                 : 1166016752
File name           : r
File name length    : 2
Reason              : 0x00000100: File create
Time stamp          : 16-03-2025 07:40:05
File attributes     : 0x00000010: Directory
File ID             : 00000000000000000002000000048043
Parent file ID      : 00000000000000000002000000048041
Source info         : 0x00000000: *NONE*
Security ID         : 0
Major version       : 3
Minor version       : 0
Record length       : 80
```

You can see the journal entries related to renaming and creating. There will be similar journal entries for delete operations.

Note: There could be a large number of journal entries (1000s or even millions) based on the activities on your system. Hence, it is best to store the output in a file for further analysis. During learning, you can press Ctrl+C to break the output after a few seconds.

Due to the number of journal entries, it is impossible to analyze these manually within a short time. There are specialized tools that can be used in such circumstances.

Checking volume shadow copies for older copies

Windows VSS feature uses shadow copies to store previous file versions, which are very useful for recovering deleted files. Windows **Volume Shadow Copy Service (VSS)** is a built-in feature that creates point-in-time snapshots of files, even if they are in use. These snapshots allow backup applications and system restore tools to access consistent versions of files without interrupting normal operations. VSS is often used for system restore, retrieving previous versions of files, and by backup utilities. In digital forensics, it can provide access to historical copies of data that may have been deleted or altered on the live system.

We can check the VSS by using the Volume Shadow Copy Service administration tool or **vssadmin** as follows:

```
vssadmin list shadows
```

When you run this command, you will see an output similar to the following:

```
C:\> vssadmin list shadows
vssadmin 1.1 - Volume Shadow Copy Service administrative command-line tool
(C) Copyright 2001-2013 Microsoft Corp.

Contents of shadow copy set ID: {0ea58511-b8c6-490c-a6d9-df3b0103d7fd}
   Contained 1 shadow copies at creation time: 05-03-2025 11:06:58
      Shadow Copy ID: {00987250-b9df-444f-88f5-8b38747e7305}
         Original Volume: (C:)\?\Volume{3fd5af64-801f-4848-86fd-ff6662108975}\
         Shadow Copy Volume: \?\GLOBALROOT\Device\HarddiskVolumeShadowCopy4
         Originating Machine: DESKTOP-633GPQP
```

```
        Service Machine: DESKTOP-633GPQP
        Provider: 'Microsoft Software Shadow Copy provider 1.0'
        Type: ClientAccessibleWriters
        Attributes: Persistent, Client-accessible, No auto release, Differential, Auto recovered

Contents of shadow copy set ID: {7a37d45c-81ff-4bca-8e9d-3f2fd97ee223}
   Contained 1 shadow copies at creation time: 10-03-2025 11:02:00
      Shadow Copy ID: {8bed36b6-5c42-4d2e-a493-3c2a30e549bb}
         Original Volume: (C:)\?\Volume{3fd5af64-801f-4848-86fd-ff6662108975}\
         Shadow Copy Volume: \?\GLOBALROOT\Device\HarddiskVolumeShadowCopy5
         Originating Machine: DESKTOP-633GPQP
         Service Machine: DESKTOP-633GPQP
         Provider: 'Microsoft Software Shadow Copy provider 1.0'
         Type: ClientAccessibleWriters
         Attributes: Persistent, Client-accessible, No auto release, Differential, Auto recovered

Contents of shadow copy set ID: {594ccf18-8b81-4bbd-b5a2-7c7db81525bc}
   Contained 1 shadow copies at creation time: 10-03-2025 11:02:55
      Shadow Copy ID: {18449213-e73c-4a55-b022-b52f9dbea16b}
         Original Volume: (C:)\?\Volume{3fd5af64-801f-4848-86fd-ff6662108975}\
         Shadow Copy Volume: \?\GLOBALROOT\Device\HarddiskVolumeShadowCopy6
         Originating Machine: DESKTOP-633GPQP
         Service Machine: DESKTOP-633GPQP
         Provider: 'Microsoft Software Shadow Copy provider 1.0'
         Type: ClientAccessibleWriters
         Attributes: Persistent, Client-accessible, No auto release, Differential, Auto recovered

Contents of shadow copy set ID: {751f543b-8c39-4317-930d-cf963ad8014c}
   Contained 1 shadow copies at creation time: 10-03-2025 11:03:53
      Shadow Copy ID: {faaf6cb0-3088-488e-8481-750bf1c0874a}
         Original Volume: (C:)\?\Volume{3fd5af64-801f-4848-86fd-ff6662108975}\
         Shadow Copy Volume: \?\GLOBALROOT\Device\HarddiskVolumeShadowCopy7
         Originating Machine: DESKTOP-633GPQP
         Service Machine: DESKTOP-633GPQP
         Provider: 'Microsoft Software Shadow Copy provider 1.0'
         Type: ClientAccessibleWriters
         Attributes: Persistent, Client-accessible, No auto release, Differential, Auto recovered

Contents of shadow copy set ID: {8c479ff7-9c18-4766-ae8d-c79fe0413d92}
   Contained 1 shadow copies at creation time: 16-03-2025 22:25:51
      Shadow Copy ID: {2443de01-4fb6-4b37-a147-87757831a535}
         Original Volume: (C:)\\?\Volume{3fd5af64-801f-4848-86fd-ff6662108975}\
```

```
        Shadow Copy Volume: \?\GLOBALROOT\Device\HarddiskVolumeShadowCopy8
        Originating Machine: DESKTOP-633GPQP
        Service Machine: DESKTOP-633GPQP
        Provider: 'Microsoft Software Shadow Copy provider 1.0'
        Type: ClientAccessibleWriters
        Attributes: Persistent, Client-accessible, No auto release, Differential, Auto recovered

C:\>
```

When trying to recover a file, we can create a discovery link using `mklink` to the volume shadow copy as follows. While running the following command, ensure that you use one of the shadow volume names listed by the preceding command:

```
mklink /d C:\ShadowCopy \\?GLOBALROOT\Device\HarddiskVolumeShadowCopy4
```

Activity

Attempt the following activities before the next recipe:

- Understand the meaning of each of the properties in the journal entries.
- Analyze how these journal entries can be used to create a timeline of the activities on the system.
- Link a VSS to a directory and check what are the information you see in the directory.

Recipe 51: Performing hash calculations

A file hash is a unique digital fingerprint generated by applying a cryptographic algorithm (e.g., MD5, SHA-1, SHA-256) to a file's contents. Such a generated hash is also called a checksum. The resulting hash value remains consistent unless the file is altered. Even a minor change in a file's content can produce a significant alteration in its hash value, which may serve as an indicator of malicious activity.

Hashes are used very frequently in digital forensics to ensure file integrity by detecting modifications. Hashes are also generated before and after forensic acquisition to verify data integrity. Hashes can also be used to verify the recovered files against the original hashes.

Interesting fact: **Well-known cybersecurity services like VirusTotal check hashes or checksums against known malware samples to determine whether a given payload is malicious.**

Let us look at how we can use PowerShell to compute hashes of files in Windows. In Linux, hash utilities are either part of the system or can be installed easily. In Windows, PowerShell provides a simple way to do that.

Note:

- **Compatibility: Windows**
- **License considerations: Part of the operating system**

Recipe

Let us first use PowerShell to generate the hash of a file as follows:

```
PS C:\> Get-FileHash C:\Work\Passwords.txt

Algorithm       Hash                                                                   Path
```

```
---------        ----                                                            ----
SHA256           AABF9D741E4E6FDB3593B59A84B0391E9A01224206F569351DD2F4C000C8836F   C:\Work\
Passwords.txt
```

This, by default, uses SHA256. If you want to use any other algorithm for hash calculation, you can pass it as a parameter as follows:

```
PS C:\> Get-FileHash C:\Work\Passwords.txt -Algorithm SHA1

Algorithm        Hash                                                            Path
---------        ----                                                            ----
SHA1             97D53627EFCC76906869BC3D08ADE3C4452176E0                        C:\Work\
Passwords.txt
```

Many other frequently used tools can help you with hash calculation. `HashMyFiles` from `NirSoft` can help you calculate the hash by right-clicking on any file.

Another example is `HashCalc`, which also provides the option to compute the hash and verify/compare it. You can look at its GitHub repository to understand how it works. `HashCalc` can be used to generate a checksum using various hash algorithms, generate hash based on a **hash-based message authentication code** (HMAC) key, and work with various file formats.

Note: If you want to create a small command-line tool with the functionalities we discussed so far, you can do it with a basic knowledge of programming and a few lines of code.

Note: Many frequently used cybersecurity utilities are the main reason behind the compromise of systems. Attackers may look for such utilities and create a malicious version of them. You may end up using a compromised version of the utility that can pose a threat to your system. Hence, verify the source before you download any such utilities. Better yet, always use a separate test system for all your digital forensic needs, and do not share that system with anything that can impact your work in case of a compromise or data loss.

Activity

Attempt the following activities before the next recipe:

- Read about various hashing algorithms, such as MD5, SHA1, SHA256, SHA512, etc.
- Analyze how SHA256 is better for file integrity verification than SHA1.
- Write a PowerShell command to compare two hashes.

Detecting data tampering with hashes

Comparing hashes is one of the key ways we can use to identify the integrity of files. They can be used for checking the signs of compromise by the enterprises if they collect hashes of important files periodically.

They can also be used during digital forensic investigations to verify the integrity of evidence as it is passed to various stakeholders as part of the chain of custody. The chain of custody is broken if the integrity of the evidence is compromised, and the evidence may not be permissible in the court of law. Hence, during the evidence acquisition period, hashes are calculated for every piece of digital evidence.

Let us look at a summary of how hashes or checksums can detect data tampering as follows:

Scenario	Hash changes	Forensic interpretation
Exact file copy	No	The file is identical.
File renamed	No	File name was changed, but the content is identical.
Metadata changes (e.g., Timestomping)	No	Only metadata like timestamp modified.
File modified (added/deleted bytes)	Yes	Content was altered.
Malware injected in the file	Yes	The file was tampered.

Table 6.8: *How hashes/checksums can detect data tampering*

Recipe 52: Working with Windows File Recovery tool

Windows File Recovery tool is a command line application from Microsoft that can be used to recover accidentally deleted files in internal and external storage devices. It may also be useful to identify the deleted file in a disk image during digital forensic analysis.

Note:

- **Compatibility: Windows**
- **License considerations: Free software used**

Recipe

The **Windows File Recovery** tool is not pre-installed. Before we continue with this recipe, install the tool from the **Microsoft Store**, as shown in the following figure:

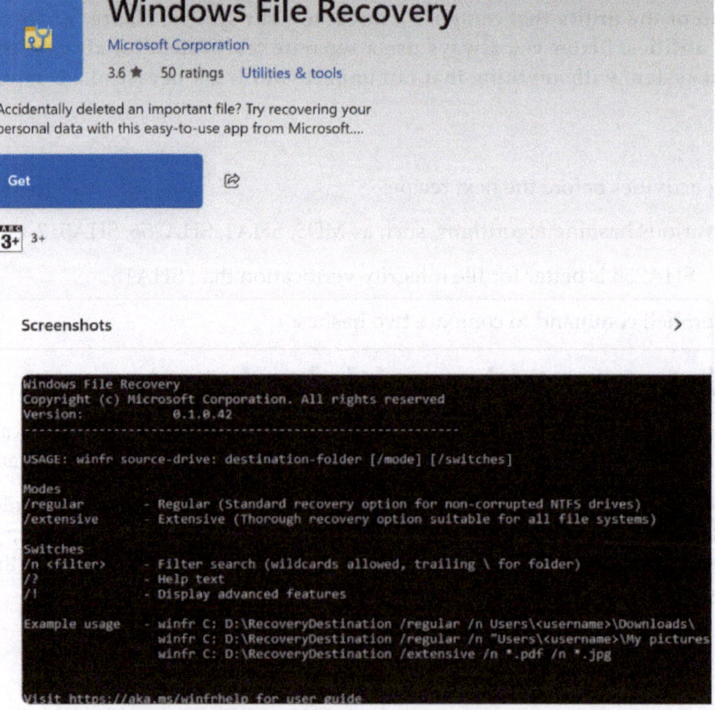

Figure 6.7: *Installing Windows File Recovery tool from Microsoft Store*

Once you have installed the tool, you can run it on a disk volume to recover all deleted files or specific files as per the following examples. You need to give a destination folder where the files will be recovered:

Command	Details
`winfr C: D:\Recovery /n \.docx`	Recover recently deleted Microsoft Word files.
`winfr C: D:\RecoveredFiles /extensive`	Recover all deleted files using Extensive mode, which performs a deep scan for all deleted files.
`winfr C: D:\RecoveredFiles /segment /n .pdf /n .jpg`	Recover deleted PDF and JPG files using segment mode.
`winfr C: D:\RecoveredFiles /segment /n \.xlsx /y:Documents /u /n 2023-01-01..2023-12-31`	Recover all deleted Microsoft Excel files within a date range.
`winfr E: D:\USB\Recovery /extensive`	Recover files from a USB disk.

Table 6.9: Important Windows File Recovery tool commands

Note: Recovery operation is a slow process as it scans the entire disk. This is also a very resource-intensive operation.

Activity

Attempt the following activities before the next recipe:

- Find out the difference between regular and extensive switches of the Windows File Recovery tool.
- Check the Windows File Recovery tool's help to understand how to use wildcards for searching for files.

Recipe 53: Recovering lost data and deleted files using WinHex

WinHex is a **hexadecimal** (or **hex**) editor that can be used to analyze the disk at a low level and recover data. Since editors like WinHex work directly at the disk level, they can be used to recover files from corrupted files or volumes with corrupted metadata and MBR. Such editors can be used to recover files from external media storage, like digital camera cards. Hence, as a digital security analyst, WinHex and other similar tools can be extremely useful.

Note:

- **Compatibility: Windows**
- **License considerations: Free for learning, with limited capabilities**

Recipe

WinHex Editor can be downloaded from **https://www.x-ways.net/winhex/index-m.html.** As usual, any tool like this should be used only on a computer dedicated to digital forensic work.

Once you have downloaded the `winhex.zip` file, extract it and run `winhex.exe`. After that, you can open any file to analyze its raw content. The hex editor shows the hex values and their text values side by side, as shown in the following figure:

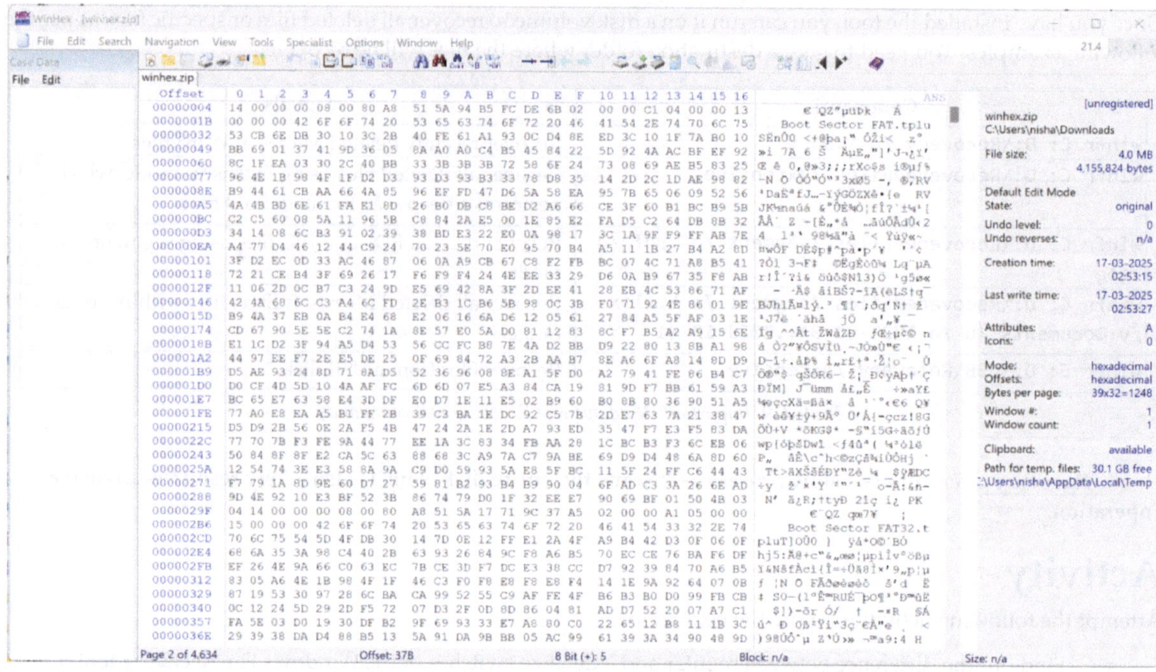

Figure 6.8: Using WinHex editor to hex edit a file

Caution: **Hex editors work at the raw file level, and hence, any change done to the file may corrupt the file. When using such hex editors, always keep a backup of the files you are working with. When working with system files, use only a copy of the system file.**

Activity

Attempt the following activities before the next recipe:

- WinHex editor is used best with cases. A case can be used to group and analyze various artifacts related to a digital forensic investigation case. Create a new case from the **File** menu and then add multiple files to be analyzed.
- Open a file and then search for a specific string and integer values in the file.

Working with Windows Registry

Let us first understand what the Windows Registry is. Windows Registry is a central, hierarchical database that stores configuration settings for Windows and many applications. It contains crucial information about hardware, software, user preferences, system settings, and more. It is vital for Windows' operation and application functionality.

Since the Windows Registry is at the center of everything that happens in Windows, it contains valuable forensic artifacts for timeline reconstruction and malware investigation. Digital forensic techniques focusing on Registry audit and analysis can provide us with valuable information about various forms of system compromise.

Windows Registry is used in the following ways:

- **Windows operating system**: Accesses the Registry constantly for settings and configuration and uses it to track installed applications, startup programs, user activity, and device connections.

- **Applications**: Applications store and retrieve their settings and preferences.
- **Users**: They rarely interact directly, but some advanced troubleshooting or customization might involve Registry editing.

The Registry consists of five root keys (hives), each storing different types of system and user data as follows:

Registry hive	Purpose
HKEY_LOCAL_MACHINE (HKLM)	Stores system-wide configurations, drivers, services, and installed programs.
HKEY_CURRENT_USER (HKCU)	Stores user-specific settings, browsing history, application usage, and settings for the currently logged-in user.
HKEY_USERS (HKU)	Stores all user profiles on the system.
HKEY_CLASSES_ROOT (HKCR)	Contains file type associations and registered applications.
HKEY_CURRENT_CONFIG (HKCC)	Stores current hardware profile information and configuration.

***Table 6.10**: Hives in Windows Registry*

Apart from these top-level hives, you also need to be aware of keys and values. Keys are subfolders within hives, organized in a tree-like structure. Values are individual settings within keys, like named variables with data.

Let us look at the two most common Windows Registry tools: regedit, which comes with Windows, and Registry Explorer, which is a free external tool. Once you become comfortable with these tools, you can also explore other tools, like RegRipper, that provide similar functionalities.

Recipe 54: Exploring Windows Registry

Let us look at using two ways to explore the structure of a Windows Registry as follows:

- **Registry Editor** (or **regedit**) is the default Registry editor supplied with Windows. It provides a simple and hierarchical view of all the hives of the Registry with an option to create, edit, and modify various entries.
- Registry Explorer is a Registry viewer from *Eric Zimmerman*, who is known for the best tools in the digital forensics world. Registry Explorer can be downloaded from Eric Zimmerman's website at **https://ericzimmerman.github.io/** or from Eric Zimmerman's website. It provides options like searching, multi-hive support, plugin support, and so on.

Note:

- **Compatibility: Windows**
- **License considerations: Free software used**

Recipe

Let us use regedit to explore the Windows Registry through the following steps:

1. First, run **Registry Editor as Administrator**. It shows the hives present on this computer. Now, you can expand any of the hives to see more details under them, as shown in the following figure:

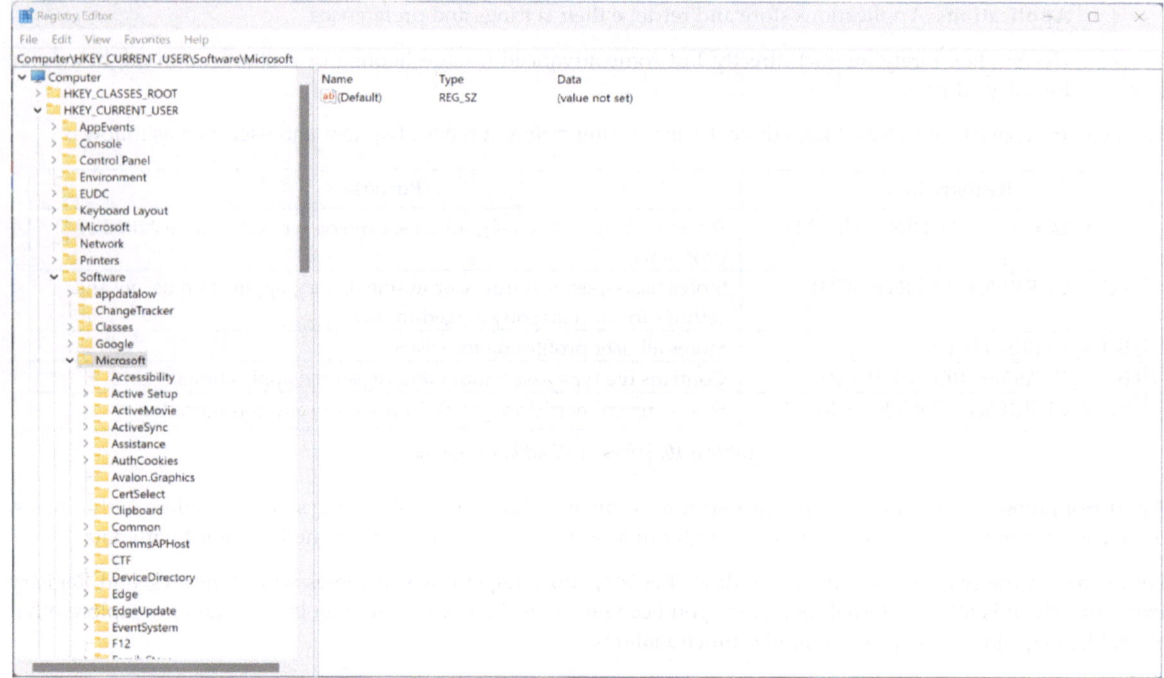

***Figure 6.9:** Windows Registry Editor with an expanded key*

The Registry Editor provides a simple way to explore the Windows Registry with features like find, export, import, etc.

2. Now, let us use Registry Explorer. From the preceding link, download the file **`RegistryExplorer.zip`** and extract it. It can now be used as a standalone program without the need for installation.

   Note: You need .Net Desktop Runtime installed to run this application. If you get an error from the program, install this package.

   Click on **`RegistryExplorer.exe`** to run it as administrator. You will see a blank screen with nothing loaded. After that, from the menu, click on **File | Live System | SOFTWARE** to load the **SOFTWARE** hive. You can see the **Live System** option only if you have run Registry Explorer as Administrator.

3. Explore various screens of Registry Explorer. You can see that the information provided by Registry Explorer is much more detailed than what is given by RegEdit, including deleted values. You can also expand each of the keys and find more details about them by right-clicking and selecting **Technical details**, as shown in the following figure:

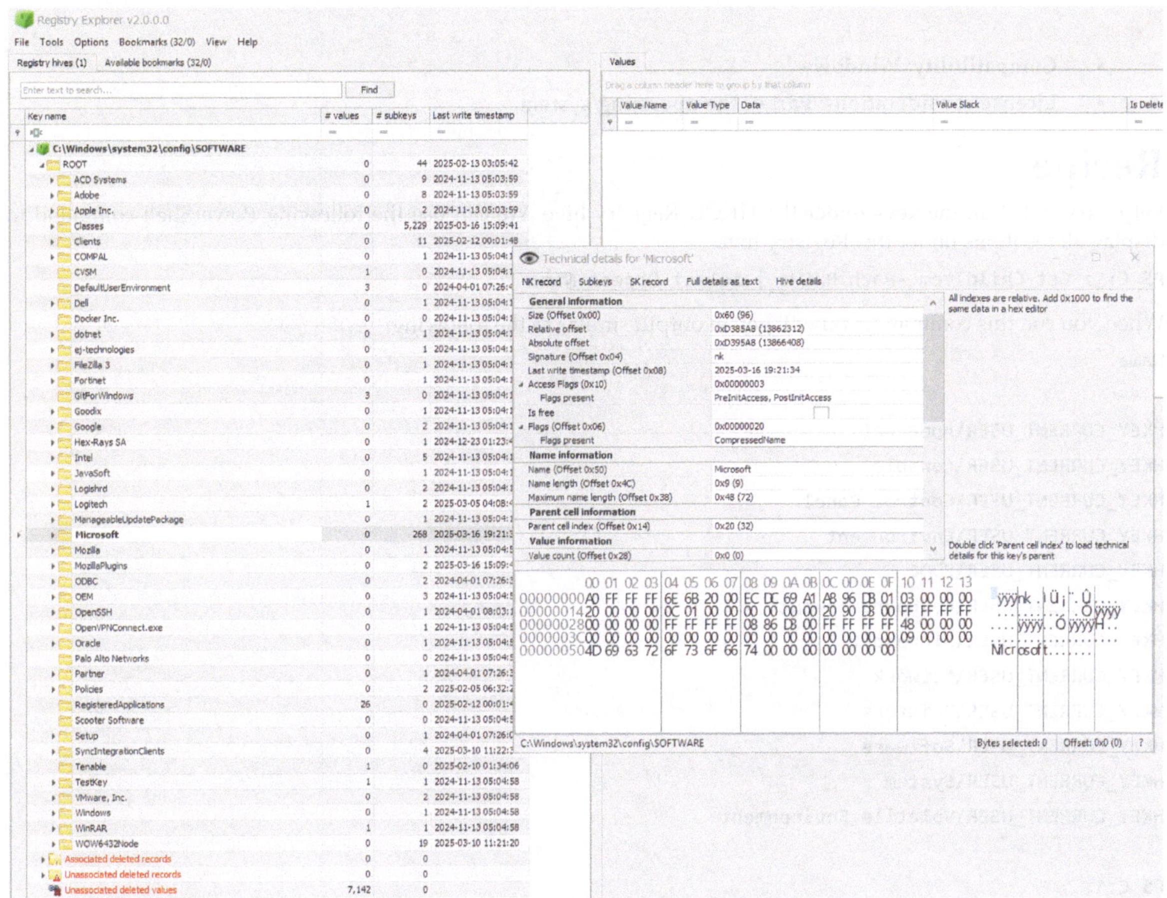

Figure 6.10: Working with Registry Explorer

Registry Explorer also provides you with the option to bookmark the Registry key for faster access at a later time.

Activity

Attempt the following activities before the next recipe:

- Search for a key using the **Find** option (**Edit | Find**) in Registry Editor.
- Explore various options of Registry Explorer and list the key differences that can help a digital forensic analyst.
- Registry Explorer provides a list of common bookmarks in the **Available bookmarks** tab. Check how you can use these bookmarks to reach the key in one click.

Recipe 55: Listing Registry keys and values

While using the Registry tools can provide you with an easy way to inspect the Windows Registry, knowing how to use PowerShell to do the same gives you a great advantage. Using PowerShell, you can automate many tasks of working with the Registry and, hence, find it very convenient for repeated tasks.

Note:

- **Compatibility: Windows**
- **License considerations: Part of the operating system**

Recipe

Let us try to list all the keys under the HKCU Registry hive. We can use the following PowerShell command to display all the items under this Registry hive:

```
PS C:\> Get-ChildItem -Path HKCU: | Select-Object Name
```

When you run this command, you will get an output similar to the following:

```
Name
----
HKEY_CURRENT_USER\AppEvents
HKEY_CURRENT_USER\Console
HKEY_CURRENT_USER\Control Panel
HKEY_CURRENT_USER\Environment
HKEY_CURRENT_USER\EUDC
HKEY_CURRENT_USER\Keyboard Layout
HKEY_CURRENT_USER\Microsoft
HKEY_CURRENT_USER\Network
HKEY_CURRENT_USER\Printers
HKEY_CURRENT_USER\Software
HKEY_CURRENT_USER\System
HKEY_CURRENT_USER\Volatile Environment

PS C:\>
```

Activity

Attempt the following activities before the next recipe:

- We used **`Select-Object Name`** in the preceding example. Try using **`Select-Object Name`** and observe what are the details you see and how they are useful information for digital forensics.
- Modify the above command to print a list of keys from other hives.
- Modify the above command to print a list of keys under Microsoft **`HKCU:\Microsoft`**.

Recipe 56: Generating logs for Registry changes

While enabling file audit in a recipe in this chapter, we saw various other audit options. One of them was **Audit Registry**. Let us use this option to enable the auditing of any unwanted Registry changes.

Note:

- **Compatibility: Windows**
- **License considerations: Part of the operating system**

Recipe

Let us enable file Registry auditing. To do that, follow the following steps:

1. To enable audit for Registry changes, first run **Local Group Policy Editor** (`gpedit.msc`) and go to **Computer Configuration | Windows Settings | Security Settings | Advanced Audit Policy Configuration | System Audit Policies**.
2. Under this, click on **Object Access** and then enable **Audit Registry**. What we are trying to say is that whenever a specific path in the Windows Registry is changed, we need to generate logs.
3. Now perform any Registry changes, e.g., adding a key, and check **Event Viewer** for the audit logs for the Registry.

Caution: **Windows operating systems and almost every application access the Registry and perform changes continuously. Hence, restrict the Registry auditing needs to specific areas in the Registry to avoid generating 1000s of logs.**

Activity

Attempt the following activities before the next recipe:

- We enabled audit for Registry changes that can log any change in the Registry. Find a way to restrict it to one hive or a few keys.
- Observe the Event ID for the Registry audit logs and understand the details that are associated with it.

Recipe 57: Checking USB device history from Registry

An attacker may use a USB device to carry the malicious payload and install it on the target system. Hence, as part of digital forensic evidence collection, details about the USB device's activities are also collected.

Note:

- **Compatibility: Windows**
- **License considerations: Part of the operating system**

Recipe

Let us look at various places in the Registry where installed USB devices' details and USB device history are available:

Registry location	Information stored
`HKEY_LOCAL_MACHINE\SYSTEM\CurrentControlSet\Enum\USB`	Subkeys for each connected USB device, listed by Vendor ID \ and **Product ID (PID)**. It can also be used to extract advanced properties.
`HKEY_LOCAL_MACHINE\SYSTEM\CurrentControlSet\Enum\USBSTOR`	List of storage-related USB devices with details like device name (manufacturer and model), serial number (if available), driver version, installation date, etc.
`HKEY_LOCAL_MACHINE\SYSTEM\MountedDevices`	List of all the mounted devices, useful to correlate when a USB device was connected and what drive letter it received.

***Table 6.11**: Registry keys for checking USB device history*

Note: Not all of them may be available in all the systems. Hence, checking all of them is important. If you want to collect the preceding information in an automated way, you can use reg query followed by the path of the key, similar to the following:

```
reg query "HKEY_LOCAL_MACHINE\SYSTEM\MountedDevices"
```

Activity

Attempt the following activities before the next recipe:

- Attach a USB device, e.g., a thumb storage drive, to your computer and run the preceding command. Check if you see this activity in the preceding Registry locations.
- Now, detach your USB device and run the preceding command. Check if you see this activity in the history.
- System logs are generated when the USB device is connected or disconnected. Find out the specific Event IDs for events related to USB devices.

Recipe 58: Working with users and groups

Windows users and groups contain crucial forensic evidence, including login activity, privilege escalation, account modifications, and unauthorized access. Investigators analyze these artifacts to detect malicious activity, privilege misuse, and account manipulation.

Note:

- **Compatibility: Windows**
- **License considerations: Part of the operating system**

Recipe

Let us look at various PowerShell commands to work with users and groups on Windows that can be used during digital forensic evidence collection and analysis as follows:

Command	Purpose
`Get-LocalUser`	List all users.
`Get-LocalGroup`	List all groups.
`Get-LocalGroupMember -Group "Administrators"`	List all the members of the group *Administrators*.
`Get-LocalUser | Select-Object Name, LastLogon`	Check last logins for users.
`Get-WmiObject Win32UserAccount | Select Name, SID, LocalAccount, Status`	Find recently created or modified accounts.
`Get-ADUser -Filter  -Property Name, LastLogonDate`	Check **Active Directory (AD)** users. It will work only if the computer is part of an AD domain.
`Get-EventLog -LogName Security -InstanceId 4728`	Check if a user was added to the Administrator group.
`Get-EventLog -LogName Security -InstanceId 4672`	Check for user privilege assignments.
`Get-EventLog -LogName Security -InstanceId 4624 | Where-Object { $\.Message -match "Logon Type:\s+10" }`	**Detect remote access (RDP)** usage.
`Get-EventLog -LogName Security -InstanceId 4740`	Check for account lockouts due to failed login attempts.
`Get-EventLog -LogName Security -InstanceId 4720`	Check for deleted user accounts.

Table 6.12: PowerShell commands for working with users and groups

Activity

Attempt the following activities before the next recipe:

- Write a command to get the list of all the members of the group User.
- Investigate if there are Registry keys that store information about users and groups and various activities on them.

Recipe 59: Working with the Device Manager

Windows Device Manager is a system utility that displays and manages the hardware devices connected to a computer. It provides details about installed drivers, connected peripherals, USB devices, network adapters, and system components.

You can access Windows Device Manager in the following ways:

- From the **Computer Management** widget.
- By directly launching **Device Manager**.

The following figure shows the Windows Device Manager screen after it is opened:

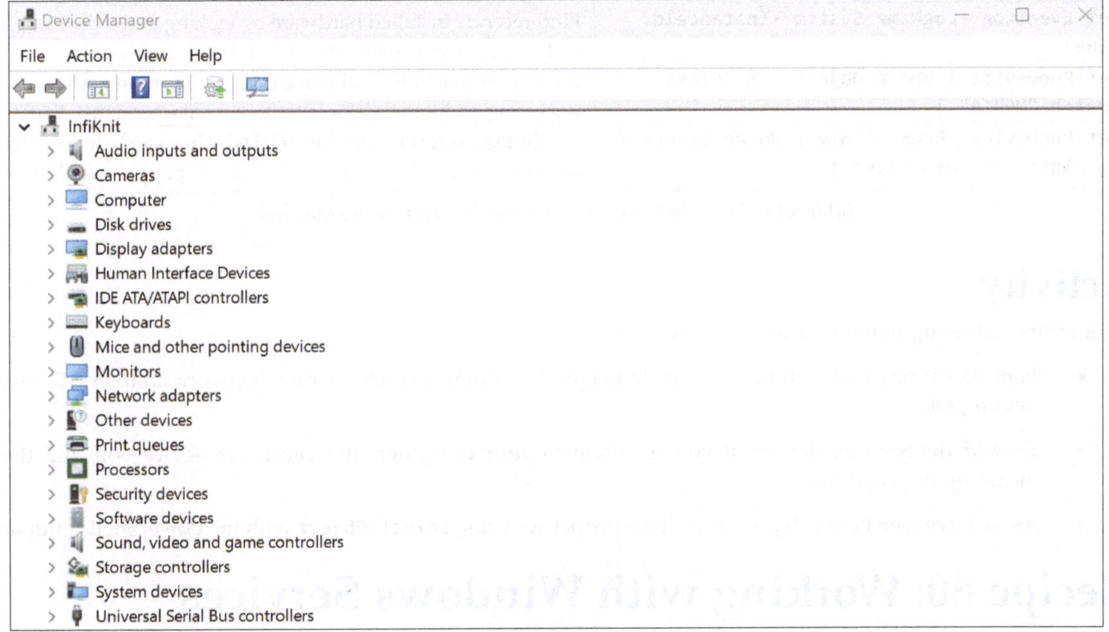

***Figure 6.11:** Windows Device Manager*

Since Device Manager manages all the devices and their versions, firmware, installation dates, and many other aspects, it can allow digital forensic investigators to track device history and usage details. Let us look at how we can do that.

Note:

- **Compatibility: Windows**
- **License considerations: Part of the operating system**

Recipe

In this recipe, we will look at the automation aspect of the information we can get from the Device Manager using PowerShell.

Note: As a rule, any information in Windows that you can access manually can also be accessed using PowerShell. We will use this capability of PowerShell to access details about various devices managed by the Device Manager.

Let us look at a few PowerShell commands that can give you a lot of insights into various devices from a digital forensics point of view:

Command	Purpose
`Get-NetAdapter | Select-Object Name, InterfaceDescription, Status`	List all network adapters. Useful for detecting unauthorized network adapters.
`Get-WmiObject Win32_NetworkAdapter | Where-Object { $_.NetConnectionID }`	Get all virtual adapters like VPNs, proxies, etc.
`Get-WmiObject Win32_PnPSignedDriver | Select-Object DeviceName, DriverVersion, InstallDate`	Extract device installation logs with details about the device name, driver version, and installation date.
`Get-EventLog -LogName System -InstanceId 20001`	Find recently installed hardware by looking at the device installation events with event ID 20001, if it exists.
`Get-PnpDevice | Where-Object { $_.Class -match "MEDIA" }`	List connected audio and video devices. This can help in analyzing additional devices that may have been installed.
`Get-PnpDevice -PresentOnly | Where-Object { $_.Class -eq "HIDClass" }`	List **human interface devices (HIDs)**. They can help identify keyloggers or malicious input devices that appear as HIDs.

***Table 6.13**: PowerShell commands for working with Device Manager*

Activity

Attempt the following activities before the next recipe:

- Explore various folders under Device Manager, like Computer, Disk drive, Network adapters, Software devices, etc.
- Expand the Security devices if you see them in your computer, and check the device you find there, including its properties.
- As we have seen before, try to print all the properties using `Select-Object` with the PowerShell command.

Recipe 60: Working with Windows Services

Windows Services are background processes that perform specific functions within the operating system. They include the service for the operating system and its various add-ons and applications, as well as the services added by various applications installed on the system.

Hence, for forensics professionals, analyzing Windows services offers insights into both legitimate and malicious activities occurring within a computer system. This analysis can be crucial for understanding how a certain software interacts with the system, identifying potential malware presence, and reconstructing events leading up to a security incident.

Note:

- **Compatibility: Windows**
- **License considerations: Part of the operating system**

Recipe

If you want to check all the services on the Windows system, you can type Services in the start menu and launch it. You can also check the services as an embedded widget inside the Computer Management widget. These are excellent ways to check the list of services, including running and disabled services. However, if you want to collect this information in a simple way, we need to use a command-line option.

Let us find a few ways to collect the list of services using PowerShell:

Command	Details
`Get-Service`	Get the list of all the services.
`Get-Service | Where-Object {$_.Status -eq "Running"}`	Get the list of all the running services.
`Get-WmiObject Win32_Service`	Retrieve comprehensive information about all services, including their properties like start mode, process ID, state, etc.
`Get-Service -Name <ServiceName> | Format-List *`	Get detailed information about a service.

***Table 6.14**: PowerShell commands for working with services*

Using one of the preceding examples, let us find out detailed information about one of the services, Task Scheduler:

```
Get-Service -Name "Task Scheduler" | Format-List *
```

When you run the preceding command, you will get an output similar to the following:

```
PS C:\Windows\system32> Get-Service -Name "Task Scheduler" | Format-List *

Name                : Schedule
RequiredServices    : {RPCSS, SystemEventsBroker}
CanPauseAndContinue : False
CanShutdown         : True
CanStop             : True
DisplayName         : Task Scheduler
DependentServices   : {NaturalAuthentication}
MachineName         : .
ServiceName         : Schedule
ServicesDependedOn  : {RPCSS, SystemEventsBroker}
ServiceHandle       :
Status              : Running
ServiceType         : Win32OwnProcess, Win32ShareProcess
StartType           : Automatic
Site                :
Container           :

PS C:\Windows\system32>
```

Sometimes, you may need to export the list of all the services to a CSV file. We can use the following command to do just that:

```
Get-WmiObject Win32_Service | Select-Object Name, DisplayName, StartMode, State, PathName |
Export-Csv -Path "ServicesList.csv" -NoTypeInformation
```

The preceding command creates a CSV file **ServicesList.csv** with the given columns. You can experiment with this command to add more columns as needed.

Activity

Attempt the following activities before the next recipe:

- Write a PowerShell command to get a list of all the services with a specific keyword.
- Write a PowerShell command to get a list of all the stopped services.
- What are the other columns you can save in the CSV file in the preceding command?
- Try **Select-Object** instead of selecting the specific column names. What type of details do you see for each service?

Recipe 61: Working with certificates

A digital certificate is an electronic file that proves the authenticity of a website, user, device, or server using cryptography and the **public key infrastructure** (**PKI**), ensuring secure communication and data exchange.

Such digital certificates can be used for the following:

- Encryption communication.
- Authenticating users for secure logins.
- Digitally signing documents, emails, and software.
- Digitally sign code, like PowerShell and Python code.
- Digital sign drivers and applications for secure execution.

Windows can manage these digital certificates used for authentication, encryption, digital signatures, code signing, and many other purposes. These certificates are issued by a **Certificate Authority** (**CA**) and are part of PKI. Let us become familiar with the Windows Certificate application that does all these.

Forensic analysts examine such collected certificates to detect unauthorized access, fake root CAs, and cryptographic abuse. Some certificate abuses by the attackers include fake Root CA attacks, code-signing abuse, **Transport Layer Security** (**TLS**) impersonation, and **Secure Sockets Layer** (**SSL**) **adversary-in-the-middle** (**AiTM**) attacks.

> Note:
> - **Compatibility: Windows**
> - **License considerations: Part of the operating system**

Recipe

You can launch the certificate application from the **Start** menu. The certificates application looks like the following:

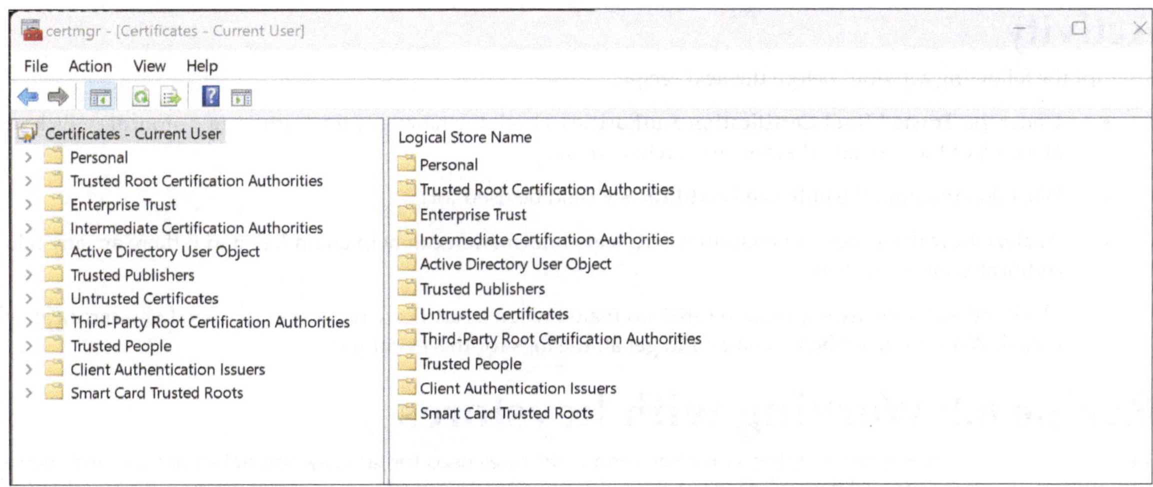

***Figure 6.12**: Windows Certificate Manager application with current user's certificates*

From the preceding screen, you can manage all the certificates on your computer. You can also perform operations like importing and exporting certificates, finding certificates, and much more.

You can extract the list of all the personal certificates (present under the **Personl** folder) by using the following PowerShell command:

```
Get-ChildItem -Path Cert:\CurrentUser\My
```

The output will be similar to the following:

```
PS C:\work> Get-ChildItem -Path Cert:\CurrentUser\My

   PSParentPath: Microsoft.PowerShell.Security\Certificate::CurrentUser\My

Thumbprint                                Subject
----------                                -------
D3C2585C30924D8D2DA1061CEBBE47DFF6E0FBA7  CN=8824a2e8-ec18-44ea-800b-8830f23b43d9


PS C:\work>
```

The path **Cert:\CurrentUser\My** corresponds to the personal certificates of the user and can also be seen under the **Personal** folder in the certificate application. Similarly, we can use various folder paths to get the corresponding certificates. For example, you can use the following command to get the list of all the Root CA certificates:

```
Get-ChildItem -Path Cert:\LocalMachine\Root
```

Note: While collecting the certificate information as digital forensic evidence, it may be a good idea to collect all the information of each certificate and not just the list of certificates.

Activity

Attempt the following activities before the next recipe:

- Under the **Trusted Root Certification Authorities**, check the names of the Certificate Authorities. Pick up at least 2 of the CAs and do more research on them.
- What do you think the untrusted certificates would be used for?
- Analyze how this process of collecting certificate information can help us understand if there are any fake certificates on the system.
- The Windows Security log event ID 4887 is created when a certificate request is approved or a certificate is issued. Write a PowerShell command to get all the logs for this event ID.

Recipe 62: Working with keystores

A keystore is a secure storage for cryptographic keys and certificates used for tasks like digital signatures and secure communication, often accessed through the Java Keytool or similar utilities. You can also think of it as a database or file that holds cryptographic keys (private and public) and associated certificates.

Windows uses the **Cryptographic API** (**CAPI**) and Windows **Cryptographic Next Generation** (**CNG**) for key management.

Note:

- **Compatibility: Windows**
- **License considerations: Part of the operating system**

Recipe

Private keys are stored securely in the Windows Keystore, protected by **Data Protection API** (**DPAPI**). They can be accessed from the following locations:

Key type	Location
User keys	`C:\Users\<User>\AppData\Roaming\Microsoft\Crypto\RSA`
Machine keys	`C:\ProgramData\Microsoft\Crypto\RSA\MachineKeys`
System keys	`C:\Windows\System32\Microsoft\Crypto\SystemKeys`

Table 6.15: Locations of private keys

You can extract the private keys using the following PowerShell command:

```
Get-ChildItem -Path Cert:\CurrentUser\My | Where-Object { $_.HasPrivateKey }
```

The output will be similar to the following:

```
PS C:\Windows\system32> Get-ChildItem -Path Cert:\CurrentUser\My / Where-Object { $_.HasPrivateKey
}


   PSParentPath: Microsoft.PowerShell.Security\Certificate::CurrentUser\My

Thumbprint                                   Subject
----------                                   -------
```

```
D3C2585C30924D8D2DA1061CEBBE47DFF6E0FBA7  CN=8824a2e8-ec18-44ea-800b-8830f23b43d9


PS C:\Windows\system32>
```

If you want to see all the information about the key, the following command can be used:

```
¨Get-ChildItem -Path Cert:\CurrentUser\My | Where-Object { $_.HasPrivateKey } / Select-Object *
```

Now, we can use the following command to export a single certificate for further analysis:

```
Export-Certificate -Cert (Get-ChildItem -Path Cert:\CurrentUser\My | Select-Object -First 1)
-FilePath C:\temp\cert.cer
```

The prior command will export the key as the `.crt` file in the preceding directory.

Activity

Attempt the following activities before the next recipe:

- Under the **Trusted Root Certification Authorities**, check the names of the CA. Pick up at least 2 of the CAs and do more research on them.
- What do you think the Untrusted Certificates would be used for?
- We exported a single private certificate in this recipe. Modify the command by looking at the documentation to export all the certificates or specific certificates.

Recipe 63: Analyzing update history

Microsoft regularly releases Windows updates to address security vulnerabilities and application issues. These updates are critical for keeping systems secure and running efficiently. For digital forensic analysts, examining the details of installed updates can provide valuable insights, such as whether the system was up to date, when the last updates were applied, and whether missing patches may have exposed potential attack vectors. This information helps in reconstructing the circumstances of a cybercrime and identifying how an attacker may have exploited the system.

Note:

- **Compatibility: Windows**
- **License considerations: Part of the operating system**

Recipe

Run the following command as administrator to get the list of Windows update history:

```
wmic qfe list brief
```

The output will look similar to the following:

```
C:\>wmic qfe list brief
Description       FixComments  HotFixID   InstallDate  InstalledBy            InstalledOn  Name
ServicePackInEffect  Status
Update                        KB5049624               NT AUTHORITY\SYSTEM   3/16/2025
Update                        KB5027397                                     12/4/2023
Update                        KB5033055               NT AUTHORITY\SYSTEM   1/19/2024
Security Update               KB5053602               NT AUTHORITY\SYSTEM   3/16/2025
```

```
Update                     KB5052107          NT AUTHORITY\SYSTEM  3/16/2025

C:\>
```

Activity

Attempt the following activities before the next recipe:

- Instead of the **brief** option, try the **full** option and observe the details you get from this command.
- Read the **Windows Management Instrumentation Command-line** (**WMIC**) documentation and understand what the option *qfe* stands for.

Conclusion

In this chapter, we explored digital forensics on Windows systems. We learned how to collect critical system information, analyze logs using Event Viewer and PowerShell, inspect file systems, and work with disk partitions and Registry entries. We also learned to enable auditing, analyze deleted files, and generate hashes to verify file integrity. Important tools like Registry Explorer, fsutil, Get-EventLog, and PowerShell commands were covered to perform various forensic tasks efficiently.

Windows logs, Registry, certificates, user and group information, and audit policies can reveal valuable clues during a digital forensic investigation. Forensic professionals must be familiar with native Windows tools and commands to extract this information while preserving evidence.

Whether analyzing user activity, detecting suspicious changes, or recovering deleted files, Windows provides powerful capabilities for digital investigation. Practicing these techniques regularly helps build confidence and expertise. As cyberattacks get more sophisticated, knowing how to trace and analyze evidence on Windows systems becomes an essential skill for every cybersecurity professional.

In the next chapter, we will explore various recipes for digital forensics for networks.

Questions

1. What is the purpose of the systeminfo command in Windows?
2. How can you list all local user accounts on a Windows machine?
3. What does the net accounts command show?
4. How is Event Viewer helpful in digital forensics?
5. Name three types of logs available under Windows Logs.
6. What is the use of PowerShell's Get-EventLog command?
7. Which Event ID represents a successful login?
8. Which log records PowerShell command usage?
9. What is a MACB timestamp?
10. What is the function of the NTFS file system?
11. How does NTFS differ from FAT32 and exFAT?
12. How can you identify the file system type of a drive?
13. What does Get-ChildItem display when used on a folder?

14. Which command helps you view the update history of Windows?
15. What is a journaling file system?
16. How can you recover deleted files from the Recycle Bin using PowerShell?
17. What are shadow copies in Windows?
18. How can audit logs help detect unauthorized file access?
19. What tool can be used to recover deleted files using a GUI?
20. What information can be gathered from Device Manager forensics?
21. How can you use PowerShell to list installed services?
22. What is the role of the Windows Registry in forensic analysis?
23. What Registry hive stores system-wide configuration?
24. How can you list Registry keys using PowerShell?
25. What command is used to generate a SHA256 hash of a file?
26. Where are private keys stored in Windows?
27. How can certificate abuse be detected using forensic analysis?

Points to remember

- systeminfo reveals detailed system metadata useful for profiling.
- Event Viewer centralizes logs from various system components.
- Security logs are critical for tracing authentication and access events.
- Application logs help detect malicious or unusual application behavior.
- PowerShell commands Get-EventLog can be used to automate log retrieval and analysis.
- Audit logs can be enabled to track file and Registry access.
- NTFS supports features like journaling, encryption, and ACLs.
- FAT32 and exFAT are simpler and used on older systems and removable media, respectively.
- MACB timestamps stand for timestamps modified, accessed, changed, and born, and can help reconstruct the timeline of file activity.
- Deleted files can often be recovered from the Recycle Bin or USN journal.
- Shadow copies store previous versions of files and the system state.
- Hashes are essential to ensure the integrity of digital evidence.
- SHA256 is preferred for strong integrity checks over SHA1 or MD5.
- Certificates can be viewed using PowerShell or Certificate Manager.
- Certificates and keys are stored in defined directories in Windows.
- Windows Registry is a centralized repository/database that holds essential system and user data.
- USB device history can also be retrieved from the Registry.
- Device Manager data can be extracted using Get-WmiObject.

Key terms

- **NTFS**: New Technology File System is the default file system for modern Windows.
- **FAT32**: File Allocation Table 32-bit is an older file system with a 4GB file size limit.
- **exFAT**: Extended FAT is used in USB drives and supports large files.
- **USN Journal**: Update Sequence Number journal tracks changes to files.
- **MACB**: Stands for timestamps modified, accessed, changed, and born, and are used as file activity timestamps.
- **SACL**: System access control list is used for auditing object access.
- **Auditpol**: Command-line tool to manage audit policy.
- **fsutil**: File system utility for advanced information and statistics.
- **Event Viewer**: GUI tool for viewing Windows logs.
- **Get-EventLog**: PowerShell command to fetch log entries.
- **Get-WinEvent**: Advanced version of Get-EventLog for filtered log queries.
- **MFT**: Master File Table, contains metadata about files in NTFS.
- **VSS**: Stands for Volume Shadow Copy and contains the backup copies of files and system images.
- **SHA256**: Cryptographic hash function providing 256-bit hashes.
- **WinHex**: A hex editor used for low-level disk analysis.
- **Registry**: A Hierarchical system database storing configuration settings and preferences.
- **HKLM**: Registry hive for system-wide settings.
- **HKCU**: Registry hive for the current user.
- **SID**: SID or Security Identifier is a unique ID assigned to users or groups.
- **DPAPI**: DPAPI is used to encrypt sensitive data, such as stored keys.
- **PKI**: Public key infrastructure is the system for managing digital certificates and encryption, and is used worldwide.
- **RegEdit**: Default Registry editing tool in Windows.

Join our Discord space

Join our Discord workspace for latest updates, offers, tech happenings around the world, new releases, and sessions with the authors:

https://discord.bpbonline.com

CHAPTER 7
Network Forensics

Introduction

The world runs on the network, and so is any enterprise, irrespective of their size. Many well-known attack vectors find their way to the target systems via the network. From an enterprise point of view, both proactive security and making the environment ready for digital forensic evidence collection are important for overall security and sometimes even for compliance. Hence, one has to protect one's networks as well as have enough ways to collect and analyze forensic evidence. We will look at various aspects of digital forensics in the context of networks.

Structure

In this chapter, we will cover the following topics:

- Evidence that can be collected from the network
- Recipe 64: Performing live packet capture using Wireshark
- Recipe 65: Performing network traffic analysis using Wireshark
- Recipe 66: Offline analysis of PCAP files
- Understanding voice forensics
- Recipe 67: Performing voice forensics using Wireshark
- Recipe 68: Identifying anomalies by monitoring network activities
- Understanding security information and event management
- Recipe 69: Checking wireless configuration changes
- Understanding indicators of compromise from network logs
- Network security best practices
- Web application forensics and log analysis

Objectives

In this chapter, we will focus on various aspects of digital forensics for the network. We will look at the types of live and offline analysis that network engineers and digital forensic analysts can perform using Wireshark. As part of this chapter, we will also cover areas like voice forensics that play a key part in digital forensic investigations. Towards the end of the chapter, we will understand what **indicators of compromise** (**IOCs**) are and how they can help secure the network. Finally, we will cover a few aspects around best practices for network security and the relationship between network forensics and web application forensics.

By the end of this chapter, you should be able to perform live packet captures in your network and analyze offline packet captures from various sources. You will also be able to relate to various security-related signals in the network and apply them during digital forensic analysis.

Evidence that can be collected from the network

Most attack vectors pass through networks. Hence, it is logical to collect as much evidence as possible from various network components during a cybercrime or cybersecurity incident investigation. As a corollary, every organization should collect evidence from the network regularly so that it can be used as evidence if needed.

In enterprise networks (on-premises corporate networks), various network-based evidence can be collected to investigate incidents. Familiar sources include network devices like firewalls, routers, **intrusion detection system (IDS)**, **intrusion prevention system (IPS)**, etc. Sources also include logs, traffic captures, and authentication records. These help investigators trace malicious activities, identify affected systems, and attribute actions to users. Full network traffic capture, including payloads (if unencrypted), is Ideal for reconstructing sessions, recovering transferred files, and performing detailed protocol analysis.

In cloud environments (such as AWS, Azure, and Google Cloud), networking is virtualized, but many of the same evidence types exist in log form. Cloud providers offer logging services that record network activity, API calls, and resource access. Forensic collection in the cloud focuses on these provider logs and any captured traffic, emphasizing cloud-specific services and how to retrieve their data. It is crucial to enable and retain cloud logs in advance since many are not archived by default.

Wireless networks (particularly Wi-Fi networks using 802.11 standards) introduce unique evidence sources due to radio signals and access points. In a wireless environment, forensic evidence comes from logs and captures that describe how devices connect and communicate over the air. Special care is needed because wireless traffic can be volatile and encrypted, and the physical range of signals means unauthorized parties might participate from outside premises. Key evidence sources in wireless network forensics include device association logs, authentication records, and wireless packet captures.

Analyzing offline network evidence

Offline network evidence refers to data no longer part of live network traffic but can be extracted from stored artifacts or historical logs. These are especially useful when responding after an incident has occurred.

Let us look at a few offline network evidence that can be analyzed in the following table:

Evidence	What is it	Forensic value	Example use case
Packet capture files (PCAPs)	Stored captures of raw network packets (e.g., from tcpdump, Wireshark).	Allows reconstruction of sessions, inspection of payloads, detection of malware communication, and extraction of transferred files.	Post-incident deep dive; e.g., recover attacker's commands sent via Telnet or identify files exfiltrated via FTP.
Network flow logs (NetFlow/IPFIX)	Summarized metadata of network conversations (source/destination IPs, ports, timestamps, byte counts).	Good for timeline reconstruction, detecting unusual volumes, lateral movement, or stealthy C2 traffic.	Identify which systems talked to a known malicious IP and when, even without full content.
Firewall and router logs (syslogs)	Historical records of network policy enforcement — connections allowed, blocked, NAT translations.	Show attempted intrusions, blocked exfiltration, and allowed suspicious access.	Confirm that data was exfiltrated over port 443 despite IDS being silent.
IDS/IPS alert logs	Historical records of alerts from Snort, Suricata, or commercial systems.	Point to signatures or behaviors indicative of malware, scanning, or exploitation attempts.	Tie a suspicious PCAP to a known vulnerability exploit signature fired at the same time.

Evidence	What is it	Forensic value	Example use case
Proxy/Web filtering logs	Logs of outbound HTTP/HTTPS requests by internal users.	Helps detect malware downloads, suspicious browsing, and C2 activity.	Show a host downloaded a .zip from a known phishing domain three days prior to detection.
Domain name system (DNS) server logs	Resolved domain name queries (local DNS logs or passive DNS).	Used for identifying malware domains, **domain generation algorithm (DGA)** usage, or unusual query patterns.	Find beaconing activity by identifying recurring queries to unknown domains.
Dynamic Host Configuration Protocol (DHCP) lease logs	Historical records mapping MAC addresses to IPs over time.	Crucial for tying an IP seen in logs to a specific device at a specific time.	Identify that 10.0.0.5 was assigned to a BYOD device during a suspected data leak.
Authentication logs (e.g., RADIUS, VPN, Kerberos)	Logs of network-level authentication events, e.g., login success/failure.	Links user accounts to access patterns and helps detect credential abuse.	Verify whether a **virtual private network (VPN)** account was used from an unusual country right before a breach.
SIEM and other centralized log archives	Aggregated logs from various sources like firewalls, **Active Directory (AD)**, Intrustion Detection Systems IDSs, syslog in tools like ArkSIEM, Splunk, Elastic Stack, etc.	Acts as the unified history of events, enabling timeline reconstruction and correlation analysis.	Pivot from an IDS alert to associated AD authentication and firewall session logs.
Email gateway and SMTP logs	Stores metadata about sent/received emails, sender/recipient addresses, IPs, attachments.	Reveals spear phishing, command execution via malicious macros, or data exfiltration via email.	Prove that an internal user received and opened a malicious Excel file 2 days before lateral movement began.
Wireless infrastructure logs	Historical logs from wireless access points or controllers (associations, deauths, signal strength).	Show when/where a device connected and help investigate rogue or transient devices.	Correlate presence of a specific MAC address near a secure lab over multiple dates.
Logs from specialized tools like NetWitness, Zeek, or Bro	Parsed session logs or metadata derived from full PCAPs.	Provide rich protocol-level insights (e.g., HTTP headers, SSL certs, DNS queries).	Identify encrypted malware traffic patterns or HTTP POSTs with exfil data without needing raw packets.

Table 7.1: *Offline network evidence*

We can easily see that each of these logs provide insights into the network activities leading to a cyberattack or an incident. Hence, the more logs you can collect the better it would be for cyber forensics investigation. It is similar to finding pieces of puzzle, the more you have, the clearer the picture would be.

Note: **Malware often communicate with their servers using a C2 mechanism. Many of what we saw above can help in identifying when the infection happened, isolating such communication packets, and even identifying the extent of exposure such malware could have caused.**

Working with Wireshark

Wireshark is a free and open-source network protocol analyzer that allows you to capture and interactively browse the traffic running on a computer network in real time or offline from saved capture files (PCAPs). It supports hundreds of network protocols and runs on most operating systems (Windows, Linux, macOS).

Note: Wireshark will feel like a magic wand if you have taken time to understand all the features and become expert in it. It is probably the only tool you may need to capture network packets, analyze network traffic patterns and perform advanced level digital forensic investigations.

Let us look at the key features of Wireshark in the following table:

Feature	Details
Captures network traffic	Wireshark can record all packets flowing through a network interface.
Decodes protocols	It dissects packet content into readable layers (Ethernet, IP, TCP, HTTP, etc.).
Filters data	Investigators can apply display filters (e.g., `http.request, ip.addr == 192.168.1.10`) to isolate relevant traffic.
Reconstructs sessions	Allows reassembly of **Transmission Control Protocol** (**TCP**) streams, file transfers, and even voice calls or chat sessions.
Exports objects	Can extract files from HTTP, **File Transfer Protocol (FTP)**, **Server Message Block** (**SMB**) sessions (e.g., malware samples or stolen data).
Analyzes performance or anomalies	Highlights retransmissions, malformed packets, or unusual timing.

***Table 7.2:** Key features of Wireshark*

Wireshark is immensely useful in digital forensics. It plays a crucial role in several stages of network forensics and incident response, as illustrated in the following table:

Task	Purpose	Example
Evidence extraction	Extract malware payloads, login data, documents, or other artifacts from captured traffic.	You find an HTTP POST request with a `Content-Type: application/octet-stream`. Wireshark allows you to export that file, which turns out to be a zip archive containing a backdoor executable.
Timeline reconstruction	Rebuild the sequence of attacker actions, system interactions, or data transfers based on packet timestamps.	By following TCP streams, you reconstruct that a compromised internal host accessed a command server at 14:03, downloaded a payload at 14:05, and began beaconing at 14:07 — all of which match the suspected breach timeline.
Malware behavior analysis	Observe how malware communicates over the network, including C2 callbacks, beaconing intervals, and exfiltration methods.	A malicious binary sends periodic HTTP GET requests to `evilhost.biz/checkin.php` every 60 seconds, which Wireshark reveals through filtering with `http.request` and examining packet intervals.
Credential/PII recovery	Recover usernames, passwords, emails, or other personal data sent over insecure channels.	A telnet session was captured by following the TCP stream, you see the attacker typed the username admin and password password123, giving insight into credential reuse or brute force success.
Protocol abuse detection	Detect covert channels or abnormal use of legitimate protocols for malicious purposes.	DNS queries contain long base64-encoded strings sent to stealthdata.attacker.com—Wireshark flags the unusual size and pattern of these requests, revealing DNS tunneling.

Task	Purpose	Example
File reconstruction	Reassemble and extract files transferred over HTTP, FTP, SMB, or other protocols.	Wireshark captures an HTTP download of a resume.pdf, which turns out to contain embedded shellcode. The file is reconstructed from the capture and handed over for malware analysis.

Table 7.3: *Use of Wireshark in digital forensics*

You can launch Wireshark from the Kali Linux menu. Following is the opening screen of Wireshark:

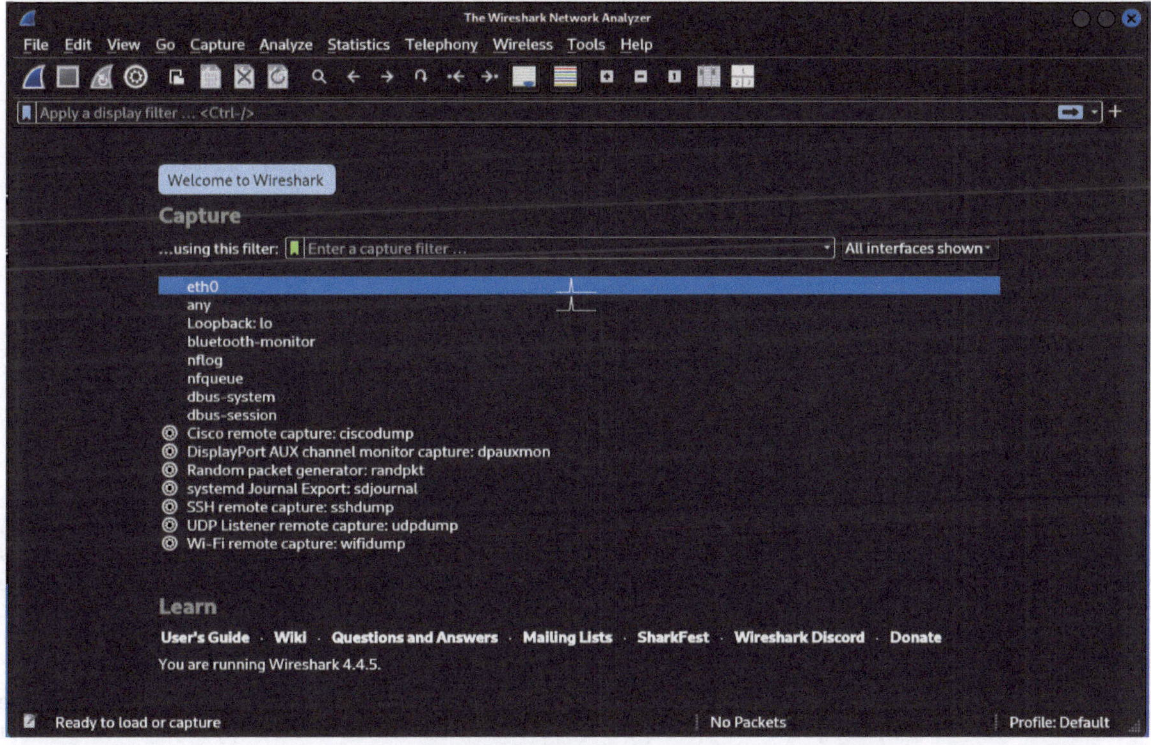

Figure 7.1: *Wireshark opening screen*

Be familiar with the features of Wireshark before starting to capture the packets. Wireshark documentation is very comprehensive and provides all the details to get started. You can also look at Wireshark's webpage for further documentations and tutorials.

Recipe 64: Performing live packet capture using Wireshark

Live packet capture using Wireshark allows investigators to monitor and record real-time network traffic as it happens. It can also help them analyze the previously recorded network activities. There are multiple ways it can help in digital forensics:

- It helps identify active connections, unauthorized access, malware communication, and data exfiltration attempts.

- It provides time-stamped evidence of network activities, crucial for reconstructing the sequence of events during an incident.
- It can capture volatile data that may be lost if not recorded immediately, such as transient attacks or session details.

Live packet captures can be done for the following scenarios in digital forensics:

Scenario	How live packet capture helps
Malware infection	Captures communication between an infected system and a **C2** server, showing IP addresses, ports, and payloads.
Data exfilteration	Detects large amounts of sensitive data being sent out to an external IP, helping trace what was stolen and when.
Insider threat	Monitors unauthorized file transfers within the network, providing evidence if an employee tries to leak confidential information.
Adversary-in-the-middle (AiTM) attack	Reveals unusual ARP traffic or forged certificates, indicating interception attempts on secure communications.

***Table 7.4**: Scenarios in which live packet capture can be done*

Note:

- **Compatibility: Linux**
- **License considerations: Free software used**

Recipe

In this recipe, let us capture live traffic using Wireshark. We will capture HTTP traffic when a website is visited.

Note: **In this recipe, we will use a non-secure demo site using HTTP. One notable site is http://www.testfire.net/, a test site from HCL AppScan, a well-known vulnerability scanner. While the login details are mentioned in this recipe for this test site, you can also get it from this site in case they change the username and password in the future.**

Follow the following procedure to capture traffic using Wireshark:

1. When you first open Wireshark, you will see various capture filters in the opening screen. These capture filters can be used to capture traffic for specific network interfaces. The first thing you may notice is that the `eth0` and `any` interfaces show a graph. This may look like the following figure:

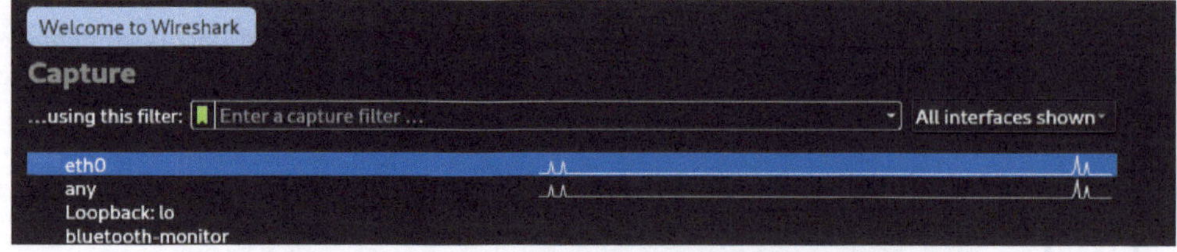

***Figure 7.2**: Network interfaces with network activity shown*

   You see this as Wireshark constantly senses the traffic, even if it is not capturing it. You will see this becoming active in case you perform a network activity, e.g., running the commands like ping or traceroute, or even opening a website in your browser.

2. Let us start capturing the packet on our test site. You can either right-click on an interface and then click on **Start Capture**, or click on the shark fin icon on the top left.

Perform the following activities:

a. Open the site **http://www.testfire.net/**

b. Once there, click on **Online Banking Login**.

c. In the login dialog, use **Username**: **`jsmith`**, and **Password**: **`Demo1234`**.

d. Stop capturing.

Your screen will look like the following:

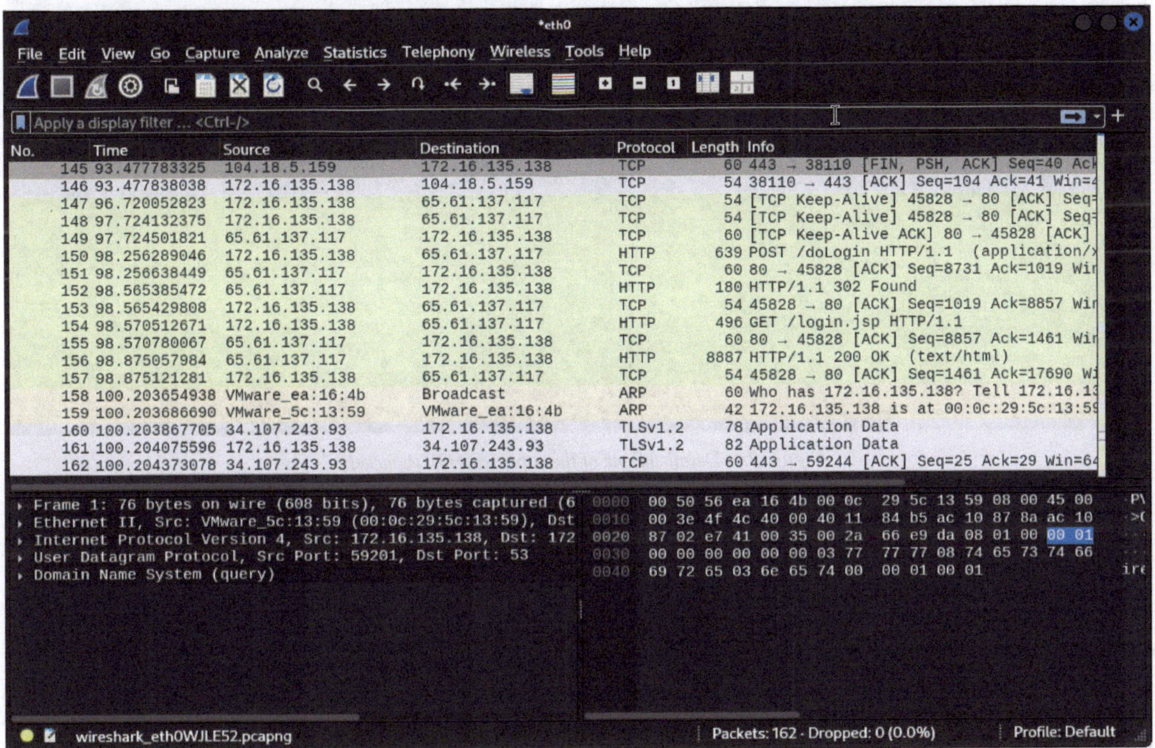

Figure 7.3: Wireshark screen with packets captured

3. Analyze various details on this screen and look at the details of a few packets. The lower half of the screen is divided into two parts: the left part shows the packet details, in this case, an HTTP packet. The right part shows the hexadecimal or hex representation of the packet's content and its text representation. Your screen may look like the following once you select a captured packet:

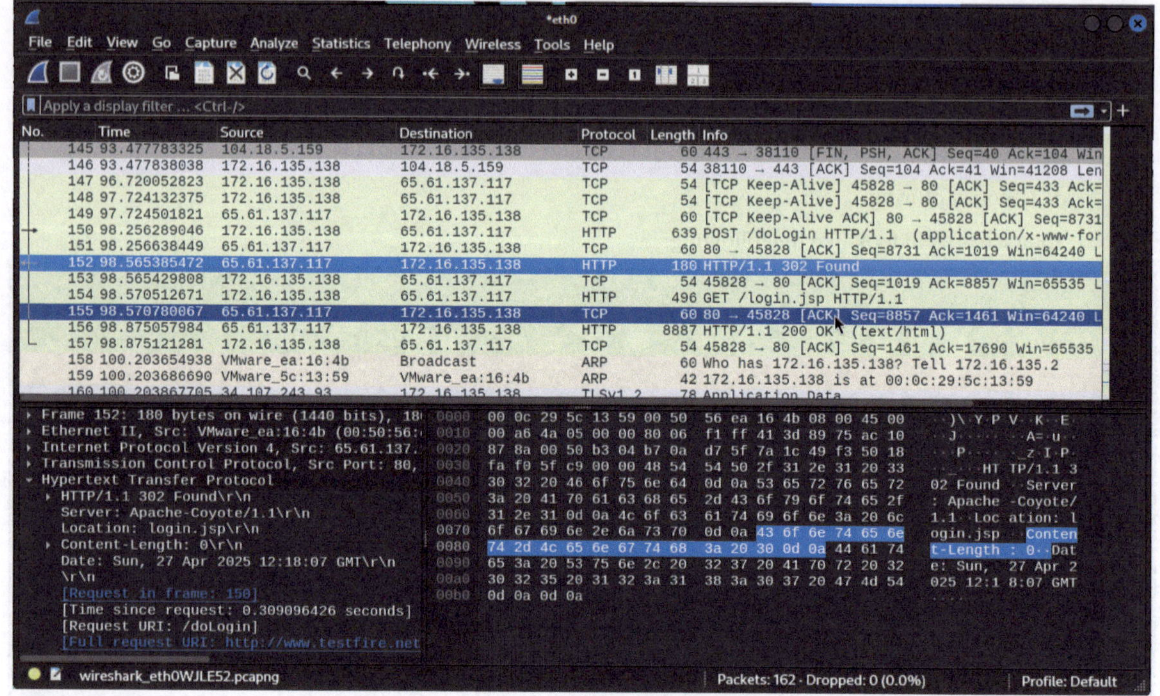

Figure 7.4: Details of one of the captured HTTP packets.

4. Let us save this network packet capture as a **.PCAP** file. This offline file can then be used for later analysis. You can save the capture by clicking on **File | Save As**, and selecting PCAP file (second option in the type).

Activity

Attempt the following activities before the next recipe:

- While you are on the opening screen of Wireshark, launch the Firefox browser inside Kali Linux. Explain why you see network activity, even though you have not opened any website.
- While you are on the opening screen of Wireshark, open any website in your browser. Observe and note down the activity show for your active network interface. Repeat the same by performing a ping to an external IP address.
- Try capturing packets while pointing your browser to a secure site (with HTTPS). Observe if you are still able to see the login and password details. Explain why is it so.
- The **File | Save** or **File | Save As**, both show PCAPNG as the default option. Read more about the **PCAP Next Generation** (**PCAP NG**) file type and understand how it is different from the PCAP file.
- Read about various other types in which the network packet capture can be saved.
- Analyze how Wireshark can capture all the packets flowing on the network, not only the packets destined for the specific/current host. Further understand how the promiscuous mode of packet capture is used to achieve this.

Recipe 65: Performing network traffic analysis using Wireshark

We saw in the last recipe how to capture HTTP traffic. Let us dive deep into analyzing what we captured in this recipe. A simple capture like this uses multiple protocols and we can analyze them step-by-step to understand the sequence of events that happened while trying to log in to a website.

Note:

- **Compatibility: Linux**
- **License considerations: Free software used**

Recipe

Let us examine the first set of packets in this network capture. If you scroll up in the list of packets, your screen may look like the following: The bottom pane has been pushed down to give more space to the packet list. Also, the size of the text font is reduced by pressing *Ctrl* -(control key and minus key). If you want to increase the font size later, you can use *Ctrl* +.

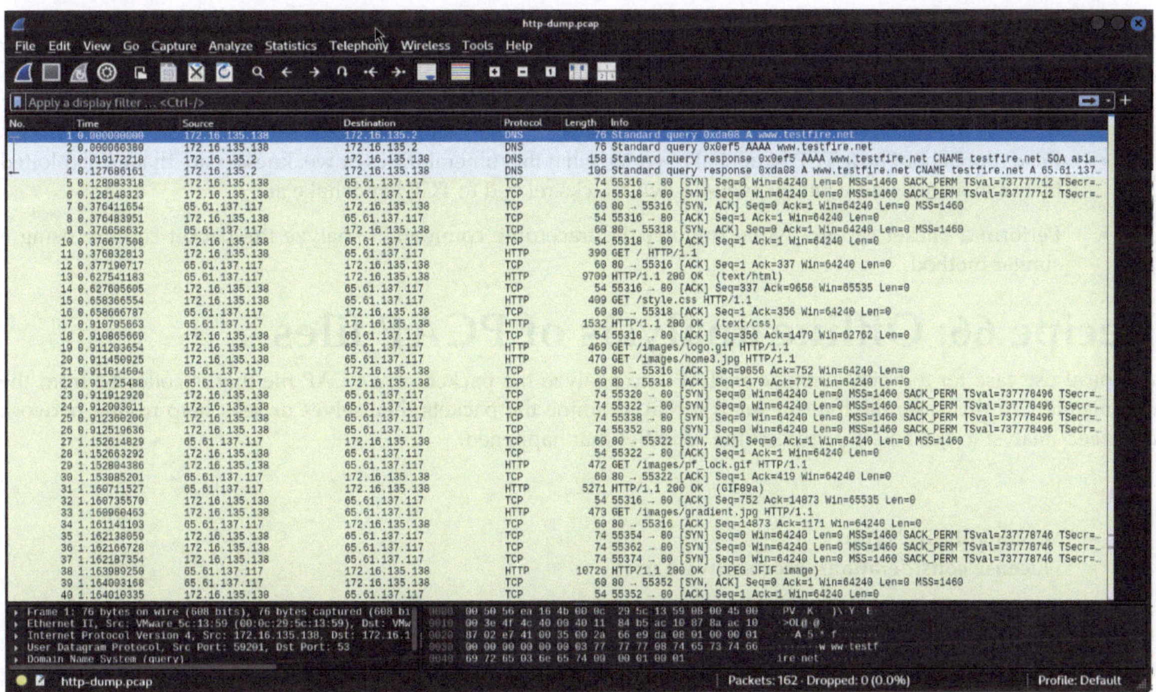

Figure 7.5: The first screen of the list of captured packets

You can see the following network activities from this packet capture:

- First, the browser performs a DNS query to query for an A record for the website. A stands for alias and is used to discover the IP address of the website domain, as per the DNS configuration of the website's domain.
- The browser gets the query response along with CNAME records.

- After that, a TCP connection is established using the default handshake mechanism. First, the browser sends a SYN request. This is followed by a SYN ACK response, and then the browser sends an ACK to acknowledge it. SYN stands for Synchronize, and ACK stands for Acknowledgement.
- Once the TCP connection is established, the browser sends a GET HTTP/1.1 request to fetch the web page and its various assets from the web server. These assets may include the HTML page, embedded images, JavaScript files, and others.
- The GET request is followed by an ACK from the destination server. A similar acknowledgement is sent after receiving a packet. Since TCP is a connection-oriented protocol, every request is acknowledged and may be retransmitted if a packet is not received, followed by the acknowledgement.
- After this, you can see various assets being fetched from the web server, e.g., `images/logo.gif`, `images/home3.jpg`, etc.
- This continues until the webpage is fully loaded.

It is very evident how important such packet captures are for understanding network activities. In case of digital forensic analysis of a cybercrime or a cyber incident, such packet captures are extremely useful resources and provide the accurate picture of network activity during the time of capture.

Activity

Attempt the following activities before the next recipe:

- Find out the importance CNAME plays for a domain.
- Read more about how TCP handshake works, what its vulnerabilities or weaknesses are that are exploited by threat actors, and what the well-known attacks related to TCP handshake are.
- Perform a packet capture while running the traceroute command. Analyze the packet capture using a similar method.

Recipe 66: Offline analysis of PCAP files

A typical use case for a digital forensic analyst is to analyze the packets in a PCAP file that is collected from the organization. In this case, the forensic analyst may examine the packets themselves or seek help from a network engineer/analyst to get a clear picture of the activities that happened.

Note:

- **Compatibility: Linux**
- **License considerations: Free software used**

Recipe

Let us open the saved PCAP and analyze it to check if we can figure out what was sent during the login activity.

Follow the following procedure to capture traffic using Wireshark:

1. First, load the PCAP file that you saved before by **File | Open**, and then select the PCAP file in your directory.
2. Now, perform a filter on all the packets captured to show only HTTP packets. You can do that by typing `http` in the filter bar and pressing *Enter*. Wireshark screen will show the filtered HTTP packets only, which is shown as follows:

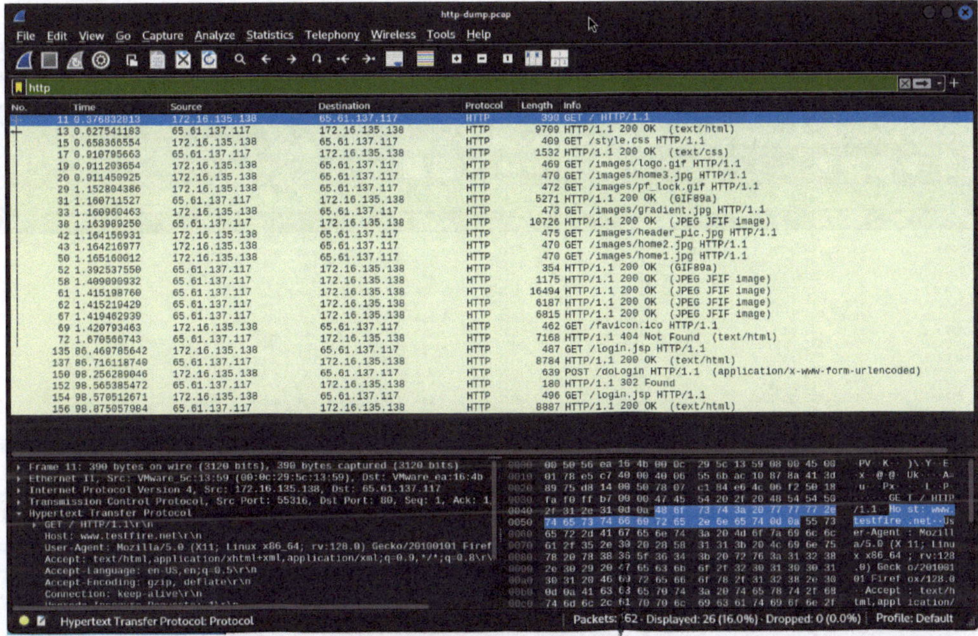

Figure 7.6: Packet capture filtered on

If you observe closely, it only shows the HTTP packets and not the entire conversation. Another way to filter it to show the entire conversation is by using the filter **`tcp.port==80`**.

3. Now, scroll down to the packet that shows **`POST /doLogin HTTP/1.1`** as follows:

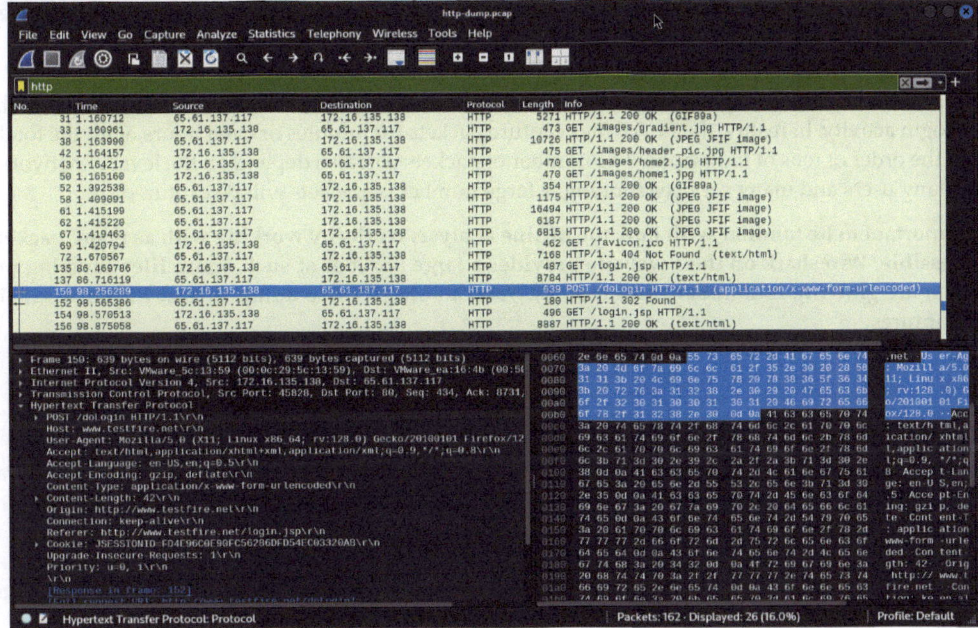

Figure 7.7: Packet with POST details for the login

4. Inspect the HTTP packet on in the bottom left window. The **Hypertext Transfer Protocol** section shows all the details about the HTTP packet including its various header information. If you scroll further down, you will see a section for the HTML form, that has the user ID and password of the login details we use:

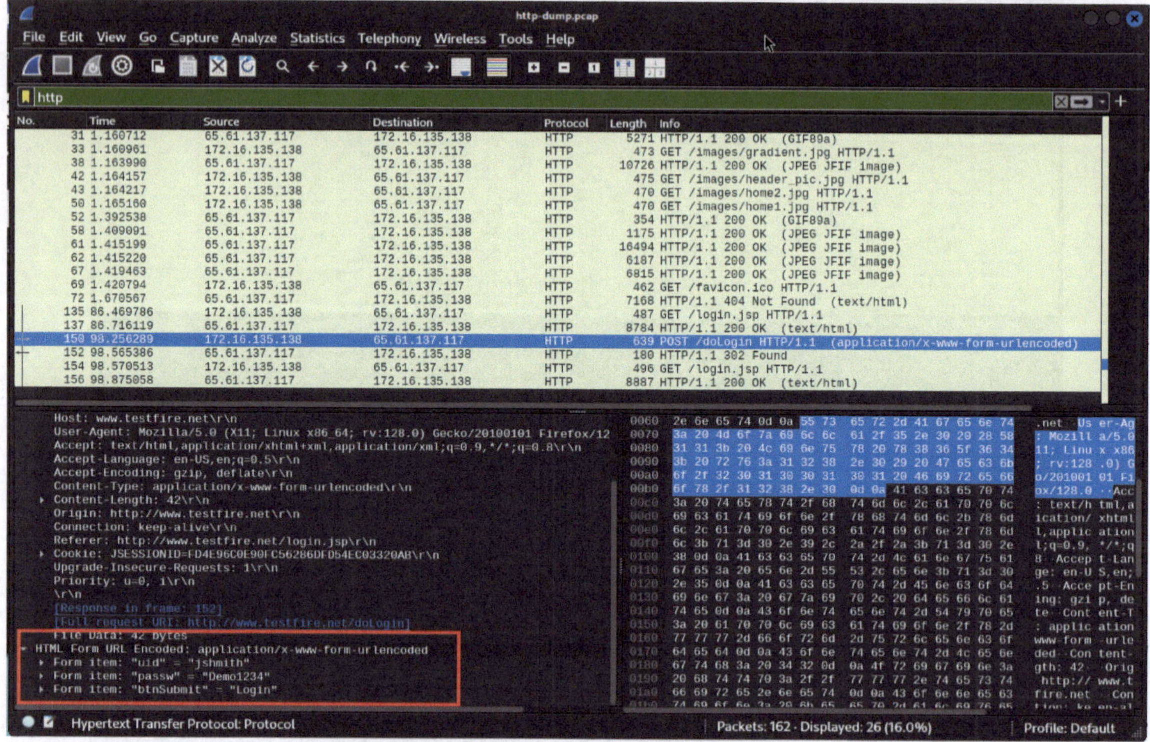

Figure 7.8: HTML Form section showing the submitted HTML form with user details

In this example, we captured only a small number of packets for a specific scenario, i.e., opening a website and performing login activity. In reality, the PCAP files capture packets for minutes or even hours, with the total number of packets in the order of tens of thousands. The number of packets will also depend on the level of network activity. If there are many users and many services running, a large number of packets will be captured.

Note: It is important to be familiar with how the offline analysis works by working with as many packet capture dumps as possible. Wireshark on their website provides a large number of such dump files covering numerous scenarios, that are growing in number continuously. You can access these dump files at https://wiki.wireshark.org/samplecaptures.

Activity

Attempt the following activities before the next recipe:

- You can automate the analysis of such PCAP files using Python. Read more about the Python libraries that can help you write very simple Python programs to perform various types of analysis.
- Try filtering the packets for DNS queries and analyze the rationale behind all the DNS queries.
- Analyze how can a digital forensic investigation can break and read the packets that are encrypted using TLS protocol.

Understanding voice forensics

Voice forensic is an important area of digital forensics that deals with the process of analyzing recorded or intercepted voice communications. This can be used to identify speakers, detect tampering and manipulations, and reconstruct conversations. This is an important process for extracting intelligence, e.g., in investigations, criminal cases, and cybercrime. Hence, voice forensics deals with and aids in the investigation of not just digital forensic cases but also conventional forensic cases.

Voice over IP or VoIP is widely used by organizations to make calls over the Internet and internal networks. Since all these packets are flowing through the network, they can also be captured along with other packets. Hence, phone calls using VoIP can be used to capture live voice data.

While voice forensic is not just about using Wireshark to capture and analyze data, Wireshark is one of the key tools used in such use cases, nevertheless. Wireshark can capture VoIP traffic [like **Session Initiation Protocol** (**SIP**) and **Real-Time Transport** (**RTP**) protocol] and carry live voice data over networks.

Note: SIP is used for creating and maintaining the VoIP session. RTP is used to deliver audio and video over IP networks in real time during a VoIP call. Hence, with the help of SIP and RTP, you cannot only carry out voice calls but also video calls and conferencing. A typical contact center uses a large number of VoIP features for functionality like call transfer, call recording, conferencing, audio playback, etc. Another protocol real-time control protocol (RTCP) works alongside RTP to provide out-of-band control, delivering statistics, quality feedback, and synchronization between media streams, and helps monitor and manage real-time audio/video transmission quality.

Wireshark can help in the following use cases in voice forensics:

Use case	Details
Capture VoIP calls	Wireshark captures SIP signaling and RTP streams which include actual voice packets.
Reconstruct audio	You can extract and play back RTP streams directly inside Wireshark or save them as audio files (`.au`/ `.wav`) for detailed analysis.
Analyze call metadata	Investigators can review caller/ callee IPs, call duration, codecs used, and call timing for evidence.
Detect VoIP fraud	Identifies unauthorized or suspicious VoIP calls, toll fraud, and spoofed call setup attempts.

Table 7.5: *Use of Wireshark in voice forensics*

Note: One of the things worth mentioning here is that only unencrypted voice can be captured. In real world audio is encrypted using scheme like forward error correction (FEC) to protect privacy. FEC itself is not an encryption method but a technique to add redundancy to data so errors can be detected and corrected during transmission. When combined with encryption, FEC ensures both privacy (via encryption) and reliability (via error correction), protecting sensitive data from interception while maintaining integrity over unreliable channels. However, if the digital forensic experts can break the encryption of the voice capture, it becomes easy to analyze it using Wireshark and other similar tools.

Tip: Having a good knowledge of Python can help you excel in voice forensics as it is extremely easy to analyze PCAP files using well-known Python libraries. This can help you getting an edge over others in the field of digital forensics.

Recipe 67: Performing voice forensics using Wireshark

Let us say we need to analyze using a voice sample for a suspicious VoIP call where the caller used social engineering techniques to get confidential details from the victim. If we get the packet capture for this conversation, we can easily do that. Such social engineering techniques are common attack vectors before a big cyberattack is carried out. Digital forensic analysts extensively use voice forensics in such cases to find definitive clues.

Note:

- **Compatibility: Linux**
- **License considerations: Free software used**

Recipe

Let us see how can be analyze a packet capture that has captured VoIP that happened in the past over the network.

Follow the following procedure to capture traffic using Wireshark:

1. First, we need a sample VoIP call packet capture dump. You can get one from **https://wiki.wireshark.org/VoIP_calls**. The same site also has a detailed description of how VoIP calls can be analyzed using Wireshark.
2. Once you have downloaded the PCAP file (e.g. `SIPCALLRTPG711.pcap`), load the file in Wireshark. You will be able to see the list of packets that were captured, shown in the following figure:

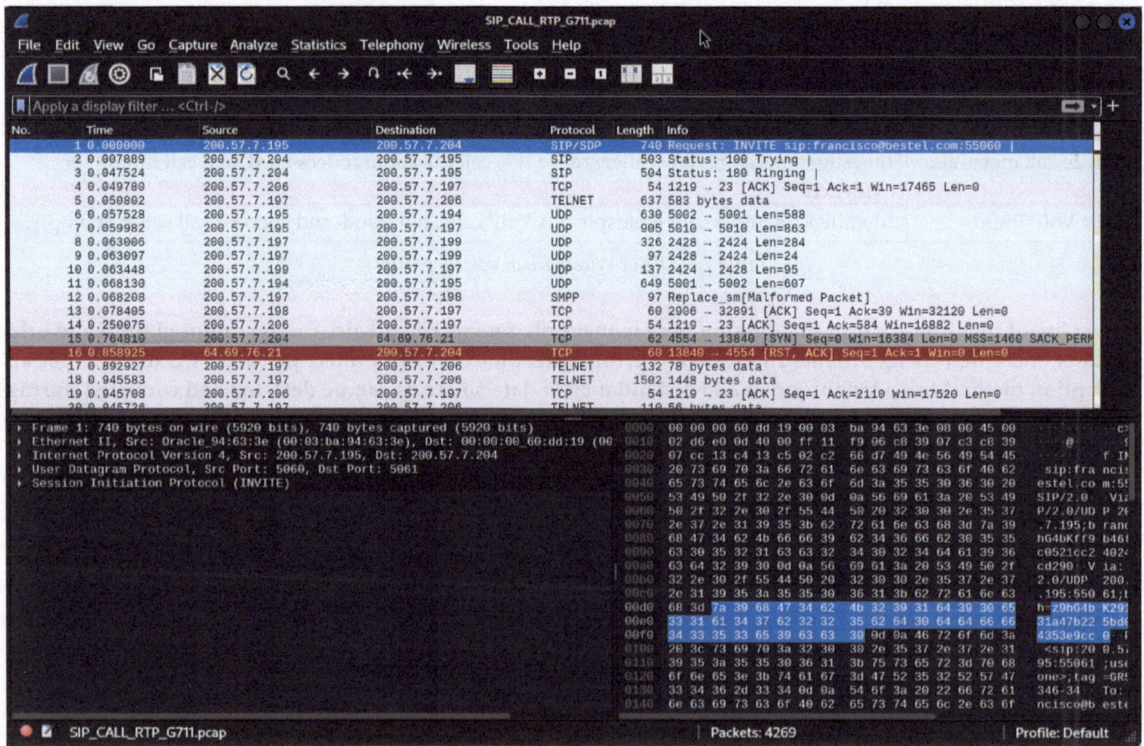

Figure 7.9: Loaded packet capture showing VoIP call packets

You can also try filtering on SIP to look at only SIP packets:

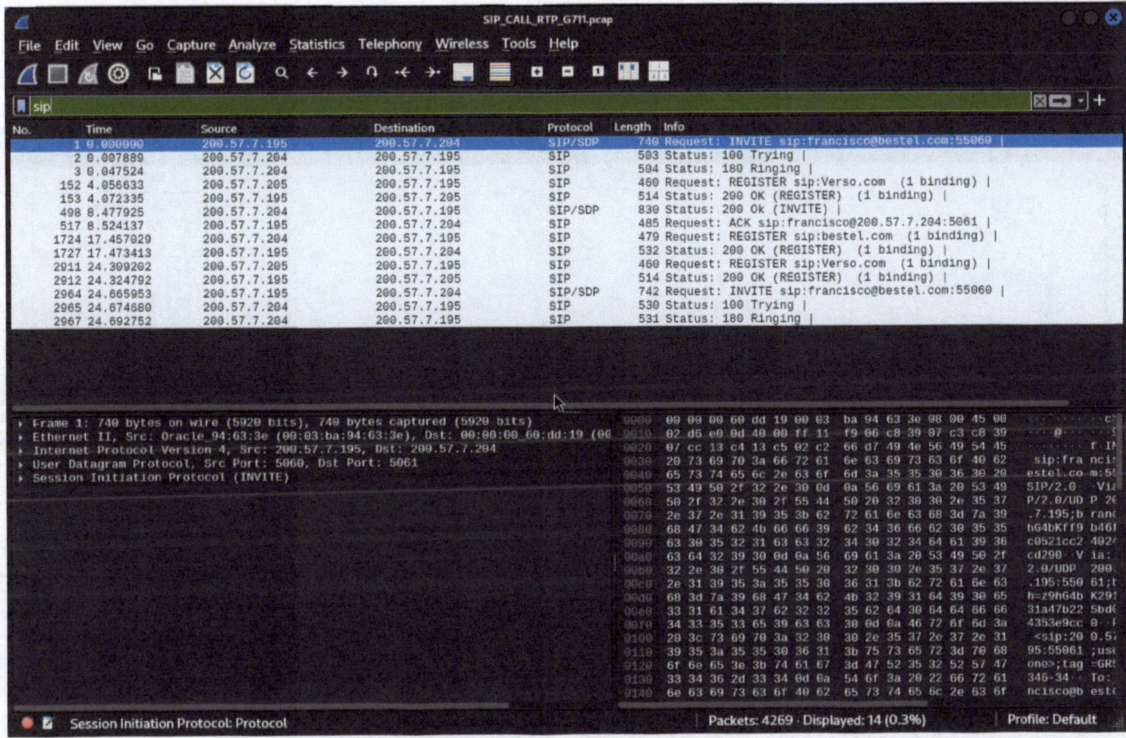

***Figure 7.10**: List of packets filtered on SIP*

3. In order to see if the packet capture, we are working with has any VoIP calls captured, click on **Telephony** | **VoIP Calls**. If your packet capture has VoIP calls or you are using a sample file from the above-mentioned website, you will see a screen similar to the following:

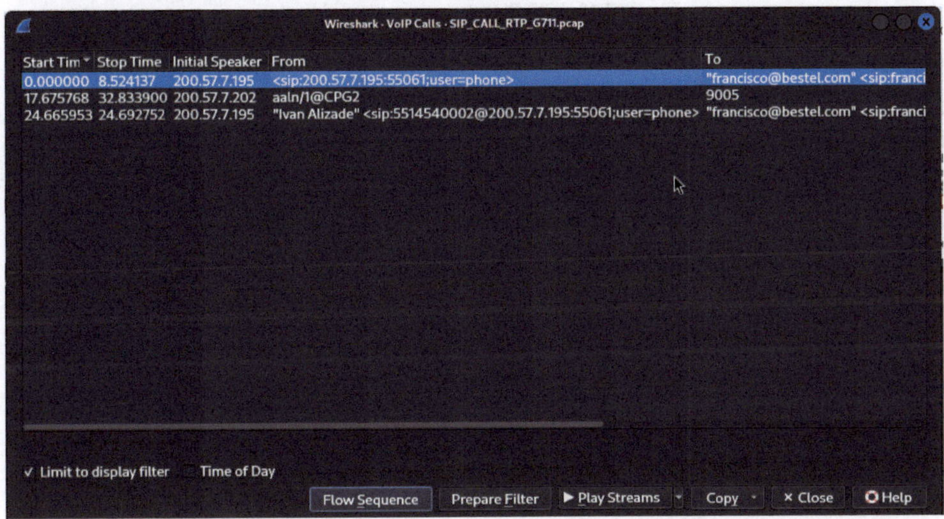

***Figure 7.11**: List of VoIP Calls discovered in the packet capture*

Note: Remove any filter from the main window before you look at the voice calls. Otherwise, you may not see all the packets related to RTP, which carries the actual media data, in this case, voice.

4. Click on the first call and then click on **Play Streams** to play the voice clip associated with this call. You will see an **RTP Player** screen like the following that shows the entire voice stream:

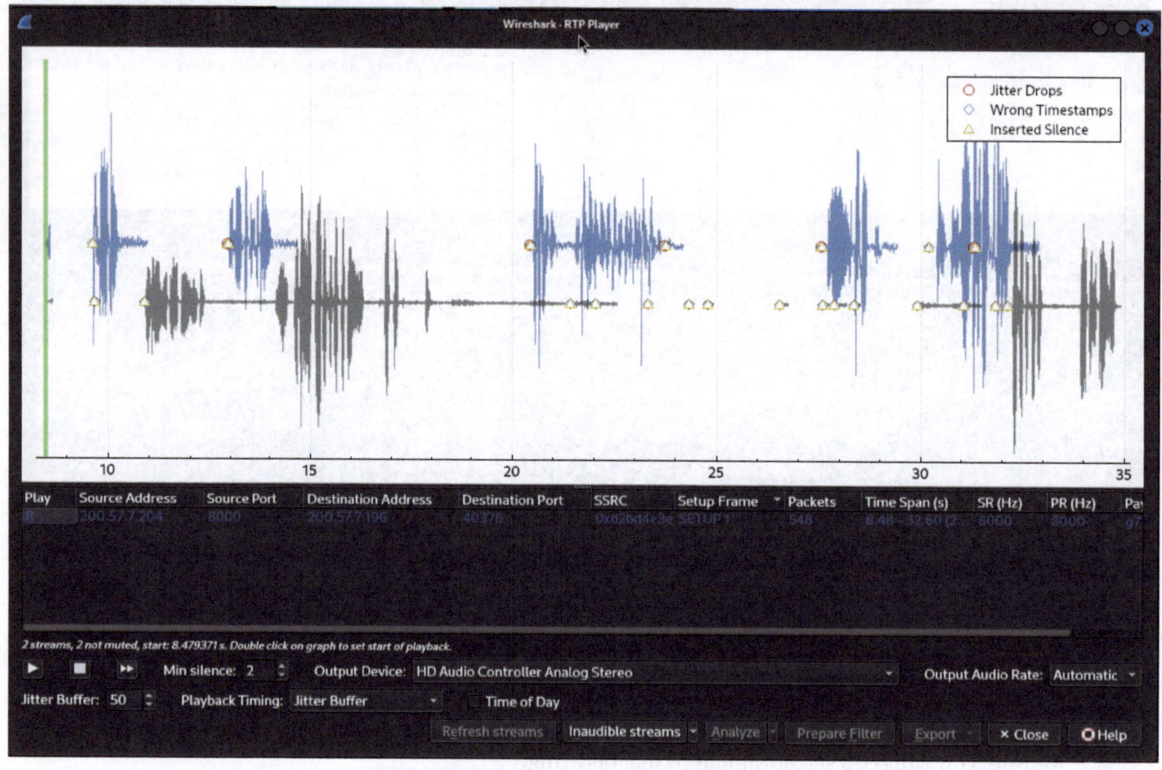

Figure 7.12: RTP Player showing the voice clip

You can even play it by click on the **Play** button in the bottom left of this player.

5. Not only that, but you can also analyze the entire SIP and RTP call flow to understand how the whole conversation took place. You can do that by clicking on the **Flow Sequence** button on the dialog shown in *Figure 7.11*. It will show a call flow like the following, which is extremely useful to analyze calls during a digital forensics investigation:

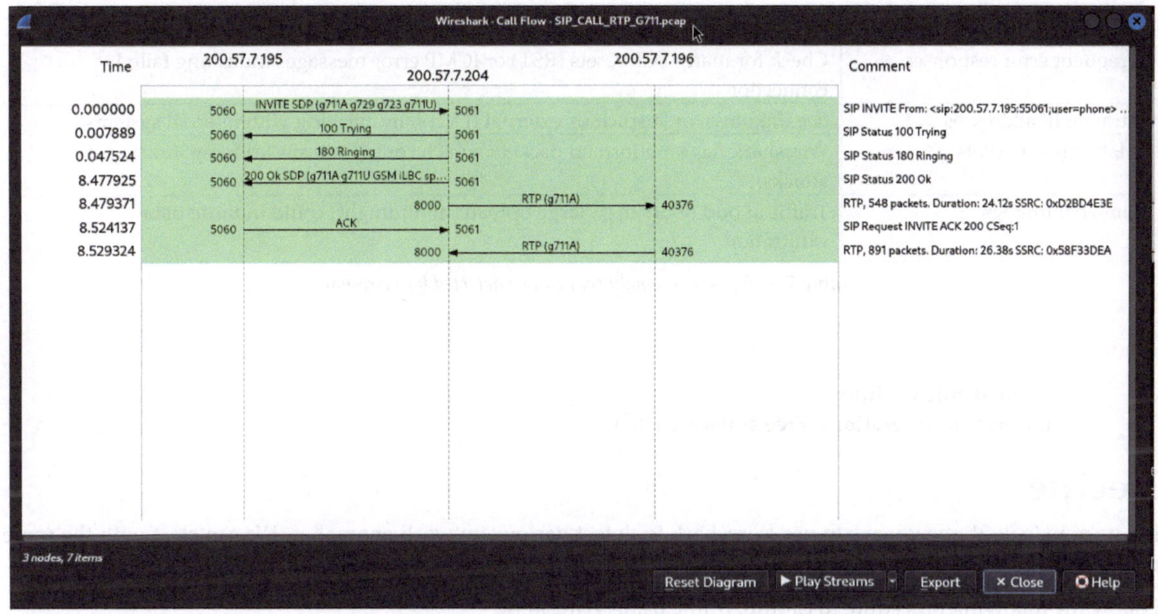

Figure 7.13: *Call flow showing SIP and RTP communication*

By now you may have already understood the power of Wireshark in voice forensics. Having an expert knowledge of Wireshark can help you carry out or aid in the overall digital forensic analysis.

Activity

Attempt the following activities before the next recipe:

- Try to make a voice call over the Internet and capture the packet using Wireshark. After that, check if you can listen to your voice call.
- Check the flow sequence for all the other conversations and figure out the differences between then in terms of call flow.
- Copy one of the call flows as YAML and paste it into a text editor. Analyze the details about the call flow as per the SIP standard. Read more about SIP to understand various directives used in the call flow.
- Find out if there is a way to export the conversation as a sound file and then analyze it using Python.

Recipe 68: Identifying anomalies by monitoring network activities

In Wireshark, we can monitor anomalies by capturing live traffic and looking for unusual patterns that differ from normal network behavior. We can achieve the same using a PCAP file in an offline mode.

We can spot many anomalies in this way. A few of them are as follows:

Anomaly type	Detection of anomaly using Wireshark
High traffic volume	Look for a sudden spike in packets or large data transfers from a single IP.
Unusual protocol or ports	Notice unexpected protocols (e.g., Telnet, FTP) or weird port numbers being used.

Anomaly type	Detection of anomaly using Wireshark
Frequent error responses	Check for many TCP resets (RST) or ICMP error messages indicating failed connections.
Strange IP addresses	See unknown or suspicious external IPs communicating with internal systems.
Malformed packets	Wireshark flags malformed packets, which could indicate scanning, fuzzing, or attacks.
Unusual timings	Traffic at odd hours (e.g., large uploads at midnight) could indicate data exfiltration.

Table 7.6: *Types of anomaly that can be detected by Wireshark*

Note:

- **Compatibility: Linux**
- **License considerations: Free software used**

Recipe

Let us now look at a few ways to use Wireshark to detect various network anomalies. We can start with the same packet capture we used for HTTP traffic to an insecure site, i.e., **http://www.testfire.net/**.

Follow the following procedure to capture traffic using Wireshark:

1. Load the PCAP file using **File | Open** as you have done before.
2. Once the PCAP file is loaded, go to **Statistics | Protocol Hierarchy**. This can show us which protocol is the most dominant portion in all the packets, as shown in the following figure:

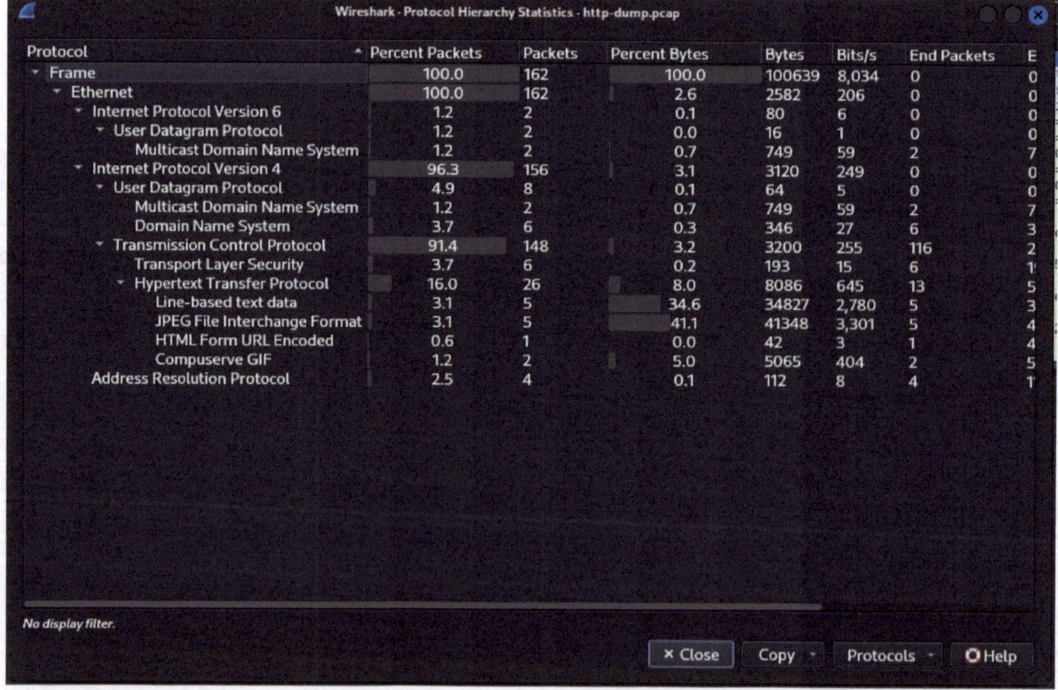

Figure 7.14: *Protocol hierarchy showing the most dominant protocol in the packet capture*

3. Next, let us look at **Statistics | Conversations** to find the top talkers, i.e., which IP address is sending and receiving the most packets. The screen will look something like the following figure:

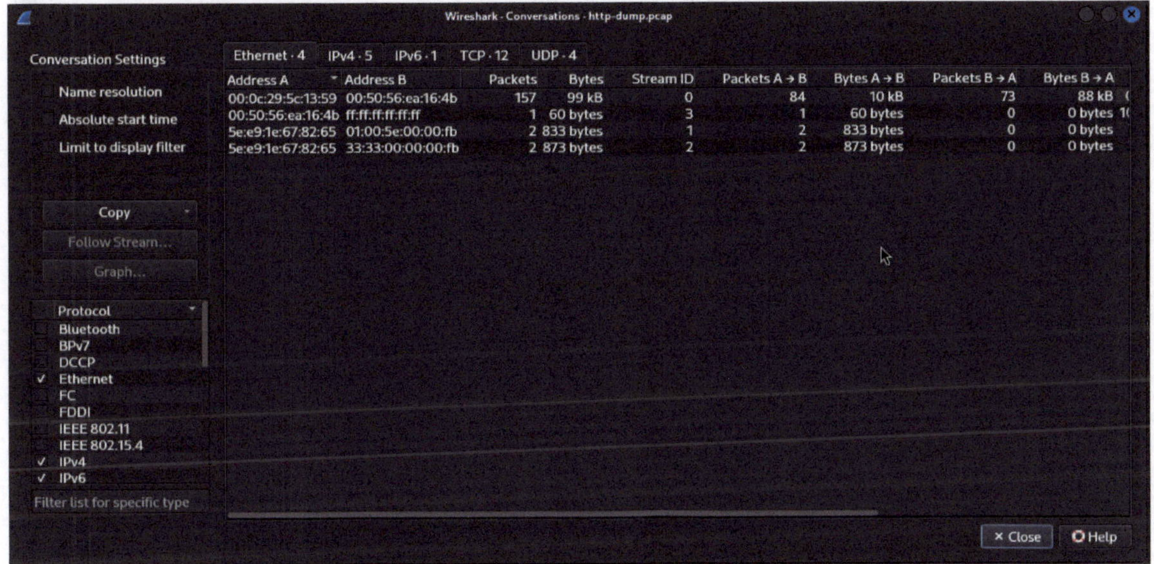

Figure 7.15: *Conversation showing the most active IP addresses*

This feature is very useful for quickly identifying IP addresses that may be talking to malicious IP addresses in a C2 model. Additionally, it can be used to quickly get protocol-level breakups of the most active IP addresses.

As you can see in this screen, we can also analyze conversations in which wireless protocols, including the protocols like Bluetooth, ZigBee, and Wi-Fi (IEEE 802.11), used in **Internet of Things** (**IoT**) devices. While these protocols may also be used in other wireless devices too, they are good place to start with if you want to analyze IoT device communication.

> Note: **This technique can be used to perform behavior analysis of an infected system in an isolated/sandboxed environment. While all the outbound packets to the C2 server will end up failing, it will immediately give details of what the malware is trying to do.**

4. We have seen flow graphs while analyzing voice packets. The same but even detailed flow graphs can be seen for all the packets under **Statistics | Flow Graph**:

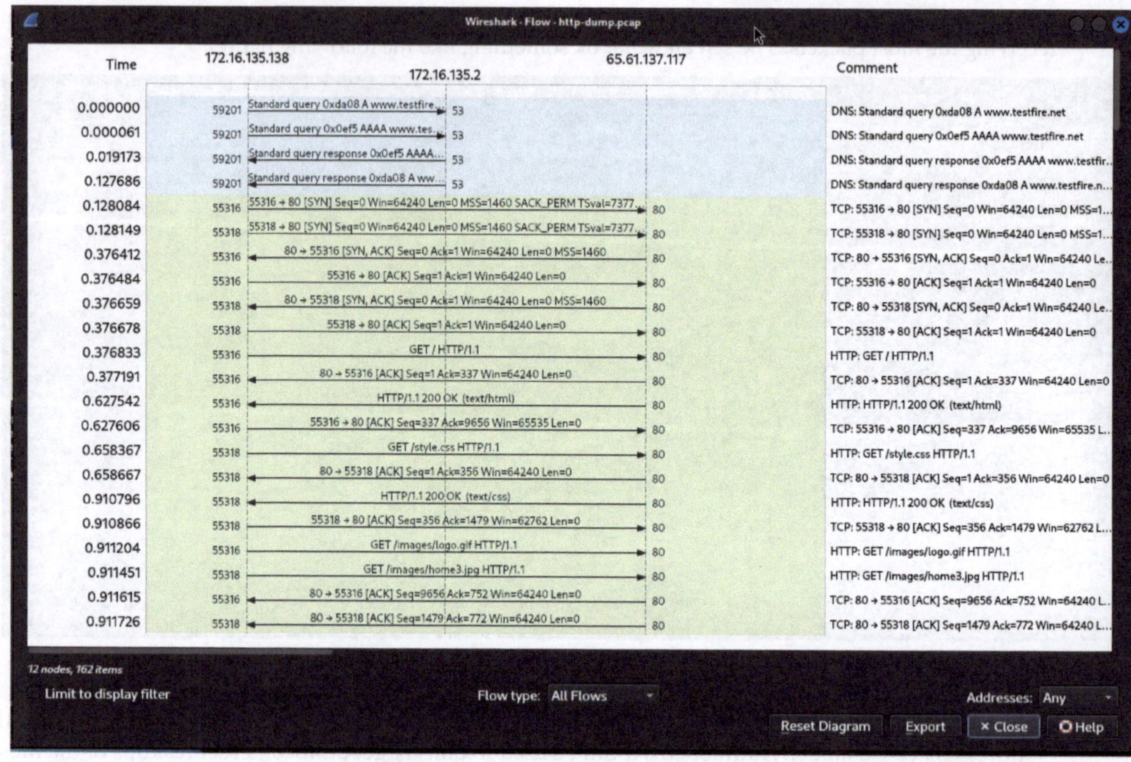

Figure 7.16: Flow graph of all the protocols

This gives a bird's eye view of the flow between various IP addresses and the protocol communication used, as is a great tool for detailed behavior analysis.

Activity

Attempt the following activities before the next recipe:

- Load the PCAP file we used for voice forensics and analyze the protocol hierarchy.
- Look at the entire flow graph and analyze the information it provides.
- Filter the flow graph on only TCP Flows and analyze how the TCP packets are flowing between various hosts.
- Read the Wireshark document to understand how can you cleverly used filters to identify anomalies like retransmissions, resets, duplicate ACKs, etc.

Understanding security information and event management

Security information and event management (**SIEM**) systems are security solutions that collect, aggregate, analyze, and correlate security event data from across an organization's IT environment, such as firewalls, servers, applications, endpoints, etc. Such a SIEM system can help provide real-time monitoring, threat detection, incident response support, and centralized log storage.

Notes: A few noteworthy examples of SIEM systems are Splunk, IBM QRadar, ArcSight, and Microsoft Sentinel. Wazuh is an open-source and extensible SIEM that is also very popular.

Use cases of SIEM in digital forensics

There are numerous use cases of SIEM in digital forensics. The following table summarizes a few of them:

Use case	Details
Incident reconstruction	Helps piece together the timeline and sequence of an attack from collected logs and alerts.
User activity monitoring	Tracks suspicious or unauthorized activities by insiders or external attackers.
Threat hunting	Supports proactive search for hidden threats using historical event data.
Root cause analysis	Helps find how a breach started (e.g., phishing email, exploited vulnerability).
Compliance and audit trails	Provides evidence for legal investigations and compliance reporting (e.g., GDPR, HIPAA).
Detection of lateral movement	Reveals if attackers are moving inside the network after initial breach.
Alert correlation	Correlates multiple smaller events into a bigger security incident (e.g., multiple failed logins as brute force attack).

Table 7.7: *Use cases of SIEM in digital forensics*

When a digital forensic analyst looks at these logs, they may need to focus on specific things while collecting evidence. Let us look at a few of them in the following table:

Evidence type	Details the analyst focuses on
Authentication logs	Successful and failed login attempts, especially from suspicious locations or times.
Access logs	Files accessed, modified, deleted especially sensitive data.
Network traffic logs	Unusual outbound traffic, command-and-control communication, data exfiltration attempts.
Endpoint alerts	Malware detections, file integrity violations, suspicious processes.
Correlated alerts	SIEM-generated incidents that combine multiple related events into one alert.
Timestamps	Accurate times of activities to build a forensic timeline.
User behavior anomalies	Deviations from normal user behavior (e.g., accessing servers they normally do not).
Changes in system configuration	Unauthorized changes to firewall rules, accounts, privileges, etc.
Threat intelligence matches	IPs, URLs, file hashes matching known threat indicators.
Persistence mechanisms	Evidence of malware setting up backdoors or autorun entries for **advance persistent threats (APTs)**.

Table 7.8: *Types of evidence digital analyst can understand with SIEM*

Note: As a corollary, all the above logs should be sent to a SIEM system so that we already have these as evidence in case of a cybercrime or cyber incident.

Sample use cases

Let us look at two scenarios that show how SIEM systems can be used for digital forensic analysis:

Scenario	Investigation
The SIEM alert shows: • 10 failed logins. • Followed by 1 successful login. • Then, a file download of 500MB to an external IP.	The forensic analyst would immediately investigate the login logs, data movement logs, network connection logs, and user session details to collect evidence of possible credential theft and data exfiltration. The logs may also show that a brute force or password guessing attempt was made.
The SIEM system generates an alert about multiple file encryption activities happening unusually fast across several machines.	This can indicate a ransomware attack in progress. The SIEM helps the forensic analyst reconstruct how the ransomware entered the system, how it spread, what files were impacted, what systems were involved, and whether any data was stolen. In such scenarios, digital forensic analysts would look for the following: • **File integrity logs**: Large numbers of file modifications in a short period (e.g., original files replaced with encrypted versions). • **Authentication logs**: If the ransomware spread using compromised admin credentials (e.g., lateral movement). • **Network traffic logs**: If connections to suspicious external IP addresses (e.g., contacting the attacker's command server) were made. • **Alert correlation**: If there were earlier small alerts (e.g., phishing email, malicious download) that triggered the chain of events. • **Persistence**: If ransomware tried to install startup entries, scheduled tasks, or backdoors.

Table 7.9: Scenarios related to digital forensic analysis with SIEM

SIEM-based digital forensic flow

A generalized SIEM-based digital forensic investigation flow will look something like the following:

Step	Signal and action
SIEM alert	• Ransomware behavior detected. • High volume of file modifications. • Suspicious process started on multiple machines.
Investigation	• Check login/authentication logs. • Analyze file system changes. • Review network traffic (external IPs, data transfer). • Correlate events from different sources (email, endpoints, servers).

Step	Signal and action
Evidence collection	• Timeline of infection and spread. • Malicious executable file hashes. • IP addresses contacted. • List of encrypted or modified files. • User accounts involved. • Persistence mechanisms created.

Table 7.10: An example of SIEM-based digital forensic flow

Note: If you want to try the entire flow of how SIEM works, even if you do not have a SIEM system, you can simulate it by various means. One of the simplest ways is to send logs to a syslog destination as discussed in Chapter 5, Digital Forensics for Linux System. You can also use free tools like SolarWinds Kiwi Log Viewer to watch syslog-based logs in real time in your test setup.

Creating logs for a SIEM system

Since SIEM systems are centralized systems receiving logs from a multitude of heterogeneous systems, there are various considerations when creating logs for SIEM systems. A few important ones are given in the following table:

Logging considerations	Details
Standardized format	Ensures SIEM can easily parse and understand events across different and heterogeneous systems. Moreover, this also ensures that minimal customizations are required to parse new logs.
Timestamp accuracy	Correct and synchronized timestamps (preferably UTC) are crucial for forensic timelines. Incorrect timestamps and drifts in timestamp may cause timeline inaccuracies as well as inability to correlate the logs.
Sufficient details	Logs need to capture source IPs, user IDs, actions performed, result status (success/failure), etc. These are important fields that are used by SIEM systems for filtering and creating reports.
Event categorization	Events need to be labeled properly, e.g., authentication event, file access event, network connection, etc. Such labels can be used by SIEM systems for categorization and easy filtering.
Minimal noise	Logging everything blindly needs to be avoided, and focus should be on meaningful events to reduce alert fatigue, which can cause one to miss important alerts. Log levels can be used to control the verbosity of logs.
Integrity and authenticity	This may apply at both the source (the system generating logs) and the destination (the SIEM system). Logs should be tamper-proof or digitally signed to ensure forensic reliability.
Scalability	Logging must not choke systems under heavy load, and hence efficient event handling is essential. This is an important aspect to capture the logs while a cyberattack is in progress, as during such times, the logs generated may be many times more than the normal working scenarios.

Table 7.11: Logging considerations for SIEM systems

Creating standardized logs can be done using two of the most common formats - syslog and CEF.

The most-used format is syslog format that is used by general logging from devices and system. Even applications can easily send logs in this format either by manually formatting it or by using a standard logging library.

An example syslog log is as follows:

```
<34>Oct 11 22:14:15 webserver sshd[12345]: Failed password for invalid user admin from 192.0.2.4
port 55874
```

Another commonly used format is **Common Event Format** (**CEF**). It has a much a better structure, hence can be used when you need well-structured security event logs that are easier for SIEM to analyze and correlate. CEF is a standardized, structured log format used by SIEM systems like ArcSight and Azure Sentinel and is designed for SIEM systems.

Example CEF log:

```
CEF:0/WebServer/SSH Service/1.0/100/Failed SSH Login/5/src=192.0.2.4 suser=admin dhost=webserver
msg=Failed password attempt
```

Knowledge of Syslog and CEF format helps a digital forensic professional in sending the logs in the standard format to SIEM systems, as well as collecting evidence that can again be analyzed by standard tools. Both of them are important for digital forensic evidence collection readiness for enterprises.

Recipe 69: Checking wireless configuration changes

There are many attacks that focus wireless networks and its components like access points, wireless controllers, etc. Hence, checking for changes in wireless configuration helps detect attacks like Rogue AP deployment, Evil Twin attacks, unauthorized Wi-Fi networks, or configuration tampering.

Note:

- **Compatibility**: **Linux**
- **License considerations**: **Free software used**

Recipe

Let us download the **Wireless LAN** (**WLAN**) sample capture file form **https://wiki.wireshark.org/Wi-Fi**, e.g., `NetworkJoinNokiaMobile.pcap`, and try to analyze various wireless packets.

Now, let us filter the WLAN packets using a special filter `wlan.fc.typesubtype == 0x08`. The screen will look something like the following, and shows Beacon frames - advertisements from APs:

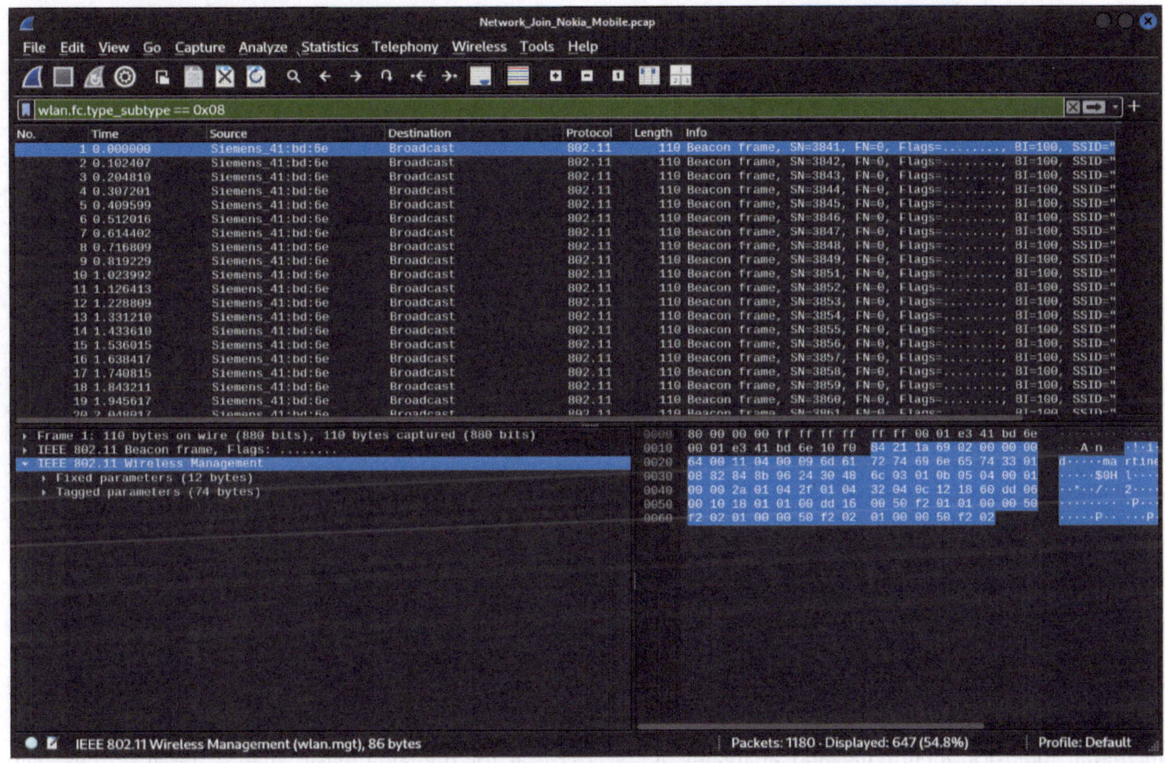

Figure 7.17: Filtered WLAN packets showing broadcast traffic

In this list of packets, one or more of the following indicate the presence of a threat:

- New of spoofed SSIDs.
- Changes in encryption, e.g., WPA2 to open.
- Different AP MAC addresses claiming to be your network (Evil Twin).

Let us say your corporate SSID is SecureNet, normally broadcasting with WPA2. Suddenly, Wireshark captures another SecureNet SSID without encryption or with a different BSSID. This could indicate a Rogue Access Point trying to lure users.

This type of information can be used by digital forensic analyst to understand if a threat actor tried to join a new rogue **access point** (**AP**) in the network and then used it as an attack vector to carry out further attacks.

Note: **There are many other ways in which wireless configuration changes can be identified. For example, logs for new AP joins, security setting changes, unexpected Beacon frames (new APs) or suspicious EAPOL frames (authentication), all can indicate malicious activities.**

Activity

Attempt the following activities before the next recipe:

- Look at other values under the **`wlan`** filter and see what else these filters can tell us about the wireless configuration changes.

- Analyze why it is not advisable to connect to open access points while on the go or while in a public place like train station or airport.

Understanding indicators of compromise from network logs

IOCs are pieces of evidence that suggest a system, network, or organization may have been attacked or breached. They act like clues or fingerprints left behind by an attacker during or after a cyberattack.

Importance of indicators of compromise in digital forensics

IOCs help security teams and forensic analysts detect suspicious activities, investigate incidents, and respond to threats more effectively. These indicators can take many forms, such as unusual IP addresses, strange domain names, unexpected file hashes, abnormal login attempts, new or unauthorized software installations, or large amounts of data being sent out of the network. Essentially, anything that stands out from normal behavior and hints at malicious activity can be considered an IOC.

For example, if a company's firewall log shows that an internal system is suddenly communicating with a blacklisted IP address in a different country, that connection could be an IOC suggesting that the system is compromised. Similarly, if antivirus software detects a known malware file signature on a server, the file hash of that malware would also be an IOC. In practice, IOCs are collected from different sources like network logs, system logs, memory dumps, or endpoint security tools. Analysts then use these indicators to detect ongoing attacks, trace back to the point of entry, and take steps to contain and eliminate the threat.

In digital forensics, identifying and analyzing IOCs is crucial for digital forensic analyst, because they help reconstruct what happened during an attack, understand the attacker's methods, and strengthen defenses against future incidents. Without paying attention to IOCs, it would be much harder to detect stealthy attacks that do not cause obvious disruptions but silently steal data or maintain unauthorized access.

Sample example to illustrate IOCs

Imagine a company's network security team notices something odd, their SIEM system reports that a server inside their network made a connection to an unknown IP address located overseas at 2:30 AM, a time when no one is supposed to be working. The analyst checks the network logs and finds the IP address is not part of any approved vendor list. This suspicious outbound connection is identified as an IOC.

Curious, the analyst digs deeper. They use Wireshark to review the network packet captures and see that the server first made a DNS query for a very strange domain name like qwertyxy12malware.com, and then, immediately, connected to the IP address found earlier. This looks highly abnormal because legitimate business software usually talks to well-known domains, not random ones. By checking the internal logs, the analyst also discovers that just before this connection, a user account had downloaded a suspicious executable file attached to a phishing email.

From that single IOC (the odd network connection), the forensic team pieces together a much bigger story:

- A user clicked on a malicious email link.
- Malware was downloaded and executed.
- The malware connected to the attacker's server to receive further instructions.

Since the IOC was caught early, the company isolates the infected server, blocks the malicious IP and domain, resets compromised credentials, and prevents a major data breach. This shows how even one IOC, like a suspicious IP or strange domain lookup, can trigger a full forensic investigation and help prevent serious damage.

Attack chain for an IOC

Let us look at the attack chain in chronological order for the previous IOC. It may look like the following:

1. Phishing email received.
2. User clicks malicious link.
3. Malware downloaded and installed.
4. Malware makes DNS query for strange domain.
5. Malware connects to attacker's C2 server.
6. SIEM detects suspicious outbound IP connection (IOC).
7. Forensic investigation triggered.
8. Server isolated, malware Removed, and credentials Reset.

This simple timeline shows how a small initial event (an odd IP connection as an IOC) uncovered the entire attack chain, allowing the forensic team to act quickly and contain the threat. A single suspicious outbound connection acted as the first clue, helping us trace the entire attack chain from phishing email to malware infection and ultimately stop the breach.

Every IOC may be dealt with in a similar fashion by the incident response team and then by digital forensic analysts.

Network security best practices

In a large enterprise, network security must be built not just to prevent attacks, but also to detect, contain, and investigate them. This requires a layered defense approach combining strong access controls, continuous monitoring, intelligent segmentation, and detailed logging. Every system must be configured with forensic readiness in mind, ensuring evidence is collected accurately and legally. Ultimately, a secure enterprise is one where prevention, detection, response, and forensic analysis work seamlessly together to protect the organization's assets and reputation.

Let us look at the most important best practices for any enterprise. These best practices can be thought of in terms of making a large enterprise secure as well as the making the enterprise ready for digital forensic evidence collection in case of a cyberattack or a cyber incident.

The following table lists the best practices for enterprises, along with forensic readiness:

Best practice	Details
Network segmentation	Dividing the network into isolated segments based on business functions limits lateral movement during breaches and makes forensic containment easier by isolating affected zones.
Strict access control	Techniques like least privilege access, using RBAC and MFA ensure forensic teams can quickly identify who accessed what and when, without ambiguity.
Centralized logging	Aggregating logs from firewalls, routers, servers, and endpoints into a SIEM system for centralized logging enables faster forensic investigations and maintains a complete, tamper-evident audit trail.
Secure configuration management	The practice of hardening devices and enforcing secure baseline configurations, and ensuring well-documented and monitored configurations, helps detect unauthorized configuration changes.
Implementation of IDS and IPS	IDSs/IPSs are specialized security products that detect and block malicious activities. Alerts from these systems provide early forensic evidence of attack vectors and timelines, which can again be sent to SIEM systems for centralized management and actions.

Best practice	Details
Traffic monitoring and traffic capture	Continuously monitoring and selectively capturing network traffic, especially on critical segments, becomes crucial forensic evidence during incident investigations. Detailed traffic capturing can also be done when a suspicious activity is detected in the network.
Threat intelligence integration	Incorporating threat intelligence feeds into network monitoring and enriching forensic analysis with external indicators (e.g., malicious IPs, hashes) improves incident response speed and accuracy.
DNS monitoring and control	Monitoring and restricting DNS traffic to prevent C2 communication and data exfiltration are important aspects of network security. DNS logs and anomalies serve as early forensic indicators of compromise.
Encryption of data in transit	Using TLS/SSL for all internal and external communications with proper encryption ensures that intercepted packets during forensic investigations are useless to attackers but meaningful to defenders with proper keys.
Regular vulnerability assessment and management	As a default practice, various network assets should be continuously scanned, patched, and prioritized for vulnerabilities. Historical vulnerability data aids forensic teams in understanding how an attacker might have exploited weaknesses.
Incident response plan with forensic procedures	Maintaining a detailed incident response plan that includes forensic evidence collection, preservation, and chain-of-custody handling ensures evidence is admissible in legal proceedings if needed.
Secure remote access	If many people connect from remote locations, implementing secure, logged remote access solutions like a VPN should be the priority. Remote access logs are critical for tracing breaches that might originate from outside the enterprise network, as many attack vectors originate from weak security policies while working remotely.
Data loss prevention (**DLP**) systems	Monitoring and controlling sensitive data leaving the network using DLP logs and events helps forensic analysts identify if intellectual property or sensitive records were exfiltrated.
Time synchronization using NTP	Synchronizing all systems and network devices to a trusted **Network Time Protocol** (**NTP**) server, as well as accurate timestamps, are essential for constructing forensic timelines during incident investigations.
Employee security awareness training	People are the weakest link in cybersecurity. Hence, staff need to be regularly trained on phishing, social engineering, and secure practices. A well-informed workforce reduces attack surfaces and provides early reporting that assists forensic readiness.

***Table 7.12**: Lists the best practices for enterprises for network forensics*

It is needless to say that collection of forensic evidence on an ongoing basis and when there is a suspicious activity in the network is important for forensic readiness. These practices are so essential that implementing even a subset of them to start with provides a much better security and forensic readiness than not having any at all.

Web application forensics and log analysis

We have seen in *Chapter 3, General Digital Forensics Techniques,* how to acquire various forensic evidence from browser. While performing digital forensics for network, web application forensics go hand-in-hand to understand the end-to-end flow of events. After all, network is what enables such web applications. Let us look at a few other general perspective related to web application forensics and how log analysis can help.

Web application forensics and network forensics

Web application forensics focuses on investigating attacks or compromises targeting web-based systems (like websites, APIs, portals, cloud applications). Network forensics focuses on capturing, analyzing, and reconstructing network traffic to detect and understand security incidents.

In real-world incidents, both must work together because:

- Web applications are accessed over a network (HTTP/S traffic, APIs).
- Network logs capture important evidence of web attacks, such as:
  - o Malicious HTTP requests.
  - o SQL injection attempts.
  - o Credential stuffing attacks.
  - o File uploads of malicious payloads.
  - o Web shell communications.
  - o Brute force attempts.

Thus, network log analysis using firewall logs, packet captures, proxy logs, load balancer logs, etc., provides critical support to web application forensics.

Note: **While we have not looked at firewall and IDS/IPS logs in this chapter, they are essential for digital forensic analysis and should be collected on a regular basis and while collecting digital forensic evidence.**

Network log analysis strengthens web application forensics

Let us look at a few ways network log analysis can help web application forensics:

Use case	Real-world example
Identify the source of attack	A web server log shows SQL errors. Firewall logs reveal that all suspicious traffic originated from IP 203.0.113.45, helping attribute the attack.
Detect web application exploits	Proxy logs capture unusual POST `/admin/upload.php` requests followed by `.php` file uploads as indicating a web shell being installed through vulnerable upload functionality.
Timeline reconstruction	PCAP files show the attacker scanning the web server, exploiting a file inclusion vulnerability, and uploading malware, all in a 10-minute window.
Credential abuse detection	Network logs show hundreds of failed login attempts to /login endpoint with different usernames and passwords from the same IP — classic brute force behavior.
Data exfiltration detection	Network packet captures reveal large HTTP POSTs containing base64 encoded customer records being sent from a compromised application to an external IP.
Spotting malware C2 channels	A malicious web shell installed through the app uses hidden HTTP traffic to communicate with the attacker. Network traffic analysis uncovers periodic, unusual requests to `/shell.php`.
Validation of forensic artifacts	If the web app logs are tampered with by the attacker, network logs can independently validate when and how requests were made to the server.

Table 7.13: *How network log analysis helps web application forensics*

Now, let us look at some real-life examples:

- **SQL injection attack investigation**: A major e-commerce site detects database errors. Analyzing Web server logs show abnormal queries like:

  ```
  /products?id=1;DROP TABLE users–
  ```

  Forensic investigation includes:

  - Network firewall logs reveal that all such requests came from a small range of IPs in a specific country.
  - PCAPs confirm that the attacker retrieved database schema details over HTTP responses.
  - Using network evidence, the forensics team reconstructs exactly what data was exposed, when, and who initiated it.

- **Web shell deployment and command injection over HTTP**: A corporate HR portal that is inaccessible from outside the corporate network is compromised.

  Forensic investigation includes:

  - Web server logs show a POST to **`/upload.php`** followed by access to a new file **`/uploads/cmd.php`**.
  - Network proxy logs captured HTTP commands being sent to **`/uploads/cmd.php?cmd=whoami`**, showing remote command execution, and command injection.
  - Packet analysis proves that the attacker maintained access for two weeks without triggering antivirus alerts.
  - Based on network forensics, the enterprise initiates incident response, removes the shell, and patches the vulnerable upload endpoint.

Conclusion

In network forensics, capturing and analyzing network activities plays a vital role in detecting and responding to cybersecurity incidents. Networks act as highways for attacks, and forensic readiness ensures organizations can reconstruct events accurately. Tools like Wireshark allow live traffic captures, protocol analysis, voice forensics, and anomaly detection. SIEM systems further enhance forensic capability by correlating logs across the enterprise. Understanding **indicators of compromise** (**IOCs**) and monitoring web applications and wireless activities also helps uncover threats proactively. Through layered security practices and comprehensive log collection, organizations can strengthen both security and forensic investigation readiness, ensuring that digital evidence is available, accurate, and usable in responding to incidents or legal actions.

In the next chapter, we will understand in detail working with processes, memory and storage.

Questions

1. What types of evidence can be collected from enterprise networks for forensic analysis?
2. What are PCAP files, and why are they important in digital forensics?
3. How can NetFlow logs be useful in network forensic investigations?
4. What is the role of Wireshark in digital network forensics?
5. How does live packet capture help during an active cyberattack?
6. What can you reconstruct by analyzing TCP streams in Wireshark?
7. What is voice forensics and how is it related to network forensics?

8. What are SIP and RTP protocols in the context of **Voice over IP (VoIP)**?
9. How can Wireshark be used to reconstruct and play a captured VoIP call?
10. What kind of anomalies can Wireshark detect during packet analysis?
11. What is the purpose of a SIEM system in cybersecurity and digital forensics?
12. How do authentication logs collected in a SIEM help during investigations?
13. What is the importance of standardized log formats like Syslog and CEF?
14. How can network logs help detect web application attacks?
15. What is an IOC?
16. How can strange DNS queries indicate possible malware infections?
17. Why is centralized logging important in an enterprise network?
18. What are examples of attacks that can be identified through wireless configuration changes?
19. How can time synchronization (NTP) impact forensic investigations?
20. What best practices make a network environment more forensic ready?

Points to remember

1. Networks are critical sources of forensic evidence during cybersecurity investigations.
2. PCAPs allow reconstruction of entire network sessions.
3. NetFlow and IPFIX provide summarized traffic metadata useful for timeline analysis.
4. Wireshark is a versatile tool for live capture and offline packet analysis.
5. TCP stream reconstruction helps understand full conversations and data flows.
6. Voice forensics relies heavily on capturing and analyzing SIP and RTP traffic.
7. Anomalous behaviors such as high data transfer, strange protocols, and malformed packets indicate compromise.
8. SIEM systems collect and correlate logs across network, endpoints, and applications.
9. Authentication, access, and traffic logs are crucial for reconstructing attack timelines.
10. Syslog and CEF formats standardize logs for easier ingestion and analysis by SIEM.
11. IOCs help detect and investigate hidden attacks.
12. DNS traffic analysis can uncover covert communication with malicious domains.
13. Wireless networks require careful forensic monitoring to detect rogue devices or Evil Twin attacks.
14. Secure remote access and segmented network architecture improve security and forensics.
15. Encryption in transit protects sensitive data but may limit packet-level forensic visibility.
16. File integrity monitoring is vital to detect ransomware or other tampering activities.
17. Regular vulnerability scanning aids in proactive breach prevention and forensic readiness.
18. Web application attacks often leave traces both in app logs and network traffic.

19. Time synchronization across devices is critical for coherent forensic timelines.
20. Employee awareness and strong incident response plans strengthen enterprise forensic readiness.

Key terms

1. **PCAP**: Packet capture file that stores captured network traffic for later analysis.
2. **Wireshark**: A network protocol analyzer tool used for live network capture and offline traffic analysis.
3. **NetFlow/IPFIX**: Network flow data formats that summarize communication metadata (such as source/destination IPs, ports, and byte counts) between hosts.
4. **VoIP**: Voice over Internet Protocol, a technology that delivers voice communications and multimedia sessions over IP networks.
5. **SIP**: Used to initiate, maintain, and terminate VoIP calls and multimedia sessions.
6. **RTP**: Carries audio and video streams over IP networks during real-time communication.
7. **SIEM** system collects, aggregates, and analyzes security logs from multiple sources for threat detection and forensics.
8. **Syslog**: A standardized message format used primarily by network devices and Unix/Linux systems for logging system and network events.
9. **CEF**: A structured, SIEM-friendly log format that helps standardize security event reporting across different devices and vendors.
10. **IOC**: Indicator of compromise, a piece of evidence or an artifact that indicates a system may have been breached or is under attack.
11. **Command and control (C2)**: A communication channel established between a compromised system and an attacker's remote server to maintain control over the infected machine.
12. **DNS**: A service that translates human-readable domain names into IP addresses.
13. **Firewall logs**: Records generated by firewall devices showing allowed, denied, or suspicious network traffic.
14. **DHCP lease logs**: Records that map device MAC addresses to assigned IP addresses at a given time, useful for tying an IP address to a specific device.
15. **Authentication logs**: Logs that record successful and failed login attempts, including information about usernames, timestamps, and access locations.
16. **Proxy logs**: Logs generated by proxy servers that capture users' web browsing activities, including URLs visited and request metadata.
17. **Network segmentation**: A security practice of dividing a network into smaller, isolated segments to contain breaches and improve traffic control and monitoring.
18. **DLP**: A set of technologies and policies that detect and prevent unauthorized transmission of sensitive data outside an organization.
19. **NTP**: A protocol used to synchronize the clocks of computers and network devices to a standard time source.

CHAPTER 8
Memory Forensics

Introduction

Analyzing processes and memory content are important aspects of analyzing a live system. They can provide a wealth of insights about the system's state at the time of acquisition, including open files, open network connections, a list of running processes, loaded Registry hives, and more. These tasks are an integral part of memory forensics and reverse engineering processes that digital forensics examiners undertake after acquiring the memory.

In this chapter, we will cover various techniques for working with volatile memory, or **random access memory (RAM)**, and analyzing it from multiple perspectives.

Structure

In this chapter, we will cover the following topics:

- Importance of process and memory acquisition
- About reverse engineering
- IOC and IOA
- Behavior analysis
- Recipe 70: Dumping memory using WinPmem
- Well-known digital forensics image formats
- Recipe 71: Dumping memory using FTK Imager
- Recipe 72: Analyzing acquired memory using Volatility
- Recipe 73: Collecting details about running processes
- Understanding process trees
- Recipe 74: Collecting process tree information
- Recipe 75: Identifying external IP addresses accessed by processes
- Recipe 76: Getting a list of strings from the memory dump
- Recipe 77: More Volatility plugins
- Recipe 78: Using Bulk Extractor to analyze RAM dumps
- Recipe 79: Collecting details about password hashes using pwdump
- Recipe 80: Extracting forensic data using OSForensics
- Recipe 81: Using sysinternals as a digital forensic toolset

Objectives

In this chapter, we will look at several ways to acquire or dump memory from a live system and then carve out various digital forensics evidence from it using multiple tools. We will also understand various key concepts of working with process and memory that are important for any digital forensics examiner assigned to such tasks.

By the end of this chapter, you should be able to dump volatile memory from a live system and analyze the dump from various angles to understand most aspects of the state of the system at the time of acquisition.

Importance of process and memory acquisition

As part of digital forensics evidence collection, process and memory acquisition is focused on capturing evidence that resides in the system's **random access memory** (**RAM**) and live running processes. Such evidence is volatile in nature and hence must be collected while the system is *live*. Hence, timeliness is of great importance.

The following table summarizes the importance of process and memory acquisition:

Acquisition task	Details
Preservation of volatile evidence	Data in memory is lost once the system is powered off. Memory acquisition allows forensic investigators to capture crucial, real-time information before it is gone.
Understanding attacker behavior	Active malware, rootkits, and remote access tools often reside in memory without leaving persistent files. Memory captures allow detection and analysis of these in-memory artifacts.
Correlation with disk forensics	Memory data can help correlate and validate disk-based artifacts, timeline events, or log files.
Live forensics capability	Enables forensics without shutting down the system, which may be critical in enterprise environments where uptime is essential.

***Table 8.1**: Process and memory acquisition tasks*

Note: The system, once powered off, is no longer considered a live system even after it is powered on later. The reason is that all the processes, memory allocation, network connections, and many other such evidence are gone or completely altered after a reboot or a power-off operation.

During the process of memory acquisition, much evidence can be collected. The most important ones are listed as follows:

Evidence type	Details
Running processes	Active programs, including hidden or malicious processes provide system state at the time of collection.
Network connections and sockets	Open ports, established connections, and remote IPs. Useful for identifying **command and control** (**C2**) communication.
Loaded modules/DLLs	Helps identify injected code or malicious libraries used by malware.
Command-line arguments	Shows how a process was executed (e.g., with suspicious flags or scripts). When this is collected along with process trees, it can be immensely useful as evidence.
Environment variables	Can contain paths, session tokens, or credentials.
Decrypted content in memory	Including in-memory plaintext credentials, encrypted files, or payloads.
Clipboard contents	Often contains copied credentials or sensitive text.
Registry hives and handles	Registry keys loaded in memory, often used by malware.
User credentials/hashes	Extracted from **local security authority subsystem service** (**LSASS**) on Windows or similar memory segments.

Evidence type	Details
Encryption keys	In-memory keys for disk/file encryption (e.g., BitLocker, ransomware payloads).
Injected code/shellcode	Evidence of process hollowing or code injection techniques.
Malware configurations	Often only available in memory, such as hardcoded IPs, domains, or triggers.
Swap files	A subset of memory that is swapped to the disk and can contain sensitive information.

Table 8.2: Evidence collected during process and memory acquisition

About reverse engineering

Reverse engineering is a process in digital forensics that refers to the analytical process of deconstructing software, binaries, or data structures to understand their inner workings. This is done without access to the original source code or documentation. In the context of processes, memory, and storage, it allows forensic analysts to uncover the behavior, intent, and structure of potentially malicious or unknown components residing in the system.

Hence, reverse engineering is particularly useful when dealing with the following:

Digital forensic task	Example goals
Malware analysis	Figuring out how a malicious process behaves.
Memory dump examination	Locating injected shellcode or stolen credentials.
Encrypted or obfuscated data	Uncovering hidden payloads or bypassing anti-forensics.

Table 8.3: Applications of reverse engineering in digital forensics

Reverse engineering is a vast area focusing on multiple goals as part of digital forensics analysis. Let us look at a few of them as follows:

Type of reverse engineering	Context	Purpose	Example use case
Static binary analysis	Storage (executables, **dynamic link libraries or DLLs**)	Understand code logic without executing.	Disassemble malware executable with IDA Pro to trace hardcoded IPs.
Dynamic analysis/runtime analysis	Memory/Processes	Observe actual behavior in a sandboxed or monitored environment.	Execute ransomware in a VM to watch file encryption patterns.
Memory analysis	RAM/Volatile memory	Identify injected code, stolen credentials, or unlinked modules.	Use Volatility to detect reflective DLL injection.
Process reverse engineering	Running processes	Understand parent-child relationships using process trees, command-line args, and loaded modules.	Reverse engineer a suspicious process showing beaconing behavior.
Data structure analysis	Files/Storage	Understand custom or proprietary data formats.	Decode a proprietary log file or encrypted SQLite blob.
Firmware or embedded device reverse engineering	Storage (IoT/OT)	Analyze firmware dumps for hidden code or hardcoded credentials in IoT and **operational technology (OT)** devices.	Dump router firmware and reverse engineer for backdoors.

Type of reverse engineering	Context	Purpose	Example use case
Malware configuration extraction	Storage/Memory	Reveal C2 URLs, campaign IDs, or botnet group info.	Extract C2 server from memory dump of botnet malware.
Encrypted payload analysis	Memory/Storage	Decrypt payloads using keys found in RAM or reverse crypto implementation.	Extract AES keys from memory to decrypt a ransomware-encrypted file.

***Table 8.4**: Types of reverse engineering*

Reverse engineering techniques like swap file analysis can also be used while analyzing processes and memory.

Let us look at a real-world example of how a digital forensics investigator may use reverse engineering to discover the threats from a suspicious executable of a compromised system:

1. A forensic investigator discovers a suspicious executable on a compromised system.
2. They statically analyze the binary in a tool like Ghidra and identify a heavily obfuscated encryption function.
3. They run the process in a sandbox, capturing memory dumps.
4. Using Volatility, they extract the in-memory decrypted configurations, revealing a list of target domains.
5. The investigator matches this data with known threat intelligence sources and attributes it to a known APT group.

IOC and IOA

While dealing with processes, memory, and storage, digital forensics analysts and investigators are frequently looking for specific indicators. They can be put into two broad groups, **indicator of compromise** (**IOC**) and **indicator of attack** (**IOA**). They are especially useful during the behavior analysis.

An IOC is a forensic artifact or piece of data that suggests a system has been compromised or attacked. These are tangible signs that malicious activity has occurred, and they help security teams detect, respond to, and investigate incidents.

A few examples of IOCs are:

- Known malicious C2 server or attack origin IP address.
- Known malicious domain used for phishing or malware distribution.
- Unique hash of a known malware binary.
- Suspicious executable dropped during compromise in the affected system.
- Presence of specific Windows Registry keys that are known to be used for persistence.
- Fake processes mimicking legitimate ones, either by a similar-sounding name or misspelling.

An **indicator of attack** (**IOA**) is a pattern of behavior or sequence of actions that suggests an attack is in progress or is being attempted. IOAs are focused on intent and method, not just evidence left behind.

A few examples of IOAs are:

- Legitimate tools like PowerShell are being abused for data exfiltration by spawning network connections.
- Office document spawning `cmd.exe` or `powershell.exe`, suggesting a macro-based malware attack.

- Unusual privilege escalation and running admin-only commands.
- Lateral movement behavior, like the use of **Windows Management Instrumentation** (**WMI**) to access other Windows systems.
- Script or binary dropped into a startup folder, suggesting an attempt to establish persistence.

Behavior analysis

Behavior analysis is a sub-discipline of reverse engineering that focuses on observing how a process, binary, or system component behaves when executed, rather than just analyzing its static code. It plays a crucial role in understanding runtime characteristics, identifying malicious intent, and uncovering obfuscation or anti-analysis techniques used by threat actors.

Behavior analysis provides context and runtime visibility in digital forensics, which is essential for detecting stealthy malware, understanding attack lifecycles, and collecting reliable forensic artifacts. When combined with static analysis and memory forensics, it forms a triad of techniques that yield a complete picture of what was done on a compromised system by the threat actors.

There are multiple reasons why behavior analysis is important during digital forensics investigations:

- Reveals actual runtime behavior not visible in static code (e.g., dynamic API resolution, unpacking routines).
- Helps detect evasive malware that only activates under specific triggers or environments.
- Identifies artifacts that get created or modified at runtime (e.g., files dropped, Registry edits).
- Supports attribution and IOC extraction by identifying network calls, C2 patterns, or exploitation techniques.
- Validates findings from static analysis and memory inspection.

This can become clearer with the examples in the following table:

Scenario	Behavior analysis activity	Use in digital forensics
Ransomware execution	Execute in a sandbox to observe file encryption patterns, file extensions used, ransom note creation.	Helps recover partial encryption keys or detect which files were targeted.
Credential stealer	Observe process injecting into lsass. exe (on Windows) or accessing browser storage.	Validates if login credentials or tokens were exfiltrated.
Persistence mechanism discovery	Monitor changes to Registry keys, startup folders, scheduled tasks.	Identifies how malware survives reboots.
Network activity logging	Inspect outbound connections, DNS queries, beacon intervals.	Extract C2 servers, exfiltration paths, and alert security teams.
Unpacking/decryption in memory	Track how packed malware decrypts payloads only in RAM.	Enables full payload recovery for static reverse engineering.
USB-based attack tool	Observe autorun behavior or hidden command execution when plugged in.	Maps how USB device triggers payloads, potentially using BadUSB or HID spoofing.
Time-based triggers or environment checks	Monitor how a sample behaves differently under VM or debugger.	Helps detect anti-forensics or sandbox evasion mechanisms.

Table 8.5: Various scenarios in which behavior analysis is useful

Behavior analysis is very useful during digital forensic investigations in the following ways:

Use case	Benefits of behavior analysis
Post-breach analysis	Understand malware that was memory-resident and left few disk traces.
Incident response	Confirm whether a suspected binary is actually harmful.
Malware family classification	Identify behavior traits linked to specific malware families.
IOC generation	Generate IOC from network, file, or process behaviors.
Legal evidence	Provide behavioral logs and demonstrations of malicious activity in court.

Table 8.6: *Various benefits of behavior analysis*

Acquiring volatile data

Let us look at a detailed view of how each of the volatile data can be acquired in both Windows and Linux.

Volatile data acquisition in Windows can be done as follows for the various data types to be acquired:

Data type	Tool/Utility	Software type	Purpose
Full RAM Dump	RAM Capturer (Belkasoft)	Freeware	Lightweight RAM capture tool.
	Magnet RAM Capture	Freeware	Compatible with many Windows versions, captures memory for analysis.
	Forensic Toolkit (FTK) Imager	Freeware/Commercial	Can capture memory and image drives.
	WinPMEM	Freeware	Part of Rekall toolkit, supports raw and AFF4 formats.
	OSForensics	Commercial	Memory capture and live response features.
Processes	tasklist, Get-Process	Built-in	View running processes (CLI/ PowerShell).
	Process Explorer (Part of Sysinternals suite)	Freeware	Advanced process inspection.
Open files/Handles	handle.exe (Sysinternals)	Freeware	Lists open handles and DLLs.
Network connections	netstat, Get-NetTCPConnection	Built-in	View active connections.
	TCPView (Sysinternals)	Freeware	GUI-based connection monitor.
Command history	doskey/history	Built-in	CLI history (limited to current session).
	PowerShell Get-History	Built-in	PowerShell history (limited).
Registry	reg export, reg query	Built-in	View or export Registry keys.
	Registry Explorer	Freeware	GUI Registry viewer and dump.
Clipboard	clip	Built-in	Basic clipboard management.
	Win32 API scripts	Freeware/Custom	Used to extract clipboard content programmatically.

Table 8.7: *Types of volatile data that can be acquired in Windows*

Let us now look at how volatile data acquisition in Linux can be done for the various data types in the following table:

Data type	Tool/Utility	Software type	Purpose
Full RAM Dump	LiME	Freeware	Kernel module to dump memory to file.
	avml (Microsoft)	Freeware	Memory acquisition for Linux systems.
	fmem	Freeware	Memory acquisition via kernel module (older).
Processes	ps aux, top, htop	Built-in/Freeware	Show running processes.
Open files	lsof	Built-in	List open files and network connections.
Network	netstat, ss, iftop, nethogs	Built-in/Freeware	Network connections and usage.
Loaded modules	lsmod, modinfo	Built-in	List or get info on kernel modules.
Command history	history	Built-in	Bash history per user.
Clipboard	xclip, xsel	Freeware	Clipboard manipulation on X11 systems.
System info	uptime, dmesg, uname, who, w	Built-in	General state and user activity.
Log analysis	journalctl, /var/log/files	Built-in	Review syslog, auth logs, etc.
Custom scripts	bash, Python, Perl	Built-in/Freeware	Scripted collection of volatile artifacts.

***Table 8.8**: Types of volatile data that can be acquired in Linux*

Dumping volatile memory or RAM

Dumping memory and acquiring volatile memory or RAM are synonymous. It is the technique used to capture the memory from a live system (while the system is still powered on after the cybercrime or cyber incident), as the volatile data in the memory disappears after the system is powered off.

Since RAM contains various highly valuable information that cannot be retrieved later from a dead system (after the system is powered off or rebooted) or its storage.

A few important insights that we can get by dumping memory are given in the following table:

Insight	Details
Detection of running malware	Malware often operates entirely in memory to evade disk-based detection. Memory dumps help identify in-memory code injection, fileless malware, and rootkits.
Retrieving encryption keys	Tools like BitLocker, VeraCrypt, and ransomware often store encryption keys in RAM. A memory dump can reveal these keys before the system is shut down.
Analysis of running processes and network connections	Investigators can view active processes, open network connections, loaded DLLs, and process trees to reconstruct attacker activity.
User activity and credentials	Passwords in clear text, clipboard contents, chat logs, and recently accessed documents may reside in RAM.
Digital evidence preservation	RAM provides real-time insight into what was happening at the moment of acquisition, which is invaluable for timeline reconstruction.

***Table 8.9**: Insights we can get from by analyzing memory dumps*

Recipe 70: Dumping memory using WinPmem

WinPmem is a well-known and easy-to-use memory acquisition tool for Windows. While WinPmem is known for acquiring memory from Windows systems, now there is a port for Linux too, called LinPmem.

Note:

- **Compatibility: Windows, Linux**
- **License considerations: Free software used**

Recipe

Let us dump the memory of a Windows system using WinPmem. Follow the following steps to complete this recipe:

1. Download the WinPmem utility by going to **https://winpmem.velocidex.com/** or directly from **https://github.com/Velocidex/WinPmem/releases.** The name of the file for x86-based Windows systems is **`winpmemminix64rc2.exe`**. Be sure to get the latest file, as a new release may come out and be released on this site.
2. Running this tool is very easy. You can open a command window as an administrator and run the following command:

```
winpmem_mini_x64_rc2.exe <path to the dump file>
```

e.g.,

```
winpmem_mini_x64_rc2.exe C:\temp\DESKTOP-879GNQP-physical-mem.raw
```

This command will start dumping the live memory of your system in the file specified, in this case **`DESKTOP-879GNQP-physical-mem.raw`** in the **`C:temp`** directory.

You will see something like this when the memory dump starts:

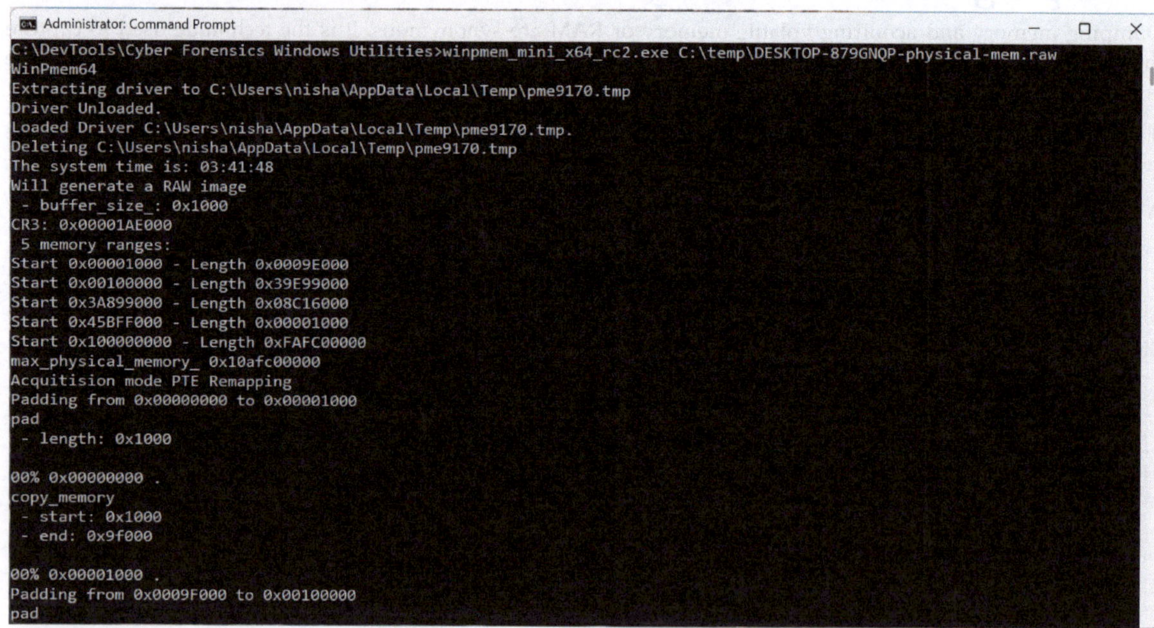

Figure 8.1: WinPmem, starting the memory dump

Once the dump is complete, you will have an output like the one shown in the following figure:

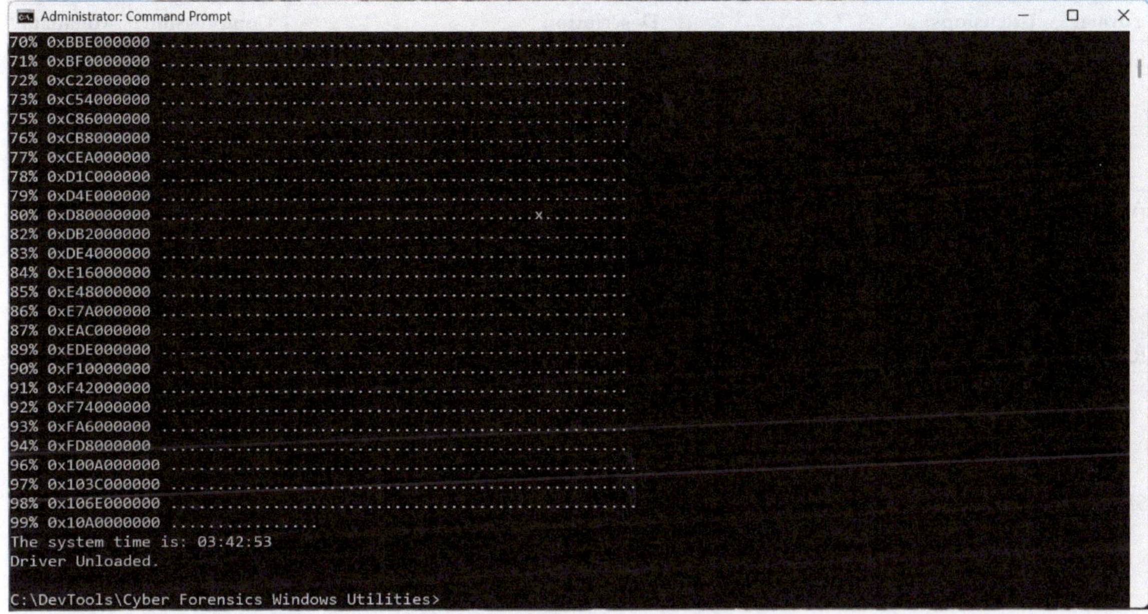

Figure 8.2: WinPmem, memory dump finished

Note: It is a good idea to have the name of the machine, or host name from where you are dumping memory, in the file name. In Windows, you can find the hostname of your machine by running the command `hostname` in the command prompt.

3. Once the preceding command is done, verify in the target directory that there is a file created with the same name.

Tip: While learning how to dump and analyze memory, work with machines with a small amount of RAM, e.g., 4 GB or 8 GB. If you have a large amount of RAM, it will take a considerable amount of time to dump memory. Moreover, the analysis will also be slower.

Activity

Attempt the following activities before the next recipe:

- Close all the running programs as much as possible on your Windows system. Now, dump the memory using WinPmem. Verify if there is a difference in the size of the memory dump.
- Use LinPmem to dump the memory of a Linux system. Verify if the size of the dump is the same as the total memory, or also include the size used by the swap file/partition.
- Analyze if you can use WinPmem directly on the target system, or if you need to use a write-blocking device.

Well-known digital forensics image formats

Whenever a digital forensic professional, like a first responder or digital forensic analyst/examiner, acquires volatile memory (RAM) or disk images, they need to use one of the well-known formats so that the image can be read and is usable with well-known tools.

Let us understand the commonly used image format. The following table lists four of these image formats:

Format	Extensions	Description	Compression	Metadata
E01	`.E01`, `.Exx`	EnCase evidence file (E01) is the most widely accepted in court due to its comprehensive logging and integrity verification. It supports compression, metadata storage, checksums, and optional encryption, making it ideal for legally sound evidence handling and courtroom presentation.	Yes	Yes
AFF	`.AFF`, `.AFD`, `.AFM`	Open-source format supporting segmented images, metadata, and optional encryption, ideal for open-source workflows, and offers extensibility. It supports metadata, compression, and encryption, and is particularly useful in research, tool development, and academic settings.	Yes	Yes
RAW	`.dd`, `.img`, `.raw`	Sector-by-sector copy of the original media without compression or metadata, which is simple and compatible but lacks metadata. It is widely supported and useful in quick or simple acquisitions but requires external logging for chain of custody.	No	No
SMART	`.S01`, `.S02`	An older, less commonly used format for Linux file systems, which includes compression and checksums in a segmented format. It is less common but still seen in certain forensic environments.	Yes	Yes

***Table 8.10**: Well-known image formats*

We will use the RAW file format in several recipes in this chapter because of its simplicity in capturing images and its compatibility with many standard digital forensics tools.

Recipe 71: Dumping memory using FTK Imager

FTK Imager is a free digital forensics tool that is used to acquire and preview forensic images of storage devices and capture volatile memory (RAM). It is part of the FTK software suite developed by AccessData and now owned by Exterro. It allows investigators to create bit-by-bit copies of drives, view files (including deleted ones), and extract digital evidence without altering the original data.

FTK Imager is a very powerful digital forensic tool that supports the following features:

Feature	Details
Disk imaging	Creates bit-by-bit forensic images of hard drives, partitions, or removable media.
Memory acquisition	Captures live RAM from Windows systems for volatile data analysis.
File system preview	Allows viewing of file structure without altering the source media.
Deleted file recovery	Displays and recovers deleted files and folders.
Hash calculation	Computes hashes (e.g. MD5, SHA1, SHA256) to verify data integrity and ensure forensic soundness.
Image mounting	Mounts forensic images as read-only volumes for quick browsing.
Export files and folders	Extracts files from images for further analysis or reporting.
Drive content search	Performs keyword searches within disk images, which is very useful during eDiscovery process.

Feature	Details
Multiple image format support	Supports E01 (EnCase), AFF, RAW (DD), and SMART image formats.
Report generation	Generates reports of acquired images and selected data.
Disk integrity verification	Verifies acquired images using hash comparison.
Bookmarking	Extracts files from images for further analysis or reporting.

***Table 8.11**: Features of FTK Imager*

Note:

- **Compatibility: Windows**
- **License considerations: Free software used**

In this recipe, we will use FTK Imager to acquire memory from a live system. We will get back to FTK Imager again in *Chapter 12, Imaging Techniques* for working with disk images. However, it would be good to be familiar with the interface of FTK Imager. While it may look very simple, FTK Imager is a feature-rich forensic tool, and it is important for everyone working in digital forensics to be acquainted with this tool.

Recipe

Let us use FTK Imager to acquire memory from a Windows system. Perform the following steps to complete this recipe:

1. While FTK Imager is free software, you still need to download it from Exterro's site after filling out a form. You can do that by going to the site **https://www.exterro.com/digital-forensics-software/ftk-imager** and clicking on the **Free Download** button. Once you fill out the form, you will get details in your email to download the software.

   Note: You would need an official email ID to register.

2. Now, install and launch FTK Imager. Once you run it, you will see the following landing screen:

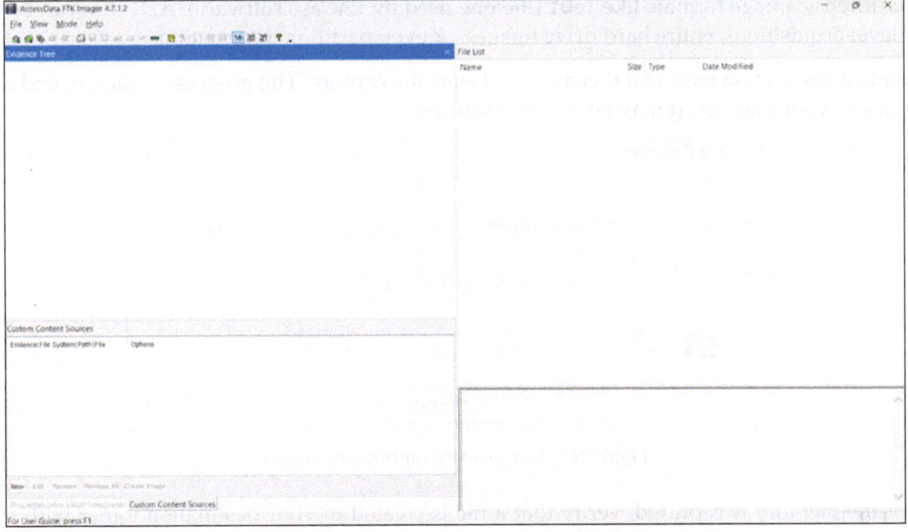

***Figure 8.3**: FTK Imager's opening screen*

The FTK Image interface is divided into multiple parts. On the left side, the evidence tree is the starting point of working with images. All the images and their hierarchy will show up as we add the images using the **Add Evidence Source** button, which is the first button on the toolbar. On the right side, in the **File List** pane, the list of files appears once we click on one of the evidence in the evidence tree.

3. To acquire an image, you can either click on the **File** menu | **Capture Memory...**, or click on the **Capture Memory** icon on the toolbar. The Capture Memory has an icon of a memory chip signifying the action.

   When you click on this option, you will see a dialog like the following. This shows the destination path and file name, if you want to capture the **pagefile**, and if you want to create the AD1 file:

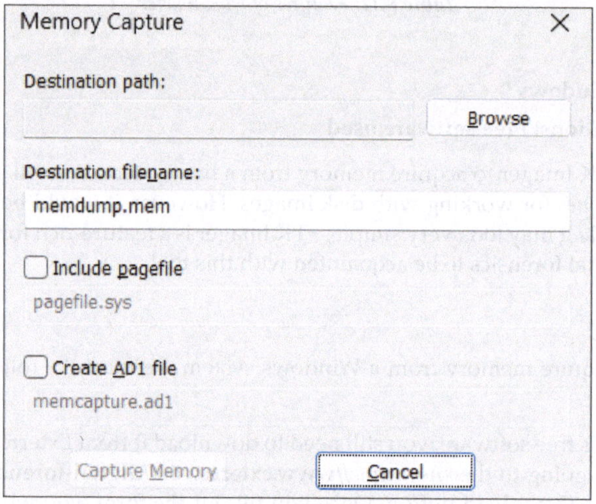

   ***Figure 8.4:** Capturing live memory using FTK Imager*

   pagefile is the swap file used by Windows, and capturing it is a good idea, as this file may have swapped memory pages that can provide additional and valuable information. AD1 is a logical image format created by Access Data's FTK Imager software. It is a proprietary format, meaning it is not as widely supported as other forensic image formats like **`.e01`** (the one used by EnCase software). AD1 files can be used to store file-level acquisitions, entire hard drive images, or even partition information.

   Provide a destination path and filename, and start the capture. The progress is shown, and depending on the size of your memory, it may take a few minutes:

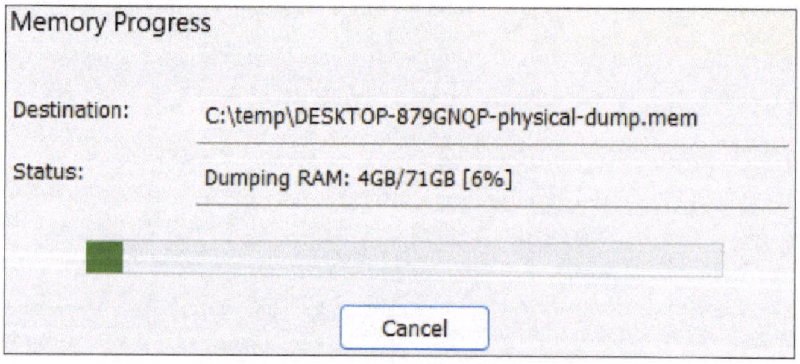

   ***Figure 8.5:** Live memory capture in progress*

4. Once the memory is captured, verify that a file is created in your destination folder with the name you provided.

Activity

Attempt the following activities before the next recipe:

- Select the **Include pagefile** option of FTK Image while capturing memory. Observe if you have gotten only one output file or additional files.
- Select the **Create AD1 file** option and observe if you get a single output file or multiple files.
- Analyze why the size of your memory dump output file is always more than the actual size of your RAM.

Recipe 72: Analyzing acquired memory using Volatility

The Volatility Framework, or volatile memory extraction framework, is the most widely used framework for extracting digital artifacts from a computer's volatile memory or RAM. It is also simply known as Volatility. Volatility provides various plugins to perform analysis of the memory dump file from Windows, Linux, and even macOS.

Note:

- **Compatibility: Windows**
- **License considerations: Free software used**

In this recipe, we will analyze the memory of a Windows system using Volatility.

Recipe

Let us analyze the memory dump file that we created before using WinPmem. You can also use the memory dump file created by FTK Imager.

Refer to the following steps to complete this recipe:

1. Open a command prompt on your Windows machine as an administrator. Change the directory to where Volatility is going to reside.
2. Now use **`git clone`** to pull the entire Volability repository from GitHub as follows. If you do not have Git installed, it can be installed very easily for Windows by downloading it from **https://git-scm.com/downloads.**

   Run the following command to clone the Volatility 3 repository from GitHub:

   ```
   git clone https://github.com/volatilityfoundation/volatility3.git
   ```

   Now we are ready to run Volatility 3 using Python.

   Note: If you do not have Git or if you do not want to clone Volatility's GitHub repository, you can also download a zip file of the entire Volatility repository from its GitHub page and extract it in a directory of your choice.

3. Now, to check if Volatility is working correctly, run the following command using Python in the directory where you cloned or downloaded Volatility 3. Depending on your installation, Python can be run using **`python`** or **`python3`**.

   ```
   python vol.py -h
   ```

   The preceding command lists all the command-line options and plugins that are supported. Volatility 3 supports a large number of plugins. You can easily appreciate that the power of Volatility lies in the analysis of volatile memory or RAM on Windows, Linux, and macOS using these plugins.

4. We are not ready to analyze the memory dump. Let us first find the details about the basic information of the Windows system where the dump was done. Change directory to your Volatility directory and run the following command:

```
python C:\temp\DESKTOP-879GNQP-physical-mem.raw windows.info
```

This command will take some time to execute based on the size of your memory dump. The output will look similar to the following:

```
C:\DevTools\volatility3>python vol.py -f C:\temp\DESKTOP-879GNQP-physical-mem.raw windows.info
Volatility 3 Framework 2.26.2
C:\DevTools\volatility3\volatility3\framework\deprecation.py:105: FutureWarning: This plugin (PluginRequirement) has been renamed and will be removed in the first release after 2026-06-01. PluginRequirement is to be deprecated. Use VersionRequirement instead.
  warnings.warn(
Progress:  100.00               PDB scanning finished
Variable        Value


Kernel Base     0xf800a9400000
DTB     0x1ae000
Symbols                 file:///C:/DevTools/volatility3/volatility3/symbols/windows/ntkrnlmp.pdb/9EF31611480D2516B9D0131E3F1D41BD-1.json.xz
Is64Bit True
IsPAE   False
layer_name      0 WindowsIntel32e
memory_layer    1 FileLayer
KdVersionBlock  0xf800aa20a870
Major/Minor     15.26100
MachineType     34404
KeNumberProcessors      8
SystemTime      2025-06-01 03:41:48+00:00
NtSystemRoot    C:\WINDOWS
NtProductType   NtProductWinNt
NtMajorVersion  10
NtMinorVersion  0
PE MajorOperatingSystemVersion  10
PE MinorOperatingSystemVersion  0
PE Machine      34404
PE TimeDateStamp        Wed Feb  5 13:37:27 2003

C:\DevTools\volatility3>
```

As you see, this output contains the basic information about the Windows system that was loaded into memory.

Activity

Attempt the following activities before the next recipe:

- You can save the basic details of the dump in a **config.json** file for speeding up the subsequent analysis of the memory dump using Volatility. Read the Volatility documentation to understand how this can be done.
- Find out what *PDB scanning* means in the preceding output and what its purpose is.
- Read more about the **--profile** option supported by Volatility. Understand how such profiles can be used to look for specific information from the memory dump.
- Read the documentation of Volatility to become familiar with other supported plugins.

Recipe 73: Collecting details about running processes

During the evidence acquisition, the running process can be directly collected from the live system. The running processes can also be collected later from a memory dump during its analysis. This provides us with insight into what was happening in the system during acquisition, and is important for incident responders, malware investigations, and other similar scenarios.

Note:

- **Compatibility: Windows**
- **License considerations: Free software used**

We have used multiple ways to get the list of processes and services using PowerShell in *Chapter 6, Digital Forensics for Windows Systems*. In this recipe, we will collect the details about the running process from the memory dump.

Recipe

Let us use Volatility to get the information about running processes from the memory dump acquired in the previous recipes in this chapter.

In order to collect the details of the running processes, we can use the following command:

```
python C:\temp\DESKTOP-879GNQP-physical-mem.raw windows.pslist
```

Note: **Make sure that you use the name of the dump file you created using either Winpmem or FTK Imager.**

The output will show all the processes that were running at the time of acquiring the memory from the live system and will look something similar to this:

```
C:\DevTools\volatility3>python vol.py -f C:\temp\DESKTOP-879GNQP-physical-mem.raw windows.pslist
Volatility 3 Framework 2.26.2
C:\DevTools\volatility3\volatility3\framework\deprecation.py:105: FutureWarning: This plugin
(PluginRequirement) has been renamed and will be removed in the first release after 2026-06-01.
PluginRequirement is to be deprecated. Use VersionRequirement instead.
  warnings.warn(
Progress:  100.00               PDB scanning finished
PID     PPID    ImageFileName   Offset(V)       Threads Handles SessionId       Wow64   CreateTime
ExitTime        File output
```

```
4       0       System  0x9c880c4cc040  280     -       N/A     False   2025-05-31 11:49:24.000000
UTC  N/A     Disabled
140     4       Secure System   0x9c880c5f4040  0       -       N/A     False   2025-05-31
11:49:19.000000 UTC  N/A   Disabled
184     4       Registry        0x9c880c5f7040  4       -       N/A     False   2025-05-31
11:49:19.000000 UTC  N/A   Disabled
696     4       smss.exe        0x9c881237c040  2       -       N/A     False   2025-05-31
11:49:24.000000 UTC  N/A   Disabled
988     892     csrss.exe       0x9c88225f0140  13      -       0       False   2025-05-31
11:49:29.000000 UTC  N/A   Disabled
872     892     wininit.exe     0x9c8825dad140  1       -       0       False   2025-05-31
11:49:29.000000 UTC  N/A   Disabled
676     856     csrss.exe       0x9c8825d4a0c0  16      -       1       False   2025-05-31
11:49:29.000000 UTC  N/A   Disabled
.
.
.
5468    1148    OfficeClickToR  0x9c88272ad080  25      -       0       False   2025-05-31
11:49:31.000000 UTC  N/A   Disabled
5460    1148    mDNSResponder.  0x9c88272af080  2       -       0       False   2025-05-31
11:49:31.000000 UTC  N/A   Disabled
5448    1148    armsvc.exe      0x9c88272a90c0  2       -       0       True    2025-05-31
11:49:31.000000 UTC  N/A   Disabled
5424    1148    svchost.exe     0x9c88272d4080  5       -       0       False   2025-05-31
11:49:31.000000 UTC  N/A   Disabled
5416    1148    svchost.exe     0x9c88272d1080  2       -       0       False   2025-05-31
11:49:31.000000 UTC  N/A   Disabled
5388    1148    svchost.exe     0x9c882729d080  7       -       0       False   2025-05-31
11:49:31.000000 UTC  N/A   Disabled
5340    1148    WUDFHost.exe    0x9c8827304080  11      -       0       False   2025-05-31
11:49:31.000000 UTC  N/A   Disabled

C:\DevTools\volatility3>
```

Since the preceding output was very large, only a part of it is shown. You can see that the output contains all the vital information of the process. The first field is the **Process ID** (**PID**), which can be used to further query the dump for more information about a specific process.

If you want to check for a specific program, you can use `findstr` to find the line with that command, like the following:

```
python vol.py -f C:\temp\DESKTOP-879GNQP-physical-dump.mem windows.pslist | findstr "chrome"
```

The output will look like the following:

```
C:\DevTools\volatility3>python vol.py -f C:\temp\DESKTOP-879GNQP-physical-dump.mem windows.pslist
| findstr "chrome"
C:\DevTools\volatility3\volatility3\framework\deprecation.py:105: FutureWarning: This plugin
(PluginRequirement) has been renamed and will be removed in the first release after 2026-06-01.
PluginRequirement is to be deprecated. Use VersionRequirement instead.
```

```
 warnings.warn(
9176    10088   chrome.exe        0x9c883b2d6080  44      -        1          False   2025-06-01
03:30:20.000000 UTC  N/A   Disabled
1872    9176    chrome.exe        0x9c883b663080  7       -        1          False   2025-06-01
03:30:20.000000 UTC  N/A   Disabled
6160    9176    chrome.exe        0x9c883b9d9080  22      -        1          False   2025-06-01
03:30:20.000000 UTC  N/A   Disabled
10288   9176    chrome.exe        0x9c883bcbd080  18      -        1          False   2025-06-01
03:30:20.000000 UTC  N/A   Disabled
15336   9176    chrome.exe        0x9c883c9230c0  11      -        1          False   2025-06-01
03:30:20.000000 UTC  N/A   Disabled
16676   9176    chrome.exe        0x9c883bfbb080  18      -        1          False   2025-06-01
03:30:25.000000 UTC  N/A   Disabled
3056    9176    chrome.exe        0x9c883c5db080  18      -        1          False   2025-06-01
03:30:25.000000 UTC  N/A   Disabled
13864   9176    chrome.exe        0x9c883c564080  20      -        1          False   2025-06-01
03:30:25.000000 UTC  N/A   Disabled
1968    9176    chrome.exe        0x9c883ad840c0  23      -        1          False   2025-06-01
03:30:35.000000 UTC  N/A   Disabled
19312   9176    chrome.exe        0x9c882c94a0c0  20      -        1          False   2025-06-01
03:30:51.000000 UTC  N/A   Disabled
10268   9176    chrome.exe        0x9c88296020c0  19      -        1          False   2025-06-01
03:30:51.000000 UTC  N/A   Disabled
13140   9176    chrome.exe        0x9c8830cc8080  18      -        1          False   2025-06-01
03:30:52.000000 UTC  N/A   Disabled
4720    9176    chrome.exe        0x9c88291130c0  19      -        1          False   2025-06-01
03:31:01.000000 UTC  N/A   Disabled
328     9176    chrome.exe        0x9c88365d6080  19      -        1          False   2025-06-01
03:31:01.000000 UTC  N/A   Disabled
10412   9176    chrome.exe        0x9c883ae240c0  18      -        1          False   2025-06-01
03:32:55.000000 UTC  N/A   Disabled
17760   9176    chrome.exe        0x9c882e3ed180  19      -        1          False   2025-06-01
03:33:27.000000 UTC  N/A   Disabled
6828    9176    chrome.exe        0x9c882ece60c0  18      -        1          False   2025-06-01
03:33:28.000000 UTC  N/A   Disabled
14512   9176    chrome.exe        0x9c883bc1e080  18      -        1          False   2025-06-01
03:33:32.000000 UTC  N/A   Disabled
12184   9176    chrome.exe        0x9c882ed680c0  13      -        1          False   2025-06-01
03:33:58.000000 UTC  N/A   Disabled
2192    9176    chrome.exe        0x9c88333cd0c0  11      -        1          False   2025-06-01
03:33:59.000000 UTC  N/A   Disabled
7260    9176    chrome.exe        0x9c8832bc50c0  9       -        1          False   2025-06-01
03:33:59.000000 UTC  N/A   Disabled

C:\DevTools\volatility3>
```

This output shows all the chrome.exe processes run by the Chrome browser at the time of the memory acquisition.

Activity

Attempt the following activities before the next recipe:

- Before acquiring the memory, start a few programs, e.g., Notepad, WordPad, etc. After that, close these programs. Now use the **windows.pslist** plugin to get a list of the processes and **findstr** to filter the output for your program.
- Find the list of processes using the memory dump by WinPmem as well as FTK Imager. Analyze if there are any differences.

Understanding process trees

A process tree is a hierarchical representation of all running processes on a system, showing the parent-child relationships between them. Each process in an operating system is usually launched by another process (its parent), and may in turn create its own child processes. The process tree visualizes this chain, helping digital forensics investigators understand the execution flow and lineage of activities on the system.

Process trees are extremely useful in incident response and in digital forensics due to the following reasons:

Use case	Details
Track attack vectors	Helps identify how a malicious process was spawned, e.g., a powershell.exe launched from winword.exe may indicate a malicious macro.
Detect abnormal behavior	Shows unusual parent-child relationships, such as a non-browser process launching a script engine, e.g., **wscript.exe** or **powershell.exe**.
Correlate events to users or sessions	By linking processes to specific users and times, investigators can reconstruct actions during a compromise.
Uncover fileless malware	Malicious scripts or code executed in memory may be visible only as suspicious child processes in the tree.
Identify persistence mechanisms	Some malware spawns multiple child processes or daisy-chains processes to stay active. A process tree can show such behavior.
Assist in timeline reconstructions	Allows analysts to track what happened in what order during a breach or suspicious activity.

Table 8.12: Use cases of process tree analysis

Let us look at the following examples to understand how process tree information may be useful:

- **Genuine process**: **cmd.exe** starts PowerShell, which, in turn, creates a network connection.
- **Suspicious process**: **cmd.exe** starting **notepad.exe** from a non-default location, which, in turn, creates a network connection.

A suspicious process tree may look like the following, as we do not expect **winword.exe** to start **powershell.exe**:

```
explorer.exe (PID 1200)
 └── winword.exe (PID 1400)
      └── powershell.exe (PID 1500)
           └── wget.exe (PID 1520)
```

Note: This is just a high-level view of how we look at the process tree information. In real life, each process may need to be examined for suspicious lineage in the hierarchy.

Recipe 74: Collecting process tree information

We can use Volatility to collect process tree information, too. Moreover, we can collect it for a specific PID to get more information about a specific process. Collecting this information can help the digital forensics examiner to get the details about the creation hierarchy of the process and help understand if the process is suspicious.

Note:

- **Compatibility: Windows**
- **License considerations: Free software used**

Recipe

Let us use Volatility to collect the process tree information. We have used the following command before to find the process list:

```
python vol.py -f C:\temp\DESKTOP-879GNQP-physical-dump.mem windows.pslist
```

This command, however, only lists each individual process and not the details about which process started it.

We can use the following command to obtain the process tree for all processes running at the time of memory acquisition:

```
python vol.py -f C:\temp\DESKTOP-879GNQP-physical-dump.mem windows.pstree
```

Activity

Attempt the following activities before the next recipe:

- Is there a way to find the process tree for any specific process or a PID? Analyze how this can be done.
- Analyze the process tree information, which is the top-level parent of all the processes.

Recipe 75: Identifying external IP addresses accessed by processes

A malicious process may communicate with the external world to help it achieve the following:

- Send telemetry information.
- Send sensitive files to a C2 system.
- Get newer updates from their server.
- Attack external IP addresses being part of a botnet.

Hence, identifying if any external connections were present at the time of memory acquisition can help understand how the malicious process was interacting with the external world.

Note:

- **Compatibility: Windows**
- **License considerations: Free software used**

Recipe

Let us use a plugin called **windows.netstat** to understand if there were any connections to the external IP addresses.

The following command can be used to get the list of all the network connections:

```
python vol.py -f C:\temp\DESKTOP-879GNQP-physical-dump.mem windows.netstat
```

When you run this command, you will see an output similar to the following:

```
C:\DevTools\volatility3>python vol.py -f C:\temp\DESKTOP-879GNQP-physical-dump.mem windows.netstat
Volatility 3 Framework 2.26.2
C:\DevTools\volatility3\volatility3\framework\deprecation.py:105: FutureWarning: This plugin (PluginRequirement) has been renamed and will be removed in the first release after 2026-06-01. PluginRequirement is to be deprecated. Use VersionRequirement instead.
  warnings.warn(
Progress:  100.00               PDB scanning finished
Offset  Proto  LocalAddr   LocalPort   ForeignAddr  ForeignPort  State  PID  Owner  Created

0x9c8825ff248  TCPv4  0.0.0.0 135  0.0.0.0 0  LISTENING  1432  svchost.exe  2025-05-31 11:49:30.000000 UTC
0x9c8825ff248  TCPv6  ::  135  ::  0  LISTENING  1432  svchost.exe  2025-05-31 11:49:30.000000 UTC
0x9c88105ffd48  TCPv4  0.0.0.0 135  0.0.0.0 0  LISTENING  1432  svchost.exe  2025-05-31 11:49:30.000000 UTC
0x9c8822a455e8  TCPv4  192.168.56.1  139  0.0.0.0 0  LISTENING  4  System  2025-05-31 11:49:30.000000 UTC
0x9c8829b6bd38  TCPv4  192.168.6.1  139  0.0.0.0 0  LISTENING  4  System  2025-05-31 11:49:43.000000 UTC
0x9c8829b6b918  TCPv4  192.168.19.1  139  0.0.0.0 0  LISTENING  4  System  2025-05-31 11:49:43.000000 UTC
0x9c8829b65cf8  TCPv4  192.168.1.8  139  0.0.0.0 0  LISTENING  4  System  2025-05-31 11:49:47.000000 UTC
0x9c8822a48b88  TCPv4  172.23.112.1  139  0.0.0.0 0  LISTENING  4  System  2025-06-01 02:07:57.000000 UTC
0x9c8826465e38  TCPv4  0.0.0.0 445  0.0.0.0 0  LISTENING  4  System  2025-05-31 11:49:31.000000 UTC
0x9c8826465e38  TCPv6  ::  445  ::  0  LISTENING  4  System  2025-05-31 11:49:31.000000 UTC
0x9c8827ef8a18  TCPv4  0.0.0.0 623  0.0.0.0 0  LISTENING  5780  LMS.exe 2025-05-31 11:49:32.000000 UTC
0x9c8827ef8a18  TCPv6  ::  623  ::  0  LISTENING  5780  LMS.exe 2025-05-31 11:49:32.000000 UTC
0x9c8827ef9938  TCPv4  0.0.0.0 623  0.0.0.0 0  LISTENING  5780  LMS.exe 2025-05-31 11:49:32.000000 UTC
0x9c8827ef93b8  TCPv4  0.0.0.0 902  0.0.0.0 0  LISTENING  6112  vmware-authd.e  2025-05-31 11:49:32.000000 UTC
0x9c8827ef8338  TCPv4  0.0.0.0 912  0.0.0.0 0  LISTENING  6112  vmware-authd.e  2025-
```

```
05-31 11:49:32.000000 UTC
0x9c8828df9518  TCPv4   127.0.0.1       1468    0.0.0.0 0       LISTENING       6632    Syslogd_Servic
2025-05-31 11:49:35.000000 UTC
.
.
.
0x9c882920cd68  UDPv4   0.0.0.0 59870   *       0               6704    logioptionsplu  2025-05-31
11:49:37.000000 UTC
0x9c882b35acc8  UDPv4   0.0.0.0 59871   *       0               6704    logioptionsplu  2025-05-31
11:49:37.000000 UTC
0x9c8827131ce8  UDPv4   0.0.0.0 60992   *       0               5460    mDNSResponder.  2025-05-31
11:49:31.000000 UTC
0x9c8827130e48  UDPv4   0.0.0.0 60993   *       0               5460    mDNSResponder.  2025-05-31
11:49:31.000000 UTC
0x9c8827130e48  UDPv6   ::      60993   *       0               5460    mDNSResponder.  2025-05-31
11:49:31.000000 UTC
0x9c8830043e28  UDPv4   127.0.0.1       63560   *       0       12064   APSDaemon.exe   2025-
06-01 02:08:44.000000 UTC
0x9c883004f908  UDPv4   127.0.0.1       63561   *       0       12064   APSDaemon.exe   2025-
06-01 02:08:44.000000 UTC

C:\DevTools\volatility3>
```

Since the preceding output was very large, only a part of it is shown. You can see that there are fields for **LocalAddr** (local address) and **ForeignAddr** (foreign/external address) that can help you understand the network connections being made.

Activity

Attempt the following activities before the next recipe:

- Use **linux.netstat** plugin to get the list of network connections in a Linux memory dump.
- There is a plugin called **windows.netscan**. Read the Volatility documentation to understand what it does.

Recipe 76: Getting a list of strings from the memory dump

Windows utility **sysinternals** has a tool called **strings**. This can be used to get a list of all the strings from the memory dump file. This is particularly useful for analyzing any clear text strings that may have been loaded in the memory by the attacker, e.g., passwords.

Note:

- **Compatibility: Windows**
- **License considerations: Free software used**

Recipe

To get a list of all the strings that are found in the memory dump, we can use the following command:

```
strings -o C:\temp\DESKTOP-879GNQP-physical-dump.mem > C:\temp\DESKTOP-879GNQP-physical-dump-strings.txt
```

Note: **This may create a very large file, and you may need a lot of memory to load the file in a text editor.**

Activity

Attempt the following activities before the next recipe:

- Check the strings file to identify if you can find anything useful, like passwords, IP addresses, scripts, etc.
- Analyze how we can find a list of readable strings from a raw memory dump, which is a binary file.

Recipe 77: More Volatility plugins

Volatility supports a large number of plugins that you might have already seen in the output of the command **python vol.py -h**. Let us look at a few more plugins that are very useful during digital forensic analysis.

Note:

- **Compatibility: Windows**
- **License considerations: Free software used**

Recipe

Let us look at a few more important plugins that can be used to get yet more information from a memory dump.

The following table lists such important plugins for Windows:

Plugin	Purpose
windows.imageinfo	Provides a high level summary of the memory image being analyzed.
windows.handles	Displays the list of open handles that includes files, Registry keys, mutexes, named pipes, events, windows stations, desktops, threads, etc.
windows.cmdscan	Searches the memory processes like **conhost.exe** and **csrss.exe** for the command entered by the attacker.
windows.envars	Gets the list of all the environment variables that were defined in the system.
windows.verinfo	Displays the version of all the **Portable Executable** (**PE**) files that were loaded in the memory, like **.exe, .dll**, and **.sys** files.
windows.consoles	Finds commands that were typed by the attacker in the command prompt or by using **cmd.exe**.
windows.Registry.hivelist	Finds the list of all the Registry hives that were loaded in memory at the time of acquisition.
windows.scheduled_tasks	List all the scheduled tasks that were loaded in the memory at the time of acquisition.

Table 8:13: A few important Windows plugins of Volatility

Windows utility **sysinternals** has a tool called **strings**. This can be used to get a list of all the strings from the memory dump file. This is particularly useful for analyzing any clear text strings that may have been loaded into memory by the attacker, e.g., passwords.

Activity

Attempt the following activities before the next recipe:

- Find similar plugins for Linux. Is there a parallel plugin in Linux for every plugin you found for Windows?
- Check if all these commands are also available for macOS and any other operating system you can think of.

Recipe 78: Using Bulk Extractor to analyze RAM dumps

Let us look at a useful tool during the memory analysis that automates a lot of tasks by extracting the digital forensics information in bulk. Bulk Extractor is an open-source digital forensics tool that scans disk images, memory dumps, or any raw data for artifacts like email addresses, URLs, credit card numbers, IP addresses, and more. It is fast, forensic-safe, and designed to extract bulk data that might be useful in investigations.

Note:

- **Compatibility: Windows**
- **License considerations: Free software used**

Recipe

Let us use Bulk Extractor to analyze our memory dump file. Follow the following steps to complete this recipe.

1. Let us first download Bulk Extractor. It can be downloaded from its GitHub page at **https://github.com/simsong/bulk_extractor/wiki/Installing-bulk_extractor**. Zip format is preferred as it has a standalone file that doesn't need to be installed.

   Note: **Bulk Extractor is installed as a default tool in Kali Linux. While using Windows-based Bulk Extractor, or any other such tools, ensure that you always look at the authenticity of the source of the file.**

2. Run the Bulk Extractor from the command line without any parameters to get various supported options:

```
C:\DevTools\Cyber Forensics Windows Utilities>bulk_extractor64.exe
imagefile not provided
bulk_extractor version 2.0.2: A high-performance flexible digital forensics program.
Usage:
  bulk_extractor [OPTION...] image_name

  -A, --offset_add arg          Offset added (in bytes) to feature locations
                                (default: 0)
  -b, --banner_file arg         Path of file whose contents are prepended to
                                top of all feature files
  -C, --context_window arg      Size of context window reported in bytes
                                (default: 16)
  -d, --debug arg               enable debugging (default: 1)
  -D, --debug_help              help on debugging
  -E, --enable_exclusive arg    disable all scanners except the one specified.
```

```
                                        Same as -x all -E scanner.
  -e, --enable arg                      enable a scanner (can be repeated)
  -x, --disable arg                     disable a scanner (can be repeated)
  -f, --find arg                        search for a pattern (can be repeated)
  -F, --find_file arg                   read patterns to search from a file (can be
                                        repeated)
  -G, --pagesize arg                    page size in bytes (default: 16777216)
  -g, --marginsize arg                  margin size in bytes (default: 4194304)
  -j, --threads arg                     number of threads (default: 8)
  -J, --no_threads                      read and process data in the primary thread
  -M, --max_depth arg                   max recursion depth (default: 12)
      --max_bad_alloc_errors arg
                                        max bad allocation errors (default: 3)
      --max_minute_wait arg             maximum number of minutes to wait until all
                                        data are read (default: 60)
      --notify_main_thread              Display notifications in the main thread after
                                        phase1 completes. Useful for running with
                                        ThreadSanitizer
      --notify_async                    Display notificaitons asynchronously (default)
  -o, --outdir arg                      output directory [REQUIRED]
  -P, --scanner_dir arg                 directories for scanner shared libraries (can
                                        be repeated). Default directories include
                                        /usr/local/lib/bulk_extractor,
                                        /usr/lib/bulk_extractor and any directories
                                        specified in the BE_PATH environment variable.
  -p, --path arg                        print the value of <path>[:length][/h][/r] with
                                        optional length, hex output, or raw output.
  -q, --quit                            no status or performance output
  -r, --alert_list arg                  file to read alert list from
  -R, --recurse                         treat image file as a directory to recursively
                                        explore
  -S, --set arg                         set a name=value option (can be repeated)
  -s, --sampling arg                    random sampling parameter frac[:passes]
  -V, --version                         Display PACKAGE_VERSION (currently) 2.0.2
  -w, --stop_list arg                   file to read stop list from
  -Y, --scan arg                        specify <start>[-end] of area on disk to scan
  -z, --page_start arg                  specify a starting page number
  -Z, --zap                             wipe the output directory (recursively) before
                                        starting
  -0, --no_notify                       disable real-time notification
  -1, --version1                        version 1.0 notification (console-output)
  -H, --info_scanners                   report information about each scanner
```

```
  -h, --help                     print help screen

C:\DevTools\Cyber Forensics Windows Utilities>
```

3. Now, let us run with our memory dump file as follows:

```
bulk_extractor64.exe C:\temp\DESKTOP-879GNQP-physical-dump.mem -o C:\temp\extract
```

After running this command, Bulk Extractor starts carving out various information from the dump file and writes it to the output directory mentioned after the `-o` option. This process takes a considerable amount of time to complete, and progress information is displayed on the screen. During this time, Bulk Extract scans the image and finds a lot of information like URLs, emails, visiting cards, binary compiled files, and directories.

Note: Running Bulk Extractor may result in several antivirus warnings while it carves various information found in the dump and stores it on the file system. It is best to run Bulk Extractor for any memory dump into an isolated system that is not used for anything critical except for digital forensic purposes.

Activity

Attempt the following activities before the next recipe:

- Transfer the memory dump file to the Kali Linux file system. Use Bulk Extractor in Kali Linux to analyze the memory dump.
- Identify other use cases of Bulk Extractor that can help us use it as a reconnaissance tool.

Recipe 79: Collecting details about password hashes using PwDump

During the collection of digital forensic information from a live system, we may often need to collect the password hashes of the local account. This can then be analyzed or even cracked to find out the password that was used.

PwDump can be used to output the Windows **Lan Manager (LM)** and **NT Lan Manager (NTLM)** password hashes of local user accounts from the **Security Account Manager (SAM)** database and from the Active Directory domain's user cache on the operating system.

Note: PwDump is widely used to perform both the famous pass-the-hash attack, and can also be used to brute force users' passwords directly. In order to work, it must be run under an Administrator account or be able to access an Administrator account on the computer where the hashes are to be dumped. PwDump could be said to compromise security because it could allow a malicious administrator to access users' passwords.

Note:

- **Compatibility: Windows**
- **License considerations: Free software used**

Recipe

Let us use PwDump to print the password hashes of the local account. Perform the following steps to complete the recipe:

1. First, we need to download the PwGen binary. It can be downloaded from **https://github.com/Seabreg/pwdump.** There are many other places from where it can be downloaded, and hence, be sure of the source of the file before downloading it. Be sure to download the zip file of the entire repository.

2. You can run PwDump in two ways. You can run it by right-clicking on the file `PwDump7.exe` and clicking on **Run as Administrator**. You can also run it directly from a command prompt that is run as an administrator.
3. When you run the program, you will see that it prints all the password hashes for the local accounts found on the system.

The password hashes are not shown here due to their confidential nature.

Note: **All the digital forensic tools downloaded from the Internet should be used only in an isolated system that is not being used for anything critical except for digital forensic purposes.**

Activity

Attempt the following activities before the next recipe:

- Create a new local user. Run PwGen7 again to see if this user's hash is dumped.
- Create two local users with the same password. Run PwGen7 again and verify if both users have the same hashes or if they differ.

Recipe 80: Extracting forensic data using OSForensics

OSForensics is a comprehensive digital forensic investigation tool developed by PassMark Software. It enables forensic analysts to acquire, index, search, and analyze digital evidence from computers, storage devices, and memory dumps. It combines many common forensic functions into a single, user-friendly interface, making it suitable for both professionals and learners.

OSForensics supports a wide range of forensic tasks, from disk imaging to memory analysis, making it an all-in-one solution for incident response and forensic investigation. It can assist with tasks such as file system and disk imaging, keyword and index search, file carving and recovery, RAM analysis, hash matching, timeline and event analysis, email and browser artifact parsing, Registry and system information extraction, drive signature comparison, and even case management.

While OSForensics is not a tool that can do it exclusively, it is something digital forensics professionals can use to make their analysis, eDiscovery, and reporting tasks easy. It is a rich and aggregated toolset for many digital forensics tasks we have learned so far.

Typical usage of OSForensics includes, but is not limited to:

- Analyzing a compromised computer for malware or exfiltration.
- Investigating insider threats or IP theft by tracing user activity.
- Recovering deleted documents or chat history in legal or HR cases.
- Matching files against known contraband or leak signatures via hash databases.
- Rapid triage and reporting in corporate incident response scenarios.

Note:

- **Compatibility: Windows**
- **License considerations: Trial software used**

Recipe

Let us use OSForensics to work with processes and memory, and hence get comfortable with one more very useful tool while working with memory forensics. Follow the following steps to complete this recipe:

1. First, download OSForensics from **https://www.osforensics.com/**. Once downloaded, proceed with installation.

   Note: The trial versions of software may be suitable for learning purposes, but should not be used for any commercial activity. Always read the licensing terms before you use any trial software, and use the software as per the terms and conditions.

2. Launch OSForensics. Your opening screen will look like the following:

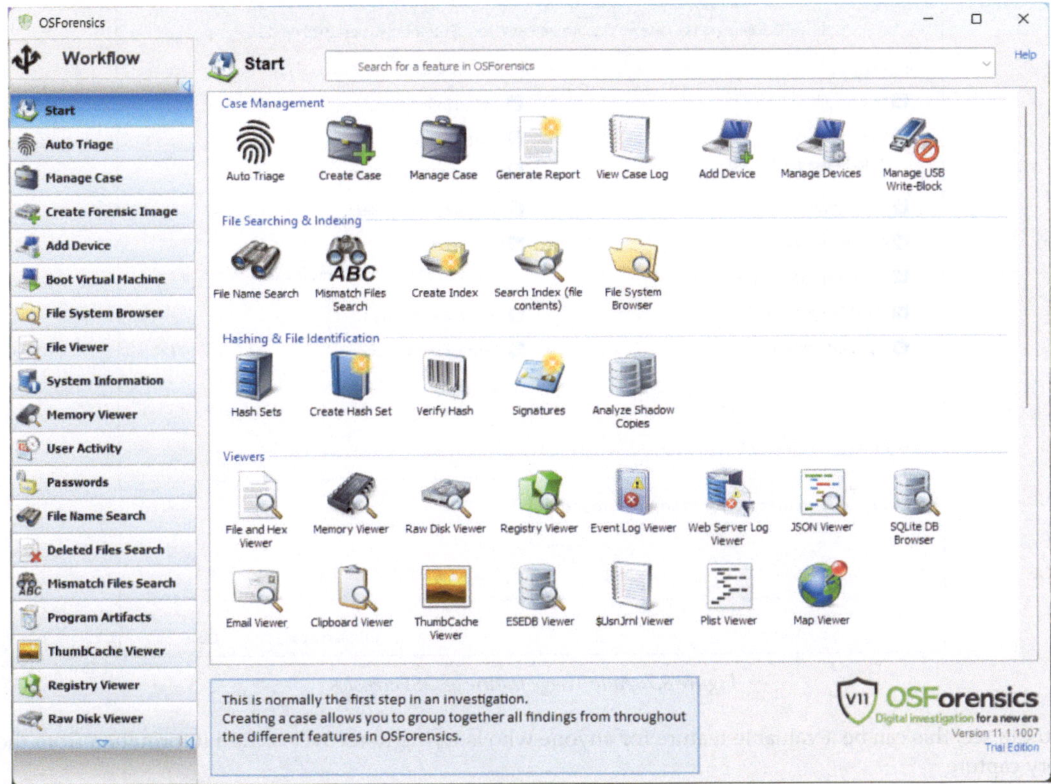

Figure 8.6: OSForensics main page

   Become familiar with various features of OSForensics.

3. Next, perform the following tasks using OSForensics:

   a. Create a new case with the description of the case.

   b. Under **Memory Viewer**, under the **Live Analysis** tab, export the process details for `Registry.exe`.

   c. Under **Memory Viewer**, use **Static Analysis** to perform the static analysis of the memory dump we created before. Note how OSForensics uses Volatility to perform memory analysis. You can perform the same task by using the option **Analyze Memory with Volatility** under Housekeeping section on the main screen.

   d. Use the **File Name Search** feature to search for files matching specific patterns.

4. Next, click on the **Auto Triage** feature on the main screen. Since we have used the memory dump to analyze a few things, OSForensics automatically uses this dump as a reference and provides a list of scan options for the figure:

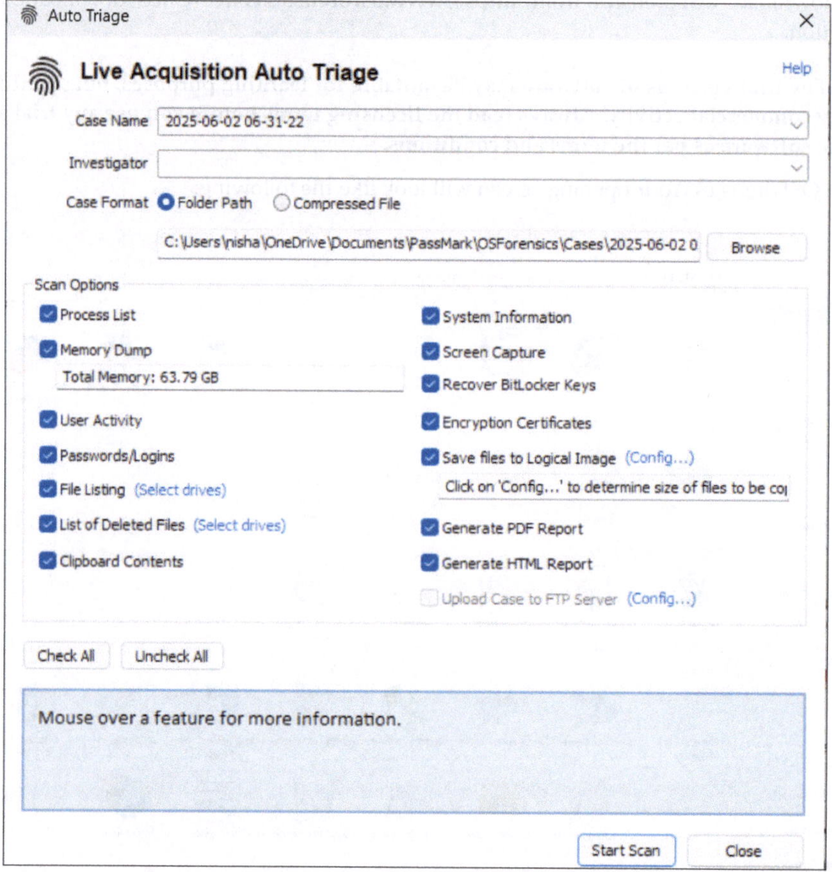

***Figure 8.7:** Auto Triage feature of OSForensics*

As you can see, this can be a valuable feature for anyone who is trying to recover or find information from the live memory capture.

Note: **Auto Triage is a resource-intensive activity. Hence, running this requires a large amount of memory and CPU. If you are using a virtual machine (VM) to test this, ensure you resize it accordingly. In real-life conditions, this is always executed on dedicated high-end hardware.**

Activity

Attempt the following activities before the next recipe:

- What is the use of creating a case when working with digital forensics analysis?
- Use the various viewers that are supplied with OSForensics, like Registry Viewer, Event Log Viewer, Email Viewer, and become familiar with their use cases.

- We have discussed the Windows Shadow Copy feature in *Chapter 6, Digital Forensics for Windows Systems*. Use the **Analyze Shadow Copy** feature of OSForensis to understand how to work with the shadow copies stored on the system.
- Go back to the *Behavior Analysis* section of this chapter and find out how many of the tasks listed can be achieved using OSForensics.

Recipe 81: Using Sysinternals as a digital forensic toolset

Windows Sysinternals is a suite of advanced system utilities developed by *Microsoft* (originally by *Mark Russinovich*) to help power users, administrators, and forensic investigators monitor, diagnose, and troubleshoot Windows systems. These tools provide deep insight into system internals, including process activity, file usage, Registry changes, and network behavior.

Sysinternals tools are widely used in live forensics and incident response because they offer real-time visibility into Windows system activities without requiring installation, making them suitable for volatile evidence collection and non-invasive investigations.

Sysinternals Suite is a free tool published by Microsoft that can be installed from the Microsoft Store widget of Windows.

The site **https://learn.microsoft.com/en-us/sysinternals/** has a comprehensive list of all the tools that are part of the Sysinternals Suite. They include file and disk utilities, networking utilities, process utilities, security utilities, system information tools, and many other miscellaneous tools.

Note:

- **Compatibility: Windows**
- **License considerations: Free software used**

Recipe

We have used the **strings** utility before, which is also a part of Sysinternals. Let us use a few more tools to become familiar with the Sysinternals suite.

If you want to see a simple and detailed view of all the running processes, you can use the command-line tool **pslist**. The following are a few ways to use **pslist**:

Command	Purpose
pslist	Provides a simple list of running processes.
pslist -m	Provides a list of running process along with their memory details.
pslist -t	Show the process tree of the running processes.
pslist -x	Show the list of running processes along with memory and thread information.

***Table 8.14:** Important pslist commands*

The utility TCPView provides the current view of all the TCP connections. When you run this utility, you will see a screen like the following that shows a lot of details about the connections opened by each of the processes:

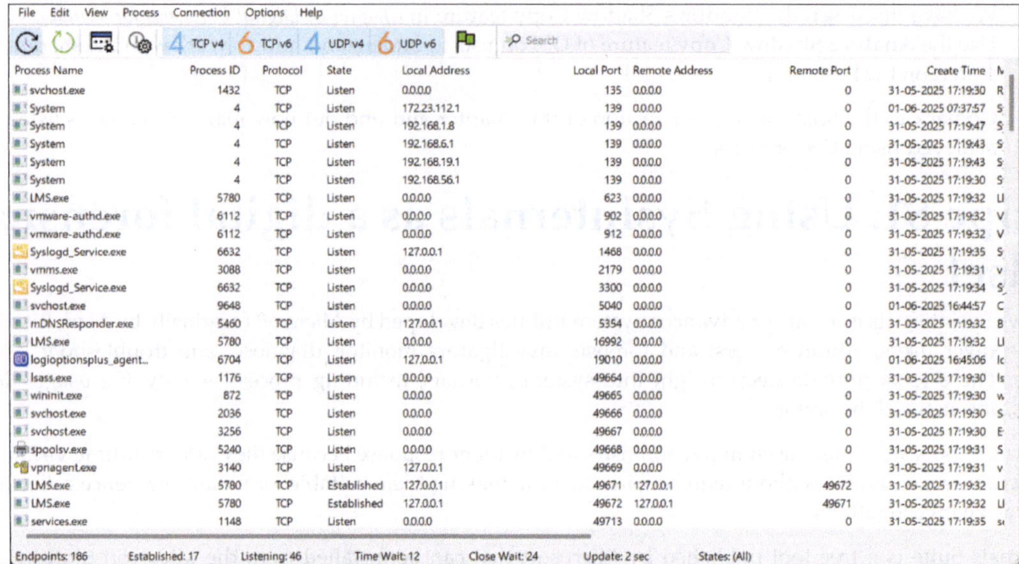

Figure 8.8: TCPView tool of Sysinternals Suite showing all the TCP connections

You can also export all the details to be analyzed later.

Finally, let us use an important utility called Process Explorer. Process Explorer shows the currently running process, their hierarchy, and many other details as shown in the following figure:

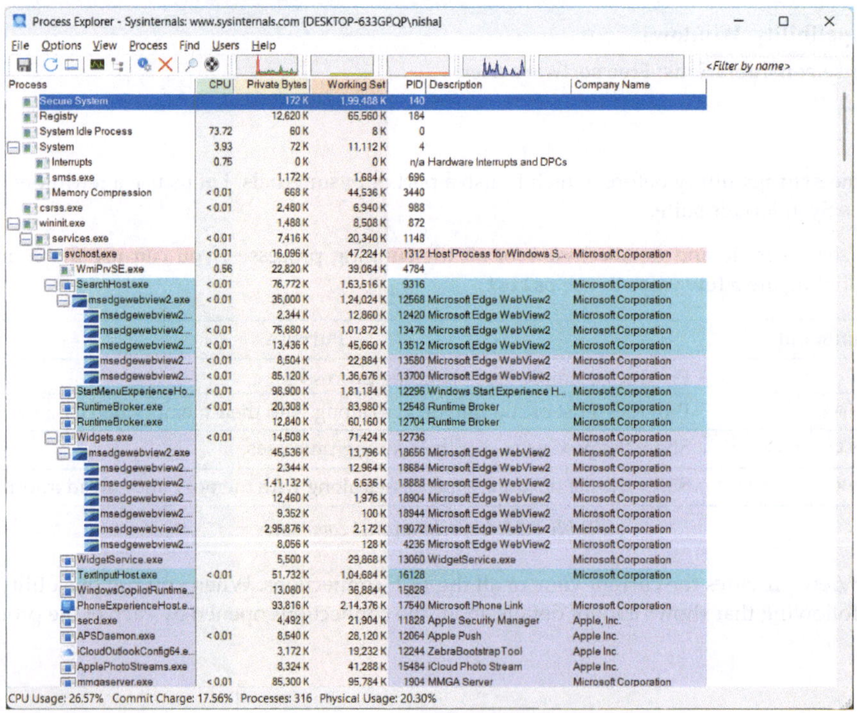

Figure 8.9: Process Explorer tool of Sysinternals Suite showing the running process and process tree

You can also check if a suspicious process is malware by verifying the process on **VirusTotal.com**, the top site for malware checks, as shown in the following figure:

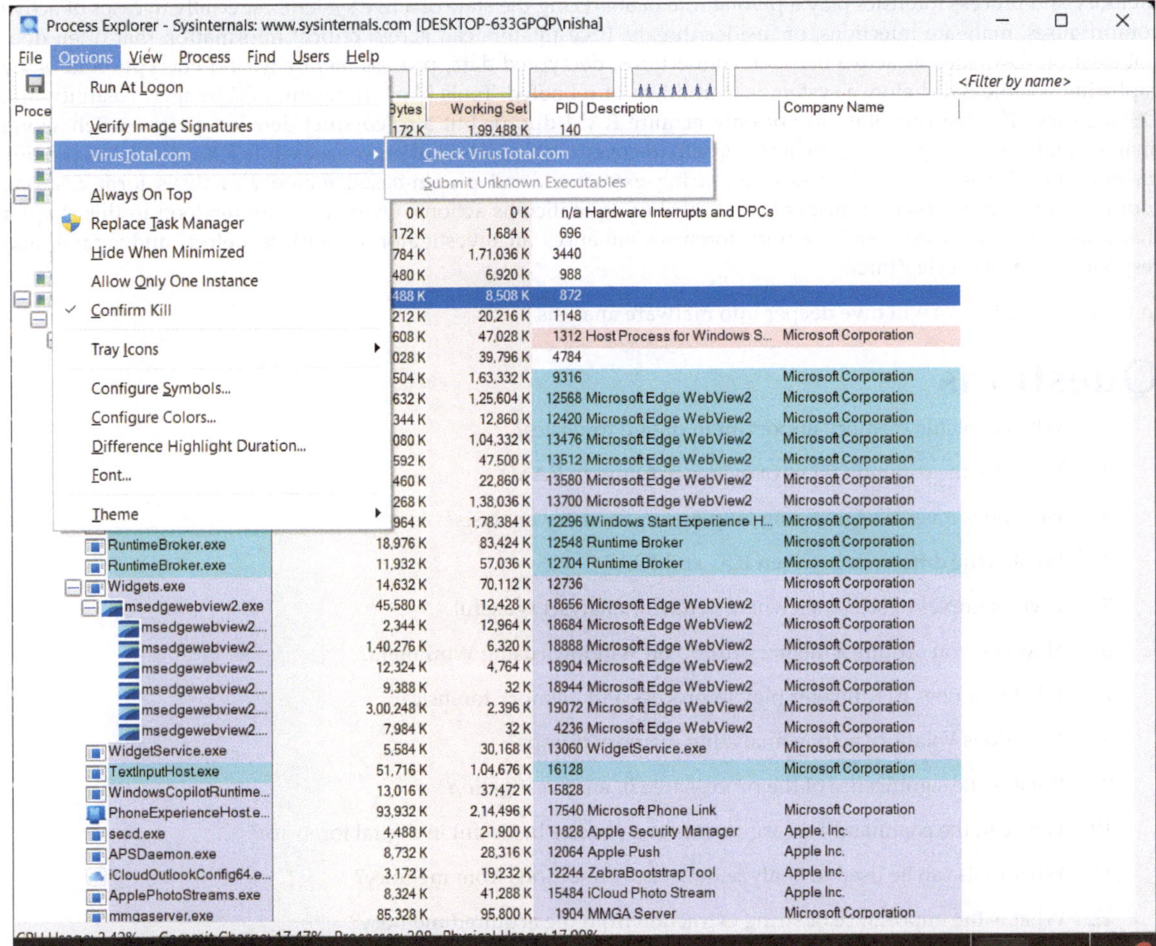

***Figure 8.10**: Process Explorer tool of Sysinternals Suite showing a suspicious process using VirusTotal.com*

Activity

Attempt the following activities before the next recipe:

- Use the **pslist** command-line tool provided with Sysinternals to print all the processes for an executable, e.g., chrome.exe.
- Explore all the other tools listed on the website of Sysinternals and be familiar with them.
- Process Explorer provides a way to create Mini Dump and Full Dump for processes. These dump files are created with the **.dmp** extension. Find out what the use of such dump files is and how they can be analyzed.
- Check a process on **VirusTotal.com** as shown in the preceding figure and observe the type of information you can see.

Conclusion

Memory and process forensics play a pivotal role in analyzing the state of a live system, especially in cases of active compromises, malware infections, or insider threats. Investigators can access critical information that often does not exist on disk, such as active network connections, decrypted data, process hierarchy, and encryption keys, by capturing volatile data before a system is shut down or rebooted. Tools like WinPmem, FTK Imager, Volatility, and OSForensics offer the capability to not only acquire RAM dumps but also conduct detailed analysis. Behavioral analysis and reverse engineering techniques help uncover the true intent of processes, while IOCs and IOAs provide insights into threat activity. Process trees, string extraction, and plugin-based memory analysis form a strong foundation for reconstructing incidents and attributing malicious actions. Overall, we understood in this chapter that mastering the process and memory forensics enhances an investigator's ability to detect, understand, and respond to complex cyber threats.

In the next chapter, we will dive deeper into malware analysis.

Questions

1. Why is volatile memory important in digital forensics?
2. What are the common types of evidence found in RAM?
3. How does reverse engineering help during memory analysis?
4. What is the difference between IOC and IOA?
5. Give examples of scenarios where behavior analysis is useful.
6. How can you acquire a memory dump on Windows using WinPmem?
7. What role does FTK Imager play in process and memory forensics?
8. How does Volatility help in analyzing memory dumps?
9. What is the significance of the process tree in an investigation?
10. How can the command-line arguments of a process be useful in digital forensics?
11. What tools can be used to analyze network connections from memory?
12. What is the importance of string extraction from the acquired memory?
13. How is OSForensics different from Volatility?
14. What can be extracted using the Bulk Extractor tool?
15. What are the things you should perform before the analysis of acquired memory?
16. Explain the use of windows.pslist and windows.pstree plugins.
17. How can the contents of a clipboard be useful in forensic analysis?
18. What is the role of environment variables in memory analysis?
19. Why is it important to analyze the parent-child relationships between processes?
20. How can digital forensics professionals use Sysinternals tools in live forensics?

Points to remember

- Volatile memory holds key evidence that is lost when the system shuts down.
- RAM analysis helps uncover live malware, encryption keys, and user activities.
- Process acquisition enables an understanding of what was running at the time of capture.
- WinPmem and FTK Imager are common tools to dump memory.
- Volatility provides plugin-based analysis of memory dumps.
- Reverse engineering helps understand unknown binaries and malware.
- IOCs are specific artifacts. IOAs are behavioral indicators.
- Behavior analysis provides runtime insights into processes and malware.
- Process trees help map the execution lineage of suspicious activities.
- Tools like pslist and pstree provide detailed information and process hierarchies.
- netstat and netscan plugins show active and past network connections.
- The Strings command can reveal plain-text passwords, scripts, and configurations.
- Bulk Extractor can extract emails, URLs, IPs, and other metadata from the RAM.
- pwdump can extract password hashes from memory.
- OSForensics integrates multiple analysis functions into a single interface.
- Well-known image formats are E01, AFF, and RAW, while SMART is also being used in some cases.
- Environment variables can reveal paths, tokens, and system state.
- Registry and DLLs in memory can help identify malware artifacts.
- Swap files may also contain sensitive remnants of RAM content.
- Sysinternals tools are essential for live system inspection.
- Always verify and hash memory dumps before and after analysis.
- Use sandboxing for behavior analysis to avoid system compromise.
- Process injection and hollowing often only appear in RAM.
- Case management tools like in OSForensics can help document everything during forensic analysis.

Key terms

- **Volatile memory**: Temporary memory (RAM) that is lost when the system powers off.
- **RAM Dump**: A complete capture of the contents of system memory.
- **WinPmem**: A memory acquisition tool for Windows (and Linux via LinPmem).
- **FTK Imager**: A tool used to capture memory and create disk images.
- **Volatility**: A memory analysis framework supporting multiple OS platforms.
- **IOC**: Tangible artifact of malicious activity.

- **IOA**: Behavior or sequence suggesting an ongoing attack.
- **Process tree**: Hierarchical structure showing parent-child process relationships.
- **Behavior analysis**: Runtime observation of a program's activity.
- **Reverse engineering**: Analyzing a binary to understand its function and logic.
- **Pagefile**: Windows swap file used to extend memory.
- **E01**: EnCase forensic image format.
- **AFF**: Open-source image format.
- **RAW/DD**: Uncompressed disk or memory image format.
- **SMART**: An older forensic image format with metadata and compression.
- **Registry Hive**: A logical group of keys, subkeys, and values in the Windows Registry.

Join our Discord space

Chapter 9
Malware Forensics

Introduction

Malware, short for malicious software, refers to any software intentionally designed to cause damage to a computer, server, client, or network. It encompasses various types like viruses, worms, trojans, ransomware, spyware, adware, rootkits, and more. In digital forensics, malware is often a central artifact of interest, and its presence usually suggests unauthorized activity or a security breach.

In this chapter, we will look at various aspects of analyzing malware to help in digital forensic analysis. While this chapter predominantly focuses on analyzing malware using Windows, most of these techniques apply to other operating systems like Linux and macOS. Wherever possible, activities are added to help you gain parallel knowledge in other operating systems.

Structure

In this chapter, we will cover the following topics:

- Introduction to malware forensics
- Recipe 82: Analyzing Microsoft Word and Excel document structure
- Recipe 83: REMnux as a malware analysis distro
- Recipe 84: Analyzing Microsoft Word and Excel documents using Oletools
- Static analysis of malware
- Recipe 85: Static analysis of malware
- Recipe 86: Reverse engineering and analyzing malware using Ghidra
- Identifying malware from the running processes
- Recipe 87: Using Sysinternals tool to analyze malware
- Using Windows Event Logs to analyze malicious activities
- Rootkits and advanced persistent threats
- Recipe 88: Identifying rootkits
- Recipe 89: Analyzing suspicious files using VirusTotal

Objectives

We have looked at various digital forensics techniques so far for collecting evidence, analyzing it, and even understanding their attack vectors. A lot of evidence that is collected may be malware. We will first understand what malware is, its various forms, and the methods for identifying it. We will then utilize various industry-standard tools to analyze the malware. We will work with multiple document types as well as binary files using these tools. By the end of this chapter, you will have the skills and confidence to analyze any malware presented to you and determine the appropriate next steps.

Introduction to malware forensics

Malware forensics can be considered a branch of digital forensics focused on the identification, analysis, and understanding of **malicious software** (**malware**) found during an investigation. The main objectives are to determine the following:

- How did the malware infiltrate the system?
- How did it impact the system (payload, data exfiltration, persistence)?
- Who may have created or deployed it?
- How to prevent further compromise?

It involves acquiring infected systems, isolating malware samples, and then using reverse engineering, static/dynamic analysis, and correlation with threat intelligence to understand malware behavior.

Common forms of malware

Let us look at the common form of malware that we may encounter during digital forensics evidence collection and analysis:

Malware type	Details	Risk level	Relevance in digital forensics
Virus	A piece of code that attaches itself to clean files or programs and spreads through user interaction (e.g., opening an infected file), often damaging data.	Medium	Important for tracing user-initiated infections and identifying compromised files or programs.
Worm	A standalone malware that replicates automatically and spreads over networks, often exploiting vulnerabilities to propagate without human action.	High	Useful in analyzing network-level propagation, identifying patient zero, and isolating compromised endpoints.
Trojan Horse	Malware disguised as a legitimate application that performs malicious activities like opening backdoors or stealing data once installed by the user.	High	Central in phishing-related forensics. Helps identify social engineering techniques and dropped payloads.
Ransomware	Encrypts files or entire systems and demands a ransom payment for the decryption key, often causing severe data loss or business disruption.	Very high	High-priority in forensic investigations. Critical to trace encryption mechanisms, find ransom notes, and potentially recover keys or trace payments.
Spyware	Secretly monitors user activity and collects sensitive information such as keystrokes, browsing habits, or credentials, often sending it to a remote server.	High	Can uncover credential theft, espionage activity, and data leakage paths through memory and network analysis.
Adware	Unwanted software that displays advertisements, typically bundled with freeware or shareware. May track user activity or redirect browser sessions.	Low	Low forensic value unless found to be part of a larger malware campaign or used for click fraud or surveillance.
Rootkits	Hides itself and other malicious components by modifying OS or kernel-level functions, making detection and removal difficult.	Very high	Requires advanced memory and kernel forensics to uncover. Used to hide long-term **advanced persistent threat** (**APT**) activity.

Malware type	Details	Risk level	Relevance in digital forensics
Fileless malware	Operates in memory without leaving traditional file artifacts on disk, often uses scripts (e.g., PowerShell) and exploits native tools (e.g., LOLbins).	Very high	Demands volatile memory analysis and behavioral logging. Evades most traditional detection tools.
Backdoor	Installs hidden remote access channels into systems, allowing attackers to bypass authentication and maintain persistent access.	High	Valuable for uncovering post-exploitation persistence mechanisms and lateral movement strategies.
Keyloggers	Captures keystrokes to collect credentials, private messages, or input data, typically logging it to local or remote locations.	Very high	Helps identify stolen credentials and communication with external command-and-control servers.

***Table 9.1**: Common forms of malware*

Ways to identify malware

Let us understand the key ways to analyze and identify malware before we get into the recipes of a few of them. The following table lists such techniques along with the skills needed by a digital forensic professional working on such tasks:

Digital forensic technique	Details	Skills needed
Antivirus/EDR logs analysis	Use alerts and logs from antivirus or **endpoint detection and response (EDR)** tools to detect known malware by signature, heuristics, or behavior.	Familiarity with EDR tools (e.g., CrowdStrike, SentinelOne), understanding of log correlation, malware signature analysis.
Hash comparison	Compute hash values (MD5, SHA256, etc.) of suspect files and compare them with databases like VirusTotal, NSRL, or threat intelligence repositories to identify known malware.	File hashing, use of hash databases, **Open-Source Intelligence (OSINT)** querying (e.g., VirusTotal, Hybrid Analysis).
Static analysis	Analyze the binary or script without executing it, look at strings, headers, import tables, or embedded resources to find indicators of malware.	PE file structure knowledge, use of tools like strings, PEiD, **Detect It Easy (DIE)**, Ghidra, etc.
Dynamic analysis	Execute the malware in a controlled sandbox environment to observe behavior such as file creation, Registry edits, process injection, or network calls.	Virtualization, sandboxing (e.g., Cuckoo), use of Sysinternals tools, Process Monitor, Wireshark, etc.
Memory forensics	Analyze RAM dumps to identify injected code, malicious processes, or fileless malware that may not appear in disk images.	Memory acquisition (FTK, WinPmem), tools like Volatility, Process Explorer, etc.
Network analysis	Monitor and analyze network traffic to detect anomalous connections, such as beaconing to C2 servers, data exfiltration, or unexpected ports/protocols.	Packet analysis (Wireshark/tcpdump), protocol decoding, NetFlow/SIEM log interpretation.

Digital forensic technique	Details	Skills needed
Log analysis	Examine logs (e.g., system, application, firewall, IDS/IPS) for anomalies like unusual user activity, script execution, or login attempts.	Log parsing (e.g., grep, LogParser, PowerShell-based methods), understanding of Windows/Linux event logging, SIEM tools.
File integrity monitoring	Detect unauthorized changes to files or system binaries over time by comparing checksums or timestamps.	Use of **File Integrity Monitoring (FIM)** tools (e.g., Tripwire), scripting for hash baseline comparisons, understanding of system file structures
Using **Yet Another Recursive Acronym (YARA)** rules	Apply YARA pattern-matching rules to files, memory, or network streams to detect known or unknown malware families based on unique strings or binary patterns. YARA is exception in flexibility and extensibility.	Writing YARA rules, pattern recognition, regex and binary pattern skills, malware family profiling.
Heuristic and behavior-based detection	Identify malware based on suspicious behavior (e.g., privilege escalation, code injection) rather than known signatures.	Threat modeling, behavior profiling, knowledge of attack techniques (e.g., MITRE ATT&CK), sandbox behavior interpretation.
Artifact correlation	Correlate multiple artifacts (e.g., dropped files, Registry entries, scheduled tasks) to build a profile of the malware's presence and timeline of execution.	Timeline analysis, use of DFIR suites (e.g., Autopsy, X-Ways), Registry forensics, process execution chain analysis.
Reverse engineering	Disassemble or decompile malware binaries to understand their inner workings, encryption logic, or persistence mechanisms.	Use of IDA Pro, Ghidra, Assembly language, understanding of Windows API and malware obfuscation techniques.

Table 9.2: Ways to identify malware

Considering a digital forensic examiner while working with malware

When handling malware, a digital forensic examiner must carefully consider several factors to ensure that all investigative guidelines are observed and that the collected evidence remains admissible in a court of law. The table below outlines these key considerations:

Consideration	Details
Environment isolation	Always perform malware analysis in an isolated and secure environment, such as a sandbox, air-gapped VM, or forensic workstation. This prevents accidental propagation or host contamination.
Chain of custody	Maintain a clear and documented chain of custody for all malware-related evidence (files, memory, logs). Each transfer or access must be logged to ensure legal admissibility.
Safe handling	Avoid executing malware on production or internet-connected machines. Disable autorun features, use write blockers when necessary, and handle media cautiously to prevent infection spread.

Consideration	Details
Proper acquisition	Acquire full disk images and volatile memory using forensically sound methods. Avoid booting or altering the infected system directly to preserve original state and volatile data.
Documentation	Thoroughly document every action taken, including tools used, timestamps, hash values, and analysis decisions. This ensures repeatability and supports legal proceedings if needed.
Tool validation	Use validated and widely accepted forensic and malware analysis tools. Verify tools' hashes and check compatibility with the malware's execution environment (e.g., OS or architecture).
Threat intelligence integration	Leverage public and private threat intelligence feeds to correlate malware indicators (e.g., hashes, IPs, domains) with known campaigns or malware families.
Legal compliance	Ensure the forensic examination complies with applicable cyber laws, data privacy regulations (e.g., GDPR, IT Act), and organizational policies to avoid legal complications.
Behavioral profiling	Analyze malware behavior (e.g., file drops, Registry modifications, network traffic) and map it to frameworks like MITRE ATT&CK to understand the attack chain and attacker goals.
Preserve original malware sample	Always keep a read-only, untouched copy of the original malware sample. Conduct all analyses on duplicates to ensure forensic soundness and enable re-analysis if needed.
Use of timestamps and Timelines	Correlate file creation/modification times, log entries, and network events to build a timeline that illustrates the malware's lifecycle on the infected system.
Collaboration with incident response teams	Work closely with SOC/IR teams to ensure the forensic findings feed into containment and remediation strategies, and that incident context is preserved.
Anti-forensics awareness	Be aware of anti-forensics techniques used by malware such as timestomping, encryption, log deletion, and environment-aware evasion. These may impact evidence integrity.
Cross-platform considerations	Understand malware behavior on multiple platforms (e.g., Windows, Linux, macOS, Android) as some malware exhibits OS-specific behavior or propagation strategies.

***Table 9.3**: Considerations for a digital forensic examiner while working with malware*

Understanding YARA rules

In today's world of digital forensics, no discussion is complete without YARA rules if we are talking about malware forensics.

YARA is a pattern-matching tool used by malware analysts and digital forensic investigators to identify and classify malware samples based on patterns (signatures) found in binaries, memory, or files. It works by defining rules that contain strings, conditions, and metadata that describe characteristics of known malware. These rules are then used to scan files or memory dumps to detect threats.

YARA rules are used by many tools due to their rich set of features that can help in malware analysis. A few of the key features of YARA rules include the following:

YARA rules feature	Details
Rule-based detection	YARA uses a rule syntax to define malware patterns using strings and logical conditions.
String matching	Supports matching text, hexadecimal, and regular expression strings.
Logical conditions	Allows use of and, or, not, of, any, all, at, in, etc., to define detection logic.
Metadata support	Enables analysts to add information such as author, description, date, and references to each rule.
Modular rules	Rules can be grouped into modules, reused, and inherited using include and import.

YARA rules feature	Details
Memory and file scanning	Can scan both files on disk and live/volatile memory dumps (e.g., via Volatility).
Tagging and classification	Rules can be tagged (e.g., APT, Trojan, Infostealer) for better organization and filtering.
Tool integration	Integrates with malware sandboxes (Cuckoo), memory forensics tools (Volatility), and AV engines.
Cross-platform support	YARA runs on Windows, Linux, and macOS, and can be used via CLI or embedded in Python scripts.

Table 9.4: Key features of YARA rules

The YARA rule is also widely used because it is very efficient in scanning large sets of files or memory without consuming significant resources.

Note: Since many well-known malware analysis tools use YARA Rules, if you are planning to make a career in malware forensics, it is important to be an expert in this area.

Let us look at a few examples of YARA rules. The following is a basic structure of how a YARA rule may look for detecting malware:

```
rule ExampleMalwareDetection
{
    meta:
        author = "Analyst01"
        description = "Detects Example Malware based on string signatures"
        reference = "https://example.com/malware-sample"
        date = "2025-06-04"

    strings:
        $string1 = "malicious_function_name"
        $string2 = "cmd.exe /c powershell"
        $hex_pattern = { 68 65 6C 6C 6F 00 }   // hex for "hello\0"

    condition:
        any of ($string*) or $hex_pattern
}
```

The preceding rule can flag files containing at least two strings indicative of PowerShell obfuscation, a common tactic in fileless malware, in the following example:

```
rule PowerShellObfuscation
{
    meta:
        description = "Detects obfuscated PowerShell commands commonly used in malware"
        author = "Nishant_K"
        date = "2025-06-04"

    strings:
        $ps1 = "Invoke-Expression"
```

```
        $ps2 = "IEX"
        $ps3 = "FromBase64String"
        $ps4 = "System.Reflection.Assembly::Load"

    condition:
        2 of ($ps*)
}
```

Based on these details, we can use YARA rules in the following scenarios:

Use case	Details
Scanning files	Find malware in folders or archives.
Memory analysis	Volatility plugin yarascan applies YARA rules to memory dumps.
Sandbox detection	Tools like Cuckoo use YARA to tag malware behavior.
SIEM/Threat hunting	Integrated into advanced SOC workflows for automatic insights into threat around malware.

***Table 9.5:** Scenarios in which YARA rules can be used*

Let us look at one more example of how YARA rules can be used to detect Base-64 encoded payloads in PowerShell scripts:

```
rule Base64EncodedPayload
{
    meta:
        author = "Nishant_K"
        description = "Detects suspicious Base64 payloads often used in PowerShell malware"
        category = "fileless"
        date = "2025-06-04"

    strings:
        $base64_string1 = /[A-Za-z0-9+/]{200,}==/  // suspicious long base64 strings
        $base64_string2 = "FromBase64String"
        $ps_invoke = "Invoke-Expression"

    condition:
        $base64_string1 and ($base64_string2 or $ps_invoke)
}
```

The preceding rule detects scripts that use large base64 strings along with commands typically used to decode and execute them (e.g., FromBase64String, Invoke-Expression). Such patterns are typical in obfuscated or fileless malware.

Once such YARA rules are written, they can be used to detect malware in the following format:

```
yara -r your_rule.yar suspicious_file.exe
```

E.g.,

```
yara -r Base64EncodedPayload.yar suspicious_file.exe
```

When multiple YARA rules are used to analyze a suspicious file using a script-based automation, the real power of YARA rules is realized.

Interesting fact: **Many well-known malware analysis software use YARA rules behind the scenes, which is completely transparent to end users and even to security professionals. Some examples of such software or sites are VirusTotal, CrowdStrike, Google Security, Carbon Black from Broadcom, and many more.**

Recipe 82: Analyzing Microsoft Word and Excel document structure

Microsoft Office programs like Word, Excel, and PowerPoint are very popular and are used by a majority of people around the world. Currently, the file extensions `.docx`, `.xlsx`, `.pptx` are the extensions that are used by MS Word, MS Excel, and MS PowerPoint. They replace the older binary formats (`.doc`, `.xls`, `.ppt`) and are fundamentally zip archives that contain structured XML and media files.

Tip: **We can make use of the fact that Microsoft Office documents are inherently zip archives to analyze them without using any specialized tool.**

All the Microsoft Office document files can be used as a good medium for spreading malware. Let us look at the following table to understand how they can contain malware:

Technique	Details	Common indicators
Macros (`.docm`, `.xlsm`)	Embedded **Visual Basic for Applications (VBA)** scripts that execute on events like document open or close.	AutoOpen macro, Shell, CreateObject("WScript.Shell").
Dynamic data exchange (DDE)	Fields that execute system commands when links are updated.	DDEAUTO, PowerShell command launched via DDE field. Automatic DDE or DDEAUTO is a well know Microsoft Outlook DDE Attack.
Embedded **objects/object linking and embedding (OLE)**	Files like `.exe`, `.js`, or `.hta` embedded in the document.	Suspicious ObjectPool entries or embedded content in XML.
External links / remote templates	XML references to external malicious templates or content.	TargetMode="External" in `.rels` files, external `.dotm` link.
Parsing vulnerabilities	Crafted XML or malformed zip content exploiting vulnerabilities in Office or viewers.	Unusual XML tags, malformed relationships, or zip bomb behavior.

Table 9.6: How Microsoft Office document files may contain malware

Note:

- **Compatibility: Windows**
- **License considerations: Part of the operating system**

Recipe

Let us analyze MS Word (`.docx`) and MS Excel (`.xlsx`) files. First, you need to create sample files with some content. For the Excel file, add a few sheets and add content in each of the sheets. After that, follow the given steps to complete the recipe:

1. Let us first take the Word file, e.g., `sample.docx`, and rename it to `sample.zip`. You may have to use the Command Window in Windows if the extension is not shown.

2. Now, extract this zip file and see the contents of the directory. You can also use a text editor program like Sublime Text, TextPad, or VS Code to view the entire structure of the directory after extraction. The directory structure may look like the following:

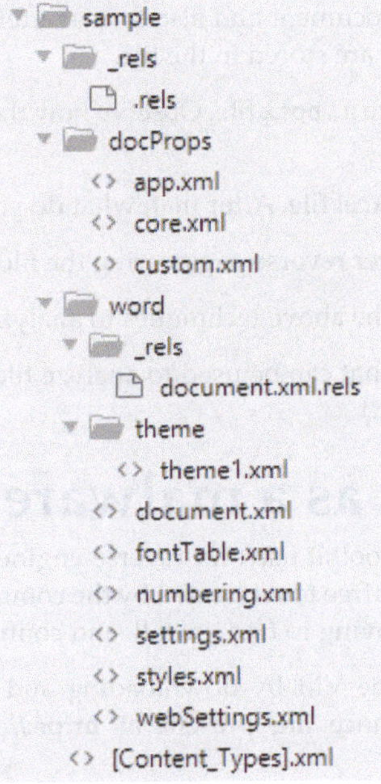

***Figure 9.1**: Structure of a Microsoft Word document*

3. You can easily see that most of the internal elements of the MS Word document are made up of various XML files and various media files.

   These are important components in the directories we can see:

Component	Details
`_rels/`	Relationship data (e.g., links between files).
`docProps/`	Document properties (title, author, etc.).
`word/`, `xl/`, `ppt/`	Main content folders for Word, Excel, PowerPoint respectively. For example, **`word/document.xml`** contains the main body content of the `.docx` file.
`[Content_Types].xml`	Lists file types and their MIME content.
`customXml/`	Custom data (often exploited for malicious macros or payloads).

***Table 9.7**: The basic structure of Microsoft Office documents*

   With this information in mind, look at each of the files.

4. Try extracting the file, modifying some content, zipping the directory, and then changing the extension back to its original value. Verify if it works, and you can see the changes made in the original document.

   Ensure that you do not zip the outside directory, but zip all the files inside the **sample** directory. Otherwise, there would be a root-level **sample** directory inside the zip file, which would break the structure of the `.docx` file.

5. Repeat the same process for the **`sample.xlsx`** file that you have created and bring out the differences between the structure of the `.docx` and `.xlsx` files.

Activity

Attempt the following activities before the next recipe:

- Add a few images to the Word document and also format a few lines as headings. Now, re-analyze to see how media and other formatting are stored in the file.
- Using the same technique, analyze a `.pptx` file. Observe how the structure of the `.pptx` file is different from the .docx and `.xlsx` files.
- Password-protect a sheet in an Excel file. After that, what do you see if you want to unzip the zip file?
- Add a macro in the Excel file. After reverse engineering the file, where do you see the macro?
- Using infected file samples, use the above techniques to analyze the files.
- Look for a similar tool in Linux that can be used to analyze files for MS Office and other Office Programs (e.g., OpenOffice, LibreOffice, etc.)

Recipe 83: REMnux as a malware analysis distro

REMnux (**https://remnux.org/**) is a Linux toolkit used for reverse-engineering and analyzing malicious software or malware. It provides a curated collection of free tools created by the community. They can be used by digital forensic analysts to investigate malware without having to find, install, and configure the tools.

REMnux can be best used as a standalone VM by downloading and installing the Virtual Appliance file. The instructions for using the virtual appliance are present at **https://docs.remnux.org/install-distro/get-virtual-appliance.**

REMnux can also be configured on an existing Kali or Ubuntu machine. The instructions for starting from scratch in such a machine are present at **https://docs.remnux.org/install-distro/install-from-scratch.**

Note:

- **Compatibility: Windows**
- **License considerations: Free software used**

Recipe

Let us download and configure REMnux, and then use it to analyze a malware sample. Follow the following steps to complete this recipe:

1. First, download the VirtualBox OVA file for REMnux from **https://docs.remnux.org/install-distro/get-virtual-appliance**. The OVA file is a self-contained virtual machine based on Ubuntu 20.04 at the time of writing.

   Note: **You can also download the general OVA that can be used in hypervisors like VMware Workstation. Irrespective of which one you use, after installation, it is a good idea to update the distribution using `apt-get update`, followed by `apt-get upgrade`.**

2. Once the download is complete, import it into VirtualBox.
3. Now, start the VM. Once prompted for a password, use remmux/malware. You have now installed and logged into REMnux VM. Let us now use this to analyze a PDF file.

   You can first download a PDF malware sample from MalwareBazaar (**https://bazaar.abuse.ch/**) using the search term **`tag:pdf`**. This will show a larger number of files of type PDF. Ensure you are working on them only in a sandboxed environment or in an isolated REMnux VM, as they are real malware files.

Note: Each file from MalwareBazaar is protected by a simple password. You need to provide that password while unzipping the file. Also, exercise caution while working with malware downloaded from MalwareBazaar or elsewhere in an isolated environment that does not contain critical or valuable data.

4. Let us first use a Python utility PDFiD (**pdfid.py**) to analyze a PDF file as follows:

```
root@remnux:/home/remnux/Downloads# pdfid.py
b710ae59bc996a099ca491f6d32fef2d8d5fa25f266d590e4a7a13f81ab2b432.pdf

PDFiD 0.2.8 ./b710ae59bc996a099ca491f6d32fef2d8d5fa25f266d590e4a7a13f81ab2b432.pdf
 PDF Header: %PDF-1.7
 obj                    36
 endobj                 36
 stream                 16
 endstream              16
 xref                    1
 trailer                 1
 startxref               1
 /Page                   6
 /Encrypt                0
 /ObjStm                 0
 /JS                     0
 /JavaScript             0
 /AA                     0
 /OpenAction             1
 /AcroForm               0
 /JBIG2Decode            0
 /RichMedia              0
 /Launch                 0
 /EmbeddedFile           0
 /XFA                    0
 /URI                    4
 /Colors > 2^24          0

root@remnux:/home/remnux/Downloads#
```

While the above output may not look like much, it does indicate that there are many objects embedded in the file.

5. Let us now use another tool to further analyze this PDF file. We can use **peepdf** for this purpose as follows:

```
root@remnux:/home/remnux/Downloads# peepdf
b710ae59bc996a099ca491f6d32fef2d8d5fa25f266d590e4a7a13f81ab2b432.pdf

File: b710ae59bc996a099ca491f6d32fef2d8d5fa25f266d590e4a7a13f81ab2b432.pdf
MD5: dffdd99fc42f0ae88b61fe588a025221
```

```
SHA1: f684d990d5522511a78d5fbc129c60ba755d2f7b
SHA256: b710ae59bc996a099ca491f6d32fef2d8d5fa25f266d590e4a7a13f81ab2b432
Size: 134609 bytes
IDs:
        Version 0: [ <2b51f03f0630c89dea9da977dedf0e8d> <2b51f03f0630c89dea9da977dedf0e8d>
]

PDF Format Version: 1.7
Binary: True
Linearized: False
Encrypted: False
Updates: 0
Objects: 36
Streams: 16
URIs: 2
Comments: 0
Errors: 0

Version 0:
        Catalog: 36
        Info: 34
        Objects (36): [1, 2, 3, 4, 5, 6, 7, 8, 9, 10, 11, 12, 13, 14, 15, 16, 17, 18, 19,
20, 21, 22, 23, 24, 25, 26, 27, 28, 29, 30, 31, 32, 33, 34, 35, 36]
        Streams (16): [5, 11, 13, 15, 17, 19, 21, 22, 23, 24, 27, 28, 31, 32, 33, 35]
        Encoded (15): [5, 11, 13, 15, 17, 19, 21, 22, 23, 24, 27, 28, 31, 32, 33]
        Objects with URIs (2): [8, 9]
        Suspicious elements (2):
                /OpenAction (1): [36]
                /Names (1): [36]

root@remnux:/home/remnux/Downloads#
```

Now we are getting somewhere. This tool shows suspicious elements apart from a few other things that may need attention. Moreover, this also displays all the checksums of the PDF file, which can be directly pasted into **VirusTotal.com** to determine if the document is malicious.

6. The next step is to use tools like PDF parser (**`pdf-parser.py`**) on the REMnux machine to parse the PDF to a text file, and then analyze it to find out suspicious things like embedded URLs. Let us see one of them in the upcoming example.

   You can use the following command to parse the PDF file:

   ```
   pdf-parser.py ./b710ae59bc996a099ca491f6d32fef2d8d5fa25f266d590e4a7a13f81ab2b432.pdf >
   pdfparser.txt
   ```

   Out of the output file, the following is one of the areas of interest for us, which shows an embedded URL that looks suspicious:

```
obj 8 0
 Type: /Annot
 Referencing: 10 0 R

  <<
    /Type /Annot
    /Subtype /Link
    /Rect [112.440591 484.865787 352.440591 533.956696]
    /P 10 0 R
    /NM (0001-0000)
    /M "(D:20220617215004+02'00')"
    /F 4
    /Border [0 0 0]
    /A
      <<
        /S /URI
        /URI (http://evacdir.com/clapton?QXV0b0NBRAQXV=&ZG93bmxvYWR8WFg0TkRkdlpIeDhNV-
FkxTlRRM09UZzRPWHg4TWpVNU1IeDhLRTBwSUZkdmNtUndjbVZ6Y3lCYldFMU1VbEJESUZZeUlGQkVSbDA=da-
vin.hyundai&infringes=logo&route=morath)
      >>
    /H /I
```

7. Finally, we can use CyberChef to perform a detailed analysis of the PDF file. First, run the following from the command line:

```
Cyberchef
```

From the CyberChef window, you can now open a file or directory as input and analyze it using various recipes on the left side.

Activity

Attempt the following activities before the next recipe:

- Paste one of the checksums, e.g., the SHA1 checksum, in **VirusTotal.com** and observe if this file comes out as malicious.
- Read the REMnux documentation (**https://docs.remnux.org/**) to understand the tools that can be used to analyze PE files.
- Check the REMnux documentation for static analysis of Android APK files and try at least one tool like `apktool`.

Recipe 84: Analyzing Microsoft Word and Excel documents using Oletools

We used a bunch of tools from REMnux in the last recipe to analyze PDF files. REMnux is a great collection of tools that can be used for malware analysis in the most commonly used file types. Oletools is one of such tools that is part of REMnux and can be used to analyze **Object Linking and Embedding** (**OLE**) objects that are embedded in the MS Office files, e.g., scripts, macros, etc.

We will now use Oletools to analyze a malicious **.docx** file. Post that you can analyze a malicious **.xlsx** file using the same method.

Note:

- **Compatibility: Windows**
- **License considerations: Free software used**

Recipe

Let us analyze a .docx file using Oletools. Since **.docx** files may contain embedded images and even macros (in the form of code or scripts), it is important to analyze such files during the digital forensics examination. Follow the following steps to complete this recipe:

1. First, let us download a malicious MS Word (**.docx**) sample from MalwareBazaar (**https://bazaar.abuse.ch/**) by searching for files using the string **tag:docx**. Extract the file as usual using the password provided during the download.

2. Next, we will use the tool **oleid** to analyze the file we have downloaded as follows:

```
oleid 082e2764b7a09854d20e2f34e343917e36a6938a2cd376c901b4fe6e461498f2.docx
```

The output will look similar to the following. If there are risks associated with the file, it will show up in the table:

```
Filename: 082e2764b7a09854d20e2f34e343917e36a6938a2cd376c901b4fe6e461498f2.docx
--------------------+--------------------+----------+--------------------------
Indicator           |Value               |Risk      |Description
--------------------+--------------------+----------+--------------------------
File format         |MS Word 2007+       |info      |
                    |Document (.docx)    |          |
--------------------+--------------------+----------+--------------------------
Container format    |OpenXML             |info      |Container type
--------------------+--------------------+----------+--------------------------
Encrypted           |False               |none      |The file is not encrypted
--------------------+--------------------+----------+--------------------------
VBA Macros          |No                  |none      |This file does not contain
                    |                    |          |VBA macros.
--------------------+--------------------+----------+--------------------------
XLM Macros          |No                  |none      |This file does not contain
                    |                    |          |Excel 4/XLM macros.
--------------------+--------------------+----------+--------------------------
External            |0                   |none      |External relationships
Relationships       |                    |          |such as remote templates,
                    |                    |          |remote OLE objects, etc
--------------------+--------------------+----------+--------------------------
```

Figure 9.2: Details provided by oleid after analysis of a PDF file

3. We can also use **olevba** tool to find out if there are any **Visual Basic for Applications (VBA)** or XML macros in the document as follows:

```
root@remnux:/home/remnux/Downloads# olevba
082e2764b7a09854d20e2f34e343917e36a6938a2cd376c901b4fe6e461498f2.docx
XLMMacroDeobfuscator: pywin32 is not installed (only is required if you want to use MS
Excel)
olevba 0.60.2 on Python 3.8.10 - http://decalage.info/python/oletools
===============================================================================
FILE: 082e2764b7a09854d20e2f34e343917e36a6938a2cd376c901b4fe6e461498f2.docx
```

```
Type: OpenXML
No VBA or XLM macros found.

root@remnux:/home/remnux/Downloads#
```

Activity

Attempt the following activities before the next recipe:

- Using the same method and analyzing an `.xlsx` file.
- Do you think that `.pptx` (PowerPoint files) can also be malicious? If yes, use the same method to analyze a `.pptx` file.
- Look at other `ole` tools that are supplied in REMnux distro and check the type of additional information they can provide.

Static analysis of malware

Static analysis is the process of analyzing a file without executing it. It is important in malware forensics when we may want to inspect a suspicious binary in a safe, controlled, and offline manner.

Before we get into the recipe for analyzing malware, let us first understand what a **Portable Executable** (**PE**) is. PE is the file format used by Windows for executables (`.exe`), dynamic link libraries (`.dll`), and other binary files such as drivers (`.sys`). It is based on the **Common Object File Format** (**COFF**) and contains all necessary information for the Windows OS loader to manage the executable code.

Since such PE files are frequently infected by viruses or modified PE files that are actually malware planted into the machine, static analysis of such files can reveal a lot. Hence, during malware forensics, static analysis plays a major role.

Let us look at what static analysis can reveal in such executables:

Aspect	What static analysis can reveal
File metadata	Compiler used, timestamps, file size, hash values.
PE structure	Section names and sizes (`.text`, `.data`, etc.), various anomalies, etc.
Imports/Exports	Functions and APIs used (e.g., CreateRemoteThread, WinExec).
Packers/Obfuscation	Signs of packing or compression (e.g., UPX, ASPack, and other such methods).
Strings	Hardcoded IPs, URLs, commands, Registry paths, C2 addresses.
Entropy	High entropy, possible encryption/compression (malware trait).
Anti-analysis techniques	Calls to IsDebuggerPresent, FindWindow, GetTickCount, obfuscation, and other anti-debugging techniques.
IOCs	File names, suspicious DLLs, unusual sections.
Signature issues	Invalid or absent digital signatures.
Threat intelligence	Known malware hash matches, embedded domains, etc.

Table 9.8: *Insights revealed by static analysis*

Tools like PEStudio can also be used to analyze basic details of non-PE files, like PDF files. Since one can embed malicious content in PDF files, too, such tools may come in handy during the analysis of such digital evidence.

Recipe 85: Static analysis of malware files using PEStudio

There are two frequently used tools for analyzing such PE files, PEiD and PEStudio. PEiD is a legacy but still useful tool used to detect packers, cryptors, and compilers for PE files. PEStudio is a powerful and modern static analysis tool for Windows executables.

While you may find PEiD available for download from many sources, it is advisable to use it on an isolated machine only, as it is legacy software and may not be available from authentic sources.

Tip: **Another important aspect we need to consider is that while it is important to work with real malware to get a first-hand knowledge, it is not always practical to do so if you are using your computer for other purposes too. In such cases, look for synthetic files that are created to mimic the malware behavior by developers and research organizations without the inherent risk.**

Note:

- **Compatibility: Windows**
- **License considerations: Free software used**

Recipe

Let us use PEStudio to become comfortable with static analysis of PE files. Perform the following steps to complete this recipe:

1. First, let us download the PEStudio. PEStudio Basic, which is sufficient for starting with static analysis of PE files and analyzing malware, can be downloaded from **https://www.winitor.com/download.** This is a zip file and does not need any installation.

2. Once you have downloaded the PEStudio, you can run it by clicking on the PEStudio executable. PEStudio loads up and shows the initial screen, which looks like the following. You can drag-and-drop a file or open a file for analysis:

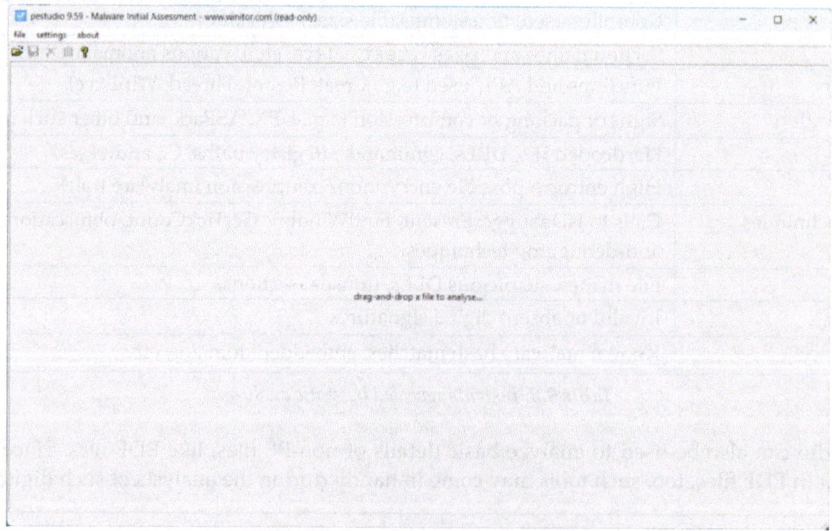

Figure 9.3: Opening screen of PEStudio

3. Now let us analyze a file using **pestudio**. In this case, we can use one of the browser forensic utilities that we have used before, as shown in the following figure:

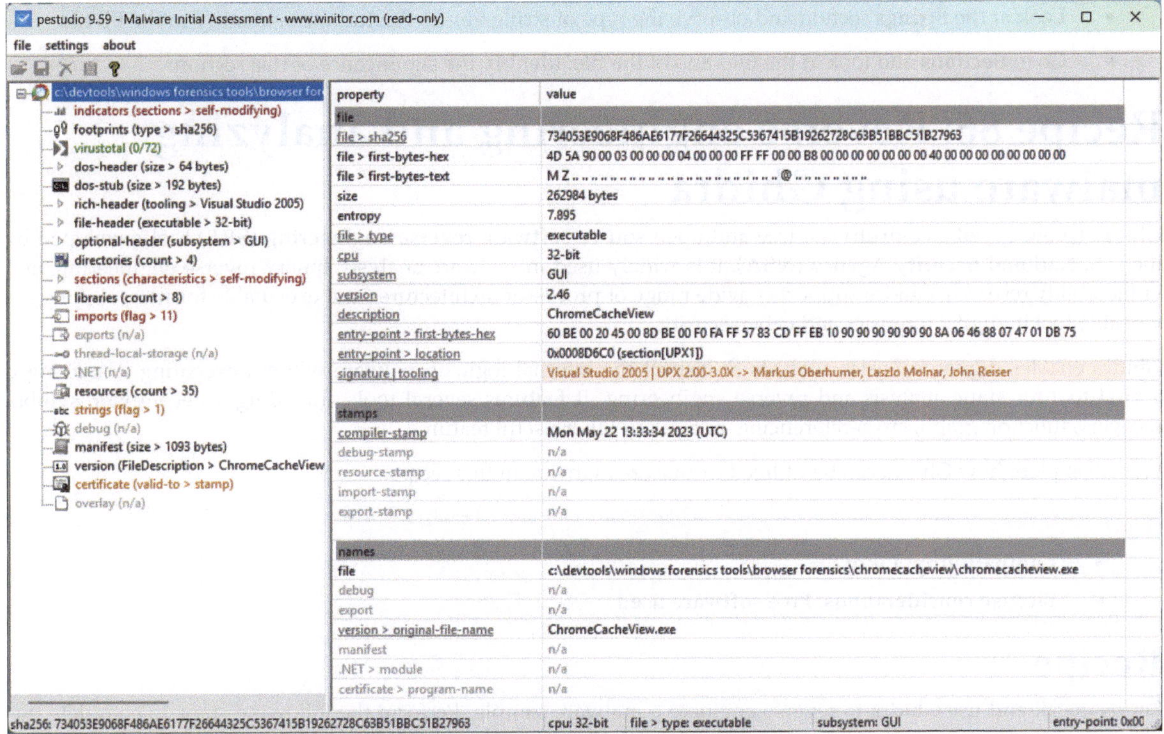

Figure 9.4: Details of file analysis in PEStudio

> **Note: In this case, we are analyzing an old file that does not contain any malware. However, since the file may be working directly using low-level system calls, it may get flagged as one having issues, or at least PEStudio thinks so. This may also be the reason antivirus programs flag some of these utilities.**

4. Look at each of the sections on the left side to understand various indicators and their significance. For example, the libraries section displays the list of **Dynamic Link Libraries** (**DLLs**) that are being loaded by the executable.

> **Note: IDA Pro from hex-rays (https://hex-rays.com/ida-pro) is a powerful disassembler, decompiler, and debugger, that is also used to reverse engineer files and analyze them for malware and other threats. This is a versatile tool of choice for digital forensics professionals for analyzing embedded systems, mobile applications, or complex multi-platform software. IDA Free (https://hex-rays.com/ida-free) can be used to start with IDA and learn it before you may want to use the Pro edition. As a digital forensics professional, this is another tool you can master.**

Activity

Attempt the following activities before the next recipe:

- Perform analysis of a **.dll** file using PEStudio. Observe the differences you see while analyzing a **.dll** file.
- Understand how PEStudio classifies the indicators and what they signify.

- Look at the **virustotal** section and look at various engines PEStudio checks for providing a score. Analyze what a high score can mean for a file.
- Look at the **Strings** section and observe the type of string values PEStudio can identify in the PE file.
- Go to **Sections** and look at the file ratio of the file. Identify the significance of this section.

Recipe 86: Reverse engineering and analyzing malware using Ghidra

Ghidra (pronounced Gee-druh) is a free and open-source **software reverse engineering** (**SRE**) tool developed by the U.S. **National Security Agency** (**NSA**). It is widely used in malware analysis, binary reverse engineering, and vulnerability research. Ghidra supports a wide range of processor architectures and executable formats, making it a versatile tool in digital forensics and cybersecurity.

Ghidra enables digital forensics analysts to inspect the internal logic of malware without executing it, making it a vital tool for static analysis and reverse engineering. It features several tools, including a decompiler, symbol recovery, function graph, cross-referencing, and many other useful features.

We will explore how Ghidra can be utilized to analyze malware in this recipe.

Note:

- **Compatibility: Linux**
- **License considerations: Free software used**

Recipe

Let us install and use Ghidra to reverse engineer a malware sample. Perform the following steps to complete this recipe:

1. First, let us install Ghidra if it is not pre-installed on your Kali Linux instance. In order to install Ghidra, run the following command:

   ```
   apt-get install ghidra
   ```

   Ghidra installs a lot of dependencies and will take a while to install. Using **apt-get** is a simple way to install Ghidra. In case you do not want to install it and directly run using the binaries, then you can do that by installing Java first and followed by running it from the release file. Look at **https://github.com/NationalSecurityAgency/ghidra** for more information.

   Note: **Ensure you have at least 1.5 GB of space on your Kali Linux VM to install Ghidra and its dependencies, like Java.**

2. Once installation is complete, launch Ghidra from the Kali Linux menu. After you accept the user agreement, you will see a screen similar to the following:

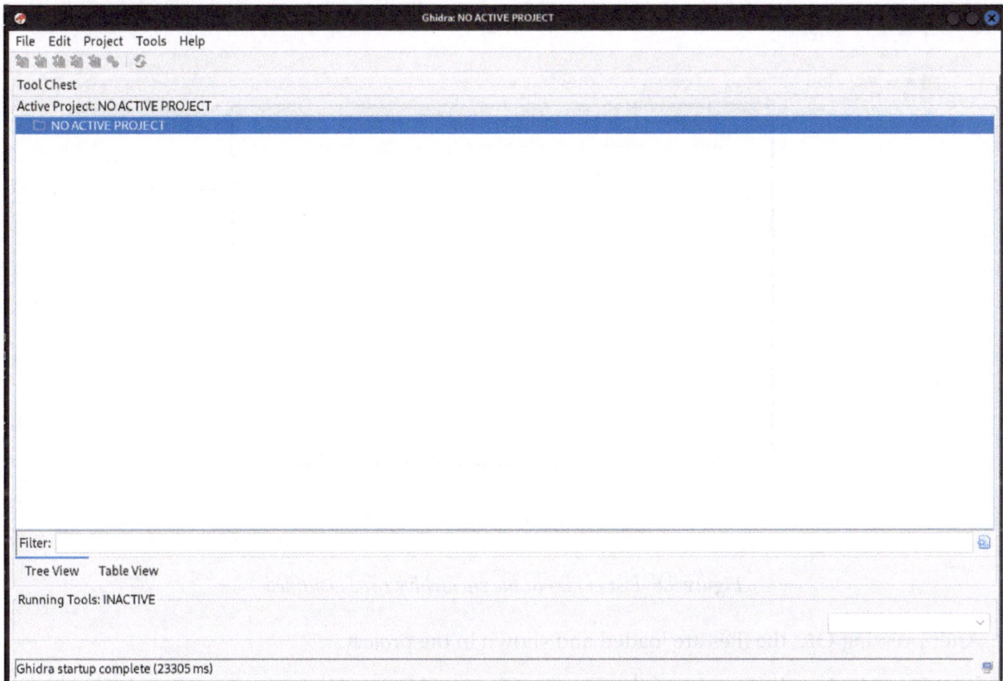

Figure 9.5: Opening screen of Ghidra

If Ghidra is launched for the first time, you will just see this screen (after the initial **Tip** popup). If you have used Ghidra before, then it will also show the previous project.

3. Let us create a new project by clicking on **File | New Project**, and selecting the first option, i.e., **Non-Shared Project**. In the next screen, provide the project directory and the name of the project.

4. Once you are done providing the preceding details, the name of the project is updated in the Ghidra screen. Now, let us add a file that we want to analyze. We can do that by dragging and dropping the malware sample file to the Ghidra window.

5. First, go to **MalwareBazaar (https://bazaar.abuse.ch/)** and download one of the samples uploaded recently. The sample file downloaded has the hash/ checksum of the file as the file name.

Caution: **Ghidra should only be used in an isolated or sandboxed environment to analyze malware samples. Do not use Ghidra to analyze malware on a computer that is also used for anything critical.**

Now, drag and drop that file into the Ghidra window. You may see a screen like the following figure. If you have a zip file containing multiple files, Ghidra will prompt you to perform a batch import. Irrespective of that, the instructions are easy to understand and follow:

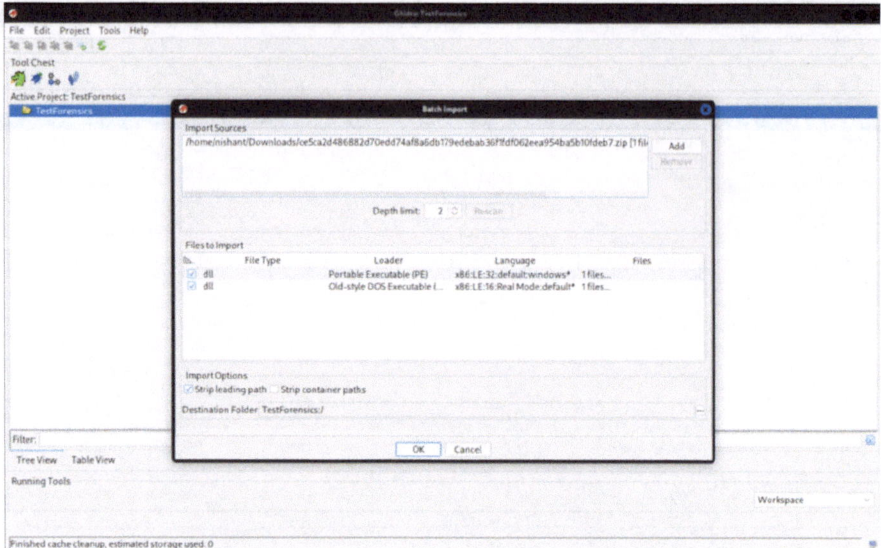

Figure 9.6: List of files in the zip archive to be identified

After pressing **OK**, the files are loaded and shown in the project.

6. When you double-click on any of the files, it will show the file in the default analysis tool, which is part of Ghidra. This tool decompiles the binary file (in this case, a `.dll` file, which is a type of PE file) and shows the listing in assembly/machine language and the decompiled high-level language program, e.g., C. The following figure shows these details:

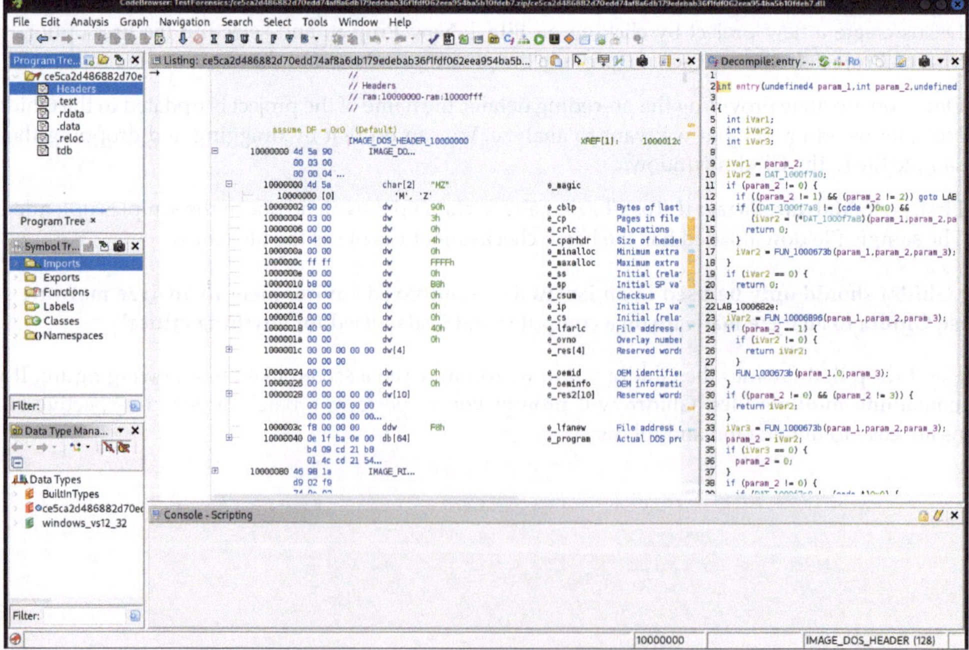

Figure 9.7: Ghidra screen with details about reverse engineering of the file

Ghidra is an important tool in the toolkit of any digital forensic analyst, and it takes time to get used to it. You can become comfortable with it by analyzing many malware samples.

Activity

Attempt the following activities before the next recipe:

- Right-click on any of the `.dll` or `.exe` files and select **About Program,** and understand various details that are shown in the pop-up window.
- There is an option **Open with Emulator** in the context menu that is displayed on right-clicking. What do you think this option can be used for?
- In the **CodeBrowser** (the tool launched that shows the details of the file) click on **Analysis** | **Auto Analysis**. Look at various options for analysis and try analyzing using specific analyzers.

Identifying malware from the running processes

In Windows-based systems, malware often disguises itself as legitimate processes or hides entirely using techniques like process hollowing, DLL injection, or rootkit-based stealth. Hence, identifying malware from running processes is a critical step in digital forensics and incident response, especially during live system analysis or memory forensics.

Let us look at a few ways in which malware disguise them in the following table:

Indicator	Details
Typosquatting	The name of the process has similar looking characters used or they sound similar, e.g., **`explorre.exe`**, **`svch0st.exe`**, **`winupdate.exe`**.
Non-standard location	The process is loaded from a non-standard location even if the name is legitimate, e.g., **`C:UsersPublic`**, **`%TEMP%`**, **`AppDataRoaming`**.
Double extension	Windows may be configured to hide well-known extensions, and hence this simple technique may be used as a decoy to convince people to open them, e.g., **`invoice.pdf.exe`**.
Suspicious command line argument of the running process	Malicious processes may try to run enumeration and other such techniques as part of the command line arguments. One such example is following where the process is trying to get the details of the user and the network interfaces: **`cmd.exe /c "whoami && ipconfig"`**
Unknown process with open TCP connection	While the process does not appear in the process list, connections are open to unknown or well-known blacklisted IP addresses.

Table 9.9: *Ways in which malware disguise themselves*

> Tip: **In the simplest stealth technique, malware can hide in plain sight by mimicking system process names with minor misspellings or unusual casing.**

Suspicious parent-child relationship is one of the best ways to investigate malware from running process details. The following are simple examples of suspicious parent-child relationships between running processes. In all such cases, one needs to do further analysis on typosquatting, non-standard location, etc:

- `winword.exe | powershell.exe`
- `svchost.exe | cmd.exe or calc.exe`
- `notepad.exe | powershell.exe`

Recipe 87: Using Sysinternals tool to analyze malware

As we discussed before in *Chapter 8, Dealing with Processes and Memory*, Windows Sysinternals is a suite of advanced system utilities to help power users, administrators, and forensic investigators monitor, diagnose, and troubleshoot Windows systems. Sysinternals tools are especially effective for dynamic malware analysis and incident response, allowing digital forensic professionals to quickly detect, trace, and document malware behavior on live systems.

Let us look at two of the important tools that can be used to analyze malware and suspicious processes.

Note:

- **Compatibility: Windows**
- **License considerations: Free software used**

Recipe

Let us first use Sysinternals Suite's Process Explorer to check if a running process is malware. In order to do so, you need to select any process in the Process Explorer. After that, go to **Options** | **VirusTotal.com** | **Check VirusTotal.com**, as shown in the following figure:

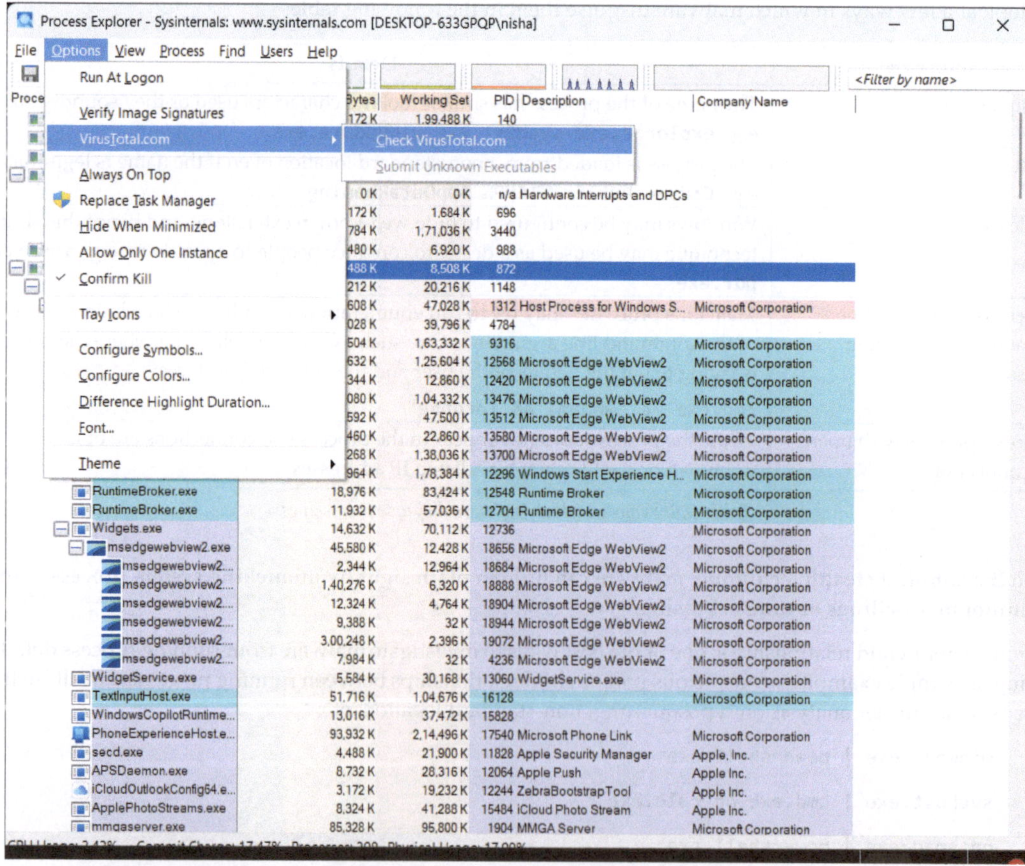

Figure 9.8: Process Explorer tool of Sysinternals Suite showing a suspicious process using VirusTotal.com

Once you click on this option, it submits the hash of the process to **VirusTotal.com**. After some time, you will see a score appearing in a new column that can be used to understand if the running process is malware.

Next, we can use Process Monitor, which is also a very good utility. This utility gives a different view than Process Explorer and can be used to closely monitor live processes.

If you look at the figure below, Process Monitor provides options like **Search Online** to search for the process name, **Stack** to get the process stack, **Count occurrences** to count the number of processes of the same type, and many other options:

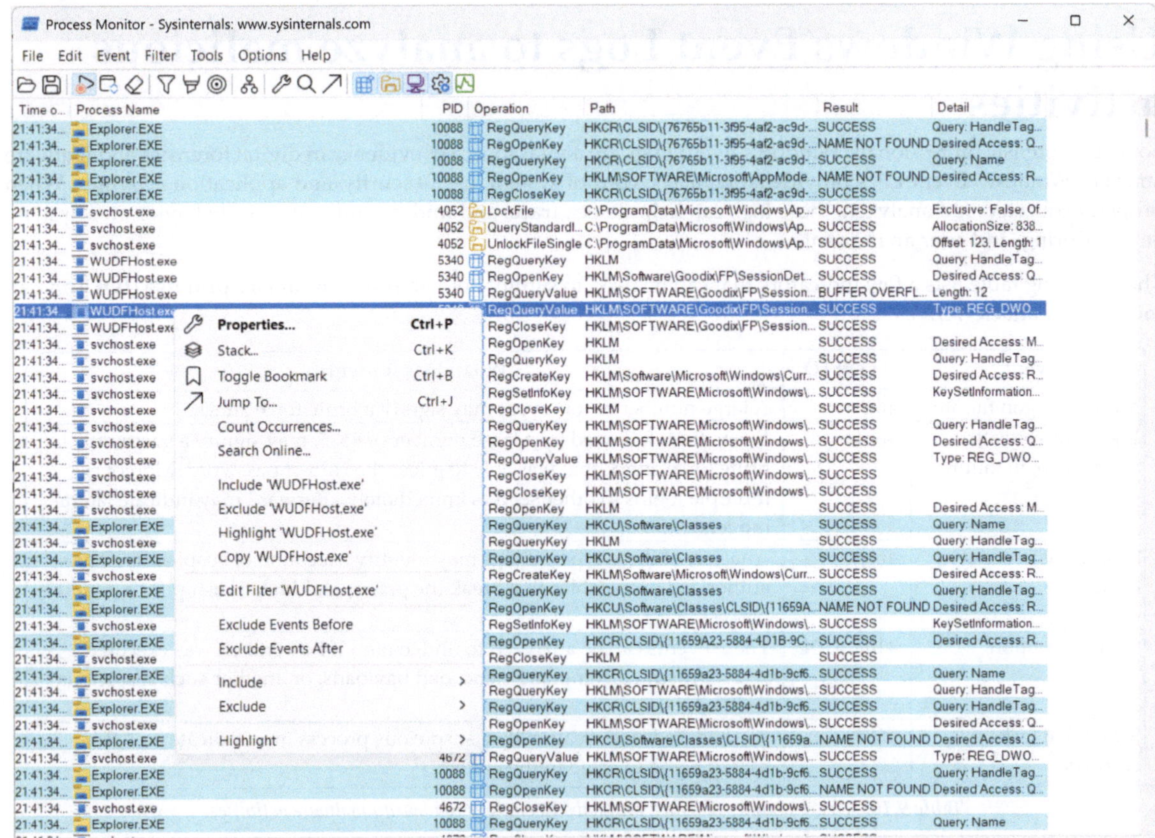

Figure 9.9: Identifying a malicious process using Systeminternals Process Monitor

These tools are hence very useful during live forensic analysis of the system.

There are other tools like Autoruns, TCPView, and SigCheck that can help with complex analysis scenarios. One can use this tool in a similar fashion, given as follows:

1. Use Process Explorer to check the process tree to find unknown parent-child chains and suspicious command lines.
2. Using Process Monitor, one can then find more details in the command line, Registry modification, etc.
3. Using Autoruns, one can find the paths to the autorun process pointing to the malicious executable files that are posing as a genuine process.
4. Then, using TCPView, connections to outbound C2 servers can be found.

5. Finally, using SigCheck (a command-line tool), the signature of the malware executable file can be verified.

Activity

Attempt the following activities before the next recipe:

- Try checking various processes using VirusTotal.com and see the details you find at the site.
- Look at the options provided by Process Monitor under the **Tools** menu and try out Network Summary to find details of the network events.

Using Windows Event Logs to analyze malicious activities

For cyber forensic professionals, Windows Event Logs are a vital source of evidence in digital forensics and malware analysis. Windows Event Logs provide a detailed record of system, user, security, and application activities. When properly collected and analyzed, these logs can help detect, trace, and understand malicious behavior on a system, before, during, and after an incident.

The following table lists a few indicators that can be used to signify both an **indicator of compromise** (**IOC**) and an **indicator of attack** (**IOA**):

Event	Event ID	What does it identify
Multiple logon failure	4625	A large number of this event may signify a brute force attack.
Logon success after multiple login failure	4624	Event 4624, followed by a large number of 4625, may signify a successful brute force attack that was able to guess the correct password. Moreover, multiple logins to other servers immediately afterward may indicate lateral movement.
Suspicious process creation	4688	Analysis of these types of logs may identify execution of suspicious or un-authorized executables that break the parent-child relationship for a genuine process.
Script execution	4103, 4104	These events can be analyzed to understand if PowerShell was executed with obfuscated commands, encoded payloads, or another such suspicious command line.
Scheduled tasks creation	4698	A scheduled task creation by a suspicious process may indicate an APT/ rootkit being injected in the system.

***Table 9.10**: A few examples of using Windows Event logs to identify malware activities*

Rootkits and APTs

Rootkits are a type of stealthy and malicious software designed to gain and maintain privileged access to a computer system while actively hiding their presence from users and traditional security tools. They operate by manipulating core system functions and intercepting calls to the operating system, often embedding themselves in kernel-level components, drivers, boot loaders, or even firmware.

Unlike typical malware, the primary goal of a rootkit is concealment; it enables threat actors to covertly control systems, execute commands, monitor activity, or deploy additional payloads without detection.

The presence of a rootkit poses significant challenges in digital forensics and incident response. Rootkits can hide running processes, files, Registry keys, network connections, and even tamper with system logs, making traditional tools unreliable for detecting anomalies. This stealth capability severely undermines system integrity, prolongs the persistence time of threat actors, and increases the difficulty of identifying, containing, and eradicating threats.

In critical environments, such as enterprise servers or industrial control systems, rootkits can facilitate long-term espionage, data exfiltration, and sabotage while evading conventional antivirus or endpoint detection systems. Their detection typically requires memory forensics, raw disk analysis, and specialized tools that bypass or inspect below the operating system's API layer.

Hence, as part of digital forensics analysis, rootkit analysis is an intrinsic part of the overall process. Due to it being closely related to APT, rootkits should be given sufficient investigation.

Recipe 88: Identifying rootkits

Identifying rootkits in Windows can be challenging for digital forensics professionals due to their ability to hide processes, files, Registry entries, and network activity. However, a combination of behavioral indicators, forensic techniques, and specialized tools can help uncover their presence.

Due to the evasive nature of rootkits, we look at indirect signs of their presence. Let us look at a few indicators of rootkit infection:

Category	Indicator
System instability	Frequent crashes, **blue screens (BSOD)**, unexplainable reboots.
Unusual activity	High CPU usage with no visible processes, unauthorized service and scheduled jobs creation.
Discrepancies in system views	File or process seen in memory but not in task manager or Process Explorer or vice-versa.
Suspicious network connections	Outbound traffic to unknown IPs, especially from hidden processes.
Failed security tools	Antivirus tools not running, disabled security center, logs being wiped.
Persistence without evidence	Malware returns after cleaning, but no persistence method visible in autoruns or scheduled jobs.
Abnormal boot behavior	BIOS or UEFI settings changed, unsigned drivers loaded early during boot.
Registry anomalies	Unusual entries in Run, Services, or Drivers32 keys, often obfuscated or empty-named.

***Table 9.11**: A few indicators of rootkits*

Note:

- **Compatibility: Windows**
- **License considerations: Free software used**

Recipe

Let us look at a few things as part of this recipe to develop the skills for identifying rootkits:

Task	Insights
Take a memory dump using WinPmem or FTK Imager.	N/A
Compare process listing using Process Explorer, Process Monitor, and Volatility (pslist and psscan).	A discrepancy in the list of processes may indicate the presence of rootkits.
Compare the list of loaded drivers from Windows vs the one from Volatility.	If the loaded drivers are not in the driver list, it may indicate the presence of APT and a rootkit may be hiding the driver entry.
Analyze network activitys by using netstat, TCPView and Volatility (netstan).	A discrepancy in the list of network connections and activities may indicate the presence of rootkits.

***Table 9.12**: List of tasks for identifying rootkits*

Activity

Attempt the following activities before the next recipe:

- Search for rootkits in MalwareBazaar using the tag `tag:rootkit` and download a few samples. Use the techniques discussed in this chapter, including VirusTotal, to confirm if the malware is indeed a rootkit.

  Note: **Ensure that you use an isolated environment for this activity due to the potential risk that may come with malware samples.**

- Identify ways to perform a Registry scan and analysis to find if an APT or rootkit is hiding somewhere.
- Use the Volatility `malfind` plug-in to identify if there is injected code or unlinked modules.

Recipe 89: Analyzing suspicious files using VirusTotal

VirusTotal (**https://www.virustotal.com/**) is a free online service that analyzes files, URLs, IPs, and domains using multiple antivirus engines, sandbox environments, and threat intelligence feeds. It is widely used in malware analysis, digital forensics, threat intelligence, and incident response to identify and share IOCs. VirusTotal also automatically shares these threats with the security community.

We have been downloading malicious file samples from MalwareBazaar in many recipes in this chapter. We have also worked with tools like Process Explorer, PDFiD, etc., that interface with VirusTotal to give a score from various sources.

Let us now also look at how to analyze a malware file using its hash as well as by using the binary file itself.

Note:

- **Compatibility: Windows**
- **License considerations: Part of the operating system**

Recipe

In this recipe, we will use VirusTotal to identify if the given hash and binary represent a malicious payload. Follow these steps to complete this recipe:

1. First, from *Recipe 83, REMnux as a malware analysis distro,* copy the SHA1 sum of the PDF file we worked with. Paste it in `VirusTotal` search box and click on **Search**:

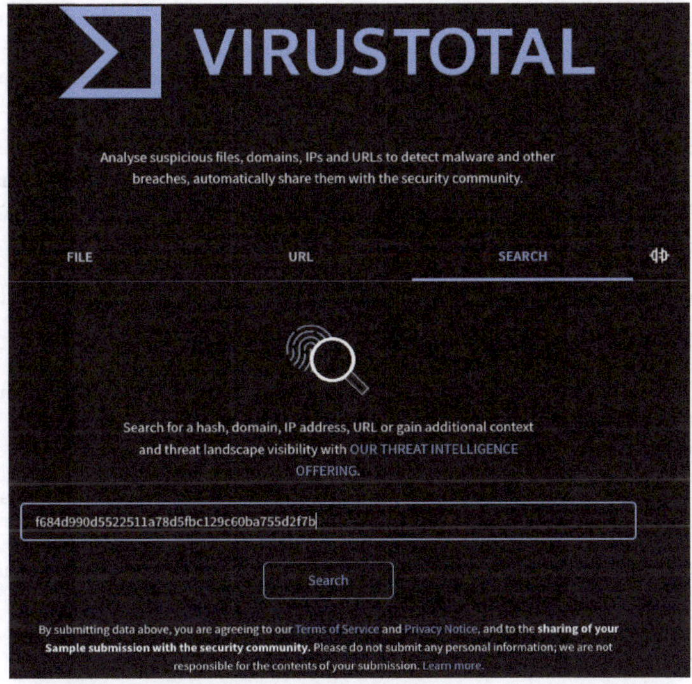

Figure 9.10: Using hash to search for potential malware in VirusTotal

2. In the search result page, you can see that this hash indeed represents malware. This is clear from the score given by various engines and the cumulative score given by VirusTotal. In this case, it basically means that 32 out of 64 engines reported this file as malicious:

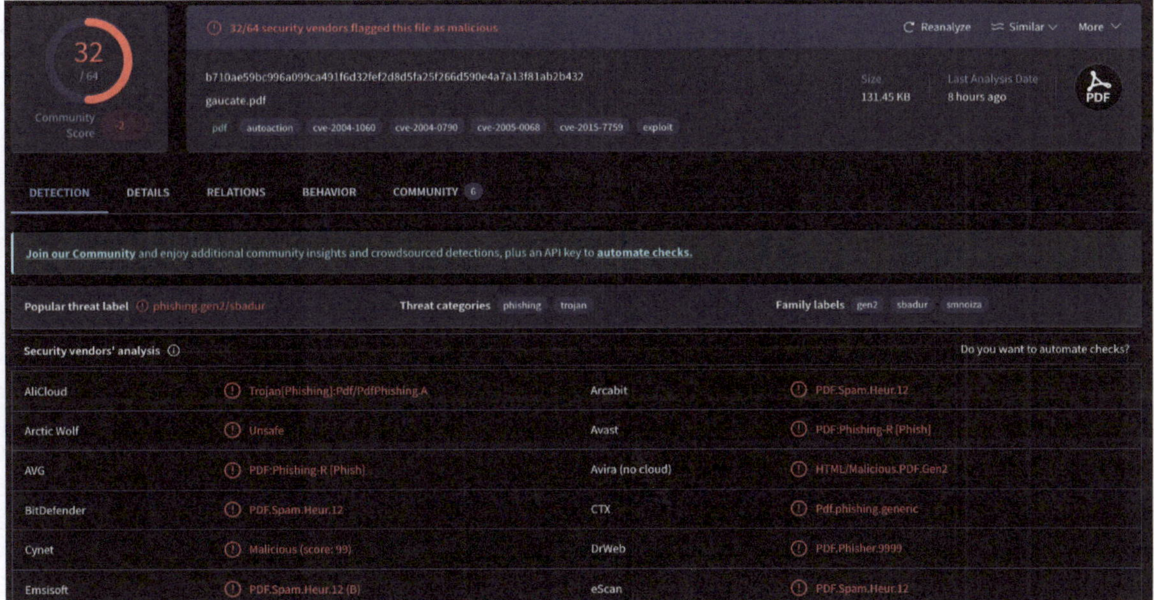

Figure 9.11: Details of malware show in VirusTotal

3. Now, let us see if we can also identify if the given file is malware by uploading the file directly. Go to the **File** tab on VirusTotal's home page, and choose and upload a file. VirusTotal will take a while to analyze the file and will take you to the same page as we saw above while uploading the hash. This confirms that both of them represent the same malware.

4. Hover your mouse on the icon on the immediate right side of the **Search** tab on the home page. This is the **Automate** option of VirusTotal. When you click on it, it will take you to the **VirusTotal API Overview** page. Here you can learn about how to automate threat intelligence and incident response tasks using VirusTotal API.

Activity

Attempt the following activities before the next recipe:

- Download a malware sample from VirusTotal. Now, find the SHA256 hash of the malware after unzipping the sample. In the **Search** tab of VirusTotal, paste this hash and click on **Search**. Verify that you see the same file that you downloaded before.
- Identify from the VirusTotal database if there can be any other malicious file types than those we used so far in this chapter.
- Read more about the various insights VirusTotal API provides under the IOC Reputation and Enrichment category.

Conclusion

Malware analysis plays a vital role in digital forensics, helping digital forensic investigators understand how malicious software infiltrates systems, what it does, and how to prevent future incidents. We used both static and dynamic analysis techniques to dissect malware, trace its origin, assess its behavior, and gather evidence for legal proceedings. We also utilized tools such as PEStudio, Ghidra, YARA, and Sysinternals to uncover hidden threats, including those that attempt to evade detection.

Whether it is a document-based malware, a rootkit, or fileless malware, proper analysis in isolated environments ensures both safety and accuracy. Understanding how malware works is the first step toward building better security systems and ensuring justice in cybercrime cases.

In the next chapter, we will understand how to work with digital forensic cases.

Points to remember

- Malware refers to malicious software intended to harm or exploit systems.
- Common types include viruses, worms, Trojans, ransomware, spyware, rootkits, and more.
- Static analysis inspects files without executing them.
- Dynamic analysis runs malware in a sandbox to study its behavior.
- YARA rules help detect malware based on string or binary patterns.
- Microsoft Office documents can contain embedded malware via macros or OLE objects.
- Tools like PEStudio reveal structural information about PE files.
- REMnux is a specialized Linux distro for malware analysis.
- Ghidra is used for reverse engineering malware binaries.

- Sysinternals tools like Process Explorer help identify live threats.
- Fileless malware resides only in memory, avoiding disk artifacts.
- Heuristics and behavioral analysis can detect unknown malware.
- Analyzing logs helps identify script execution and suspicious tasks.
- Rootkits hide malware presence and require memory forensics for detection.
- VirusTotal aggregates scan results from multiple engines.
- Reverse engineering is useful to decode obfuscated payloads.
- Tools like Oletools extract macro and OLE information from Office files.
- High entropy in a file suggests compression or encryption.
- Cross-checking hash values against known malware helps validate suspicions.
- Memory dumps are crucial in detecting fileless and injected malware.

Key terms

- **Malware**: Malicious software designed to harm or exploit a computer system.
- **Static analysis**: Examining a file's content without executing it to identify malicious patterns.
- **Dynamic analysis**: Running malware in a controlled environment to observe behavior.
- **YARA**: A tool for identifying malware using rule-based pattern matching.
- **PE File**: Portable Executable file format used in Windows for executables, DLLs, etc.
- **REMnux**: A Linux distribution loaded with malware analysis tools.
- **Ghidra**: An NSA-developed reverse engineering tool for binary analysis.
- **VirusTotal**: An online platform that scans files and URLs using multiple antivirus engines.
- **Process Explorer**: A Sysinternals tool to inspect running processes in real-time.
- **Process Monitor**: A tool for tracking Registry, file system, and process/thread activity.
- **Entropy**: A measure of randomness in a file. High entropy may indicate encryption or obfuscation.
- **Rootkit**: Malware that hides its presence and maintains privileged access.
- **Fileless malware**: Malware that resides in memory and does not write to disk.
- **Indicators of compromise (IOCs)**: Artifacts like hashes, IPs, and file names used to detect malware.
- **Heuristic analysis**: Detecting malware based on behavior rather than signature.
- **Office Macros**: Scripts embedded in MS Office files, often exploited by malware.
- **Object Linking and Embedding (OLE)**: Technology that allows embedding of objects like scripts into Office documents.
- **Autoruns**: A Sysinternals tool that shows programs configured to run during startup.
- **TcpView**: A tool to inspect active TCP/UDP connections on a system.
- **SigCheck**: Command-line utility to verify the digital signatures of executables.

- **WinPmem**: Tools for memory acquisition used in live forensics.
- **Volatility**: A memory forensics framework used to extract artifacts from RAM dumps.
- **Hash**: A digital fingerprint of a file (e.g., MD5, SHA1) used for integrity and identification.
- **Sandbox**: Isolated environment for safely running untrusted programs.
- **Advanced persistent threat (APT)**: A stealthy, prolonged cyberattack often involving rootkits.

Questions

1. What is malware, and how is it different than other threats?
2. How does a Trojan horse typically infect systems?
3. What does ransomware do once it infects a computer?
4. What is the goal of a rootkit?
5. What is fileless malware?
6. Which forensic technique analyzes malware without executing it?
7. What is the role of YARA rules in malware detection?
8. How are macros used in document-based malware?
9. What are IOCs, and how are they different from IOAs?
10. What is a suspicious parent-child process relationship in Windows?
11. How can you detect malware using Windows Event Logs?
12. What are the components of a PE file?
13. What is the purpose of analyzing a file's entropy?
14. How can VirusTotal help in malware analysis?
15. What is the danger of analyzing malware in a production environment?

Join our Discord space

Join our Discord workspace for latest updates, offers, tech happenings around the world, new releases, and sessions with the authors:

https://discord.bpbonline.com

Chapter 10
Working with Digital Forensics Cases

Introduction

As part of working with digital forensics cases, digital forensics professionals need to keep all the evidence organized, cross-reference it, do auto analysis to some extent, and also generate rudimentary reports to aid in their analysis. In this chapter, we will look at various essential aspects of working with such digital forensic cases.

Structure

In this chapter, we will cover the following topics:

- Understanding digital forensic case
- Core elements of a digital forensic case
- Triaging
- Organizing various evidence for a case
- Recipe 90: Understanding Autopsy tool
- Recipe 91: Creating a case and ingesting evidence artifacts
- Recipe 92: Visualizing and reporting using Autopsy
- Chain of custody
- Recipe 93: Understanding The Sleuth Kit
- Recipe 94: File system timeline creation by Plaso
- Adding details about anti-forensics techniques used

Objectives

While working with evidence as part of the digital forensics investigation, a digital forensics professional may be required to work with a structured approach to dealing with and organizing the evidence. We will look at how we can create a case using tools like Autopsy and ingest various evidence. We will also understand how to visualize the results in the form of timelines and rudimentary reports. By the end of this chapter, you will become familiar with working with and handling digital forensic cases.

Understanding digital forensic case

A digital forensic case refers to a structured investigation involving the identification, collection, preservation, analysis, and reporting of digital evidence. It is initiated when there is suspicion or confirmation of a cybercrime or security incident involving digital devices (e.g., computers, mobile phones, servers, IoT, cloud systems).

These cases may be criminal, civil, corporate, or regulatory in nature and usually involve identifying:

- What happened during the incident or cybercrime?
- Who was responsible?
- How did it happen, and what attack vectors were used?
- What digital evidence supports the conclusion?

It often starts when a suspicious activity is reported or detected (e.g., via an alert, a whistleblower, a compliance audit, or even a police raid), triggering a need for forensic professionals to examine digital systems such as laptops, phones, servers, cloud environments, or IoT devices.

In such cases, digital forensics helps in establishing the timeline and method of cybercrimes that can help support criminal prosecution or civil litigation. Digital forensics can also help meet compliance and audit requirements and even prevent future attacks by identifying root causes.

Note: A digital forensics case may have law enforcement and digital forensics professionals working together in tandem. Such digital forensics professionals may not have any legal background, but can bring their technical know-how to help in the analysis and investigation of the case based on the evidence collected.

Core elements of a digital forensic case

Let us look at the core element of any digital forensic case, a digital forensic professional working on the case may care about:

Core element	Details
Incident trigger	This is the starting point of the investigation. It may be a cyberattack alert, a whistleblower report, an unusual system behavior, or a legal request. The trigger defines the initial scope and urgency of the case.
Legal authority and scope	Forensic actions must be authorized legally, through search warrants, internal company approvals, or court orders. This ensures evidence is collected lawfully and is admissible in court or compliance audits.
Identification of evidence sources	This involves locating where relevant digital evidence may reside, such as computers, mobile devices, cloud storage, USBs, or network logs. It includes defining primary and secondary data sources to be analyzed.
Acquisition and preservation	Forensic imaging and data capture are done using write-blockers and tools like FTK Imager or dd. Evidence must be collected using forensically sound methodologies to ensure its authenticity, prevent any modification or contamination, and preserve its integrity throughout the process.
Hashing and chain of custody	Hash functions (MD5/SHA256) are used to verify data integrity before and after analysis. The **chain of custody (CoC)** logs who accessed the evidence, when, and for what purpose, ensuring accountability and admissibility.
Forensic analysis	The actual examination of data includes recovering deleted files, analyzing file systems, examining logs, timeline generation, and identifying artifacts. This phase often uses tools like Autopsy, Sleuth Kit, Volatility, etc.
Timeline reconstruction	Analysts reconstruct the sequence of events to understand what happened and when. It includes correlating logs, file timestamps, user activity, and system changes to build a cohesive narrative.
Interpretation of findings	This step involves correlating technical findings to the case objectives. Analysts must interpret what the artifacts mean in context, e.g., presence of malware, evidence of data theft, user actions, etc.

Core element	Details
Reporting and documentation	Findings must be documented in a structured report including summaries, methodology, tools used, timelines, and evidence details. Reports should be understandable by legal teams and decision-makers.
Presentation and testimony	In some cases, forensic professionals may be required to present findings in court or internal hearings. This involves clear communication of technical evidence and withstanding cross-examination.

Table 10.1*: Core elements of a digital forensic case*

Working with a case

Digital forensic investigations call for deep technical expertise and exceptional attention to detail to accurately interpret and analyze the evidence. The following tables show a few examples of the role of cyber forensic professionals while working on such cases:

Case	Details	Role of digital forensics professionals	Example possible outcome
Insider data theft at a bank	A senior analyst is suspected of leaking customer data to a competitor via personal USB drives and email.	Autopsy and USBDetective can be used to examine USB history, extract email headers and attachments, and analyze recent file access patterns.	Confirmed multiple USB transfers and unauthorized email usage. Employee terminated and evidence submitted to legal.
Ransomware attack in healthcare/ medical institution	Systems across multiple departments are encrypted. Incident triggered by patient data unavailability.	Volatility can be used to analyze memory dumps and Plaso/ log2timeline for the event timeline. Ransomware samples can be isolated with tools like Cuckoo Sandbox.	Attack vector identified as malicious Excel attachment. **indicator of compromise** (**IOC**) shared with teams like **Computer Emergency Response Team** (**CERT**) and recovery process initiated.
Compromised web server	A government web server is found hosting unauthorized phishing pages targeting financial services.	Sleuth Kit can be used to analyze a disk image. Web server logs, like Apache logs, can be traced for IP traces. Deleted malware payloads can also be recovered from the disk image.	Attacker IPs traced to external **virtual private network** (**VPN**). Server hardened and logs handed to law enforcement for further action.
Mobile evidence in harassment case	A student files a complaint involving threatening messages and images sent over WhatsApp.	Mobile data can be extracted using MobSF and Autopsy's Android modules. Autopsy's iLEAPP module can be used for analyzing iOS artifacts. Timeline can be created using TimeSketch.	Deleted images and threatening messages recovered. Evidence helped secure a restraining order.
Firmware tampering in **industrial control system** (**ICS**)	An operator reports unusual behavior in **programmable logic controllers** (**PLCs**) in a factory.	Engineering workstation can be examined with Autopsy, configuration files can be extracted, and firmware binaries can be extracted using Binwalk for analysis.	Unauthorized firmware identified. Employee VPN logs confirmed insider sabotage. Case handed over to HR/legal.

Case	Details	Role of digital forensics professionals	Example possible outcome
IP theft from source code repo	A developer is suspected of copying code from a confidential project to a personal Git repo before resigning.	Tools like GitInspector and Autopsy can be used to analyze commit history and browser usage. Command history and file transfer logs can be recovered.	Confirmed source code was cloned to external Git repo. Legal case initiated and **non-disclosure agreements (NDAs)** enforced.
Digital fraud in e-commerce	An internal audit reveals payment mismatches and unauthorized refunds processed via admin access.	Log correlation using ELK Stack, forensic timeline via Plaso, and access log review with GoAccess can be used.	Forensic artifacts tied refund activity to one admin account. Criminal complaint filed.
Phishing email investigation	Employees report suspicious emails impersonating the IT department requesting credentials.	Email headers can be analyzed, and Autopsy can be used to trace downloaded payloads.	Email traced to spoofed domain. Payloads identified and blacklisted. Awareness training conducted.

Table 10.2: *Role of cyber forensic professionals while working on a case*

Triaging

The concept of triaging came from the early 19th century from military medicine. It is used by medics on the battlefield for assessing wounded soldiers and prioritizing treatment based on the severity of injuries. This helps them make decisions like who needs immediate attention to survive, who can wait, and who is beyond help.

This means that the process of triaging can bring together multiple stakeholders to make a collective decision while focusing on the most important things.

Triaging in digital forensics is the process of quickly assessing and prioritizing digital evidence to determine what is important, what needs to be examined first, and what can wait. This is similar to how doctors handle patients in an emergency room. They check who needs immediate attention and who can wait. Similarly, forensic professionals use triage to identify which files, systems, or devices may contain the most critical evidence.

Note: **Whether on the battlefield or in a forensic lab, triaging is about smart prioritization under pressure.**

During a triage process, digital forensics investigators would generally do the following:

- Connect suspicious media (disk, phone, image) to the analysis system. Use write-blocking devices whenever needed.
- Run triage tools to search for recently accessed files, web history, device logs, communication logs like email and chat, and suspicious or known-malicious files.
- Mark and extract artifacts of interest for full analysis.
- Decide on the next steps, such as conducting deeper disk imaging, acquiring memory, or isolating the device.

Note: **Triaging is not always possible, especially in surprise raids in hostile environments where the first responder may need to collect as much evidence as possible in high-pressure situations.**

Organizing various evidence for a case

As part of any digital forensic investigation or analysis, a large amount of evidence is involved. This evidence is collected by first responders, can be carved out of the evidence provided (e.g., from an image), or can be collected later as part of the e-discovery process.

Hence, it is extremely important for the digital forensic professionals working on the case to ensure that the evidence is organized properly. Evidence organization involves creating a systematic structure where every item collected, examined, or reported is traceable, well-documented, and easily retrievable.

While every organization or team working on digital forensics cases may have its own processes and set of tools, there are a few best practices that anyone can adopt.

The following table discusses a list of such best practices that one should be aware of:

Best practice	Details
Maintain CoClogs	Record every handoff, access, and transfer of evidence with time, date, and person. Whenever possible, take videos of handoffs and any other such actions.
Use unique IDs for evidence	Assign a consistent naming and numbering convention across all evidence artifacts.
Use read-only media for storage	Read-only media prevents accidental tampering. It also helps in preserving admissibility in court.
Hash all files	Generate and store MD5/SHA256 hashes to verify evidence integrity before and after analysis. Also, records should be maintained for the generation of such hashes.
Separate originals from working copies	Always analyze copies of evidence, and store originals securely and untouched. The original should not be accessible by more than a few authorized people.
Document every step	Use notebooks, log files, or digital case notes to record all actions performed during acquisition and analysis.
Use case management tools	Tools like Autopsy, DFIRTrack, or CaseNotes help track, tag, and comment on evidence throughout the lifecycle.
Use standardized reporting	Use consistent language and structured formats for all the reports to ensure readability and legal acceptance.
Use safe cloud storage	In case evidence need to be stored using cloud infrastructure, use cloud storages that use data redundancy, encryption and security to preserve the integrity and organization of the data.

Table 10.3: Best practices for organizing evidence and reporting

It is evident that one would need to have various processes, templates, and tools to effectively organize various evidence. This becomes even more important when the digital forensics team or organization works on multiple cases simultaneously. Templates like CoClogs, evidence intake form, reporting templates, and hash validation sheets come in handy during the entire investigation. All of these templates can also be digitized, but with tight control on who can modify them.

Tools for working with cases

There are several open-source and commercial tools that can be used for working with the cases. We have already discussed two such tools so far. These are:

- Autopsy, which offers a quick preview of drives and highlights suspicious files (e.g., images, documents, emails, browser history).
- Bulk extractor that scans disk images and memory images to extract key artifacts (e.g., email addresses, URLs, credit card numbers) for quick review.

There are other tools that are used to create forensic images of storage media (disks, memory, etc.) without altering original data. Two such tools are FTK Imager and dd.

Let us look at a quick snapshot of the categories of tools used while working with digital forensic cases. We will also look at a few examples of each of these tools:

Tool category	Purpose	Example
Evidence acquisition	Used to create forensic images of storage media (disks, memory, etc.) without altering original data.	FTK Imager, dd.
Memory forensic	Used for acquiring and analyzing RAM (volatile memory).	WinPmem, Volatility framework.
File system and artifact analysis	Used to extract, analyze, and interpret files, logs, metadata, and other digital artifacts.	Autopsy, The Sleuth Kit, Bulk Extractor, ExifTool, YARA.
Timeline and log analysis	Tools that help create activity timelines or analyze logs.	Plaso/log2timeline, Eventlog Explorer.
Mobile forensics	Tools for analyzing smartphones and mobile apps.	**Mobile Security Framework (MobSF)**, Autopsy.
Network forensics	Tools for analyzing network traffic and logs.	Wireshark, TCPDump, Zeek (Bro).
Triage and live response	Tools for quickly collecting relevant artifacts to chart the next course of actions.	Autopsy, Bulk Extractor, GRR Rapid Response.
Case management and reporting	Tools for documenting, tagging, and organizing forensic investigations.	Autopsy, DFIR-IRIS.

Table 10.4: *Various tools for working with cases*

Recipe 90: Understanding Autopsy tool

We have been mentioning the Autopsy tool several times in the book so far. Autopsy is a free and open-source digital forensics platform used to investigate hard drives, memory dumps, mobile data, and other digital evidence. Autopsy is the **graphical user interface (GUI)** built on top of **The Sleuth Kit (TSK)**, which is a powerful set of command-line tools for digital forensic analysis of disk images and file systems. Autopsy is widely used by law enforcement, corporate investigators, and academic labs.

Note:

- **Compatibility: Windows**
- **License considerations: Free software used**

Autopsy is installed in Kali Linux by default and can be launched as a web application rather than a desktop application. We will go ahead with the Windows version as it is easier to work with and understand.

Recipe

In this recipe, we will install the Autopsy tool and understand its basic elements. Perform the following steps to complete this recipe:

1. Download Autopsy **from https://www.autopsy.com/download/**and install it.
2. Once installed, launch Autopsy. After the splash screen, you will see the following screen:

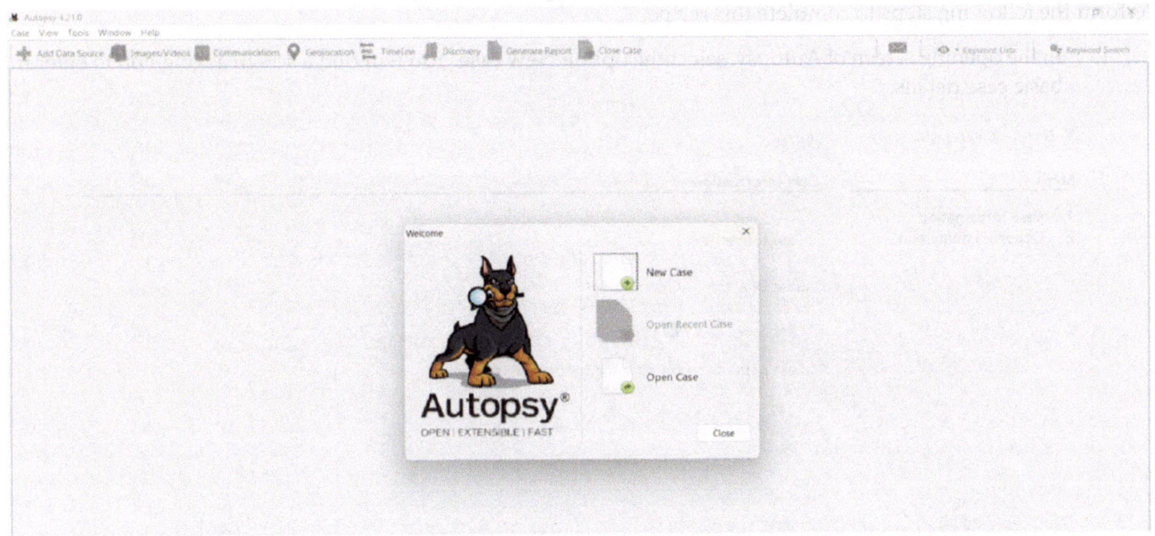

***Figure 10.1**: Autopsy opening screen*

Since Autopsy workflows are case-driven, it asks you to either start with a new case or open an existing case.

3. Click on each of the enabled options, explore, and become familiar with the interface.

4. Go to the Autopsy's installed path and look at the type of tools and plugins present in the autopsy directory. See if you can recognize any of these tools that are used internally by Autopsy.

Activity

Attempt the following activities before the next recipe:

- Install Autopsy on a Linux distribution like Ubuntu. Verify if the user interface is the same.
- Read the Kali Linux and Autopsy documentation to understand how to use them.

Recipe 91: Creating a case and ingesting evidence artifacts

Each case in Autopsy is a directory on the disk where all the evidence artifacts of the case are stored. This evidence can be added while starting a new case in Autopsy or later throughout the life cycle of the case. In this recipe, we will start by creating a new case and then add a few pieces of evidence to it.

Note:

- **Compatibility: Windows**
- **License considerations: Free software used**

Recipe

In this recipe, we will create a new case for digital forensic analysis and then add a few pieces of evidence to it. All the steps need to be run with administrator privileges.

Perform the following steps to complete this recipe:

1. In the opening screen of Autopsy, select the option **New case**. You will find a screen asking you to enter the basic case details:

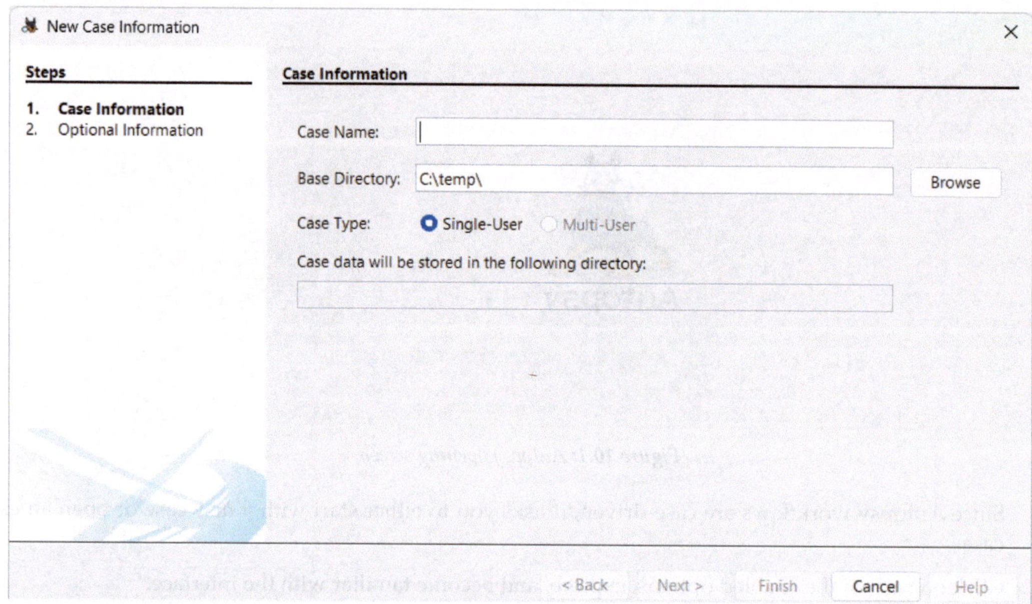

***Figure 10.2:** Autopsy case creation, adding basic case information*

2. In the **Case Name**, enter the name of the case and then set the **Base Directory**. The **Base Directory** is where the database of this case is managed by Autopsy, as shown in the following figure:

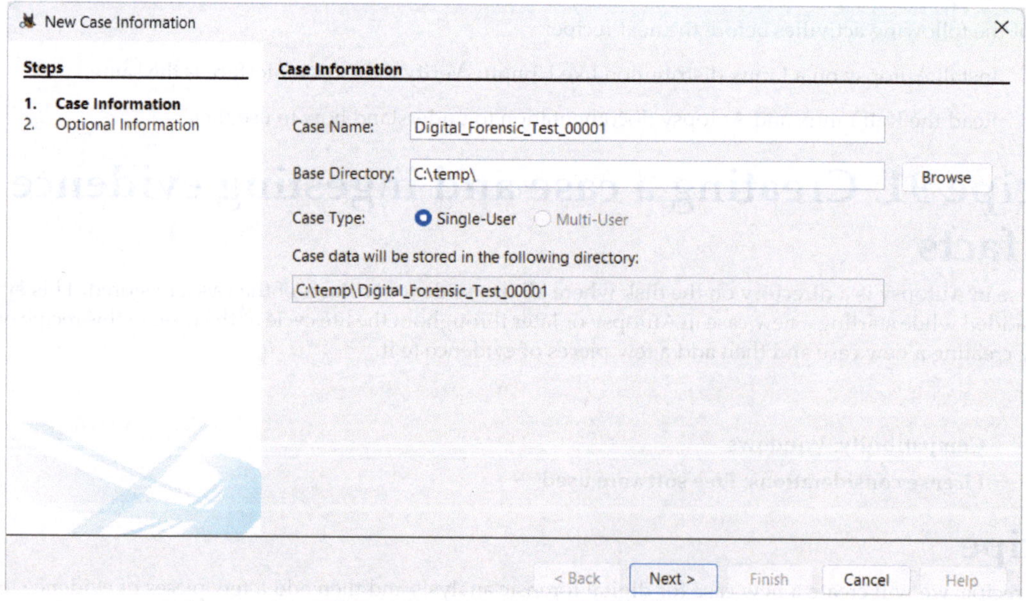

***Figure 10.3:** Autopsy case creation, adding case information*

The case type can be only **Single-User** for the community edition of Autopsy, which gives you enough exposure to understand working on cases.

In the next screen, you can enter other information like the case number of the court case and the details of the examiner. These are important details that will be stored as metadata of the case:

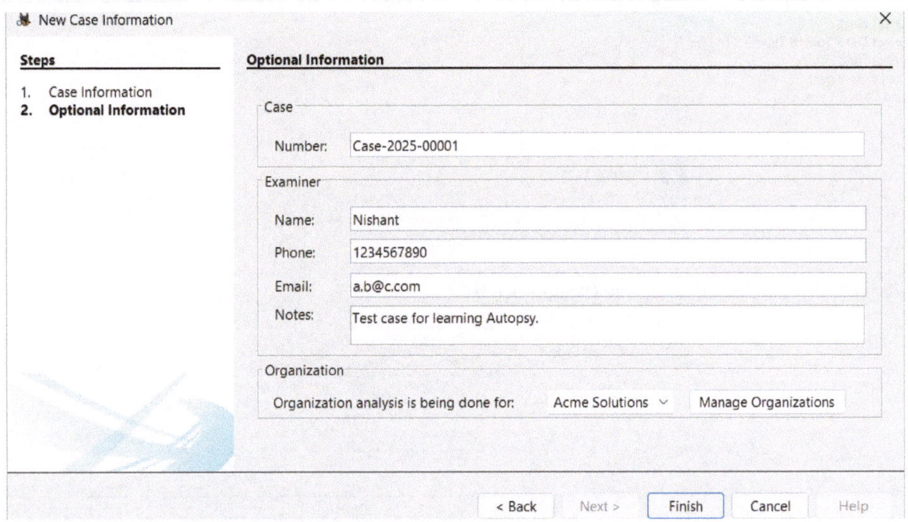

***Figure 10.4**: Autopsy case creation, adding optional information*

You can also enter the details of the organization for which the analysis is being done. It could be a law enforcement department or a private company that would have hired you to perform the analysis. Click on **Manage Organizations** to manage the organizations you may be working with, and then select the appropriate organization.

3. After you click on **Finish**, you are taken to the screen to add the data source, which is an optional step. This screen allows you to add a data source right away in the case, as shown in the following figure. You can also do it later by clicking on the **Add Data Source** button on the menu bar of the tool:

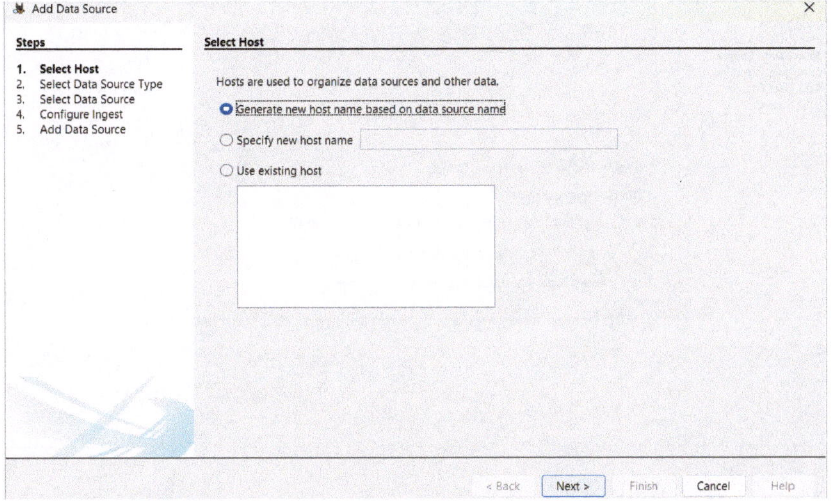

***Figure 10.5**: Autopsy case creation, Add Data Source, Select Host*

If you select the default option and then click on **Next**, the next screen shows you a list of types of evidence that can be added:

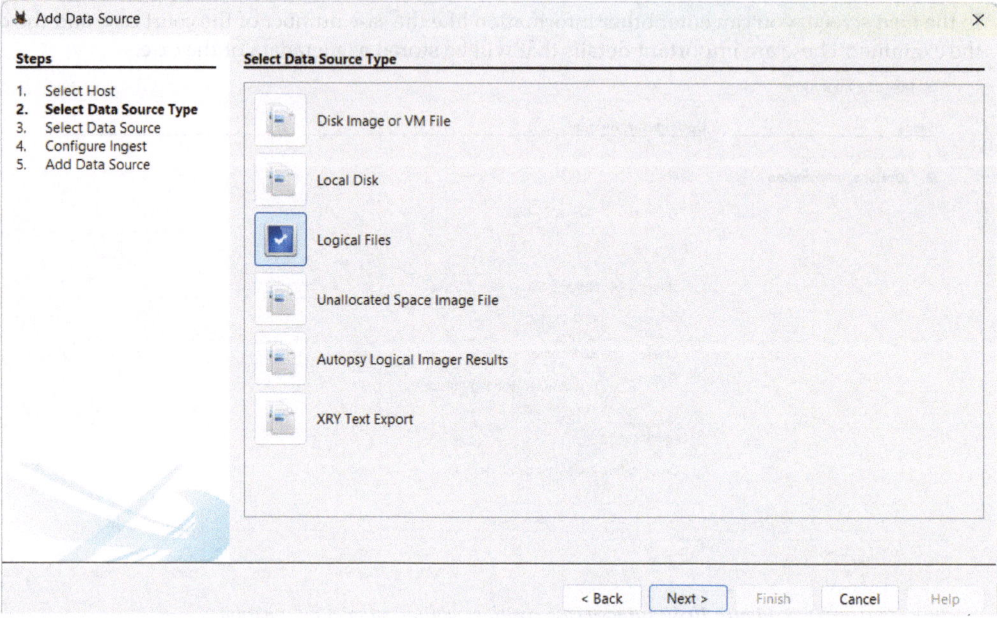

Figure 10.6: Autopsy case creation, Add Data Source, Select Data Source Type

You can appreciate that this list of data source types can cover all the types of evidence that can be added.

Let us continue with the default option, i.e., **Logical Files,** and click on **Next**. In the next screen, you can add all the files and folders on your machine that you want to be part of the case. You can also include various timestamps as part of the data source:

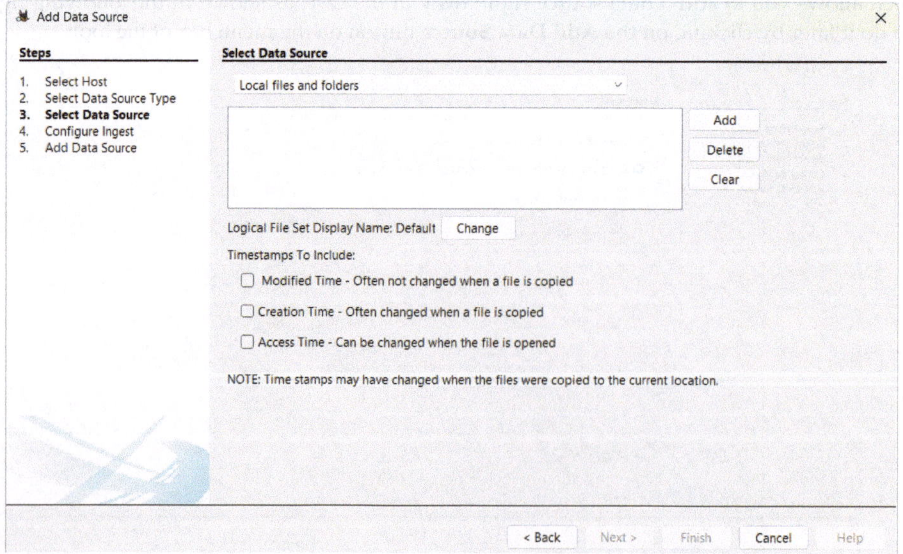

Figure 10.7: Autopsy case creation, Add Data Source, Select Data Source

Note: This is the time to go back and refresh your knowledge about MACB timestamps, which stand for modified, accessed, changed, and birth (or created).

4. You can now add the local files and folders location where you have stored the evidence, change the display name of the data source, and select the timestamps to include:

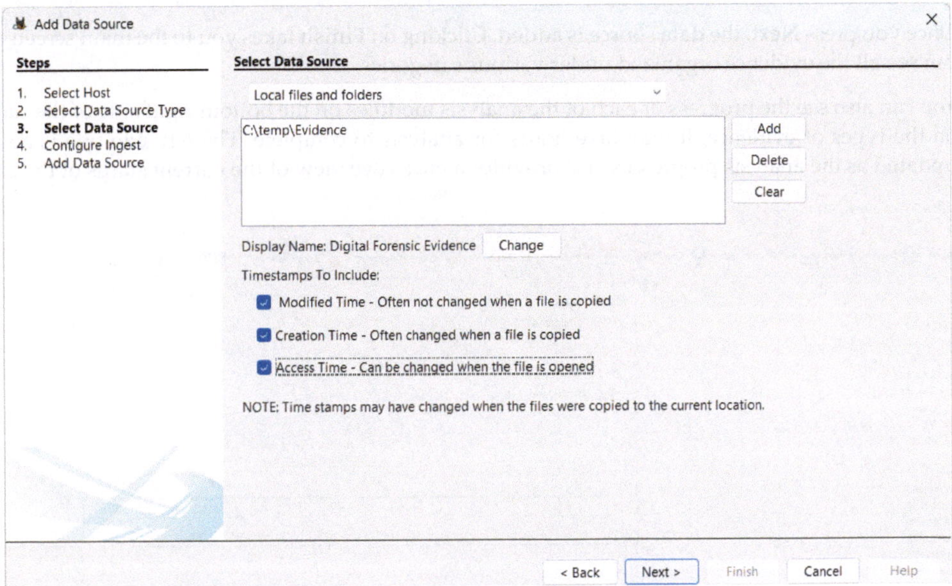

Figure 10.8: Autopsy case creation, Add Data Source, Select Data Source

Once you add the local files and folders location, you can move forward by clicking on **Next**. In this screen, you can select which ingest module to run on the data source. Autopsy, by default, provides many ingest modules that automatically analyze the data source and provide the results:

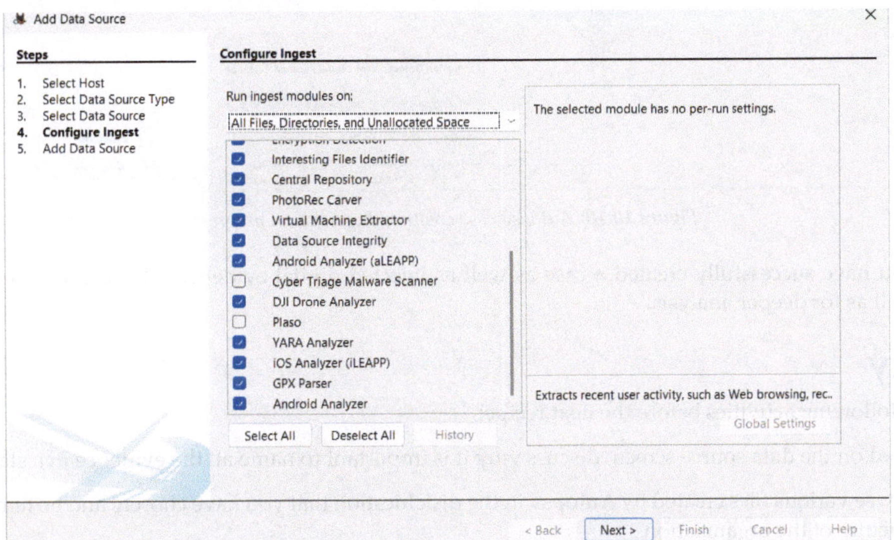

Figure 10.9: Autopsy case creation, Add Data Source, Configure Ingest

For example, Email Parser parses for email addresses, Picture Analyzer looks for pictures in various evidence, and Plaso is used for the creation of timelines. Plaso parser, when enabled, can take a lot of time for analysis and hence may not be apt for quick triaging. **Cyber Triage Malware Scanner** is available for a separate license.

Look at what each of the modules does in the Autopsy documentation.

5. Once you press **Next**, the data source is added. Clicking on **Finish** takes you to the main screen, where you can see all the evidence organized under various categories.

   You can also see the progress of each of the analysis modules on the bottom right side of the screen. Based on the types of evidence, it may take hours for analysis to complete. The left side tree is automatically updated as the analysis progresses and provides a bird's eye view of the current status of the analysis:

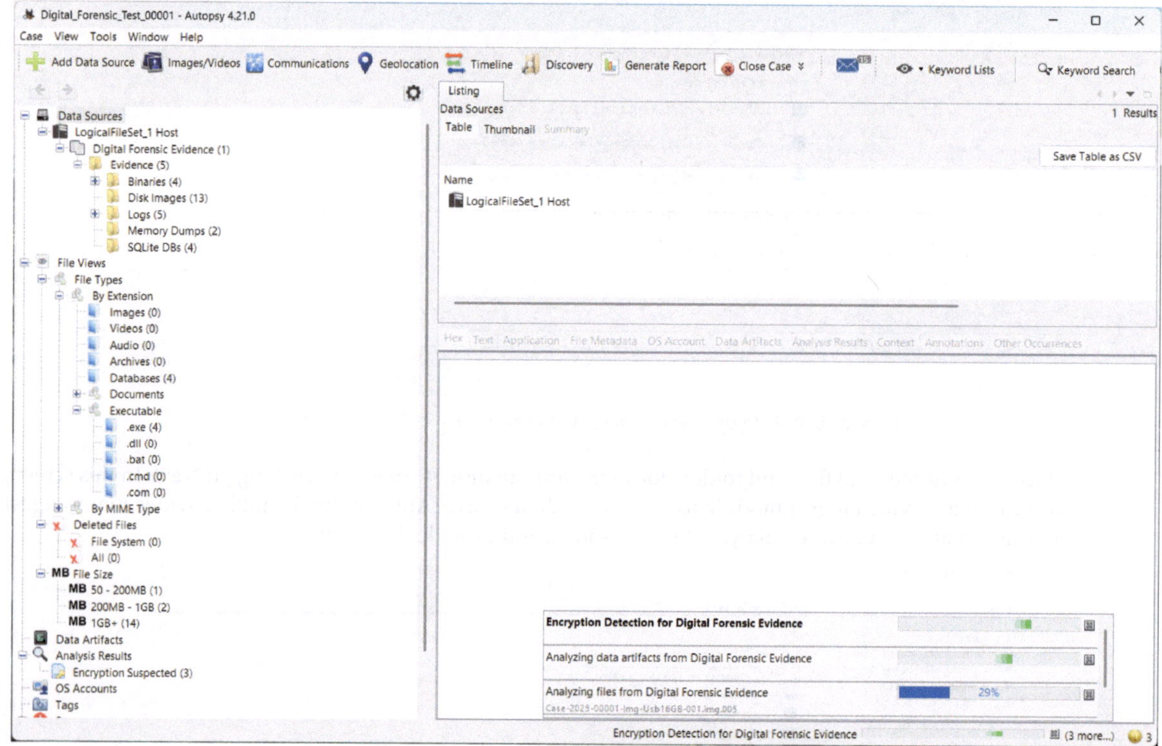

***Figure 10.10**: Autopsy case creation, Ingestion in progress*

With this, you have successfully created a case as well as injected digital evidence. This can be used for triaging activity as well as for deeper analysis.

Activity

Attempt the following activities before the next recipe:

- Based on the data source screen, discuss why it is important to name all the evidence in a standard way.
- Browse various files created by Autopsy in the disk location that you have chosen, and be familiar with the structure of the organization.

- You will find that Autopsy automatically creates a file called **`autopsy.db`** in the root of your folder. This is a SQLite database. Use a SQLite DB browser tool that we have used before to open this database and understand the structure of the organization.
- Dump the memory of a machine using FTK Imager and then add the dump file to the case. Observe if Autopsy automatically analyzes the image and the content inside it.
- Create a few files in a USB drive and delete them. Take an image dump of a USB drive using FTK Imager and add it to the case. Observe if Autopsy automatically analyzes the image and the content inside it.

Recipe 92: Visualizing and reporting using Autopsy

In any digital forensic case investigation/analysis, stakeholders need to understand a summary of the case or visualize it in such a way that it can be used to make decisions on the next course of action. Once the evidence is ingested and analyzed by Autopsy, it has various ways to do just that.

Note:

- **Compatibility: Windows**
- **License considerations: Free software used**

Recipe

Let us use Autopsy to check the timelines of the evidence files ingested visually, and also create a rudimentary report of the case:

1. **Checking timelines**: First, click on the **Timeline** option at the top of the Autopsy screen. You will see a timeline of all the events in the evidence provided. You can also use the zoom out and zoom in buttons to look at the timeline for a specific time duration. This provides a clear view of visualizing the timeline and focusing on the investigation accordingly.

   The following figure shows the timeline view of Autopsy:

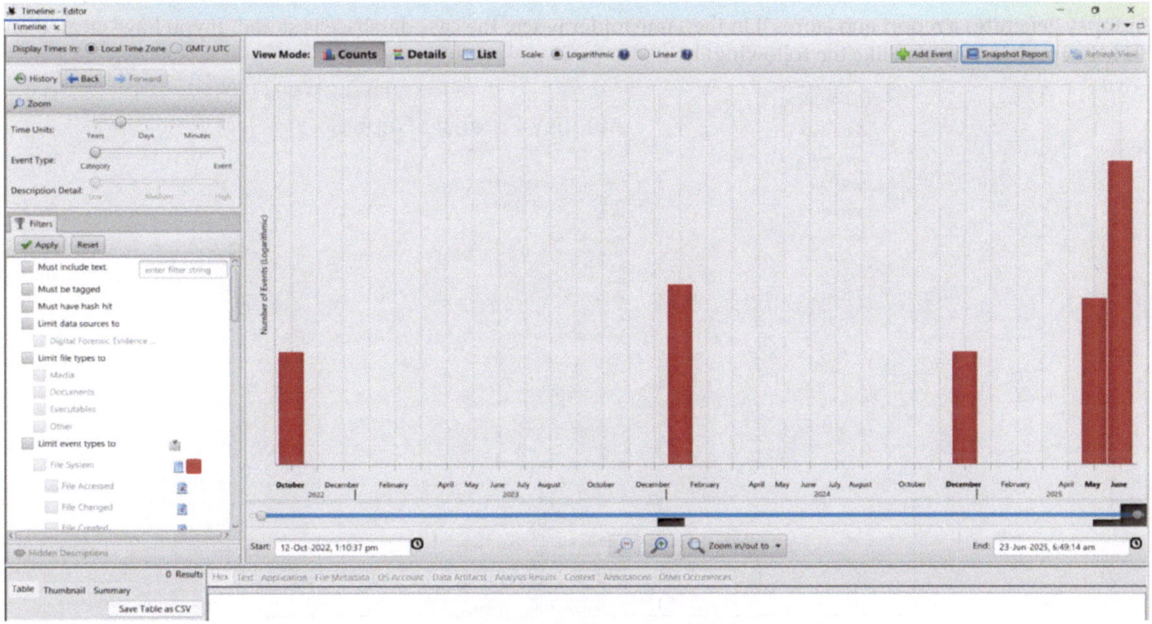

Figure 10.11: Autopsy timeline

You can also use various filters to get the timeline view you require. Moreover, the **Details** and **List** views give an additional way to visualize the timelines.

2. **Generating a rudimentary report**: In order to generate a simple report from Autopsy, click on the **Generate Report** option in the top bar. In the pop-up window, confirm the type of reports you want to generate. Press **Next** to select data sources or any other options based on the type of report you have selected:

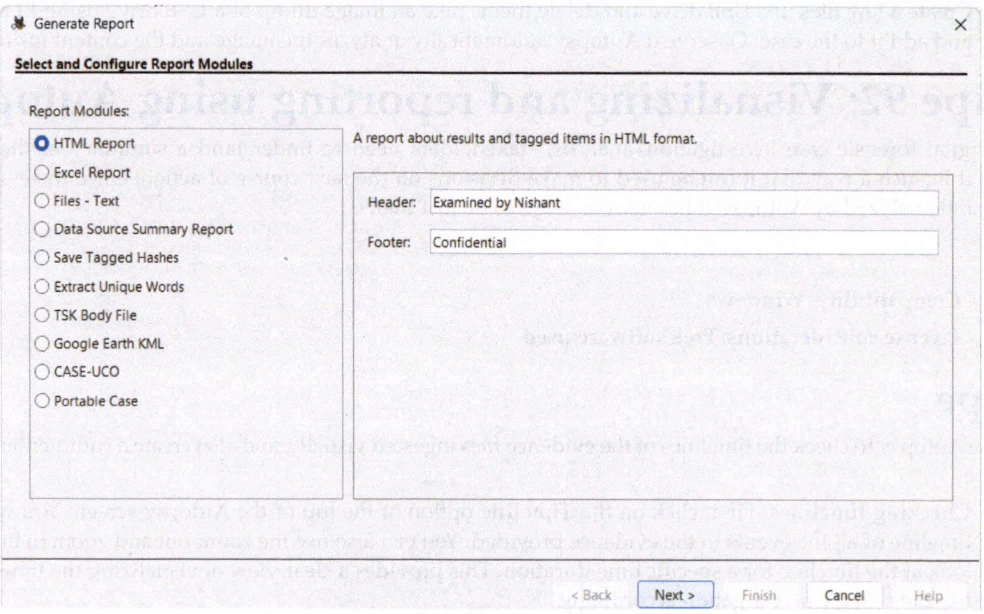

Figure 10.12: Generating a report

Autopsy generates a report and stores it in the same folder where the case database is stored. If you have created an HTML report, it may look like the following:

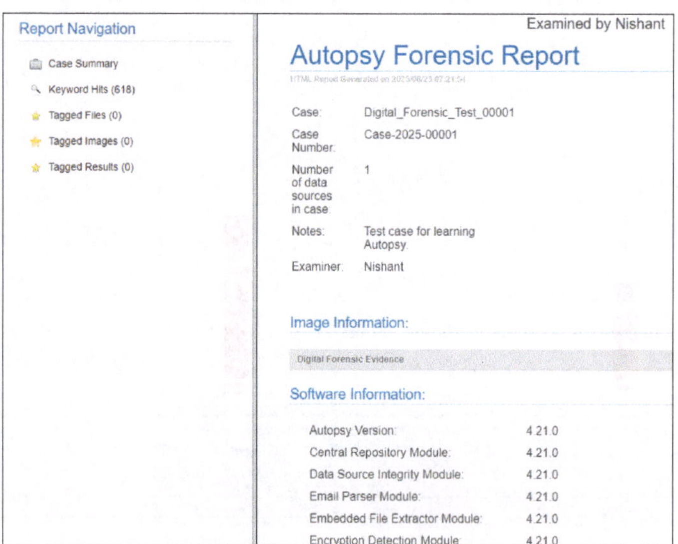

Figure 10.13: A sample generated report

Please note that this example shows a very rudimentary report. Based on the types of evidence analyzed, this report would be a very detailed report that can be used as part of the investigation and prosecution.

Activity

Attempt the following activities before the next recipe:

- Click on the **Discovery** option in the main window of Autopsy and become comfortable searching for images, videos, documents, and domains based on various options and filters. Discuss how this feature can be used during the eDiscovery process.
- Add a few more pieces of evidence and analyze them. Once the analysis is complete, check if the report now shows the details of the new evidence that you added.

Chain of custody

We discussed CoC in *Chapter 1, Introduction to Digital Forensics*. Let us dive a little deeper into the intricacies of this very important concept.

CoC refers to the documented and unbroken process that shows the seizure, custody, control, transfer, analysis, and disposition of digital evidence from the time it is collected until it is presented in court.

CoC is important due to the following:

Reason	Details
Ensuring evidence integrity	It helps verify that the digital evidence has not been tampered with, altered, or replaced throughout the investigation.
Maintaining legal admissibility	A well-documented CoC is crucial for evidence to be accepted in court. Any break can lead to the dismissal of evidence.
Establishing accountability	Tracks who handled the evidence, when, and for what purpose, ensuring every action is attributable and traceable.
Supporting forensic best practices	It aligns with international forensic standards and audit requirements, thereby upholding professional credibility.

***Table 10.5:** Importance of CoC*

Hence, while working on any digital forensics case, the following key elements need to be maintained for CoC records to be built and maintained:

- Unique evidence ID.
- Description of the evidence.
- Date, time, and location of collection.
- Name and signature of collector.
- Each transfer includes the time/date and signatures.
- Purpose of transfer or examination.

By now, you would have already realized that we used most of these elements while creating the case and while adding a data source. This is one of the advantages of using standard tools like Autopsy, as they automatically build and document such metadata that will be useful later.

Recipe 93: Understanding The Sleuth Kit

As we discussed in the previous recipe in this chapter, **Understanding Autopsy tool**, The Sleuth Kit or TSK is the engine that performs the low-level forensic tasks like parsing file systems (FAT, NTFS, ext), recovering deleted files, analyzing metadata, and more. Autopsy provides the dashboard and the UI that is used to present the results from TSK in a user-friendly graphical interface, adds automation features, integrates modules (like email analysis, keyword search), and supports case management.

> Note: **File Allocation Table (FAT) and New Technology File System (NTFS) are file systems for Windows operating systems that are used to organize and store data and provide ways to access them. While FAT (specifically FAT32) is an older, simpler system with broad cross-platform compatibility but limited features, NTFS is Microsoft's modern, journaling file system offering advanced features like security, file compression, larger file size support, and better fault tolerance.**

Autopsy adds workflow enhancements, such as tagging, reporting, and plugins, making it easier to manage a full digital investigation. However, when you load a disk image into Autopsy, it internally calls TSK utilities (like **`fls`**, **`istat`**, **`imgstat`**, etc.) to extract and process data.

While Autopsy provides all the features provided by the underlying TSK, it is a good idea to learn using the command line interface provided by TSK. This comes in handy for the automation of various digital forensic analysis tasks that cannot be provided by the GUI-based interface of Autopsy.

TSK also enables digital forensic investigators to identify and recover evidence from images acquired during incident response or from live systems.

> Note:
>
> - **Compatibility: Windows**
> - **License considerations: Free software used**

Recipe

In this recipe, we will understand how to work with **TSK**. Perform the following steps to complete this recipe:

1. First, let us download TSK from **https://www.sleuthkit.org/sleuthkit/download.php**. Windows binaries are basically a zip file that contains everything and can be run directly from a folder. There is no need to install anything.
2. Look at the files present in the bin directory of the extracted zip file. There are many utilities present in this directory; each of them can be used independently by the investigators.
3. Let us try a few tools on the evidence you have collected and used before while working with Autopsy. The following table has a list of such tools that can be run from the command line, considering our image file name is **`diskimage.dd`**:

Tool	Details	Example command
`fsstat`	Displays detailed file system metadata information (e.g., type, block size, laysout).	Identify the type of partition: **`fstat -t diskimage.dd`** View NTFS metadata from the disk image: **`fsstat -f ntfs diskimage.dd`** View FAT32 metadata from the disk image: **`fsstat -f fat32 diskimage.dd`**

Tool	Details	Example command
`fls`	Lists files and directories in a file system, including deleted entries.	Recursively list all files with paths including deleted entries: **`fls -r -m / diskimage.dd`**
`mmls`	Displays partition layout of a disk image.	List all partitions and their offsets: **`mmls diskimage.dd`**
`tskimageinfo`	Provides the basis information about the image like encryption, encryption type, whether it is supported by TSK and so on.	Print the image information of the image: **`tskimageinfo diskimage.dd`**
`tskloaddb`	Loads image metadata into a SQLite database. The file then can be used for further analysis with Autopsy.	Prepare a SQLite DB for analysis: **`tskloaddb diskimage.dd`**

Table 10.6: *Commonly used TSK commands*

Tip: **In order to use the command line tool part of TSK, add the full path of the bin directory to the Windows path environment variable.**

Activity

Attempt the following activities before the next recipe:

- Read the documentation of TSK to understand the purpose of other utilities supplied in the bin directory and try them out.
- What other similar tools, like TSK, can you think of that are capable of doing the same tasks?

Recipe 94: File system timeline creation by Plaso

A timeline of the file system is useful to understand the order of creation, deletion, and modification of various files. This is one of the key tools created to aid in digital forensics analysis, supporting digital forensic investigators and analysts in correlating the large amount of information found in logs and other files within the image of an average computer.

Plaso (**https://github.com/log2timeline/plaso**) is one of the important tools that can be used to create a super timeline from an image. We will use this tool to create a timeline of our disk image.

Note:

- **Compatibility: Linux**
- **License considerations: Free software used**

Recipe

Let us use Plaso to create a timeline of all the files present in our disk image of a USB drive. We will use this in Kali Linux as it is easier to install and use Plaso there. Follow the following steps to complete this recipe:

1. Install the Plaso package by using the following commands:

```
apt-get update
apt-get install plaso
```

2. Once Plaso is installed, run the following command to check if Plaso is working properly:

```
plaso-log2timeline --info
```

This command prints information about all supported plugins, parsers, output modules, etc., and is useful to understand the capabilities of Plaso.

Now run the following command to get the timeline of the disk image, considering the disk image name is **diskimage.dd**:

```
plaso-log2timeline --storage-file timeline.plaso diskimage.dd
```

Based on the size of the disk image, it will take some time to create the timeline file.

3. The timeline we got preceding is not in sorted order. Hence, we need to use the following command to get a sorted timeline in a CSV format by using the following command:

```
plaso-psort -o L2tcsv -w timeline.csv timeline.plaso
```

The **L2tcsv** in this command means Log2Timeline CSV file. Once the command has finished, it will create a **timeline.csv**. This file now has a sorted timeline that provides an excellent view of the sequence of events that could have occurred on the system in chronological order.

> Tip: **If you have the image file stored in Windows and you do not want to copy it to Linux again for analysis, one of the best options is to use Kali Linux using Windows Subsystem for Linux (WSL), which gives a simple way to run Linux in Windows. WSL also provides full access to files in Windows from the familiar Kali Linux shell.**

Activity

Attempt the following activities before the next recipe:

- Look at various options supported by Plaso. Use the firefoxcache parsers to parse Firefox's cache dump.
- Look at the list of parser plugins Plaso supports. Understand how Plaso can be used to parse various artifacts from an Android image.

Adding details about anti-forensics techniques used

Anti-forensic techniques are deliberate methods used by threat actors to hinder, mislead, or completely obstruct digital forensic investigations. These techniques are designed to erase traces of activity, manipulate evidence, or delay detection, thereby reducing the chances of attribution or prosecution.

Common anti-forensic methods include:

- **Timestomping**: It is where file timestamps are altered to confuse event timelines, and secure deletion or file wiping, which overwrites data to make recovery impossible.
- **Log manipulation or deletion**: It is often employed to hide login sessions, command executions, or network activity.
- **Encryption and steganography**: Threat actors utilize these methods to conceal data within files or images, making detection more challenging without the decryption keys or prior indicators.
- **Obfuscation**: Obfuscation tools like packers, crypters, and runtime encryption are used to disguise malware, while memory-only malware and fileless attacks avoid disk writes altogether.

Additionally, attackers may disable or tamper with system auditing, destroy volume shadow copies, or use alternate data streams and obscure file locations to hide payloads.

While working with cases, digital forensic analysts should be vigilant for such techniques by analyzing inconsistencies, unexpected gaps, system anomalies, and by using timeline correlation, Registry analysis, and cross-source artifact validation to detect signs of tampering and possible anti-forensic techniques used.

Let us look at a few examples of the suspicious markers that signal that anti-forensic techniques were used:

- Abnormal timeline patterns much before the time of the incident.
- Deleted / missing recent documents or cleaned histories.
- Suspicious keyword searches in the browsing history and in the operating system.
- Unallocated space with deleted files that are not recognized.
- Log file headers with missing content, or logs in the log file that are not in the correct chronological sequence.
- Absence of common user activities (browsing, document access) in otherwise populated systems.

Such details, when observed, should be added to the digital forensic analysis report. A more in-depth analysis of such anti-forensic techniques may require a more sophisticated tool, including AI-enabled tools.

Conclusion

Working with digital forensic cases involves a structured, methodical, and legally sound approach to collecting, analyzing, and reporting digital evidence. We looked at the importance of understanding the lifecycle of a digital forensic case, from incident trigger to final reporting. We also covered critical components, including CoC, triage, evidence acquisition, the use of tools such as Autopsy and Sleuth Kit, and the importance of organizing and managing digital evidence. A key takeaway from this chapter is that every action taken by a forensic analyst must preserve the integrity and admissibility of the evidence. We also learned how modern forensic tools help create timelines, extract meaningful artifacts, and effectively visualize findings. Digital forensic professionals can build legally admissible, technically sound case narratives that support investigations, compliance, and litigation efforts by applying these concepts learned.

In the next chapter, we will focus on various techniques used in mobile forensics.

Points to remember

- A digital forensic case begins with an incident trigger, like an alert or legal request.
- CoC ensures evidence integrity and legal admissibility.
- Evidence must be acquired using write-blockers and verified with hashing.
- Forensic analysis involves artifact recovery, log examination, and timeline creation.
- Triaging helps prioritize evidence in high-pressure or large-scale investigations.
- TSK is the command-line backend used by Autopsy.
- Organizing evidence includes labeling, hashing, separating originals, and logging all steps.
- Read-only media should be used to avoid evidence modification.
- CoC must log every access and action on evidence.
- Autopsy's ingest modules automate analysis of pictures, emails, browser data, etc.
- Anti-forensic techniques aim to obscure evidence through deletion, encryption, or tampering.
- Anomalous timestamps or missing logs may indicate anti-forensics.
- Report writing should be structured, readable, and technically sound.
- Cross-referencing multiple sources enhances investigative accuracy.

- Digital forensic professionals may be required to testify or present findings in court.

Key terms

- **Digital forensic case**: A structured investigation into a cybercrime or digital incident involving evidence collection, analysis, and reporting.
- **Chain of custody**: A documented process tracking every access and transfer of digital evidence to ensure its integrity and admissibility.
- **Triaging**: The process of prioritizing digital evidence based on importance and relevance to the investigation.
- **Autopsy**: A GUI-based digital forensic tool that integrates multiple modules for case management, analysis, and reporting.
- **TSK**: A collection of command-line tools used for forensic analysis of disk images and file systems.
- **FTK Imager**: A tool used to create forensic images of storage devices without modifying the original data.
- **Plaso**: An open-source framework used to generate timelines from forensic artifacts using a variety of parser plugins.
- **Timeline reconstruction**: The process of organizing events in chronological order to understand the sequence of activities in a case.
- **MACB timestamps**: File metadata showing modified, accessed, changed, and birth (created) times.
- **Write-blocker**: A hardware or software tool that prevents a device from being altered during acquisition.
- **Volatility**: A memory forensic framework used to analyze RAM dumps for malicious activity.
- **Evidence hashing**: Creating cryptographic hash values to verify that digital evidence has not been altered.
- **Anti-forensics**: Techniques used by threat actors to hide or tamper with evidence to mislead investigators.
- **Alternate data stream (ADS)**: A feature in NTFS that allows data to be stored outside the main file content, often used to hide malicious payloads.
- **Ingest modules**: Autopsy components that analyze added data sources automatically for relevant forensic artifacts.
- **SQLite**: A lightweight database format used by Autopsy to store case metadata and analysis results.
- **Case management tool**: Software tool used to track and organize evidence, actions, and reporting throughout the forensic investigation.
- **Data source**: The input to a forensic case, such as disk images, memory dumps, or logical files.
- **Reporting**: The process of documenting forensic findings in a structured and legally admissible format.
- **Timestomping**: An anti-forensic method where file timestamps are modified to mislead timeline analysis.

Questions

1. What is a digital forensic case, and when is it initiated?
2. Explain the significance of maintaining a chain of custody.
3. What is the role of timeline reconstruction in forensic investigations?
4. Name any three core elements of a digital forensic case.
5. Describe the concept of triaging in digital forensics.
6. List at least three tools used for digital evidence acquisition.
7. How does Autopsy assist in handling digital forensic cases?
8. What are MACB timestamps, and why are they important?
9. Define the role of forensic imaging tools, such as FTK Imager or dd.
10. What are some best practices for organizing forensic evidence?
11. How does Plaso assist in timeline creation?
12. Describe a scenario where anti-forensic techniques might be used.

CHAPTER 11
Mobile Forensics

Introduction

Mobile devices, including smartphones and tablets, are ubiquitous and are used by nearly all individuals, including criminal actors. During law-enforcement operations such as crime-scene raids, mobile devices are routinely seized along with other physical evidence. In many cases, even routine criminal activities involve the use of mobile phones or leave behind a digital footprint through communications such as messages, emails, application data, and location records. As a result, the forensic examination of mobile devices has become a critical component of modern digital investigations, which we will study in this chapter.

Structure

In this chapter, we will cover the following topics:

- Need for mobile forensics
- Acquiring images and app files for learning
- Acquiring iOS images and app files
- Android and iOS architecture
- Android techniques for mobile forensics
- iOS techniques for mobile forensics
- Understanding endpoint detection and response
- Understanding the Android file system
- Anatomy of an APK file
- Anatomy of an AAB file
- Lifecycle of AAB and APK files
- Recipe 95: Extracting APK file to learn its structure
- Recipe 96: Using Autopsy to scan an APK file
- Recipe 97: Using Autopsy to scan an Android image
- Recipe 98: Using Android Studio for Android forensics
- Recipe 99: Using Logcat with live Android device
- Using Mobile Security Framework
- Recovering deleted files from Android forensic image
- Challenges in mobile forensics

Objectives

Knowledge of mobile forensics techniques is essential for digital forensics professionals due to their applicability during crime investigation. In this chapter, we will create a conceptual understanding of mobile forensics, as well as work with tools that individuals can use. We will first start with various concepts about mobile forensics that apply to both Android and iOS devices. After that, we will understand the anatomy and lifecycle of **Android Package Kit** (**APK**) and **Android App Bundle** (**AAB**) files. Once we are familiar with these concepts, we will use tools like Autopsy and Android Studio to work with mobile forensics for Android devices. Though mobile forensics for iOS devices is not straightforward without full access to the device or an unencrypted backup, we will look at various techniques that can be used for iOS devices.

By the end of this chapter, you will become familiar with many important concepts of mobile forensics that are relevant in solving cybercrimes as well as conventional crimes.

Need for mobile forensics

Mobile forensics is a branch of digital forensics focused on the recovery, analysis, and preservation of digital evidence from mobile devices, such as smartphones, tablets, GPS devices, and wearables. This process typically involves:

- Acquiring data from a device without altering it.
- Recovering deleted or hidden data.
- Analyzing communication logs, apps, files, and location data.
- Ensuring the chain of custody and evidence integrity.

Mobile forensics encompasses a range of mobile operating systems, primarily Android and iOS, and historically included platforms such as Windows Mobile. It also employs specialized tools like Cellebrite UFED, Magnet AXIOM, MOBILedit, Oxygen Forensics, etc., many of them being commercial and highly sophisticated tools.

Importance in cybercrime and cyber incidents investigation

When a conventional or cybercrime is committed in today's world, there is a high chance that it has a digital trail. Most of these digital trails also involve some sort of mobile device, e.g., a smartphone.

Let us look at a few key reasons why mobile forensics plays an important role in solving crime in today's world:

Aspect	Importance of mobile forensics
Ubiquity of mobile devices	Most individuals use smartphones extensively, making them rich sources of evidence in both cyber and physical crimes.
Communication evidence	Mobile devices often contain emails, SMS, messaging apps (WhatsApp, Telegram, iMessage, WeChat, etc.), call logs, message logs, and contact lists that are crucial in tracing communication patterns.
Location tracking	GPS logs, geotagged images, and app location data help place suspects at crime scenes or track movements.
App data and artifacts	Apps (banking, social media, ride-sharing) can provide transaction records, communication, and other digital footprints relevant in cybercrimes like fraud, stalking, or phishing.
Deleted data recovery	Even deleted content can be recovered using forensic techniques, which is essential when suspects try to hide or wipe evidence.

Aspect	Importance of mobile forensics
Cloud synchronization	Many devices sync data with cloud services, mobile forensics can link local data with cloud evidence during incident analysis.
Insider threats and espionage	In corporate or state-level espionage, mobile devices may hold leaked documents, screenshots, or communication with external actors.
Cyber incidents	For ransomware, phishing, or social engineering attacks launched or executed via mobile apps or SMS, mobile forensics helps trace initial vectors of compromised devices.

Table 11.1*: Importance of mobile forensics*

In a nutshell, mobile forensics plays a critical role in modern digital investigations, given the pervasive use of mobile devices in everyday life. Whether it is cyberstalking, financial fraud, intellectual property theft, or coordinated cyberattacks, analyzing mobile devices provides invaluable insights into user behavior, communication patterns, and location history, often serving as key evidence in court proceedings and incident response.

Mobile forensics provides vital evidence in digital investigations where mobile devices are central to the communication, planning, or execution of cyber and real-world crimes. It complements other branches of forensics and is essential in cybercrime, corporate investigations, legal proceedings, and incident response scenarios.

Using mobile forensics in digital forensic investigation

Mobile forensics is an integral part of digital forensic investigations, particularly when mobile devices are suspected of being involved in committing or facilitating a crime, which is almost always the case nowadays. Investigators use mobile forensics to:

- Extract data from mobile devices (physically, logically, or via cloud sync).
- Analyze the content, such as call logs, messages, app data, browser history, multimedia files, and geolocation data.
- Recover deleted or hidden data using forensic tools.
- Correlate findings with other digital evidence, like computer forensics or network logs.
- Preserve evidence in a forensically sound manner (maintaining chain of custody).
- Generate reports suitable for presentation in courts or regulatory investigations.

Let us look at a few real-world use cases where mobile forensics plays an important role in investigations:

Crime	Details	Role of mobile forensics
Cyberstalking	A victim reports persistent stalking via social media and messaging apps.	Extracted and analyzed messages, call logs, app activity, and location data can be used to identify the suspect and patterns of harassment.
Corporate espionage	An insider leaks confidential data to a competitor.	Analysis of messaging apps, file transfers, and cloud sync history can be used to reveal unauthorized data transmission via mobile.
Ransomware coordination	Ransomware attacks were coordinated using encrypted messaging apps.	Decrypted and analyzed data from a suspect's phone can be used to uncover the command chain and crypto wallet used for ransom payments.
Drug trafficking ring	Mobile devices were used to communicate with dealers and clients.	GPS logs, text messages, and call records can be used to establish links between multiple suspects and trace drug delivery routes.

Crime	Details	Role of mobile forensics
Hit-and-run investigation	The accused denied being at the scene.	Location data, step counters, and image metadata from the phone can be used to confirm presence near the scene at the time of incident.
Digital fraud like phishing	A phishing scam targeted victims via SMS.	Suspect's device can be analyzed to trace phishing messages, fake sites visited, and stolen credentials stored locally.

***Table 11.2**: Real-world use cases of mobile forensics*

Android is no longer restricted to mobile phones

Android's evolution beyond mobile phones, into smart TVs, wearables, automotive systems (Android Auto), IoT devices, and even embedded systems, has significantly expanded both the cybersecurity threat landscape and the scope of digital forensics.

The following table provides the implications of Android beyond mobile devices:

Aspect	Details
Expanded attack surface	More device types (TVs, watches, cars) running Android means more endpoints for attackers to target.
Inconsistent security models	Many devices do not receive timely updates, use modified **Android Open-Source Project** (**AOSP**) builds, or lack Google Play's security features.
Insecure IoT deployments	Smart devices with Android often expose open ports, weak auth, or outdated firmware.
Supply chain vulnerabilities	Custom Android forks and vendor-specific components can introduce hidden backdoors or insecure apps.
Physical access threats	Devices like smart TVs or infotainment systems are often left unattended, enabling USB-based or local attacks.
Cross-device propagation	Malware may spread across Android devices sharing the same Google account or network, e.g., from watch to phone to TV.

***Table 11.3**: Applications of Android beyond mobile devices*

Hence, with the advent of such an expansion into consumer space where security may not be the first consideration, a broader capability to collect, correlate, and analyze data from diverse Android devices is an important aspect of digital forensics. Similar techniques that are used for a smartphone can also be used for these smart devices.

Acquiring images and app files for learning

Acquiring Android and iOS images for digital forensics can be challenging due to encryption, device security policies, and legal restrictions. Still, there are practical methods and tools to obtain useful datasets, especially for training, simulation, and tool validation. Let us look at a few ways by which we can acquire images and files for our testing and learning purposes.

Acquiring Android images and app files

For Android devices, the following can be used:

Acquisition type	Details
Physical image acquisition	Can be done either by rooting the devices or by specialized forensic tools. This allows a bit-by-bit copy including deleted files.
Logical image/backup	Can be performed without root for most user-accessible data. Tools like Magnet Acquire, Oxygen Forensics, OSForensics, and **Mobile Device Investigator** (**MDI**) are commonly used. **Android Debug Bridge** (**ADB**), which is part of the Android **software development kit** (**SDK**), can also be used.
Community datasets	Public forensic images for various Android versions are available for training, analysis, and tool validation purposes.

***Table 11.4:** Acquiring Android images and app files*

Acquiring iOS images and app files

For iOS devices (e.g., iPhone and iPad), the following can be used:

Acquisition type	Details
Physical image acquisition	Challenging due to Apple's hardware encryption. Physical imaging (full disk) is generally only feasible on older devices or if the device is jailbroken and the passcode is known, which is now becoming rare. This is one of the key challenges for forensic labs when they receive an iOS device as part of the evidence.
Logical image/backup	iTunes backup and other 3rd party software-based backups are the best bet when dealing with iOS devices. If the backups are unencrypted, they can provide extensive forensic artifacts from the device.
Unencrypted images	Complete, unencrypted images of modern iOS devices are generally not available due to Apple's strong encryption and secure enclave. Datasets might exist for legacy devices or simulated test images, but these are rare for current iPhones.
Community datasets	Forensic images based on older versions of iOS are available for download from various sources for training purposes.

***Table 11.5:** Acquiring iOS images and app files*

Use of backups for digital forensics training

Android and iOS backups (i.e., logical images produced via OS or forensic tools) can be valuable for forensics training and are commonly analyzed in professional and educational courses. They provide app data, SMS, call logs, media, and, in some cases, encrypted secrets, but usually not deleted or low-level system artifacts, which are only available from physical images.

While backups do not include the full raw disk, they include plenty of practical evidence for training and simulate many real-world investigative scenarios. A lot of content, like app data, media, settings, messages, call logs, photos, contacts, etc., is available in such a type of backup and can help us understand.

Tip: **As a digital forensic practitioner, if you want to get into the area of mobile forensics, having a bunch of Android and iOS devices that are not your primary device but are still used actively can be easily used for training and demonstration purposes. You can also acquire old phones from your friends and family and from the market. However, always ensure and respect the privacy and confidentiality of the data, as many such phones may not have been wiped clean and can still contain users' data.**

Using public forensic images

This is another viable option for mobile forensics practitioners. A few places from where you can get such images are as follows:

Source	Details
Digital Corpora	Digital Corpora (**https://digitalcorpora.org/**) provides public images, including cell phone dumps, for use in computer forensics educational research. Please note these images may be very large and will also need excellent resources for analysis.
Mobile Security Framework (MobSF)	MobSF is a security research platform for mobile applications on Android, iOS, and Windows Mobile. It can be utilized for various purposes by digital forensic researchers and practitioners, such as mobile application security, penetration testing, malware analysis, and privacy analysis. You can download various files that are scanned by other users from **https://mobsf.live/recent_scans/**. Please be aware that the files may contain malware and other cyber security threats.
NIST CFReDS	NIST CFReDS, or Computer Forensic Reference DataSet Portal (**https://cfreds.nist.gov/**), provides a lot of datasets for digital forensics, including those for mobile phones.

Table 11.6: *List of a few public forensic image sources*

Note: We will use a few artifacts from the sources mentioned in the preceding table for this chapter. However, as the principles and tools used in digital forensics would be the same irrespective of the place from which the images are acquired, please feel free to use other sources. As usual, when dealing with public images and files, ensure that you do not use your primary machines for working with them.

Android and iOS architecture

Android and iOS are the top two mobile operating systems in today's world. While both are very popular, they are inherently very different in terms of their architecture.

Android architecture

The Android architecture is a layered framework built on top of the Linux kernel, designed to support a wide range of hardware and application environments. At its core is the Linux kernel, which manages low-level device operations such as memory, process, and power management. Above it, the **hardware abstraction layer** (**HAL**) allows Android to interface uniformly with diverse hardware components. The **Android Runtime** (**ART**) executes application bytecode using **ahead-of-time** (**AOT**) and **just-in-time** (**JIT**) compilation, operating alongside native libraries that provide low-level system functionality.

The Application Framework exposes essential services and APIs (e.g., activity management, notifications) to developers. Finally, user-facing applications, including both system and third-party apps, run in isolated sandboxes, ensuring security and stability. This modular structure enables Android to be flexible, scalable, and portable across smartphones, tablets, TVs, and IoT devices.

Android architecture is based on the Linux kernel and is organized in five main layers from bottom to top as follows:

Layer	Description
1. Linux Kernel	Hardware abstraction, device drivers (e.g., display, camera, battery, radio).
2. HAL	Interface between hardware drivers and system services.
3. ART and Libraries	Core Java libraries and ART (replaces Dalvik) to run apps.

Layer	Description
4. Application Framework	Manages UI, resources, activities, telephony, content providers, etc.
5. Applications	System and third-party apps (APK), all run in sandboxed user space.

***Table 11.7**: Layers in Android architecture*

iOS architecture

The iOS architecture is a tightly integrated stack designed by Apple, combining a Unix-based core with advanced app and user interface capabilities. It begins with the Core OS layer, built on the XNU kernel, which provides essential low-level services like memory management, security, and device drivers. Above this, the core services layer delivers foundational APIs for data management, networking, and location. The media layer enables rich audio, video, and graphical output through frameworks like Metal and Core Animation. At the top, the cocoa touch layer powers the user interface and application environment, managing gestures, multitasking, and the application lifecycle.

This highly controlled architecture ensures optimized performance, strict security, and seamless integration across the Apple ecosystem, including iPhones, iPads, and wearable devices.

iOS uses a Unix-like Darwin core and is structured in four abstraction layers from bottom to top, shown in the following table:

Layer	Description
1. Core OS layer	Kernel (XNU), drivers, file system, power management, low-level security.
2. Core services	Fundamental system services (SQLite, iCloud, networking, location services).
3. Media layer	Graphics, audio, video, image processing (OpenGL, Metal, Core Audio).
4. Cocoa touch	App-facing API, handles touch, gestures, UI, and app lifecycle.

***Table 11.8**: Layers in iOS architecture*

Android techniques for mobile forensics

While most think of mobile phones and tablets, Android runs on a wide range of devices. They not only include smartphones and tablets, but also devices like smart watches, set-top boxes, streaming devices, car infotainment systems, **point of sale** (**PoS**) devices, and even **Internet of Things** (**IoT**) devices.

While we are not discussing other devices powered by Android apart from mobile devices, as a mobile forensics practitioner, it is a good idea to spend some time understanding how to collect evidence and analyze it.

Let us look at a few key techniques that are used while dealing with Android devices:

Technique	Details
Logical acquisition	Used to extract files, databases, call logs, messages, photos, and other app data through direct access in debug mode, Android's APIs, Android Studio without accessing raw memory. It is faster and can access most data, but may miss deleted data.
File system acquisition	Can be used to capture complete file system structure, including hidden/system files, providing more evidence than logical acquisition.
Physical acquisition	Creates a bit-by-bit copy of the entire storage (e.g., NAND flash), and can recover deleted files, but often requires a rooted device or specialized hardware tools.

Technique	Details
Chip-off forensics	Involves physically removing the flash memory chip and reading it directly with hardware tools. Used when the device is locked/damaged.
Android Debug Bridge (**ADB**) extraction	Utilizes developer debugging mode to extract data. It is, however, limited by permissions and device state. The device need to be in debug mode as well.
Cloud data acquistion	Collects synced data from associated Google accounts, app cloud backups, and services like Google Drive or Photos.
App-based data parsing	Uses tools to analyze popular apps' internal databases of installed applications. They can include databases like SQLite that are easy to analyze if acquired. Many applications like WhatsApp, Facebook, etc. may have encrypted databases.

Table 11.9: *Key techniques used in Android forensics*

iOS techniques for mobile forensics

Mobile forensics for iOS devices is generally taken up by advanced digital forensics labs and researchers due to the level of security from all perspectives - hardware, software, and Apple ecosystem. However, mobile forensics for iOS devices also has a role to play in digital forensics, especially when the password of the device is known, or unencrypted backup or cloud backups are acquired.

Let us look at a few techniques for mobile forensics for iOS devices and whether they can be carried out by a general digital forensics practitioner or require an advanced lab:

Technique	Details	Possible by general practitioner	Required advanced lab
Logical acquisition	Used to extract user data accessible through normal APIs and backups (contacts, call logs, messages, media, some app data). Often done via iTunes backup or forensic tools (e.g., Cellebrite UFED, Magnet AXIOM).	Yes	No
Backup acquisition	Creates a local encrypted or unencrypted iTunes backup, which can be parsed for messages, app data, and settings. Encrypted backups yield more data (Wi-Fi creds, website history).	Yes	No
File system acquisition	Used to extract the complete file system from the device using jailbreaking or authorized tool exploits; includes system files and some deleted data remnants.	Only if jailbreak possible.	Yes
Full physical acquisition	Used for bit-by-bit copy of NAND storage, recovering deleted files and all partitions.	Only possible on older devices (e.g., A4–A11 chips) or with vulnerabilities like checkm8.	Only possible on older devices (e.g., A4–A11 chips) or with vulnerabilities like checkm8.
CheckM8-based acquisition	CheckM8 tools provide exploit-based acquisition for iPhones with A5–A11 SoCs, and can be used to extract the full file system and some keychain data even without a passcode.	Only possible on older devices and with sophisticated tools and skills.	Only possible on older devices and with sophisticated tools and skills.

Technique	Details	Possible by general practitioner	Required advanced lab
Cloud data acquisition	Can be used to gathers iCloud-synced data (contacts, calendars, photos, backups, app data) using account credentials or legal requests to Apple.	With credentials and consent. Apple may not give access even after a legal order or subpoena.	With credentials and consent. Apple may not give access even after a legal order or subpoena.
App data extraction	Can be use to parse app containers (WhatsApp, iMessage, Mail, etc.) from device or backup. Decryption of protected data often needed.	Can be used to parse only unencrypted and local app data.	Needed for encrypted and protected data, but may need tools that are not accessible to all except government agencies.
JTAG/ISP extraction	Chip-level direct memory access by tapping into debugging interfaces or solder points and can bypass OS-level security on some devices.	No	Yes, but the result may not be positive for newer devices.
Chip-off forensics	Involves physically removing NAND chip and reading it directly.	No	Yes, but extremely rare for iPhones due to encryption tied to hardware keys.
Volatile memory (RAM) acquisition	Capturing live memory to extract encryption keys, passwords, or in-use data.	No	Yes, requires device to be unlocked and special tools.
Passcode bypass / brute Force	Can be used to exploit vulnerabilities or hardware methods to bypass the lockscreen and brute force passcodes without triggering wipes.	No	Yes but may not work for newer devices.

Table 11.10: *Key techniques used in iOS forensics*

Interesting fact: **The Apple A5 is a 32-bit system on a chip (SoC) designed by Apple Inc., part of the Apple silicon series, and manufactured by Samsung. This was used in older versions of Apple devices up to around 2016. The A series of Apple SoCs, e.g., A16, A17, and A18, is still prevalent but is much hardened and secure.**

In a nutshell, due to the built-in security at all levels, iOS devices may not be easy to work with unless the mobile forensics investigators already have access to the pass code or have consent from the owner of the device.

Understanding endpoint detection and response

Endpoint detection and response (EDR) is a cybersecurity solution focused on monitoring, detecting, investigating, and responding to suspicious activities and threats on endpoints (e.g., laptops, desktops, mobile devices, and servers).

EDR solutions continuously collect and analyze data from endpoints using techniques like:

- Real-time behavior monitoring.
- Threat intelligence correlation.
- Automated and manual incident response.
- Alerting and forensics data collection.

Role of EDR in reducing cyber risks

While EDR solutions are often costly and complex to implement, they provide a multitude of benefits for large enterprises that are often susceptible to various cyber risks. Let us look at a few ways in which EDR can help reduce such potential cyber risks:

Benefit of EDR	Details
Real-time threat detection	Identifies malware, ransomware, lateral movement, and suspicious processes as they happen.
Automated response mechanisms	Quarantines files, kills malicious processes, or isolates endpoints instantly reducing attacker dwell time.
Automatic forensic visibility	Provides rich context (process tree, network connections, file changes) for in-depth incident investigations.
Reduced **mean time to respond (MTTR)**	Rapid detection and containment lowers the time and impact of a breach.
Threat hunting features	Enables proactive identification of **advanced persistent threats (APTs)** using collected telemetry.
Compliance and audit capabilities	Maintains logs and reports that aid in compliance with GDPR, HIPAA, ISO 27001, etc.
Insider threat mitigation features	Detects unauthorized access, privilege abuse, or suspicious insider behavior.

***Table 11.11**: Use of EDR in reducing cyber risks*

XDR as an evolution of EDR

Extended detection and response (XDR) is a holistic evolution of EDR, integrating threat data across multiple security layers, such as endpoints, networks, cloud, emails, and identities, to provide correlated threat detection, investigation, and response.

XDR brings together signals from various solutions, like the following, providing a much more comprehensive view of security posture:

- EDR
- **Network detection and response (NDR)**
- Email security
- Cloud workload protection
- Identity providers (e.g., Azure AD, Okta)

While XDR provides a much higher level of security, this is not a solution for everyone. Most of the time, an EDR solution may suffice for most enterprises. Let us look at a few key differences between EDR and XDR in the following table:

Aspect	EDR	XDR
Scope	Focuses on endpoint data only.	Correlates across multiple layers (endpoint, network, cloud, email, identity).
Data correlation	Limited to endpoint telemetry.	Cross-domain data fusion for broader context.
Visibility	Isolated endpoint-centric.	End-to-end visibility across enterprise.

Aspect	EDR	XDR
Threat detection	May miss multi-vector or lateral attacks.	Better at catching complex, multi-stage attacks.
Response capability	Endpoint-specific actions.	Coordinated response across different tools/systems.
Complexity	Easier to deploy, but limited.	Broader coverage, may require tighter integration.

Table 11.12: Key differences between EDR and XDR

In short, EDR helps detect and respond to threats on endpoints, improving cyber resilience by minimizing threat impact. On the other hand, XDR expands this approach, correlating signals across multiple domains, resulting in better visibility, faster detection, and unified response to complex cyber threats. Both play critical roles in a layered defense strategy, with XDR offering a more integrated, next-gen approach to modern enterprise security.

Role of EDR in mobile forensics

EDR tools, while costly and complex to implement, can provide numerous benefits for mobile forensics evidence collection and investigation. While EDR is not a replacement for dedicated mobile forensic acquisition, it is a powerful complement, especially for the following:

- Ongoing monitoring and detection on managed mobile endpoints.
- Providing logs and artifacts is crucial for rapid, effective forensic investigations.
- Enabling incident response actions that both contain threats and preserve evidence.

Traditional forensic imaging tools are still needed to extract full device data, bypass encryption, or work with devices not covered by EDR, particularly for iOS and non-managed Android devices. EDR may also not be very useful for **Bring Your Own Device** (**BYOD**) scenarios when permitted in the organization.

Understanding the Android file system

Android file system is a Linux-like file system with a lot of elements and principles taken from Linux. However, it is customized to the needs of the mobile device.

The following table shows the high-level structure of the Android file system:

Directory	Description
`/`	Root directory. Base of all file system hierarchy. Not user-accessible, unless rooted.
`/system`	Contains OS binaries, system apps, and libraries. Read-only after boot.
`/data`	App data and user data. Encrypted by default. Each app gets its own subdir.
`/cache`	Temporary files like **over the air** (**OTA**) updates, downloaded package metadata.
`/sdcard`	User-accessible storage (or internal storage), and is used to store media, downloads, documents, etc.
`/storage`	Mount point for all external storage (e.g., SD cards, USB).
`/vendor`	Device-specific drivers and HALs (added by manufacturer).
`/dev, /proc, /sys`	Virtual/Kernel directories for devices, processes, and system info.
`/boot`	Bootloader, kernel, and RAMDisk. Typically not mounted after boot.
`/recovery`	Special partition for factory reset or firmware flashing.

Table 11.13: Basic structure of Android file system

The following hierarchy is a good representation of the Android file system:

```
/
├── boot                 # Boot partition (kernel + ramdisk)
├── system               # Core Android OS and system apps
│   ├── app              # System apps
│   ├── bin              # System binaries
│   ├── etc              # System config files
│   └── lib              # Native libraries
├── data                 # User-installed apps and user data
│   ├── data
│   │   └── com.app.package   # App-specific private data
│   ├── user
│   │   └── 0                # Primary user profile
│   └── media
│       └── 0   # Internal/primary storage equivalent to /sdcard
├── cache       # Temporary cache files
├── recovery    # Recovery partition (used for updates/resets)
├── misc        # Misc. system settings and info
├── vendor      # Hardware/device-specific binaries and drivers
├── storage
│   ├── emulated
│   │   └── 0 # Internal user-accessible storage (a.k.a. /sdcard)
│   └── external_SD  # Physical SD card (if present)
├── mnt
│   └── sdcard       # Mount point for SD cards
├── sdcard           # Symlink to /storage/emulated/0
├── Android
│   ├── data         # App-written external data
│   └── obb          # App expansion files (e.g. game data)
```

From a mobile forensics insights point of view, the following are important:

- Forensic data is mostly in **`/data/data/`** and **`/sdcard/Android/data/`**.
- Full access requires root access (or rooting) or exploitation of recovery/custom ROMs.
- File timestamps, app databases (e.g., SQLite databases), media files, and logs are crucial artifacts that are carved out from various directories.

Anatomy of APK and AAB files

Let us first understand the two most common file types used in Android: **Android Package** (**APK**) and **Android App Bundle** (**AAB**) files. The relation between APK and AAB files lies in the fact that both are part of the Android app packaging and deployment process, but they serve different purposes in the lifecycle of an app.

Previously, APK files were directly submitted to Google Play (new name for Google Play Store) for publication. This meant that one had to submit multiple APK files for different target devices. Now AAB is the source bundle submitted to Google Play, and APK is the output generated from that bundle automatically by Google Play, tailored to specific devices.

Note: The structure of APK and AAB files may change based on the newer versions of Android OS. Hence, what we are discussing in this section is subject to change. However, the overall structure and types of files and assets may remain similar.

Anatomy of an APK file

An APK file is a zip archive containing the following:

File/folder	Description/purpose
`AndroidManifest.xml`	Declares app components, permissions, activities, etc.
`classes.dex`	Compiled bytecode for the Android Runtime (Dalvik/ ART).
`resources.arsc`	Precompiled resources (strings, layouts, etc.).
`res/`	Raw resources (images, XMLs, layouts), non-compiled.
`lib/`	Native libraries (.so) for different CPU architectures.
`assets/`	Raw files used by app (read at runtime).
`META-INF/`	Certificates and signature files.
`kotlin/`	Kotlin runtime libraries (if app uses Kotlin).
`kotlin-tooling-metadata.json`	Kotlin compiler metadata (optional).

Table 11.14: Structure of APK file

Since it is a zip file, it can be extracted using unzip or other similar utilities to see all the files and folders.

Anatomy of an AAB file

An AAB file is also a zip archive, but it follows a different structure. We can think about AAB in terms of containing all the possible configurations. APK is what runs on the target Android devices.

A typical AAB file contains the following:

File/folder	Description/purpose
`base/`	Base module, contains core app code (similar to APK structure).
`feature/ folders`	Optional modules (dynamic features or language packs).
`assets/, res/, etc.`	Like APK, per module.
`manifest/`	AndroidManifest for each module.
`dex/, lib/`	Compiled code and native libs (like APK but per module).
`BUNDLE-METADATA/`	Contains metadata like bundle version, signing info.
`ModuleProtocol.proto`	Protobuf file describing module relationships.

Table 11.15: Structure of AAB file

Since AAB files also follow the zip file structure, they can also be extracted using unzip or other similar utilities to see all the files and folders.

Lifecycle of AAB and APK files

Let us first understand how APK files are generated by Google Play from the AAB files that are submitted by developers. Following is a list of high-level steps in the lifecycle of AAB and APK files:

- Developers build an AAB file using Android Studio or command-line tools.
- They upload the AAB to the Play Store.
- Google Play uses the AAB to generate optimized APKs using a tool called bundletool.
- These APKs are split and created for the target device configuration (language, screen size, CPU architecture, etc.), based on the source assets uploaded.
- Only the relevant APKs are installed on the user's device to reduce size and improve performance.

Note: **The way Google Play uses the bundle tool to create APKs, a threat actor can do the same after adding malicious code to the APK. Once done, the APK file is then shared with unsuspecting users in the form of free or cracked versions of games and utilities that are otherwise costly. Sometimes, threat actors also share the APKs posing as the latest version of the well-known apps with additional features or security.**

Recipe 95: Extracting APK file to learn its structure

One of the best ways to understand the structure of an APK file is to extract one yourself. You can acquire sample APK files from various sites and GitHub repositories, including those listed before in this chapter.

Note:

Compatibility: OS Independent

License considerations: Free software used

Recipe

As mentioned before, the APK files are basically zip files, and hence unzipping them using one of the compatible utilities should be sufficient to see the structure of the file.

Follow the following steps to complete this recipe:

1. Acquire an APK file. Let us say we have the APK file called `sample.apk`.
2. Now, rename the `sample.apk` to `sample.zip`. Your operating system may ask for confirmation while doing so.
3. Now use a zip extraction utility to unzip the file. This can be done by the operating system's built-in utility or from the command line using third-party utilities. For example, for Windows, you can right-click on the zip file and click on **Extract All...**.
4. You should now see all the files under the APK file, as we previously discussed.

Activity

Attempt the following activities before the next recipe:

- Inspect the file `AndroidManifest.xml` at the root of the APK file carefully and analyze how this file can be used to mask any malicious content in the APK. Do the same with the files under `/lib`.
- There is a file under the `/` called `classes.dex`, which is compresses made up of all the Java classes in the application code. Use a utility called **dex2jar** to convert it into a jar, then extract the class files from the jar using the `jar` command. After this, try to decompile the extracted `.class` files to understand what they are doing.

Recipe 96: Using Autopsy to scan an APK file

We have used Autopsy as a versatile tool in the previous chapter for working with digital forensic cases. We will use Autopsy again in this recipe to analyze the sample APK file. This can also help with quick triaging based on what is found inside the APK file.

Note:

- **Compatibility: Windows**
- **License considerations: Free software used**

Recipe

Let us use Autopsy to analyze the APK file that we renamed to a zip file, say **`sample.zip`**. Follow the following steps to complete the recipe:

1. Add a new data source by clicking on the **Add Data Source** button on the menu bar. In the Window that comes up:
   a. Use the default option for the **Select Host** step.
   b. Select **Logical Files** for the **Select Data Source Type** step.
   c. In the next step, **Select Data Source**, click on **Add,** and select the zip file. Click on Next.
2. In the **Configure Ingest** step, select the ingest module that you need to use for analyzing the zip file. Choosing a lot of modules may result in longer analysis time:

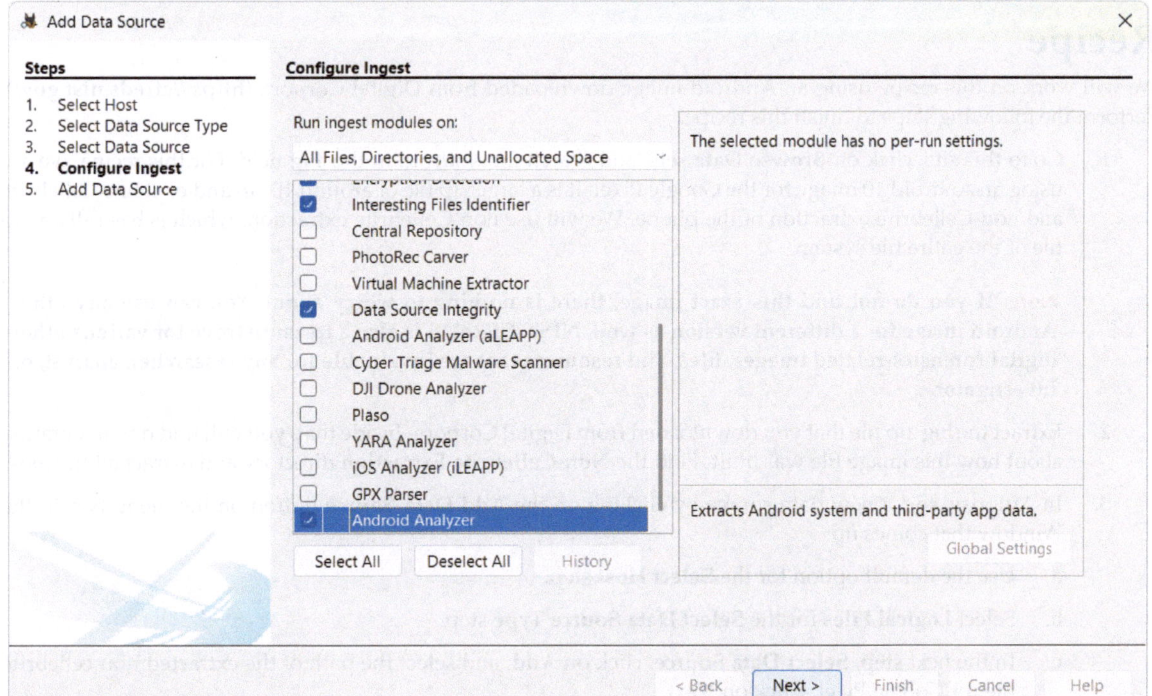

Figure 11.1: Ingest modules in Autopsy

> Interesting fact: **The Android Analyzer module of Autopsy wraps the Android Logs Events And Protobuf Parser (ALEAPP) tool and creates Autopsy artifacts with the results by analyzing Android databases and files. This works on both physical images and logical file sets.**

3. Press **Next**. The new data source is added, and analysis begins. The left side tree is updated as the ingest modules are executed and the data source is analyzed.

Activity

Attempt the following activities before the next recipe:

- List down the new insights you got from Autopsy versus analyzing manually by unzipping the APK file.
- Read Autopsy's Android Analyzer Module documentation to understand what artifacts this module can analyze.

Recipe 97: Using Autopsy to scan an Android image

Since the digital forensic analysts can discover a lot of data, including call logs, messages, app data, browser history, multimedia files, geolocation data, and much more, scanning an Android image becomes an essential part of mobile forensics. Let us understand in this recipe how we can scan an entire Android image using Autopsy.

> Note:
>
> - **Compatibility: Windows**
> - **License considerations: Free software used**

Recipe

We will work on this recipe using an Android image downloaded from Digital Corpora (**https://cfreds.nist.gov/**). Perform the following steps to finish this recipe:

1. Go to this site, click on **Browse Data** sets, and search for Android in the **Tag** field. For this recipe, we are using an Android 10 image for the Google Pixel. It is a large zip file of around 10 GB and contains Cellebrite and non-Cellebrite extraction of the phone. We will use non-Cellebrite extraction, which is basically a zip file of the entire file system.

   > Note: **If you do not find this exact image, there is nothing to worry about. You can use any other Android image for a different version as well. NIST CFReDS is also a treasure trove for various other digital forensics-related images, files, and resources that are invaluable for any researcher, analyst, or investigator.**

2. Extract the big zip file that you downloaded from Digital Corpora. Inside that, you will find documentation about how this image file was built. Find the **Non-Cellebrite Extraction** directory and extract all the files.
3. In Autopsy, add a new data source by clicking on the **Add Data Source** button on the menu bar. In the Window that comes up:
   a. Use the default option for the **Select Host** step.
   b. Select **Logical Files** for the **Select Data Source Type** step.
   c. In the next step, **Select Data Source**, click on **Add**, and select the path of the extracted non-cellebrite file for Google Pixel. Click on **Next**.
4. In the **Configure Ingest** step, select the ingest module that you need to use for analyzing the zip file. Choosing a lot of modules may result in longer analysis time.

5. The analysis will take some time based on the size of the image file and show the results in the hierarchical structure of the left side of the Autopsy window.

   Once the analysis is complete, you may see something like this, which shows that Autopsy was able to figure out a lot of data artifacts like call logs, a large number of SQLite files, emails, phone numbers, WhatsApp database files, and much more:

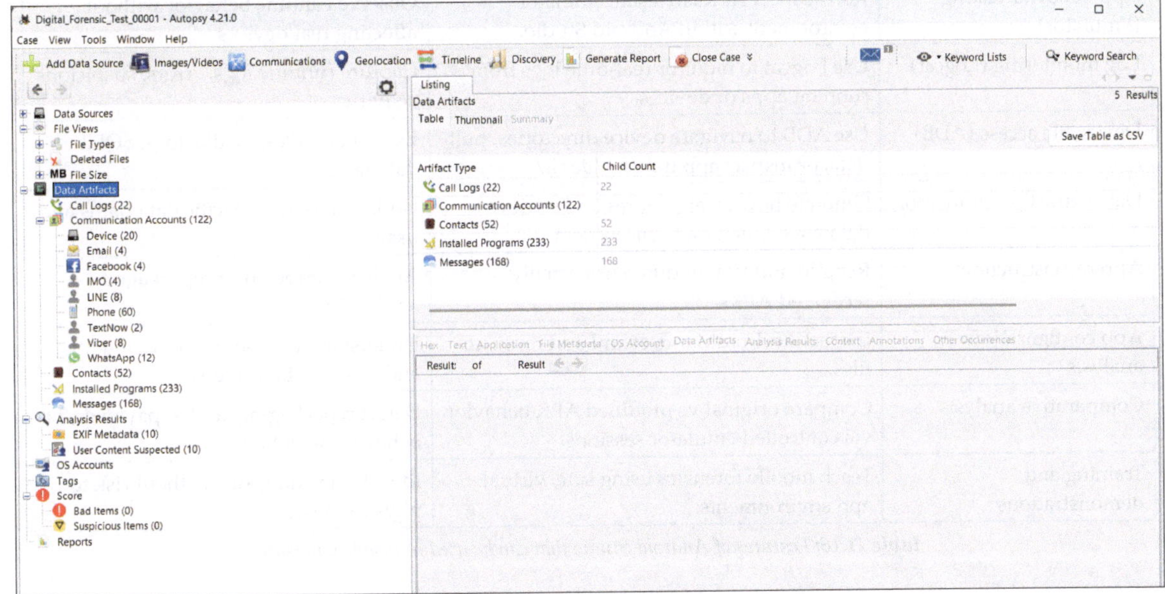

Figure 11.2: Analyzed artifacts are shown in Autopsy

Activity

Attempt the following activities before the next recipe:

- List down all the artifacts Autopsy is able to carve out of the Android image file.
- Analyze a few SQLite database files found by Autopsy using the SQLite database tools we have learned so far.
- Analyze if it is possible to see the deleted files in the extracted files zip we used. Why and why not?

Recipe 98: Using Android Studio for Android forensics

Android Studio is the official **integrated development environment** (**IDE**) for building Android applications, developed by *Google*. It provides tools for coding, debugging, testing, and deploying Android apps. It includes a powerful code editor, Android emulator, device log viewer (Logcat), and integration with tools like ADB and Gradle. While Android Studio is primarily a development tool, it can be very useful in digital forensics investigations involving Android devices, especially when dealing with app analysis, file system navigation, and emulator-based testing, and device interaction via ADB.

The following tables create a strong case for why a mobile forensic investigator would like to use Android Studio:

Use case	Description	Forensic objectives
APK inspection	Open and examine decompiled APK source code, manifest, and resource files.	Identify malicious permissions, components, or behaviors.
App behavior testing (Emulator)	Run suspect APKs in a safe emulator environment within Android Studio.	Observe runtime behavior without affecting real devices.
Log monitoring (Logcat)	Use Logcat to monitor real-time logs from running apps or devices.	Capture runtime logs, errors, suspicious activity.
Device file access (ADB)	Use ADB to navigate device directories, pull data, or inspect app data in `/data/`.	Extract app files, media, logs, SQLite databases.
Data extraction simulation	Simulate how an app stores and retrieves data via emulator and file system.	Understand app-specific data paths and usage.
App reconstruction	Rebuild and test modified or partially recovered APKs.	Analyze tampered or repackaged applications.
App configuration analysis	Inspect AndroidManifest.xml and resource files.	Understand app permissions, intents, and broadcast receivers.
Comparative analysis	Compare original vs modified APK behavior via controlled emulator sessions.	Detect repackaging, added payloads, or behavior deviation.
Training and demonstrations	Teach mobile forensics using safe, virtual app environments.	Ideal for training labs without risk to physical devices.

***Table 11.16**: Features of Android Studio that can be used in mobile forensics*

Note:

- **Compatibility**: **OS Independent**
- **License considerations**: **Free software used**

Recipe

In this recipe, we will use Android Studio to connect to an Android phone and perform various operations like accessing the files and checking the logs.

Follow the following steps to complete this recipe:

1. First, we need to download Android Studio from **https://developer.android.com/studio**. Android Studio is available for Windows, macOS, and Linux. So, no matter what your favorite operating system is, you will have a consistent Android forensic experience while working with Android Studio.
2. Once downloaded, follow the installation instructions to install it. Once installed, Android Studio will ask to download files for components like **Android Virtual Device** (**AVD**) and other libraries. This may take some time to complete due to the size of the initial download.
3. Once all the components are installed, Android Studio will start. You can go ahead and create a new project or open an existing one. You can also clone a code repository. In this case, we can just start with a new project for testing a few tools. From the welcome page, if you click on **More Actions**, you can also debug an APK.

4. Let us start by analyzing the APK file we used before. Clicking on the option to analyze the APK file in **More Actions**, Android Studio automatically opens the APK file, extracts everything, and even decompiles all the **`.class`** files found in the **`.dex`** file. The screen will look like the following figure, which shows the entire project created out of this APK:

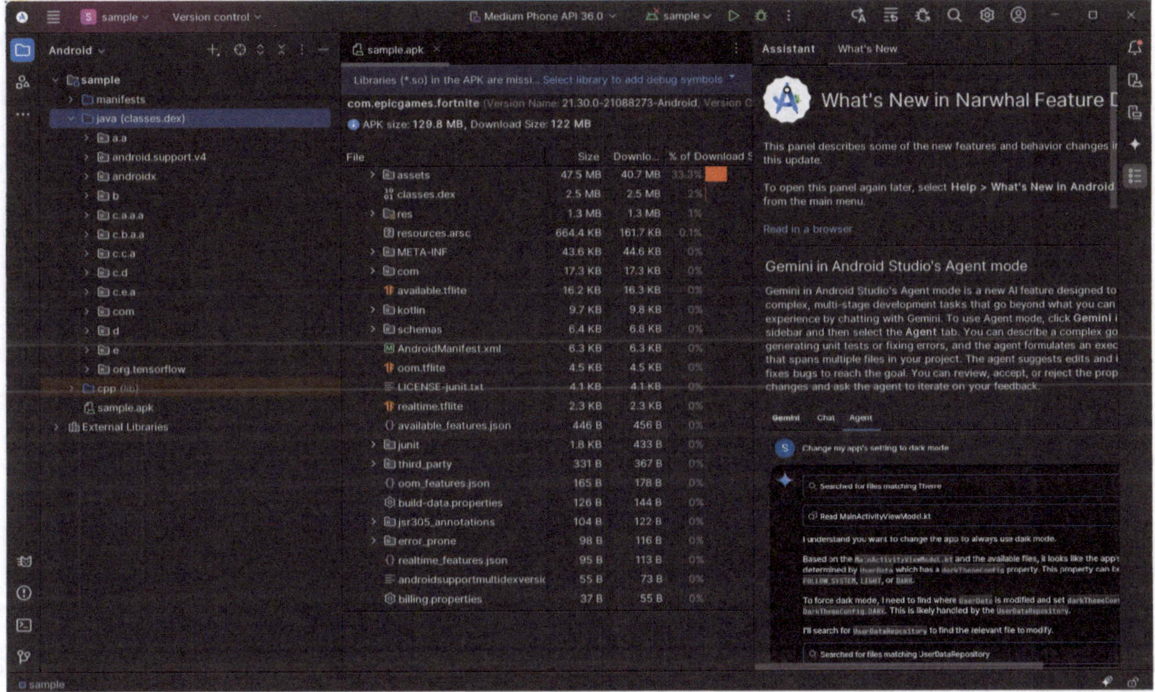

Figure 11.3: Android Studio showing various artifacts in the extracted APK file

Android Studio significantly simplifies APK analysis by providing built-in extraction, decompilation, and inspection capabilities. Not only that, but you can also analyze the behavior of the application by running it in an emulator.

5. Let us now connect an Android phone to the Android Studio. For this, first you need to ensure that debugging is on in your Android phone. Once you connect the phone to your laptop, it will appear in the list of devices under **Device Manager**. You may have to find it in the Android SDK window if you are using it for the first time. Clicking on the three dots in the name of the phone and then clicking on **Open in Device Explorer**, the entire file system is shown on the screen as shown in the following figure:

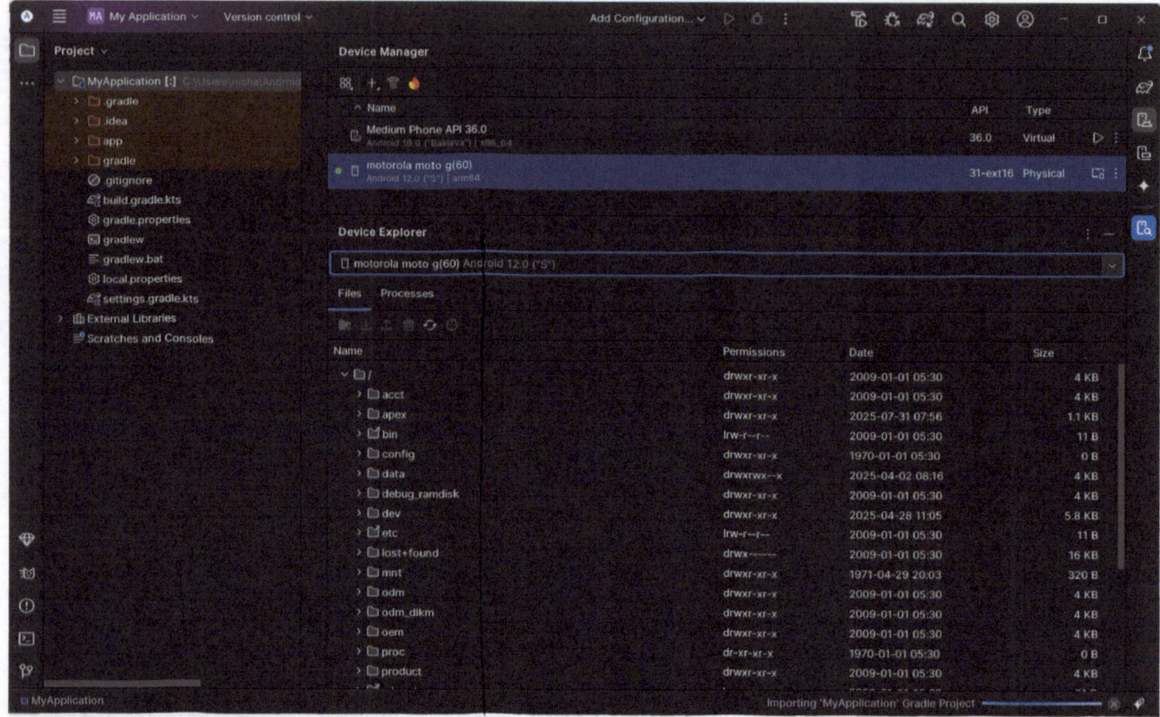

***Figure 11.4:** Accessing device's file system in Android Studio*

By now, you must appreciate the fact that Android Studio is a very versatile tool for working with Android devices and APKs.

Activity

Attempt the following activities before the next recipe:

- Analyze the APK file and list down various components found by Android Studio.
- Analyze the DEX file decompiled by Android Studio. Check if you can see the Java files for the .class files.
- List down all the artifacts you can retrieve from your phone. Also, analyze the significance of all these features.

Recipe 99: Using Logcat with live Android device

Logcat is a built-in tool in Android Studio (and Android SDK) that displays real-time system logs from an Android device or emulator. These logs include information about system events, app activity, crashes, garbage collection, network access, and much more. It is essentially a diagnostic console used for debugging, but it is extremely useful in mobile forensics for observing app behavior and extracting volatile evidence.

Logcat is a highly valuable tool in Android mobile forensics due to its ability to capture real-time system and application-level logs. It can be used to capture the following types of evidence:

Types of evidence	Examples
App behavior tracking	Logs showing app crashes, API calls, network requests.
Timestamps	Precise time markers for events like user actions or background tasks.
Intent logging	Details of system and custom intents (inter-process communication).
Broadcast receiver logs	Helps identify received system-level events (e.g., boot complete, SMS).
Login/session tracking	Logs of login events, token exchanges, user session lifecycle.
Network activity	API endpoints accessed, request/response codes, errors, and more.

***Table 11.17:** Features of Logcat*

Note:

- **Compatibility: OS Independent**
- **License considerations: Free software used**

Recipe

In Android Studio, click on the **Logcat** icon (the icon is a cat icon) while your phone is shown in the list. Remove any filter if applied. Now, you can see all the logs that are generated by the system and various apps installed, as shown in the following figure:

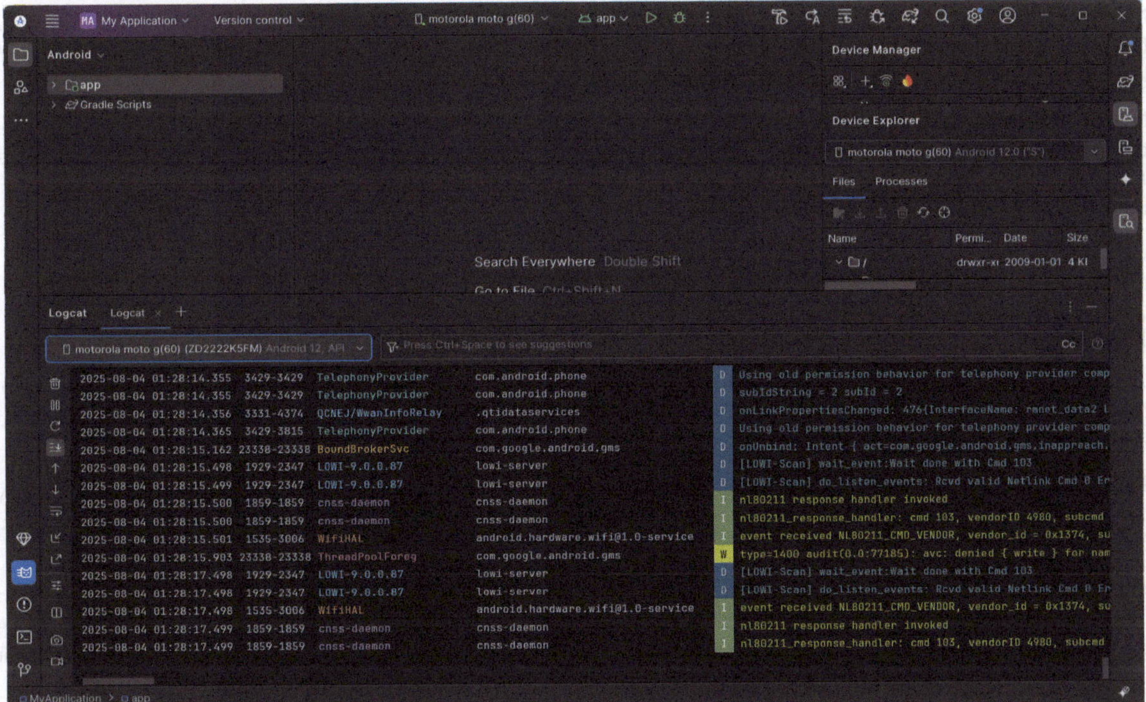

***Figure 11.5:** Using Logcat to access system and application logs*

If you monitor carefully, you will see logs related to battery service, charging, Wi-Fi, network, and many other things, basically everything that is happening in the device.

A digital forensic investigator can use Logcat to get logs in real time for a phone that is under investigation. The same thing can be done for an app running in a simulator, which is a sandboxed environment provided by the AVD of Android Studio.

Activity

Attempt the following activities before the next recipe:

- Find a way to export all the Logcat logs to a file. What file format is it?
- Apply a filter for specific types of logs, e.g., Wi-Fi logs.

Using Mobile Security Framework

Mobile Security Framework (**MobSF**) is a research platform designed for assessing the security of mobile applications across Android, iOS, and Windows Mobile. It supports various use cases, including mobile application security testing, penetration testing, malware analysis, and privacy assessments.

MobSF provides a wide range of capabilities for analyzing both Android and iOS applications. Its Static Analyzer supports popular mobile binaries such as APK, IPA, and APPX, as well as source code. The Dynamic Analyzer supports Android and iOS apps, enabling interactive instrumented testing, runtime data inspection, and network traffic analysis. Additionally, MobSF integrates smoothly into DevSecOps or CI/CD pipelines through REST APIs and CLI tools, helping to strengthen security workflows efficiently.

MobSF can be used offline without the need for sending data to an external site, and hence works great for digital forensics labs as well as individual investigators/researchers. More details about MobSF can be found at **https://github.com/MobSF/Mobile-Security-Framework-MobSF**.

MobSF also has an online analyzer just like Virustotal at **https://mobsf.live/**, where you can upload mobile images to analyze them. Moreover, MobSF API provides a great way to automate analysis or perform specific analysis tasks. The API Docs at **https://mobsf.live/api_docs** is a great place to start with MobSF API and also for developing an understanding of mobile forensics in general.

Recovering deleted files from Android forensic image

Commercial tools like Cellebrite UFED and Magnet Acquire can be used to acquire a forensically sound image. Such tools are generally used by government forensic labs and other research labs due to the cost and the process behind acquiring such tools.

The same applies to recovering deleted files and carving all the evidence present on such an image. We have already used Autopsy to carve out evidence in a logical backup of the phone. However, the open-source, community, and free tools have very limited support for working with forensic images of phones.

This should not stop you from understanding the inner workings of the mobile operating systems, including their file organization, how they maintain the data, and what types of logs and events are generated. While understanding the principles and approach to mobile forensics takes time, mastering how to use a tool is a much easier job for digital forensic practitioners.

Challenges in mobile forensics

While mobile forensics is an exciting area of digital forensics and is indispensable in solving cybercrime, mobile forensics professionals often face many challenges. Let us look at a few such challenges in the following table:

Challenge	Details
Device and OS fragmentation	Thousands of manufacturers and models with varying hardware and Android versions make a one-size-fits-all forensic method impossible.
Security measures	Encryption (full-disk and file-based), Secure Boot, and hardware-backed keystores hinder physical acquisition.
Lock screen and biometrics	PIN, pattern, fingerprint, and face locks can block forensic access without bypass methods.
Rooting restrictions	Newer Android versions and security patches limit rooting, which is often needed for deep data access.
Rapid OS updates	Frequent updates can change internal file structures, affecting tool compatibility.
Data in encrypted apps	Apps like Signal, WhatsApp, and Telegram encrypt local storage, making extraction harder.
Cloud dependency	Some data resides only in the cloud, requiring legal procedures to access.
Anti-forensic techniques	Malware or advanced users can use secure wiping, encryption, or obfuscation to destroy evidence.
Limited RAM access	Volatile data acquisition is time-sensitive and difficult if the device is locked or auto-suspends.

Table 11.18: *Challenges in mobile forensics*

Working with iOS devices has additional challenges, apart from the preceding challenges. They are summarized in the following table:

Challenge	Detail
Hardware based encryption	Hardware-based encryption tied to a unique device key using UID key, that is used to secure biometric and authentication data.
Tight control on pairing	Tightly controlled hardware-OS pairing. Additional pairing secured by OTP.
Secure Enclave Processor (SEP)	iOS SEP handles the security of features such as Touch ID, Face ID, Apple Pay, etc. The SEP is its own chip on the logic board, tied to the mobile phone and does not work if the iOS image is restored on another device.
Root/Jailbreak limitations	Jailbreaks required for deep access. Fewer jailbreaks available for modern iOS devices.
Other built-in security	Security features that can disable the phone after a specific number of attempts, strong end-to-end encryption for data like messages and health data, and many more such features.

Table 11.19: *Challenges in mobile forensics involving iOS devices*

Note: At the time of writing this book, the latest iOS version is iOS 26. Before this re-versioning strategy by Apple, the previous version was 18.x. At this time, most digital forensics labs are only able to break the encryption of up to iOS 14, and that too, not without using the most complex and costly software that not everyone can have access to. This will probably give you an indication of how tough it is to work with iOS images and other iOS devices (iPhone, iPad, etc.) as part of a digital forensic investigation.

Conclusion

Mobile forensics has become an indispensable part of modern digital investigations due to the pervasive use of mobile devices in both cyber and traditional crimes. Phones, tablets, and other Android/iOS-based devices store critical evidence in the form of communications, app data, geolocation records, and even deleted or hidden content. The field involves specialized acquisition techniques, e.g., logical, file system, physical, chip-off, and cloud-based approaches, while always ensuring evidence integrity and chain of custody.

For Android, forensic techniques range from ADB-based extraction to physical imaging, while iOS presents tougher challenges due to strong encryption, Secure Enclave, and limited jailbreak availability. Practitioners also rely on tools like Autopsy, Magnet AXIOM, Cellebrite UFED, and MobSF for analysis. EDR solutions further complement investigations by providing real-time monitoring and logs.

Despite its utility, mobile forensics faces challenges like OS fragmentation, rapid updates, encryption, and anti-forensic tactics. For investigators, mastering both the technical knowledge of mobile architectures and the practical skills to use forensic tools is essential. Ultimately, mobile forensics bridges the gap between digital evidence and criminal attribution, playing a central role in solving today's complex cases.

In the next chapter, we will look at various imaging techniques that are used to acquire logical and physical images.

Questions

1. What is mobile forensics, and why is it important in modern investigations?
2. How do mobile devices act as sources of evidence in conventional crimes?
3. What are the primary acquisition methods in Android forensics?
4. Why is rooting important for certain Android forensic techniques?
5. Explain the challenges in extracting data from encrypted mobile apps.
6. What makes iOS forensics more difficult compared to Android?
7. Describe the SEP and its forensic implications.
8. What challenges are posed by device fragmentation in Android?
9. What is Logcat, and how is it useful in forensic investigations?
10. How does Android Studio support forensic analysis of APKs?
11. What is the significance of APK and AAB files in Android forensics?
12. What is MobSF, and how can it be used in forensic investigations?
13. What role does EDR play in mobile forensics?
14. Explain the importance of maintaining chain of custody in mobile forensics.
15. Give two examples of crimes where mobile forensics played a central role.

Points to remember

- Mobile forensics focuses on the recovery, analysis, and preservation of digital evidence from mobile devices.
- Evidence sources in mobile forensics include SMS, emails, call logs, app data, media files, and geolocation data.

- Android and iOS are the dominant mobile OS platforms, each with unique forensic challenges.
- Logical acquisition extracts user-accessible data but may miss deleted files.
- Physical acquisition captures full memory, enabling recovery of deleted data.
- File system acquisition retrieves hidden and system files without full disk imaging.
- Chip-off and JTAG techniques are advanced methods for damaged or locked devices.
- **Android Debug Bridge** (ADB) allows the extraction of files via debugging mode.
- Cloud acquisition retrieves synced data from Google or iCloud accounts.
- App analysis often involves parsing SQLite databases.
- iOS devices employ strong encryption tied to hardware-based UID keys.
- Secure Enclave protects sensitive authentication and cryptographic data on iOS.
- iTunes backups (especially unencrypted) are a key source of iOS forensic evidence.
- Jailbreaking is often required to access deeper iOS file systems.
- EDR provides real-time monitoring, threat detection, and forensic visibility.
- XDR integrates multiple data sources (endpoint, cloud, network) for better context.
- Android Studio helps analyze APK files and monitor device activity with Logcat.
- APK and AAB files contain app code, resources, and configurations.
- Chain of custody ensures the admissibility of mobile evidence in court.
- Deleted data can often be recovered from physical or file system acquisitions.
- Anti-forensic techniques (secure wipe, obfuscation) can hinder investigations.
- Legal and privacy considerations are critical in accessing cloud-stored data.

Key terms

- **Mobile forensics**: A branch of digital forensics focusing on the extraction and analysis of evidence from mobile devices.
- **Logical acquisition**: Extraction of user-accessible data such as contacts, messages, and media without accessing raw memory.
- **File system acquisition**: Collection of the complete file system, including hidden and system files.
- **Physical acquisition**: Bit-by-bit copy of a device's memory, enabling deleted file recovery.
- **Chip-off forensics**: Physically removing and reading the device's memory chip for direct data access.
- **Joint Test Action Group (JTAG) acquisition**: Using debugging interfaces to extract memory content from devices.
- **Android Debug Bridge (ADB)**: Command-line tool for accessing and extracting data from Android devices.
- **Android Package (APK)**: File format containing Android application code, resources, and metadata.
- **Android App Bundle (AAB)**: Modern Android app distribution format; Play Store generates APKs from AABs.

- **Secure Enclave Processor (SEP)**: Dedicated coprocessor in iOS handling encryption keys and biometric data.
- **UID Key**: Hardware-based encryption key unique to each iOS device, binding data to hardware.
- **iTunes backup**: Logical copy of iOS device data; unencrypted backups provide rich forensic artifacts.
- **Jailbreaking**: Process of removing iOS restrictions to gain deeper system access.
- **Cloud acquisition**: Retrieval of synced mobile data from cloud services (Google Drive, iCloud).
- **App sandboxing**: Security model isolating each app's data from others.
- **Logcat**: Android log viewer for real-time system and application event monitoring.
- **Android studio**: Official IDE for Android development, also useful for app and forensic analysis.
- **Mobile Security Framework (MobSF)**: Tool for static and dynamic analysis of Android and iOS apps.
- **Endpoint detection and response (EDR)**: Security solution monitoring endpoint activities and aiding forensic investigations.
- **Extended detection and response (XDR)**: Evolution of EDR, correlating data across endpoints, cloud, and networks.
- **Chain of custody**: Documentation ensuring the integrity and admissibility of forensic evidence.
- **SQLite database**: Common database format used by mobile apps to store messages, logs, and settings.
- **Anti-forensics techniques**: Techniques used by suspects or malware to wipe, encrypt, or hide data.
- **Community forensic datasets**: Publicly available forensic images and datasets used for training and research.

Join our Discord space

Join our Discord workspace for latest updates, offers, tech happenings around the world, new releases, and sessions with the authors:

https://discord.bpbonline.com

Chapter 12
Imaging Techniques

Introduction

Imaging techniques lie at the core of the work performed by digital forensic professionals, including first responders and forensic analysts. Such techniques are used to work with live imaging and dead imaging. Imaging is used for the acquisition of evidence, as well as for creating a working copy by a cyber forensic investigator/examiner.

Several imaging techniques have already been introduced implicitly in earlier chapters. We will look at multiple additional aspects of imaging techniques used in such situations by cyber forensic experts in this chapter.

Structure

In this chapter, we will cover the following topics:

- Imaging techniques covered so far
- Importance of imaging
- Types of imaging and their usage
- Creating a forensic disk in Linux
- Recipe 100: Creating forensic disk images using dd
- Recipe 101: Dumping a Linux swap partition using dd
- Creating a forensic disk in Windows
- Recipe 102: Understanding FTK Imager
- Recipe 103: Creating forensic disk images using FTK Imager
- Recipe 104: Verifying forensic disk created using FTK Imager
- Preparing disk image for examination
- Recipe 105: Mounting and analyzing disk images
- Best practices for organizing evidence using FTK Imager

Objectives

Imaging techniques are at the core of a cyber forensic investigator or examiner's day-to-day work. Hence, expert knowledge of imaging techniques is essential for digital forensics professionals due to its applicability during crime investigation.

We have implicitly looked at many imaging techniques before this chapter. In this chapter, we will deep dive into imaging in Linux and Windows environments. First, we will look at the types of imaging done during the cybercrime investigation. After that, we will look at multiple techniques to perform imaging in Linux and Windows environments. Finally, we will understand how a disk image can be prepared for examination and what the best practices are for organizing evidence.

By the end of this chapter, you will become familiar with the acquisition of images and working with master evidence media and making working copies from another image.

Imaging techniques covered so far

Since imaging is so intrinsic to digital forensics, we ended up covering a big part of it already in the previous chapters. To recap, we have already covered the following techniques so far:

- In *Chapter 8, Memory Forensics*, we understood how to use **Forensic Toolkit** (**FTK**) Imager to acquire an image of the volatile memory.
- In *Chapter 10, Working with Digital Forensic Cases*, we use **The Sleuth Kit** (**TSK**) to identify and recover evidence from images acquired during incident response or from live systems. An implementation of TSK called PyTSK does the same thing.
- In *Chapter 11, Mobile Forensics*, we used Autopsy to analyze phone images downloaded from public sources.
- In both *Chapter 10* and *11*, we used Autopsy to analyze images and other digital forensic evidence.

While you may already be comfortable using FTK Image to perform the image acquisition tasks, we will cover details about using FTK Imager to acquire an image of connected disks.

Importance of imaging

Imaging is the process of creating a complete, bit-for-bit copy of a digital storage device such as a hard drive, SSD, USB, or memory card, including not only active files but also deleted data, unallocated space, slack space, and system areas that may contain hidden artifacts.

Such forensic images serve as a replica of the original evidence, verified through cryptographic hash functions like MD5, SHA1, or SHA256 to prove integrity, and are essential because direct examination of a suspect's device risks altering timestamps, metadata, or even overwriting deleted files, which could render the evidence inadmissible in court.

Knowledge of imaging techniques is critical for digital forensic professionals because it ensures they can preserve the evidence in a sound manner, maintain the chain of custody, and comply with legal standards. Imaging also allows multiple examiners to work on identical copies of the same evidence without touching the original, making it possible to use a wide range of forensic tools for analysis, from file recovery and timeline reconstruction to malware detection and encrypted volume analysis. Digital forensic professionals also need to understand different imaging formats, such as raw (dd) for universality, E01 (EnCase) for compression and metadata support, or AFF for advanced handling, as well as techniques like live imaging when dealing with running systems and memory capture.

Without mastery of imaging, forensic investigators would lack the ability to preserve digital evidence reliably, defend their methods in court, or extract the full scope of potentially crucial data that lies beyond what the operating system exposes. Thus, imaging is not just a technical skill but the foundation of trustworthy digital forensic practice.

Types of imaging and their usage

As we discussed before, imaging means creating a forensic copy of a digital device so that investigators can examine it without altering the original evidence. The way this image is acquired depends on the state of the system at the time of collection.

Broadly, forensic professionals use two main types of imaging, namely, live imaging and dead imaging. Both have their own usage scenarios, advantages, and limitations. Live imaging is useful for capturing volatile data from a running system, but risks altering the evidence, while dead imaging provides a more controlled and legally robust copy of static storage devices. Digital forensic professionals must be skilled in both methods to choose the right approach based on the case scenario. Let us look at both of them one by one.

Live imaging

Live imaging is performed when the system is powered on and running, and investigators acquire data while it is still active. This is often used when shutting down the machine is not possible, such as in cases where critical processes, volatile data (including RAM contents, encryption keys, and running malware), or live databases must be preserved. Live imaging captures volatile memory and sometimes even active network connections, giving insight into what was happening at the time of acquisition. However, it has limitations: running processes may overwrite the evidence, and the act of imaging itself can alter system state.

Example, in a corporate intrusion investigation, live imaging may be used to acquire the contents of RAM to recover an attacker's encryption keys or chat fragments before they disappear upon shutdown.

Dead imaging

Dead imaging is performed when the system is powered off, and the evidence media (such as a hard drive or SSD) is removed and connected to a forensic workstation, usually through a hardware write-blocker. This is the more traditional and preferred method forensically because it avoids altering the live system and ensures a static, verifiable copy of all disk sectors, including deleted files, slack space, and unallocated areas. Dead imaging is considered more forensically sound and easier to defend in court since the acquisition process does not interfere with running processes.

Example, in a fraud investigation, investigators may seize a suspect's laptop, power it down, remove the hard disk, and create a bit-by-bit forensic image using FTK Imager or dd with a write-blocker.

Creating a forensic disk in Linux

Forensic disk imaging means making a bit-for-bit copy of a storage medium (HDD, SSD, USB, memory card) while preserving all metadata, deleted data, and unallocated space. Linux provides several tools capable of performing forensic disk imaging efficiently, many of which are both lightweight and reliable.

Let us look at a few common tools for creating a forensic disk in Linux:

Tool	Details
`dd`	This native Linux utility creates a raw image file by reading every block from the device. It is minimal and available on almost all Linux systems.
`dcfldd`	This is a forensic-oriented enhancement of the dd command. It adds features like built-in hashing (MD5, SHA1, SHA256), progress indicator, splitting images into fixed sizes, and error logging. It was developed by the U.S. Department of Defense Computer Forensics Laboratory, which is reflected in its name.
`dc3dd`	This tool is an improved fork of dd created by the U.S. DoD Cyber Crime Center (DC3). It offers hashing, logging, progress updates, and better error handling. It is often used when dd is too bare-bones, but a raw image format is still desired.
`Guymager`	Guymager is a **graphical user interface (GUI)** based Linux tool for forensic imaging. It supports AFF, **expert witness format (EWF)**, and raw formats. It automatically calculates multiple hashes (MD5, SHA1, SHA256), creates reports, and is much easier for less experienced investigators.

Table 12.1: *List of common forensic disk creation tools in Linux*

As is true with tools used for any other area of digital forensics, it is important to be comfortable with one or two key tools that can serve one's purpose. However, on certain occasions, the usage of a tool depends on what is available and what can be installed in a restricted environment.

Tip: Use `dd` when you need a trusted, universal, court-defensible raw image with minimal dependencies. Use specialized tools (`dcfldd`, `dc3dd`, `Guymager`, `ewfacquire`) when you need extra features like hashing, progress monitoring, splitting, and reporting.

Recipe 100: Creating forensic disk images using dd

The dd command in Linux is a low-level utility used for copying and converting raw data. It works directly on files, block devices, or partitions and is often used for tasks such as backups, disk cloning, creating bootable USB drives, or wiping data.

The dd command is one of the earliest and simplest tools used to acquire forensic disk images. Due to its simplicity and low-level operation of bit-by-bit copy, dd can be used to perform a variety of tasks during digital forensics analysis.

A typical **dd** command looks like the following:

```
dd if=<input_file> of=<output_file> [options]
Where:
if: input file/device (e.g., /dev/sda, /dev/zero, an ISO file)
of: output file/device (e.g., another disk, partition, or file)
Frequently used options are:
bs: block size (number of bytes copied at a time).
count: number of blocks to copy.
```

Let us look at a few ways dd can be used to create a forensic disk image in this recipe.

Note:

- **Compatibility**: Linux
- **License considerations**: Free software used

Recipe

The following dd commands are used to perform disk imaging-related tasks. Each of them may be useful while acquiring images as well as while creating a forensically sound copy of the acquired evidence for analysis purposes:

Purpose	dd command
Create a disk image of connected disk, considering it is mounted on `/dev/sda`.	`dd if=/dev/sda of=/home/user/disk.img bs=4M`
Create a disk image of a swap partition, considering it is mounted on `/dev/sda5`.	`dd if=/dev/sda5 of=swapimage.dd bs=4M status=progress`
Write an ISO (`ubuntu.iso`) to a mounted USB drive.	`dd if=ubuntu.iso of=/dev/sdb bs=4M status=progress`
Backup the **master boot record** (**MBR**), that is first 512 byte of the disk.	`dd if=/dev/sda of=mbrbackup.img bs=512 count=1`

Purpose	dd command
Restore the MBR **Caution:** This is a destructive operation that may make your computer no more bootable by overwriting the MBR.	`dd if=mbrbackup.img of=/dev/sda`
Partial acquisition of disk image, e.g., 1 GB, with block size (bs) of 1MB and count of 1024.	`dd if=/dev/sda of=/mnt/evidence/partial.img bs=1M count=1024`
Memory dump or raw memory acquisition.	`dd if=/dev/mem of=/mnt/evidence/memdump.dd bs=1024`

Table 12.2: Various dd commands

Based on your preference, you can have **.dd** or **.img** as your image extension. In both cases, the image created is a raw bit-by-bit copy image.

Caution: **A wrong output file (like /dev/sda) can overwrite your entire disk. Hence, always double check the dd command before running it.**

Activity

Attempt the following activities before the next recipe:

- Copy an **ISO** file to a USB disk and confirm if you can boot/install from that disk.
- Create a copy of an ISO file into another file. Use various checksum tools to confirm if it is a forensically sound copy.
- Dump the first 100MB of any disk to an image file using dd.
- Acquire MBR image using dd. Use various forensic tools discussed so far to analyze the content of the image.

Recipe 101: Dumping a Linux swap partition using dd

As we discussed *in Chapter 5, Linux Forensics*, a swap file or swap partition is a space on the disk used as virtual memory when RAM is full. When physical memory is exhausted, Linux moves inactive pages of memory from RAM to swap to free up RAM for active processes. Swap can also be used for hibernation, where the contents of RAM are written to swap so the system can restore its state on reboot.

Swap files or partitions are used in most modern operating systems to support virtual memory management. Since they contain a portion of the memory in the form of serialized memory pages, they can be used to discover a subset of what was running in the main memory or RAM.

While swap helps the system handle memory overflow, it may store sensitive data, including passwords, encryption keys, chat and document fragments, and other artifacts. Programs offloaded to the swap leave behind evidence of user activity. Some of these may be recoverable, as even after process termination, data may linger in swap until overwritten.

Let us look at how to dump the swap file to the disk in this recipe.

Note:

- **Compatibility: Linux**
- **License considerations: Free software used**

Recipe

Now, since we understand various **dd** commands, let us use dd to dump a swap partition in a raw image file. In order to do that, let us first understand which partition is used to store the swap file. We can do that using the **swapon** command as follows:

```
┌──(root㉿forensics)-[~]
└─# swapon --show
NAME      TYPE      SIZE USED PRIO
/dev/sda5 partition 975M   0B   -2
┌──(root㉿forensics)-[~]
└─#
```

We now know that **/dev/sda5** is being used as a swap partition. We can now use the **dd** command to dump this partition into a file to create a forensic image:

```
dd if=/dev/sda5 of=swap_image.dd bs=4M status=progress
```

The prior command will show the progress of the dumping and then show the final results of the operation. The output will look similar to the following:

```
┌──(root㉿forensics)-[/home/nishant]
└─# dd if=/dev/sda5 of=swap_image.dd bs=4M status=progress
994050048 bytes (994 MB, 948 MiB) copied, 11 s, 90.0 MB/s
243+1 records in
243+1 records out
1022361600 bytes (1.0 GB, 975 MiB) copied, 11.4523 s, 89.3 MB/s
┌──(root㉿forensics)-[/home/nishant]
└─#
```

The generated file is now a forensic image of the swap volume. This can now be used for performing various analysis tasks by using tools that are part of Kali Linux as well as advanced image analysis tools.

Caution: **Be careful when dumping an entire partition into a file, as the file size will match the disk partition size. If you do not have enough space, you may run out of disk space, which can disrupt applications.**

Activity

Attempt the following activities before the next recipe:

- Use the dd command to dump the swap partition with a block size of 1M instead of 4M. Analyze if this makes any difference.
- Add a small-sized new disk to your virtual machine or physical machine. Now trying to dump that disk to a file. Note down your observations.

Creating a forensic disk in Windows

Linux provides excellent tools like dd and its variants to create forensic disks. However, in Windows environments, digital forensic professionals generally cannot rely on native OS commands (like **dd** in Linux). Instead, investigators use dedicated forensic imaging tools that can interact with raw disk devices safely, often with built-in hashing, metadata capture, and reporting.

One of the most common tools that can be used in Windows is FTK Imager from AccessData, which is now owned by Exterro. This is a GUI-based tool and is widely used in digital forensic labs. There are many other commercial tools like Encase Imager, X-Ways Forensics Imager, OSForensics Imager, Magnet ACQUIRE, etc. that are widely used based on the need and budget.

Since commercial tools often involve significant licensing costs, it is important to be proficient with at least one reliable free tool, such as FTK Imager. Once a digital forensic professional understands one of these tools and the process of acquiring and analyzing images, they can switch to any other tool very quickly.

Recipe 102: Understanding FTK Imager

FTK Imager is a forensic imaging and preview tool developed by AccessData (now owned by Exterro) that allows investigators to create exact, forensically sound copies of digital media such as hard drives, USBs, and memory cards while ensuring the integrity of the evidence through hashing and verification. It is useful because it not only acquires forensic images in multiple formats like raw (dd), EnCase (E01), and AFF, but also allows examiners to preview the contents of a drive or image without altering the original data, perform targeted acquisitions, recover deleted files, and generate detailed reports with hash values for court admissibility.

Its key features include write-blocked acquisition, built-in MD5/SHA1 hashing, support for segmented and compressed images, the ability to mount and view images in a read-only mode, and the generation of comprehensive documentation that strengthens the chain of custody.

Note: **The free version of FTK Imager is widely considered good enough for most digital forensic professionals, as it covers core imaging and previewing needs, provides reliable hashing and verification, and integrates smoothly with other forensic analysis tools. This makes it a trusted and practical solution for both lab work and field investigations.**

Some of the key features of FTK Imager useful for acquiring or creating forensic images are as follows:

- It is a GUI-based, easy-to-use tool with a minimal learning curve.
- It supports creating raw images (`.dd`), EnCase format (`.E01`), and AFF. Hence, the image can be analyzed by industry-standard tools.
- It performs MD5/SHA hash verification during acquisition.
- It can be used to acquire full disk, logical volumes, or even live RAM. This makes it a versatile one-stop solution for most forensic labs.

Note:

- **Compatibility: Windows**
- **License considerations: Free software used**

Recipe

Once you launch FTK Imager, you will see a screen like the following:

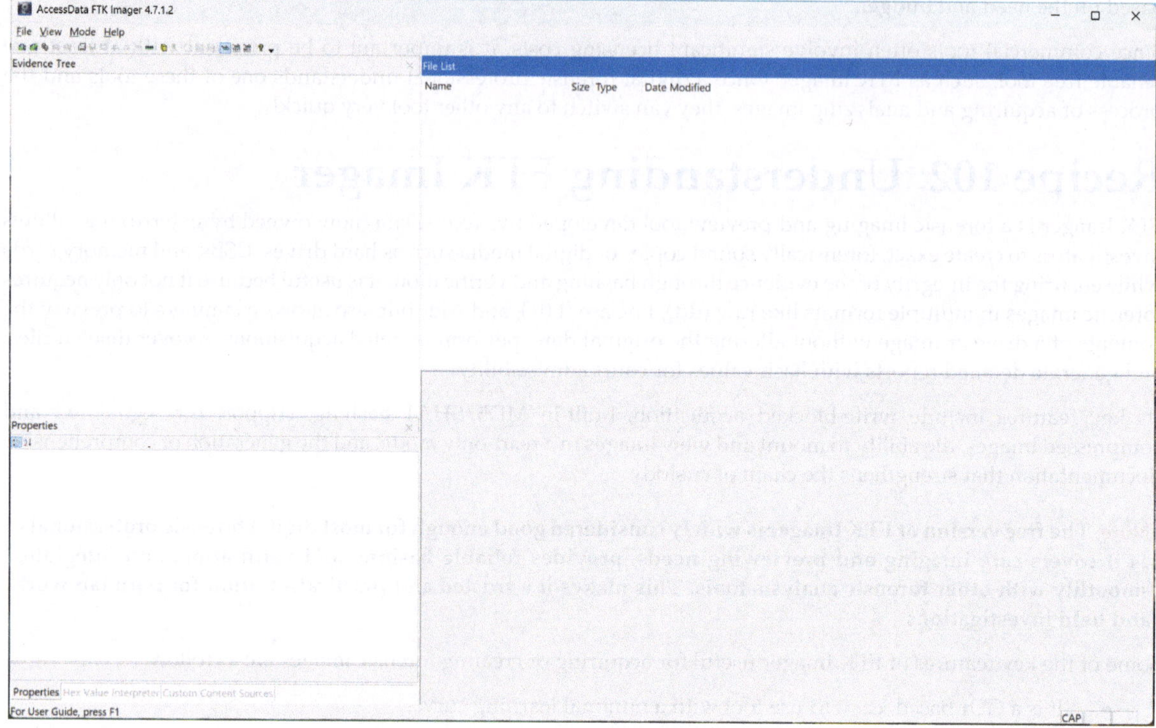

Figure 12.1: Landing screen of FTK Imager

In this screen, there are multiple distinct panes:

- On the top left, there is an **Evidence Tree** view where all added evidence items are displayed.
- On the bottom left, the properties of the selected evidence is displayed.
- On the top right, the list of files for a selected directory is displayed.
- On the bottom right, the file content itself is displayed.

Apart from this, there is a toolbar at the top with the most important actions supported by FTK Imager.

Activity

Attempt the following activities before the next recipe:

- Explore the features tied to each of the icons in the toolbar, especially the option for dumping live memory.
- Understand what the modes are in which FTK Imager can be used from the **Mode** menu.

Recipe 103: Creating forensic disk images using FTK Imager

Learning how to create a forensic disk in Windows is essential for every digital forensics professional to preserve digital evidence in a way that ensures accuracy, integrity, and legal admissibility. This is also important, as directly examining a suspect's drive risks altering or destroying crucial data such as deleted files, metadata, or hidden artifacts.

Investigators need a reliable method to capture a bit-for-bit image of the original media, along with verifiable hash values, so they can work on copies while the original remains untouched. FTK Imager is well suited for this task because it provides a trusted, forensically sound way to acquire complete or targeted disk images, supports multiple evidence formats, automatically generates MD5/SHA1 hashes for verification, and produces detailed reports for chain of custody, all through an easy-to-use interface that makes it effective for both professional labs and field work.

In this recipe, we will go through a step-by-step process to create a forensic disk.

Note:

- **Compatibility: Windows**
- **License considerations: Free software used**

Recipe

We will create a forensic disk of a USB disk. Since it takes a lot of time to dump a disk, it is advisable to use a small USB disk, e.g., 4-8 GB, for this recipe.

Follow the following steps to complete this recipe:

1. First, connect your USB drive to your computer. Ensure you can see it in the list of disks. Also, ensure that the disk is not empty.
2. Once the USB drive is connected, click on **File** | **Create Disk Image**. In the next dialog box, select **Physical Drive** as shown in the following figure:

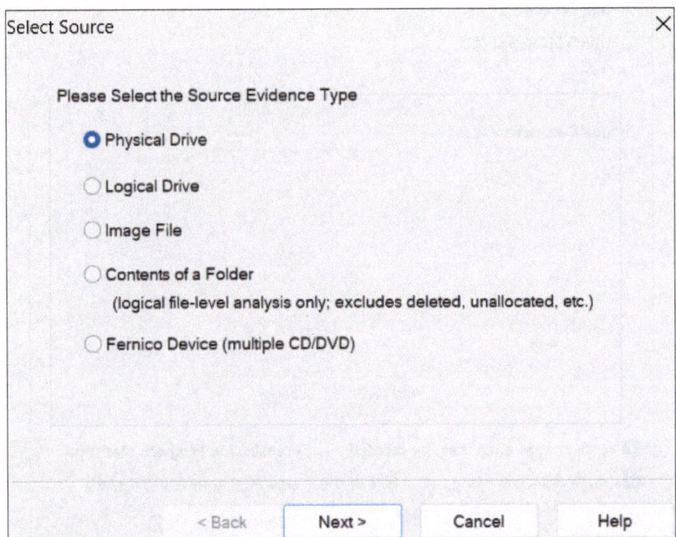

Figure 12.2: *Creating forensic disk images using FTK Imager, Select source evidence type*

3. In the next screen, select the source drive that you want to image. This list shows all the physical drives connected to the computer. You need to choose the USB drive as shown in the following figure:

Select Drive
Source Drive Selection
Please select from the following available drives:
\\.\PHYSICALDRIVE2 - Sony Storage Media USB Device [15GB USB]
< Back
Finish
Cancel
Help

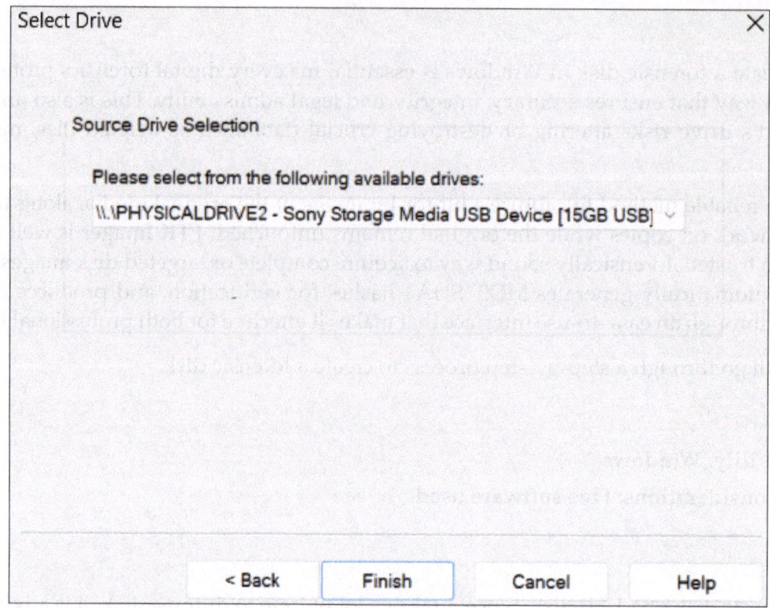

***Figure 12.3**: Creating forensic disk images using FTK Imager, Source drive selection*

Click on **Finish**.

4. In the next dialog box, **Create Image**, we need to add the destination of the exported image. Click on **Add...** to proceed as shown in the following figure:

Create Image
Image Source
\\.\PHYSICALDRIVE2
Starting Evidence Number: 1
Image Destination(s)
Add...
Edit...
Remove
Add Overflow Location
Verify images after they are created
Precalculate Progress Statistics
Create directory listings of all files in the image after they are created
Start
Cancel

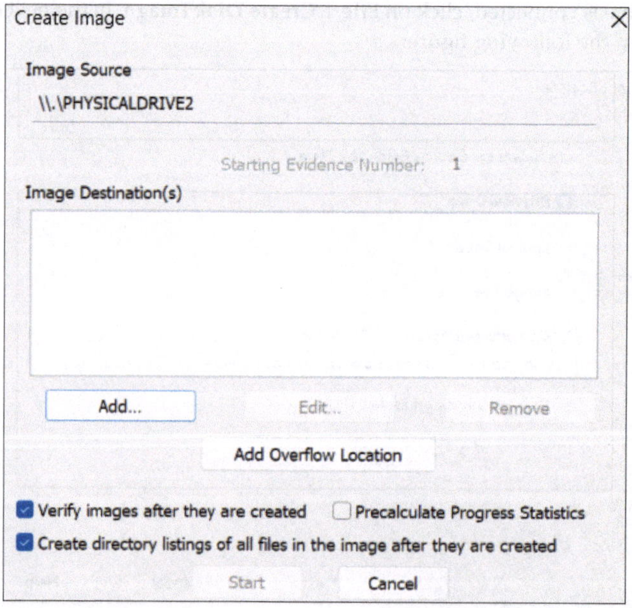

***Figure 12.4**: Creating forensic disk images using FTK Imager, Add image destination*

This will result in a series of dialogs. In the next dialog, the image type can be selected. The three most common image types are as follows:

- **Raw (dd)**: Sector-by-sector, no compression.
- **E01 (EnCase)**: Compressed, supports metadata, widely used in court.
- **Advanced Forensic Format** (**AFF**).

In this dialog, select **E01** to create an image of EnCase format, from the dialog shown as follows:

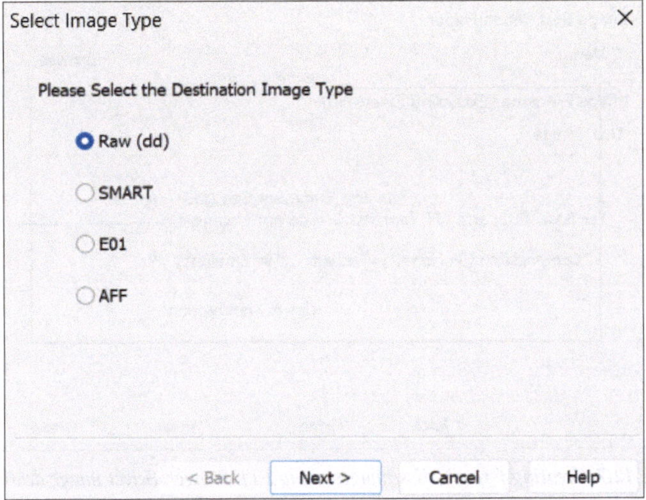

Figure 12.5*: Creating forensic disk images using FTK Imager, Select image type*

Click on **Next**.

5. Since every image that is acquired is related to a case under investigation, FTK Imager asks for information about this evidence item. Following is a sample of the type of information that can be entered for this evidence item:

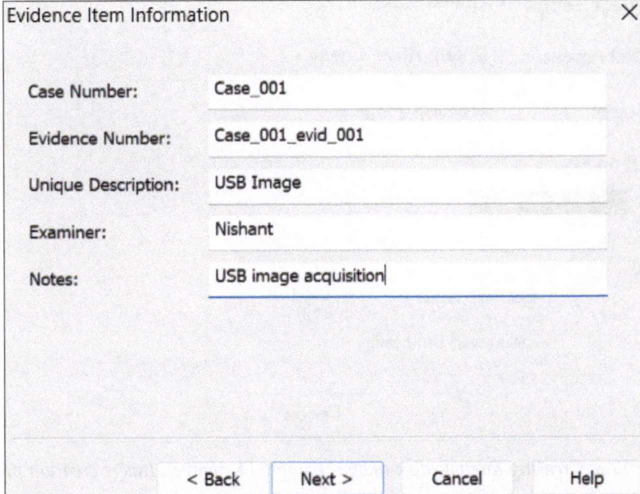

Figure 12.6*: Creating forensic disk images using FTK Imager, Evidence item information*

Once the evidence item information is entered, click on **Next**.

6. Finally, we need to enter the destination folder in the next dialog.

   In this screen, enter `0` so that the image is not fragmented, i.e., it will be a single exported file. You can leave compression to the default or decrease it for faster acquisition:

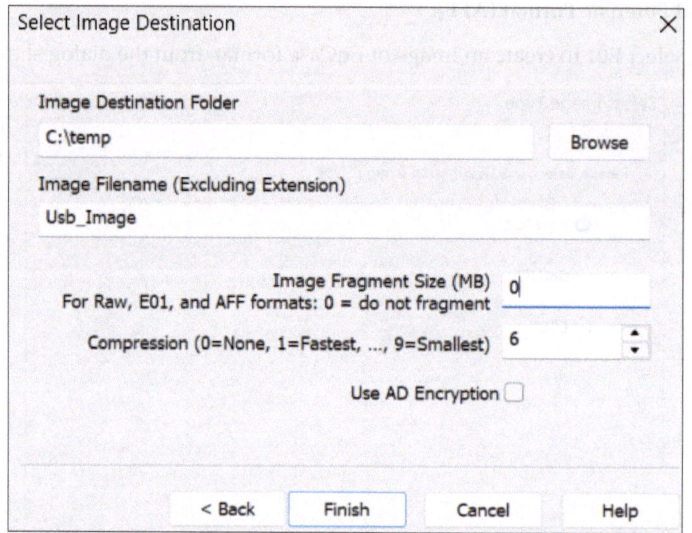

***Figure 12.7:** Creating forensic disk images using FTK Imager, Select image destination*

   Click on **Finish** once done.

7. Now, FTK Imager starts creating the image of the USB drive as shown in *Figure 12.8*. This process may take a significant amount of time, depending on the size of the source media, as shown in the following figure:

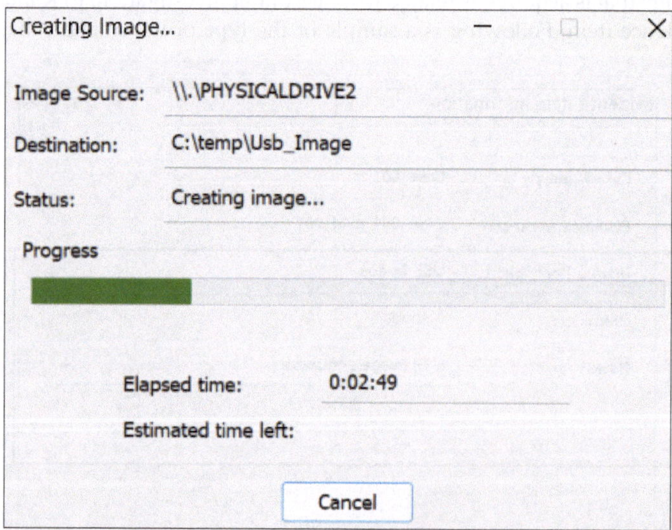

***Figure 12.8:** Creating forensic disk images using FTK Imager, Image creation progress*

Once the image is created, FTK Imager also verifies it based on whether you selected the option to verify the image in *step 3*:

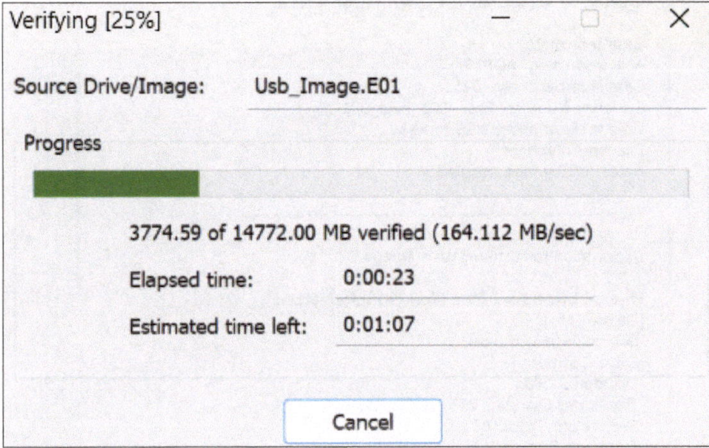

***Figure 12.9**: Creating forensic disk images using FTK Imager, Image verification post creation*

Once the verification is done, the result is shown. It will be good to store this information for later reference:

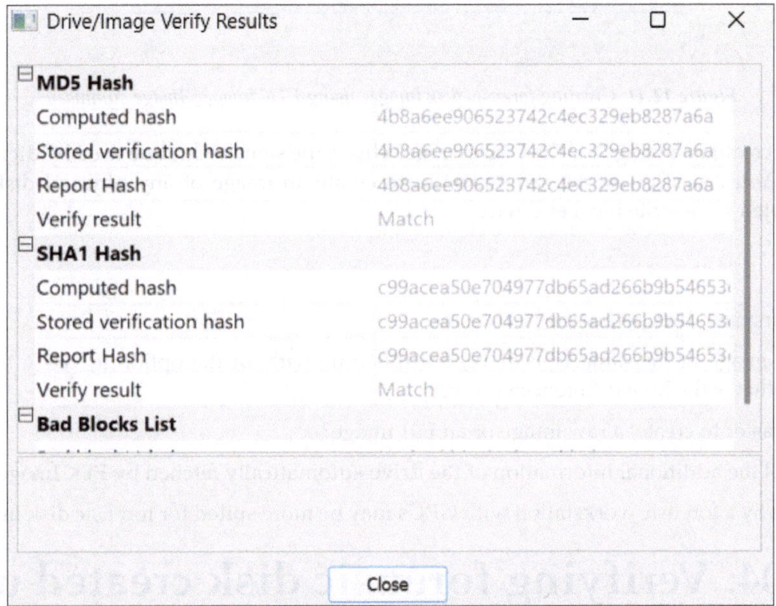

***Figure 12.10**: Creating forensic disk images using FTK Imager, Image verification results*

Finally, FTK Imager shows the image summary with a lot of important details. This information should also be stored for later reference:

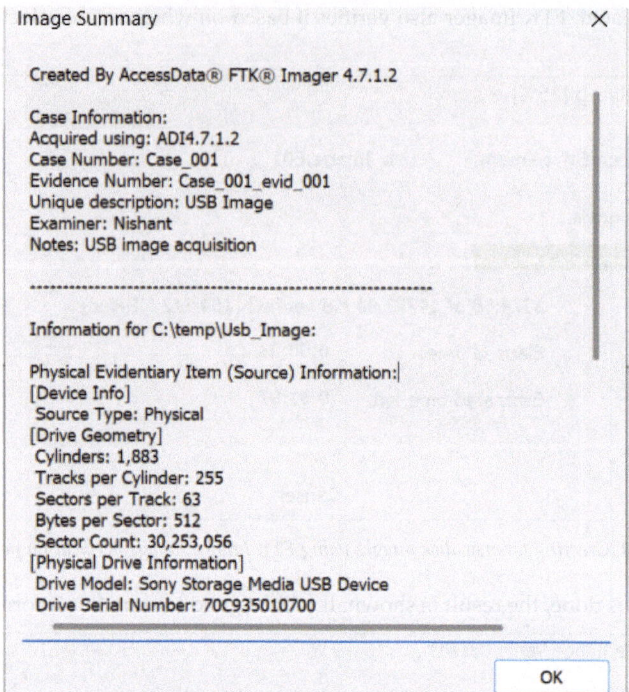

***Figure 12.11**: Creating forensic disk images using FTK Imager, Image summary*

With this, you have created an image for the USB storage. This is the same technique used by digital forensic experts around the world. You can also use the same process to create an image of any physical disk, be it part of the computer or connected via a write blocker device.

Activity

Attempt the following activities before the next recipe:

- Create an image of the same USB drive, but this time without the option to verify the image once it is created. What is the time difference you see?
- Which is faster to create, a raw image or an E01 image?
- Identify all the additional information of the drive automatically fetched by FTK Imager.
- Analyze why a forensic workstation with GPUs may be more suited for forensic disk image creation tasks.

Recipe 104: Verifying forensic disk created using FTK Imager

We created an image for a USB disk in the last recipe. Now, let us verify if we can add this image as evidence to FTK Imager. Moreover, we need to check whether the image contains the same files as those on the USB drive.

Note:

- **Compatibility: Windows**
- **License considerations: Free software used**

Recipe

In order to verify the USB disk image we just created, launch FTK Imager. Once open, go to **File | Add Evidence Item...** to add an evidence item. In this case, it is the disk image that we created in the last recipe.

Once you add the evidence, you can see the USB image appearing in the **Evidence Tree** with all the details of what was on the USB disk, as shown in the following figure:

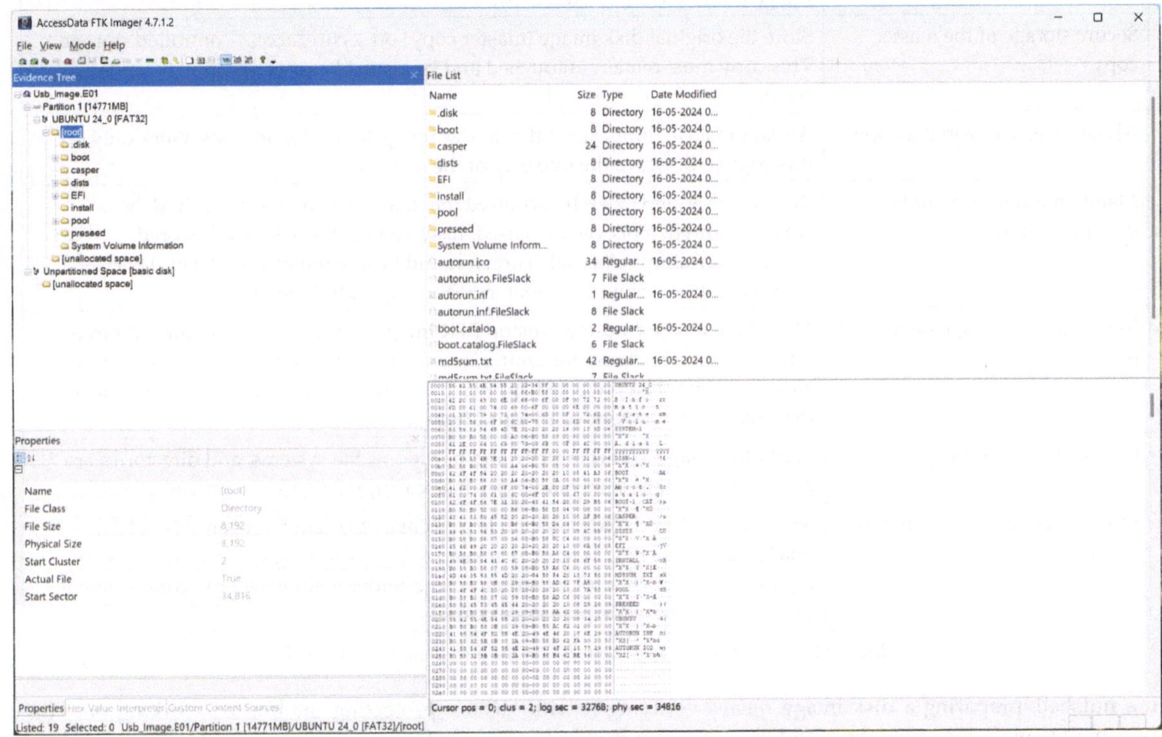

***Figure 12.12:** Details of the evidence in FTK Imager*

Verify a few files to confirm if you can open and view them. Compare the content of the same file from the USB drive and verify if they are the same.

Activity

Attempt the following activities before the next recipe:

- Try to change the content of any file. Observe if FTK Imager allows this.
- Try to delete any file or directory from the evidence tree. Were you able to complete this operation?
- Add the physical drive directly as evidence and export the hash of all the artifacts. Now do the same for the image file we created. Compare the resulting hash files to confirm if they are the same.

Preparing disk image for examination

As part of a digital forensic investigation, when a disk image is given to you, several things need to be done before the image can be examined. These are done to ensure the image is valid, consistent, and handled according to forensic standards.

Let us look at the key things that must be done before the disk image is examined:

Task	Details
Verify integrity with hashes	Compute cryptographic hash values (MD5, SHA1, or SHA256) of the disk image, immediately after acquisition and compare them with the original drive's hash, which was calculated during the initial acquisition. Matching values prove the image is an exact, unaltered copy.
Secure storage of the master copy	Store the original disk image (master copy) on secure, access-controlled storage. This copy must remain untouched and be available for verification if needed in court.
Always create a working copy	Always make a duplicate of the master image to use for analysis. Work only on this copy to preserve the integrity of the master.
Maintain chain-of-custody documentation	Record every step like who acquired the image, when was it acquired, how was it acquired, tools versions used, hash values, and where it is stored. When uncertainty exists, all actions should be documented in detail. This documentation ensures transparency and legal admissibility.
Mount or load image safely and in read-only mode	Mount the image read-only (using FTK Imager, Autopsy, etc.) or import it into forensic software. Avoid mounting it in a way that allows writes, which could alter metadata. The preferred approach is to use a hardware-based write-blocker to prevent any unintended modifications.
Check file system integrity	Verify the image loads correctly and partitions, file systems, and directories are accessible. Document any issues such as corrupted sectors or unreadable areas.
Prepare case folder for analysis output	Set up a structured folder system (e.g., **`/Case123/Acquisition`**, **`/Case123/Analysis`**, **`/Case123/Reports`**) to keep notes, exported evidence, and reports organized. Consistent folder structure and folder and file naming convention is the key to create self-explanatory outputs.

***Table 12.3**: List of things to be done before the disk image is examined*

In a nutshell, preparing a disk image means verifying it with hashes, protecting the master, working only on a copy, maintaining documentation, and ensuring safe read-only access before starting analysis. This process should be followed every time there is a change of hands in the chain-of-custody, and ensures the examination is both technically sound and legally defensible.

Recipe 105: Mounting and analyzing disk images

A forensic workstation is a specialized computer system designed and configured to perform digital forensic tasks such as evidence acquisition, preservation, analysis, and reporting. Unlike regular computers, it is hardened, controlled, and equipped with forensic-grade hardware and software to ensure the integrity of digital evidence.

At a minimum, a forensic workstation may consist of the following:

- Hardware write-blockers to connect suspect media in read-only mode, e.g., Tableau, for **Serial Advanced Technology Attachment** (**SATA**), **Integrated Drive Electronics** (**IDE**), **Non-Volatile Memory Express** (**NVMe**), USB, and SD cards.
- Specialized hardware with high-performance CPU and RAM (for large datasets, memory dumps, malware analysis), and large storage arrays (often RAID) for evidence storage.
- Multiple interfaces and ports to connect a variety of devices, or respective hardware adapters.

- Forensic software like FTK Imager, Encase Imager, Autopsy, Volatility, IDA Pro, Ghidra, Sleuth Kit, Bulk Extractor, etc., most of which we have discussed about in the previous chapters.

Let us look at the process of mounting a disk image and analyzing it using a forensic workstation using write blocker and FTK Imager.

Note:

- **Compatibility: Windows**
- **License considerations: Free software used**

Recipe

In order to analyze a disk image using such a forensic workstation, we can follow the following steps. You should be able to use these steps to mount and analyze any such disk image from public sources, as well as what is given to you as part of the investigation:

1. **Preparation**: Before we analyze a forensic disk image, we need to ensure the forensic workstation is ready and we only have read-only access to the acquired image. In rare cases, while analyzing directly from the original evidence drive, we need to ensure that it is connected via a hardware write-blocker.
2. **Launch FTK Imager and add evidence item**: Launch FTK Imager. Once open, go to **File** | **Add Evidence Item...**, to add evidence item. In this case it is the disk image that we can add as an evidence item.

   In the next dialog box, that lists the source evidence type, select **Image File** as shown in the following figure:

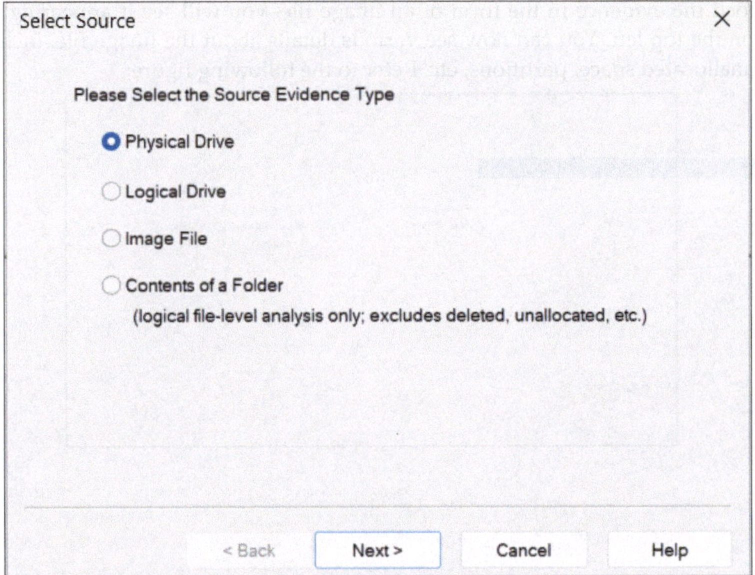

***Figure 12.13**: Mounting and analyzing disk images, select source evidence type*

   Browser to the read-only image file or the select the device attached via write blocker, as relevant. After that click on **Finish**. Refer to the following figure:

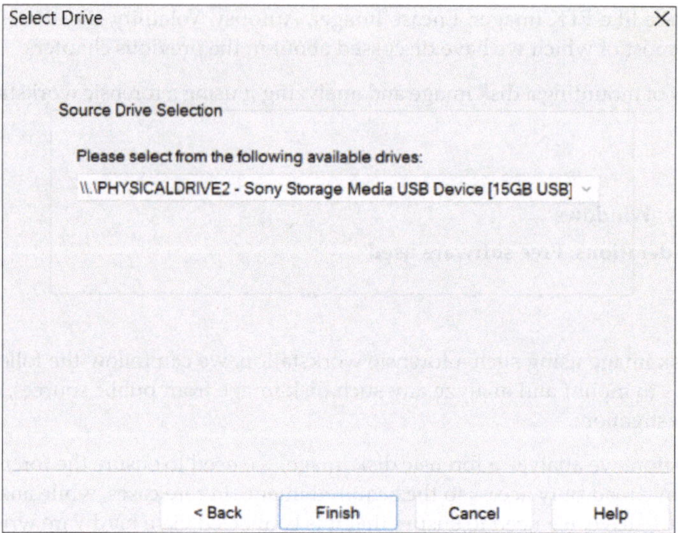

Figure 12.14: Mounting and analyzing disk images, Select drive

Note: In case you are connecting through a write-blocker, then you can also choose physical drive as an option.

Once you load the evidence in the form of an image file, you will see it appearing under the **Evidence Tree** pane on the top left. You can now see various details about the image file, including the filesystem hierarchy, unallocated space, partitions, etc. Refer to the following figure:

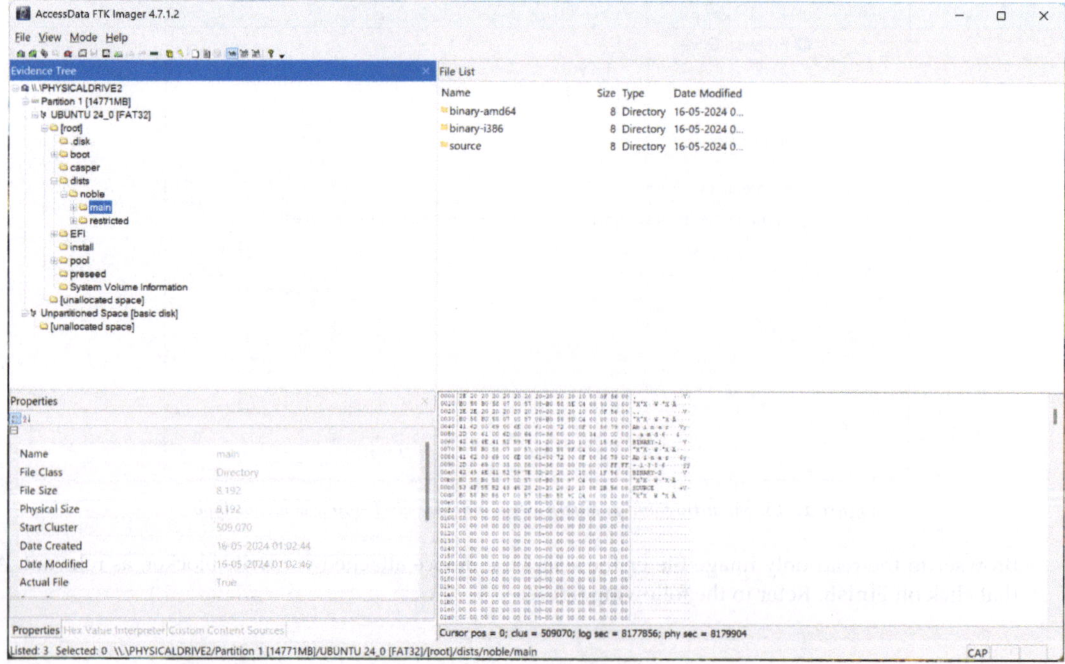

Figure 12.15: Mounting and analyzing disk images, show file list for a folder

You can also see the file list in context on the right pane based on what you have selected on the evidence tree. You can also see the file preview by clicking on a file listed in the file list pane.

3. Now, let us try out these few operations with this loaded evidence:
   - You can preview the files by clicking on a file in the file list.
   - You can search for keywords across the entire image.
   - You can recover deleted files.
   - You can also export the evidence by right clicking on a file/folder.
   - You can inspect the raw binary content of the file in the hex format, which may be useful for malware analysis.

Activity

Attempt the following activities before the next recipe:

- Create a checklist of items to go through before analyzing any image to avoid accidental writes or data integrity-related changes.
- What are the ways do you think chain-of-custody can be kept intact while using such a forensic workstation?

Best practices for organizing evidence using FTK Imager

While working with a few evidence may not be much of a hassle, when working with complex cases with a large number of evidence, it may be important to understand the considerations for organizing the evidence.

Since FTK Imager is a tool of choice for most digital forensic professionals, let us look at a few best practices for organizing evidence using FTK Imager, though these are general rules and will apply to any other tool as well:

Best practice	Details
Think like a librarian	Treat every piece of evidence as a book in a library. If you do not label and shelve it properly, you will lose track of it later. This includes giving your image files meaningful names (e.g., `Case123LaptopE01` instead of image1), and storing them in clearly labeled folders by case number and device type.
Keep originals and working copies separate	Never touch the original disk/image once acquired. Make at least two forensic images: • One master copy, stored securely, untouched. • One working copy, which is the one you actually analyze.
Document everything	FTK Imager gives you a nice report after acquisition that contains the hash values, device details, and examiner notes. It is a good practice to export this list on a regular basis to keep the details of the hash of each of the files. This is a good way to prove that nothing has changed. Apart from that, documentation should be done to keep the chain-of-custody intact whenever evidence changes hands.

Best practice	Details

Use consistent folder structures	As part of the acquisition, using a consistent folder structure does not leave anything for guess work. For example, a simple and reliable structure may look like the following:
	`Case_123/`
	`Acquisition/`
	`Disk1_Laptop_E01/`
	`Disk2_USB_DD/`
	`Reports/`
	`Analysis/`
	`Exports/`
	`Notes/`
	This way, anyone on the team knows where to find acquisition files, reports, and analysis output.

Hash and verify	FTK Imager can easily compute the hash after acquisition. These hash values should always be saved along with other artifacts and notes. These hash values act as a cryptographic fingerprint of the evidence. Later, if questioned in court, the examiner can prove this image is exactly the same as when we acquired it.

***Table 12.4**: Best practices for organizing evidence using FTK Imager*

Conclusion

Imaging techniques form the foundation of digital forensics, ensuring that investigators can acquire and analyze evidence without compromising its integrity. Through both live and dead imaging methods, forensic experts can preserve data from running systems or offline devices, depending on the case requirements.

Linux offers command-line utilities like dd, dcfldd, and dc3dd, along with GUI-based tools like Guymager, while Windows relies on specialized imaging software such as FTK Imager. These tools enable the capture of entire disks, partitions, or even volatile memory, with built-in verification through hashing to ensure authenticity.

Preparing disk images for examination requires careful validation, maintaining a chain of custody, creating working copies, and documenting every step of the process. A forensic workstation, equipped with hardware write-blockers and specialized software, is essential for safely mounting and analyzing these images.

Ultimately, a strong understanding of imaging techniques is indispensable for digital forensic professionals, enabling accurate evidence preservation, legally defensible analysis, and confident investigative decision-making.

In the next chapter, we will look at all the aspects of what **digital forensics and incident response** (**DFIR**) is and how it is used in digital forensics during crime investigation.

Questions

1. What is imaging in digital forensics, and why is it important?
2. Explain the difference between live imaging and dead imaging.
3. Provide one example scenario where live imaging is necessary.
4. Provide one example scenario where dead imaging is preferable.

5. Why is hashing important during the imaging process?
6. What risks exist when imaging without a write-blocker?
7. Describe how the dd command works in Linux for imaging.
8. What is the role of dcfldd or dc3dd compared to dd?
9. Why is swap partition acquisition relevant in digital forensics?
10. What are the advantages of using FTK Imager in Windows?
11. How does FTK Imager ensure evidence integrity?
12. Why should forensic professionals create both a master copy and a working copy?
13. What steps are required to prepare a disk image for examination?
14. What is a forensic workstation and why is it different from a regular computer?
15. What are some best practices for organizing evidence in FTK Imager?

Points to remember

1. Imaging creates a bit-for-bit copy of a digital device, preserving all data.
2. Live imaging captures volatile data but risks altering the system state.
3. Dead imaging is performed on powered-off systems and is more defensible in court.
4. Hashing (MD5, SHA1, SHA256) is essential to verify image integrity and for maintaining chain-of-custody.
5. Linux tools for imaging include dd, dcfldd, dc3dd, and Guymager.
6. Windows forensic imaging is usually done with FTK Imager, EnCase, or similar tools.
7. FTK Imager supports raw (dd), E01, and AFF formats.
8. Swap partitions can hold sensitive residual data such as passwords or keys and hence become key evidence.
9. Always use a write-blocker while working with images to prevent accidental writes to evidence media.
10. Chain of custody documentation must be maintained at every stage.
11. A forensic workstation provides specialized hardware and software for safe analysis.
12. Imaging is the first step before recovery, analysis, or reporting.
13. Memory imaging is critical for capturing volatile artifacts like keys or live malware.
14. Forensic imaging ensures court admissibility by preserving authenticity.
15. Device identifiers should always be double-checked in commands like dd to prevent accidental overwrites.

Key terms

- **Imaging**: The process of creating a bit-for-bit copy of a digital storage medium.
- **Live imaging**: Acquisition performed while the system is running to capture volatile data.
- **Dead imaging**: Acquisition performed on a powered-off system using write-blockers.
- **dd**: A native Linux utility that creates raw bit-for-bit images.

- **dcfldd**: A forensic-enhanced version of dd with hashing and logging features.
- **dc3dd**: A forensic imaging tool developed by DoD cyber crime center with improved error handling and hashing.
- **Swap partition**: Disk space used as virtual memory, which may contain sensitive data.
- **Write-blocker**: A hardware or software tool that prevents any modifications to evidence media.
- **FTK Imager**: A forensic imaging and preview tool for Windows that supports multiple formats and automatic verification.
- **EnCase format (E01)**: A compressed forensic image format that includes metadata and is widely accepted in court.
- **Advanced Forensics Format (AFF)**: An image format with advanced handling and metadata support.
- **Hash value**: A digital fingerprint (MD5, SHA1, SHA256) used to verify image integrity.
- **Chain of custody**: Documentation process that tracks the handling of evidence from acquisition to presentation in court.
- **Forensic workstation**: A specialized computer system equipped with forensic tools and write-blockers for secure analysis.
- **Master copy**: The original forensic image created during acquisition, stored securely and never modified.
- **Working copy**: A duplicate of the master image used for actual analysis.
- **Unallocated space**: Disk space not currently assigned to files but potentially containing recoverable data.

Chapter 13
Digital Forensics and Incident Response

Introduction

As part of evidence reporting and presentation, a **digital forensics and incident response** (**DFIR**) document is used. DFIR itself is a highly specialized field in digital forensics, requiring extensive experience and expertise across multiple domains, as well as effective reporting capabilities. It is a combined practice of identifying, investigating, and responding to cybersecurity incidents such as data breaches, malware infections, or unauthorized access. Organizations use DFIR to minimize damage and prevent future cybersecurity incidents. In this chapter, we examine the key aspects of DFIR and the structure and purpose of DFIR reports.

Structure

In this chapter, we will cover the following topics:

- Need for accurate reporting
- Digital forensics and incident response
- Events and incidents
- Digital forensics and incident response report
- Recipe 106: Creating forensic reports using FTK Imager
- Recipe 107: Creating forensic reports using Autopsy
- Recipe 108: Creating reports from other forensic tools
- Implementing post-incident recovery procedures

Objectives

Digital forensics and incident response (**DFIR**) is a specialized domain within cybersecurity that blends two critical disciplines: digital forensics and incident response. As digital forensics professionals, the ability to investigate, respond to, and recover from cyberattacks while preserving evidence for legal, regulatory, or internal use is an important skill to acquire. We will discuss this aspect of digital forensics in detail in this chapter.

By the end of this chapter, readers will be familiar with leveraging forensic artifacts and reports from multiple tools to support the DFIR process and produce defensible DFIR reports.

Need for accurate reporting

The need for accurate reporting in digital forensics cannot be stressed enough. The goal of every digital forensic investigation is to identify, analyze, and document all relevant aspects of a cybercrime and present the findings in a legally admissible manner. Moreover, findings need to be presented in a format that is admissible in the court of law.

The same applies to the decisions taken by the top management of the business, for example, in terms of whether it is worth spending more money to strengthen the security posture of the organization. Thus, accurate reporting serves as a critical bridge between technical findings and business or legal decision-making.

The following are the key points that bring out the need for accurate reporting as part of digital forensic investigation:

Key need	Details
Clarity	Investigators may work for weeks, but the report is what managers, lawyers, or courts will actually see.
Legal validity	If evidence is going to court, only a properly documented and error-free report can stand as proof.
Accountability	Shows exactly what was done, how evidence was handled, and prevents doubts about tampering.
Learning and prevention	Reports help organizations understand what went wrong and how to stop it happening again.

Table 13.1: *Key points for accurate reporting*

Various reporting techniques

Reports can take different forms depending on the intended audience. Digital forensic reports may vary greatly based on whether it is the technical team, management team, or legal team.

Let us look at a few common reporting techniques that are used during the digital forensic investigation:

Reporting technique	Details	Focus and goals
Executive summaries	Short, business-focused overviews. Needed by executives, legal, and management teams.	Explain what happened, why it matters, and next steps without technical jargon.
Technical reports	Detailed, step-by-step documentation of methods, tools, and findings. Essential for validation and legal defensibility.	Provide full technical accuracy so another expert can replicate or verify results.
Timeline reports	Chronological reconstruction of events (e.g., login | file copy | log deletion). Needed to visualize attacker behavior.	Show how the incident unfolded and identify gaps in monitoring or response.
Visual reports	Diagrams, charts, and attack-path visualizations. Needed for mixed or non-technical audiences.	Make findings easy to understand at a glance, highlight weaknesses, and support decision-making.
Chain of custody reports	Formal record of who handled evidence, when, and under what conditions. Legally required in most cases.	Ensure evidence integrity and make it admissible in court or regulatory reviews.
Lesson learned reports	Post-incident reviews highlighting strengths, weaknesses, and improvements. Needed for organizational growth.	Capture what worked and what did not to refine policies, playbooks, and defenses.
Court-submitted reports	Structured forensic reports submitted as part of legal proceedings. Must be factual, unbiased, and based strictly on evidence.	Present findings in a clear, defensible, and legally admissible way for judges, juries, and lawyers.

Table 13.2: *Common reporting techniques*

One key observation from the preceding table is that not all reports are intended for legal or judicial audiences. Reporting is done on an ongoing basis as part of the investigation.

Another key thing about reporting is that the court-submitted reports are different from technical or executive reports. They must follow strict legal standards. The language used must be objective, concise, and free of speculation. They also often include a chain of custody, timeline evidence, and expert witness statements.

Digital forensics and incident response

DFIR is a specialized domain within cybersecurity that blends two critical disciplines, i.e., digital forensics and incident response. Together, both of these practices ensure that organizations can investigate, respond to, and recover from cyberattacks while preserving evidence for legal, regulatory, or internal use.

Digital forensics is the scientific discipline concerned with the identification, collection, preservation, analysis, and interpretation of digital evidence to answer questions such as who did what, when, and how. Incident response is the structured process of detecting, containing, eradicating, and recovering from cybersecurity incidents to minimize impact.

When a security breach occurs, DFIR teams act swiftly to contain the threat, assess impact, recover affected systems, and collect evidence necessary to determine root cause and attribution.

Key components of DFIR

There are two key components of DFIR, namely, digital forensics and incident response.

Digital forensics

Digital forensics is the investigative backbone of DFIR. It requires precision and adherence to strict methodologies so that findings are legally sound and can withstand scrutiny in court. Let us look at it in detail:

- **What it does**: Examines file systems, logs, memory dumps, and network traffic to reconstruct attacker actions.
- **Primary goal**: Determine what happened, how attackers gained access, what was stolen or altered, and who may be responsible.
- **Key principles**: Evidence must be collected under a strict chain of custody, ensuring that it has not been tampered with and is admissible in legal proceedings.

Incident response

Incident response is the action-oriented side of digital forensics. It focuses on speed, coordination, and mitigation. It is a structured approach to managing and mitigating a cyber threat as it unfolds, prioritizing speed to minimize damage. Let us look at it in detail:

- **What it does**: Detects intrusions, isolates affected systems, prevents lateral movement, and restores operations.
- **Primary goal**: Contain the immediate threat, eradicate malicious presence, and return the organization to safe operations as quickly as possible.
- **Key principles**: Guided by an **incident response plan** (**IRP**) that outlines predefined steps for handling different types of incidents [e.g., ransomware, insider threats, **distributed denials of service** (**DDoS**).

DFIR lifecycle

DFIR activities often follow structured models such as the **National Institute of Standards and Technology (NIST)** Computer Security Incident Handling Guide (SP 800-61) or ISO/IEC 27043 Incident Investigation Principles. A typical lifecycle includes the following:

- **Preparation**: Develop policies, train staff, identify critical assets, and build an incident response toolkit.
- **Detection and analysis**: Monitor for suspicious activity, identify incidents, and assess their scope and severity.
- **Containment**: Limit the spread of the threat (e.g., isolating infected hosts or disabling compromised accounts).
- **Eradication**: Remove the root cause (e.g., malware, malicious users, exploited vulnerabilities).
- **Recovery**: Restore systems, validate security, and resume business operations.
- **Post-incident review**: Conduct a lessons-learned exercise to improve readiness and strengthen defenses.

Importance and benefits of DFIR

DFIR is vital because it provides organizations with both immediate response capabilities and long-term resilience. The key benefits of DFIR are as follows:

- **Minimizes impact**: Rapid response reduces downtime, reputational harm, and financial loss.
- **Identifies root cause**: Forensics pinpoints the initial attack vector so it can be patched.
- **Strengthens defenses**: Post-incident reviews feed into better security controls and staff awareness.
- **Provides legal evidence**: Properly preserved evidence supports court cases, insurance claims, and compliance audits.
- **Meets compliance needs**: Many regulations (GDPR, HIPAA, PCI-DSS) mandate incident reporting and investigation, which DFIR enables.

In short, DFIR ensures that cybersecurity incidents become opportunities to learn and improve, rather than just chaotic emergencies.

Events and incidents

An event is any observable occurrence within a system, network, or digital environment that is captured and logged by security or operating systems. However, an incident is a confirmed or suspected security breach, policy violation, or malicious activity that threatens the **confidentiality, integrity, or availability (CIA)** of systems or data.

In order to understand, let us use a simple example:

- **Event**: A door was opened.
- **Incident**: A door was forced open at 2 AM by an intruder.

Every incident qualifies as an event; however, not every event constitutes an incident. However, not every event may be an incident. **Incident response (IR)** focuses time and resources on confirmed incidents or high-risk suspicious events.

Events can be escalated to incidents using an alerting mechanism. Let us understand how that is done using another example:

- **Event**: Raw data (e.g., login attempt).
- **Alert**: Event flagged by security control (e.g., 5 failed logins lead to a brute force alert).
- **Incident**: Validated and investigated issue (e.g., confirmed account compromise).

In digital forensics, events represent the individual system or network activities such as logins, file accesses, or process executions, forming the raw evidence used to reconstruct a timeline of actions. Analysts correlate these events from logs, registries, and artifacts to understand user or attacker behavior. An incident, on the other hand, is a verified or suspected security breach or policy violation that triggers the forensic investigation. Events provide the granular data that help identify, validate, and analyze an incident. Together, they allow digital forensic investigators to trace the root cause, assess impact, and produce defensible evidence for legal or organizational reporting.

Skills required for a career in DFIR

In *Chapter 1, Introduction to Digital Forensics,* we discussed job roles in digital forensics. DFIR, as a specialized part of digital forensics, offers many other job opportunities like forensic investigator, incident responder, SOC analyst, threat hunter, incident manager, and so on.

A typical progression while focusing on DFIR would look like this: **SOC Analyst** | **Incident Responder** | **Forensic Investigator** | **DFIR Manager**. However, based on the types of use cases and investigations one works with, all sorts of career paths are possible.

To build a successful career in DFIR, technical expertise alone is insufficient. One requires a variety of skills, including soft skills and analytical skills. Let us look at the key skills required for a DFIR career:

Skill area	What it involves	Relevant to DFIR
Technical skills	Knowledge of OS (Windows, Linux, macOS, iOS, Android), networks, forensic tools (EnCase, **Forensic Toolkit** (**FTK**), Autopsy, Magnet AXIOM and many others), memory forensics (Volatility, Rekall), malware analysis, cloud/IoT forensics.	Provides the hands-on ability to collect, analyze, and interpret digital evidence from diverse environments.
Analytical skills	Ability to correlate logs, spot anomalies, reconstruct timelines, and identify **indicators of compromise** (**IOCs**).	Helps investigators connect the dots and rebuild attacker activity to *understand who, what, when,* and *how*.
Soft skills	Clear communication, precise documentation, teamwork, and the ability to brief executives, lawyers, and technical teams. A balanced combination of assertiveness, clarity, and professional articulation.	Ensures findings are understood, defensible, and actionable for both technical and non-technical audiences.
Certifications and training	Various relevant certifications and training in offensive security, digital forensics and vendor-specific programs.	Validates expertise, ensures continuous learning, and keeps professionals up to date with evolving threats.

Table 13.3*: Skills required for a DFIR career*

In order to be ready for the DFIR role, the digital forensics professional must be hands-on in areas like disk forensics, memory forensics, network forensics, log analysis, malware analysis, cloud forensics, and IR. While incident response is not covered in this book, all the other areas have pretty deep and wide coverage.

Digital forensics and incident response report

Let us now become familiar with a DFIR report. DFIR reports are typically comprehensive documents, often developed collaboratively and reviewed through multiple iterative cycles before being shared with stakeholders. Moreover, such a report undergoes multiple review and update cycles before being published to the concerned stakeholders.

A typical report may contain information like the following:

Report section	Information
Cover page	Case number/reference. Title (e.g., digital forensics and incident response report). Name, designation, and organization of the investigator. Date of submission. Confidentiality statement.
Executive summary	Brief overview of the incident or case. Scope of investigation (systems, devices, timeframes). High-level findings (e.g., unauthorized access confirmed, data exfiltration occurred). Purpose of the report (to assist the court in establishing facts).
Case details	Case identifier/docket number. Parties involved (e.g., plaintiff, defendant, organization). Legal authority under which evidence was collected (court order, corporate investigation, etc.).
Investigator information	Name, qualifications, certifications. Role in the investigation. Statement of impartiality (confirming unbiased reporting).
Scope and methodology	What evidence was examined (devices, files, logs, memory, etc.). Tools and techniques used (FTK Imager, EnCase, Autopsy, Volatility, etc.). Methodology followed (e.g., ISO/IEC 27043, NIST guidelines). Assurance that forensic best practices were applied (write blockers, hashing, validated tools).
Chain of custody	Table showing evidence ID, description, who collected it, dates/times, transfers, and current custodian. Demonstrates evidence integrity and prevents challenges in court.
Findings	Clear, factual observations supported by evidence. **Example**: At 10:15:32 UTC, user jdoe logged in remotely from IP 192.168.1.25. File `salaries.xlsx` was copied to a USB drive (serial: XYZ123) at 10:20:45 UTC. Screenshots, hash values, or log excerpts may be included. **Avoids speculation**: It relies exclusively on verifiable, evidence-based facts.
Timeline of events	Chronological list of key events reconstructed from logs, memory, or artifacts. **Example**: **10:02:11**: Remote login attempt succeeded (RDP). **10:05:44**: File access detected. **10:10:07**: Event logs cleared.

Report section	Information
Conclusion	Concise statement summarizing the overall outcome. **Example**: The investigation confirms unauthorized access on June 5, 2025. Evidence indicates that sensitive data was exfiltrated via USB device. **Does not speculate on motive**: Leaves interpretation to the court.
Appendices	Tool validation reports. Glossary of technical terms (to help non-technical readers). Additional screenshots, logs, or hashes. References to standards used (ISO, NIST, SANS guidance).

***Table 13.4**: DFIR report format*

The key traits of reports that are submitted to a court of law should be:

- **Factual**: No assumptions or guesses.
- **Objective**: No emotional or biased language.
- **Structured**: Easy for lawyers and judges to follow.
- **Defensible**: Another expert should reach the same conclusion using the same data.

Tools used in creating DFIR report

Investigators and other professionals rely on a mix of acquisition, analysis, and reporting tools during the DFIR process. Let us look at the most important tools used in DFIR. We have already covered many of them in the previous chapters:

Tool	Examples	Purpose
Evidence acquisition	FTK Imager, dd (Linux), Cellebrite UFED	Copy data from computers, mobiles, or drives without changing it.
Forensic analysis suites	EnCase, Autopsy, Magnet AXIOM, SIFT Workstation	Examine collected evidence, search keywords, recover deleted files, build timelines.
Incident response platforms	Velociraptor, GRR, CrowdStrike Falcon	Collect evidence including process tree live from many systems at once and help with fast containment.
Memory and malware forensics	Volatility, Rekall, REMnux	Analyze running processes, memory dumps, or malware behavior.
Case management and reporting	Monolith, Lima, NIMBUS	Keep track of evidence, chain of custody, and generate formal reports.

***Table 13.5**: Common tools used for creating DFIR report*

A combination of these tools enables digital forensic investigators to progress from raw data acquisition to evidence analysis and, ultimately, structured reporting.

Note: **Many of the tools in the preceding table are commercial tools. However, it may be possible to acquire a trial license for learning purposes. Refer to the licensing policies of each of these tools before you use them.**

Recipe 106: Creating forensic reports using FTK Imager

We have used FTK Imager multiple times in this book so far, with a detailed recipe for creating a forensic disk image in the previous chapter.

FTK Imager itself is an evidence acquisition and preview tool, not a full analysis platform. It produces verifiable, court-admissible artifacts that become the foundational evidence section of your overall digital-forensics report.

FTK Imager can be used to acquire the following:

- Case metadata (examiner name, case number, description, date/time).
- Imaging logs containing acquisition start/end times, tool version, and hash verification results.
- MD5/SHA-1/SHA-256 hashes for both the source media and the resulting image files.

As part of this recipe, we will perform several tasks that generate key artifacts used in the final digital forensic report.

Note:

- **Compatibility: Windows**
- **License considerations: Free software used**

Recipe

Let us perform the following task that adds to the overall forensic report:

1. Create a forensic disk image using a USB or a hard disk mounted using a write blocker device. Use a physical drive as an option while acquiring this evidence.

   Once you are done, confirm you can see the following in the same directory where the image was exported:

   - Image summary with case information and physical evidence metadata.
   - A directory listing of the image acquired.

2. Create a disk image using a directory. You can select this option in the **Select Source** dialog. This is good only for logical acquisition and does not acquire metadata or other important artifacts like unallocated space and deleted files.

   Once you are done, confirm you can see the following in the same directory where the image for the directory was exported:

   - Image summary with case information and metadata of the directory.
   - A directory listing of the image acquired.

3. Create a disk image using the **Logical Drive** option. In the next screen, choose a logical drive available on your machine. This is also a very important option for acquiring images and creating a forensic report that can be used as part of the overall report.

Once you are done, confirm you can see the following in the same directory where the image for the directory was exported:

- Image summary with case information and metadata of the logical drive, e.g., Google Drive.
- Directory listing of the image acquired.

Note: Image acquisition using a logical drive can also be used to acquire Google Drive mounted on the same machine, thereby giving access to additional evidence.

Activity

Attempt the following activities before the next recipe:

- Check the image summary file after you acquire the **Contents of a Folder** as the source. List down the metadata that is exported by FTK Imager.
- Bring out the importance of creating an image using a logical drive.
- Find out if you can acquire a drive for any other service apart from Google, e.g., OneDrive.

Recipe 107: Creating forensic reports using Autopsy

Autopsy is a full-featured digital forensic investigation platform (built on The Sleuth Kit).

While FTK Imager focuses on evidence acquisition, Autopsy handles analysis, correlation, and reporting. Autopsy can generate automated forensic reports and also allows analysts to create manual case notes, tags, and result summaries that appear in the final report.

In this recipe, we will look at various reports that can be generated from Autopsy.

Note:

- **Compatibility: Windows**
- **License considerations: Free software used**

Recipe

Let us generate a few important reports from Autopsy that can be used as part of the overall forensic report through the following steps:

1. Open an existing case that we created before, or create a new case. Add at least a few local directories and a mobile image (with artifacts like SMS, images, etc.) as data sources.
2. Now, click on the **Timeline** button on the toolbar. This shows the timeline of all the files in the case. Click on the **Snapshot Report** to get the timeline graph snapshot report. Now, click on **List** to change the view to list view. Click on the **Snapshot Report** to get the timeline list snapshot report.
3. From the main window, in the list of files, tag a few files and add comments. Tagging can be done by right-clicking on any file in the list and provides an excellent way to add case-specific tags and comments.
4. From the main window, now click on the **Generate Report** button. In the next screen, select the report type. In the next screen, select all the data sources that need to be included in the report. In the next screen, click on **Finish**. This generates a detailed report of all the artifacts along with the tags you added.

Activity

Attempt the following activities before the next recipe:

- Try the **Geolocation** option in Autopsy. What information can you see here that can be reported?
- Explore how you can create your own project-specific tag from Autopsy.

Recipe 108: Creating reports from other forensic tools

As part of this book, we got familiarized with a large number of digital forensic tools. FTK Imager and Autopsy are the tools that digital forensic investigators may use on a daily basis. Let us go back to a few more of them and understand how they can be used to create parts of reports that can add up to the overall DFIR reports.

Note:

- **Compatibility**: **Windows/Linux**
- **License considerations**: **Free software used**

Recipe

Let us go back to a few tools and techniques we have used before and generate various reports from each of them. This is also an opportunity to revise the tools we have learned and use them from the perspective of creating DFIR reports, as shown in the following table:

Chapter	Technique	Report/evidence
General Forensic Techniques	Browser forensics	Export browser history as evidence. Export reports using specialized tools like **ChromeCacheView**, **ChromeHistoryView**, and **BrowsingHistoryView**.
General Forensic Techniques	Capturing audit logs	You can export audit logs on both Windows and Linux using either built-in or other utilities to help understand the timeline of the events.
Linux Forensics	Identifying deleted files	Output of tools like **find**, **lsof**, **extundelete**, all of them can be used as simple reports.
Linux Forensics	Capturing command history	The history command can provide an excellent output to add to the DFIR report.
Windows Forensics	Checking system information	A simple command like **systeminfo** can provide a lot of valuable information to be included in the DFIR report.
Windows Forensics	Working with Windows events	Event reports of all type in Windows provide an excellent snapshot in the timeline of the cyberattack and other incidents.
Network Forensics	Packet capturing	Packet capture and their filtered and exported formats provide excellent evidence for any case, especially when it can also be correlated to other artifacts and reports.
Memory Forensics	Analyzing memory	Tools like Volatility provide numerous plugins to export various artifacts from memory, each of them adding to the overall report.
Memory Forensics	Using digital forensics toolsets	Tools like OSForensics and sysinternals act as digital forensic toolsets and provide many insights that can be exported in the form of simple reports.
Malware Forensics	Analyzing malware	Any report from malware analysis tools and distributions like REMnux, pestudio, Ghidra, and sysinternals are indispensable for overall reporting.
Mobile Forensics	Scanning Android images	Tools like Android Studio and MobSF can be used to export various evidence while analyzing Android images.

Table 13.6: *Creating part of DFIR report using various tools*

Activity

Attempt the following activities before the next recipe:

- Most tools generate heterogeneous reports in their own proprietary formats. Are there ways to normalize them into a format that is consistent with the DFIR report?
- Find out if there are ways to automatically generate such reports using the command line or any other automation option for each of the tools.
- Create a DFIR report using the techniques we learned in the network forensics chapter.

Implementing post-incident recovery procedures

Post-incident recovery is the final operational phase in the DFIR lifecycle. This phase focuses on safely restoring systems, validating their integrity, and improving the organization's resilience for future incidents.

The core objectives of this phase are as follows:

Objective	Details
System restoration	Bring compromised systems back online safely using clean, verified images or backups.
Validation	Ensure systems are free of malware, unauthorized changes, and backdoors before reintroduction.
Control hardening	Apply patches, configuration fixes, and improved monitoring.
Documentation	Capture forensic and operational evidence of the recovery process.
Knowledge feedback	Update IR playbooks, detection rules, and awareness training.

***Table 13.7**: Core objectives of post-incident recovery*

In order to achieve these key objectives, we need to perform many steps. Many of the following key steps are taken by the respective organizations and teams, like the incident response team, SOC analysts, forensic analysts, etc. Let us understand these key steps in the following table:

Activity	Responsible roles	Output/evidence
Confirm eradication	Incident response team, SOC analyst	Verified evidence that all malware, persistence mechanisms, and compromised accounts are removed. Integrity checks, **endpoint detection and respone (EDR)** scans, and antivirus scans confirm systems are clean and safe for restoration. Verification logs and hash reports are documented.
System restoration	System administrator, forensic analyst	Systems are rebuilt from trusted images or validated backups. Data integrity is verified via checksum or hash comparison. Restoration logs and configuration baselines confirm successful and clean system recovery.
Patching and hardening	IT operations, security engineer	All OS and application patches applied and vulnerable components remediated. Security configurations aligned with CIS/NIST benchmarks. Credentials rotation may also need to be done.
Validation in quarantine	Forensic analyst, network engineer	Recovered systems pass AV, integrity, and vulnerability tests in isolated VLAN. Network logs should show no malicious traffic. Validation and vulnerability reports to confirm readiness for controlled production reintroduction.

Activity	Responsible roles	Output/evidence
Controlled reintroduction	ir lead, system owner, soc team	Systems are gradually restored to production under heightened monitoring. SIEM and EDR telemetry should confirm normal activity. Business owners validate operational stability and sign off for full restoration.
Data integrity verification	Database administrator, application owner	Database and file integrity verified against last known good state. Business data is consistent and free from tampering. Validation reports demonstrate **recovery time objective (RPO)/recovery point objective (RTO)** compliance and data authenticity.
Post-recovery monitoring	SOC analyst, operations team	Continuous monitoring detects no residual or new threats. **security information and event management** (**SIEM**) correlation and EDR dashboards confirm normal behavior. Monitoring summaries and alert reviews are archived for audit.
Documentation and chain of custody update	Forensic lead, IR manager	All recovery actions, timestamps, and responsible personnel documented. Chain of custody updated with recovery evidence. Logs, screenshots, and signed reports stored for forensic and legal review.
Post-incident review (lessons learned)	IR manager, CISO, stakeholders	Formal review identifies root cause, procedural gaps, and improvement areas. Findings are documented in post-mortem report. Updated detection signatures and workflow changes approved.
Continuous improvement	Security governance, training lead	Lessons learned integrated into IR playbooks, awareness training, and red/blue team exercises. Updated procedures and controls enhance overall organizational resilience and DFIR maturity.

***Table 13.8**: Key steps in post-incident recovery*

Conclusion

DFIR represents the convergence of two essential cybersecurity disciplines: forensics and incident management. While digital forensics focuses on the meticulous collection, preservation, and analysis of evidence, incident response emphasizes timely detection, containment, eradication, and recovery from cyberattacks. Together, DFIR enables organizations to respond quickly while maintaining the evidentiary integrity required for legal and regulatory processes.

Accurate reporting forms the backbone of DFIR by translating complex technical findings into actionable intelligence for executives, legal teams, and law enforcement, translating complex technical findings into actionable intelligence for executives, legal teams, and law enforcement. We also looked at tools such as FTK Imager and Autopsy for assisting investigators in generating credible, reproducible evidence and structured reports. As part of this, we also understood the importance of differentiating between events and incidents, as well as the skill sets required for DFIR professionals. Finally, we learned that implementing a structured post-incident recovery procedure ensures that lessons learned feed back into improved defenses.

In summary, DFIR transforms cyber incidents into opportunities to strengthen organizational resilience, ensure accountability, and reinforce trust.

In the next chapter, we will look at cloud forensics, which is another important area of digital forensics, given the ubiquity of various cloud platforms.

Questions

1. What is DFIR, and why is it important in modern cybersecurity operations?
2. How do digital forensics and incident response complement each other?
3. Why is accurate reporting critical in digital forensic investigations?
4. Explain the difference between an event and an incident with suitable examples.
5. What are the typical sections included in a DFIR report?
6. How does the chain of custody ensure evidence admissibility?
7. Describe the DFIR lifecycle as per NIST or ISO standards.
8. What tools are commonly used for evidence acquisition and reporting in DFIR?
9. How can FTK Imager contribute to the creation of forensic reports?
10. What types of reports can Autopsy generate as part of DFIR analysis?
11. Which key skills are required for professionals pursuing a career in DFIR?
12. What are the major objectives of a post-incident recovery procedure?
13. How does documentation support post-incident activities and compliance?
14. Why should lessons learned be included in the DFIR process?
15. How does DFIR help organizations strengthen their overall security posture?

Points to remember

- DFIR combines digital forensics (investigation) and IR (action).
- Accurate reporting ensures findings are defensible, clear, and legally valid.
- Not every event is an incident.
- Incidents are verified security breaches.
- DFIR reports must be factual, objective, and reproducible.
- Chain of custody maintains evidence integrity throughout investigation.
- The DFIR lifecycle includes preparation, detection, containment, eradication, recovery, and lessons learned.
- Post-incident recovery validates restored systems and strengthens defenses.
- Communication and documentation are as vital as technical analysis.
- DFIR professionals need technical, analytical, and soft skills.
- Legal admissibility depends on proper procedure and documentation.
- DFIR turns every breach into a learning opportunity for resilience.

Key terms

- **DFIR**: Integration of digital forensics and incident response to investigate, mitigate, and recover from cyber incidents.
- **IR**: A structured approach to detecting, containing, eradicating, and recovering from cybersecurity incidents.
- **Event**: Any observable activity within a system or network, such as a login, file access, or process execution.
- **Incident**: A confirmed or suspected breach, attack, or policy violation that impacts the confidentiality, integrity, or availability of information systems.
- **Chain of custody**: A documented process showing how evidence was collected, transferred, and stored to maintain its integrity and legal admissibility.
- **Forensic image**: A bit-by-bit copy of digital media acquired for investigation without altering the original evidence.
- **Hash value**: A unique cryptographic checksum used to verify the integrity and authenticity of forensic evidence.
- **Timeline analysis**: A method of reconstructing digital events in chronological order to understand system or attacker activity.
- **Incident recovery**: The process of restoring affected systems to a verified, secure state following an incident.
- **Eradication**: The step in incident response where malware, backdoors, or compromised accounts are completely removed from the environment.

CHAPTER 14
Cloud Forensics

Introduction

When conventional crimes or cybercrimes are committed, cloud environments are frequently involved as part of the attack surface or evidence trail. When a cybercrime is committed against cloud-native applications, we need to identify the attack vectors in the cloud application and the underlying cloud platform. As organizations increasingly migrate workloads, data, and applications to the cloud, traditional forensic techniques become insufficient because data no longer resides on local, physical devices. The data is virtualized, distributed, and often spans multiple jurisdictions. As a result, cloud forensics has become an essential extension of modern digital forensics.

In this chapter, we will understand various aspects of cloud forensics. We will discuss various aspects of cloud forensics using well-known public clouds. However, these principles also apply to other deployment models, such as private cloud, hybrid cloud, multi-cloud, and so on.

Structure

In this chapter, we will cover the following topics:

- Introduction to cloud computing
- Well-known deployment model in the cloud
- Widely-used public clouds
- Shared responsibility model in the cloud
- Need for cloud forensics
- Collecting forensic evidence using cloud CLI utilities
- Recipe 109: Creating user for collecting forensic evidence from AWS
- Recipe 110: Configuring AWS CLI using access keys
- Recipe 111: Collecting digital forensic evidence from AWS
- Recipe 112: Snapshotting a disk volume on AWS
- Recipe 113: Connecting Azure CLI to Microsoft Azure
- Recipe 114: Collecting digital forensic evidence from Azure
- Recipe 115: Snapshotting a disk volume on Azure

Objectives

With the exponential growth and maturity of cloud computing, many organizations are going cloud native. Moreover, organizations are migrating to the cloud or at least using the cloud for some use cases. This chapter examines the cybersecurity challenges introduced by cloud environments and explains why cloud forensics has become indispensable, and how digital forensics for cloud becomes indispensable. We will discuss the well-known service model and deployment model of cloud. After this, we will understand why we need cloud forensics. This will be followed by recipes for collecting various evidence from AWS and Azure.

By the end of this chapter, readers will be familiar with the core concepts of cloud computing and the role of cloud forensics, including the use of AWS CLI and Azure CLI to automate forensic evidence collection.

Introduction to cloud computing

The cloud refers to a model of delivering computing resources, such as servers, storage, databases, networking, software, and analytics, over the internet (*the cloud*) instead of running them locally on a personal computer or on-premises data center. In simpler terms, instead of buying, installing, and maintaining hardware and software yourself, you rent computing resources from a provider such as **Amazon Web Services** (**AWS**), Microsoft Azure, or **Google Cloud Platform** (**GCP**).

Cloud computing refers to the on-demand use of shared, configurable computing resources to perform computing tasks without direct management of underlying infrastructure. It provides on-demand access to a shared pool of configurable resources (e.g., servers, storage, networks, applications) that can be rapidly provisioned and released with minimal management effort.

Cloud computing revolutionizes IT by delivering elastic, scalable, and cost-efficient computing resources via virtualization. While customers retain ownership of their data, they share security responsibilities with providers. This paradigm shift improves agility and global accessibility but demands stronger data governance, encryption, access control, and compliance awareness to mitigate the expanded attack surface and data sovereignty risks.

Well-known service models in the cloud

A service model in cloud computing defines which computing resources or services are provided to the customer and how much of the underlying stack is managed by the provider versus the user. Examples include IaaS, PaaS, and SaaS, representing layers of abstraction from infrastructure to complete applications. Let us look at each of these models in detail, including the responsibilities of the provider and the customer.

Note: **Many other service models may be flavors of these models. However, at a high level, the following service models cover all the important ones. FaaS and CaaS are relatively new to the cloud computing paradigm.**

Infrastructure as a service

IaaS provides fundamental computing resources such as virtual machines, storage, and networking over the internet. Users can install and manage their own operating systems and applications while the provider manages the underlying hardware and virtualization. It offers high flexibility and scalability for organizations needing custom environments.

Let us look at the key characteristics of IaaS:

Characteristic	Details
Purpose/definition	Provides virtualized computing resources like servers, storage, and networking on demand.
Provider responsibility	Physical infrastructure, hypervisors, and core networking.
Customer responsibility	**Operating system** (**OS**) configuration, middleware, applications, data, and access.
Key advantages	Flexible, scalable, pay-per-use. Good for custom environments.
Common examples	AWS EC2, Microsoft Azure VM, Google Compute Engine, **Oracle Cloud Infrastructure** (**OCI**) Virtual Machine

Table 14.1: Key characteristics of IaaS

Platform as a service

PaaS delivers a complete development and deployment platform that includes infrastructure, operating systems, and runtime environments. Developers can focus on building and running applications without worrying about server management or scalability. It accelerates development cycles and supports continuous integration and deployment workflows.

The following table provides the key characteristics of PaaS:

Characteristic	Details
Purpose/definition	Offers a complete development and deployment environment in the cloud abstracting away infrastructure management.
Provider responsibility	Infrastructure, OS, runtime, and middleware.
Customer responsibility	Application code, data, user administration, and user access.
Key advantages	Faster app development, no need to manage servers or OS, and auto-scaling.
Common examples	Google App Engine, Azure App Service, AWS Elastic Beanstalk, AWS **Relational Database Service (RDS)**, Heroku.

Table 14.2: *Key characteristics of PaaS*

Software as a service

SaaS provides fully functional, ready-to-use software applications accessible via a web browser. The provider handles everything, from infrastructure and maintenance to updates, while users simply configure and use the software. It is well-suited for end-users who require rapid access to business applications without installation or maintenance overhead.

The following table provides the key characteristics of SaaS:

Characteristic	Details
Purpose/definition	Delivers fully functional applications accessible via the web. Users consume the app directly.
Provider responsibility	Everything, from hardware to app management and updates.
Customer responsibility	End-user data, configurations, and access permissions.
Key advantages	No installation or maintenance, subscription-based, accessible anywhere.
Common examples	Microsoft 365, Salesforce, Zoho Suite, Dropbox, Zoom, Gmail

Table 14.3: *Key characteristics of SaaS*

Function as a service or serverless

FaaS allows users to run code functions in response to events without managing servers or infrastructure. The provider automatically handles provisioning, scaling, and runtime management. It is highly cost-effective for microservices and event-driven applications since billing is per execution. They may be known by different names in different cloud platforms, e.g., function, Lambda, etc.

Let us look at the key characteristics of FaaS in the following table:

Characteristic	Details
Purpose/definition	Executes event-driven functions without managing servers. Code runs only when triggered.
Provider responsibility	Underlying infrastructure, runtime, and scaling.
Customer responsibility	Application logic (functions) and triggers.
Key advantages	Highly scalable, cost-efficient, ideal for microservices.
Common examples	AWS Lambda, Azure Functions, Google Cloud Functions

***Table 14.4**: Key characteristics of FaaS*

Container as a service

Container as a service (**CaaS**) provides a platform to deploy, manage, and orchestrate containers using technologies like Docker and Kubernetes. It enables faster application deployment, scalability, and portability across environments. This model is popular for DevOps and modern microservices architectures.

The following table provides the key characteristics of CaaS:

Characteristic	Details
Purpose/definition	Provides container orchestration and management platform using Docker or Kubernetes.
Provider responsibility	Infrastructure and orchestration engine (e.g., K8s).
Customer responsibility	Container images, application code, scaling rules.
Key advantages	Portability, faster deployment, DevOps-friendly.
Common examples	**Google Kubernetes Engine** (**GKE**), AWS EKS, Azure AKS.

***Table 14.5**: Key characteristics of CaaS*

Well-known deployment model in the cloud

A deployment model defines where cloud infrastructure is hosted and who has control over its management and security. For example, public, private, hybrid, or multi-cloud, determining factors like ownership, accessibility, and security responsibility.

Let us look at each of these deployment models in detail.

Public cloud

The public cloud is a shared environment where computing resources are owned and operated by third-party providers and delivered over the internet. It offers high scalability, cost efficiency, and global accessibility. However, users have limited control over infrastructure and must rely on the provider's security and compliance measures.

The following table discusses the key attributes of public cloud:

Attribute	Details
Definition and scope	Cloud resources (compute, storage, network) provided over the internet and shared across multiple tenants.
Ownership and control	Owned and operated by third-party providers like **Amazon Web Services** (**AWS**), Microsoft Azure, or **Google Cloud Platform** (**GCP**).

Attribute	Details
Use case scenarios	Startups, **small and medium-sized enterprises** (**SMEs**), and enterprises needing scalability and cost savings.
Advantages	Low cost, elastic scaling, global accessibility.
Challenges and limitations	Limited control, compliance complexity, potential vendor lock-in.
Examples	AWS, Microsoft Azure, Google Cloud Platform.
Security risks	• Multi-tenancy risks (data leakage between tenants). • Misconfigured storage buckets. • Insecure APIs. • Dependency on the provider's security posture. • Data residency and sovereignty issues.

***Table 14.6**: Key attributes of public cloud*

Private cloud

A private cloud is dedicated to a single organization and can be hosted on-premises or by a third-party provider. It provides greater control, customization, and data security, making it suitable for industries with strict compliance requirements. The trade-off is higher cost and management overhead compared to public clouds.

The following tables discuss the key attributes of private cloud:

Attribute	Details
Definition and scope	Dedicated infrastructure for a single organization, either on-premises or managed by a vendor.
Ownership and control	Owned or leased by one organization.
Use case scenarios	Enterprises with strict regulatory, security, or data control needs.
Advantages	High control, customization, regulatory compliance.
Challenges and limitations	High cost, requires in-house expertise and maintenance.
Examples	VMware vCloud, OpenStack, Azure Stack, AWS Outposts.
Security risks	• Insider threats. • Misconfigured virtualization environments. • Weak access controls. • Patch management lapses. • Data loss due to poor backup policies.

***Table 14.7**: Key attributes of private cloud*

Hybrid cloud

The hybrid cloud combines private and public cloud environments, enabling data and applications to move between them seamlessly. This model provides flexibility, sensitive workloads can stay on-premises while less critical tasks run in the public cloud. It optimizes cost and performance but introduces complexity in integration and security management.

Let us look at the key attributes of hybrid cloud:

Attribute	Details
Definition and scope	Integration of public and private clouds enabling workload and data portability.
Ownership and control	Joint control between organization and provider.
Use case scenarios	Workloads requiring on-prem data control and cloud scalability.
Advantages	Flexibility, optimized resource usage, scalability.
Challenges and limitations	Complex configuration, integration, and policy enforcement.
Examples	AWS Outposts + AWS Cloud, Azure Arc, Google Anthos.
Security risks	• Data transfer vulnerabilities between environments. • Inconsistent IAM and encryption policies. • Shadow IT risks. • Cloud misconfiguration due to complex setup.

Table 14.8: *Key attributes of hybrid cloud*

Multi-cloud

Multi-cloud refers to using multiple public cloud providers simultaneously for different services or workloads. It avoids vendor lock-in and allows organizations to use the best capabilities of each provider. However, it requires strong governance and interoperability management across platforms.

Let us understand the key attributes of multi-cloud in the following table:

Attribute	Details
Definition and scope	Use of multiple public cloud providers for redundancy, optimization, or avoiding vendor lock-in.
Ownership and control	Managed by organization; services sourced from different providers.
Use case scenarios	Large enterprises balancing risk or needing specialized cloud services.
Advantages	Vendor independence, fault tolerance, best-of-breed capabilities.
Challenges and limitations	Complex management, data synchronization challenges, cost tracking.
Examples	• Cross-cloud identity and access management issues. • Inconsistent security controls. • Data exfiltration risks during cross-cloud sync. • Monitoring blind spots.
Security risks	Combination of AWS + Azure + GCP, or any of the other **co-location** (**colo**) and local clouds.

Table 14.9: *Key attributes of multi-cloud*

Community cloud

A community cloud is shared by several organizations with common goals, such as security, compliance, or mission objectives. It is jointly managed and can be hosted by one of the participants or a third party. This model balances shared cost and governance with alignment to specific community standards.

The following tables discuss the key attributes of community cloud:

Attribute	Details
Definition and scope	Shared infrastructure between organizations with similar regulatory or operational goals.
Ownership and control	Jointly owned or managed by the community or a trusted third party.
Use case scenarios	Governments, research groups, financial or healthcare consortiums.
Advantages	Shared cost, compliance alignment, collaboration friendly.
Challenges and limitations	Complex governance, shared accountability, cost distribution issues.
Examples	• Shared responsibility ambiguity. • Insider threats across member orgs. • Access control mismanagement. • Compliance enforcement inconsistencies.
Security risks	Government Research Cloud, Health Cloud, CJIS Cloud Consortium.

***Table 14.10**: Key attributes of community cloud*

Widely used public clouds

Public cloud providers deliver on-demand computing resources, i.e., servers, storage, databases, networking, analytics, and now even AI, over the internet. While AWS, Microsoft Azure, and GCP dominate globally, others, such as **Oracle Cloud Infrastructure** (**OCI**), IBM Cloud, and several regional providers (like Alibaba Cloud and Tencent Cloud), serve specific industries or geographies. Each provider has distinct strengths, pricing models, and ecosystems, catering to diverse business and compliance requirements.

Note: **We have looked at the most used cloud providers at the time of writing. New cloud providers come out all the time. While they may have a small learning curve, the underlying principles across the cloud providers remain the same.**

Let us look at each of them in detail.

Amazon Web Services

AWS is one of the first and largest public cloud platforms. AWS pioneered IaaS and PaaS offerings with the broadest global reach. It provides extensive services for compute, storage, networking, machine learning, and serverless architectures. Typical businesses that use AWS include startups, SaaS companies, enterprises, and government agencies. Many large-scale streaming services operate on AWS infrastructure.

From a security point of view, AWS uses a shared responsibility model, end-to-end encryption, AWS Shield for DDoS, **identify and access management** (**IAM**), CloudTrail, and extensive compliance.

Microsoft Azure

Azure integrates tightly with Microsoft's enterprise ecosystem, making it ideal for organizations using Windows Server, Active Directory, or Microsoft 365. It supports a wide range of hybrid and enterprise-grade workloads with strong compliance frameworks. Azure is a preferred cloud platform for many organizations, particularly those already invested in Microsoft's enterprise ecosystem. Typical businesses include enterprises that use Windows Server, .NET, and Microsoft 365, as well as various government agencies.

Azure has enterprise-grade security provided by Azure Security Center, Sentinel (SIEM/SOAR), Defender for Cloud, and AD-based identity management.

Google Cloud Platform

GCP excels in data analytics, machine learning, and container orchestration. It is favored for innovation-driven workloads, AI/ML development, and scalable web or mobile applications. GCP is used by tech startups, analytics-driven companies, gaming, media, and AI research companies.

GCP has state-of-the-art security using BeyondCorp Zero Trust model, built-in encryption, strong IAM and audit capabilities, and Titan security chips.

Oracle Cloud Infrastructure

OCI targets enterprise and mission-critical workloads, especially for Oracle databases and ERP systems. It is known for predictable performance, strong **service level agreement** (**SLAs**), and optimized database-as-a-service capabilities. Although OCI entered the public cloud market later than its competitors, it has rapidly expanded its capabilities and adoption. Financial institutions, telecom, and enterprises using Oracle ERP or databases are the key users of OCI.

OCI provides layered defense with Oracle Cloud Guard, encryption by default, identity federation, and compliance with PCI-DSS and GDPR.

IBM Cloud

IBM Cloud focuses on hybrid cloud, AI (Watson), and regulated industries. It offers both bare-metal and virtualized options, with deep expertise in security and compliance for finance and healthcare. IBM Cloud, while not preferred by tech startups, has a role to play in very large enterprises. Banking, insurance, and healthcare sectors, government agencies with high compliance needs, are the users of IBM Cloud.

IBM Cloud provides IBM Hyper Protect Services for confidential computing, FIPS 140-2 Level 4 HSM, and extensive compliance certifications.

Alibaba Cloud

Alibaba Cloud (regional leader, Asia-Pacific) dominates in China and Southeast Asia, offering scalable e-commerce and AI services. It caters to businesses expanding into the Asian market and supports compliance with local data regulations. Typical businesses of Alibaba Cloud include E-commerce, logistics, fintech, and regional enterprises.

It offers Anti-DDoS, Cloud Firewall, and encryption compliance with China's Cybersecurity law.

Tencent Cloud

Tencent Cloud (regional leader, China) serves gaming, media streaming, and social platforms with strong integration into Tencent's ecosystem (e.g., WeChat, QQ). It is popular among digital entertainment and online service companies in Asia. Typical businesses of Tencent Cloud include gaming, media, social, and AI-based startups in Asia.

Tencent Cloud also provides robust security controls aligned with regional regulatory requirements. It adheres to Chinese regulatory frameworks; provides WAF, DDoS protection, and data encryption services.

Shared responsibility model in the cloud

In the last section, we saw that all the public clouds have pretty good security features and controls in place. Therefore, it is essential to understand the factors contributing to the growing number of cloud security threats and exposures.

The shared responsibility model in cloud computing defines how security and compliance duties are divided between the cloud provider and the customer. It ensures clarity about who is responsible for what across the cloud stack, covering physical infrastructure, virtualization, operating systems, data, and access controls. At a high level, the provider secures the cloud itself (data centers, networking, hardware, hypervisors), and the customer is responsible for securing what they put in the cloud (data, users, configurations, and access policies).

Let us look at the breakdown of various responsibilities under the shared responsibility model in the following table:

Area	Cloud provider's responsibility	Customer's responsibility
Physical security	Securing data centers, hardware, and global infrastructure.	None (handled fully by provider).
Network security (Core)	Protecting backbone network, hypervisors, and virtualization layers.	Configuring firewalls, **virtual private clouds (VPCs)**, and security groups correctly.
OS and middleware	Managed by provider in PaaS/SaaS; shared in IaaS.	Patching, hardening, and maintaining guest OS if using IaaS.
Applications	Managed in SaaS (e.g., Salesforce, Office 365).	Building secure applications and enforcing secure APIs.
Data protection	Encryption tools and secure storage provided.	Encrypting sensitive data, key management, and access control.
IAM	Provide IAM tools and authentication services.	Define roles, enforce MFA, and manage user permissions.
Compliance	Maintain infrastructure certifications (ISO, SOC, GDPR).	Ensure workloads and configurations align with applicable laws.

***Table 14.11**: Various responsibilities under the shared responsibility model*

Let us now look at the cloud provider-specific examples for the shared responsibility model in the following table:

Cloud provider	Responsibility under the shared responsibility model
AWS	AWS secures the infrastructure (e.g., EC2 hosts, S3 storage systems), while the customer secures data and configuration. For example, AWS provides encryption using **key management system (KMS)**, but the customer must enable bucket policies and access control in S3.
Microsoft Azure	Azure secures physical hosts and network fabric, while customers must configure **network security groups (NSGs)**, Azure AD roles, and patch their VMs. In Azure PaaS (e.g., App Service), Microsoft manages the OS layer.
OCI	Oracle secures hardware, storage, and virtualization, while customers control network isolation, database encryption settings, and user privileges. In autonomous database, Oracle automates much of the security patching.
GCP	Google secures infrastructure and hypervisors, but customers manage IAM policies, service account permissions, and data classification. GCP's BeyondCorp model reinforces Zero Trust, but customer misconfiguration remains a top risk.
IBM Cloud	IBM provides secure enclaves (e.g., Hyper Protect) and compliance tools, but customers need to configure security controls like application-level security, data encryption, and identity federation. It is designed for high-compliance workloads but still customer-managed above the hypervisor.

Cloud provider	Responsibility under the shared responsibility model
Alibaba Cloud	Alibaba secures data centers and platform services, but customers must set **resource access management (RAM)** policies, network ACLs, and DDoS configurations. Misconfiguration remains a common customer risk.
Tencent Cloud	Tencent handles infrastructure and compliance under Chinese law, but customers must secure API access, service permissions, and application security. Businesses using gaming or media workloads must integrate additional DDoS and access-layer protections.

Table 14.12: *Cloud provider specific examples for the shared responsibility model*

With the discussion around the shared responsibility model, we can now understand that digital forensics is a vital aspect for being ready for evidence collection, as well as in the event of an exposure or a cyberattack.

As we discussed so far, the shared responsibility model ensures security is collaborative. In this model, the cloud providers handle the foundation, and customers secure their implementation. Failures in applying this model correctly are a frequent cause of cloud security breaches, typically due to customer misconfigurations rather than provider vulnerabilities. Proper understanding and implementation of this model are essential for maintaining cloud security and compliance across all platforms.

Need for cloud forensics

Cloud forensics is a specialized branch of digital forensics focused on investigating, collecting, and analyzing digital evidence from cloud environments (e.g., AWS, Azure, GCP, OCI, IBM Cloud, etc.). As organizations increasingly migrate workloads, data, and applications to the cloud, traditional forensic techniques become insufficient because data no longer resides on local, physical devices. The data is virtualized, distributed, and often spans multiple jurisdictions.

Consequently, cloud forensics is no longer optional for organizations operating in cloud environments. It is an essential capability for any enterprise operating in the cloud. It ensures visibility, accountability, and recoverability in multi-tenant, dynamic environments.

Without it, enterprises risk data loss, regulatory penalties, reputational damage, and prolonged exposure to undetected cyber threats.

The key reasons for the need for cloud forensics are as follows:

Reason	Detail
Decentralized and shared infrastructure	Cloud data can reside in multiple data centers across regions. Forensic investigators must handle multi-tenant environments and identify which data belongs to which entity.
Ephemeral and elastic resources	Virtual machines, containers, and serverless functions can be short-lived or transient. Without timely forensic readiness, valuable evidence (e.g., logs, memory, metadata) can vanish when instances terminate. This could make it impossible to reconstruct an incident.
Complex logging and visibility	Logs are spread across multiple layers, application, hypervisor, API gateway, and service level. Cloud forensics ensures logs are preserved, correlated, and analyzed properly. This can also help later to create a timeline of events, which is essential while investigating a cybercrime or an incident.
Legal and compliance requirements	Many frameworks (e.g., GDPR, HIPAA, ISO 27001, SOC 2) mandate incident investigation and accountability for data breaches. Cloud forensics supports audit trails and regulatory reporting. Without cloud forensics, organizations handling personal, financial, or healthcare data may face non-compliance penalties under these frameworks if they cannot produce digital evidence or an audit trail after a breach.

Reason	Detail
Incident response integration	Forensics in the cloud helps security teams respond to breaches, ransomware, or insider attacks by identifying intrusion vectors, compromised assets, and data exfiltration paths. Without forensic readiness, incident responders lack the visibility needed to isolate compromised assets, restore systems safely, and verify that threats are eradicated, extending recovery time and costs.
Attribution and accountability	Forensics provides traceability, i.e., linking an attack to a specific account, IAM role, or cloud resource modification, which is essential for both technical remediation and legal proceedings. In cases involving insider threats, IP theft, or cross-border cybercrime, a lack of cloud forensics capability prevents legal attribution. It may also invalidate evidence in court due to improper handling of the chain of custody.

***Table 14.13**: Need for cloud forensics*

Collecting forensic evidence using cloud CLI utilities

Each of the public clouds we discussed so far provides a vast array of services. Forensic evidence should be collected in a repeatable and automated manner to ensure consistency and defensibility. This is where cloud-provider **command-line interface** (**CLI**) utilities become essential. They can be used to automate a variety of tasks for forensic evidence collection from a digital forensic investigator's or a system administrator's machine.

Let us look at the CLI utilities supported by each of the widely used clouds in the following table:

Cloud	CLI utility	Installation instructions and details
AWS	aws	**https://aws.amazon.com/cli/**
Azure	az	**https://learn.microsoft.com/en-us/cli/azure/**
GCP	gcloud, gsutil, bq	**https://docs.cloud.google.com/sdk/docs/install**
OCI	oci	**https://docs.oracle.com/en-us/iaas/Content/API/Concepts/cliconcepts.htm**
IBM Cloud	ibmcloud	**https://cloud.ibm.com/docs/cli?topic=cli-install-ibmcloud-cli**

***Table 14.14**: CLI utilities for widely used clouds*

All these CLIs support scripting, logging, and automation, making them essential for **digital forensics and incident response** (**DFIR**) in cloud environments. They enable investigators to collect, preserve, and correlate evidence, such as audit trails, snapshots, and logs, while maintaining reproducibility and chain of custody.

Install the CLI for one or more clouds you are using, using the installation instructions from the link in the preceding table. Once installed, configure them for your account.

Note: **Do not use your root/admin account or any user account to run these CLI tools. It is recommended to create a new role, e.g., ForensicRole, and an account in that role with the least privilege that provides read-only access to properties, logs, etc., and provides you permission to create copies, snapshots, etc.**

In the following recipes, we will use AWS CLI and Azure CLI for cloud forensics-related use cases with AWS and Microsoft Azure, respectively. Once you have become comfortable with them, you can use the CLI tools of other clouds like OCI, GCP, and IBM Cloud to collect cloud forensic evidence.

Recipe 109: Creating user for collecting AWS forensic evidence

In this recipe, let us create a role and assign the role to a user for collecting forensic evidence from AWS using AWS CLI.

You need to have an AWS account, and you should be comfortable working with the AWS Console as prerequisites to this recipe.

Note:

- **Compatibility: AWS**
- **License considerations: Requires subscription. Free services and trial periods apply.**

Recipe

Perform the following steps to complete this recipe:

1. In the AWS Console, open IAM. Click on **User groups** under **Access management**. The existing user groups are displayed in the list.
2. Click on the **Create group** button on the top right. In the next screen, assign a name to the group, e.g., **ForensicGroup**.

   In the same screen, add permissions, filter by **AWS managed - job function**. Select **ReadOnlyAccess**, as shown in the following figure. This would give read-only access to all the services:

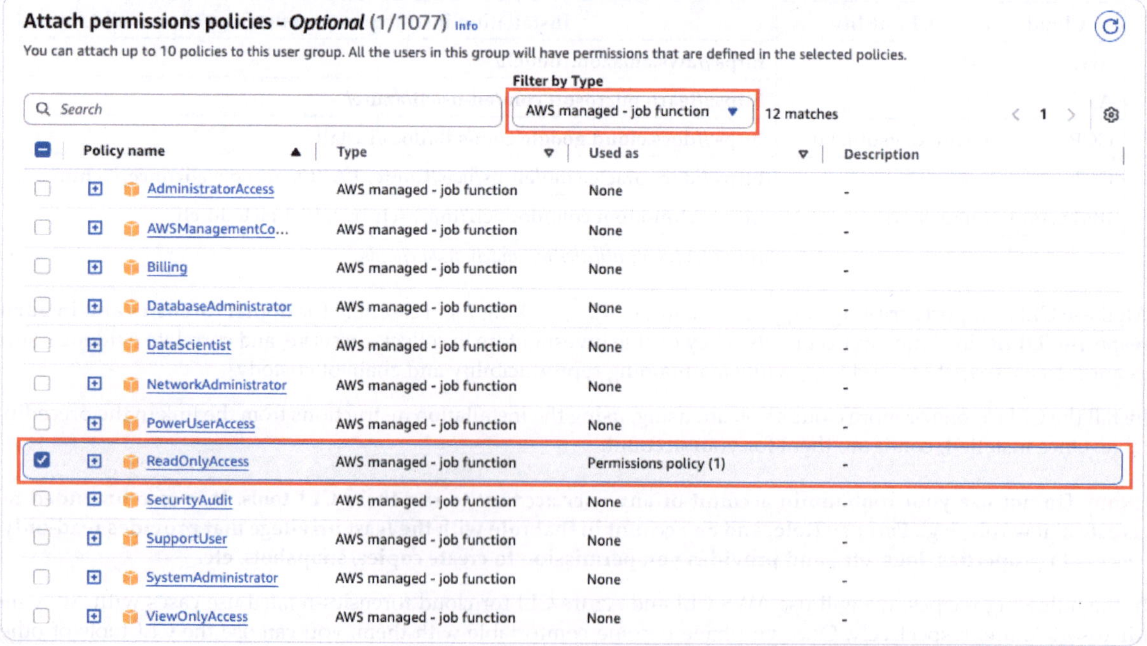

Figure 14.1: Attach permissions policies from the list of policies screen

Click on the **Create user group** button to create the user group.

3. This user group only has read-only access to services. Let us assign a snapshot permission to this group so that the user assigned to this group can create a snapshot of EC2 instances. To do that, click on the group name in the list of user groups, click on the Permission tab, and then click on **Add Permissions** | **Attach policies**. In this screen, search for **`snapshot`**, select the permission policy as shown in the following figure, and then click on the **Attach policies** button to finish adding the policy:

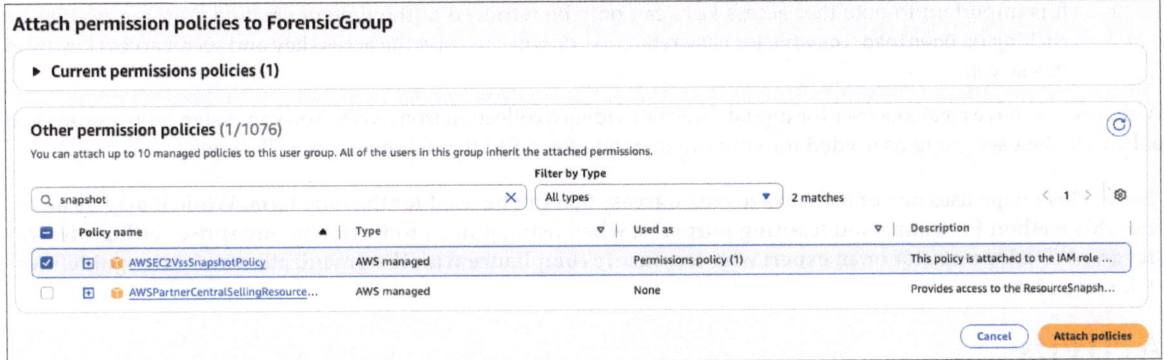

Figure 14.2: Attach permissions policies to the user group

4. Once you are done, verify that your group looks like the following:

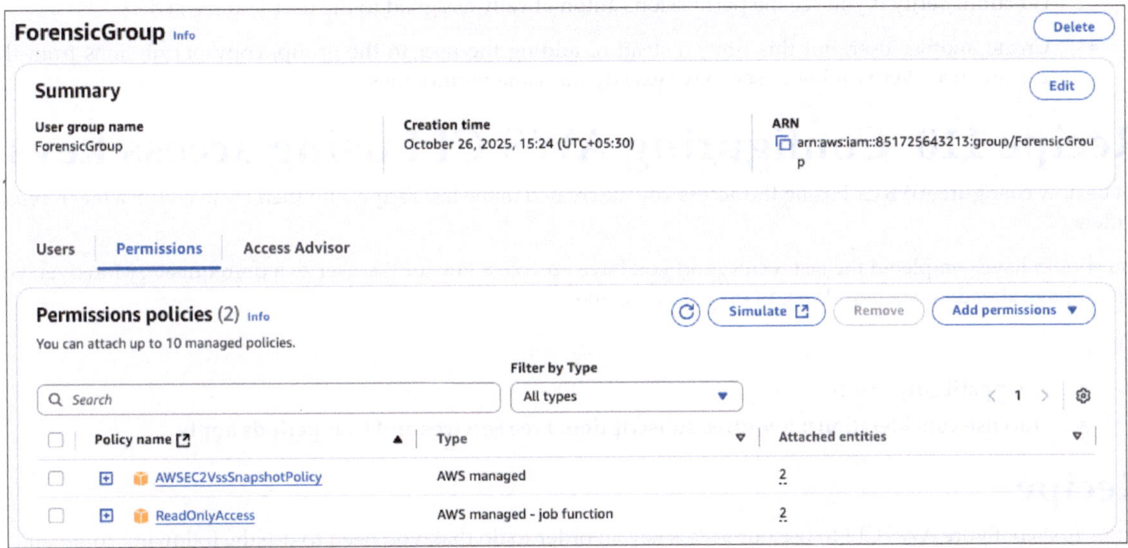

Figure 14.3: User group after attaching the permission policies

5. Now, let us create a user and assign the user to this group. To do that, click on **Users** on the left list under **Access management**, click on **Create user**, and provide a user name, e.g., forensic. In the next screen, select **Add user to the group** in the permission options, and select the group we just created, viz., **ForensicGroup**. Click on the **Next** button to go to the **Review and create** screen, and then click on **Create user** to create the user and assign the user to the group.

6. While the user is created, we cannot use the user yet. For that, you need to go to the user page, click on the **Security credentials** tab, and choose one of the ways this user accesses AWS through CLI. In this case, let us add an access key by clicking on **Create access key** under **Access keys**.
7. In the next screen, select the first option, i.e., **Command Line Interface (CLI)** under use case. Click on **Next** after checking the checkbox below. In the next screen, set a tag, e.g., **forensic-access-key**, and then click on the **Create access key** button to create the access key.
8. It is important to note that access keys can only be retrieved at the time of creation. You can do that by clicking on `Download .csv` file for easy reference, or you can copy the access key and secret access key from this screen.

With this, you have created a user for digital forensic evidence collection from AWS. You can assign more permission policies to the user group as needed for your organization for cloud forensic evidence collection.

Note: **This recipe uses one of the ways to create access that can be used for the long term. While it may be ok to use this method for testing and learning purposes, when using it in a production or enterprise setting, always let an AWS administrator or an expert who can ensure compliance with the organization's security guidelines take care of it.**

Activity

Attempt the following activities before the next recipe:

- Add one more permission policy SecurityAudit to the created group by filtering by **AWS managed - job function**. Verify if you see the permissions automatically assigned to the user you created.
- Create another user, but this time, instead of adding the user to the group, copy permissions from the existing user. Verify if both users have exactly the same permissions.

Recipe 110: Configuring AWS CLI using access keys

Let us now configure AWS CLI using the access key we created in the last recipe, and then try to collect a few forensic evidence.

You should have completed the last recipe, and you have an access key for the user as a prerequisite. Moreover, you should have already installed AWS CLI on your machine.

Note:

- **Compatibility**: **AWS**
- **License considerations: Requires subscription. Free services and trial periods apply.**

Recipe

Let us first configure AWS CLI to use our access key. In order to do that, you need to use the following command:

```
aws configure
```

Now provide the details as shown in the output. For the output format, you can just press *Enter* or enter **`text`**:

```
┌──nishant@Ivy ~
└─$ aws configure
AWS Access Key ID [None]: < redacted >
AWS Secret Access Key [None]: < redacted >
Default region name [None]: ap-south-1
```

```
Default output format [None]: text
┌─nishant@Ivy ~
└─$
```

Tip: If you have set the output format to `json`, all the output will be shown in the JSON format. If you have selected `text` as the output format, then you can always use `--output json` option to get the output in JSON format.

Activity

Attempt the following activities before the next recipe:

- Understand the AWS CLI options by running **`aws help`**. Also, try help for a specific command, e.g., **`aws iam help`**, and **`aws iam list-users help`**.
- Run **`aws --version`** to see the version of AWS CLI.

Recipe 111: Collecting digital forensic evidence from AWS

Now that you have configured AWS CLI, it is time to collect a few important evidence from AWS. In this recipe, we will collect a list of users, a list of groups, and a list of VMs to become comfortable working with AWS CLI. After that, you should be able to collect most information by looking at the AWS CLI reference that comes with the tool, or that is published by AWS.

Note:

- **Compatibility: AWS**
- **License considerations: Requires subscription. Free services and trial periods apply.**

Recipe

In this recipe, we will collect many evidence across AWS services. Follow the steps below to complete this recipe. **`xxxxxx`** is used in many places to redact sensitive information like account ID:

1. First, let us check the list of all the groups in the AWS account. To do this, you can use the command **`iam list-group`** as shown:

   ```
   aws iam list-groups
   ```

   IAM is the service we are using in this context. Your output will look similar to the following:

   ```
   GROUPS      arn:aws:iam::8517xxxxxx13:group/ForensicGroup          2025-10-26T09:54:07+00:00
   AGPA4MTWN5XGWKC23NTZS    ForensicGroup    /
   ```

   You can see here that the group we created is listed. This means when we run it regularly, we can find any new group that might have been created by the threat actor.

2. Now try the same using **`-- output json`** option. Your output will look similar to the following:

   ```
   {
       "Groups": [
           {
               "Path": "/",
               "GroupName": "ForensicGroup",
   ```

```
                "GroupId": "AGPxxxxxx5XGWKC23NTZS",
                "Arn": "arn:aws:iam::8517xxxxxx13:group/ForensicGroup",
                "CreateDate": "2025-10-26T09:54:07+00:00"
            }
        ]
}
```

3. Now, let us try to list the users we created. You can run the following command to get the list of users in JSON format:

```
aws iam list-users --output json
```

Your output will look similar to the following:

```
{
    "Users": [
        {
            "Path": "/",
            "UserName": "forensic",
            "UserId": "AIDA4MTWN5XGQxxxxxx4F",
            "Arn": "arn:aws:iam::8517xxxxxx13:user/forensic",
            "CreateDate": "2025-10-26T10:02:48+00:00"
        }
    ]
}
```

You can already realize by now how handy this command will be to find out the deviation from the existing user list.

4. Let us now move to the **virtual machines (VMs)**. In AWS, **Elastic Compute Cloud (EC2)** service is one of the ways to create VMs. VMs can be created, or their properties can be modified by a threat actor during a cyberattack. Hence, collecting information about the VMs and comparing them with the baseline is absolutely important as part of cloud forensics.

Note: Before you try out the EC2 commands, you need to have at least one running EC2 instance in your account. You can create a small (e.g., t2.micro) instance for testing purposes.

Let us first list the instances by running the following command:

```
aws ec2 describe-instances
```

The output contains all the details of all the instances. You can verify these details from the EC2 pages as well.

While these details are good, if we need to get a much more formatted list, then we need to supply specific attributes of the details. Furthermore, we can also use the `--output table` to get a much formatted output as follows:

```
aws ec2 describe-instances --query "Reservations[*].Instances[*].[InstanceId, State.Name,
InstanceType, PrivateIpAddress, Tags[?Key=='Name'].Value|[0]]" --output table
```

The output of the preceding command will look similar to the following output in a formatted tabular format:

```
----------------------------------------------------------------------
|                        DescribeInstances                           |
+---------------------+---------+-----------+--------------+-----------------+
|  i-05f6aa8b6dxxxxxx0 |  running |  t2.large  |  172.31.33.43 |  mongodb-test  |
|  i-02703dd7fexxxxxxd |  stopped |  t2.medium |  172.31.42.65 | CTF1           |
|  i-07735e9fa8xxxxxxf |  stopped |  t2.medium |  172.31.39.20 | CTF2           |
+---------------------+---------+-----------+--------------+-----------------+
```

5. Finally, let us see if we can collect logs from AWS using AWS CLI. Many AWS services have their own logs. Moreover, the logs can be sent to CloudWatch for real-time monitoring and analysis purposes. We can first get the list of logs groups by running the following command:

```
aws logs describe-log-groups --output json
```

The output may look similar to the following:

```
{
    "logGroups": [
        {
            "logGroupName": "foresic-test-logs",
            "creationTime": 1761479645803,
            "retentionInDays": 7,
            "metricFilterCount": 0,
            "arn": "arn:aws:logs:ap-south-1:8517xxxxxx13:log-group:foresic-test-logs:*",
            "storedBytes": 0,
            "logGroupClass": "STANDARD",
              "logGroupArn": "arn:aws:logs:ap-south-1:8517xxxxxx13:log-group:foresic-test-
logs"
        }
    ]
}
```

You can now perform a bunch of tasks on this log group. For example, you can get the logs for a specific log stream under this group. You can also export the logs to AWS S3 for future reference and preservation.

By now, you can see how easy it is to use AWS CLI to get details of everything from AWS. The commands are simple to construct and are very logical. You can also control the amount of details you need for evidence collection or simply for audit purposes.

Activity

Attempt the following activities before the next recipe:

- Try to get all the details of a group and a user by using one of the **iam** commands. Refer to AWS CLI's help to understand the relevant command that can be used.
- For each of the commands described in this recipe, redirect the output to a file for future reference.
- Get details of all the stopped VMs by using their instance IDs.
- Read the AWS documentation to understand where else you can collect logs.

Recipe 112: Snapshotting a disk volume on AWS

We have seen so far that AWS CLI is extremely useful to automate the evidence collection tasks. In case of a cyberattack, one may have to create a copy of the disk volume attached to an EC2 instance for further analysis. This can also be done by using AWS CLI. In this recipe, we will create a snapshot of the disk volume for an EC2 instance.

Note:

- **Compatibility: AWS**
- **License considerations: Requires subscription. Free services and trial periods apply.**

Recipe

In order to create a snapshot of the volume of an instance, first, we need to get a few details about the instance. We can do that by querying the instance ID and details about the volume as follows:

```
aws ec2 describe-instances \
  --filters "Name=instance-state-name,Values=running" \
  --query '
    Reservations[].Instances[].{
      InstanceId: InstanceId,
      Name: Tags[?Key==`Name`]|[0].Value,
      AvailabilityZone: Placement.AvailabilityZone,
      RootDeviceName: RootDeviceName,
      Volumes: BlockDeviceMappings[].{
        DeviceName: DeviceName,
        VolumeId: Ebs.VolumeId
      }
    }' \
  --output json
```

The output of the preceding command will look similar to the following:

```
[
    {
        "InstanceId": "i-05f6aa8xxxxxx2b30",
        "Name": "mongodb-test",
        "AvailabilityZone": "ap-south-1a",
        "RootDeviceName": "/dev/sda1",
        "Volumes": [
            {
                "DeviceName": "/dev/sda1",
                "VolumeId": "vol-0fdc81xxxxxx9c7f3"
            }
        ]
    }
]
```

We have all the required information to create a snapshot. The following command can be used to create a snapshot:

```
aws ec2 create-snapshots \
  --instance-specification InstanceId=$INSTANCE_ID,ExcludeBootVolume=false \
  --description "$DESC" \
  --copy-tags-from-source volume \
                                                             --tag-specifications
"ResourceType=snapshot,Tags=[{Key=Case,Value=DFIR},{Key=SourceInstance,Value=$INSTANCE_ID}]"
```

The actual command may look like the following, where description and instance ID are updated. Ensure that you update the instance ID from the describe-instance command in this command to create snapshot:

```
aws ec2 create-snapshots \
  --instance-specification InstanceId=i-05f6aa8xxxxxx2b30,ExcludeBootVolume=false \
  --description "Forensics snapshot of i-05f6aa8xxxxxx2b30 on $(date -u +%F)Z" \
  --copy-tags-from-source volume \
  --tag-specifications "ResourceType=snapshot,Tags=[{Key=Case,Value=DFIR},{Key=SourceInstance,Value
=i-05f6aa8xxxxxx2b30}]"
```

The command will exit right away. However, the snapshot operation will take a while to complete. Once done, you can verify if the snapshot is created properly and if the details are also set as per the command we used.

Tip: **If you get an error that the user is not authorized to perform this operation, check the permissions given to the user group. You can do that by going to Add permission | Create inline policy, then choose the EC2 service and provide all the permissions for snapshot operations.**

If your command is successful, you will see an output like the following:

```
SNAPSHOTS       Forensics snapshot of i-05f6aa8b6d4c72b30 on 2025-10-26Z        False   851725643213
snap-0d36dfb47148d3c4f  2025-10-26T12:37:03.618000+00:00 pending vol-0fdc81adfe4c9c7f3  30

TAGS    SourceInstance  i-05f6aa8b6d4c72b30

TAGS    Case    DFIR
```

Verify the Snapshots page in EC2 and confirm if the snapshot creation is in progress.

Activity

Attempt the following activities before the next recipe:

- Identify the cause of why the permission we assigned while creating users did not work for creating a snapshot.
- Describe how the created snapshot can be used as a forensically sound copy of the disk volume.

Recipe 113: Connecting Azure CLI to Microsoft Azure

In this recipe, we will use a default subscription, e.g., pay-as-you-go to configure the Azure CLI with Microsoft Azure.

You need to have a Microsoft Azure account, and you should be comfortable working with the Azure Console as a prerequisite to this recipe.

Note:

- **Compatibility: Microsoft Azure**
- **License considerations: Requires subscription. Free services and trial periods apply.**

Recipe

Perform the following steps to complete this recipe.

1. Once you have installed Azure CLI, run the following command:

```
az login
```

2. A browser will be opened automatically where you need to log in to your Azure account. Once you complete the login, Azure CLI will save the details, and the command will exit.

3. Verify that Azure CLI is configured properly to use your account by running the following command, which lists all the resource groups:

```
az group list --output table
```

The output of this command will look something like the following:

```
┌─nishant@Ivy ~
└─$ az group list --output table
Name                             Location       Status
-------------------------------  -------------  ---------
wp-xxxxx-website_group           centralindia   Succeeded
NetworkWatcherRG                 centralindia   Succeeded
AzureBackupRG_centralindia_1     centralindia   Succeeded
xxxxx-qa                         centralindia   Succeeded
┌─nishant@Ivy ~
└─$
```

Activity

Attempt the following activities before the next recipe:

- Run **az help** command to get the list of commands available with Azure CLI. Which ones do you think are self-explanatory?
- There are a few commands that are marked as experimental in the list of commands. Get more information about these commands.
- Create a restricted account in Azure that has restricted access to collect forensic data and perform operations during forensic evidence collection. Perform **az logout** and then **az login** to reconfigure Azure CLI to use this account.

Recipe 114: Collecting digital forensic evidence from Azure

In the last recipe, we connected to our Azure subscription. Now, let us try to collect a few important evidence from Azure so that you become comfortable working with Azure CLI. The principle behind collecting evidence remains the same as what we saw while working with AWS. After completing this recipe, you should be able to collect most information by looking at the Azure CLI reference that comes with the tool, or that is published by AWS.

Note:

- **Compatibility: Microsoft Azure**
- **License considerations: Requires subscription. Free services and trial periods apply.**

Recipe

In this recipe, we will collect many evidence across Azure services using Azure CLI. Perform the following steps to complete this recipe. **xxxxxx** is used in many places to redact sensitive information like an account ID:

1. First let us list all the resources inside a resource group. A resource group in Azure is used to group together related resources, e.g., for a specific application.

   Run the following command to list the resources inside a resource group. In this example, you need to specify a resource group name as per your Azure account:

   ```
   az resource list --resource-group      wp-xxxxx-website_group --output table
   ```

   The output will look similar to the following:

   ```
   Name                                                          ResourceGroup          Location
   Type                                              Status
   -----------------------------------------------------  -------------------  ----------
   --  -------------------------------------------  --------
   wp-xxxxxx-website                                                    wp-xxxxxx-website_group
   centralindia  Microsoft.Compute/virtualMachines
   wp-xxxxx-website_OsDisk_1_fb67c3ccba6344228901435d2541789b      WP-XXXXX-WEBSITE_GROUP
   centralindia  Microsoft.Compute/disks
   wp-xxxxx-website_key                                  wp-xxxxx-website_group  centralindia
   Microsoft.Compute/sshPublicKeys
   wp-xxxxx-website_group-vnet                           wp-xxxxx-website_group  centralindia
   Microsoft.Network/virtualNetworks
   wp-xxxxx-website-ip                                   wp-xxxxx-website_group  centralindia
   Microsoft.Network/publicIPAddresses
   wp-xxxxx-website-nsg                                  wp-xxxxx-website_group  centralindia
   Microsoft.Network/networkSecurityGroups
   wp-xxxxx-website/AzureNetworkWatcherExtension                      wp-xxxxx-website_group
   centralindia  Microsoft.Compute/virtualMachines/extensions
   wp-xxxxx-website460                                   wp-xxxxx-website_group  centralindia
   Microsoft.Network/networkInterfaces
   vault696                                              wp-xxxxx-website_group  centralindia
   Microsoft.RecoveryServices/vaults
   ```

   This list shows many resources, including virtual machines, SSH keys, virtual network, public IP address, and much more.

   Note: The az tool supports output in JSON, YAML, table, tab separated value (TSV), and many other formats.

2. Let us list only the virtual machines inside a resource group by running the following command:

```
az resource list --resource-group wp-xxxxx-website_group --resource-type Microsoft.Compute/
virtualMachines --output table
```

The output will look similar to the following:

```
Name              ResourceGroup          Location      Type                                  Status
-------------     -------------------    -----------   ---------------------------------     ---
-----
wp-xxxxx-website  wp-xxxxx-website_group  centralindia  Microsoft.Compute/virtualMachines
```

Now, in order to list all the virtual machines in the account, we can use the following command:

```
az vm list --output table
```

The following command can show all the details of all the VMs. In this case, it is preferable to show the details in JSON format:

```
az vm list --show-details --output json
```

3. Let us now list all the users in the Azure account. We can do as follows:

```
az ad user list --output table
```

The preceding command will list all the users in the Azure **Active Directory** (**AD**) account. The output is now shown due to its confidential nature. However, all the details listed under Users in Azure can be shown, including details for specific users.

4. Let us now see how to find all the sign-in activities for any user. Azure has excellent logs for every user if the organization is using Microsoft 365. Azure acts as the directory service for all the users and hence has information like login time, location of access, etc., which is extremely valuable in case of a cyberattack or incident. You can see these logs under **Users | Sign-in** logs in the Azure console. We can also use the following command to get these logs:

```
az ad signin list --output table
```

Note: The preceding command needs the plugin module `AzureADPreview` to be installed. This can only be installed through PowerShell. Another option is to use the Microsoft Graph API, but that needs a premium subscription.

These sign-in logs also contain logs for Azure CLI. You can see that in the Application column.

As we saw with AWS CLI, working with Azure CLI is also very easy. The commands are simple to construct and are very logical. You can also control the amount of details you need for evidence collection or simply for audit purposes.

Activity

Attempt the following activities before the next recipe:

- Update the `az` command to output only specific columns, just like we did with AWS CLI.
- Modify the `az vm list` command to list only the running VMs.
- Find out the ways various logs can be collected from Azure.
- Modify the preceding commands to save the output into files for future reference.

Recipe 115: Snapshotting a disk volume on Azure

We have seen so far that Azure CLI is extremely useful to automate the evidence collection tasks. In case of a cyberattack, one may have to create a copy of the disk volume attached to a virtual machine for further analysis. In this recipe, we will create a snapshot of the disk volume for a virtual machine.

Note:

- **Compatibility: Microsoft Azure**
- **License considerations: Requires subscription. Free services and trial periods apply.**

Recipe

In this recipe, first we will get the details of all the disks attached to a VM and then snapshot the disks. Refer to the following steps to complete this recipe:

1. First, let us get the list of all the disks attached to the VM. This command needs us to supply the VM name and the resource group:

```
az vm show \
  --name <vm-name> \
  --resource-group <resource-group-name> \
  --query "storageProfile.{OSDisk:osDisk, DataDisks:dataDisks}" \
  --output json
```

The command updated with the VM name and resource group will look like the following:

```
az vm show \
  --name wp-xxxxxx-website \
  --resource-group WP-xxxxxx-WEBSITE_GROUP \
  --query "storageProfile.{OSDisk:osDisk, DataDisks:dataDisks}" \
  --output json
```

The output will look similar to the following:

```
{
  "DataDisks": [],
  "OSDisk": {
    "caching": "ReadWrite",
    "createOption": "FromImage",
    "deleteOption": "Detach",
    "diffDiskSettings": null,
    "diskSizeGb": 30,
    "encryptionSettings": null,
    "image": null,
    "managedDisk": {
      "diskEncryptionSet": null,
        "id": "/subscriptions/fa480b5c-xxxx-4467-xxxx-ca8f076c5a09/resourceGroups/wp-
xxxxxx-website_group/providers/Microsoft.Compute/disks/wp-xxxxxx-website_OsDisk_1_
fb67c3ccba6344xxxxxx435d2541789b",
```

```
            "resourceGroup": "wp-xxxxxx-website_group",
            "securityProfile": null,
            "storageAccountType": "StandardSSD_LRS"
          },
          "name": "wp-xxxxxx-website_OsDisk_1_fb67c3ccba6344228901435d2541789b",
          "osType": "Linux",
          "vhd": null,
          "writeAcceleratorEnabled": null
        }
      }
```

We have all the information required to snapshot the disk of the VM. The snapshot can be taken by the following command:

```
az snapshot create \
  --resource-group WP-xxxxxx-WEBSITE_GROUP \
        --source      /subscriptions/fa480b5c-xxxx-4467-xxxx-ca8f076c5a09/resourceGroups/wp-xxxxxx-website_group/providers/Microsoft.Compute/disks/wp-xxxxxx-website_OsDisk_1_fb67c3ccba6344xxxxxx435d2541789b \
  --name forensic-test-snap-20251026 \
  --tags Purpose=Forensics CreatedBy=DFIR \
  --output table
```

Be sure to update the preceding command with the details shown in the previous output. Once you run this command, Azure starts creating a snapshot of the disk supplied in the `az snapshot` command and provides the details of the snapshot as the output. You can verify if the snapshot has been taken from the VM by visiting **Compute Infrastructure | Disk + images | Snapshots**.

Activity

Attempt the following activities before the next recipe:

- Describe how the created snapshot can be used as a forensically sound copy of the disk volume.
- Modify the `az snapshot` command to snapshot all the disks attached to the VM.

Conclusion

In this chapter, we understood that cloud forensics extends classical DFIR into environments where data, compute, and networks are virtualized, distributed, multi-tenant, and ephemeral. Since evidence can disappear when instances terminate or containers reschedule, forensic readiness, pre-enabling audit logs, immutable exports, and least-privilege collection roles are as important as post-incident response.

The shared responsibility model prevalent in the cloud means providers secure the cloud (physical, hypervisor, core networking) while customers must secure and preserve what they deploy (configurations, identities, data, keys, logs).

Real-world cloud forensic investigations may span IaaS, PaaS, SaaS, FaaS, and CaaS environments, significantly expanding the scope and complexity of evidence collection.

When implemented effectively, cloud forensics delivers visibility, attribution, containment guidance, and compliance evidence at cloud scale and speed.

Questions

1. What distinguishes cloud forensics from traditional on-prem forensics?
2. How does the shared responsibility model vary across IaaS, PaaS, and SaaS during investigations?
3. Why is forensic readiness essential in elastic and serverless environments?
4. List three risks that multi-tenancy introduces for evidence handling.
5. Compare volume snapshots vs. disk images in cloud contexts.
6. Which IAM misconfigurations most commonly enable compromise, and how do you detect them?
7. How do you baseline cloud resources for later anomaly detection?
8. How do you preserve evidence from short-lived containers or functions?
9. Explain tagging strategies that aid case management and e-discovery.
10. What legal/jurisdictional issues can arise when acquiring cross-region data?
11. How do object-store versioning and immutable tiers support forensics?
12. When is live response preferable to shutting down an instance?

Points to remember

- Forensic readiness on the cloud should be planned in advance before incidents by enabling logs, object versioning, and least-privilege forensics roles.
- Cloud provider's CLIs and APIs can be used to automate acquisitions, and ensure every command is timestamped and tagged.
- Evidence should be preserved first and analyzed later by creating snapshots and capturing object versions as early as possible.
- Every acquisition should be treated as evidentiary by hashing artifacts, documenting steps, and maintaining an unbroken chain of custody.
- Logs can be collected proactively from containers and serverless platforms because their artifacts are highly ephemeral.
- Log and snapshot retention periods can be aligned with legal and regulatory requirements for each operating region.
- Baseline inventories and configurations can be created to quickly spot anomalous resource creations or changes.
- First responder privileges should be separated from production administration and never use root or long-lived high-privilege keys.
- It is important to tag every artifact with a CaseID, source, time, and handler to ensure complete traceability throughout the case.
- Snapshot integrity can be preserved by computing hashes and mounting copies read-only before any examination.
- Investigation findings can be circled back into hardening efforts by improving IAM policies, logging coverage, and detection rules.

- Evidence collection can be rehearsed with various exercises and drills to reduce response time and mistakes during real incidents.

Key terms

- **Cloud forensics**: DFIR practices adapted to cloud environments, leveraging provider APIs, logs, and snapshots.
- **Control plane**: Provider management layer where API calls configure cloud resources; a primary evidence source.
- **Data plane**: The path where user data flows and is processed (e.g., VM disks, object stores).
- **Shared responsibility model**: Division of security duties between provider and customer across service models.
- **IaaS**: Infrastructure services (VMs, storage, networks) where the customer manages OS and above.
- **PaaS**: Managed platforms that abstract OS/runtime; customer focuses on code and data.
- **SaaS**: Fully managed applications; customer controls data, config, and access.
- **FaaS/Serverless**: Event-driven functions with provider-managed runtime; highly ephemeral evidence.
- **CaaS**: Managed container orchestration (e.g., Kubernetes) with container-centric evidence sources.
- **Multi-tenancy**: Shared underlying infrastructure across customers; isolation and leakage risks.
- **Forensic readiness**: Pre-incident posture enabling rapid, defensible evidence collection.
- **Snapshot**: Point-in-time copy of a disk/volume created via provider APIs.
- **Object versioning**: Keeping prior versions of objects in storage to support recovery and forensics.
- **Immutable storage (WORM)**: Write-once, read-many storage preventing tampering with preserved evidence.
- **IAM**: Identity and access management for roles, policies, and permissions.
- **Instance metadata**: Per-VM context (roles, IPs, tokens) useful for live response.
- **Ephemeral Resource**: Short-lived compute/storage entities (spot VMs, pods, functions).
- **Evidence tagging**: Applying metadata (CaseID, Source, Hash) to artifacts for tracking.
- **IaC**: Declarative resource definitions (e.g., Terraform) assisting baselining and diffs.

Join our Discord space

Join our Discord workspace for latest updates, offers, tech happenings around the world, new releases, and sessions with the authors:

https://discord.bpbonline.com

Index

A

B

C

D

E

R

S

T

U

V

W